MW00559453

Dispute Processes
ADR and the Primary Forms of Decision-making

Third Edition

This wide-ranging study considers the primary forms of decision-making – negotiation, mediation, umpiring, as well as the processes of avoidance and violence – in the context of rapidly changing discourses and practices of civil justice across a range of jurisdictions. Many contemporary discussions in this field – and associated projects of institutional design – are taking place under the broad but imprecise label of Alternative Dispute Resolution (ADR). The book brings together and analyses a wide range of materials dealing with dispute processes, and the current debates on and developments in civil justice. With the help of analysis of materials beyond those ordinarily found in the ADR literature, it provides a comprehensive and comparative perspective on modes of handling civil disputes. The new edition is thoroughly revised and is extended to include new chapters on avoidance and self-help, the ombuds, Online Dispute Resolution and pressures of institutionalisation, as well as offering a section including classroom role plays, and making extended suggestions for further (open-access) reading.

Michael Palmer is Emeritus Professor of Law at the University of London's School of Oriental and African Studies (SOAS). He is also Senior Research Fellow at the Institute of Advanced Legal Studies (IALS) and at the Hong Kong Institute of Asia-Pacific Studies (HKIAPS) at the Chinese University of Hong Kong. His publications are mainly in the field of comparative legal studies and give particular attention to Chinese law, both traditional and modern. Michael has been Joint Editor of the *Journal of Comparative Law* for more than a decade and is also Editor of the journal *Amicus Curiae*. He is a barrister at Serle Court and at McNair Chambers. He has been a special adviser to the Attorney-General of Hong Kong, the Office of the UN High Commissioner for Human Rights and the European Commission, and also recently served as (very probably) the first western dean of a mainland Chinese law school.

Simon Roberts (1941–2014) was Professor of Law at the London School of Economics and Political Science (LSE). A renowned legal anthropologist, his early career included two years' teaching in Malawi in the 1960s and three years as Adviser on Customary Law to the Botswana Government (1968–1971). He authored the seminal work *Order and Dispute: An*

Introduction to Legal Anthropology (1979, with a second edition in 2013), a study of law, order and dispute settlement and how they are conceptualised and socially founded. His analysis drew inter alia upon field research among the Kgatla in Botswana and later encouraged his work on issues in dispute processes in jurisdictions such as England and Wales. His most recent book was *A Court in the City: Civil and Commercial Litigation in London at the Beginning of the 21st Century* (2013), based on his ethnographic research at the Mayor's and City of London Court. This study examined the work of the court in sponsoring dispute settlement. He continued to teach ADR at the LSE long after retirement. Simon also served on the Lord Chancellor's family law advisory board which assisted in preparations for the Family Law Act (1996) and was General Editor of the *Modern Law Review* from 1988 until 1995. In 2011, Simon was elected an Honorary Fellow of the LSE.

The Law in Context Series

Editors: William Twining (University College London),
Maksymilian Del Mar (Queen Mary, University of London) and
Bronwen Morgan (University of New South Wales).

Since 1970 the Law in Context series has been at the forefront of the movement to broaden the study of law. It has been a vehicle for the publication of innovative scholarly books that treat law and legal phenomena critically in their social, political and economic contexts from a variety of perspectives. The series particularly aims to publish scholarly legal writing that brings fresh perspectives to bear on new and existing areas of law taught in universities. A contextual approach involves treating legal subjects broadly, using materials from other social sciences, and from any other discipline that helps to explain the operation in practice of the subject under discussion. It is hoped that this orientation is at once more stimulating and more realistic than the bare exposition of legal rules. The series includes original books that have a different emphasis from traditional legal textbooks, while maintaining the same high standards of scholarship. They are written primarily for undergraduate and graduate students of law and of other disciplines, but will also appeal to a wider readership. In the past, most books in the series have focused on English law, but recent publications include books on European law, globalisation, transnational legal processes, and comparative law.

Books in the Series
Acosta: *The National versus the Foreigner in South America: 200 Years of Migration and Citizenship Law*
Ali: *Modern Challenges to Islamic Law*
Alyagon Darr: *Plausible Crime Stories: The Legal History of Sexual Offences in Mandate Palestine*
Anderson, Schum & Twining: *Analysis of Evidence, 2nd Edition*
Ashworth: *Sentencing and Criminal Justice, 6th Edition*
Barton & Douglas: *Law and Parenthood*
Baxi, McCrudden & Paliwala: *Law's Ethical, Global and Theoretical Contexts: Essays in Honour of William Twining*
Beecher-Monas: *Evaluating Scientific Evidence: An Interdisciplinary Framework for Intellectual Due Process*
Bell: *French Legal Cultures*
Bercusson: *European Labour Law, 2nd Edition*
Birkinshaw: *European Public Law*
Birkinshaw: *Freedom of Information: The Law, the Practice and the Ideal, 4th Edition*
Broderick & Ferri: *International and European Disability Law and Policy: Text, Cases and Materials*
Brownsword & Goodwin: *Law and the Technologies of the Twenty-First Century: Text and Materials*
Cane & Goudkamp: *Atiyah's Accidents, Compensation and the Law, 9th Edition*
Clarke: *Principles of Property Law*
Clarke & Kohler: *Property Law: Commentary and Materials*

Collins: *The Law of Contract, 4th Edition*

Collins, Ewing & McColgan: *Labour Law, 2nd Edition*

Cowan: *Housing Law and Policy*

Cranston: *Legal Foundations of the Welfare State*

Darian-Smith: *Laws and Societies in Global Contexts: Contemporary Approaches*

Dauvergne: *Making People Illegal: What Globalisation Means for Immigration and Law*

Davies: *Perspectives on Labour Law, 2nd Edition*

David: *Kinship, Law and Politics: An Anatomy of Belonging*

Dembour: *Who Believes in Human Rights?: Reflections on the European Convention*

de Sousa Santos: *Toward a New Legal Common Sense: Law, Globalization, and Emancipation*

Diduck: *Law's Families*

Estella: *Legal Foundations of EU Economic Governance*

Fortin: *Children's Rights and the Developing Law, 3rd Edition*

Garton, Probert & Bean: *Moffat's Trusts Law: Text and Materials, 7th Edition*

Garnsey: *The Justice of Visual Art: Creative State-Building in Times of Political Transition*

Ghai & Woodman: *Practising Self-Government: A Comparative Study of Autonomous Regions*

Glover-Thomas: *Reconstructing Mental Health Law and Policy*

Gobert & Punch: *Rethinking Corporate Crime*

Goldman: *Globalisation and the Western Legal Tradition: Recurring Patterns of Law and Authority*

Haack: *Evidence Matters: Science, Proof, and Truth in the Law*

Harlow & Rawlings: *Law and Administration, 3rd Edition*

Harris: *An Introduction to Law, 8th Edition*

Harris, Campbell & Halson: *Remedies in Contract and Tort, 2nd Edition*

Harvey: *Seeking Asylum in the UK: Problems and Prospects*

Herring: *Law and the Relational Self*

Hervey & McHale: *European Union Health Law: Themes and Implications*

Hervey & McHale: *Health Law and the European Union*

Holder & Lee: *Environmental Protection, Law and Policy: Text and Materials, 2nd Edition*

Jackson & Summers: *The Internationalisation of Criminal Evidence: Beyond the Common Law and Civil Law Traditions*

Kostakopoulou: *The Future Governance of Citizenship*

Kreiczer-Levy Destabilized Property: *Property Law in the Sharing Economy*

Kubal: *Immigration and Refugee Law in Russia: Socio-Legal Perspectives*

Lewis: *Choice and the Legal Order: Rising above Politics*

Likosky: *Transnational Legal Processes: Globalisation and Power Disparities*

Likosky: *Law, Infrastructure and Human Rights*

Loughnan: *Self, Others and the State: Relations of Criminal Responsibility*

Lunney: *A History of Australian Tort Law 1901–1945: England's Obedient Servant?*

Maughan & Webb: *Lawyering Skills and the Legal Process, 2nd Edition*

McGlynn: *Families and the European Union: Law, Politics and Pluralism*

Mertens: *A Philosophical Introduction to Human Rights*

Moffat: *Trusts Law: Text and Materials*

Monti: *EC Competition Law*

Morgan: *Contract Law Minimalism: A Formalist Restatement of Commercial Contract Law*

Morgan & Yeung: *An Introduction to Law and Regulation: Text and Materials*

Nicola & Davies: *EU Law Stories: Contextual and Critical Histories of European Jurisprudence*

Norrie: *Crime, Reason and History: A Critical Introduction to Criminal Law, 3rd Edition*

O'Dair: *Legal Ethics: Text and Materials*

Oliver: *Common Values and the Public-Private Divide*

Oliver & Drewry: *The Law and Parliament*

Palmer & Roberts: *Dispute Processes: ADR and the Primary Forms of Decision-Making, 1ˢᵗ Edition*

Palmer & Roberts: *Dispute Processes: ADR and the Primary Forms of Decision-Making, 3ʳᵈ Edition*

Picciotto: *International Business Taxation*

Probert: *The Changing Legal Regulation of Cohabitation, 1600–2010: From Fornicators to Family, 1600–2010*

Radi: *Rules and Practices of International Investment Law and Arbitration*

Reed: *Internet Law: Text and Materials*

Richardson: *Law, Process and Custody*

Roberts & Palmer: *Dispute Processes: ADR and the Primary Forms of Decision-Making, 2ⁿᵈ Edition*

Rowbottom: *Democracy Distorted: Wealth, Influence and Democratic Politics*

Sauter: *Public Services in EU Law*

Scott & Black: *Cranston's Consumers and the Law*

Seneviratne: *Ombudsmen: Public Services and Administrative Justice*

Seppänen: *Ideological Conflict and the Rule of Law in Contemporary China: Useful Paradoxes*

Siems: *Comparative Law, 2ⁿᵈ Edition*

Stapleton: *Product Liability*

Stewart: *Gender, Law and Justice in a Global Market*

Tamanaha: *Law as a Means to an End: Threat to the Rule of Law*

Turpin & Tomkins: *British Government and the Constitution: Text and Materials, 7ᵗʰ Edition*

Twining: *General Jurisprudence: Understanding Law from a Global Perspective*

Twining: *Globalisation and Legal Theory*

Twining: *Human Rights, Southern Voices: Francis Deng, Abdullahi An-Na'im, Yash Ghai and Upendra Baxi*

Twining: *Jurist in Context: A Memoir*

Twining: *Karl Llewellyn and the Realist Movement, 2ⁿᵈ Edition*

Twining: *Rethinking Evidence: Exploratory Essays, 2ⁿᵈ Edition*

Twining & Miers: *How to Do Things with Rules, 5ᵗʰ Edition*

Ward: *A Critical Introduction to European Law, 3ʳᵈ Edition*

Ward: *Law, Text, Terror*

Ward: *Shakespeare and Legal Imagination*

Wells & Quick: *Lacey, Wells and Quick: Reconstructing Criminal Law: Text and Materials, 4ᵗʰ Edition*

Zander: *Cases and Materials on the English Legal System, 10ᵗʰ Edition*

Zander: *The Law-Making Process, 6ᵗʰ Edition*

International Journal of Law in Context: A Global Forum for Interdisciplinary Legal Studies

The *International Journal of Law in Context* is the companion journal to the Law in Context book series and provides a forum for interdisciplinary legal studies and offers intellectual space for ground-breaking critical research. It publishes contextual work about law and its relationship with other disciplines including but not limited to science, literature, humanities, philosophy, sociology, psychology, ethics, history and geography. More information about the journal and how to submit an article can be found at http://journals.cambridge.org/ijc

Dispute Processes

ADR and the Primary Forms of Decision-making

Third Edition

MICHAEL PALMER
SOAS and IALS University of London

SIMON ROBERTS
London School of Economics and Political Science

CAMBRIDGE
UNIVERSITY PRESS

CAMBRIDGE
UNIVERSITY PRESS

University Printing House, Cambridge CB2 8BS, United Kingdom

One Liberty Plaza, 20th Floor, New York, NY 10006, USA

477 Williamstown Road, Port Melbourne, VIC 3207, Australia

314–321, 3rd Floor, Plot 3, Splendor Forum, Jasola District Centre, New Delhi – 110025, India

79 Anson Road, #06–04/06, Singapore 079906

Cambridge University Press is part of the University of Cambridge.

It furthers the University's mission by disseminating knowledge in the pursuit of
education, learning, and research at the highest international levels of excellence.

www.cambridge.org
Information on this title: www.cambridge.org/9781107070547
DOI: 10.1017/9781107707467

First edition © Michael Palmer and Simon Roberts 1998
Second edition © Simon Roberts and Michael Palmer 2005
Third edition © Michael Palmer and Simon Roberts 2020

This publication is in copyright. Subject to statutory exception
and to the provisions of relevant collective licensing agreements,
no reproduction of any part may take place without the written
permission of Cambridge University Press.

Second edition 2005
Reprinted 2008
Third edition 2020

Printed in the United Kingdom by TJ International Ltd, Padstow Cornwall 2020

A catalogue record for this publication is available from the British Library.

Library of Congress Cataloging-in-Publication Data
Names: Palmer, Michael J. E., 1944– author. | Roberts, Simon (Simon A.), author.
Title: Dispute processes : ADR and primary forms of decision-making / Michael Palmer, University of
London; Simon Roberts, London School of Economics and Political Science.
Description: Third edition. | Cambridge, UK ; New York, NY : Cambridge University Press, 2020. |
Series: The law in context series | Includes bibliographical references and index.
Identifiers: LCCN 2020010873 (print) | LCCN 2020010874 (ebook) | ISBN 9781107070547
   (hardback) | ISBN 9781107687578 (paperback) | ISBN 9781107707467 (epub)
Subjects: LCSH: Dispute resolution (Law)
Classification: LCC K2390 .P35 2020 (print) | LCC K2390 (ebook) | DDC 347/.09–dc23
LC record available at https://lccn.loc.gov/2020010873
LC ebook record available at https://lccn.loc.gov/2020010874

ISBN 978-1-107-07054-7 Hardback
ISBN 978-1-107-68757-8 Paperback

Cambridge University Press has no responsibility for the persistence or accuracy
of URLs for external or third-party internet websites referred to in this publication
and does not guarantee that any content on such websites is, or will remain,
accurate or appropriate.

To the Memory of Simon Roberts

Contents

Preface   *page* xv

1 Introduction   1
   Preliminaries   1
   Transformations in the Common Law World   2
   Civilian Parallels   8
   The Comparative Scene   10
   Legal Reform Initiatives, the Role of ADR and Normative Pluralism   11
   The Nature and Scope of this Book   12

2 Cultures of Decision-making: Precursors to the Emergence of ADR   17
   Introduction   17
   Ideals of Informal Justice   18
   The Establishment of Formal Justice   19
   The Religious Impulse towards Informalism   25
   The Political Impulse towards Informalism   27
   The Ethnic Impulse towards Informalism   33
   The Occupational Impulse towards Informalism   34
   Territorial Identity and the Impulse towards Informalism   37
   Family and Kinship   42
   Legal Reform, Pluralism and Informalism   44
   Self-regulation   46
   Temporal Dimensions   48
   Conclusions   49

**3 The Debates around Civil Justice and the Movement towards
    Procedural Innovation**   51
   Introduction   51
   The Debates of the 1980s   55
   The Subsequent Trajectory of the ADR Movement   61
   Reiterating the Critiques of Informalism   67
   The Direction of ADR   70

4   Disputes and Dispute Processes   73
Introduction   73
Typologies of Response   75
Reconstructing a Panorama of Decision-making   79
Conclusions   99

5   Development of Disputes, Avoidance and Self-help   101
Introduction   101
The Genesis of Disputes   102
Characterising Dispute Responses   104
Avoidance: Its Forms and Close Relatives   106
Violence and Its Forms   113
Conclusions   122

6   Negotiations   123
The Nature of Negotiation   123
Intra-party and Multi-party Negotiations   127
The Processual Shape of Negotiation   132
Power in Negotiation   138
Strategy in Negotiation   139
Representative Negotiations   146
Ethical Issues in Negotiation   148
Conclusions   152

7   Mediation   153
Introduction – The Nature of Mediation   153
The Mediator in the Negotiation Process: The Processual
Shape of Mediation   163
The Late Twentieth-century Re-institutionalisation of Mediation   167
Conclusions   190

8   Umpiring: Courts and Tribunals   191
Introduction   191
Government and Dispute Institutions   192
The Legitimation of Third-party Decision-making   194
The Role of Courts   197
The Heterogeneity of Court Practice   200
Contemporary Transformations in the Common Law World   201
The Popular Element in Courts   209
Tribunals   210
Conclusions   211

9   Umpiring: Arbitration   213
Introduction   213
Arbitration – Court-linked   216
Arbitration – International   217

Processual Styles in International Arbitration from
a Comparative Perspective   219
Conclusions   223

10   Hybrid Forms and Processual Experimentation   225
Introduction   225
Settlement as Civil Justice   230
Negotiation-related Innovations   234
Mediation-related Innovations   238
Refurbishing Umpiring   246
Conclusions   270

11   The Ombuds and its Diffusion: From Public to Private 273
Introduction   273
The Growing Importance of the Ombuds   274
Two Kinds of Ombuds   277
Public Law Ombuds   279
Organisational Ombuds   280
Sectoral Ombuds   281
Transplanting the Ombuds to China?   284
Conclusions   285

12   Online Dispute Resolution and its Diffusion: From Private to Public   287
Introduction   287
ODR and ADR   288
ODR Systems   291
Regulation   294
ODR: The Flourishing in China   295
The Emergence of E-courts   297
Conclusions   300

13   Institutionalisation of ADR   301
Introduction   301
Informal and Formal Justice Reconsidered   303
The Mixed Message of the 'Multi-door Courthouse'   306
Woolf's Doors   308
What Happened to Naming, Blaming and Claiming?   308
Formalisation and its Contexts   312
Formalisation and the Routinisation of Charisma?   317
Harmony and Deformalisation in China?   319
Conclusions   320

14   Reflections   323
Introduction   323
The Contemporary Scene   324
Lawyers and ADR   325

The Changing Nature of the Court   326
The Future   327

Appendix A: Some Role Plays   331
References   347
Further Reading   367
Recommended Viewing   393
Index   405

Preface

This book grew out of more than two decades of teaching 'Alternative Dispute Resolution' for postgraduate students in law at the University of London, as well as many years of research and writing in this field by both of us. The approach taken in assembling the study is intentionally wide-ranging and comparative so that it can be read not only in its own right but also as a broader, contextualising companion to more conventional and jurisdiction-specific ADR texts. The present study is also informed by the view that litigation and adversarial proceedings should no longer be seen as the paradigmatic processes of decision-making in our civil justice systems. Looking first at the sources of 'ADR' ideas and the debates which have surrounded the rise of alternative approaches to dispute resolution, we then move on to examine the primary forms of decision-making: negotiation, mediation, umpiring and also avoidance and force. This is followed by an examination of the emergence in contemporary Anglo-American practice of the fusions of the foundational modes of decision-making that are generally referred to as hybrid or mixed processes, as well as by consideration of other important contemporary developments.

In putting together this book, we have been given generous help by others. William Twining persuaded us to write this in the first place, and has throughout remained a source of wise counsel. Marian Roberts has helped not only by teaching family disputes for our students but also by providing consistent support and excellent advice. Maria-Frederica Moscati has also been a constant source of advice and encouragement, as have Patricia Ng, Chen Yongzhu, Amy Kellam, Lin Yang, Li Jing and Cong Wanshu. Last, but by no means least, there are the many students who gave enthusiastic and critical response to our first and second editions, and whose observations have helped to make the third edition a better book.

Michael Palmer and Simon Roberts

1

Introduction

'impressed with command, we see little else.'

C. Geertz *Negara* (1982: 121)

'there probably exists no social unit in which convergent and divergent currents among its members are not inseparably interwoven.'

G. Simmel *Der Streit* ([1923] trans. 1955: 15)

'the charismatic message inevitably becomes dogma, doctrine, theory, reglement, law or petrified tradition.'

M. Weber *Economy and Society* ([1917] 1978: 1122)

Preliminaries

This book, *Dispute Processes: ADR and the Primary Forms of Decision-making*, principally concerns disputes and the processes relied on to deal with disputes in many societies around the world. It is more than ten years since the publication of the second edition of our efforts to understand and explain these two central concerns, and during this past decade or so awareness of the advantages of providing a variety of processes for seeking and securing civil justice has greatly increased. A steadily expanding number of jurisdictions have introduced reforms intended to put in place multiple processes for managing and resolving disputes, thereby giving disputants a greater degree of choice of process for pursuing their grievance. Negotiation, mediation, umpiring (including in modified forms), innovative hybrid methods and so on have become better understood and more widely relied on, not only within jurisdictions but also across geographical borders so that, for example, the European Union now actively encourages the use and recognition of 'alternative' modes of dispute resolution. Indeed, the meaning of the 'A' in the acronym for 'Alternative Dispute Resolution' namely, 'ADR', is now perhaps better understood to mean 'Appropriate', so that many commentators now also speak of 'Appropriate Dispute Resolution', or simply 'processual pluralism'. Moreover, ideas significantly encouraged by ADR and civil justice reform have seeped into neighbouring legal fields perhaps most noticeably in areas of restorative criminal justice and 'Truth and Reconciliation'.

It is therefore even more important than ever for students of law to engage with the developing theoretical and practical field of dispute processing, including in particular ADR. Moreover, we take the view that enhancing the understanding of, and sharpening the skills used in, such processes as negotiation and mediation is also invaluable in enhancing our personal capacity to relate to each other and to solve problems better, so that it is also important for students of other disciplines to appreciate the value of ADR. We have learned from our students that role plays in class help all sorts of student to grasp these benefits more effectively, and some role plays we use in our teaching are therefore included in an Appendix to this book for the first time. Students have also told us that they enjoy reading the extracted materials which we provided in quite considerable number in earlier editions, allowing the commentators to 'speak for themselves'. However, the ever-growing availability of material online has encouraged us to reduce such materials so as to create space to broaden the scope of the book and thereby cover important new developments in the rapidly evolving field of dispute resolution.

These developments are taking place not only because both the practice of dispute resolution and the theorising about disputes and their management are continuing to evolve and to be diffused but also because the context in which the field has emerged is changing and encourages new responses. The international economy (coincidentally) suffered a significant downturn several years after the publication of the last edition, generating among many other things demands for better ways to handle financial disputes involving aggrieved small investors, as well as leaving many people more impoverished. The world of legal services is shifting, becoming more globalised on the one hand, and suffering from reductions in legal aid, governmental intolerance of lawyers' dissenting voices in many parts of the globe and other difficulties on the other. The use of violence in its many forms, including terrorism, as a way of resolving differences at various levels, appears to be strengthening rather than abating. Environmental degradation, ethnic tensions, gender inequalities and injustices, the difficulties of containing infectious disease, the growth of transnational organised crime, and the abuse of human rights seem to be more serious than they were a decade ago. The search for solutions to such problems should include a willingness to learn from dispute resolution discourse and practice as explicated in, for example, this book.

Transformations in the Common Law World

Everywhere, there are disagreements between neighbours, family members, affines, colleagues and others. The manner in which quarrel situations are characterised, and the ways in which the particular modes of response are regarded, vary from society to society – indeed, also from group to group within any given society. The nature of disputes, the appropriate responses to disputing situations, and the remedies considered proper are inevitably informed by fundamental social values and even cultural identity. This is the starting point for the examination of dispute processes provided in this book, which also locates current enthusiasms for 'alternative' modes of resolving disputes – especially those found in the United States and other parts of the Anglo-American common law world – in a wider comparative framework.

Forty years ago we could have said with reasonable confidence, in the common law world, what the principal institutions of public disputing 'were'. Over a long period, judges and lawyers had progressively become central, well-defined agents of public dispute management. The former held out the beautiful promise of an authoritative third-party decision; the latter, as both advisers and champions, presented themselves as essential companions along the arduous route of litigation.[1] With the increasing dominance of courts in an evolving public sphere as the nation state solidified, and the parallel emergence of lawyers as a specialised service profession, other institutionalised forms of disputing had receded in importance. For example, ordeals and duelling had ceased to be a recognised part of disputing cultures in the West. Mediation, too, had been elbowed aside and hidden in the background,[2] even if it was always 'there' as an irreducible element of any context in which more than two agents are involved.[3]

We should nonetheless be cautious as to how we present this picture of 'formal justice'. First, it is easy to exaggerate the extent to which a discrete 'public' sphere, characterised by a distinctive rationality and actively shaping a subordinate 'private' sphere, had ever historically evolved.[4] In this respect, we need to recall that the relationship of the courts to government in common law jurisdictions has always been a distinctive and ambivalent one. In England, for example, there is not now, and never has been, a career judiciary. In recent times, the higher ranks of the judges have been recruited exclusively from the legal profession, with appointment representing the ultimate career stage of the successful lawyer. While elaborate ritual, including the conferment of knighthood in the case of the higher judiciary, marks the transition from barrister to judge, and some formal distance is subsequently maintained between judges and former colleagues, judges remain socially very much part of the professional group from which they emerge. They will be 'Benchers' of their Inns and remain part of long-established networks of information exchange and support, including those centred on the chambers in which they formerly practised as advocates. These networks cross generations, beginning

---

[1] Max Weber recognised an extraordinary degree of reliance upon the legal profession for everyday matters in the common law world, when he noted the English layman's propensity to relate to the law 'by retaining once and for all a solicitor as his legal father confessor for all contingencies of life' (Weber, [1917] 1978: 891).

[2] For the way this transformation progressed in early modern France, see Castan (1983).

[3] See the seminal discussion of the 'triad' in Simmel ([1908] trans. 1950) 138–44 and 145–69. See also Simmel 'The Quantitative Conditioning of the Group' ([1908] trans. 2009a: 53–128).

[4] This point can perhaps be made particularly strongly in relation to Habermas' 'system'/ 'lifeworld' opposition (Habermas, 1981).

in the great 'public' schools, continuing in the older universities and subsequently in the London clubs (of which the Inns of Court are today in some
senses a variant).[5] So the courts are perhaps just as accurately seen as the apex
of the legal profession as they are a specialised branch of government.

A second caution must concern the manner in which civil courts have
historically been employed, notably the use made of their procedural arena by
lawyers. Until the 1970s the courts on the whole conceived their role quite
narrowly, as one of providing trial and judgment. Pre-trial interventions
were largely devoted to making sure the landscape did not change too much
before trial, otherwise leaving the parties to proceed at their own pace. But
while this narrow approach that common law judges traditionally took to their
role may appear to draw a clear line between solutions achieved through
negotiated agreement and authoritative third-party determination, this concealed something that had for generations gone on beneath the surface.
Lawyers, conceptualising virtually their entire role in dispute management
as 'litigation', had long used the framework provided by civil procedure as
the primary arena for their attempts to 'settle', so that the process of dispute
resolution in effect became one of 'litigotiation'.[6] It is a common place that
in English and other common law civil jurisdictions only a tiny proportion of
proceedings commenced ever reach trial, let alone judgment. So, through this
clandestine use of civil process as an arena for negotiations, two apparently
different modes of decision-making had long shared a single procedural route
(one historically devised for the safe achievement of judgment). Some elements
of this picture were closely attended to in legal scholarship. The principal
form of research in the growing number of university law schools consisted
of commentary upon the decisions of superior courts.[7] Other areas, including
the greater part of lawyers' contentious work – the out-of-court management of
dispute processes – were virtually uncharted.[8]

At the beginning of the second half of the twentieth century this distinctive
culture of public disputing, under which courts treated their role as the
delivery of judgment while a dominant legal profession used litigation as
a vehicle for strategies of late settlement, appeared securely entrenched.
Indeed, the growing state provision of welfare and a steady increase in rights
consciousness further encouraged reliance on litigation and the courts. But
during the last three decades, the certainties represented in this apparently
well-established universe were swept away right across the common law world.

---

[5] The pattern of 'network' recruitment also gives rise to problems of gender and ethnic under-
representation in both the judiciary and the bar. The most sustained efforts to broaden access are
to be found in the decision to allow solicitors to represent clients as advocates in the High Court,
and perhaps to serve as judges. See Griffith (1997) for an exploration of the social provenance of
the judiciary.
[6] See Galanter (1984).
[7] See Murphy and Roberts (1987).
[8] Note some important exceptions: Johnstone (1967); Abel-Smith and Stevens (1967).

Over that relatively brief period, the known identities of the 'court' and the 'lawyer' were placed in question and the 'mediator' re-emerged as a major, if ill-defined, figure. Central strands of this transformation to an overt 'culture of settlement' have been advanced, as noted above, under the fugitive *leitmotiv* of Alternative Dispute Resolution, with its universal acronym, 'ADR'.[9]

Characterising this new world and identifying the forces that have shaped it is not altogether straightforward even if at the heart of it lies a burgeoning culture and ideology of 'settlement' across the whole spectrum of dispute institutions.[10] It could almost be said that, in ideological terms, there has been a reversal of priorities as between two foundational processes, 'judgment' and 'agreement'. Of these two, the first – linked to the potent symbol of the Blind Goddess – long represented the *beau idéal* of public justice. The second, although represented in the powerful and beautiful image of the handshake, never enjoyed ideological parity and was seldom even articulated as an objective of public justice.

In England and Wales, recognition by the legal professions that the sponsorship of settlement was an explicit, official objective of the public justice system came only in the 1990s. Statements of this aspiration appear in the Heilbron/Hodge Report of 1993[11] and then in the Interim and Final versions of the 'Woolf' Report, followed by the introduction in 1999 of new 'CPR' or Civil Procedure Rules.[12] In the handling of civil cases, judicial 'case management' has become prescribed and its overall purpose identified as encouraging settlement of disputes at the earliest appropriate stage, and, where trial is unavoidable, to ensure that cases proceed promptly to a final hearing (of limited duration). Thus, 'settlement' is presented as the primary objective of the courts, with adjudication relegated to an auxiliary, fall-back position. So 'settlement' itself becomes the preferred route to civil justice – an astonishing reversal.[13] Continuing evolution of the civil justice system now includes

---

[9] The phrase 'alternative dispute resolution' creeps into general use in the North American literature in the years around 1980, having perhaps been used first by Sander (1976).

[10] 'Settlement' is used here in the general sense of the search for negotiated, consensual agreement as opposed to resort to a third-party decision. The approach to settlement seeking found in practice may bear little relation to the foundational idea of consensual decision-making through a bilateral exchange. While the rhetoric of voluntary agreement is retained, settlement in the lawyer's sense can well be, perhaps is typically, the culmination of a bruising process, characterised by secrecy and suspicion, in which one party's representatives have successfully wasted the other to the point at which the latter decides reluctantly, perhaps facing the inevitable, that she or he has got to give up.

[11] *Civil Justice on Trial: The Case for Change* (London: Justice 1993).

[12] *Interim Report to the Lord Chancellor on the Civil Justice System in England and Wales* (London: Lord Chancellor's Department, 1995), and *Access to Justice: Final Report to the Lord Chancellor on the Civil Justice System of England and Wales* (1996) HMSO, London. The Civil Procedure Rules are available at www.legislation.gov.uk/uksi/1998/3132/contents/made, accessed 3 December 2019.

[13] Lord Woolf has also encouraged the use of settlement in resolving administrative disputes that come before the courts in England and Wales, although this possibility was not taken up in his

a projected move to extensive reliance on online dispute resolution (ODR) (Briggs, LJ, 2016).

This shifting balance between the ideologies of 'command' and 'joint decision-making' has been reflected in institutional terms through three closely linked developments. The first of these can be loosely described as the arrival of the 'new professionals' in dispute resolution. In most common law jurisdictions, specialist groups have emerged over the last three decades, in both the not-for-profit and the private sectors, offering facilitatory help with joint decision-making. The members of these groups, who generally identify themselves as 'mediators', thus provide services that compete only indirectly with lawyers.

A second strand of these developments has been represented in parallel, more or less contemporaneous initiatives within the courts to move beyond adjudicative roles to sponsorship of settlement. These initiatives, visible earliest in North America, have been driven by contradictory imperatives: both the attribution of a primary value to party decision-making and a more general ambition towards 'case management'.

reports on the state of civil justice (1995; 1996). In several leading judgments, Lord Woolf declared in robust language that the emphasis on ADR and other reforms introduced by the 1998 Civil Procedure Rules should also govern administrative cases. Indeed, in the Cowl case (*Cowl v Plymouth City Council* [2001] EWCA Civ 1935), which concerned an effort by local residents of a residential care home to secure a judicial review of a decision by the local government to close down their care home, he stated: 'the importance of this appeal is that it illustrates that, even in disputes between public authorities and the members of the public for whom they are responsible, insufficient attention is paid to the paramount importance of avoiding litigation whenever this is possible. Particularly in the case of these disputes both sides must by now be acutely conscious of the contribution alternative dispute resolution can make to resolving disputes in a manner which both meets the needs of the parties and the public and saves time, expense and stress.' And: 'The appeal also demonstrates that courts should scrutinise extremely carefully applications for judicial review in the case of applications of the class with which this appeal is concerned. The courts should then make appropriate use of their ample powers under the CPR to ensure that the parties try to resolve the dispute with the minimum involvement of the courts. The legal aid authorities should cooperate in support of this approach.' However, this policy is not one that has found widespread support among senior members of the judiciary. The then Lord Chancellor declared in 1999 that there are natural limits to the role of mediation in public law cases: 'Some unstinting admirers of ADR assert that all disputes are suitable for ADR, and can benefit from it. I doubt that such unlimited enthusiasm does much to help promote wider use of ADR in the long run. Courts have a vital – indispensable – part to play in the resolution of many categories of dispute. It is, at best, naïve to claim that mediation and its alternatives can adequately equate to this role ... consider the issues of cases which set the rights of the individual against those of the State ... this is an extremely sensitive area, which must be approached with extreme care. I think the use of ADR in administrative cases is of necessity limited' (Irvine, 1999). It might be added here that the development in the late twentieth century of the 'regulatory state' – involving a process of privatisation, contracting out and supervision by a regulator of important areas of the economy – in the hope of smaller government but enhanced protection for consumers and others, has also had an impact on administrative dispute resolution, perhaps most notably through the development of a policy emphasis on greater use of tribunals and a reduced reliance on the administrative courts: see Scott (2010: 26); Rawlings (2010: 302).

Yet a third strand has subsequently become visible in responsive, defensive movements of recovery on the part of the lawyers. The arrival of the new professionals in dispute resolution, and the growing readiness of the courts to become involved in settlement processes, combined to encourage lawyers to re-examine their own practices. This process of re-examination has led lawyers both to move beyond advisory and representative roles towards non-aligned interventions, and to develop new specialist techniques in aid of their settlement strategies.

While the new professionals initially promoted mediation as promising a 'third way' between external, hierarchically imposed decisions and representation by legal specialists, clear boundaries between these three strands of development did not last long. The boundaries were blurred, first, through the new professionals being drawn into association with public justice through court-sponsored mediation schemes and, second, through the incorporation of 'mediation' in the evolving practice of lawyers.

The heterogeneous nature of these practice developments has not prevented each of these strands laying claim to, and coming to be associated with, the shared label of 'Alternative Dispute Resolution' (ADR). As noted above, this term seems to have been used first by Professor Frank Sander in a paper to the Pound Conference in 1976 (Sander, 1976), a meeting largely attended by lawyers and judges, explicitly concerned with renovating court processes. So ADR cannot be seen as a label only associated with the movement of escape and resistance from lawyers and the courts. ADR in a narrow sense originated very much as something lawyers decided to do and judges to participate in and encourage. Indeed, the identification of courts as sites and sponsors of ADR processes was powerfully expressed in the notion of a 'multi-door' courthouse – a key symbol of the new approach to civil justice that is 'ADR', and one that also emerged from Frank Sander's contributions to the Pound Conference – reflecting the former dominance of courts in the common law world as *the* institutions of dispute resolution.[14]

The complex, interwoven nature of these developments – the routinisation or institutionalisation of the 'charismatic' messages of ADR – is clearly reflected in contemporary scholarship around dispute processes. The considerable body of writing now found under the label of 'alternative dispute resolution' – and the university courses which are important consumers of this discourse – has been largely produced by lawyers. So this writing must by no means be read as a literature 'just' about alternatives to lawyers and courts. Indeed, it would not be an exaggeration to say that the literature of ADR has come to reside to a substantial extent within the discourse of law. Alongside this literature is a struggle between different professionals to associate themselves with an emergent image supposedly attractive to client groups,

---

[14] And see Palmer (2014a) on the impact of the 'multi-door courthouse' ideal in encouraging processes of institutionalisation of ADR, an issue further discussed in Chapter 13.

with lawyers seeking both to resist but also to incorporate ADR into their practice. ADR remains significantly relocated close to legal norms, institutions and actors.

Civilian Parallels

When we turn to civilian jurisdictions, the major themes of processual transformation that we have noted here are all present: the re-emergence of institutionalised mediation, procedural reform of public justice systems and consequent accommodations within the legal professions. But the emergent picture is very different, for two linked reasons. First, in continental jurisdictions the common law culture of using civil process as an arena for strategies of late settlement was never replicated. Second, the late twentieth-century shift in the common law courts towards a managerial approach did not need to take place.

The continental judicial apparatus, inherently more bureaucratic and hierarchical than that found in common law systems, has traditionally given judges a much more active role to play in litigation so that, for example, 'delegation of any procedural step to outsiders is inappropriate or even repugnant. Private procedural enterprise is . . . almost an oxymoron in the lexicon of hierarchical authority' (Damaška, 1986: 56). In preparatory proceedings, judges of lower standing are charged with collecting factual material and preparing it as written evidence for their superiors. The evidence thus gathered and presented forms the basis for the written case file that is developed through a series of stages that culminates in the final public proceeding, the trial. The central position of the judge – or, better, the hierarchy of judges – dealing with a civil case gives civil litigation a different processual shape (Markesinis, 1990), one which has not generated the same pressure for reform experienced in common law jurisdictions.

Nevertheless, the judiciary in civilian systems has not necessarily been expected to give priority to adjudication in its handling of a civil case. For example, the courts in Germany which have for some time been bound by the Code of Civil Procedure to 'promote at every stage of the legal procedure a consensual settlement', are encouraged by practice-related writings to adopt a 'peace-making function' and are pressured by heavy caseloads to engage in settlement activities (Röhl, 1983: 2–3). Moreover, since the early 1960s there have been developments in Germany to promote informalism in some of the areas of social life that in common law jurisdictions have also been considered appropriate for ADR mechanisms. In particular, there have been operating for some forty years extra-judicial 'conciliation boards', designed to process disputes between consumers and producers, professionals and their clients, and so on (Eidemann and Plett, 1991). In France, too, efforts have been made to adopt ADR mechanisms to enhance the machinery of civil justice. Indeed, as long ago as the French Revolution the use of a *juge de paix* as a mediator was made obligatory for many kinds of civil disputes, and although this was not felt to be a particularly helpful device, it was not abandoned until 1975. For the resolution of certain kinds of administrative disputes, the French introduced in 1973 the *Médiateur de la République*, an ombudsperson system designed to deal with complaints raised by citizens against public bodies. In addition, in some areas of France, the mayor appoints a 'district mediator' in order better to deal with complaints against local administration. Moreover, reformed civil procedure law has encouraged judicial mediation of civil disputes. Labour and family disputes appear to be the most commonly mediated types of disagreement.[15]

Arguably, the developments towards ADR in the civilian world have largely taken place in part as a result of a diffused inspiration from the ADR movement in the Anglo-American common law world. In civilian jurisdictions in Europe, academic writings on the nature of new ADR approaches to civil justice being introduced in the common law world appear to have been an important catalyst for a growing recognition that ADR is a viable and valuable alternative to litigation and adjudication. As a result, in Germany for example, in the late 1990s legal practitioners began to develop enthusiasms, 'although current litigation reforms are heavily focused on reducing court waiting lists through court related mediation schemes' (Alexander, 2002: 110). In addition, in 2008, the European Directive on Mediation (2008/52/EC)[16] put in place a common framework for cross-border mediation within the European Union, and in so doing stimulated the wider acceptance of mediation in member states, especially as they were required to implement the Directive by May 2011. As a result, many member states with civilian legal traditions which had hitherto not seen a significant expansion of ADR processes took the opportunity to encourage appreciation of the value of providing a greater range of dispute resolution possibilities, especially more use of mediation. Other states, such as Germany and France, have gone further and introduced new laws and regulations on mediation, going well beyond the basic requirements of the Directive itself.[17]

---

[15] The existence and potential for informalism in the civil justice systems of jurisdictions within the civilian tradition was stressed in the essay by Mauro Cappelletti identifying the rise of ADR as a third wave – after legal aid reforms and court focused reform ranging from small claims courts to class actions – in the 'Access to Justice' movement: 'whereas – in the last two centuries or so – Western civilisations have glorified the ideal of fighting for one's rights (Jehring's famous Kampf um's Recht), we should recognise that in certain areas a different approach – one that I used to call "co-existential justice" – might be preferable and better able to assure access to justice' (1993: 287).

[16] Directive 2008/52/EC of the European Parliament and of the Council of 21 May 2008 on certain aspects of mediation in civil and commercial matters. Available at: http://eur-lex.europa.eu/legal-content/en/ALL/?uri=CELEX%3A32008L0052, accessed 3 December 2019.

[17] See, generally, Hopt and Steffek (2013). For Germany, see Tochtermann (2013), and for France, see Deckert (2013).

Elsewhere in the world, local legal cultures which have 'modernised' their legal systems at least in part by a process of diffusion and adaptation of 'western law' have not necessarily cast aside traditional legal culture's emphasis on mediation and other forms of extra-judicial dispute resolution in their efforts at refurbishing civil justice. Thus, for example, in the case of China, many of the efforts at legal system reform have since the late nineteenth century been focused on transplanting into China laws and institutions from, initially the civil law tradition and then the socialist branch of the civil law tradition (Palmer, 2009). But this has not in itself significantly reduced a long-standing emphasis on the use of negotiation and mediation as preferred forms of dispute resolution and transitional exchanges. Indeed, in the case of China the last decade or so has seen an extraordinary re-emphasis on mediation not only in community dispute resolution processes and other extra-judicial systems but also in the manner in which courts handle cases and official agencies deal with complaints (Fu and Palmer, 2017). The general policy has been to encourage reliance on mediation in dispute decision-making in order to assist in the promotion of a more harmonious society, and to ensure greater social and political stability in a period of rapid economic change.

The Comparative Scene

These transformations in the practice of public dispute management – in particular in the common law world as noted above – coincided with a moment when legal scholarship was both becoming much more sensitive to the social sciences and taking on a broader comparative view. This growing sensitivity was signalled in the language through which some academic lawyers, and a few legal practitioners, began to talk about conflict. In the course of self-conscious attempts by lawyers to theorise disputes, the terms of conversation shifted from 'cases', 'litigation' and 'judges', to 'disputes', 'dispute processes' and 'interveners' (see Abel, 1973). This shift at the same time involved a growing familiarity with the ethnography of dispute processes to which leading Anglo-American social anthropologists contributed in the years following the Second World War (Gluckman, 1955; Bohannan, 1957; Turner, 1957; Gibbs, 1963; Gulliver, 1963; 1971). This exposure of lawyers to other cultures led sometimes to explicit 'borrowing' in the formulation of projects of domestic reform (Danzig, 1973), but more generally growing comparative awareness prompted expansive reflection on 'complementary' and 'alternative' arrangements at home (see Sander, 1976). Central to this growing concern was a return of attention to the primary processes of negotiation and mediation. One of the most robust explorations of disputing in this field is Philip Gulliver's study *Disputes and Negotiations*, a processual analysis of negotiations fashioned from a wide variety of cross-cultural case studies. It highlights the sequences inherent in negotiation and mediation, the importance of the parties' views of the dispute resolution process, and shows that 'patterns of interactive behaviour in negotiations are essentially similar despite marked differences in interests, ideas, values, rules, and assumptions among negotiators in different societies' (1979: xv).

Legal Reform Initiatives, the Role of ADR and Normative Pluralism

Within the common law world, a process of diffusion of the emerging experience of North America with ADR resulted in important procedural reforms in many jurisdictions, sometimes directly, sometimes more indirectly by means of the reforms introduced in England and Wales as a result of the recommendations of Lord Woolf (1996).[18] We have noted too that the developments towards ADR in the civilian world were significantly encouraged by a diffused inspiration from the ADR movement in the Anglo-American common law world.

Elsewhere, too, ADR is slowly being incorporated into legal reform projects – including by means of international assistance for developing countries. But, somewhat paradoxically, the extent of this incorporation has been limited by conventional approaches to legal development. International legal assistance programmes continue to focus primarily on improving courts and introducing legal codes in the recipient countries – an enthusiasm for building up formal legal institutions that rests uncomfortably with the benefits that ADR is perceived to bring in the donor states themselves. So, while in the legal systems of North America and Europe complaints and reforms have focused on the problems generated by a perceived flood of litigation, the social divisiveness of litigation and court proceedings, and the rapacious activities of self-interested lawyers – the predators and parasites of modern society, as Galanter (1994) has suggested the public view them – the foundations of these elements are concurrently promoted in legal development programmes. At the same time, there is a certain irony – indeed an incongruity – in teaching contemporary forms of ADR to the very societies whose own traditions of community-based, extra-judicial dispute resolution have served as a key inspiration for the development of alternatives to conventional civil process in the Anglo-American common law world. It was, for example, after a visit to a local Chinese community mediation committee in Shanghai during an official visit to China in 1981,[19] that Chief Justice Warren Burger advised the legal professions in the United States to consider adopting ADR-type reforms for enhancing access to civil justice in the United States (1982).

A further complication is that even within common law jurisdictions committed to ADR-type reforms, increasing social heterogeneity, often associated with the development of migrant diasporic communities, has encouraged

---

[18] As for example in the case of Hong Kong, where the Chief Justice's Working Party on Civil Justice Reform (2001) advised that the Woolf reforms were an appropriate template.

[19] See, for example, Ge Jun (1996).

a demand for state recognition of dispute resolution methods grounded in the entrenched cultures of the migrant communities, sometimes creating potential conflicts with the laws of the host state.[20] With increasing ethnic and cultural complexity, the extent to which a minority culture should be allowed to regulate its affairs – especially disputes – within the community may become an acute issue. To what extent should the state recognise and even enforce minority community decisions made in terms of the values of the minority culture rather than the norms of state law? There are several reasons why this may be problematic. For one thing, the family may well be at the heart of this issue, as it embodies the cultural (and perhaps also religious) identity of the minority and yet family life is also an area of society in which the host state is likely to have a strong public policy interest. For another, the norms of the minority culture may be seen as infused with unacceptably discriminating values, including use of violence, especially in relation to women and children.

The Nature and Scope of this Book

These various developments within and surrounding civil justice reveal a range of contradictory, but entangled, agendas and projects. So where to go, when 'ADR' itself turns out to be a fugitive label, attached to a disparate group of evolving practices? It seems to us that the place to begin is with a close look at three primary processes – negotiation, mediation and umpiring. A sociologically informed understanding of these processes appears indispensable to forming a clearer view of the complex, culturally specific developments in different jurisdictions. Chapters 5, 6 and 7, built around these foundational processes, form the core of this book. The approach here thus takes us away from an exclusive concern with what lawyers and judges do in and around the trial, and from the analysis of legal doctrine – subjects which have traditionally preoccupied law schools in the common law world.

So, this book offers a wide-ranging examination of the primary processes of dispute resolution, how a variety of parties and complexities of issues (arising out of such characteristics as multiplicity of problems and ties between disputants, financially complicated transactions, civil rights, environmental welfare or other public policy concerns, a need for scientific or technological evidence, multiple causation and responsibility, matters of social and cultural identity, and so on) may complicate dispute resolution efforts, and how – in the common law civil justice reforms of recent years in particular – syncretic and innovative processual forms are created and elaborated by drawing upon coalescing key dimensions of several of the primary forms.

As we stressed in both the first and second editions of this book, we try to secure a balance between theory and practice of dispute resolution, and while

---

[20] See, for example, Chotalia (2006).

the book does not offer skills training per se it is hoped that those studying it will nevertheless gain insights that will help them to be more skilful and effective in managing disputes. A negotiator or mediator who understands the nature of dispute resolution decision-making processes will achieve better outcomes than those who lack them.

The book also offers a non-jurisdiction specific examination of what we consider to be processual forms of dispute resolution found in many societies around the world. As ADR has developed primarily in the common law world as a movement and practice of civil justice reform, we tend to draw more on the recent experiences of the common law world. However, we also try to contextualise these developments in a broader examination, which includes the idea that the ADR movement should be looked at in the larger context of 'informal justice' ideals, and that wider perspective draws upon the authors' own empirical research into African and Chinese societies respectively and their interest in comparative legal studies.[21] Encouraged by this broader and contextualising perspective, we examine in some detail areas of disputing that are not ordinarily considered in depth by conventional ADR texts, including the emergence of disputes, the use of force (including, for example, domestic violence) and avoidance in response to emerging disagreements, the rapid diffusion of the ombuds, the relationship between ADR and notions and practices of 'ODR' (Online Dispute Resolution) and processes of institutionalisation. This perspective also encourages us to take into account the importance of the disputants' perspective, and the important fact that in many societies around the world recourse to dispute resolution processes outside courts is the norm, and reliance on litigation and adjudication is in a real sense the 'alternative'.

The principal theoretical underpinnings for this study, as we have suggested above, are to be found in the seminal work of Philip Gulliver on negotiation (and, by extension, mediation) and joint decision-making. This approach – sometimes explicitly, sometimes implicitly – is drawn upon in mediation training programmes around the world, especially those in which facilitative mediation (see Chapter 7) is encouraged. The Gulliver understanding of the negotiation process is one which sees negotiation as the exchange of information and learning, compromise and co-ordination, so that joint decisions are reached. This, in turn, involves two component processes, one cyclical and the other developmental. The cyclical process is one of repeated exchange of information between the parties, evaluation of such information, and a resulting adjustment of expectations and preferences which continue throughout the unfolding phases of dispute resolution. The second process is developmental, consisting of a series of stages in which the parties narrow their differences in a manner that is sometimes antagonistic sometimes more

---

[21] See, for example, Comaroff and Roberts (1986); Roberts, Simon (2013); Palmer (2014a); 2017; Fu and Palmer (2017).

conciliatory to the point where they reach agreement and, possibly, implement it. Of course, as Gulliver acknowledges, power, norms (legal and otherwise) and the social and cultural contexts of the negotiations may well also impact on these two processes: 'negotiations do not occur in a socio-political vacuum. They are intricately enmeshed in ongoing, wider social processes that constitute their essential environment and to which negotiations themselves often contribute and often modify' (Gulliver, 1988: 249). In addition, we should not assume 'finality and completeness. Outcomes vary tremendously in their degree of settlement and, in any case, it is generally impossible to know this until some time after the negotiations are over' (Gulliver, 1979: 78–9). The 'resolution' of the instant dispute does not necessarily mean that the dance of disagreement has come to an end.

In looking more specifically at the contents of the book, we prepare the way for understanding the primary processes and the emergence of ADR in Chapter 2, which sketches in the cultural and historical background to contemporary institutional change. Chapter 3 then introduces important debates around 'informal justice' and the critiques of 'settlement' that have accompanied the rise of the ADR movement. Here a notable feature of the landscape we are examining has been the quality and intensity of the critiques that some seemingly common-sense prescriptions and practice initiatives have evoked. Chapter 4 looks at the nature of disputes, and at how disputes are created, and then draws in the typology of dispute processes that informs the subsequent shape of the book. In Chapter 5 we further explore the nature of disputes and look at the two ends of the spectrum of possible societal responses to disputes, namely, avoidance on the one hand and use of force on the other (giving particular attention to the social problem of domestic violence), and include analysis of the ideologies (of harmony, of violence) that often surround each of these two responses when they are given official blessing.

In Chapters 6 and 7 we turn to the primary processes of negotiation and mediation. Bringing these to the centre of the stage, we are deliberately concerned to avoid the law school's historic preoccupation with what judges and lawyers do at and around the trial. That preoccupation almost inevitably marginalised the activities of the parties themselves – most notably, those predominantly bilateral processes through which decisions were and still are typically reached at stages before resort to legal specialists. Beginning with negotiation underlines the fact that this mode of decision-making is common to everyday life and to the instance of dispute, providing the site of transition between them. At the same time, concentration on roles involving authoritative determination, on the one hand, and partisan advisory and representative activity, on the other, has left little room for a serious examination of the impartial, facilitatory interventions of the mediator.[22]

---

[22] For English law students – and for many of those elsewhere in the common law and civilian worlds – this approach involves a radical break from the universe of understanding within

With Chapter 8, on umpiring processes, we are inevitably brought back to the familiar terrain of superior court litigation and its formal goal of judicial determination. But we are concerned to locate these in a wider context of third-party decision-making as a whole. Chapter 9 explores the nature and significance of arbitration, a private form of umpiring concerned primarily though not exclusively with commercial disputes. Then, in Chapter 10, we consider the very extensive hybridisation of processes that has accompanied contemporary procedural change. This concern continues in Chapter 11, which looks at the ever-expanding importance of the ombuds. Chapter 12 offers an examination of ODR, a development that owes much to the development of online shopping, but has now come knocking on the door of the courts, and also offers potential to transform the very nature of these institutions.

Chapter 13 deals with the broad pattern of institutionalisation of the ADR movement over the past three decades, and extends our consideration of some of the developments examined in Chapter 10 on hybridisation of process to explore related issues such as the impact of the notion of the 'multi-door courthouse'. For comparative purposes, the changes taking place in China are briefly explored.

We conclude, in Chapter 14, with a tentative look at the possible continuing evolution of alternative dispute resolution, speculate on its implications for enhancing access to justice, and in the light of the evidence presented in the preceding chapters consider the extent to which criticisms levelled against the processes of ADR in the 1980s and 1990s remain valid today.

which dispute processes have been traditionally located. Our own students have repeatedly drawn our attention to the need for a different approach. The case for a change in emphasis in North American legal education was forcefully expressed by Derek Bok in his seminal essay, 'A Flawed System of Law and Practice Training' (1983). See also Menkel-Meadow's examination of the main arguments in favour of changing understandings in her robust and insightful analysis of the development of ADR (2003). An excellent panoramic analysis of the field, with an emphasis on North America, is to be found in Menkel-Meadow, Love, Schneider and Moffitt (2019).

2

Cultures of Decision-making: Precursors to the Emergence of ADR

Introduction

In this chapter we begin by marking out, in broad schematic terms, the larger background to the emergence of ADR in the latter part of the twentieth century. This apparently abrupt shift towards what we have loosely identified as a 'culture of settlement' came at the end of a long period during which the lawyer and the judge had emerged as central figures in disputing. The entrenchment of institutions of formal justice, closely associated with the maturity of the nation state, resulted in other foundational institutional forms being marginalised and lost sight of. But these institutional forms, and the values associated with them, were always somewhere in the picture; and as Auerbach (1983), Abel (1982a; 1982b) and Nader (1986) have suggested, a panoramic view would show something of an episodic alternation between values of 'formalism' and 'informalism'. Some sense of this larger picture, inevitably casting doubt upon contemporary claims to radical innovation, provides a necessary context for understanding the contemporary transformation of disputing under the *leitmotiv* of Alternative Dispute Resolution.

While, as we shall see in Chapter 3, self-conscious efforts to 'find a better way' (Burger, 1982) of dealing with civil disputes have in part shaped the ADR movement, co-option by government, large business interests and expansive professional agendas are also important in the movement's emergence and growth. The largely unchallenged critiques of 'informal justice' appearing at the beginning of the 1980s deserve careful examination today.

Two other related themes, articulated across a range of societies, inform the ADR movement. The first holds that there is a necessary tension between formal law and justice. The second claims that disputing institutions are there to secure outcomes that go beyond providing remedies for the parties themselves. So, these institutions are there: to maintain social order; to avoid conflict; to restore harmony; to achieve equality and to express communal identity. As Auerbach has emphasised, the rejection of legal processes as an appropriate mode of decision-making in the context of disputes is often part of an attempt to develop or retain a sense of community: 'how to resolve conflict, inversely stated, is how (or whether) to preserve community'

(1983: 4). We argue here that this impulse may manifest itself in a variety of specific contexts – religious, political, territorial, ethnic and occupational seem to be the most important of these. These values often constitute a counter-tradition to legalism or what Santos has labelled the 'neoclassical model' of law (1982: 256).

Ideals of Informal Justice

A 'model' of informal justice invariably contains a number of identifiable core elements that are seen as superior to orthodox, formal justice. These include the development of processes and associated institutions that are:

- non-bureaucratic in structure and relatively undifferentiated from society, relying on small, local fora, which – unlike large legal bureaucracies – can get to grips with the social relationships of the parties;
- local in nature and, for example, rely on local rather than professional or official languages;
- accessible to ordinary people, and not dependent on the services of ('expensive') professionals;
- reliant on lay people as third-party interveners, perhaps with some – but not a great deal – of training, and who are preferably unpaid;
- outside the immediate scope of official law, and reliant instead on local standards of conduct and common-sense thinking;
- based on substantive and procedural 'rules' that are vague, unwritten, flexible and good common sense – so that 'the law' does not stand in the way of achieving substantive justice in the 'instant' case; and
- intent on promoting harmony between the parties and within local communities, in part because they get to the 'real' underlying cause of the problem(s), in part because they search for outcomes mutually acceptable to the parties rather than the strict application of legal rules and in part because they carry an ethic of treatment.

We would argue that there is in *every* legal system some line of thinking which manifests these principles of informalism to a certain extent. Even within our current legal practice, professional jokes may reflect such values, albeit in a negative manner – for example, 'any lawyer can achieve justice; it really takes a good litigator to achieve an injustice'.

In contrast, in centralised legal systems a dominant ideological strand typically stresses perceived values of formal justice, for dispute resolution through law and legal institutions. The values or elements that are, to a greater or lesser degree, given emphasis include:

- specialised bureaucratic mechanisms that are differentiated from society so that such mechanisms can make good, independent and technically correct decisions;

- professionals with relevant expert knowledge and the capacity to articulate and to enforce the law;
- an impartial, publicly available official law (typically, that of the state) that may be imposed on the parties, and which is interpreted in terms of the bounded discourses of law;
- clear, fair procedures, and as concerned with procedural justice as with substantive justice, because due process is a key element in the rule of law; and
- the authority of the state, with court able to compel the parties to accept that authority.

But, argue proponents of informalism, these ideals of formal justice may well come to act as a barrier to the provision of substantive justice. For example, with reference to adversarial proceedings:

> the effect of our exaggerated contentious procedure is to give the whole community a false notion of the purpose and end of law. If law is a mere game, neither the players who take part in it nor the public who witness it can be expected to yield to its spirit when their interests are served by eroding it. The courts, instituted to administer justice according to the law, are made agents or abettors of lawlessness (Pound, 1906: 406).

Thus, the growth of the modern ADR 'movement' by no means exhausts the history of the search for alternatives, and this growth is itself understood better in a broader historical context. If the time scale is expanded sufficiently then even in the common law world we may see that it is state-organised adjudication that is the real novelty – in England, for example, the Royal Courts only began functioning in the twelfth century. Moreover, any historical understanding should surely also encompass the experiences of dispute resolution mechanisms of more than northern Europe and North America.

The Establishment of Formal Justice

Since the arrival of political authority in the form of the state, the provision of dispute resolution mechanisms has been bound up with the ambition of those in power to govern. By and large, the preference of the state has been to provide processes and institutions that we would want to characterise as formal, with litigation and adjudication central to the state-sponsored system of civil justice. But, even as these formal systems of justice were being created, there were those who argued against them or who sought to modify their full rigour, or who simply looked for other ways to solve their differences.

In pre-Imperial China, for example, there was by the third century BC, if not before, already an important ideology of legal formalism and strong state power. This ideology, known as 'Legalism' (*Fajia*), arose in part as a reaction to Confucian thinking on disputes and their treatment – thinking which emphasised the importance of harmony, moral leadership, education and self-sacrifice. The emergence of Legalism thus resulted in a marked dichotomy in Chinese legal philosophy between 'Legalist' and 'Confucian' schools. This dichotomy has persisted, in modified form, through to the present day. The Legalists have persistently advocated a strong centralised state, operating with a comprehensive set of law codes, and a rigorously administered hierarchical system of courts designed to enforce the rules of Imperial statutory law. These rules should be unambiguous and comprehensible, and applicable with equal force to all subjects regardless of their social status. Those who break the law should be given appropriately stern punishment. Equipped with this philosophy, as well as a large and efficient army, the State of Qin unified China in 221 BC and installed itself as China's first dynasty. But the reign of the Qin was extremely authoritarian in nature and therefore short-lived, and Legalism was abandoned as the official state philosophy by the succeeding dynasty, the Han (206 BC–AD 220), in favour of Confucianism. This alternative body of thought remained the prevailing creed in Chinese society until the toppling of the Qing dynasty in the early years of the twentieth century.

The Confucianist approach to law and morality has been resolutely to maintain that a formal 'law-based' approach encourages parties to be adversarial, strategically pursuing their rights at the expense of substantive justice. Much better, therefore, for the state to ensure order and continuity in social life by means of a ruler whose personal conduct is so superior that his subjects would be inspired to emulate his virtuous example. Ordinary people would have no need for law, and when involved in a dispute the good subject would not stand on his or her rights but, rather, 'yield' so that lawsuits could be avoided. This avoidance of state-administered justice was also perceived by ordinary people to be appropriate for other reasons, and a distrust of litigation was expressed in a wide range of popular aphorisms: for example, 'let householders avoid litigation, for once you go to law there is nothing but trouble', or 'win your lawsuit, lose your money', or 'even an upright magistrate has difficulty in deciding family disputes', or 'nine [disputes] out of ten are settled by mediation' (van der Sprenkel, 1962: 135–6).

The origin of formal justice in the Roman polity is not fully documented (Stein, 1999: 3), but a measured view is that 'in very early times . . . it is likely that the Romans had recourse to ordeals or battle or oath taking as a means of settling disputes' (Stein, 1984: 27). Initially, the Roman state was a theocracy in which legal matters were put in the hands of a college of pontiffs serving as a judicial council, and where 'from the first a clear distinction was drawn between the procedure meant to secure the adjustment of private claims and the process by which penal pronouncements were made' (Greenidge, 1971: 8). Following the establishment of a Republic in the late sixth century BC, the Roman community showed considerable concern with maintaining social order and resolving disputes. The Law of the Twelve Tables reflected these concerns and attempted to demarcate the boundaries of self-help and other forms of unilateral force, and to stipulate the procedural requirements that a party had to meet in order to secure assistance from the state institutions for dispute settlement:

> in particular, the Twelve Tables dealt with the details of legal procedure, what a citizen could do to help himself without invoking a court and what he had to do to start court proceedings. In the early republic there were few state officials to help an aggrieved person get redress for injuries which he claimed to have suffered and he had to do a lot for himself to activate the legal machinery. In certain cases self-help was tolerated, since the community was not yet strong enough to eliminate it. The Twelve Tables show, however, a determination to institutionalize such cases and keep them within strict limits (Stein, 1999: 4).

The development of a state-controlled civil process continued, although it seems that up to the mid-second century AD if not beyond: 'the average Roman lawsuit ... was [still] one in which the plaintiff either commanded physical superiority over the defendant, or was at least a good match for him' (Kelly, 1966: 20).

In other important respects, too, the slowly emerging system of state justice did not fully displace 'alternative' forms. Instead, processes originating in pre-existing Italian society persisted; these included, in particular, the use of communal humiliation of an offending party by a stratagem known as *flagitatio*. Moreover, in the system of civil litigation that did develop, very considerable scope was still allowed for a 'culture' of settlement, as the observations of Kelly indicate:

> The ancient Italian custom of 'popular justice' ... seems to have been known and practised at least up to the end of the Republic, and very likely well into the Empire. ... In primitive Italian society the gaps [in the normal processes of law] were filled by the popular condemnation of a wrongdoer, which may originally have taken the form of mob justice and the forcible expulsion by flogging of the culprit from the community; later the forcible expulsion was replaced by a communal disgracing of the offender [known as *flagitatio*]. This communal disgracing took the form of an organized shouting of insulting words in the offender's presence ... with a view to compelling him to make good or compensate for some disgraceful act (most often the non-payment of a debt) ... Not altogether removed from this field of thought and behaviour is the permission accorded by the XII Tables to a person whose witness has failed to appear in court to go to the witness's house and shout ... in front of it ...

> The literary evidence seems to show that it was a living custom into the Empire. There is no doubt that it must reflect a state of affairs in which the processes of law were inadequate to ensure the righting of all wrongs ... [Moreover] In the system of classical Roman law, as in that of our own, the rules relating to the settlement or compromise of actions do not form a separate chapter. In both systems the subject, despite its enormous practical importance, lies more or less concealed within a structure of more general notions; in English

law, the doctrine of consideration; in Roman, the rules about formless pacts and stipulations. The words *transactio, transigere,* &c., with the meaning of settlement of an action, occur frequently in the writings of classical jurists, but it does not appear that the concept of *transactio* enjoyed any special treatment before the publication of Justinian's *Codex* and *Digest,* wherein respectively imperial constitutions and a number of juristic texts from the most miscellaneous sources are gathered into separate titles under the rubric *De transactionibus* ...

A question which requires some attention is that of the stages at which *transactio* was possible. It is clear, in the first place, that there was no obstacle to the conclusion of a settlement before the beginning of proceedings; ...

Even after the proceedings had been begun by the summoning of the defendant by the plaintiff (*in ius vocatio*) a settlement must still have been possible; ... it is certain that a settlement reached by the parties in the course of the proceedings before the praetor was valid, and indeed the praetor actively encouraged such a solution; it was to some extent his duty to induce the parties to compose their differences ...

Finally, in this connexion there is the question whether *transactio* was possible after a decision had been given by a *iudex* ... and there can be no doubt that the occasion to make such settlements arose commonly in the Roman world, as it does in our own (Kelly, 1966: 21–3, 132, 147, 148 and 150).

In England, the process of state-building began well in advance of the Norman conquest of 1066, and the new Anglo-Norman rulers continued to build up the authority of the English monarchy, a process leading, inter alia, to the establishment under Henry II in the second half of the twelfth century of a system of national courts with broad powers of original jurisdiction and operated in a bureaucratic manner by justices appointed by the king. The various kinds of royal court were administered in a unified style.

Each court was run and its judgments made by a relatively small number of justices. It held daily sessions, often during specific periods of the year (terms). The Common Bench and the King's Bench held daily sessions during the four law terms each year. The General Eyre held continuous daily sessions in the counties it visited but did not divide its work up by terms until the reign of Edward I and then only in the largest counties it visited. Assize justices held sessions only at three specified times of the year under legislation of 1285. Each court kept a written record of the business it transacted. The court normally only heard such civil litigation as it had been specifically authorised to hear, and the authorisation normally took the form of a royal writ (an 'original writ') addressed to the local sheriff, instructing him to summon the defendant to answer a specific plea in a specific court on a specific date ... and to 'return' the writ to the court where the plea was to be heard. Quasi-bureaucratic royal courts of this type were an innovation of the reign of Henry II and differ markedly from the type of court which had previously been the norm in England. In the older type of court judgements were normally made by a relatively large group of suitors whose obligation to perform this function was derived not from appointment by the king but from tenure of land in the area where the court exercised jurisdiction. Such courts normally only held sessions lasting for a day or less at more or less regular intervals. They did not keep any written record of their proceedings nor did they require any written authorisation from the king for hearing litigation (Brandt, 1997: 112).

Nevertheless, the bulk of civil litigation continued to be carried out in lower courts and 'most litigation initiated in these various lower courts was none the less determined there or settled out of court' (Brandt, 1997: 110).

Moreover, for some types of civil dispute, pre-existing institutions continued to flourish as the preferred specialised forum for settling differences between the parties. For example, the boroughs possessed their own courts in which the burgesses, the citizens of the borough, were able to bring suit. These courts did not exercise criminal jurisdiction, which was a matter for the king's authority, but they did become important sites for laws governing trade and commerce, for the boroughs were themselves centres of trading and commercial activity. The royal law dealt with such matters as real estate, as this was an area of regulation that concerned the landed aristocracy. In contrast, the borough law more firmly reflected the interests of the merchant, and its courts dealt with many disputes between merchants and artisans. As a result, borough courts were partly responsible for the development of commercial law, and their utility was such that they were able to resist the intrusions of the royal tribunals for many centuries. Indeed, the borough courts, which also helped to lay the foundations for the subsequent development of equitable procedures and remedies (Murray, 1961), were not the whole story, for in addition there were ad hoc disputing mechanisms in the great fairs that the boroughs often hosted. During these events it was customary for the borough court to be entirely or at least partly suspended in favour of the so-called 'Piepowder' Courts. These market fair courts were so-called by reference to the French term '*pieds poudrés*' or the 'dusty feet' of merchants travelling to the fair and the members of the court going about their dispute resolution business in the market. They are known to have existed from well before the Norman conquest of 1066 and were not formally abolished until the Administration of Justice Act 1977, although by the seventeenth century most of their powers had been shifted to the system of regular courts, largely as a result of urban development, more settled populations and the attendant growth of more organised trading systems.

> In these great fairs disputes would arise in the course of bargaining that would have to be settled before the wayfaring traders went their several ways, and temporary courts for this purpose have existed in England from the earliest times. In cases where the ordinary borough courts were not held during fair time, their place would be taken by these tribunals ... The fair courts have always been known in England as Courts of Piepowder (Cole, 1905: 377).

Cole's analysis of the functioning of these borough courts focuses on those found in Bristol, in its time one of the greatest trading centres in England.

By the fourteenth century another distinctive form of borough court had emerged, namely the court of the Tolzey, its name being derived from the old term used to designate the place where tolls, which played a significant role in early trading, were collected. The Tolzey was, as a result, something of a gathering place for merchants and therefore also a very convenient location for a commercial court. With urban growth and more established trading systems, it steadily grew in importance, absorbing a number of other foci of local courts, including the Piepowder courts. Abolished in 1971, a significant part of its effective decision-making was that the judge's decision was final – no appeals were allowed (Cole, 1905).

So, even a cursory examination of the emergence of the Royal Courts of Justice reveals a world in which many litigants, preferring the local knowledge and expertise of local dispute-settlement institutions, relied on these local institutions rather than the royal courts to handle their grievances, and even when invoking the system of royal justice to pursue their grievance, the parties were inclined to settle when they perceived settlement to be in their best interests.

A broadly similar pattern of pluralist socio-legal ordering emerged with the spread of European economic power and political authority in the nineteenth and early twentieth centuries, in many parts of Africa and Asia resulting in the subordination of local society to colonial rule and its new forms of government, economic relations and systems of law. A common pattern was for the colonial state not only to monopolise criminal prosecutions but also to introduce 'Western-style' civil justice for more important and larger disputes, and in which colonial settlers, traders, missionaries and others might have an interest. The focus here was on adjudication. For less significant civil disputes, and especially those involving the indigenous population that raised issues of 'customary' law – itself a product of local social ordering and colonial ideology – the colonial state allowed issues to be dealt with by more traditional-based dispute resolution processes, which often emphasised negotiation and mediation. And in the post-colonial situation, efforts to restore pre-colonial law and institutions have in many places been made not only in order to assist in the elimination of alien laws and processes introduced by the former colonial rulers but more recently also to try to deal with serious issues arising out of the collapse of political authority and the formal legal system in failed states such as Afghanistan and Rwanda.

Take, for example, the widespread use of the *gacaca* or local community courts in Rwanda following the bloody civil war of 1994 in order to handle the many cases involving alleged perpetrators of genocide. The formal criminal justice system lacked the capacity to handle the many problems, as there were more than 100,000 alleged culprits of murders, rape and torture and many of the judges who would have tried these defendants had themselves been murdered in the civil war. As a result, the Rwandan government adopted the traditional *gacaca* local court system of community justice – *gacaca* referring to the ideal of 'justice among the grass'. This system thus was intended to reduce the case load of the ordinary courts and speed up the handling of cases of the many persons who were being held in detention. The *gacaca* was and is primarily a local dispute resolution institution, with an ideal of members of the 'court' sitting on the grass together in order to listen to and consider the issues that come before them. The community justice ideals also include local healing regeneration of moral standards and ready access to justice. Confidence in the system is enhanced by its visibility, as respected community leaders solve on the *gacaca* and the proceedings may be observed by local residents (Sarkin, 2001: 157–9).

The Religious Impulse towards Informalism

The impulse to provide forms of dispute resolution that operate outside or alongside the legal system of the state is further manifested in a number of quite specific contexts in which emphasis is placed on the importance of dealing with trouble situations within the community, thereby avoiding the state and its legal institutions. Here the emphasis is typically placed on decision-making processes other than adjudication with its claims of certainty, legal rights and independence. One such context is the religious community, most obvious in the case of sectarian organisations that seek to establish and maintain a distinctive religious association that offers a moral order and social formation outside ordinary society, which is perceived to be deeply flawed and even corrupt. These alternative, often 'utopian', communities may be created by religious impulse alone, or encouraged by the experiences of migration and attendant ethnic discrimination. The alternative systems of dispute handling offered to members are thus one part of a more general withdrawal or separation from ordinary society. Community rules may even bar members from recourse to state courts, as in the case of Chinese lineages or clans – which existed, inter alia, as mechanisms for the perpetuation of the memory of the founding ancestor and the performance of ancestor worship: 'one who takes the case into court without submitting it to the clan organization, even if justice is on his side, should also be penalized for having forgotten that the other party who has wronged him is a fellow clan member and a descendant from the same origin' (Wang Liu, 1959: 157).

Examples abound, but some of the most persistent strains of informalism can be found in the Protestant sectarian tradition. In North America, for example, Auerbach has demonstrated that during the colonial period formal legal institutions played a relatively minor role in dispute settlement because the colonists were hostile to any external interference that challenged the religious and social values of the local communities. Courts and commercial arbitration[1] then came to play an increasing role in handling disputes as a

---

[1] We view arbitration not as an alternative but, rather, as a private form of umpiring and therefore processually very similar to adjudication. See Chapter 9.

result of increases in trade and commerce during the first part of the eighteenth century. But a fresh impetus towards alternatives was provided by the development of utopian communities in the first half of the nineteenth century – again, often inspired by religious ideals as in the case of the Shakers, the Mormons and so on. Auerbach argues that the 'counter tradition to legalism', in particular mediation, was, however, impossible to sustain in the face of the ever-growing pressures of greater economic and social integration, increasing immigration and secularisation (in particular, declining church membership). He points out that the first generation of New England colonial settlers consisted primarily of Protestant congregational communities based on covenants with God and with each other and in which Christian values of brotherly love were important. Having left England in order to escape what they saw as the problems of individual greed, social decline and the impure Anglican Church, they hoped to create a new society based on a 'perfectionist' communal vision of brotherly love. There exclusivist communities cherished the ideal of resolving their own differences and disliked the notion of lawyers being involved in the process of adjustment and reconciliation. Lawyers would, in their view, undermine the religious, communal and consensual ethos of the process of healing (Auerbach, 1983: 19–21).

But amongst some communities of believers, the religious impulse to informalism has persisted right through to the present day. In her important study of the Baptists of 'Hopewell', a county situated close to Atlanta, Georgia in the southern United States, Carol Greenhouse provides an insightful account of the continuing impact of religious belief on disputing behaviour in the mid-1980s. Her examination shows the importance of the Baptist belief that the 'saving power' of Christ is available to all in equal measure, and this egalitarianism restricts the overt expression of conflict. The specific basis for this restriction is that unexpected and untoward events are to be seen as opportunities for spiritual development rather than for an assertion of rights and interests or expressions of anger, because it is assumed Jesus' plans are made with everybody's interest taken into account. A verse from Romans is used to state the value succinctly: 'avenge not yourselves . . . I will repay, saith the Lord' (13: 19). So, to accept Jesus is to refuse to act on such negative feelings. And where there is nonetheless real potential for conflicts, within the group a range of verbal strategies is employed so as to avoid escalation of tensions – narratives and gossiping, joking, duelling with scripture, prayer, and so on. In tensions in relations with outsiders, however, such techniques have limited effectiveness as the parties do not share the same religious understandings. In such cases, Baptist believers are still encouraged to hold back, to yield, for by declining to allow overt disputing, they confirm their own beliefs and commitment to faith, and see themselves as bearing witness to the other party. Because such non-believers do not belong to the community of God, they have a potentially dangerous corruption influence and thus should be resisted. This commitment to harmonious relationships is not, it is acknowledged, easy. There is an ever-present temptation to pursue one's own interests in contemporary society, and responses to trouble situations are in danger of being self-interested. However, by not engaging in adversarial conduct, the Baptist believers reinforce their sense of community and their commitment to Christian values. At the same time, there are appropriate sanctions for those who nevertheless indulge in offensive conduct. Such persons are characterised as suffering from a spiritual defect, and their conduct is to be corrected by kind but firm advice, or by avoidance. And the incidents of tensions are not seen in terms of cases or rules, but of salvation – or, if conflict persists, by damnation (Greenhouse, 1989: 108–18).

The Political Impulse towards Informalism

The close association between the state and formal justice, and the tendency to domination of the system of formal justice by ruling classes, encourages those who reject the prevailing social order, and who wish to create a more just political community, either by withdrawal in whole or part from mainstream institutional life or by popular revolution, to create alternatives for the hand-ling of disputes.

There is, for example, the well-documented Philadelphian working-class organisation that developed in the late 1860s under the title 'Knights of Labour'. This was a kind of general trade union that aimed to move the American value system away from materialism in the direction of greater moral worth, as well as to improve the pay and conditions of its members. In the eyes of the leaders and many of the members of this organisation, the conventional court structure seemed weighted against working people, dealing out overly severe punishment in criminal cases and proving inaccessible in civil cases in which a working-class person was the plaintiff. An 'alternative' system of dispute resolution was established for members, but one that, as the movement became more firmly institutionalised, came to model itself on the official court system so that it both lost the advantages of informalism and incurred the wrath of the authorities who viewed it as a threat to state power. Nevertheless, at the high point of its development the Knights' court system consisted of some 8,000 tribunals dealing with problems in more than 3,000 communities, and it apparently proved very popular as a result of its good work in settling disagreements between working people. As a result, it clearly stands out as a precursor for later attempts at developing 'alternatives' (Garlock, 1982).

More generally, the development of socialism in the twentieth century encouraged ideals of informalism, with attempts being made in a wide variety of societies to create a new system for resolving disputes that would no longer serve the interests of the bourgeoisie but, instead, incorporate the will of the masses and assist in the construction of a socialist society. Writing in the early 1980s, but with the experience of the Portuguese revolution of 1974 in mind, Santos characterised this search for informal or 'popular' justice in the following terms:

> Historical analysis of the most important revolutionary crises in modern times leads us to a concept of popular justice in which the following elements tend to be present. It is class justice; that is, it appears as justice exercised by the popular classes parallel to or in confrontation with the state administration of justice. It embodies alternative criteria of substantive legality or at least alternative criteria for the interpretation and enforcement of pre-existing legality. It is based on a concrete notion of popular sovereignty (as opposed to the bourgeois theory of sovereignty) and thus on the idea of direct government by the people. Consequently, it requires that judges be democratically selected by the relevant communities and act as representative members of the masses, who are autonomously exercising social power. It operates at a minimum level of institutionalization and bureaucratization (a non-professional justice with very little division of legal labour and immune to systematic rationality). Rhetoric tends to dominate the structure of the discourse mobilized in the processing and settlement of conflicts. Formal coercive power may or may not exist, but when it does it tends to be used in interclass conflicts for the punishment of class enemies, whereas educative measures tend to be favoured in intraclass conflicts. In sum, popular justice in a revolutionary crisis is a form of 'revolutionary law in action', the embryo of a new power structure, though popular justice is less comprehensive than revolutionary legality since it is restricted to revolutionary actions that directly confront the judicial decision-making apparatus of the state (Santos, 1982: 253–4).

These observations help us to understand, for example, the extraordinary experiments in civil (and indeed criminal) justice undertaken by the Chinese Communist Party (CCP) in areas of China 'liberated' by the revolutionaries prior to the creation of a People's Republic throughout China in 1949. Essentially, the comrades carrying out 'legal work' in the pre-1949 'Liberated Areas' sought to create a system of justice that was socialist in nature but not necessarily in the image of that developed in the Soviet Union. Instead, it had to be adapted to local Chinese conditions. On the basis of traditional values and practices of dispute resolution, the CCP thus experimented with ways of incorporating traditional approaches into its emerging system of popular justice. This approach was called, after the judge who played the most role in its development, the 'Ma Xiwu Judicial Style' (*Ma Xiwu Shenpan Fangshi*). Among the most distinctive features of this system were on-the-spot trials and circuit tribunals – so that the courts could have direct contact with the masses, gather evidence themselves, draw in local people to assist in the processes of settling disputes and educate the masses through their participation in the trial proceedings. In addition, a system for appointing 'people's assessors' was created in which lay members of the community were invited onto the bench by the invitation of the court, or by election by local organisations, or by nomination by an appropriate body (for example, nomination by a trades union in employment dispute cases, or the women's association in divorce cases). In this way, the court could benefit from the lay but sometimes specialised knowledge of the assessor, while the assessor could supervise judicial work in the name of 'the people' and increase the possibility of publicity for laws and policies. Furthermore, the importance of both extra-judicial and judicial mediation was stressed as this would 'strengthen the unity of the people', reduce litigation and enhance production. One of the key features of informal justice that was not in this system was, however, disassociation from state power – this was a very hands-on system, with the CCP authorities in firm control, running a system in parallel with the state legal system of the Nationalist Government.

Civil justice policy, rules and practice in the present-day People's Republic of China (PRC) strongly emphasises the role of mediation in civil cases. The principal Chinese term for mediation, *tiaojie*, bears a broad meaning and in China's socialist legal system often represents a highly evaluative process in which the parties are subjected to considerable pressure to settle, despite the existence of formal rules requiring consent. The emphasis on mediation, and the style of mediation promoted, owes much to the 'judicial' thought and practice of Ma Xiwu, a key figure in Communist Party attempts to combine socialist revolution with administrative consolidation during the late 1930s and the early 1940s in a large area of northwest China mainly controlled by the revolutionary forces of the CCP and known as the 'Soviet Border Region' (formed out of substantial areas of Shaanxi, Gansu and Ningxia Provinces). Although Ma's influence is now in decline, he played a vital role in the development of ideas of informal justice within China's socialist legal system, and in the decisive years of revolution enabled the Party to avoid excessive reliance in legal work on the institutions and experience of the Soviet Union.

Ma was born on 8 January 1899 into a peasant family in Bao'an County (now, Zhidan County) in Shaanxi Province. He began his career as a socialist revolutionary in 1930, formally joined the CCP in 1935, and played an active role in the creation of the Soviet Border Region. Although possessing only limited legal training, Ma specialised in legal issues and developed what became known as the 'Ma Xiwu Adjudicatory Style' (*Ma Xiwu Shenpan Fangshi*), incorporating many principles of informal justice, including an emphasis on mediation. After 'Liberation' in 1949, he rose to become a Vice-President of the Supreme People's Court and a member of the National People's Congress (China's main parliamentary body). He died in 1962, following serious illness.

A key feature of Ma's approach, which persists today, is 'mediation first, adjudication second' (*xian tiaojie, hou shenpan*). Although the provisions of the 1991 Civil Procedure Law of the PRC do not make mediation mandatory prior to trial, its use in local settings, as well as by courts before and during both original and appellate proceedings was encouraged by Ma and has continued to be stressed, albeit with some modification, since the late 1970s in the post-Mao era of reform. Ma's efforts, which were an integral part of the CCP's more general attempt to develop a system of people's justice in pre-Liberation China, were primarily focused on civil cases – most of which consisted of disputes over land rights and divorce – in the Border Region. Reliance on mediation on the primary mode of decision-making was regarded by Ma as democratic practice (*minzhu shijian*) integral to the judicial system being created by the CCP as part of a general policy of 'the mass line' (*qunzhong luxian*). Under the latter policy, the Party abandoned the elitist leadership style of unyielding ideology and rigid Party discipline that had been reasonably effective in urban areas. In its place the Party introduced a more devolved approach that mobilised the often poorly educated and apathetic peasantry by allowing for a degree of popular participation in the shaping of policies and the making of decisions. In keeping with this revised approach, emphasis was placed on the need in legal work not only to stress mediation but also to keep procedures informal and uncomplicated.

Ma developed a considerable reputation for being a skilled decision-maker in his handling of both civil and criminal cases in circuit hearings he conducted while serving as a Special Commissioner (*zhuanyuan*) and head of a branch court in the Border Region. In the course of his work, Ma encouraged the development of a system of 'on-the-spot' trials (*jiudi shenpan*) and 'circuit tribunals' *(xunhui fating*, or *paichu fating*). Both procedural innovations were (and still are) intended to enable ordinary people to enjoy greater access to, and direct contact with, the courts, to enhance the understanding by the 'masses' of policy and law, and for the courts to be able to handle cases with the active, direct involvement of local people. Traces of the policy of engagement with the masses can perhaps also still be found in a system of inspectors sent out periodically by the National People's Congress to investigate the enforcement of laws and related issues at the local level.

One particular case handled by Ma that continues to be characterised within China as embodying some of key elements in his approach is that of obstruction to the marriage between Zhang Po'er and Feng Peng'er. When Zhang and Feng were still very young, their parents entered into a traditional contract of marriage in which the youngsters were to marry as soon as they had grown up. Difficulties arose when the girl's father later promised his daughter's hand in marriage to a third party. Zhang and Feng then fell in love, complicating matters further. Zhang and his family 'kidnapped and married' (*qiangqin*) the young Ms Feng, whose father then secured a local court declaration that the marriage was invalid. The local community, unhappy at this outcome, asked Ma to settle the matter. Ma is reported to have talked with the parties, especially the young girl, as well as with local officials, neighbours and kinsfolk, gathering evidence and opinions in preparation for a new trial. At that event, held in front of the entire local community, a new judgment was put together, approving the marriage on the ground that it accorded with the principle of freedom of marriage.

The style of decision-making promoted by Ma stressed the importance of making people's justice accessible to ordinary people, and avoiding reliance on the services of legal experts. In addition to placing an emphasis on extra-judicial mediation, Ma's approach assumed that the courtroom was not necessarily the best place for dealing with disputes. Instead, the court should be seen as an institution that could be in session anywhere – in particular, through the system of on-the-spot trials and circuit tribunals, in the social setting of the dispute. Thus, a good judge is one who follows the mass line by adhering to certain basic principles: 'conduct hearings on the spot, adhere to no formality, carry out in depth investigation and research, connect with the masses, [and thereby] work out a solution to the problem (*jiudi shenpan, bu ju xingshi, chenru diaocha yanjiu, lianxi qunzhong, jiejue wenti*)' (Zhang, 1983: 41). The model judge gets out of her or his 'cave dwelling' (*yaodong*) or office, and investigates a dispute where it has occurred, involving local people, so as to be able to investigate the background to the dispute, and to understand better the psychology of the parties. Such a judge also brings in locally esteemed persons to carry out 'persuasion and explaining work' (*shuofu he jieshi gongzuo*), tries to get all the relevant parties involved in the case to analyse the situation and to come up with solutions, and schedules and locates the hearings so that they do not interfere with the productivity of the masses. The style of adjudication promoted by Ma embraced the understanding that had been achieved within the local community through a mixed process in which failed mediation – or a decision that mediation was not the appropriate decision-making process in the instant case – was followed by a hearing conducted in front of the 'masses' and a decision then made on the basis of a simple majority by the assembled crowd. If adjudication is necessary then the judge should display an earnest attitude so that the parties accept the judgment without too much unhappiness. (Zhang, 1983: 41; Ma, 1955: 90–1).

During the 'Yan'an Period' (1935–1945), when the CCP was engaged in a broad 'united front' (*lianhe zhanxian*) with anti-Japanese forces and generally more cooperative in its relations with non-Party elements, mediation came to be given a principal role in resolving civil disputes. This pre-eminence remains an integral feature of the PRC's approach to civil justice.

Although he gained the affectionate epithet of 'Blue Sky' (*Ma Qingtian*) a traditional Chinese term symbolising an honest, upright magistrate, Ma stressed the value of informal processes. With his active encouragement, extra-judicial mediation was developed as the primary means of resolving disputes among the people. Ma also highlighted the virtues of lay persons as third-party decision-makers, asserting that when it came to dispensing people's justice 'three old peasants are better than a local judge' (*sange nongmin lao ding ge difang guan*) (Zhang, 1983: 46, 79). Ma's stress on the value of using lay people as third-party interveners was incorporated into the Party's ideological device of the 'model' and the virtues of these heroic figures thereby extolled. Although often unpaid and with little formal training, these skilled figures were praised for their efficiency and sense of public duty, and held up as shining 'Folk Model Mediators' (*minjian tiaojie mofan*) to be emulated by others. A number were quasi-political figures – for example, the heads of the mass-line institution of the local Peasant Association – indicating the close link that such figures were also expected to enjoy with Communist Party authority.

Ma also encouraged reliance on colloquial, everyday language in handling civil cases, stressing that it was important to 'use reason to persuade' (*yi li fu ren*). He praised the work of a 'heroic' mediator, Du Liangyi, especially in the latter's apposite use of traditional Chinese colloquialisms to change parties' attitudes. A wife-beater who claimed that he was driven to violence by his wife's mismanagement of family affairs was told that while he could admonish his children in front of others, it was better to 'instruct his wife on the pillow' (*renqian jiaozi, zhenshang jiao qi*). A middleman who took sides with a wealthy landlord brokering a land deal was admonished with the customary idiom that 'all middlemen are born of one mother, and see each other as flesh and blood' (*tianxia fanzi yi nang sheng, fanzi kanjian fanzi qin*), praised with the advice that 'blessed is the man who bestows benevolence' (*zuoxia en'de chang yao dang fuhan*) and encouraged to promote reconciliation with the suggestion that 'the wealthy do not fight with the poor' (*fu bu he pin dou*) (Jiang, 2000).

While Ma's approach stressed the importance of operating within the parameters of law and official policies, it also contained a strong emphasis on local standards of conduct and common sense. Today, it tends to be seen by reformist minded civil proceduralists in China as giving insufficient attention to the application of law – although it is also recognised that in the difficult revolutionary situation of the Border areas, the system of formal laws and regulations was very thin and often quite inadequate for deciding cases in terms of the direct application of legal norms. There was a strong didactic element in the mediation process promoted by Ma, as that process was designed not only to resolve difference between the parties but also to spread understanding and acceptance of party policy and regulations, as well as to promote harmony generally.

This harmony could be realised through Ma's approach in part because his methodology was able to identify the 'real', underlying cause of the problems, in part because it created outcomes mutually acceptable to the parties and in part because it carried an ethic of treatment. Underlying Ma's style was the idea that the social function of litigation is to avoid or end disharmony by resolving the fundamental problems underlying a dispute. A flexible approach to the application of law also helped to ensure that policy goals and ethical standards were properly realised. Sometimes local actors combined forces with a 'parental hand' or 'blue sky mandarin' in local settings in order to formulate a decision that was acceptable to both the masses and the disputing parties. This approach remains embedded in China's current civil procedure law, and is relied on by many rural courts in handling disputes relating to marriage, inheritance, adoption, debt and other relatively routine civil matters. In this way, substantive justice can be achieved – and not defeated – by the legal system.

Although primarily influential in the area of civil justice, Ma's thinking and practical work extended to criminal matters, where he also assisted in the development of a distinctively Chinese socialist style of decision-making. In this area, he encouraged – as a parallel to the mediator in the handling of civil cases – the use of people's assessors (*renmin peishenyuan*) as lay judges. A lay element was also promoted in evidence gathering, with judges advised to rely on the masses for collecting material evidence, albeit with a degree of scepticism given that the masses lacked adequate understanding of investigatory techniques. He also advised that 'adjudicators' (*shenpanyuan*) must understand adequately, and focus on the difference between the masses and the enemy, and 'protect the masses as a heavenly-bestowed duty' (Zhang, 1983: 9), thereby promoting the role of courts as instruments of class justice. One dimension of this emerging system of class justice in Ma's hands was that minor criminal offences, which had not been carried out by a class enemy, were amenable to the judicial style that he advocated for handling civil cases – that is, a combination of mediation and adjudication (Zhang, 1983: 45). On the other hand, Ma was aware of the dangers of excessive informalism, and in the handling of serious criminal cases believed in holding open trials, prohibiting torture and corporal punishment, and obtaining reliable evidence (especially by means other than torture). Many of the reports of his work in criminal cases involved his intervention as a kind of trouble-shooter who was able to correct an injustice created by the incompetence of ordinary officials.

The Ethnic Impulse towards Informalism

Although often overlapping with religious communities, ethnic minority communities too have sometimes felt the strong need to close out the outside world and to enjoy a degree of local sovereignty or control over their own affairs. Indeed, where a distinctive ethnic group has been created by the process of migration, and is therefore perceived by other local people as something of a body of outsiders, its members (and especially its leaders) may feel the strong need to withdraw from mainstream society in order to avoid prejudiced attitudes and discriminatory conduct. In the case of the Chinese diaspora, such withdrawal often took the form of retreat into Chinatowns, urban enclaves within which they developed a tightly knit community, and where leadership was provided by office holders in the major voluntary associations that the Chinese migrants had established, with this leadership settling disputes, controlling deviant conduct, and providing assistance for the less well off. In the United States, Chinese migrated in steadily increasing numbers until 1882, when federal law introduced new barriers to such immigration in response to white hostility that included mob violence. It was not until many decades after that the Chinese-Americans felt able to integrate more firmly with mainstream society.

Doo Leigh-wai noted that in these Chinese communities, as is often the case elsewhere, the principal style of mediation was highly evaluation – or 'didactic' in his terms – directed at determining fault and virtue in the conduct of the parties in disputes, although it became less coercive and judgemental as time progressed. But initially at least, community elders adopted an authoritarian and coercive style of mediatory intervention, and their encouragement or imposition of specific outcomes was backed not only by moral righteousness but also by ostracism and economic boycott. The power of community leaders depended in large part on the semi-closed nature of the community, lack of employment opportunities outside the community and inequalities of wealth within the communities.

They used this power to stress community harmony and to emphasise hierarchy and status, rather than recognising the validity of parties' claims. As time passed, however, and Chinese migrants better integrated in wider society, the approach to dispute resolution necessarily changed. Disputants could now resist the imposition of didactic mediation, perhaps taking their case to court or seeking some other avenues to justice, and the style of mediation where it was employed necessarily changed, becoming more voluntary and patient in ethos (Doo, 1973: 652–4).

A broadly similar pattern of change induced by declining community homogeneity may be observed in the approach to resolving disputes relied on by the Jewish Conciliation Board of New York. The board initially comprised a rabbi, a lawyer and a lay representative – typically a businessperson who brought to the proceeding 'real world' experience and 'common-sense'. Although loosely modelled on the rabbinical court, proceedings were very informal, varied in style from case to case, and were often infused with emotion, flattery and apology. The resulting settlement agreements were, however, made formal by being expressed in terms that accorded with the provisions of the American Arbitration Association Standard agreement, so that if so required an agreement could be enforced by the state courts. By the 1960s, the Board's case load was more than 1,000 cases annually, and necessarily many of these were dealt with informally, without a hearing of the full Board. But with the passage of time, as immigrants became more integrated with and acclimated to wider society, the Board gradually lost its distinction appeal so that by the end of the century many of its functions were taken over by community social services (Rosen, 2006; 45–6).

The Occupational Impulse towards Informalism

Within various kinds of economic institutions, too, there is often a feeling that certain kinds of economic activity give rise to particular kinds of problem, and also a preference for self-governance that tends to encourage specialised modes of dispute resolution. Some indication of this was given above in our discussion of fairs and borough courts in England. But such tendencies are found across a whole range of societies, and one institution in which they were prominently located was the urban guild, which, from Europe to Imperial China, often dominated the urban social landscape. The guild was an association in which members engaged in the same line of commerce or craft joined together in order to protect members' businesses from outside competition and control their conditions of business in such matters as standard of product, methods of sale and employment relations. Guilds were often religious brotherhoods, dedicated to specific saints, with their regulations urging members to follow a strict religious way of life, and their rules (including those relating to economic activities) might well be expressed in religious terms. The guilds were by and large self-regulating, especially when their rules had been approved by the state authorities. An assembly of guild leaders would consider alleged violations of rules and impose penalties. The ultimate punishment was expulsion from the guild. Only criminal offences were excluded from the jurisdiction of the guild. Various kinds of pressure encouraged the handling of disputes – both between guild members and between members and their workers – within the guild. Disputes impeded business or production, and therefore needed to be dealt with quickly. Taking a dispute to court often meant delay and, as important, possible revelation of trade secrets and other matters best kept from the eyes of outsiders. Commercial and employment relationships were important, sometimes complex, and often more significant than assertion of legal rights. In such circumstances, mediation and arbitration within the guild were almost everywhere the preferred processes for handling disputes.

Although the power of guilds in Europe declined from the fifteenth century onwards as a result of the growth of the state, improvements in communications, expanding trade and, subsequently, the industrial revolution, the commercial preference for arbitration, mediation and other extra-judicial modes of dispute handling continued. In the United States, the transition from colonial to modern society involved the decline of 'geographical, religious and ideological boundaries of community' and their replacement by commercial bonds which generated their own communitarian values including a stress on commercial arbitration. The ending of slavery and the need to create new kinds of economic relations in the South was an additional significant complication. In Europe, too, there was a persisting preference amongst merchants for commercial arbitration and self-regulation. Later, with the development of labour unrest towards the end of the nineteenth century and the maturing of the industrial revolution, in both the United States and Europe special approaches were also needed for the resolution of employment disputes. These included industrial arbitration. And with the development of organised labour, arbitration and mediation came to serve as important mechanisms for collective bargaining. Here, the technical issues that are often involved, the fact that the parties are well-informed and practiced opponents, and the large constituencies that the negotiating parties often have behind them, make mediation and arbitration especially suitable processes.

Van der Sprenkel describes in some detail a similar situation among Chinese urban guilds in nineteenth-century China, noting how these guilds disseminated their regulations by posting them publicly on felicitous red paper. Such rules dealt with issues such as working hours, apprenticeships, product quality, prices and weights, merchant share and dispute resolution rules. The latter required disputes to be settled within the guild, so as to avoid unwelcome external – especially official – intervention into the affairs by the guild, to promote instead internal cohesion and contact, and to maintain the good reputation of the guild. Those members who resisted their control, and took their case to the local magistrate's court, would be subject to a public reprimand and denied a hearing in the event of a future grievance. Other sanctions included fines, especially by means of a mandatory and expensive feast for guild members that was thought to serve both as a punishment and a mode of reintegration with the community of the guild. For more recalcitrant members, however, the ultimate response was expulsion from the guild, which meant to all intents and purposes, that the deviant member could no longer continue in business (Van der Sprenkel, 1962: 92–4).

In the United States in the nineteenth century, according to Auerbach, the Civil War of 1861–1865 was a major watershed in the general pattern of dispute resolution. Prior to the Civil War, alternative dispute settlement was valued in terms of its place in community justice. After the Civil War, it was reduced to an argument for judicial efficiency, and became an external instrument of social control. This transformation had a lasting impact, as well as immediate consequences. In the aftermath of the Civil War, newly freed slaves were pushed into new employment contracts for work on the plantations. While these 'agreements' were nominally consensual in reality they were compulsory. The Freedmen's Bureau, a government agency specially created in order to regulate the change from slavery to freedom, handled many of the resulting disputes, but in so doing failed to see the importance of the serious bargaining power imbalances between the former plantation masters and their newly freed slaves. Arbitration tribunals were also tried, but these gave too much emphasis on the formal principle of freedom of contract, and their composition favoured the employers. As a result, 'the diversion of disputes from the formal court system (where blacks, palpably disadvantaged, had no right to testify until 1866) to arbitration had few discernible benefits for the freedmen. Informality, in a social setting of disparate power relations, inevitably served the interests of the dominant group'(Auerbach, 1983: 59).

In the subsequent rapid urbanisation and industrialisation of the United States, arbitration became an increasingly important process, both as a means of facilitating negotiations between employer and employee, and for handling labour grievances. The reliance on arbitration was specifically encouraged by the National Labour Relations Act 1935. Although it now takes many forms and has been institutionalised in various ways, it often retains a distinctive ethos, as Van Wezel Stone has pointed out:

> A third view of arbitration is that it is not a mirror image of litigation but rather a method for applying norms and resolving nonjusticiable disputes that arise within a self-regulating normative community. In the *self-regulation view*, the distinctive value of arbitration is not that it can enforce laws, but that it can enforce fairness norms that were not presently embodied in law. This view is based on the insight that face-to-face communities generate their own fairness norms for certain types of situations, and that community elders know and can apply these norms better than a court can.

> Traditionally, arbitration has been designed to permit arbitrators to blend internal fairness norms with the norms of the larger community in order to reach results that are neither compelled by the law nor inconsistent with it, but fair in the context of the particular dispute. Arbitration originated as a form of dispute resolution for use within craft and merchant guilds to resolve disputes between members. These trade groups set their own norms of conduct and business standards, and established their own dispute resolution procedures to resolve disputes that might arise. Disputes that arose often blended allegations of breach of contract with allegations of violation of customary norms. Arbitrators were expected to resolve them by applying both the parties' own contracts and informal customary norms of the trade. The self-regulation view of arbitration counsels courts to support this aspect of arbitration, when arbitration constitutes and enhances the normative life of the workplace community (Van Wezel Stone, 2001: 468–71).

Territorial Identity and the Impulse towards Informalism

An additional and important context within which strong impulses for informalism may emerge is the local community. Of course, these may well be overlapping with other forms of community or social organisation, religious, ethnic, political and so on. But a recurrent and sometime distinguishing feature of such impulses is a concern to create or restore a sense of identity between the individual and the local community or neighbourhood, and an 'empowerment' of local people.

Indeed, contemporary moves are visible across a wide range of jurisdictions both to develop community justice, especially neighbourhood mediation, and to link it with the public justice system. These developments, however, must recall the powerful, and largely unchallenged, critiques of informal justice that were developed at the beginning of the 1980s (Abel, 1982b; Auerbach, 1983; Freeman, 1984) and which are dealt with in some detail in Chapter 3. Suffice it to state here that those analyses argued that informality of process and the diversion of disputes towards alternatives to adjudication seldom improved the position of the disadvantaged, but tended rather to entrench inequality and increase opportunities for coercion and manipulation. They revealed the limitations of innovatory dispute institutions as empowering schemes and as means of reconstituting community or social solidarity. They also underline the potential complexity of agendas for the recovery or transplanting of 'traditional' modes of dispute resolution.

In Britain, the much later emergence of interest in 'alternatives' on the part of those responsible for running the public justice system has enabled them to consider the North American experience in developing their plans. While attention is paid to ADR in Lord Woolf's 1995 and 1996 proposals for the renovation of the civil justice system as a whole, it is notable that he comes out strongly against using ADR as a channel of deflection to reduce court loads and against mandatory mediation. Nevertheless, the past decade has seen a flourishing growth in community mediation programmes in the United Kingdom, as both voluntary associations and local government have followed the United States' example and increasingly committed themselves to providing such schemes in order to address problems of neighbour disputes, family quarrels, homelessness and juvenile misconduct.

Thus, the 'romance' of community dispute resolution, is another persisting force shaping preferred approaches to dispute resolution, although the precise form and function such systems take varies from context to context. Perhaps one of the best known such 'informal justice' systems in the Anglo-American common law world is to be found in the San Francisco Community Board (SFCB) system established in the late 1970s. The SFCB is not only important in its own right but also has been the inspiration for many other programmes and training models. As Merry and Milner have stressed, it 'continues to stand for a grass-roots vision of mediation ... [and] ... espouses [ideals of] neighborhood organization, empowerment, and self-government'(1993: 11). In keeping with these values, the SFCB system tries to avoid contact with the courts, to be autonomous but grounded in the local community, and to promote justice and harmony locally by using mediation to deal with the family and neighborhood troubles that it typically handles. In this way, it aspires not only to offer better processes of dispute resolution but also to encourage civic responsibility and good neighbourliness in local society, offering 'a fundamentally different and potentially transformative style of thinking about conflict, where communication and the expression of feelings replace force and violence' (Merry and Milner, 1993: 13). The SFCB system clearly faces challenges: the probably much diminished sense of 'local' community in the contemporary urban setting, the unclear nature of community 'values', the difficulties of funding and organising such schemes where they clearly exist outside the formal legal system, and the competing visions of 'community' that are held by many of the relevant actors. Above all, it faces many of the processual difficulties that arise when attempts are made to develop an informal system of justice in the contemporary world:

How much legal pressure should be exerted to bring plaintiffs and defendants to the table? Should mediation be a specialized mechanism for handling certain kinds of cases referred by the court or a new form of authority outside the court altogether. Should mediators define the authority they exercise as derived from the court through, for example, 'oaths of confidentiality' administered by a judge or as derived from a self-governing community? Some forms of community mediation incorporate the discourse and symbols of law, while others endeavor to rely on that of the community, or therapy, or of relationships. SFCB is important in this debate because it has in the past deliberately resisted any contact with state law (Merry and Milner, 1993: 14–15).

Auerbach takes a somewhat more negative view of the community mediation initiatives and 'social justice in the courts experiments', especially those sponsored by the US Department of Justice in response to the call of the Pound Conference to engage in new approaches to civil justice. In the case of Dorchester programme, the law reformers involved in the experiments were committed to new approaches, hoping to secure community participation in dispute-settlement processes, and to do so in a spirit of healing and reconciliation rather than isolation and punishment. Despite this commitment, and high neighbourhood visibility, approval and cost-free services, Dorchester residents continued to ignore the mediation on offer in Dorchester's neighbourhood justice centres, and only participated in community mediation where their choice was made for them in the form of a court referral. In Auerbach's view, a key problem was the absence of a viable community that would underpin the new system:

> The fragility of the Dorchester community empowered the local district court and undercut mediation as an alternative. In an atomistic social environment, only the court possessed sufficient coercive power to secure the compliance of disputing parties. Mediation was an unfamiliar process in Dorchester. Mediators, although local residents, were 'strangers with known values.' Above all, mediation required a social context of intimacy, reciprocity, and permanence that was conspicuously missing in Dorchester, as in other American urban neighborhoods. The choice of forum, in Dorchester as elsewhere, reflected the degree of neighborhood cohesion. In a Boston inner-city neighborhood near Dorchester, for example, black and white residents, lacking a sustaining network of community supports, readily took their disputes to court; while their Chinese neighbors, who depended upon community relationships for employment and social interaction, went to court with considerable reluctance. Dorchester and Dedham were only miles apart, but the possibilities for communal dispute settlement without law, so evident in the seventeenth century, were all but obliterated in the twentieth. Alternative dispute settlement served as a tenacious metaphor for missing elements of community in American cities, but there was little in urban life to sustain it as a functioning process. All signs pointed to the same conclusion about urban justice: 'Life rather than logic makes self-referred mediation as unpalatable to Americans as it is attractive to the peoples of other cultures.'

The new urban mediation alternatives contradicted virtually every prerequisite for informal justice that comparative anthropology and American history provided. Communities played no role in their design or implementation. The site-selection process suggested that community fragmentation, not community cohesion, was the primary criterion. Rochester, Dorchester, and Harlem, to cite three early recipients of mediation programs, all had recently experienced acute tension and overt conflict – and, significantly, signs of incipient political activism among community residents, which government officials and legal professionals preferred to stifle, through formal or informal means. Legal institutions hovered over the new mediation programs; virtually every project, by design, received the overwhelming preponderance of its referrals from criminal justice agencies. With legal coercion permeating the mediation process, few neighbors brought their disputes to neighborhood justice centers. An indigenous community practice had come to serve the interests of the state legal system in promoting the efficient processing of criminal complaints (Auerbach, 1983: 131–5).

As we have noted, when the CCP attempted to develop its own distinctive approach to dispute resolution in the 1930s, it built on the entrenched tradition of mediation but at the same time politically transformed it into a process for using disputes as part of its efforts to re-order Chinese Society and encourage popular support for and implementation of Communist Party policies (Lubman, 1967). Much of the system of 'people's mediation' (renmin tiaojie) as it came to be known was and still is focused on the local community. Writing in the mid-1960s, Lubman emphasised that there was 'undeniably much mediation within the new collectivities for residence and work which the Communists have fashioned in reordering Chinese society' (Lubman, 1967: 1285). The felt need to emphasise local community has continued and indeed intensified in the post-Mao reform period, and has become particularly pronounced over the past fifteen years or so. The community-based system, which is now focused on the village rather than the production brigades of pre-reform days, and the enterprise rather than the work unit, still has dispute resolution by means of mediation as a central concern. The urban residential district, has recently been reformed by a series of measures culminating in the 2010 People's Mediation Organizational Law. In a recent analysis of these developments, Wu Yuning observes that there is much continuity in the way people's mediators handled their disputes.

> The goal of people's mediation is clearly specified in the law as that of 'timely to resolve disputes among the people and maintain social harmony and stability' (Art. 1). The expression, 'disputes among the people', places a limit on the range of the disputes that people's mediation may handle. Several decades ago, Cohen stated that 'these disputes among the people in the great majority of cases concern land, housing, timberland, water utilization, marriage, debts, and other questions'. This statement is still valid today. The public prefers to use the traditional social network mediation to solve disputes that involve relatively

minor interests and risks, and non-purely monetary disputes. Typical types of dispute dealt with include marriage and family disputes, neighbor disputes, agricultural production disputes, and other disputes involving compensation for minor harm. Disputes that are most suitable for mediation include those where the disputants have long-term, multidimensional relationships with one another, preferably in a union built upon spontaneous, informal collaboration, where the interests of the disputants are often overlapping and intertwined, and the disputes involve relatively few interests or risks (Wu Yuning, 2017: 39–40).

At the same time, its political functions have been intensified, and in many respects the emphasis on the importance of community mediation is one which reflects a felt need to improve tight social control in a rapidly changing society in which there is growing turbulence and unrest:

> The purpose of the 2010 law is clearly indicated by Wu Aiying, the then Chinese Minister of Justice: 'While China is experiencing profound social and economic changes, various kinds of social conflicts are also emerging [. . .] Mediation should be the first line of defense to maintain social stability and promote harmony'. Indeed, this law came into being at a time when China had seen (and continues to see) a surge of social contradictions and conflicts, manifested by numerous popular grievances, collective complaints, and negative incidents, such as suicides, violent acts, protests, demonstrations, and riots. These incidents have posed serious threats to social stability and state control. In response to this social disorder, the CCP propagandizes a 'harmonious society' (*hexie shehui*). One of the strategies used is the promotion of people's mediation, with a hope that this will alleviate social conflicts before their escalation to mass incidents. This harmony ideology, however, is not without criticism. With its heavy focus on social stability and propaganda, this ideology may promote 'intolerance for conflict' in a society, and an 'intention to prevent the expression of discord rather than to deal with its cause' (Wu Yuning, 2017: 40).

And Professor Wu concludes,

> Though it has had something of a fluctuating history post-1949, civil mediation remains one of the most popular dispute resolution methods in China today. Even in the post-Mao reform era when laws and the rule of law are emphasized, informal, community-based mediation outside courts has continued to be a central method of dispute resolution. Entering the new century, the people's mediation has seen a more vigorous approach, with top-down support, better funding and better staffing with more highly educated, more skillful, and less politicized mediators. As long as people's mediation continues to be a mechanism through which an acceptable outcome can be fairly prompted, with less cost, lower pressure, more convenience, and greater flexibility, it will remain an ideal of social justice in China. And, as long as people's mediation continues to be seen as a good method with which to resolve conflicts and stabilize the society, it is likely to retain official support and keep evolving and adapting to the changing problems and times (Wu Yuning, 2017: 29, 30 and 38).

Family and Kinship

Finally, we examine the ways in which 'communities' created by the family and broader-based kinship groupings characterise themselves as relatively or even absolutely autonomous areas for resolving disputes between members, albeit sometimes incorporating and overlapping with territorial and religious impulses. In many societies around the world, maintaining harmony in the family and in more extended kinship groupings is an important value and one that is considered by family and kinship group elders to be more important than the laws and justice offered by the state, and indeed it is such an important value that kinship may come to serve as metaphor for group solidarity, including self-regulation, as in the case of criminal enterprises such as the Mafia and their families.

In stateless societies, kinship is perhaps the most important organising principle for structuring and regulating social relations, and dispute resolution within the family and localised kinship group is necessarily predominant. However, within societies with states and formal legal systems, the preference is to settle trouble situations within a circle of kin and by means of informal processes that take fully into account family and kinship norms and values. In Imperial China, for example, not only did the rules of local lineages often expressly forbid members from taking their disputes to court (as did their urban counterparts, the guilds, as we have noted above), but statutory law also explicitly discouraged family members from litigating their cases in court.[2] And if they got to court, local magistrates were warned by popular stories to resist any temptation to accept and handle them. Nevertheless, in a range of situations, the retention of informal authority to resolve kinship and family disputes 'at home' could be found, and was often an important element in the ideology of kinship. Thus, for example, in many parts of patrilineal China, it was the maternal uncle – the brother of the husband's mother – who was regarded as the most appropriate mediator of a matrimonial dispute, as his membership of a different descent line suggested a disinterest in the family's troubled affairs. In short, family life was seen as a profoundly private sphere over which the state should not necessarily have much control.

Another powerful example is provided in Barton's seminal account of a Philippines people, the Ifugao, which included analysis of Ifugao dispute resolution.[3] Although the Ifugao had well-developed dispute resolution procedures,

---

[2] Of the Ten Great Abominations identified in Imperial Chinese statutory law, the penal code stipulated that 'the seventh is called Lack of Filial Piety. (This means to bring suit against, or to curse, one's Paternal grandparents, or one's parents, or one's husband's paternal grandparents, or parents' (Jones, 1994: 15–16). This was not simply a rule of procedure: to bring suit against close kin, especially patrilineal kin, was one of the most serious criminal offences in Imperial Chinese statutory law, breaching a basic principle of filial duty (*xiao*).

[3] Roy F. Barton (1883–1947) was an educationalist who first went to the Philippines in 1906, and lived for a decade with the Ifugao as, in effect, a colonial officer in the United States Civil Administration (which saw itself preparing the Philippines for eventual independence). For

including the use of skilled third-party intervention, Barton's account also highlights the central value of avoiding external party intervention in the handling of quarrels within the family:

The Family in Relation to Procedure

124. Family unity and cooperation. The mutual duty of kinsfolk and relatives, each individual to every other of the same family, regardless of sex, is to aid, advise, assist, and support in all controversies and altercations with members of other groups or families. The degree of obligation of the various members of a family group to assist and back any particular individual of that group is in direct proportion: first, to the kinship or the relationship by marriage; second, to the loyalty the individual in question has himself manifested toward the family group, that is, the extent to which he discharges his obligations to that group.

The family is without any political organization whatever. It is a little democracy in which each member is measured for what he is worth, and has a voice accordingly in the family policy. It is a different body for every married individual of the whole Ifugao tribe. There are a great many relationships that complicate matters. An Ifugao's family is his nation. The family is an executive and a judicial body. Its councils are informal, but its decisions are none the less effective. The following rules and principles apply to the family and to individuals in the matter of procedure.

Brothers of the blood can never be arrayed against each other. They may fall out and quarrel, but they can never proceed against each other. This is for the reason that their family is identical (before marriage at least), and a family cannot proceed against itself. Cousins and brothers of the half-blood ought never to be arrayed against each other in legal procedure. In case they should be so arrayed, the mutual kin try to arrange peace (Barton, 1919: 92).

In the contemporary world, too, we find specialised forms of third-party intervention which are specifically focused on family relations, as Marian Roberts has powerfully observed. In her analysis of the unfolding discourses and practices of family mediation, she notes the difficulties created by defensive exercise of parental authority, the difficult decision on how best to take into account children's interests, and so on, and how these have encouraged a move towards greater use of therapy-based techniques for dealing with intra-family disputes. As we shall see later in the book, this poses problems for the practice of mediation as more traditionally understood and applied in the family context, as mediation and family therapy are forms of intervention that bear differing objectives, process, methods and theoretical assumptions: understanding of family mediation could be seriously distorted by the grafting onto it of the assumptions and techniques of family therapy, and of family systems theory in particular (Roberts, Marian, 2014b: 112–15).

much of this time he served as Supervising Teacher of Ifugao Sub-Province, and he held this position until his return to the US in 1916.

A further complication is the nature of the family relationships that are the subject of disagreement and dispute is changing in many parts of the world. Contemporary family life takes multiple forms. There is now a clear distinction between married life and the life of a couple, two notions that were previously closely linked. Today, people increasingly shape their own common life, with or without marriage, with or without cohabitation, in different- or same-sex relationships, and with varying ideas about financial arrangements. This means innovative forms of third party intervention may be needed when couples have disagreements, possibly leading to relationship break up and regrouping in new configurations. Thus, for example, recourse to mediation may be especially suitable for such situations because the law has not kept up with changing social realities in a number of jurisdictions and because the parties want to keep their disagreement private. Mediation offers a suitable option but may be complicated by and need innovative adjustments in style to take into account intra-family power imbalances, sharp contrasts in attitudes between the parties on their family arrangements, and issues of parenting in a legal environment which offers insufficient guidance on the position of children.[4]

Legal Reform, Pluralism and Informalism

In the United States, the growing dissatisfaction with the formal justice system at the end of the nineteenth century resulted in a number of significant attempts made during the period 1900–1930 to develop alternative dispute-settlement mechanisms. These were given jurisprudential inspiration by Roscoe Pound in his firm condemnation of the 'sporting theory of justice' (Pound, 1906). In Pound's view the adversarial approach to justice found in common law systems promotes an excessively instrumental attitude to law, and discouraged disputants from making concessions on the basis of shared values. Auerbach traces subsequent North American moves to informalism in the early years of this century. But in addition to the development of concili-ation centres described by Auerbach, efforts were made to reform courts by making them more efficient through the application of scientific management principles, and socially responsive by the introduction of specialised chambers for dealing with particular kinds of case – domestic relations, juveniles, small

---

[4] See Moscati (2014); (2015) and (2017). The style of family mediation in the area of LGBT couples needs to take into account some of the distinctive characteristics of this social grouping including 'different styles of communication and negotiation, different attitudes towards sex and relationships, different expectations of intimacy, and perhaps different expressions of conflict than opposite-sex couples' (Hanson, 2006: 305). A particularly serious issue that may arise, and which family mediators need to be aware of, is when one of the LGBT partners may have resisted coming 'out' or even to have come to terms with their sexuality. Another problematic area is domestic abuse, which may include threats by one party to 'out' – their counterpart. In the case of lesbians, partners' experiences have shown that the intense intimacy of the relationship may create problems – that require skilful mediatory handling – in the transformation of the relationship from togetherness and autonomy. A straight mediator who becomes familiar and sensitive to LGBT issues may then be as effective as a LGBT mediator in handling LGBT cases.

claims and so on – often relying on mediation as the principal process for decision-making, as Harrington (1982) has emphasised. That process of reform continued beyond the Second World War, and was given particular impetus by the emergence of the 'access to justice' movement described in Chapter 3.

In some ways, this movement of reform involved infusing formal legal institutions with ideas and processes drawn from community mediation and other informalist agencies. As Auerbach has noted, some of these initiatives were more successful than others:

> Conciliation was part of a package of reforms designed to alleviate procedural injustices that bore down most heavily upon the urban poor. Along with legal aid, small-claims courts, and public defenders, it was intended to undercut the claim that justice was available only in proportion to the ability to pay for it. The modern conciliation movement began in 1913 in Cleveland, where a conciliation branch of the municipal court was authorized to assist litigants who were unable to obtain lawyers to settle their small claims. All claims for thirty-five dollars or less were entered on the conciliation docket; parties were encouraged to appear before a municipal judge without lawyers; in the absence of formal legal procedure, the judge, relying upon an 'appeal to common sense' to resolve the disagreement, tried to arouse amicable feelings and suppress fighting instincts. Conciliation procedure was voluntary and formless, intended to encourage disputants to compromise their differences. Judgments rested entirely upon the consent of the parties; if conciliation failed, the dispute went to trial.
>
> The conciliation idea spread slowly during the next decade. The Cleveland plan provided a model for Chicago, where a similar program was implemented two years later. In New York, the state bar association endorsed conciliation as an alternative to what one member described as 'the hell of litigation.' In Phila-delphia, the Municipal Court established a special division for conciliation, small claims, and legal aid. And in Iowa, controversies involving less than one hundred dollars were consigned to conciliation at the discretion of the judge. The presence of lawyers was discouraged; the object was 'to get the parties themselves to meet and talk over their differences' (Auerbach, 1983: 96–7).

A growth in arbitration, by contrast, was driven by commercial concerns, especially in New York and the preference for self-regulation unhindered by the unwelcome presence of law and lawyers.

Harrington's analysis of 'delegalisation' as reform offers a succinct charac-terisation of some of the early efforts at court reform. These included the development of specialised tribunals dealing with small claims, family issues, minor tort, juvenile delinquency and so on, and in which the presiding judge could adopt informal procedures and employ robust case management powers. Also case flow was shaped by the decisions of the municipal courts' presiding judge. These tribunals were called 'socialised courts', and their case handling was intended to reflect principles of 'diagnosis, prevention, cure, education'. In particular, the domestic relations courts were an institutionalisation of informal dispute processing, and taking up the juvenile court philosophy of social justice they applied it to cases of wife abandonment, illegitimacy, failure to support, offences against minors and custody disputes (Harrington, 1982).

Despite these aspirations, the specialised courts came in for significant criticisms after 1940, with the courts being denigrated as appendages of trad-itional judicial institutions and as failing to fulfil their intended role as genuine alternatives to the adversarial process, as well as over-complicating court organisation. Yet even after court reform in the 1950s and 1960s aimed, inter alia, at a more centralised court organisation, the social justice influences have persisted, so that Harrington was still able to observe in the early 1980s that minor disputes were channelled into processes that emphasised therapeutic intervention by trained lay citizens. Individuals, assisted by mediators, were encouraged to reach an agreement on how best to adjust their future conduct in order to avoid or prevent conflict. Problems such as violence against women, neighbourhood quarrels, and landlord-tenant disagreements were individual-ised so that the social injustices underpinning many disputes were depoliticised or ignored, and the resolutions were internalised by the individualised form of participation. Conflict in this setting is absorbed into a rehabilitative model of minor dispute resolution.

Harrington concluded with the suggestion that the social justice influenced approach continues to be infused with contradictions and to promote state power over civil society, albeit less directly than it once was. Discretion formerly applied by court officials and the police officers became the preroga-tive of mediators and arbitrators in a therapeutic setting. Delegalisation thus meant a transfer of control rather than a withdrawal of control, and neigh-bourhood justice centres actually expanded rather than reduced the impact of the state and its policies (Harrington, 1982).

Self-regulation

In more recent times, the growing ethnic heterogeneity found in many soci-eties around the world has brought into sharp relief the problems that may be created by the impetus towards self-regulation. Here, the emphasis on 'in-house dispute resolution' and a preference for what are seen as more culturally appropriate modes of dispute resolution management, may create serious difficulties for a state which allowing for a degree of normative pluralism, is committed to notions of the rule of law and human rights. Of course, not all examples are contentious, and we continue to see many bodies – financial, sporting, media, and so on – arguing that they are best placed to deal with disputes and deviant conduct in their field, and should be allowed to get on with administering their own regulatory system in a fully autonomous manner. As we shall see in a later chapter, however, dispute of their approach has – at least in the United Kingdom – been one of the important factors encouraging the growth of the ombuds as a specialised dispute resolving institution. But in many other cases, there is simply an unresolved tension or uncertain state of affairs, as Tamanaha has pointed out:

> Private security forces now patrol and maintain order in gated communities, universities, places of public entertainment … public facilities … shopping malls, corporate headquarters, many small business and even public streets (neighbourhood watch). Privately owned and run (for profit) penitentiaries are handling an increasing number of prisoners. Many private organisations and institutions promulgate rules that apply to their own activities and to others within their purview. In situations of dispute, many parties choose (or are required) to bypass state court systems seen as inefficient, unreliable, too costly or too public, resorting instead to arbitration or private courts. Many of the massive slums that are ubiquitous in large cities around the world function with little or no official legal presence, beyond the purview of law and courts, often without legally recognised rights; order is maintained and intercourse conducted in these areas through other social norms, institutions or mechanisms (Tamanaha, 2008: 387).

Some of the more recent efforts to create these 'semi-autonomous fields' (Moore, 1973) have proved to be especially controversial, as worries arise about how such developments will interrelate with evolving human rights standards, rule by law values and the authority of the state. Although these issues are by no means confined to Islamic communities, social tensions have arisen over such communities perhaps more than they have over others. The prioritising of religious beliefs and relationships over commitment to the secular state is seen as an important issue by host communities so that, for example, in the case of Muslim migrants to the United Kingdom 'Muslim law is still superior and dominant over English law in the Muslim mind and in the eyes of the Muslim community' (Yilmaz, 2002: 343).

One controversial attempt to deal with this situation is the initiative in Ontario, Canada, taken in late 2003 by the Islamic Institute of Civil Justice. The Institute decided that within the overall framework of the Ontario Arbitration Act it should establish an Islamic family dispute arbitration board for Canadian Muslims. By this means, decisions by a Muslim arbitrator based on Islamic principles could be enforced in Canadian courts, assuming that such decisions were in accordance with the provisions of the Act. And the creation of such a system of dispute resolution would be consistent with the commitment to religious freedom and multiculturalism as enshrined in Canada's Charter of Rights and Freedoms.

This development was, however, subject to fierce criticism by a broad range of rights, including Muslim women's organisations, who argued that application of the principles of Sharia Law as intended in the proposal would bar many Muslim women from important personal rights guaranteed under Canadian Law. Although an important official report written in response to the highly contentious issue recommended that the proposed scheme be allowed to go ahead but with important safeguards (Boyd, 2004), the Ontarian authorities made a robust decision to respect the scheme, revising the Arbitration Act so that family dispute resolution based on non-Canadian laws and principles, including religious principles, would not have legal effect and could not be enforced by the courts.

Temporal Dimensions

The identification of informal values and processes across a range of cultural contexts is complicated by the changes that may occur over the course of time. Although there is seemingly a perpetual movement between informal principles and those of 'formal' justice, the process of development is often much more complex than a simple 'oscillating' model would allow.

The experience of China's system of people's mediation also shows clearly the manner in which changes in political climate radically affect the nature of that system. The scheme for community mediation that has been resurrected in post-Mao China does, in both form and substance, bear the imprint of the system that was replaced in the 1960s by the highly radical and politicised style of 'mediation' pursued during the Cultural Revolution. Nevertheless, this revivification is not a simple replication of the 1950s. The revived system put in place in the 1980s and 1990s was more decentralised, more professional, and placed much more firmly in a subordinate position in relation to the state courts than its 1950s predecessor.

Even within particular political and economic contexts there are pressures of institutionalisation at work that may result in changes that fundamentally transform the meaning of the institution, often with a tendency for it to become incorporated in the state system or at least to become juridified (Flood and Caiger, 1993)[5] so that 'despite its formal opposition to state law, popular justice often replicates and strengthens its language and cultural forms' (Merry, 1993: 60). An important factor here is the close connections that often exist between formal and informal justice (Abel, 1982b; Harrington, 1982). In addition, in an important commentary on 'popular justice' Peter Fitzpatrick argues further that the ideals of informal justice are rarely capable of being sustained, in large part because they are put into effect in a process which mirrors the ideology and practice of formal justice, so that the ambitions of informalism – expressed in its 'origin myth' – are only achieved with great difficulty (Fitzpatrick, 1993).

And even in China, where there is a strongly entrenched tradition of mediation in its legal culture, and attempts were made in the 1980s and 1990s to give its practitioners a genuine degree of autonomy, there have been strong pressures for mediation to serve better the interests of the CCP and the state, as Fu and Palmer have indicated:

---

[5] Menkel-Meadow's work powerfully explores some of the crucial ethical issues that such processes raise (2002). See also Chapter 7.

for China, the Party-State promotes and imposes mediation and informal dispute resolution particularly in times of crisis, perceived or real. This official promotion of mediation is strongly infused with a felt need to impose political control, justified by a responsibility to maintain stability and promote harmony. As a result, an emphasis on mediation for decision-making in the handling of disputes carries within itself the significant danger of serving as a 'turn against law'. In contrast, in a more stable and relaxed atmosphere, such as that which emerged in China in the second half of the 1990s, there is space for a more nuanced and varied approach to the handing of disputes. In the case of the PRC, the more self-confident Party-State of twenty years ago felt able to tolerate and even to promote rule-based adjudication through an autonomous legal process. And it did so as part of a larger endeavor to develop the rule of law. The Chinese leadership of Hu Jintao and Wen Jiabo (2002–03 to 2012–13) came, however, to rely extensively on mediation and other ad hoc, and highly politically charged, measures so as to maintain order and promote harmony. Under the umbrella of this policy, disputants were to be persuaded, suppressed and even bribed to swallow their grievances, withdraw their claims or simply end their disputes. Legal and extra-legal actors were encouraged – and often required – to bypass legal rules and procedures in the interests of political expediency and achieving proper impact in 'resolving' disputes. In promoting what was referred to as 'grand mediation' (*da tiaojie*), the distinction between legal and extra-legal processes was intentionally blurred and indeed became quite fuzzy. In the eyes of the Party-State, disputes were disruptive and should be prevented and ended as soon as they had occurred (or even before they had become manifest) (Fu and Palmer, 2017: 2).

Conclusions

The various contexts within which informal principles of justice have often been found reveal a widespread and persistent tendency to create alternatives to adjudication, or at least modified forms of adjudication, for handling disputes. Despite considerable cultural diversity and variations over time, we can often see a strong impulse to create institutions that rely on modes of decision-making other than adjudication for handling disputes. A general aversion to state-based formal justice, or religious, political, ethnic or territorial forces, or a felt need to refurbish courts and other agencies of formal justice are perhaps the most common contexts – sometime enclaves – within which ideologies and practices of informal justice have most readily taken hold. The contemporary ADR movement is thus backed by quite firm historical credentials, and given this experience it is perhaps surprising that current efforts across a range of jurisdictions – but especially in the Anglo-American common law world – to encourage greater attention to the value of the key processes of informal justice, namely negotiation and mediation, have met stiff and sometimes fierce resistance. In Chapter 3 we attempt to identify and explain the main strands of this criticism.

3

The Debates around Civil Justice and the Movement towards Procedural Innovation

Introduction

Across common law jurisdictions generally, the decades since 1960 have seen native institutions of civil disputing subject to more or less continuous re-examination and renovation. This process has taken place against the background of a particular jural inheritance, of which three foundational elements stand out. First is the historical dominance of state-sponsored adjudication, and hence of litigation, in the theory and practice of civil justice in the common law world. Second is the extent to which, as litigation has acquired a privileged status as the approved mode of dispute resolution, lawyers have through its practice achieved over generations a near monopoly over dispute management. The nature of this monopoly is only fully revealed when it is remembered that judicial appointment represents the ultimate career stage for the successful lawyer. Third is the manner in which lawyers have utilised civil procedure as the vehicle for their negotiation strategies, bringing about the profound entanglement of 'settlement' and 'litigation'. Behind an ideology under which settlement remains virtually invisible and submerged, it is in practice pursued through use of the procedural framework prescribed for bringing a dispute to trial and judgment.

Disenchantment with this distinctive culture of disputing has generated some complex, overlapping conversations, for the most part recognisable earliest in the United States. These conversations have varied in pace and direction from one jurisdiction to another and are not readily subjected to generalisation. But, at the risk of over-simplification, they can at first be reduced to three broad discussions: one about the conditions of availability of 'judgment'; another about the corresponding merits of 'settlement'; and a third around the search for 'alternative' forms.

The first of these conversations could probably be traced back to the very emergence of adjudication, to a time when the earliest kings and other rulers were struggling to establish a steering role. But for our purposes we can locate its recent origins in the 1960s and the 1970s. It was then articulated as an 'access to justice' movement. It represented the contemporary expression of primordial concerns about the costs, delays and general inaccessibility of adjudication, and called for quicker, cheaper, more readily available judgment with procedural informality as its hallmark. This was thus a conversation directed towards the renovation of adjudication – Mauro Cappelletti and Bryant Garth were at the centre of this reform effort, as we shall see below (1978a).

The second conversation, emerging during the 1970s, problematised adjudication itself, pointing to the advantages of 'settlement' (Burger, 1976; Bok, 1983). In a fierce critique of existing arrangements, Derek Bok analysed the factors which in his view underlie 'the blunt, inexcusable fact that [the United States], which prides itself on efficiency and justice, has developed a legal system that is the most expensive in the world, yet cannot manage to protect the rights of most [of its] citizens' (1983: 574). He concluded:

> Over the next generation, I predict, society's greatest opportunities will lie in tapping human inclinations toward collaboration and compromise rather than stirring our proclivities for competition and rivalry. If lawyers are not leaders in marshaling cooperation and designing mechanisms that allow it to flourish, they will not be at the center of the most creative social experiments of our time (1983: 583).

In the mid-1970s a third conversation began to develop which looked beyond the renovation of adjudication and arguments about the merit of settlement through lawyer negotiations to the possibilities of 'complementary' and 'alternative' forms. Auerbach identifies the 1976 National Conference on the Causes of Popular Dissatisfaction with the Administration of Justice (the Pound Conference) as 'the decisive moment in the legalization of informal alternatives' (1983: 123), and that Conference seems also to have been the first occasion on which Frank Sander used the term 'alternative dispute resolution' (Sander, 1976). We have already noted in Chapter 1 how this shift was signalled in a fundamental change in the way academic lawyers, and to some extent practitioners, began to talk about conflict. We saw there how new ways of thinking about disputes were linked to a growing sensitivity on the part of lawyers to the social sciences, and in particular to anthropological studies of dispute.

This exposure of lawyers to other cultures sometimes led to explicit 'borrowing' in the formulation of projects of reform (Danzig, 1973), but more generally growing comparative awareness prompted expansive reflection on 'complementary' and 'alternative' arrangements at home (see Sander, 1976). It is notable that in much of this conversation the court still remains the pivot around which discussion proceeds, as it is in Sander's seminal proposal of the 'Multi-Door Courthouse', as we shall explore below (and in Chapter 13).

In the 'access to justice' analysis offered by Cappelletti and Garth, it is pointed out that until the early twentieth century little attention was given to addressing the problem of 'legal poverty', a systemic weakness characterised as 'the incapacity of many people to make full use of the law and its institutions' (Cappelletti and Garth, 1978b: 183). Formal, but not necessarily effective, access to justice for the individual was considered to be sufficient. As Deborah

Rhode observes, 'access to law was considered a basic right, but access to lawyers was not' (2004: 47). But pressures emanating from the growth of the welfare state, increasing social complexity, and in reaction to the many injustices created by Fascist authoritarianism in the first half of the twentieth century, made it difficult to sustain this 'laissez-faire' attitude. There was a fundamental transformation in values so that not only was the important belief in human rights incorporated into governance and law, but affirmative action by the state was seen as essential in order to ensure that these important rights could be enjoyed by all. The right of effective access to justice was finally recognised as being crucial for the enjoyment of these newly recognised social and individual rights. So, in the second half of the twentieth century, argued Cappelletti and Garth, effective access to justice should be regarded as a fundamental value: 'the most basic requirement – the most basic "human right" – of a modern, egalitarian legal system which purports to guarantee and not merely proclaim, the legal rights of all' (1978a: 9).

In response to this situation, a major innovation – or 'wave' to use Cappelletti and Garth's metaphor (1978b: 196) – was to use the provision of legal aid in order to facilitate greater equality of access to lawyers and courts so as to eliminate the unacceptable inequality between aggrieved citizens who could not afford to hire lawyers, pay court costs, and meet other financial burdens in pursuing their claims through the formal legal system and those whose private wealth enabled them to pursue their cases through the courts. Litigation needed to be made more affordable for underprivileged members of society, in particular the impoverished and the inexperienced – those whom Galanter characterises as the 'one-shotters'[1] – and a major way to achieve this was by extending legal aid to such persons. A subsequent history of this experiment would show that many states which embraced this reform found it too expensive to sustain and it was given steadily reduced governmental financial support.

A second wave of the access to justice movement was to introduce various kinds of procedural reform to the litigation and judicial processes so that the legal systems could more effectively hear grievances and deliver rights to all. The creation of law centres, the development of public interest litigation and class actions, the provision of pro-bono legal services, the expansion of small claims courts, the use of simplified procedures and so on were innovations intended to strengthen the role of the courts in delivering more equal access to justice. One important dimension of this wave was its efforts to deal with what

---

[1] 'One-shotter' is a term introduced by Galanter to refer to an individual, commercial entity, or organisational unit that has little experience of dealing with legal institutions such as courts, whose power and influence is weak, and whose involvement in litigation is probably limited to the case at hand. In contrast, the 'repeat-player' is often a legal professional with extensive case experience including awareness of local jurisdictional rules, knowledge of relevant officials, and the professional practices within which proceedings are contextualised (Galanter, 1974).

Cappelletti and Garth identified as 'diffuse' interests[2] such as those found in areas such as environmental welfare and consumer protection where many individuals may perhaps share the same grievance and where there is often a strong public interest dimension – and in many cases, no clear procedural track that can encompass the various concerns and interests.

But in addition to these efforts to achieve more effective access, Derek Bok took the view that what was also needed was a new approach to legal education. In his essay 'A Flawed System of Law and Practice Training', Bok argued that there was a real need for reforms in teaching and in research if the basic problems in the civil justice system were to be properly addressed (1983: 582–3). Rather than preparing students for legal combat, training them 'to think like a lawyer', and focusing analysis on the decisions of superior courts, law schools might better educate their students and prepare them for practice (the real world) by teaching them about the 'voluntary mechanisms that might enable parties to resolve various types of disputes ... without going to court in the first place' (1983: 582). This would mean that law schools should be encouraged to develop 'the gentler arts of reconciliation and accommodation'. Moreover, to the extent that more conventional legal education is maintained, students as future 'leaders of the bar' should be studying the manner in which a legal system might be pushed in the direction of creating simpler rules, less costly legal proceedings, and greater legal protection for the economically disadvantaged and socially vulnerable. The goal should be to extend legal protection to the poor and disadvantaged so that they 'can defend their interests without being exploited or having to go to court' (1983: 583). Writing some thirty years later on issues of higher education in the United States, Bok concluded that law schools have only responded in a relatively limited fashion to the need for reform which he had identified:

> At one time, law schools were criticized for concentrating too much on the analysis of appellate cases and the reasoning of judges while neglecting other legal institutions, such as trial courts and administrative agencies, and alternative ways of settling disputes, such as mediation, arbitration, and negotiation. By now, law schools have succeeded in introducing these previously neglected subjects into the curriculum. However, faculties have been slower to give adequate attention to the full range of skills students require to become effective practitioners (Bok, 2013: 275).

Building on the innovative reform of courts that had taken place from the 1930s onwards, discussed in the previous chapter, in which courts were redesigned so as to provide substantive expertise in areas such as family

---

[2] By diffuse interests is meant 'collective or fragmented interests such as those in clean air or consumer protection. The basic problem they present – the reason for their diffuseness – is that either no one has a right to remedy the infringement of a collective interest or the stake of any one individual in remedying the infringement is too small to induce him or her to seek enforcement action' (Cappelletti and Garth, 1978b: 194).

problems, juvenile misconduct and so on, Sander argued for the introduction of a more innovative procedural approach. On the one hand he argued for greater use of sequenced, combined, processes: 'in situations involving disputing individuals who are engaged in a long-term relationship. The process ought to consist initially of a mediational phase, and then, if necessary, of an adjudicative one. Problems that would appear to be particularly amenable to such a two-stage process are disputes between neighbors, family members, supplier and distributor, landlord and tenant' (Sander, 1976: 126). On the other hand, the legal system needs to provide disputants with a flexible and diverse array of dispute resolution processes that might be brought together effectively in the form of a dispute resolution centre such as a 'Multi-door Courthouse' which would include not only traditional litigation but also ombuds mediation, a range of evaluative methods, arbitration and a malpractice screening panel. It was Sander's hope – matching to a significant degree the hopes of Derek Bok – that 'once these patterns begin to take hold, the law schools, too, should shift from their preoccupation with the judicial process and begin to expose students to the broad range of dispute resolution processes' (Sander, 1976: 132). It would seem, however, that the impact on the courts was more forceful than on legal education, so that one commentator takes the view that in the United States '[t]he MDC concept has dominated the design of dispute resolution systems in . . . trial courts for the past 25 years' (Edwards, 2013: 321).

The Debates of the 1980s

A notable feature of these three 'movements' – towards the renovation of civil justice, the sponsorship of consensual decision-making and a search for 'alternatives' – was the nature and power of the critiques which they evoked. These critiques, though delivered from a range of very different positions in ideological terms, shared a common starting point in identifying what was seen as the beginning of a major shift in the wider socio-political landscape within which dispute processes were located. Over a long period, culminating after the middle of the twentieth century, government had become progressively differentiated, creating 'public' and 'private' spheres, each characterised by distinctive processes and rationalities. The most powerful institutions had evolved as formal institutions in the public sphere. Among these powerful institutions were the courts; with the consolidation of government's involvement in the management of disputes had come a conception of 'public justice', presented as the delivery of authoritative third-party determinations. In the late 1970s, the process showed signs of going into reverse, breaking down the hitherto apparently clear distinction between the 'public' and the 'private'. One early commentator, Richard Abel, presented this shift as an expansion of state power under which the mode changes from open coercion to covert manipulation, from 'command' to 'inducement' (Abel, 1980). Correspondingly, this shift was reflected in dispute institutions in a growing emphasis upon state sponsorship of 'settlement'.

Working on an even larger canvas, Boaventura de Sousa Santos argued that the state was now 'expanding in the form of civil society' and, predicted that this would take place through a 'dislocation of power from formal institutions to informal networks' (Santos, 1980: 391, 392). In the area of dispute institutions, this general transformation would be reflected in an expansion of state power as, through informalisation, the state sought to co-opt the private sphere and 'to integrate the sanctioning power of ongoing social relationships' (Santos, 1980: 391). Santos summed up his analysis, with its echoes of Althusser and Foucault, with the forecast that state and non-state would come 'to look more and more alike and it is not absurd to predict the development of a face-to-face state' (Santos, 1980: 391).

In contrast with these forecasts informed by Marxist and Post-Modern perspectives is the contemporary account of this forthcoming transformation offered by Gunther Teubner from within the paradigm of neo-systems theory (Teubner, 1983). Starting from Luhmann's assumption of 'functionally differentiated society', Teubner appears to leave 'government' right out of the picture. Developing a conception of 'reflexive law', he forecast a new evolutionary stage in which law becomes 'a system for the co-ordination of action within and between semi-autonomous social subsystems'. With this integrative function of 'furthering reflexive processes in other social subsystems', attempting 'the control of self-regulatory processes' (1983: 281), Teubner predicted that 'reflexive law, now just an element in a complicated mixture of legal orientations, may emerge as the dominant form of post-modern law' (1983: 246). So, while the story is told in terms of self-generating systems of communication rather than of state power, the emergent transformation is in many ways strikingly close to that envisaged by Abel and Santos.

Early Critiques of 'Informalism'

Against this background of a perceived, apparently large-scale, shift in the nature and reach of state power and law, two broad critiques of corresponding changes in the nature and direction of dispute institutions emerged. One critique, exemplified in Richard Abel's *The Politics of Informal Justice* (1982c; 1982d), identified a range of linked problems associated with moves towards 'informalism'. The second, formulated by Owen Fiss in a terse but powerful polemic, 'Against Settlement' (1984), opposed any further move to deflect disputes away from adjudication.

The Politics of Informal Justice

Richard Abel begins by arguing that the growth of informal institutions generally constitutes an expansion, rather than a contraction, of state power; so that what may appear at first sight as a reduction in state activity is in reality likely to represent covert expansion. State sponsorship of a neighbourhood justice scheme, for example, exposes more conduct to review, increases governmental expenditure and co-opts a voluntary sector initiative. There is simply a change in the mode of state domination as the overtly coercive agency of the court is replaced by covert, ideological penetration through community mediation schemes, with 'the state co-opting the sanctioning power of on-going social relationships'.

Abel goes on to argue that beneath the rhetoric of consensus, informal, settlement-directed approaches to the management of disputes simply massage, neutralise and suppress conflict. As a result, the disadvantaged are left worse off, getting less than they would under adversarial, adjudicatory processes. Some of the problems stem from the relaxation of the procedural safeguards associated with formal adjudication that generally occurred with the move to informalism. Intervening third parties are left free to engage in coercive and manipulative action. At the same time, the removal or relaxation of procedural safeguards typically operates in the interest of stronger, institutional litigants rather than the disadvantaged. The latter find themselves left with poorer quality substitutes for adjudication. Abel pointed out that the creation and use of informal institutions and processes by the capitalist state strongly echoes colonialism and its nineteenth- and early twentieth-century strategy of indirect rule which claimed to respect and support indigenous authority but, in effect, created subservience. Moreover, the business world too creates dependency and subordination through setting up a host of specialised complaint procedures – not only processes such as labour arbitration for dealing with production disputes, but also consumer grievance channels so as to contain consumer discontent when substandard products have been purchased. The effect is that the consumers essentially remain passive and unchallenging, and even when they are able to voice their grievances they do so in a controlled way. Business may, for example, appear superficially generous with policies of unconditional returns for unsatisfactory merchandise. But the reality is that the marginal cost of such services for the producer is both small and predict-able, and in any event is in effect paid for by the consumers as a whole through increased prices. Some informal institutions such as small claims court and landlord tenant courts, even when explicitly set up to assist the disadvantaged, undergo functional transformation so that they come to serve the interests of creditors and landlords. Moreover, even in informal institutional settings experience is important. Although businesses may feel more comfortable with invoking the authority of the court in pursuing their interests, informal pro-cesses also favour the experienced, repeat players. The complainant is often a one-shotter who struggles to cope with the experience manoeuvring of the repeat playing business defendant. Without the protection of the state authority because of the limited jurisdiction of such institutions and processes, 'laws specially designed to protect and benefit the disadvantaged, such as those protecting the consumer, are ignored' (Abel, 1982c: 198).

Overall, Abel thus argues that the position of disadvantaged litigants is seldom improved, and typically worsened, where state-sponsored or business-encouraged informal procedures are substituted for formal adjudication. There is a certain irony in the fact that this work, lying at the heart of the critical legal studies movement, has in the last resort to be read as a heroic rescue, if not quite a celebration, of judgement.

Contemporary critiques of these embryonic transformations did not forecast an entirely unrelenting story of domination. The corresponding potential for oppositional strategies of resistance is emphasised in Jürgen Habermas' discussion in *Theorie des kommunikativen Handelns* (1981), where he points to the potential of the shift to secure the communicative and decision-making procedures of the 'lifeworld', as against those of 'system':

> The place of law as a medium is to be taken by procedures for settling conflicts that are appropriate to the structures of action oriented by mutual understanding – discursive processes of will-formation and consensus-oriented procedures of negotiation and decision-making ... From the perspective of social theory, the present controversy ... can be understood as a fight for or against the colonization of the lifeworld. (1981 [trans. 1987]: 371)

Against Settlement

The response to proposals, such as those of Derek Bok, that more disputes should be deflected from the court in the direction of settlement, was just as vigorous. Here the attack comes from those who see a paramount beauty in adjudication. The classic statement appears in Fiss' article 'Against Settlement' (1984). One plank of the Fiss argument echoes the critique of informalism in pointing to the propensity of 'settlement' to underline disparities of power between disputants. Imbalances of power shape the processes of grievance construction, the perception and progress of a dispute, and understandings of the likely outcomes. Fiss worries about settlement, inter alia, because of the impact of imbalances of power on the processes involved:

> By viewing the lawsuit as a quarrel between two neighbours, the dispute resolution story that underlies ADR implicitly asks us to assume a rough equality between the two parties. It treats settlement as the anticipation of the outcome of trial and assumes that the terms of the settlement are simply a product of the parties' prediction of that outcome. In truth, however, settlement is also a function of the resources available to each party to finance the litigation, and these resources are frequently distributed unequally. Many disputes do not involve a property dispute between two neighbours but rather concern a struggle between a member of a racial minority and a municipal police department over alleged brutality, or a claim by a worker against a large corporation over work-related injuries. In these cases the distribution of financial resources, or the ability of one party to pass along its costs, will inevitably 'infect' the bargaining process and settlement will be at odds with a conception of justice that seeks to make the wealth of the parties irrelevant (1984: 1076).

Fiss highlights three major ways in which disparities in resources – that is, power differentials – can influence the process of settlement, often adversely impacting on the interests of ethnic minorities, subordinated employees, and other disadvantaged persons. First, the financially less well-off litigant may be less capable than his or her opponent of gathering and analysing the information necessary in order to gain a reasonably accurate picture of the probable outcome of the litigation. Second, the poorer party may need the damages she or he seeks and, as a result, be induced to settle in order to accelerate payment. Third, the poorer disputant may be forced to settle precisely because she or he lacks the resources to finance litigation. The better-resourced party is able to anticipate the poorer party's costs as if the case were to be tried fully, and decrease her or his offer by that amount, so that 'the indigent plaintiff is a victim of the costs of litigation even if he settles' (1984: 1076).

Overshadowing Fiss' concern with the impact of power imbalances on individual litigants, his central objection to settlement lay in the assertion that a move away from the court would compromise key legal and political values. In a fundamental apology for adjudication, Fiss presents the role of judges in resolving disputes as secondary to their function of restating important public values. The centrality of adjudication is reasserted by presenting judgment as the means through which the core repertoire of norms in society is publicised and refurbished. With the substitution of settlement, the opportunity for the courts to articulate central values is lost, and as these values fall from public attention the stability of the polity is compromised. Thus a broader appreciation of the nature of adjudication is needed. The dispute may be private, but there is a public interest in how it is best resolved. Adjudication uses public resources, and those who adjudicate are publicly appointed officials whose intended role is 'not to maximize the ends of private parties, nor simply to secure the peace, but to explicate and give force to the values embodied in authoritative texts such as the Constitution and statutes: to interpret those values and to bring reality into accord with them. This duty is not discharged when the parties settle.' In contrast, when parties agree to settle, while they may secure peace they do not necessarily secure justice, and this is not in the public interest (Fiss, 1984: 1085–6).

The arguments against settlement put forward by Fiss met with a vigorous response. In particular, McThenia and Shaffer countered in the following terms: 'Fiss's argument rests on the faith that justice is usually something people get from the government. He comes close to arguing that the branch of government that resolves disputes, the courts, is the principal source of justice in fragmented modern American society' (1985: 1660). McThenia and Shaffer (1985) argue that Fiss too easily assumes that the ADR movement is one that wants to secure peace at any price and that is why Fiss is opposed to settlement and other party negotiated outcomes. In their view, Fiss also takes this simplistic view because he views the matters that often come before courts in America as inappropriate for ADR, for one or more reasons. Thus, there may be distributional inequities.

Or it may be difficult to secure authoritative consent or settlement. Perhaps continued supervision following judgment is necessary. Or perhaps there is a genuine need for an authoritative interpretation of law. Moreover, Fiss offers too simplistic a characterisation of disputes – as arguments between two neighbours, one of whom has vastly superior bargaining power over the other – and this enables him to characterise litigation as superior to settlement, because litigation is a way to equalise bargaining power.

And, it is argued against Fiss, the process of reconciliation is much more likely to be one in which the anger of broken relationships is confronted rather than avoided, and in which healing demands not a truce but confrontation. Instead of 'trivialising the remedial process', settlement exalts that process. Rather than 'reducing the social function to one of resolving private disputes', the process of settlement draws on important substantive community values. Settlement is sometimes a beginning, and is sometimes a postscript, but it is not the essence of the enterprise of dispute resolution.

> The 'real divide' between us and Fiss may not be our differing views of the sorts of cases that now wind their way into American courts, but, more fundamentally, it may be our different views of justice. Fiss comes close to equating justice with law. He includes among the cases unsuited for settlement 'those in which justice needs to be done, or to put it more modestly, where there is a genuine social need for an authoritative interpretation of law.' We do not believe that law and justice are synonymous. We see the deepest and soundest of ADR arguments as in agreement with us. Justice is not usually something people get from the government. And courts (which are not, in any case, strangers) are not the only or even the most important places that dispense justice (McThenia and Shaffer, 1985: 1165).

Fiss retorts that it is McThenia and Shaffer who have misunderstood the ADR movement. Overly infused with a spirit of religious commitment they have, in his view, added a layer of meaning to ADR that is in reality simply not present – the goal of reconciliation. The reality is, continues Fiss, that litigation (and therefore also settlement) is resorted to by the parties when there is little possibility of genuine reconciliation, and so addresses a different kind of situation. Rather than dwelling on a somewhat romanticised understanding of community-based and often religious-infused antecedents of the contemporary ADR movement,[3] we should focus on the stark realities of the 'modern American community' and regard ADR as an unwelcome deregulation movement that frees powerful private actors to pursue self-interest free of community normative values. Adjudication, in contrast:

> is a social process that uses the power of the state to require the reluctant to talk and to listen, not just to each other, but also to judges . . . who must in turn listen and talk to the parties. These public officials are the trustees of the

---

[3] As explored in Chapter 2 above

community. They are given the power to decide who is right and who is wrong and, if need be, to bring the conduct of the parties into conformity with the norms of the community. What we need at the moment is not another assault on this form of public power, whether from the periphery or the center, or whether inspired by religion or politics, but a renewed appreciation of all that it promises (Fiss, 1985: 1672).

There is a strong Durkheimian concern in this plea for society to recognise the role of the courts in refurbishing and restating collective norms and thereby promoting social solidarity, overcoming thereby some of the deep racial and class divisions of society in the contemporary United States.

We should note also that the various critiques noted above all centre around questions of power. Comparing them, it is important to keep in view the different ways of conceptualising power – already marked out in classical social theory – that they adopt. Abel's discussion treats power as located at the level of structure, highlighting problems of stratification, issues of class and gender and of the domination enjoyed by large corporations. Looked at in this way 'power' may be concealed from, and unexamined by, the actors. Santos' characterisation of power in terms of heterogeneous, ramifying networks is foretold in the work of Althusser and Foucault. At a different level, Fiss' discussion of power locates it, in Weberian terms, at the level of human agency: the capacity of the particular actors to make others do what they would not otherwise have done. But, as we have pointed out above, there is also a strong Durkheimian echo in his insistence on the irreducible role of cosmology in securing social order.

The Subsequent Trajectory of the ADR Movement

From the end of the 1970s the discussion of alternatives began to be translated into institutional shape. In the broadest, schematic terms three things started to happen, more or less concurrently, in most common law jurisdictions. First, the emergence of new, embryonic professional groups offering institutional-ised help for party negotiations away from the surveillance of the courts and legal profession; secondly, moves on the part of lawyers to re-model areas of legal practice, including a growing readiness to assume non-aligned facilitatory roles; and, thirdly, a re-definition of the role of civil courts under which the active sponsorship of settlement becomes a primary responsibility.

The 'New Professionals' in Dispute Resolution

The growth of ADR in the 1980s and beyond encouraged the emergence of new specialised agencies offering a range of dispute management services in most common law jurisdictions. These agencies have not attempted to do the things which lawyers have traditionally done in the way of advisory and representative intervention. In offering mediation and some novel dispute management techniques they compete only indirectly with lawyers in holding out the possibility of an alternative route. This development took place earliest in the United States, where pioneering agencies included a National Institute of Dispute Resolution (NIDR) and the Society of Professionals in Dispute Resolution (SPIDR),[4] alongside more specialised groupings (for example, the Academy of Family Mediators). This institutional growth, which shows all the signs of disciplinary specialisation and the emergence of an autonomous profession, is accompanied by an emerging regulatory framework surrounding such matters as selection, training, accreditation and standards of practice.

Parallel developments can be found in Australia,[5] Canada and the United Kingdom, notably in the family, community and commercial spheres. In England, initiatives are visible both in the voluntary and the private sectors. In the former sector, the main institutional growth has been in 'family' and 'community' mediation. In the case of family mediation, the most extensive example is provided by the range of local agencies grouped together under the umbrella of National Family Mediation (NFM).[6] In the private field, NFM is matched by the smaller Family Mediators' Association (FMA). Important initiatives in the community, neighbourhood and restorative justice spheres have taken place under the co-ordination of Mediation UK. The Centre for Dispute Resolution (CEDR), founded in 1990, offers a full range of ADR procedures, predominantly catering for commercial disputes. ADR services are also offered across a broad range of disputes by a number of other agencies, most prominently by IDR (Europe) Ltd, a company established in 1989. In outlining these initiatives, the line in institutional terms between lawyers and the new professionals in dispute resolution has often been difficult to draw. This, for example, IDR (Europe) Ltd is effectively a solicitor's organisation, drawing its mediators from a network of member law firms; and the foundation of CEDR was co-sponsored by the Confederation of British Industry (CBI) and several large commercial law firms. So, while something of a distinctive role of 'dispute resolution professional' acting variously as arbitrator, mediator, facilitator, ombuds and counsellor, could be said to have now emerged, in reality legal practice qualifications are still often seen as an important attribute of that role.

---

[4] Now the Association for Conflict Resolution, claiming to represent more than 6,500 professionals in dispute resolution.

[5] Fully discussed in Astor and Chinkin (2002).

[6] Here some sixty services are providing facilitative support for parties wishing to retain control over decision-making in the period around and following family breakdown. NFM services encourage the parties to use lawyers in an advisory capacity and recognise that where mediated negotiations are unsuccessful, more extensive reliance on legal expertise will probably follow.

The Re-modelling of Legal Practice

The arrival of the new professionals was certainly seen by the lawyers as a challenge to their monopoly position in dispute resolution; but a far greater threat – and stimulus to change – was presented by the courts' new determination to sponsor and police settlement. But in a direct sense, the ADR movement was also something that lawyers constructed for themselves. Its very vocabulary and conceptual shape were first sketched in by an academic lawyer, Frank Sander, in his seminal paper to the Pound Conference in 1976. Essentially, ADR has meant two things for lawyers in the common law world: first, the development of specialised client-management devices involving them in non-aligned and advisory roles; second, the growing aspiration to mediate (in many cases claiming this new role as part of legal practice). An important outgrowth of ADR for lawyers has also been the establishment of private and voluntary sector corporations offering dispute resolution services. JAMS Endispute Inc. provides an example of the former and the CPR Institute of Dispute Resolution an example of the latter.

Lawyers in England for the most part responded slowly to the developments noted in the preceding section, and their involvement was initially confined to the field of family disputes. Here their attempt to compete with the new professionals in dispute resolution can be traced back to the formation of Solicitors in Mediation in 1985. This body, initially consisting of five solicitors with practices in family law and the former Training Officer of the National Family Conciliation Council, began to offer 'mediation' in child-related and property disputes. The experiment quickly acquired official approval and was followed by the formation of the FMA under the wing of the Law Society in 1988. Under the scheme operated by the FMA, a solicitor may co-mediate with another professional with experience in marital or family work in helping 'couples cope with the legal, financial and emotional problems of separation and divorce, as well as arrangements for children'.[7] This includes assisting parties 'to work out proposals for settlement' and reach joint decisions in the context of family breakdown.

The English Bar immediately responded to the initiative represented by Solicitors in Mediation with its own scheme for a joint consultancy role under which expert advice could be offered to both parties from a neutral standpoint. In 1985, the Family Law Bar Association announced that it was establishing a 'Conciliation Board' to administer a 'Recommendation Procedure' designed 'to give the parties the benefit of an impartial, confidential and economical recommendation how to settle their differences'. Under this procedure, barristers offer neutral opinions on financial issues submitted to them by the solicitors to the respective parties. This procedure, conceived 'in the hope that

---

[7] See FMA, 'About Family Mediation', available at https://thefma.co.uk/about-family-mediation/, accessed 6 January 2020.

the intervention of a neutral, and experienced outsider might nudge the parties towards a settlement', has not been widely used. Those operating the scheme indicate that advisory opinions have been sought in not more than a handful of cases each year.[8]

By the end of the 1980s lawyers had begun to show an active, proprietorial interest in ADR across a wider field of disputes. One early sign was the formation of IDR (Europe) Ltd. This company, established in 1989, initially drew its mediators from solicitors working in a network of twenty-four member firms. The CEDR, again, was largely a creature of some major commercial law firms.

During 1991, both the Bar and the Law Society hastened to sponsor major reports on ADR. These reports, prepared by Henry Brown for the Courts and Legal Services Committee of the Law Society and the Committee under Lord Justice Beldam for the Bar Council, heralded ADR as something new and important, and identified central roles for lawyers in ADR processes. One major recommendation of the Beldam Report proposed a scheme of court-linked mediation to operate in county courts across a wide range of civil disputes. The proposal was that 'facilitatory mediation' should be offered to litigants at an early point in the court process. In mapping out a pilot scheme, the Committee argued that the role of mediator would most appropriately be filled by lawyers. The Committee offered the view that 'it may be preferable to choose the mediators from those with litigation experience who are barristers or solicitors and to arrange their supplementary training in mediation *so far as may be necessary*' (emphasis added). The report concluded: 'We would suggest that legal mediators should be chosen from lawyers with at least seven years' post-qualification experience' (1991: 11).[9]

By the end of the 1990s, these moves on the part of lawyers to occupy non-aligned advisory and mediatory roles had gained momentum. Increasing numbers of lawyers, in both the commercial and private client sectors, began training as mediators. By the end of 1997, the great majority of large commercial law firms had CEDR-trained mediators among their fee-earning staff; and in many cases firms had begun to advertise ADR services in their promotional literature.

These local developments coincided with the establishment of European offices in London by JAMS Endispute and the CPR Institute of Dispute Resolution, both agencies with a claimed history of success in mediating large commercial disputes in North America. These bodies provided a model for the local emergence of several specialist associations of commercial mediators, offering their services through a central contact site. Perhaps the most prominent among these associations was and still is CEDR (Centre for Effective

[8] See Roberts, Marian (2008: 7) on the Family Law Bar Association's Conciliation Board.
[9] The Beldam plan was realised in experimental form in a London County Court Pilot Scheme – Genn (1998).

Dispute Resolution) founded in 1990 (under its original name, Centre for Dispute Resolution) as a non-profit organisation.[10] As noted above, its chief supporters and promoters have been UK businesses and law firms. Then as now it has a primary focus on resolving commercial disputes. To a lesser extent CEDR also handles consumer and other disagreements. It additionally specialises in offering mediation skills training.[11] The International Dispute Resolution Centre (IDRC) in Fleet Street provides a home for a number of dispute resolution bodies including CEDR and ResoLex.[12]

Correspondingly, on the private client side, the Solicitors Family Law Association, in response to the passage of the Family Law Act 1996, had initiated its own mediation training programme for members; and smaller groups of 'lawyer mediators', such as the British Association of Lawyer Mediators (BALM) were formed.

The Courts as Sponsors of Settlement

In trying to characterise the changes in legal culture now observable in the common law world, perhaps the first point to emphasise is that the most powerful challenge to the lawyers' traditional management of disputing has come from the courts, rather than from disenchanted clients or the emergent new professionals. As we will see in Chapters 7 and 8, a general feature of common law courts has been an increasing determination to control pre-trial processes and in doing so actively sponsor settlement, effectively regulating the terms of access to judgment.

In England, this shift is first visible in spontaneous local initiatives by judges in the family courts at the beginning of the 1980s,[13] followed in the commercial courts a decade later,[14] and then generalised for the civil courts in a Practice Direction of the mid-1990s.[15] Lord Woolf endorsed these steps in his Interim Report on *Access to Justice*, denouncing the culture of late settlement with startling candour and proposing a regime of intensive judicial 'case management'.[16] While his proposals were received critically by some litigation lawyers and commentators, Lord Woolf held to them robustly in his Final Report.[17] The revised Civil Procedure Rules, brought into force in 1999 following his Final Report, challenged the culture of late settlement in two ways: by

---

[10] See Mackie (1991).

[11] See, www.cedr.com, accessed 7 January 2020.

[12] See, www.resolex.com, accessed 15 March 2020. ResoLex presents itself as offering a team approach to resolving disputes and other aspects of the management of large and complex projects.

[13] Parmiter (1981).

[14] Commercial Court *Practice Statement* of 10 December 1993.

[15] *Practice Direction* of 24 January 1995, issued jointly by the Lord Chief Justice and the Vice-Chancellor: [1995] 1 WLR 262.

[16] See: Lord Woolf (1995), especially Chapter 3, paras. 3–11, 30–9.

[17] See Chapter 5 and Lord Woolf (1996), Chapter 1, paras. 1–17.

putting serious pressure on parties to negotiate in the pre-litigation phases of a dispute; and by introducing rigorous case management once litigation has commenced:

4. It has also been suggested that judges are not well equipped to be managers. I do not see the active management of litigation as being outside a judge's function. It is an essential means of furthering what must be the objective of any procedural system, which is to deal with cases justly. Case management includes identifying the issues in the case; summarily disposing of some issues and deciding in which order other issues are to be resolved; fixing timetables for the parties to take particular steps in the case; and limiting disclosure and expert evidence. These are all judicial functions. They are extensions backwards in time of the role of the trial judge. It should be remembered that not all judges will be acting as procedural judges. I envisage that the function of procedural judges will usually be taken by Masters and district judges, although in more complex cases Circuit judges and High Court judges will perform the task. I see case management as an enhancement of the present role of Masters and district judges, but with clearly defined objectives. Obviously there will be a need for training for both judiciary and court staff in order to improve the necessary skills. The Judicial Studies Board recognises that a substantial training effort is needed and has already begun to consider what is required. I am conscious that some procedural judges may feel that their decisions, for example on limiting evidence or the order in which issues are to be dealt with, may be overturned by the trial judge or on appeal. In the future, I hope that the team system will make for a greater partnership between all the judges in every court and ensure consistency of approach to the handling of cases and the development of case management.

. . .

16. Essential elements of my proposals for case management include:

(a) allocating each case to the track and court at which it can be dealt with most appropriately;
(b) encouraging and assisting the parties to settle cases or, at least, to agree on particular issues;
(c) encouraging the use of ADR;
(d) identifying at an early stage the key issues which need full trial;
(e) summarily disposing of weak cases and hopeless issues;
(f) achieving transparency and control of costs;
(g) increasing the client's knowledge of what the progress and costs of the case will involve;
(h) fixing and enforcing strict timetables for procedural steps leading to trial and for the trial itself.[18]

Judicial statistics soon revealed that Lord Woolf's ambition to bring about a cultural change has begun to be realised. The dramatic reduction in the

---

[18] Lord Woolf (1996), Chapter 1, para. 16.

number of starts in the civil courts showed that from the early 2000s onwards settlement is in many cases reached in the pre-litigation phase.[19]

As Hazel Genn has suggested, while on the surface the impetus for the Woolf reforms was something of a 'moral panic' of a 'crisis' in civil justice, it is likely that in reality more immediate concerns such as cutting the legal aid budget for civil cases were the real generators of reform (Genn, 2012: 399). In any event, the new approach was justified in the Woolf Reports (1995; 1996) as a felt need to overcome a lack of judicial control which gave space to skilful and aggressive litigators to use their adversarial, self-interested, strategies to delay, to increase cost, and to deliver settlement at only a very late stage in the proceedings. So, while ADR was to be promoted in the Woolf-inspired civil justice reforms, it was to be done in the context of a spirit of proportionality – complexity and costs should reflect the nature and value of the matters in dispute – and guided by greater degree of managerial control on the part of judges. Indeed, the degree of control as financially expressed in the Civil Procedural Rules embodying the reforms was greater than Lord Woolf had originally envisaged:

> The Civil Procedural Rules ... conferred on the court the authority to order parties to attempt to settle their case using ADR and the judge the power to deprive a party of their legal costs if, in the court's view, the party has behaved unreasonably during the course of the litigation. This discretion is of considerable significance when legal costs are often equal to, and may dwarf, the amount of money at stake in the dispute. The effect of the rules in relation to ADR is not to provide a direct incentive for parties to settle disputes by mediation, but to impose a future threat of financial penalty on a party who might be deemed to have unreasonably refused an offer of mediation (Genn, 2012: 402).

Reiterating the Critiques of Informalism

The early critiques of informalism and the sponsorship of settlement clearly remain directly relevant to this prolific institutional growth; and they have been vigorously reiterated, notably by Laura Nader. In an earlier monograph on the Mexican Zapotec, *Harmony Ideology* (1990), she had underlined the potential of colonial local courts as the site of *both* 'hegemonic' and of 'counter-hegemonic' strategies. But, reflecting on the ADR movement in the United States at the end of the century, she seems to move to a position much

---

[19] The Queen's Bench Division (QBD), which deals mainly with civil actions in contract and tort (but also hears more specialist matters such as applications for judicial review), appears to have been affected more than any other part of the High Court. In 1998, the year immediately prior to the introduction of the new Civil Procedure Rules based on Lord Woolf's proposals for reform, total writs and originating summons in the QBD numbered 114,984. This figure was thereafter steadily brought down, so that by 2003 it was a mere 14,191 – a reduction of 800 per cent over the figure for 1998. See Lord Chancellor's Department (1999) and Department for Constitutional Affairs (2004).

closer to that of Richard Abel. She wrote in 2002 that 'it began to look very much as if ADR were a pacification scheme, an attempt on the part of powerful interests in law and in economics to stem litigation by the masses, disguised by the rhetoric of an imaginary litigation explosion' (2002: 144).[20]

While these overarching critiques are to some extent persuasive, they only provide us with a partial understanding of contemporary moves to institutionalise 'settlement' in the common law world. First, in pointing to a fundamental shift in the strategies of state power they arguably go too far. They tend to exaggerate the extent to which a discrete 'public' sphere, characterised by a distinctive rationality and actively shaping a subordinate 'private' sphere, had ever historically evolved.[21] So we need to be cautious about endorsing the general claim about governmental change in the West. There is nothing particularly novel about those at the centre aspiring to managerial oversight of local processes. More generally, government has 'always' been ready to operate in a dual manner – by central command *and* by inducement in co-opting the local and submitting it to regulation. This was, for example, exactly the mode of government adopted in England following the Conquest in the eleventh century. More recently, this was the procedure followed under nineteenth- and early twentieth-century British colonial expansion, as local agencies were harnessed and brought into government under the policy of Indirect Rule.[22] Again the manifold regulatory arrangements involved in schemes of late twentieth-century 'privatisation' had essentially the same character.[23] In this respect, traditional conceptualisations of the 'public' and the 'private' in constitutional theory have never provided us with more than a partial handle on what is going on.

Lastly, we should recognise that there is a profoundly conservative side to the critique of 'informal justice'. We should be able to imagine 'justice' without wanting to disparage 'settlement'. It is somewhat ironic, given its origins in the Critical Legal Studies movement, that the critique of ADR seems to point us toward the recovery and celebration of 'traditional' superior court adjudication. Any such recovery and celebration, moreover, seems less and less likely to be fully realised, given the hybrid shapes towards which 'courts' across the common law world seem to be moving. The growing impact of new technologies and associated processes such as ODR also make such a restoration unlikely.

Nevertheless, in recent years there has been a positive re-evaluation of the Fiss critique of settlement. The Fiss antipathy to settlement needs to be seen in a more nuanced manner, argue a number of commentators. In the mid-1990s,

---

[20] Another of Nader's targets here was 'ADR's psychotherapy-influenced forums' (2002: 144). The early Californian experiments were explicitly modelled upon Gibbs' study of the West African Kpelle dispute processes (Gibbs, 1963).

[21] This point can perhaps be made particularly strongly in relation to Habermas' 'system'/ 'lifeworld' opposition.

[22] See, for an excellent exposition, Read and Morris (1972).

[23] See Black (1996).

David Luban (1995) reasoned that rather than throwing the Fiss baby out with the settlement bathwater, we need to acknowledge that no legal system has the capacity either to 'settle' or to 'adjudicate' all its civil disputes. Nor is a full embrace of one of these modes of decision-making at the expense of the other at all desirable. Therefore, the real issue is one of 'how much settlement' and 'how much adjudication'. Moreover, the private nature of settlement negotiation and mediation does carry within itself the potential to damage the public good – the public-private distinction that had, as we noted earlier, developed with the rise of the modern state, is something of an illusion, and important public values may well be lurking in apparently exclusively private disputes. There is also the risk of holding back the development of substantive law through judicial decision-making. Such worries could be addressed by – with appropriate safeguards – publishing mediation agreements. Finally, we should accept that there are two differing understandings of the nature of civil litigation. The first is focused on dispute resolution, and sees the court as a neutral umpire making decisions about the claims and counterclaims brought by two roughly equal parties. The parties aim to secure peace, and settlement may achieve this. The second sees civil litigation as an essential dimension of political activity, the judicial counterpart of the legislative process and democratic elections, and therefore an important arena for the explication of social values. So, for some kinds of civil case at least, the courts are the most appropriate forum for resolving disputes, namely those which involve important public values which the state has – or should have – an obligation to enforce. As Menkel-Meadow put the matter succinctly, 'when an authoritative ruling is necessary . . . Fiss is right – the courts must adjudicate and provide clear guidance for all. Racial discrimination is wrong; oppressive prison conditions are intolerable in a decently human society' (Menkel-Meadow, 1985: 500).

In another re-reading of Fiss, Amy Cohen distinguishes herself from Fiss by emphasising that as an empirical matter, it is not categorically the case that ADR processes erode public values – indeed, if we look at the very politicised use of mediation in socialist China and Cuba, for example, informal dispute resolution processes may be used quite aggressively from above to educate local communities in new social and moral values (Cohen, 2009: 1146). The issue that really concerned Fiss, in her view, was not so much the adjudication-settlement dichotomy but, rather, the distinction between moral deliberation and interest satisfaction. At the time he was writing – in the late 1970s and early 1980s – Fiss took the view that it was adjudication that was better suited to moral deliberation – in particular, in promoting continued support for the welfare state and civil rights – whereas settlement would all too readily promote the then-embryonic attempts to privatise state functions and responsibilities. In this light 'once we characterize Fiss's polemic for adjudication and against settlement as an argument for a particular kind of public morality and against an overarching market rationality currently empowered by neoliberalism, then the choice between competing institutional forms becomes less determinate, and Fiss's overarching challenge becomes more irrevocable and enduring' (Cohen, 2009: 1148). And the fundamental concern that worried Fiss was that ADR was one part of broader social efforts to 'replace law with markets as a primary means of resolving social conflict, and replace the state with citizens as the agents primarily responsible for social well-being' (Cohen, 2009: 1150). It was the view of Fiss that adjudication might serve as a force of resistance against this tide, based as it is on principles of social justice, the ideals of the welfare state, and guardianship of justice values.

In a further, and more critical re-assessment of the Fiss analysis, Fisher and Bilsky also argue that it is more important to focus on the Fiss commitment to public values and law reform than process per se, and that – like Cohen – settlement is not necessarily inimical to the promotion of rule of law values especially if it takes place in a court-related setting:

> Settlement is a mechanism that can enhance norm articulation through [for example] the collaboration of judges and parties, in both the process of factual inquiry and devising ways to reform the defendant institution. Furthermore, settlement can facilitate the creation of public spaces of deliberation and new channels of communications. Thus promoting the intrinsic values of [adjudication] (Fisher and Bilsky, 2014: 96).

The Direction of ADR

This contemporary resurgence of alternative forms is distinctive in several important ways. First has been the speed with which the new groups offering institutionalised support for party negotiations away from the surveillance and control of the legal profession have themselves become professionalised. Second has been the counter-movement of recovery under which lawyers have developed alternative forms, treating ADR as the umbrella under which they have re-modelled certain areas of legal practice. Third has been the extent to which the courts themselves have embraced ADR in their (in England at least) novel enthusiasm for sponsoring settlement. This final development points to the unprecedented extent to which the ideas associated with what, at first sight, seems a revolutionary movement have been co-opted by the legal profession and the state. All of this, most notably the embrace of ADR by governments bent on cost-cutting, must renew the concerns expressed in the 1980s critique of informalism. The converging enthusiasm of the courts for settlement, and government for saving money must bring the risk of weaker litigants being coerced into accommodation.[24] Here much will depend on the quality of the emergent regulatory frameworks within which ADR providers work; and upon the extent to which the traditional roles of lawyers and judges retain their identity.

---

[24] A recurrent theme in the writings of Menkel-Meadow (1997; 1999).

Over the past decade or more, the position has been further complicated by the development of ODR, in particular in the increasing use of ODR techniques in institutions such as the courts, ombuds and administrative authorities. Leading commentators expect that this development and the accompanying digitalisation processes will increasingly impact on the field of dispute resolution as a whole:

> ODR began its existence as 'Online ADR' and was intended to be a network-based equivalent of offline face-to-face dispute resolution processes, such as negotiation, mediation and arbitration. It attempted to mimic traditional processes but at a distance . . . In that guise, it was not a change agent in any kind of fundamental way.
>
> Despite the growth of ODR systems during this millennium, the traditional dispute resolution field has continued to view ODR as a niche area with limited relevance beyond the world of simple, repetitive online conflicts. Some of the resistance by individual mediators related to a concern over a need to learn about and use new online tools and technologies. In addition, however, there was apprehension over the possibility that ODR might indeed be something new in that it would threaten some of the values that were embedded in ADR processes . . . there is truth to this as boundaries that shape online and offline activities, relationships, concepts and values are indeed eroding as growing numbers of conflicts are being addressed through digital tools. In many respects, this parallels disruptions occurring in other information-intensive industries and professions.
>
> Growth of ODR is slowly moving it beyond the position of new tools providing efficiencies and conveniences to that of a 'disruptive' technology, one that can be expected to challenge some of the most basic assumptions governing the field and around which its logic has been organized . . . both courts and ADR mechanisms employ processes and approaches that are shaped by physical, conceptual, psychological and professional boundaries. These boundaries have allowed the dispute resolution field to deal with limited capacity, accommodate preferred values and preferences and generate institutional legitimacy. But it is precisely these boundaries that are being challenged by digital technology. As digital tools are increasingly used to assist parties in conflict, the use of predigital dispute resolution models will appear suboptimal. At the same time, alongside the challenge of growing numbers of disputes is the opportunity to use information technologies in new ways that anticipate and prevent disputes and that may not be consistent with some traditional practices (Rabinovich-Einy and Katsh, 2012: 6–7).

The progress of ADR and of ideologies of informalism have come to play an important part in the civil justice systems in many jurisdictions around the world, and yet this development has in large part taken place without convincing challenges to the powerful dissent that emerged in the 1980s. It is difficult to escape the conclusion that governments, big business defendants and the courts themselves are often willing to pressure weaker parties into accommodation through ADR processes, creating distinct possibilities of unfairness and injustice. Of course, as the re-evaluations of the Fiss critique of settlement suggest, these worries are perhaps not always justified, but it is important nevertheless for practitioners engaged in ADR, framers of regulatory standards, and the courts, when they are involved, to guard against the dangers that have been so explicitly identified. With the likely continued expansion of ODR and other digitalised dispute resolution processes, those involved in the design of new dispute resolution developments will also need to be aware of dangers of this growth for the socially disadvantaged, and seek to put in place regulatory frameworks that will ensure a fair and level playing field.[25]

---

[25] The need for effective regulation of ODR-type processes is considered further in Chapter 12.

4

Disputes and Dispute Processes

Introduction

Disputes are primarily affairs of 'naming, blaming and claiming' as Felstiner, Abel and Sarat put it (1980–1). An individual perceives herself or himself as suffering some injurious experience, identifies this as originating in a legal (or some other form of) wrong, blames someone for this and institutes a claim against that someone, setting in train a process that hopefully will put the matter to rights. A grievance that arrives at the lawyer's office thus does so with a history. The lawyer representing the parties will then reshape that history of the dispute into a form suitable for processing in the legal system, often transforming the nature of the grievance in so doing.

Lawyers represent disputes as 'cases' – discrete, bounded and pathological episodes, generated by rule-breach. They are, in everyday language, 'messes' which need to be 'cleared up'. In the lawyer's classical view they are most appropriately cleared up in a particular way, through 'litigation'. This is a process under which, ideally, evenly matched adversaries fight it out – through their legal representatives – on the level playing field of the 'justice system'. In native legal theory, litigation culminates in a final moment of adjudication in which a neutral third party reaches an authoritative determination; although, as we have already seen, lawyers have in practice come to use litigation as the vehicle for their negotiating strategies, and in so doing 'settle' the great majority of causes before judgment.

Clearly, the lawyer's view is a selective, culturally specific understanding of disputes even in the context where it originates. First, in making litigation the paradigm case, and in presenting the instance of professional management as normal, it vastly overplays the extent to which disputes – even in this culture – get anywhere near lawyers and the courts. Second, the image of evenly matched, individual adversaries is tendentious, disregarding potential inequalities of power, the fact that many disputes occur across lines of stratification, or arise as a direct consequence of the efforts of those in power to exercise a steering role. So this image disguises the extent to which conflict resides at the level of structure. In Marxist terms, for example, conflict can be seen as originating fundamentally in the clash of opposed groups over scarce resources in a stratified society. Again, the very conceptualisation of certain kinds of issue in terms of 'dispute' perhaps has an ideological aspect. This may operate both to sanitise particular instances of conflict by separating them from a context in which structural inequalities become apparent; and to mark an event as pathological and so identify it as a suitable focus for professional intervention. In a wider context, the extent to which the lawyer's folk view of conflict privileges settlement-directed talking is also problematic. While we can say that in any group you will find institutionalised means of preventing quarrels getting in the way of the essential business of everyday life – whether this is gardening, herding, cultivating, stockbroking, or whatever – sit down talking will not necessarily be central (Gulliver, 1979: 1–3).

This Durkheimian strand in social theory, in conceptualising disputes as pathological moments separate from the even flow of normal life and best dealt with by specialists, represents a contested position. As Simmel suggests at the beginning of his essay on conflict, 'there probably exists no social unit in which convergent and divergent currents among the members are not inseparably interwoven', and even if an absolutely harmonious group could be conceived in theory it 'could show no real life process' ([1908] trans. 1950: 15). Cultures also differ in the extent to which quiet harmony among the members is presented as a necessary, or even ideal, condition; loud, contentious behaviour may be admired, and quarrelling be seen as normal.[1] The presentation of disputes as discrete, bounded 'cases' is problematic in another way. In any social context, disputes are embedded in everyday life, arising from a 'past' and merging into a 'future'.

Developing a related point, the very firm line drawn in this culture between the 'legal' and the 'political', marked in the distinction between conflict associated with rule-breach (identified as pathological) and that originating in competition for resources (seen as a normal part of everyday life) is not necessarily typical. The very complex relationship between rule-breach and what may be perceived as legitimate competition is illustrated in Turner's seminal account of the devolution of political office in *Schism and Continuity in an African Society* (1957). The headship of Ndembu communities must devolve on a male member of the senior matrilineage in the village; but no detailed rules specify which member this is to be – this is a matter of individual achievement and acceptance. So whenever an existing head shows signs of growing old and losing his grip, younger members of the matrilineage compete among themselves for the headship. Bitter quarrels attend this competition, typically involving claims to wrongdoing, accusations of witchcraft and sorcery. It is only as the new head manages to establish his ascendancy that this all subsides and disappointed competitors either knuckle down under the new regime or leave the village and found their own communities. In this

---

[1] See, for example, Nader (1990: 291–308); Greenhouse (1989); and Palmer (1988).

process, claims about wrong are closely interwoven with struggles for political ascendancy and competition for resources; and given the constantly negotiated nature of Ndembu life, it is not helpful to view conflict as pathological and somehow in contrast to normal life processes – it is simply part of them.

Typologies of Response

A number of general typologies of dispute process were formulated in the theoretical literature that developed around the extensive ethnographic evidence of disputing which had accumulated by the 1960s (Llewellyn and Hoebel, 1941; Gluckman, 1955; Bohannan, 1957; Turner, 1957; Gulliver, 1963; Nader, 1965).[2] These emphasised several core oppositions: between fighting and talking ('war' and 'law'); between agreed outcome and imposed decision ('negotiation' and 'adjudication'); and between different kinds of third-party intervener (for example, 'partisan' or 'neutral') and modes of intervention (for example, 'advice' or 'decision'). The tentative typology of dispute processes or 'responses to trouble' put forward here draws upon and reacts to these attempts. We make no large claims for it; it is simply our shot for these particular purposes.

Avoidance

At one end of the spectrum lies *avoidance*. A universally encountered response to perceived wrong is to do nothing – to 'lump it' (Felstiner, 1974; 1975; Galanter, 1974). We have all, again and again, encountered situations where it has made sense to 'let it go into the net' rather than to respond – perhaps because the issue was too small, or because the overall cost of trouble would have been too great having regard to the value of the relationship concerned. In the same vein, but requiring an active step, is the decision to disengage and avoid, staying away from the person one is in disagreement with. This widely recognised way of dealing with trouble has a range of important consequences: it enables parties to 'cool it'; it signals unambiguously how unwelcome actions have been received; it may put pressure on recalcitrants to step back into line. Obviously, in many situations, total avoidance will be an impossibly costly response; but there are here almost infinite possibilities of fine tuning, allowing extensive variation in scale and severity. Subtle forms of partial withdrawal and of reduction in cooperation are often available – such as stinginess in exchange – which are enough to convey the necessary message about future conduct. The ultimate form of this response is ostracism, where members of a group temporarily discontinue all cooperation with a wrongdoer, or even expel

---

[2] And which continued thereafter – see Abel (1973); Koch (1974); and Gulliver (1971; 1979).

him, leaving him to manage on his own or seek admission to another group (Felstiner, 1974: 79–80).

Self-help

At the other end of the spectrum is *self-help*. A different, potentially costly way of dealing with conflict is to make a direct physical attack on the other party in an attempt to eliminate competition, respond to a wrong or subdue them into compliance with your wishes. On one level this can be presented as an antithesis of avoidance or talking; but a bald fighting/talking, law/war dichotomy is misleading. In any society where fighting is an accepted means of reaching an outcome, it may be expected to take on a conventionalised, restricted, even ritual form. This can be illustrated in the European 'duel', or in any number of reports of New Guinea societies where fighting takes on a heavily rule-governed form. Fighting is reduced to virtually a ceremonial procedure in Eskimo head butting and battering contests; and in the *nith* songs where violence is channelled into a song exchange. Some anthropologists have gone much further than this and treat a whole range of formalised conduct as somehow 'representing' fighting – for example, where ceremonial, competitive presentations of goods are interpreted as replacements for fighting.[3]

Talk: Public Decision-making

Dominant strands of legal theory in the West start out with a distinctive idea of the 'public' sphere in decision-making. This is a sphere represented as created and shaped by government, by definition dominated by governmental interventions (for a powerful statement of this position, see Loughlin, 2003). Within it, decision-making is overwhelmingly characterised by the mode of command and differentiated in such a manner that 'everyday' decisions and decisions in the context of 'dispute' are self-consciously separated. The limitations of this view, in a world where the now obtrusive – if embattled – nation state actually appeared rather late on the scene, need to be recognised before a broader panorama can be attempted.

Starting again, we begin with a recognition that the public sphere is 'always' present in the social world, before government and independent of emergent hierarchies, whatever degree of co-option by those aspiring to power may subsequently take place. Drawing in the contents of this space, we try to elaborate both the range of forms which 'intervention' may take and the varied shapes of hierarchy when this is present. Where the public sphere is colonised by government, the mode of 'command' must even then be relocated in a wider spectrum of interventions.

[3] See Rappaport (1967: 119, 121–3, 138–9).

The Legacy of Command

A primary linkage of decision-making to 'government' gets us off to an uncertain start when thinking about the general shapes of the social world. For as long as we lawyers can remember, our thinking about decision-making has been shaped in broad, schematic terms by images of 'the King' (or some other kind of ruler) and his surrogate 'the Judge'. Laying the very foundations of modern legal theory, Austin (1955 [orig. 1832]) built upon the centrality of command. In Maine's examination, *Ancient Law*, legal history is solidified as the story of adjudication (Maine, 1861). For Maine there were no structural changes in the process of dispute settlement over what he saw as the fundamental stages of societal development. From the primal ascendancy of the senior male agnate onwards, disputes were resolved by decision, handed down by a third party; there was no suggestion of negotiatory modes of settlement giving way to processes of third-party adjudication. The presence of a normative basis for decision-making was the key attribute of law for Maine, and the emergence of this feature heralded the transition from the pre-legal to the legal world. Third, there was the later development of specialisation as legal rules became separated off from other rules operating in society. So for Maine, social life is the product of 'government', law develops in the course of that process, and the fundamental way in which kingly power is revealed is through adjudication. Subsequently, from this emergence of specifically legal theory, attempts to theorise adjudication have dominated jurisprudence.[4] Even today, the courts remain legal theory's central preoccupation (see, for example, Dworkin, *Law's Empire*, 1986).

This way of thinking about decision-making is not peculiar to lawyers but draws on a long dominant strand of socio-political theory. Its foundations are visible in Hobbes' *Leviathan* (1651), a fundamental justification of kingship, where compliance by the subject with 'laws' commanded upon him by the sovereign is offered as the only alternative to brutish and ultimately hopeless conflict. While a less grim view of the pre-state world underlies Locke's *Two Treatises on Civil Government*, political society is still defined in terms of 'a common establish'd Law and Judicature to appeal to, with Authority to decide Controversies between them' (Locke [1690] trans. 1924: 87).

Much later, the centrality of a steering role in society was still taken for granted by Weber in *Economy and Society* ([1917] 1978). In its essentials, Weber's view of the social world was based irreducibly on a model that assumes a leader and a following – the *leiter* and the *verband*. The leader's steering role was exercised through command, a matter of one telling others what to do. In this account a particular conception of power comes into the

---

[4] Although in *The Concept of Law* (1961), Hart appeared to marginalise adjudication by identifying law as an affair of rules, MacCormick's exegesis was quick to re-present Hart's theory of law as one of adjudication (MacCormick, 1981).

picture. It becomes a matter of the chances that people will comply when being told to do things they would not otherwise have done. Realisation of such arrangements is taken to require two general conditions. First, we must assume the availability of staff capable of exercising force if necessary – 'a group of men specially empowered to carry out this function'. Second, because leaders who want to be around for a sustained period cannot rely on coercive power alone, conditions must be such that at least some members of the following regard their domination as normal, even 'right'.

These parochial folk understandings of the 'modern' West, even if they depict with at least partial accuracy the particular context in which they originate, potentially distort any broader panorama. First, the central conception of 'order' as intimately linked to 'government' – in the sense of a self-consciously exercised steering role working within a separate, dominant 'public' sphere – fixes too strong an imprint on the way we see the social world. The overall picture is misleading in that it both overstates and diminishes the place of 'government'. It overstates the role of government in portraying the shapes of the social world as the skilled, intentional achievement of those in power – making it impossible to imagine 'society' without the sovereign. It diminishes it in implying an impoverished mode of operation restricted to command.

The implications of these presuppositions for the understanding of decision-making have been far-reaching. They underlie a quite general pre-supposition that decision-making must be problematic in the absence of 'third parties' to secure it. For example, a widely held assumption of New Guinea anthropology was that negotiatory processes tend to be inherently unstable unless there are third parties capable of acting in a bridging position between the two sides. In commenting on his Jale ethnography in *War and Peace in Jalemo*, Klaus Koch argued that the prevalence of fighting could be put down to the fact that 'very ineffective methods exist to transform a dyadic confrontation into a triadic relationship which could secure a settlement by the intervention of the third party' (Koch, 1974: 159).

Although the link between 'society' and 'government' which these under-standings presuppose was challenged at an empirical level as far back as the seventeenth century, when accounts of Amerindian groups became available in the West, this knowledge was ignored, even suppressed.[5] The reality of aceph-alous society, of social groupings which cannot accurately be represented through the paradigmatic form of leader and following, was confirmed in the course of the subsequent encounter with small-scale, technologically simple societies that fell under imperial rule in the course of late nineteenth- and early twentieth-century colonial expansion. This reality was not easily accommodated

---

[5] It now seems established that one of the motivations underlying Locke's Two Treatises was a justification of the expropriation of the Amerindians involved in European settlement, in which he was directly involved. Locke's formulation of 'political society' was shaped to provide an explicit contrast with the social organisation of Amerindian groups (Tully, 1993).

to these dominant strands in social and political theory. Even for Malinowski 'order' was a problem: how did these acephalous societies hold together given the absence of 'codes, courts and constables'. His discussion in *Crime and Custom in Savage Society* was framed as an answer to that question. There his elucidation of a complex of reciprocal economic obligations linking members of Trobriand society to each other startlingly illustrated a society with limited institutionalised leadership, let alone centralised authority or the differentiated arrangements associated with government in the contemporary West (Malinowski, 1926).

Not only were these societies 'without the King', but in some of them – notably those of hunter/gatherers – explicitly 'egalitarian' understandings were combined with an absence of institutionalised hierarchy, leaving disparities of strength, speed and skill to mark the boundaries of power relations. In the case of such societies accounts abound of people quickly pouring scorn and ridicule on any individual who shows signs of aspiring to personal ascendancy, of 'telling others what to do' or exploiting their labour. The Mbuti of the Ituri forests described by Turnbull (1966), the Hadza of Northern Tanzania (see Woodburn, 1972) and the Amazonian Yanamamo (Clastres, 1977) provide exhaustively observed examples. In these cases – which include shifting cultivators – there is according to the accounts, no 'will to power', no desire to acquire wealth. Production and reproduction take place and order prevails, not only in the absence of centralised authority, but also with very limited institutionalised hierarchy within the group. As Lee insists of one such society (the !Kung San hunter/gatherers of the Kalahari): 'it is not simply a question of the absence of a headman and other authority figures but also a positive insistence on the essential equality of all people and the refusal to bow to the authority of others' (Leacock and Lee, 1982: 53). As Clastres puts it of the Yanamamo: 'no one feels the quaint desire to do more, own more, or appear to be more than his neighbour' (1977: 173). Writing of the Hadza, Woodburn (1972) describes how individuals with troublesome aspirations to leadership are simply abandoned by other members of the small, mobile groups of which this society is made up.

This is not to suggest that in these societies differences of age, gender and skill will not set up diffuse power relations. While these relations are typically of fluctuating content, shifting ramification and transitory duration, to some degree such relations will be institutionalised. In the case of the Hadza, for example, Woodburn identifies a mother and her nubile daughters as constituting one enduring grouping around which a shifting population of aspirant males will congregate.

Reconstructing a Panorama of Decision-making

Against this background, releasing 'society' from a fundamental subordination to 'government', the overall map of public decision-making has to be re-drawn. This revision requires:

- a depiction of the 'public' sphere as an emergent feature of society rather than the achievement of government;
- a recognition of *both* the 'command' and the 'bilateral exchange' as primary modes of decision-making, cutting across any distinction between private and public spheres;
- a re-exploration of triadic forms; and
- a re-examination of hierarchy beyond command.

As we have noted, in many societies the lawyer's 'native' view – and often in the wider tradition of socio-political theory underpinning it – is one in which the 'public' sphere appears as something separate from and other than society, regulating (and in some versions even creating) the rest of the social world. Whatever degree of differentiation may now be present, this prioritisation of the 'public' and the very public/private opposition that this involves is misleading. The public sphere is 'always' there in the social world. It takes its primary, simplest form wherever a third party observes/becomes involved in the bilateral exchanges of everyday interaction. At the same time, we can expect to find it marked out, spatially and symbolically – even in the smallest and most transitory social groups – in the central open space, in the area 'around the fire'. In that context it takes the form, variously described in numerous ethnographies, of a 'council' in which the members of a community meet together and see to their general arrangements – in Bailey's terms an 'arena council' (1969). Bloch's discussion of the Merina *fokon 'olona* (1971) provides an example. He describes meetings which deal with all the general arrangements of the group. They are not confined to some specialised area of competence or 'jurisdiction', but simply consist of the community 'doing something'. In such groups, decision-making may be by consensus, the meeting just breaking up as people disagree; alternatively, some form of decision by 'majority' may operate.

The public sphere in this form is there long before institutionalised office or government is present. So we need firmly to reverse the order as it were, so the public is seen as an emergent feature of the social, upon which differentiation or elaboration – in whatever form – may subsequently from time to time develop. We consider below the different forms of decision-making within such a public space. The whole space may be filled by two opposed groups; there may be others who are not directly involved and may intervene from a non-aligned stand point; there may be yet others who are not directly involved at all but merely have an interest in 'decisions being made' so that they can get back to the fields again. Others may just be 'there', watching, offering the tacit assurance that 'this is the way things are done'. The public space is obviously open to internal or external co-option, and it may well develop as the scene of hegemonic strategies; but, as Clifford Geertz warns in *Negara* (1982), we diminish it if we restrict it to the site of 'command'.

At the same time, and related to that, when we begin talking about decision-making we should make two preliminary shifts of focus. First, we need to begin by paying attention to the primary bilateral exchange as the essential springboard to more complex relations. Simmel recognised the 'dyad' as 'the simplest sociological formation, methodologically speaking ... that which operates between two elements. It contains the scheme, germ, and material of innumerable more complex forms' ([1908] trans. 1950: 122). Restoring a primacy focus on this elementary, ubiquitous mode, under which decisions are reached by those immediately engaged, without intermediaries, through cyclical processes of information exchange and learning, should not be necessary. It is only made so by a dual historical process: the overwhelming attention given by lawyers to third-party decisions in the form of adjudication; and the parallel entrenchment of professional, partisan representation.

Second, we need to go back again and look at the 'triad', recognising the importance of this elementary form of the 'public' sphere as something that is always there in the social world. As Simmel noted, dyads 'have very special features' but 'the addition of a third person completely changes them' ([1908] trans. 1950: 138). But at the same time the triad has to be prised apart from any necessary association with hierarchy – particularly hierarchies of command – for as Geertz has warned us, and as we noted at the very beginning of Chapter 1, 'impressed by command, we see little else' (Geertz, 1982: 121). The dominant, exhaustive image of the leader and following has made dyadic processes appear somehow insecure, even incomplete, and has also harmfully constrained the ways in which we think about third-party intervention.

Taking this forward, we need to explore public decision-making in four primary directions. First, we need to restore the reality of stable arrangement in the absence of institutionalised triadic form, let alone the presence of command. Second, we need to re-explore the possibilities of the triad, turning away from the assumption of 'command'. Third, we need to explore command from the start, stripping away strong institutional shapes. Lastly, we need to look at institutionalised command as part of a wider complex of interventions.

The Shapes of Public Decision-making

While the 'public' sphere is always there in the social world, constituted by the presence of the triad in Simmel's sense, public decision-making need not *necessarily* be characterised by a triadic form. The public sphere may simply represent an immobile but supportive backdrop against which primary processes of decision take place. It may do no more than constitute an authentic context in which A and B negotiate a joint decision, or in which A tells B 'what to do', and thus provide the arena in which dyadic relations are played out. While both of these spare models have realised, recognisable counterparts in any social scene, we need to begin by restoring joint decision-making (negotiation and the rich variations upon it) to parity with command. It has for too long been elbowed aside by the ideology that has come to characterise the nation state.

In searching for an analytical model, the varied forms of settlement-directed communication leading to decision-making may be distinguished through a range of variables. These include: the presence or absence of third-party intervention; the form of such intervention where it takes place; and the location of power in decision-making. On the basis of these variations three basic modes of settlement-directed communication may be identified: bilateral negotiation; facilitated negotiations ('mediation'); and umpiring processes. These are sketched in here as 'models' only, cut away from context and thus achieving an analytical clarity typically absent in real-life processes.

Negotiations are represented here as the simple bilateral exchange. They are processes of communication, involving the exchange of information, potentially leading to common understanding and joint decision-making. In their simplest, bilateral form two parties in dispute approach each other without the intervention of third parties and attempt to achieve an agreed outcome through information exchange and learning. The exchange and examination of information lead to the modification or consolidation of expectations to a point at which agreement is achieved. Communication continues as long as agreement is seen by both sides as possible and advantageous. The essential feature is that control over the outcome is retained by the disputants themselves, informed by their meanings and understandings. The simple contrast is with processes in which power is shared with, or transferred to, third parties.

The simple model of bilateral negotiations can be transformed in a number of ways. First, in the direction of multi-party negotiations, additional individuals or groups may enter the negotiations as parties. Second, partisans may be added in support of the principal disputants. The 'help' extended by such partisans may take numerous forms. At one end of the scale, assistance may be limited to tacit support, it may extend to advice, and further along the spectrum it may involve the partisan standing beside the principal as a member of a 'team'. The most extreme form of partisan intervention arises where the principal retreats into the background and is represented in negotiations by a partisan as 'champion'. The provenance of partisans is also variable, ranging from the friend or neighbour to the professional adviser or representative.

The intervention of partisans necessarily changes the shape of simple negotiations in a number of ways. First, the number or quality of partisans on one side or the other may alter existing configurations of power. Second, insofar as partisans take an active role in negotiations, rather than providing tacit support, some of the power over decision-making otherwise enjoyed by the parties alone will pass to them. Third, the universe of meaning within which negotiations proceed is necessarily extended and changed by the presence of partisans on either side; their understandings, their interpretations and their repertoire of norms will come to inform the process to a greater or lesser extent.

For the purposes of the next model, the basic structure of the decision-making process is changed by a presence of a third party who intervenes, in contrast to the partisan, from a position of at least apparent non-alignment to facilitate achievement of an outcome. The primary role of such a 'mediator' must be to facilitate communications between the parties, but the potential nature and range of involvement extends beyond that. While at first sight power in facilitated negotiations remains with the parties themselves, control necessarily passes to some extent to the intervener who may in some cases come to share power over the outcome. The nature and extent of facilitatory intervention varies greatly; the very term 'mediator' conceals a wide range of different activities and degrees of intervention, as we indicate in Chapter 7.

For the purposes of the third model, the essential change is that power over the outcome is transferred to some third-party decision-maker. Beyond this fundamental attribute, the nature and characteristics of umpiring are widely variable. Some are state-sponsored ('judges'), others are privately selected by the parties ('arbitrators'). Equally, the central role of judges can be perceived in a number of ways: as a compartment of 'government', exercising a steering role; as revising and keeping in public view central norms and understandings in society; as deciding individual disputes brought before them. Umpires differ also in the resources that they draw upon in decision-making. We explore all these questions in Chapters 8 and 9.[6] In the sections which follow, we look a little more closely at the three foundational forms of handling disputes that necessarily involve verbal communication between the parties, attempting in so doing to move beyond the parochial context of decision-making of the contemporary West.

Negotiations

We can identify the basic elements of the bilateral exchange across widely different socio-cultural contexts. They are as visible in the unselfconscious routines of everyday life as in the formalised, set-piece exchanges of an international conference. The fundamentals also remain constant whether the issue is uncontentious or a focus of extreme conflict. While the basic features of negotiation – as processes of communication, involving the exchange of information, potentially leading to common understanding and joint decision-making – hold steady across cultures, the form they take and the conventions under which they take place will be shaped by the specific cultural context.

Ethnographic examples of these bilateral and multi-party decision-making processes offer little support for that strand in political-legal theory that identifies such processes as inherently unstable in the absence of available, non-aligned, third-party intervention.[7] The reality of stable decision-making processes in a context which does not encourage non-aligned, third-party

---

[6] For further details see Abel's comparative essay on dispute institutions in society (1973), and Shapiro's study of courts (1981).

[7] See Koch (1974).

intervention is powerfully illustrated in Philip Gulliver's ethnography of the Arusha, *Social Control in an African Society* (1963). Before being subject to colonial rule in the nineteenth century, the Arusha were settled agriculturalists located in northern Tanzania and organised in terms of cross-cutting social organisations of lineage, age-set and territorial unit ('parish'), but without a state. The organisation of Arusha society demarcated the range of settings available in decision-making. An aggrieved Arusha could present a complaint with members of his parish, his lineage or his age-set. This enabled a grievant with a problem some freedom to choose the forum where he believed his support was strongest. However, Arusha understandings impose limitations upon this freedom to 'forum shop'. Disagreement between members of a lineage should be kept *within* the lineage and a similar feeling was expressed so far as age-mates are concerned. It goes with the idea of 'privacy' to the group that disputes between members of a single lineage should be taken to a meeting of the lineage, rather than to either of the other two agencies. Quarrels between age-mates should be similarly settled within the set to which they belong. Only where two members of the same parish who were neither age-mates nor members of the same lineage were in dispute did the parish meeting constitute an approved venue for discussion. In addition to this beyond lineage 'privacy' restriction, two further features of Arusha society determined the bilateral shape of intra-lineage decision-making. First, Arusha lineages were organised in such a way that where any two members of the lineage were in disagreement the allegiance of the remaining members is routinely deter-mined. The two ensuing groups meet and together provide the venue within which discussion and decision-making occurs. Second, for Arusha a posture of non-aligned disinterest is unbelievable. A person is on one 'side' as a partisan or the other. The idea of a 'mediator' is not available to them. Instead, discussion takes place bilaterally between the two opposed groups allied with the respective 'principals'. Room to manoeuvre in decision-making is created – even though Arusha normative understandings may be clear-cut and detailed – by the fact that such norms are approached in a transactional way and become bargaining chips rather than determinants of outcome. In the absence of 'mediators' pressure seems typically to come from within the opposed groups. These, however, seldom develop into solidary 'power' groups that might threaten social stability, as each will contain members of the same age-sets and parishes.

The 'Third Party' in Decision-making

Where we do encounter the 'third party' in decision-making, some strong native legal stereotypes – notably those of the 'king' (or 'emperor' or some other kind of ruler) and the 'judge' – need to be recognised before triadic interventions as a whole can be re-assessed. These are hierarchically positioned interveners, explicitly associated with an institutionalised role of centralised steering (and so exercising 'official' power), making imposed decisions (and so utilising the mode of 'command'). So in native legal theory, fundamental structural features of the triad, even if well marked out in sociological theory, are virtually erased. For example, the idea and the person of the 'mediator' have in many regions of the West been driven to the margins. This has resulted from a dual process: the increasing dominance of 'command' as the nation state solidified; and the emergence of lawyers as a specialist service profession. Overall we need to make the non-aligned intervener more securely theorised. In so doing we must, in particular, reverse the historical priority given to the judge and the corresponding marginalisation of 'the mediator'.

The nature of third-party intervention is inevitably closely dependent upon the socio-cultural context in which it takes place, making any attempt at generalisation hazardous. Recognising the culturally specific character of any intervention, on an analytical level we need to work along two primary planes, representing respectively:

- what interveners *do*; and
- their provenance.

Non-aligned third parties may become involved in a wide range of interventions – in constituting the means of communication (the 'go-between'), in providing advice and information, in facilitating the decisions of others (the 'mediator') and in themselves making the decisions (the 'arbitrator' and the 'judge'). Such interventions are perhaps best represented as ranged along a spectrum of progressively increasing intensity. At the minimal end is the passive observer whose mere presence sanctions bilateral decision-making. A little further along lies the 'go-between' who carries messages between two poles, setting in place the communications arrangements necessary to enable decision-making to take place. At the far end lies the legislator or the judge, making decisions to which others are subject. If we seek to make a clear analytical break along this spectrum, one way of doing so is to distinguish those interventions that facilitate the decisions of others from those that constitute the decision itself. Another way of putting the same point, is to ask where 'power' over the outcome lies – drawing a line between 'the mediator' and 'the judge'.

Looking closely at the provenance of different interveners in the context of their interventions immediately forces us to take seriously the variable elements of hierarchy and institutionalisation. Many third parties are senior, through rank or office, to those in relation to whom they intervene. They may be 'elders' in terms of kinship, feudal superiors, political leaders, dominant specialists, or even rulers. They may, on the other hand, be collateral kin, friends, neighbours, bystanders or workmates. These variables obviously affect both the modes of their intervention and the manner in which that intervention will be received.

Mediatory Interventions

While 'advice' and 'mediation' may appear analytically distinct activities, in many instances it is difficult to prise them apart. First, while much advice is delivered from an openly partisan standpoint, we can recognise the reality of the non-aligned adviser, attempting to address the parties to decision in an even-handed way. Second, the label of 'mediator' seems to conceal at least two analytically distinct modes of intervention, with quite different processual shapes. One involves a primarily facilitatory role, setting in place the communications arrangements between parties which enable them to negotiate; the other a more active dominant role, associated both with the political superior and the expert consultant (the latter is a role familiar across a wide range of contemporary professions).

The role of the mediator may be as clearly recognisable in the routine, unexamined interventions of friends and kinsmen as in those of professional specialists or political superiors. Ethnographic accounts also provide numerous cases of figures who mediate in the course of a broader role – the Nuer 'leopardskin chief' (Evans-Pritchard, 1940) and the Kalinga *monkalun* (Barton, 1919), for example. But a paradigm case where leadership in decision-making is narrowly institutionalised in the shape of the mediator is described in Philip Gulliver's ethnography of the Ndendeuli of Southern Tanzania, *Neighbours and Networks* (1971). The Ndendeuli typically reside in small kinship groups, and practice simple slash-and-burn agriculture that required cooperation within and between households. These mutual help arrangements would transform over time into ties of more generalised reciprocity, so that they also offered a pool of support if one member became involved in a dispute.

In the event of a dispute arising between two members of an Ndendeuli community, the approved method of dealing with it is for the disputants to meet together with their kinsmen for settlement-directed discussion. Third parties, who in the nature of these communities will inevitably be kinsmen or affines of the disputants, must in theory play one of two roles. They may join either disputant as a supporter (Gulliver describes such people as members of a disputant's 'action-set'), or seek to perform a mediatory function in a more or less impartial way by convening and facilitating meetings between the two groups. Gulliver found that the action-sets were built up of people with whom the disputants enjoyed the closest ties of material cooperation (e.g. if A has repeatedly helped B in his clearing and hoeing operations, and vice versa, either will expect the support of the other in the event of a dispute). Each disputant will try to secure as members of his action-set people who are influential in the community and who are listened to with respect in a meeting: sheer numbers, while important, may be matched by quality.

Mediators, on the other hand, are likely to be drawn from people with whom neither party has particularly close ties of cooperation and who stand equidistant from each in terms of kinship. Outright support in the event of a dispute strengthens the ties between the supporter and the disputant, and necessarily leads to a corresponding cooling of relations with the other party. Similarly, while successful mediation can increase prestige in the community, failure to achieve a settlement, or demonstrated partiality for one side, will be damaging. Because of this, in a small community third parties have to calculate very carefully the consequences of a particular position or alignment and judge nicely the degree of support they may extend. Each dispute leaves its mark on the community in the sense that new loyalties are established and old ones decline. Existing hostilities are similarly liable to modification.

Once a meeting has been convened, both sides outline their version of the dispute, and the competing assertions and demands will be supported by the respective action-sets. As the overall picture becomes clear, those who have adopted a neutral posture hitherto may suggest possible lines of settlement, urging both parties to give ground in such a way that their respective positions converge to a point where some agreed outcome is possible. In doing so they necessarily put a given construction on events and implicitly allocate responsibility for the dispute. At this point the supporters of each disputant may themselves urge a particular compromise and outline the merits of some course of action that a mediator has proposed. In this way a solution can speedily be reached, and the meeting end successfully. But equally the meeting may break up with the rival positions hardened in deadlock. Where this happens, another meeting has to be arranged to try again. While each disputant retains a degree of independence, once the meeting begins and his action-set has been convened he is to some extent constrained by the opinions the members express and the courses of action they favour. If influential members of the set favour a particular solution by way of settlement, and advocate it strongly, there is little the disputant can do but accept this, for otherwise his group of supporters will simply melt away if the meeting ends without a conclusion. Certainly where members of the respective action-sets are as one as to the solution to be followed, there is little the principals can do but comply.

In searching for a settlement, reference may be made to socially accepted rules, to the importance of sustaining particular social ties and to the harmony of the community as a whole. While appeal to some Ndendeuli norm must underlie any claim which one party may make against the other and many form the criteria on which a settlement is urged, such norms tend to be general and ill-defined, rather than detailed and clear-cut. This lack of clarity is illustrated in the norms relating to bridewealth and to the behaviour of the son-in-law. While Ndendeuli are clear that bridewealth must be presented on marriage, and that a good son-in-law has a duty to give material help to his wife's father, the rules do not make it clear what constitutes an adequate presentation of bridewealth, what is sufficient help to a father-in-law, or where these different responsibilities begin and end in relation to each other. The uncertainty of these Ndendeuli norms thus provides ground over which argument can range if a quarrel between a man and his son-in-law should arise.

Besides any socially approved norms which may be specifically relevant to a dispute a higher appeal may also be made to the parties that they must patch up the dispute in the interests of harmony in the group. Such an appeal will run: 'We are all kinsmen, we cannot allow this quarrel to continue and disrupt our lives.' A call like this will take on particular urgency if the quarrel persists, or if it occurs at a time when its prosecution delays vital agricultural activities.

Beyond any such appeals to norms and underlying values, political under-currents will also be present. The 'notable' who is able to form a large action-set made up of the men who are influential in the community and articulate in debate will be well-placed to achieve the more favourable settlement.

The consequences which this form of organisation has for the Ndendeuli processes of dispute settlement appear clearly in Gulliver's account. First are the limitations imposed upon third parties where they have no authority to impose a decision on the disputants. This lack of authority is underlined in instances Gulliver cites of meetings frequently breaking up without any con-clusion having been reached. Such a conclusion is only reached when the disputants themselves, however reluctantly, agree upon one. Therefore the role of third parties cannot extend beyond helping to achieve that agreement. They do this, first, by constituting a forum within which discussion may take place; second, as members of the respective action-sets, by formulating the positions of the two sides; and, third, by building the elements of a compromise out of the positions which develop. Analytically, the role of the action-set member, and that of the mediator, are distinct in this process; and in their nature will be performed by different people. But mediators are not necessarily without bias, as Gulliver's illustrations reveal. Further, members of the respective action-sets, as well as any mediator, may play a significant part in edging the respective positions closer and, finally, articulating the possible solutions implicit in the positions that have emerged. Nor should the influence of third parties in achieving a settlement be under-emphasised. Although they lack any decision-making power, their assessment of what constitutes an appropriate compromise will be hard for the parties to resist, particularly if a consensus develops between the two sets, or if a preponderance of political muscle is lined up on one side or the other. No disputant can afford to hold out for a solution which his supporters do not favour, as in the short term his support will melt away and in the longer term he will put in jeopardy future valuable cooperation.

A second general point is the flavour of bargain and compromise inherent in this settlement process. As the outcome must lie in agreement, the formula will be found in the most which each party is prepared to concede and the least she or he is prepared to accept. Under such conditions norms cannot be exclusive determinants of an outcome, and considerations such as the respective economic strength and political muscle of the different parties become important. But so far as the part played by Ndendeuli norms in the process is concerned, Gulliver argues that their very lack of clarity is of vital importance. This characteristic introduces an element of flexibility that provides leeway for successful negotiation. Were the rules clear-cut, one avenue of compromise would be unavailable.

The process of settlement here is different in two major respects from that in the Arusha case described above. First, the necessary leeway for negotiation is achieved through a different means. In the Ndendeuli case, imprecision of norms provides the needed flexibility. With the Arusha there is no lack of clarity: the rules about bridewealth or that a man inherits his father's field are crisp and unambiguous. It is the fact that the norms are seen as negotiable, as resources in the process of reaching an outcome, that provides the necessary flexibility to achieve a solution. Second, the mode of settlement is different. In the Ndendeuli case, a purportedly non-aligned mediator stands between the respective groups of supporters and helps guide them to a negotiated solution. With the Arusha, the initiative towards compromise comes from *within* the opposed groups themselves. This feature is foretold in Arusha lineage organisation. These lineages are constructed in such a way that they divide into two all the way down, with the result that in the event of conflict arising within the lineage, each member knows on which side his support is due (Gulliver, 1963: 134–40). Obviously he has discretion to exert himself strongly or remain in the background; but the 'side' he is on in any conflict within the lineage is decided for him in the principles of lineage organisation. Thus, within the lineage there is no one who *can* stand in an intermediate position and behave as a neutral mediator. Further, as we noted, there is the principle of privacy to the group that operates strongly in lineage affairs. So there are strong cultural inhibitions against someone from *outside* the lineage being drawn in to mediate.

Third-Party Decisions: The Attribute of Command

While the distinction between the mediator, who facilitates a decision, and a third party who makes one may be clear-cut on an analytic level, these two shade into one another in practice. Here the language of communication may provide only a limited guide. Particularly where those involved are in relations of hierarchy, decisions may well be couched in the form of 'advice', even tentative 'suggestion'. The key variable here is the presence or absence of leeway to accept or reject the solution identified.

Where a 'command' mode of decision-making is present in the public sphere, the degree to which this is institutionalised is variable. A paradigm case of the instantly recognisable but minimally institutionalised commander is the 'big man' who repeatedly appears in Melanesian ethnography. In the earlier literature, the 'big man' was presented in sharp contrast to 'the African chief', whose incumbency was determined by 'descent' and whose relationship with his people had a prescribed character, governed by a definite repertoire of understandings.

Big men were depicted as healthy, intelligent, energetic individuals who managed to build up followings through personal ability, by manipulating wealth in the form of pigs and other valuables. Such a following would fluctuate in size in accordance with contemporary success (rather than with kinship), falling away as vigour, luck or skill deserted him; the big man would not necessarily pass on a following to his son. No following would last longer than the big man remained able to coerce his subordinates or they continued to see advantages in continued association. In much of this ethnography, coercion was central; the big man was depicted as a commander, a transitory despot, who 'told members what to do' and would in the last resort deal with them physically, in person, when faced with opposition.

On the whole, this early picture of the Melanesian big man has survived in contemporary anthropology; he is still an 'emergent individual' rather than a member of an 'ascribed category'. It is now clear, however, that these power relations varied in character from place to place, both in expression (varying from command to advice) and in degrees of consolidation, especially in the degree to which 'family' was important (in some groups it was certainly the ambition for big men to assemble followings for their sons, who were placed in advantage by their family associations – in such cases 'descent' should be seen as one variable in the make-up of success, and was certainly not absent altogether). There is also now a clearer picture of the 'syndrome' of which 'bigmanship' forms a part: accumulation and circulation of valuables; some men marrying several wives, others none at all; sexual segregation in both work and social life.

The nature of the 'big man's' ascendancy is revealed in accounts of his part in decision-making. These suggest no clear distinction between occasions directly linked to a big man's attempts to secure his domination over another member of the group, incidents arising out of efforts to maintain and discipline a following, and cases where a big man seeks to 'resolve' quarrels between two members of that following. Moreover, responses of particular big men to quarrels have an unsystematic quality and depend upon personal style and contemporary standing; they range from direct interpersonal violence to subtle or oblique diversion. Pospisil (1958) describes big men as variously clubbing recalcitrant members with billets of wood, weeping and throwing tantrums and quietly tendering fatherly advice. Each situation is confronted as it arises; issues are dealt with ad hoc. But it is important to note that the modes of power associated with 'government' – in terms of violence and persuasion are already there before institutionalised hierarchy, even though the 'caging resources' may be much more limited in scale.

Except in the extent that some big men seek to assemble followings for their sons (at which point one encounters perhaps an elementary form of institutionalisation), these relations, grounded in the person of the possessor of economic or symbolic capital, do not involve an element of transmissibility. There is no 'position' distinct from the person; 'power' cannot be thought, even primordially, as a 'possession' or 'thing', itself, independently of economic or symbolic capital, transmissible from person to person, in life or in death.

Command Institutionalised: Towards 'the State'

If in overall human history 'government' arrived late on the scene, it has now been around a long time across many regions and the forms of ascendancy associated with the pretension to exercise a generalised steering role have been extremely varied. These transformations have taken place within the public sphere, which those aspiring to ascendancy progressively co-opt, presenting themselves to be its source as they do so.

While it may be relatively straightforward to distinguish the transitory 'big man' from the 'elder' claiming to exercise leadership on the basis of genea-logical seniority, pinning down 'kingship' and 'the state' is problematic. Ana-lytically, within the spectrum of leadership roles, a clear break seems to arise with the junction of 'rank' and 'office'. This junction is realised with the emergence of an actor having authority to make decisions concerning the general arrangements of the group, holding an office with identified responsibilities which devolves from one incumbent to another in accordance with socially accepted rules. Three elements are often important in this emergence: a close and sometimes complex relationship between 'kinship' and 'kingship'; developing 'steering' roles which may lie on the border between command and inducement; and the growth of a notion of 'legality'.

Thus, the transition between institutions founded in kinship and those transcending kinship, although presented by scholars like Fried (1967) as the pivotal moment in state formation, is complex and uncertain. While it is common for people like kings to appeal to genealogy and use the idiom of fatherhood, the link may be more than metaphorical. In some African king-doms, for example, the ruler *is* the genealogical senior member of a dominant patrilineage, and speaks of his activities in parental terms. We take here the example of the Kgatla (Tswana) rulers encountered by European explorers, traders and missionaries arriving in Bechuanaland towards the end of the eighteenth century. In this account we may see complexities in the relationship between kinship and 'kingship', the somewhat ambiguous nature of steering roles, and culturally based understanding of the notion of legality.

Each Kgatla ruler (*kgosi*) claims to be the genealogically senior member of the cluster of patrilineages of which his 'tribe' (*morafe*) was made up. The Kgatla polity was thus governed by a hereditary ruler (*kgosi*),[8] who may turn

---

[8] The state of affairs described here is that which existed in the last years of the nineteenth century, before the Kgatla state was absorbed in the Bechuanaland Protectorate. The Setswana term *kgosi* has conventionally been translated as 'chief', a usage which will be followed here.

to three different groupings for advice and help in decision-making. First, he is surrounded by a small informal council drawn by him from among his immediate senior relations (his father's and his own younger brothers, his male cousins, his maternal uncles), together with any other men who enjoy special positions of influence and trust. Secondly, he may call together all the headmen of the wards (the name conventionally given to the major administrative divisions into which the society is divided up). Finally, there may be a meeting to which all the adult male members of the society are summoned. Most everyday decisions are taken within the first of these groupings and any decision that is reached is then transmitted to the headman of each ward, who himself passes it on down the administrative hierarchy. If more serious matters have to be discussed, all the headmen are summoned; and in matters of the greatest importance all the adult males of the society may be assembled.

The procedure in a meeting at any one of these levels is very flexible, and the actual location of authority is hard to pin down. Typically, the chief raises a matter which he wishes to take action on and speaks about it for a while. Then other people present give their views. Often when a clear view emerges quickly, the chief will summarise it and propose action along that line; there will be chorused assent, and the matter is concluded. People say, though, that it is for the chief to decide; and not for the people at the meeting, whatever level this may be at. In one sense this may be true, but no chief would last long unless he enjoyed general acceptance and this would be swiftly eroded if he constantly tried to push through measures for which there was no support.

Many of the major decisions which are taken in these councils require action by large groups if they are to be carried out: in the past, if war was to be made, or the state organised for defence; today, if the cattle are to be rounded up, or if major water-works are to be dug. Where anything like this has to be done, the age-sets will be called to do it. A new age-set is formed every five years or so when the young males of the society then approaching physical manhood are gathered together and submitted to initiation procedures (including circumcision). All those initiated together form the new set; and as the new sets are successively formed over the years, those above rise in seniority. The physically hardest work, such as major building projects and (formerly) making war, are left to the members of the more junior sets.

The link between the chief and the senior man in each ward is ideally a genealogical one, for the office of chief should devolve from father to eldest son, while the younger sons of each ruler go off to form their own wards, assuming administrative control of these new sub-divisions of the main group. The Kgatla believe that their society was founded by Kgafela in the late seventeenth or early eighteenth century, and most of the forty-eight wards in the central village of Mochudi today are headed by men claiming descent from younger brothers of chiefs descended from Kgafela. A few wards whose members do not claim descent from younger brothers of former chiefs have been founded by men of groupings previously conquered by the Kgatla, or who have asked for permission to join them for defence against a common enemy. But apart from these exceptions, ward heads are senior members of the junior branches of the chief's lineage.

This system of administration is reflected at ground level in the residential organisation of the main village. At the centre is a group of homesteads occupied by men of the chief's immediate agnatic segment, and ranged around this are forty-seven other groups of homesteads, each presided over by a ward head. Thus, the ward in this sense constitutes a geographical area; and each headman ideally lives with those over whom he has administrative control and responsibility.

Within each ward there may be anything from 200 to 600 people, and the majority of the members again claim to be related in the male line to the headman. Two further sub-divisions are also generally found inside a ward. First, all the males claiming descent from a common grandfather tend to be grouped together, and within such a sub-group a minimal unit is made up of an adult married male, occupying a homestead with his wife (or wives) and children. In many wards also, there have been incorporated individuals from other tribes who have come over time to form their own descent groups under the administrative control of the headman who is a member of the major segment.

Thus, if the group is looked at from the bottom up there is first the married male heading his own household, then the group consisting of his closest male agnates, then an aggregate of such groups forming a ward, and lastly the wards together forming the total society. Kgatla society can thus be seen as an ever-growing and deepening pyramid, the base of which is extended as more males are born and rear their own families; while in its simplest form the political and administrative organisation is imposed on the lineage system like a cloak.

Kgatla see the regularities of their everyday lives as governed by a corpus of rules which they describe as *'mekgwa le melao ya Sekgatla'*, a phrase which has generally been translated as 'Kgatla law and custom'. However, this translation is misleading in two ways. First, the terms *melao* and *mekgwa* are not sharply distinguished in the way that this translation would suggest. Secondly, 'Kgatla law and custom' cannot be seen as a body of rules corresponding directly to our rules of law, because the term embraces a whole repertoire of norms of different kinds, ranging from rules of polite behaviour and etiquette, through moral imperatives and rules taken very seriously in the context of dispute, and even includes examples of what we would call legislation. Everyone, even the chief, is expected to comply with these rules in their everyday behaviour, and there is a Tswana saying: *'Molao sefofu, obile otle oje mong waone'* – 'The law is blind, it eats even its owner.' But there is not the distinct category of 'legal' rules which so clearly characterised our system. Norms governing social behaviour on a visit to someone else's homestead fall just as clearly within the overall classification as those prescribing what must be done when one man's cattle destroy another man's field of corn.

The origin of some of these rules is seen by the Kgatla to lie in long-established and adhered-to patterns of approved behaviour, others as arising out of decisions made by a chief in handling a dispute, yet others out of direct announcements made by him in what we would see as statutory form. The Kgatla would distinguish among such announcements those which simply restate and emphasise something which already forms part of 'Kgatla law and custom'; but which has perhaps become forgotten or carelessly observed. The occasion of any meeting in the chief's *kgotla* may provide an opportunity for such a reminder. On the other hand, an announcement which either expressly changes some existing rule, or which provides a new regulation to deal with some special contingency, has to be introduced with more careful preparation. The Kgatla say that when a chief wishes to make a change of this kind, he should call together the tribesmen so that the matter can be discussed. Only when he has done this, and following discussion in the *kgotla* announces a new rule, does such a rule become part of 'Kgatla law and custom'.

Although the Kgatla would say that it is for the ruler to announce a new law, most would agree that he *should not* do so unless the proposal he has already put to the *kgotla* meeting meets with approval. Where such a proposal does not attract support few would say that this prohibits a ruler from going ahead with his announcement, for there is a saying to the effect that 'The chief is law' ('*Lentswe lakgosi kemolao*'), but the chances of such a rule being generally complied with are greatly lessened.

Rules which Kgatla and other Tswana chiefs have announced in this way extend over a very broad field of subjects, including family life (e.g. how many wives a man may marry; what he must give by way of bridewealth; the age of a woman at marriage; the number of cattle payable as compensation when one man impregnates someone else's daughter); land tenure (regulations relating to the fencing of fields and the settling of uncleared land); public hygiene; and traffic regulations (e.g. to the effect that wagons must be fitted with proper brakes for going downhill).[9]

The extent to which one of these legislative announcements gets complied with depends upon the degree of social acceptance which it achieves and upon the capacity of the chief to enforce it. Some chiefs do not announce a measure until they feel that it will enjoy widespread acceptance, and in such a case enforcement presents few difficulties. Where a rule does not enjoy social approval, or where it is burdensome to comply with, much depends on the energy of the chief. If it involves such a matter as the fencing of the fields or the branding of stock, the matter can be handled through rigorous inspections and the punishment of those who fail to comply. On the other hand, chiefs who have tried to regulate family life have found this much harder to achieve.

[9] See Schapera (1943) and Comaroff and Roberts (1977).

As well as providing signposts for proper social behaviour, *mekgwa le melao ya Sekgatla* are also seen as furnishing the criteria according to which disputes should be settled where these arise. All Kgatla talk freely about these rules, and consider that they know them; there is no sense in which they are the special preserve of some particular sub-group within the society. In the context of a dispute these rules may be expressly invoked, or more frequently referred to by implication through the way in which the details of a particular claim are presented. People are taken to know the rules, and the mere claim that 'Molefe's son has impregnated my daughter' or 'Lesoka's cattle have trampled my corn' is sufficient to invoke by implication the body of rules which everyone knows to be associated with damage to crops by cattle and the impregnation of unmarried women.

As in most societies, *mekgwa le melao* differ considerably in their degrees of generality, and it is possible for them to be adduced in the context of a dispute in such a way as to conflict. Where, for example, two brothers are in dispute over who should inherit the mother's homestead, the one may invoke a general rule to the effect that close agnates should live peacefully together, whereas the other may rely on the much more detailed prescription to the effect that the youngest son should inherit the dwelling. It is where conflicting rules are relied on like this that it becomes necessary to talk about rules explicitly. Where both disputants agree as to the rules, but argue about the interpretation of facts in relation to an agreed rule, explicit reference is unnecessary.

Settlement-directed discussion is seen under all circumstances as the most appropriate way to handle a dispute. While retaliatory violence and forcible re-taking of property are tolerated within narrow limits, these never enjoy social approval. Similarly, while it is recognised that supernatural agencies may be invoked in order to establish responsibility for harm or misfortune that has been suffered, further resort to these agencies when a human is identified as responsible is strongly discouraged. Such methods are recognised as likely to exacerbate a dispute in the event of their discovery by the other party.

The agencies for handling a dispute are located in the institutional hierarchy we have already considered. Where a quarrel breaks out between two people, the Kgatla see it as their own responsibility to try and settle it between themselves through bilateral discussion; but because they realise that such negotiations may fail, and that the help of third parties may be necessary, they each keep their senior kinsmen in touch with what is going on from a very early stage. Relatively simple and recurring problems, like the destruction of crops by cattle, are typically resolved at this level; but where the matter is more serious, or where there has been a history of bad relations between the parties, the trouble may be taken directly to senior kinsmen. Under such circumstances, with tempers running high, attempts at bilateral negotiation may be avoided entirely through fear that a fight will break out.

Where bilateral attempts at settlement fail, or where they are not made through fear that they will lead to violence and a heightening of the trouble, the disputants call on their immediate kin to resolve the matter. Although the Kgatla rely heavily on their close agnates for help in disputes, trouble is seldom contained as closely within the lineage as we saw it to be in the case of the Arusha, and close maternal kinsmen are likely to be drawn in from the beginning. These approaches may culminate in private negotiations or a formal meeting at the homestead of a senior member of the lineage to which either disputant belongs. The mode of settlement attempted at this level depends upon relationship of the parties. Where they are not close kinsmen, the respective disputants typically meet with their kin in support, and then the two groups try to feel their way towards a settlement by negotiation, without anyone seeking to mediate from a bridging position. Where they are related, a senior kinsman who can claim equally close relationship to both may try to mediate from a neutral standpoint. At this level no-one is in a position to impose a decision, and if a compromise cannot be reached through negotiation, the matter has to be taken to the headman within whose ward the earlier meetings have been held.

The headman has a range of options available to him in dealing with the dispute. He may attempt to mediate directly by suggesting solutions which may possibly be acceptable to both parties; or he may send them away for further discussion with their close kinsmen if he feels that the possibilities of that avenue have not been exhausted. However, although the headman may act as a mediator if he wishes, it is also recognised that he may attempt to resolve the matter by imposing a decision. Where he does so, the parties have the choice of accepting and complying with his decision, or taking the dispute to the chief. Where the matter is taken to the chief, he hears the report of the headman who dealt with the dispute earlier and the accounts of the disputants and their respective senior kinsmen. Then, like the headman, he may attempt to mediate, or proceed directly to resolve the matter by decision. Once a decision has been given, the chief has the capacity to enforce it if necessary. Disobedience will be met with corporal punishment, the confiscation of stock or the withdrawal of land allocations. The age-set organisation provides the necessary machinery for enforcement: members of one of the more junior sets can be sent out to bring a recalcitrant individual before the chief or collect together his stock prior to confiscation (Roberts, Simon, 1979).

So, in this Kgatla example settlement-directed talk enjoys pre-eminence as a mode of handling disputes, while such means as violent self-help and sorcery are strongly disapproved. In the settlement of disputes, as in the ordering of everyday life, people are expected to follow *mekgwa le melao*; but this reper- toire of norms, ranging from the general to the particular, offers the Kgatla considerable flexibility in managing their lives and in dealing with disputes. Nor can it be accurately seen as a discrete corpus of legal rules, ranging as it does from norms of polite behaviour to mandatory statutory injunctions. Further, it does not constitute a monolithic system, as variations in content and in interpretation can be found both in different geographical areas, and at different levels in the polity's organisation.

Thus, the hierarchical organisation of the Kgatla polity is also matched in the institutionalisation of disputing, as attempts at resolution should move from the disputants themselves, to the descent group, to the ward, and finally to the *kgosi*. Further, while negotiatory and mediatory means of settlement may be attempted at all levels, these give way in the last resort to a judicial mode before a headman or the *kgosi*, while the latter has access to organised force in ensuring compliance with any decision if this should prove to be necessary.

In looking at dispute institutions in a centralised polity, we have taken a third African example. We could just as well have looked further afield as these forms have developed again and again in different geographical locations in widely different historical periods. For example, in Imperial China too, we can see manifestations of three elements discussed at length for the Kgatla: a close and sometimes complex relationship between 'kinship' and 'kingship'; developing 'steering' roles which may lie on the border between command and inducement; and culturally based notion of 'legality'. The Emperor was characterised as the 'Son of Heaven' (*Tianzi*) in early Chinese society, and ruled over 'all below the sky' (*tianxia*) by virtue of the Mandate of Heaven, bestowed by Heaven on whomever was regarded as most fit to rule. Responsible for the prosperity and security of his people by the threat of removal of the mandate through revolution (*geming*),[10] but in fact this was relatively rare and the position was hereditary, Emperors from the same family thus formed the major dynasties in traditional China. Authoritative third-party decision-making was deeply embedded in the hierarchical structure of the Imperial state. The creation of a unified state was achieved – as we noted in Chapter 2 – by the ruler of the state of Qin, who thereby installed himself as the first Emperor of a unified Chinese state. He brought with him a philosophy of Legalism, and although in due course this was abandoned as the official ideology, it nevertheless bequeathed China a system of formal legal institutions of considerable sophistication. But, despite the technical sophistication of the Imperial legal system, parties were expected wherever possible to deal with their differences outside the purview of the courts. The fundamental cultural preference was for 'lumping' grievances – that is, simply ignoring the problem – and making concessions or *rang* in order to facilitate 'resolution'. Negotiations or '*tanpan*' were embedded in concerns with 'face' or social prestige, with building networks of favours through gift giving to make the negotiation of particular issues easier. Central was the belief that individual interests and rights should not be paramount but, rather, that parties in disagreement should compromise and thereby promote social stability. Fundamental too was a cultural preference for third-party intervention in the form of mediation – not only for disputes, but also for transactions. The 'middle person' has always had an important role to play. Often such mediators were

---

[10] Literally, to deprive a ruling dynasty of the divine mandate to rule, but coming to mean revolution more generally.

local leaders – lineage or guild heads – and by the nineteenth century at least, elaborate systems had developed within the local political structure that enabled parties from different local communities to take their complaints to higher tribunals (Palmer, 1987: 79).

But parties did on occasion take their civil disputes to court, sometimes even in violation of lineage rules expressly forbidding recourse to the local magistrate, who combined executive and judicial roles and who, like the Emperor himself, was seen in parental terms – he was the 'father and mother official' (*fumu guan*). Although inclined to 'mediate' the dispute before him, or send it back to the local community for leaders to attempt to mediate again, he would if necessary impose an authoritative decision on the parties, and records of appeal and review cases show that Chinese magistrates and their judicial and administrative superiors did provide or impose outcomes in many civil disputes by the application of statutory rules, local customary norms, and a sense of justice and fairness, as well as a felt need to secure compromise if at all possible:

> The case records . . . demonstrate that magistrates were in fact guided closely by the code in adjudging civil disputes. To be sure, they preferred to defer to extrajudicial/kin mediation whenever possible, in accordance with official ideology. But when confronted in a formal court session with suits not resolved by extrajudicial mediation, they almost always adjudicated forthwith by the code. They acted, in other words, as judges and not as mediators. Indeed, the standard magistrate handbooks . . . directed magistrates to study the code closely and adjudicate accordingly. Examining actual magisterial judgments in civil cases brings into focus some of the most frequently used substatutes of the code, often buried under misleading statutes . . .

> Of the triad of principles – law, commonsense right and wrong, and peacemaking – that guided informal justice, compromise was the most important. But that is not to say that state law did not matter. The fact that imperial state sought in its representations to deny, or at least to trivialize, civil law [did not mean that] the informal justice system . . . [was] . . . unaffected by official law . . . All parties knew . . . that if and when community state failed, resort to the courts of the state might follow . . .

> [Thus, there was an] intermediate realm between formal and informal parts of the justice system. The majority of civil cases were settled without a formal court session, by a process that combined the workings of informal community mediation and magisterial opinion. Once a case entered the court system with the filing of a plaint, efforts at community mediation would be intensified. At the same time, expressions of magisterial opinion in the form of comments on the plaints and counterplaints, generally available to the litigants, provided a preliminary indication of the likely verdict of a formal court session. Informal mediations were generally worked out under the influence of such magisterial opinion (Huang, 1996: 12–13).[11]

---

[11] And see, more generally, Galanter and Cahill (1994).

Conclusions

We have used these vignettes to shift our understanding of three primary modes of decision – bilateral negotiation, mediation, umpiring – away from the parochial context of decision-making in the West. The ethnographic detail is necessary in our view to locate the possibility and reality of these foundational forms in a wider cultural context. In later chapters we look in more detail at these three forms, and then the hybrids into which they may evolve in real-life processes.

Development of Disputes, Avoidance and Self-help

Introduction

We have suggested in Chapter 4, that in many if not all societies, regardless of their location in time and space, there is an identifiable range of responses by which disputes are handled and resolution sought. In general terms, the range of these procedures and their variation can be understood within a spectrum of responses ranging from avoidance and lumping at one end to self-help, including in particular violence at the other. Between these two extremes we have identified processes that are more reliant on talking and communication, namely, negotiation, mediation and umpiring. We have also seen how these broad categories may overlap with each other. In this chapter we give consideration to the manner in which disputes emerge, and the ways in which this may affect in particular either an inert or inactive response, or on the other hand a resort to self-help.

A dispute is ordinarily a social relationship, and societies around the world offer social actors as disputants a range of possible processes that they can put into operation in order to change that relationship when 'trouble' arises. As we saw in the preceding chapter, at one end of the spectrum of responses lies avoidance, including, for example, the 'lumping' of problems, where a party with a grievance for a variety of reasons does not pursue her or his grievance, and/or unilaterally readjusts a relationship in which a dispute has arisen so that tensions are mitigated or even dissolved. At the other end of the spectrum, another important response is recourse to self-help, perhaps most notably including the use of violence, sometimes with a degree of social and legal acceptance, in response to disagreement or more serious forms of tension between the parties. Other forms of self-help may be utilised, but the choice of violence is usually a serious and significant event in the unfolding problem in the relationship between the parties.

This chapter further examines the nature and characteristics of, on the one hand, avoidance, and on the other, the threat and use of self-help for resolving 'civil' disputes. In so doing, the chapter considers social phenomena to which texts on 'alternative dispute resolution', 'civil procedure' and so on tend not to give a great deal of attention. The mainstream focus is, of course, primarily on the ordinarily more morally appropriate and legally acceptable processes of negotiation, mediation and umpiring. It may well be the case too that there is a widely held value in society in which order is considered preferable to disorder, and this too encourages concern with processes that in 'resolving' a dispute also assist in maintaining order. Resort to violence, in contrast, is oftentimes a form of conduct that strays over the borders of civil disagreement into the realm of criminal justice, moral censure, public disorder and even social instability. Moreover, of course, doctrinal analysis in the common law world tends to be focused on the application of the law by judges in decided cases and this too distracts the gaze, as recently emphasised by Cownie and Bradney (2020). Further, the importance of such 'touchline' work is arguably made more compelling in a world where there continues to be significant access to formal justice problems facing the socially disadvantaged, and where in many societies resort to violence as a mode of resolving disagreement is an increasing concern. Finally, the ineluctable processes of 'juridification' within ADR practice and accompanying discourse may also encourage us to lose sight of the compelling but sometimes competing values that encouraged the emergence of 'ADR' in the first place, namely, to encourage processes and outcomes that are suited to the parties' needs, to increase voluntary compliance with outcomes, to provide accessible, cheap and speedy fora to ordinary people with disputes, and to give the parties greater control over the process of dispute resolution so that they might, first, have a sense of ownership of their dispute and its resolution, and, second, handle disagreements better in the future, and not looking to violence or litigation as decision-making processes in disputes . The intent of this chapter is to explore the two relatively neglected forms of response – avoidance and closely associated processes on the one hand, and coercion, especially the use of violence, on the other – in order to provide a fuller understanding of the range of decision-making responses to 'trouble'. In the early days of ADR these were given much more attention in the relevant literature than they are today, and so the chapter is more a revival of concern than it is a new start.

The Genesis of Disputes

As we also noted in the previous chapter, disputes emerge through a process that Felstiner, Abel and Sarat (1980–1) characterise as 'Naming', 'Blaming' and 'Claiming'. These represent a series of processual stages in which injurious experiences may be perceived and understood in some way to be problematic (naming), and then might become grievances in the sense that the cause of the perceived injury is blamed on another person or organisation, and in due course may then be transformed by a claim against the person or organisation thought to be responsible, which is resisted, thus creating a dispute. A dispute thus arises when a claim based on a grievance (perceived or real) is rejected (either in whole or in part) by the party who is blamed for the trouble. The study of the emergence and transformation of grievous experiences into disputes means the examination of a social process and the analysis of the conditions under which injuries are unperceived or go unnoticed, as well as how people respond to the experience of injustice and conflict.

In order for disputes to emerge and therefore also remedial action to be taken, an 'unperceived injurious experience'(unPIE) must be transformed into a 'perceived injurious experience' (PIE) (Felstiner et al., 1980–1: 633). Whether someone who has been harmed in some way is able to perceive that he or she has suffered an injury is a more important issue than is commonly recognised. In addition, Felstiner and colleagues admit that there are conceptual and methodological difficulties in studying this transformation. Thus, for example, since an 'injurious experience' is any experience that is regarded as negative by the person to whom it occurs, so it may well have a strongly subjective dimension. It may be difficult, therefore, to establish who in a given population has experienced an unPIE (1980–1: 634).

The first transformation of naming – a personal acknowledgement that a particular experience has been injurious – may be the critical transformation. The next step is the transformation of a perceived injurious experience into blaming. This occurs when a person attributes an injury to the fault of another individual or social entity. Felstiner and colleagues argue that fault is necessarily one dimension of a grievance, and this means that an injurious experience is one that is viewed both as a normative violation and as likely to justify a remedial action. This is the grievant's perspective: the injured person must feel wronged and believes that something should be done in response to the injury, however politically or socially improbable such a response might be. The third transformation occurs when someone with a grievance – who blames – conveys to the person or entity believed to be responsible and asks for some remedy. This communication is called claiming. A claim is transformed into a dispute when it is rejected in whole or in part. Felstiner et al. (1980–1: 636) suggest that transformations 'reflect social structural variables, as well as personality traits'.

PIEs, grievances and disputes are subjective, unstable, reactive, complicated and incomplete. The fact that they are 'subjective' means that transformations need not be accompanied by any observable actions. A disputant may discuss her or his problem with another person and accordingly re-evaluates the conduct of the opposite party. Transformations can be little more than changes in feelings and awareness, and feelings and awareness may change repeatedly, hence the process is unstable. Since a dispute is centred on a claim and a rejection of that claim, disputes are reactive by definition. The characteristic of instability is often visible when parties engage in efforts to resolve their quarrel.

Although there is considerable overlap between the two, and while many scholars do not draw a line between the terms 'dispute' and 'conflict', we do see a broad distinction between the two. A dispute, we have argued is where a perceived grievance is blamed and claimed and rejected in whole or in part, and the grievance is based on some sense that there had been some breach of correct conduct. Conflict we see as a broader and sometimes longer-lasting phenomenon, such as struggles for political office or wage bargaining, where trouble is generated in the pursuit of an objective without any rule or standard necessarily being broken. This differs from situations where one person has physically injured another or has pursued their interest against another in a manner which is at variance with the accepted norms of the society concerned.

Characterising Dispute Responses

Efforts to depict the range of responses to an emerging dispute have been around for more than half a century. A number of general typologies of dispute process were formulated in the theoretical literature that emerged from the extensive ethnographic evidence of disputing and which had pre-ceded the emergence and development of ADR in the 1970s. These efforts influenced subsequent attempts to characterise the range and nature of responses to dispute. The early characterisations tended to be built around one or more fundamental distinctions: between fighting and talking (that is, 'force' and 'negotiation'); between agreed outcome and imposed authoritative decision ('negotiation' and 'adjudication'); between different kinds of third-party intervener ('partisan' or 'neutral') and between different styles of inter-vention ('advice' or 'decision'). In due course, slightly more elaborate mapping took place, and the resulting typologies of dispute processes or 'responses to trouble' usually placed on the spectrum the phenomena of, at one end, 'avoidance' and at the other, 'force', including 'violence'. However, these two polar responses tended not to be treated as another core dichotomy but, rather, they seem to be treated more as afterthoughts, added to provide a more comprehensive and rounded picture.

An important reason for this tendency to look at the central processes is, it might be suggested, that such processes potentially offer an identifiable and feasible resolution of the disagreement between the parties, whereas the polar extremes of avoidance and force offer much less certainty and stability in the future relations between the disputing parties. One factor that helps to explain this unpredictability is, of course, that individuals do not always want to settle their differences and thereby bring an end to a dispute. Instead, they conduct themselves with a view to future opportunities to raise their grievance. Both avoidance and force might well be part of a complicated relationship between the parties in which, in due course, there will be a revival of the dispute. Both avoidance and coercion also share a common characteristic: they are both primarily *unilateral* modes of decision-making, unlike many aspects of the more central dispute response processes, and this too may reduce predictability.

Value of Looking at 'Avoidance' and 'Violence' More Carefully

Early studies of one or both of these phenomena revealed, however, that these modes of response in dispute processes were sometimes widespread, and carried serious messages for both a better understanding of dispute processes and law reform agendas. Thus, in their seminal essay on 'Naming, Blaming and Claiming', Felstiner and colleagues (1980–1) emphasised the importance of looking at the initial stages in the emergence of a dispute. First, it is in the embryonic phase that an aggrieved person is most likely to conclude that her or his complaint is best discontinued, feeling unable or unwilling to pursue her or his grievance. Secondly, the range of behaviour encompassed in the early phases of a dispute is greater than that involved in the later stages, where the institutional milieu tends to narrow the range of options open to disputants. One implication arising from these observations is that if, for example, limited rights' consciousness and a sense of futility have led to 'grievance apathy',[1] then it is unproductive (perhaps even counterproductive) to implement civil procedural reforms which offer more equal access at the later stages of disputing, as the later stages are where inequality may have a greater impact and the disputant suffering from grievance apathy is caught up in an unfamiliar and uncomfortable world of official institutions. Thus, reforms such as legal aid, the waiver of court costs, the creation of small claims courts, and other legal reforms may have a more limited impact than they might have otherwise delivered: the horse may have already bolted, so to speak. As Felstiner and colleagues conclude:

> A theory of disputing that looked only at [the formal legal] institutions mobilized by disputants and the strategies pursued within them would be seriously deficient. It would be like constructing a theory of politics entirely on the basis of voting patterns when we know that most people do not vote in most elections (1980–1: 636).

Moreover, inadequate opportunities or a sense of futility despite a felt need to correct an injustice can lead directly to a violent outcome. This seems to worry some legal cultures more than others, so that for example, in contemporary China very early intervention by people's mediators in an emerging dispute is often justified by the claim that this will 'nip the contradiction in the bud', thereby preventing 'degeneration' of the dispute into criminal conduct involving violence. This concern also reflects a longer standing worry in Chinese legal culture, namely that oppressive conduct in a social relationship may well lead to suicide, and that in some senses this is the functional equivalent of homicide. Thus, in traditional China from the Ming dynasty onwards, it was a specific offence in the law of homicide for a person to act in

---

[1] That is, the phenomenon of the unwillingness of persons who perceive themselves to have suffered an injurious experience caused by another party to pursue their grievance against that party.

such a manner as to drive another into committing suicide. MacCormack describes the unfolding law in the following terms:

> This form of liability may be regarded as distinctive since it is not found in the main legal systems of the West: Anglo-American common law and the Roman based civilian law. The particular Chinese rules on liability for driving another to commit suicide . . . are not found prior to the Ming (1368–1644). Although there are no explicit rules on liability for suicide in the Tang code [however] this does not necessarily mean that in Tang law there were no cases in which one person might be held liable for driving another to suicide . . . In the course of its history we see a significant change in the nature of the liability. In the Ming and early Qing liability essentially was grounded upon coercive acts by which another was driven to suicide. By the middle of the nineteenth century two significant changes had occurred. First, in the important group of rules concerned with illicit sexual intercourse and offensive behaviour, the element of coercion as a requisite of liability came to be disregarded, to the extent that liability might be imposed where one person's suicide could be attributed to, was caused by, another's immoral behaviour.[2] Second, increasing parallels drawn between homicide and suicide, as well as the multiplication of cases in which the death penalty was applied, suggest that driving or even causing another to commit suicide came to be seen virtually as a category of homicide (MacCormack, 2018: 217).

Avoidance: Its Forms and Close Relatives

Introduction: Dispute Avoidance and Dispute Pre-emption

Avoidance is non-confrontation, but beyond this minimal understanding, an accurate characterisation of the processes of avoidance is perhaps not as easy as it might seem. Philip Gulliver, in searching for a definition, draws an important distinction between dispute avoidance and what he portrays as 'conflict avoidance', although the latter term is perhaps better characterised as 'dispute preemption' (1996: 126–7). He speaks to the line which Felstiner earlier drew between avoidance 'as [a form of] dispute processing . . . [and] . . . avoidance behavior adopted to prevent disputes arising in the first place' (1975: 695). Thus, dispute avoidance is evasive conduct that occurs within the circumstance of an emerging dispute between individuals or groups. This evasive conduct occurs when a disputant (whether a group or an individual) decides to take concrete action (or more or less consciously decides not to take action) that limits interaction with the other party (and, possibly, the latter's partisan supporters) after trouble has emerged. The evolving problem is thus contained by restrained action, the aggrieved party

---

[2] Though, if we take a broader view of what constitutes coercion, we might not want to agree with MacCormack's assumption that 'immoral' conduct necessarily constituted a move away from a concern with coercion in the imposition of liability for suicide, as it may be seen by the aggrieved partner as conduct which is a strong rejection of the relationship and for that reason tantamount to coercion.

sidestepping a looming confrontation of some kind, at least immediately and perhaps also long-term. This may involve forms of conduct such as 'lumping' (tolerating the injustice, though see below); ostracising the other party (perhaps individually, or collectively [sending to Coventry]); 'turning the other cheek' (refusing to respond to an injustice); and 'sidestepping' (diverting attention by refocusing the relationship on some other issue that is less or non-confrontational). We may even go so far as to characterise, as a form of avoidance, acceptance of a claim or offer that is unjustified but once accepted avoids further interaction. Or, there is the use of diversion – including sometimes diversionary force – to avoid further hostile deliberating on the substantive issues giving rise to the dispute, if not the dispute itself, and so on.

Rather strangely, when the literature on such conduct refers to concrete examples, the illustrations chosen appear to be more inclined to fall under 'dispute pre-emption' in nature. To draw on Felstiner again, his tangible examples of dispute avoidance have a strongly pre-emptive tone to them:

> adolescent children limiting contacts with their parents to perfunctory matters because matters of importance have proved too contentious, of friends curtailing their relation because of past quarrels, of consumers switching their trade from one retail merchant to another after a dispute, of casual workers (gas station attendants, waitresses, dishwashers, gardeners, housekeepers) quitting jobs because of problems with employers, of children moving out of their parents' houses because of irreconcilable values and of neighbors who visit less because of offensive pets, obstreperous children, loud parties and unseemly yards (Felstiner, 1974: 76).

This suggests that while the line between the two forms of conduct – dispute avoidance and pre-emption – in some cases may be clearly drawn, in other cases the difference might be quite difficult to identify.

In another set of observations, Gulliver also seems to conflate avoidance and pre-emption when he writes:

> Conflict avoidance may be an explicit cultural style or an implicit possibility. Thus, in some contexts it may be prescribed by formal rules which require individuals to abstain from or limit contacts with certain other persons with whom interaction is considered potentially dangerous: for instance, daughter's husband and wife's mother, or classificatory brothers and sisters. Less formally, but often in a culturally stylised way, individuals practice avoidance in order to prevent disputes arising or to minimise involvement in situations where dispute already exists or seems imminent. For example, in rural Ireland (County Kilkenny), individuals often chose not to frequent places or to engage in activities where troublesome situations and people would be encountered, or they crossed the street or took another route so as not to meet certain individuals. When unavoidable meeting occurred and straightforward ignoring was undesirable, interaction was kept to conversation on superficial topics, such as the weather or non-local gossip. In this way, people avoided intimacy or controversy or matters of importance (1996: 127).

Here too we see behaviour that lies on the penumbra nestling between avoidance and pre-emptive conduct, and suggestive of the fact that specific manifestations of these two forms of action may attempt to deal with an issue both before a dispute occurs, as well as after a grievance has been created and a dispute begins to emerge.

Preventing

For dispute pre-emption the intention is, more or less knowingly – how much less is a matter of some debate, as we shall see below – to prevent disputes occurring or to limit involvement in circumstances in which it is anticipated that a dispute might well occur. Dispute pre-emption is thus explicitly forward looking, an established part of the practice of law, and may well involve the use of legally binding contracts and other devices in a wide range of situations.[3] Thus, to give an obvious example:

> The phenomenon of a steadily increasing number of divorces in many cultures calls for a growing need for couples contemplating marriage to foresee future divergences in their married life and to try to prevent them through premarital agreements. Premarital, prenuptial, or antenuptial agreements (commonly abbreviated to 'prenups' or 'prenupts') 'describe the rights, duties and obligations of prospective spouses during and upon termination of marriage through death or divorce' . . . They are a type of mediation within the framework of Alternative Dispute Resolution (ADR), aiming at resolving disputes other than through litigation, and taking the form of contracts used by individuals who want to precisely define the disposition of their assets (Denti and Giordano, 2010).

Changing Legal Practice

Accordingly, it should be acknowledged that in various ways commercial and civil legal practice (in the common law world at least) has been drifting in the direction of dispute avoidance for some time now, making adjustments specifically intended to avoid the development of disputes. As is well known, the above-noted pre-nuptial agreements are just one form of contract preliminary intended to avert future disputing or at least to clarify the rights of the parties should disagreement arise. This is not to say that the goal of pre-emption is the sole prompter of such developments, but that it may well be an important factor. Thus, in addition to pre-emptive contract arrangements we may think of avoidance as including evolving processual innovations such as collaborative lawyering,[4] partnering, or simply better project design and management, as one leading London firm advises:[5]

---

[3] See also, for example, Brockman (1980).
[4] See, for example, Wolski (2017).
[5] See Gould (2019).

Conflict avoidance requires clear, concise, careful and proper planning of the strategy for the execution of a project. It is also about adopting a proactive conflict avoidance approach such as risk analysis, clarity in the contract documentation or partnering ... There are a number of simple steps that can be taken in order to attempt to avoid conflict. These include:

1. Good management: Proactive planning and management of future work, as well as raising early issues of concern can avoid disputes;
2. Clear contract documentation: Ambiguities in contract documents can lead to argument, disagreement and dispute. Focusing on the specific details of the particular project (rather than generalization) is important;
3. Partnering and alliancing: Building cooperation between the project participants and fostering team spirit is extremely valuable;
4. Good project management: Planning ahead and managing generally and specifically the time, money and risks associated with the project are crucial;
5. Good client management: Understanding the client's objectives and communicating issues and problems early on are fundamental;
6. Good constructor management: A regular objective assessment of progress and the costs relating to a project also involves communicating well with the constructor and dealing positively and objectively with problems that arise. Do not ignore problems in the hope that they might go away;
7. Good design team management: Good information is crucial;
8. Record keeping: Disputes can often be resolved by retrospectively considering records that have been kept during the project. However, those records are often not sufficiently detailed.

Creative Lawyering

More generally, such initiatives are part of a range of attempts at creating a professional culture of problem-solving, as Rosenberry in an understated and under-estimated essay points out:

Those in the legal profession who respond to a rapid change by broadening their repertoire of approaches for preventing and solving problems are more likely to be successful in their practices and feel more personally fulfilled. In a rapidly changing world the nature of problems change; in order to respond, one needs a box full of tools. Therefore, it is important to recognize ways to facilitate creativity and creative problem solving (2005: 424).

Some Temporal Dimensions of Avoidance

Avoidance as a process involves doing little or nothing to resolve the issues in dispute between the parties. Sometimes the approach is intended to be only *temporary*, giving a party breathing space to rethink the dispute, or to attract partisan support (popular and/or expert) or gather material resources. Avoidance may also in effect be a form of indirect pressure, intended to discomfort the other party who seeks a rapid resolution of the parties' disagreement. To this might be added the observation that delaying a response may have the additional virtue of avoiding the dispute, perhaps by allowing tempers to cool, and the parties to retreat. However, avoidance may become *protracted*, or even permanent, perhaps even being handed down to the disputants' heirs – a counterpart in a sense to feuding across generations. Then again, the disagreement itself may be slowly overlooked, and either a new, albeit circumscribed, relationship emerges between the parties, or the relationship returns to an approximation of its former state because of the common benefits it offers (Gulliver, 1996: 128).

Grievance Apathy and Lumping: Are They Avoidance?

Another important dimension to the conceptualisation of avoidance is the extent to which intention should be included in the characterisation. It is argued by Gulliver that avoidance is:

> a positive and more or less deliberate choice of strategy and action by which to deal with – to manage – the dispute. It is not merely resignation because of perceived inability to do anything in the situation as the opponent appears to be overwhelmingly stronger, or out of reach, geographically or socially, or where the costs of any conceivable action are too high (Gulliver, 1996: 128).

From this perspective what is often referred to as 'grievance apathy' and (possibly) 'lumping' would be excluded from the characterisation,

> [avoidance] is not merely resignation because of perceived inability to do anything in the situation as the opponent appears to be overwhelmingly stronger, or out of reach, geographically or socially, or where the costs of any conceivable action are too high (Gulliver, 1996: 128).

But it is not at all easy to identify this lack of intention to get involved, and resignation in the face of overwhelming odds. They may well also be seen as casting doubt on the need for intention in the characterisation of avoidance. Structural pressures may be so overwhelming that the aggrieved person feels she or he has no choice of action. That is not quite the same as saying that there is no decision-making involved. So, our inclination is to include 'grievance apathy' and 'lumping' as often constituting forms of avoidance.

Cultural Variation?

Avoidance conceivably happens everywhere, and there are some analytical dangers lurking in the use of cultural embeddedness as an explanation for avoidance conduct. It seems likely that some societies encourage dispute avoidance more than others: some legal cultures and the institutions which are one part of such cultures may well contain policies that encourage avoidance ideologically and in practice. This may be as a preference to other forms of dispute resolution, but it might also be as the promotion of one possibility amongst a range of other socially endorsed responses to disputes (and associated phenomena such as the social conditions that lead to disputes), including some form of third-party intervention such as umpiring or mediation, or bilateral negotiation (Gulliver, 1996: 128–9).

Action and Ideology: The Avoidance Ethic and Harmony Ideology

Sometimes, it is claimed, there is a crucial moral value of avoidance that is supportive of, and reinforced by, recurrent avoidance conduct. Carol Greenhouse, for example, looks at the influence of certain forms of Christian thought in the United States, and identifies the notion of an 'avoidance ethic', which she characterises as 'an ethical preference to self-restraint' (1992: 249). This ethic of restraint represents a 'culturally appropriate means of resolving contradictions between the self-interests and the collective good' (1992: 242). In ADR discourse, the debates surrounding civil justice have sometimes characterised the legal culture of the United States as being 'litigious', but Greenhouse suggests that it can more accurately be characterised as possessing an avoidance culture. Most people attempt to avoid confrontation, and such avoidance conduct is also linked to values of individualism and self-reliance. Avoidance does not necessarily manifest itself in real conduct, but it is, however, a primary value that shapes understandings and explanations, shaping how ordinary people think about confrontation, and indeed their own cultural identity (1992: 248).

If we turn back to China, we see a very similar ethic or 'ideology' of avoidance, albeit based on apparently different ideas about the relationship between the individual and society. The Confucian concept of 'harmony' (*he*) is central to traditional Chinese disputing culture, and is a continuing influence in mainland China today. Many popular sayings emphasise the value of 'harmony'. These include 'harmony is precious' (*he wei gui*) 'harmony creates wealth' (*he qi sheng cai*), and 'peaceful families flourish' (*jia he wan shixing*) and so on.

The emphasis on harmony is entrenched in the Confucian Analects and robustly expressed in Confucius' oft-quoted revelation that 'in hearing lawsuits, I am like any other person. What is necessary, however, is to cause the people to have no litigation.' The educated gentleman would not allow himself to be drawn into a dispute against his fellows; such involvement was itself indicative of moral weakness, and if a dispute did arise, he would nevertheless rise above it by practising yielding (*rang*). The ideal Confucian society is one without litigation, and in rural China today there are local anti-litigation societies that are still given local official and popular support. People maintain ideals of harmonious interpersonal relationships based on mutual love and respect, thereby serving the greater good and benefiting society. The Confucian ideal of harmony is also linked to Daoism, and the latter philosophy's ideas about the relationship between the human world and the cosmic order.

A disturbance in society is a disruption of harmony in the cosmos. Therefore, harmony in society should be promoted actively. Today, harmony so understood is an ideal that is central to the Hu Jintao ideal of creating a 'socialist harmonious society' (*shehui zhuyi hexie shehui*).

Choice – Rational Decision-making and the Costs of Choice – the Evolutionary and 'Econocentric' Approaches

In examining the pursuit of particular strategies of dispute resolution it seems to us that the analytical perspective and the participant's perspective are sometimes far apart. In the literature on avoidance, the tendency is to see decisions about opting for this strategy in terms of individual rational choice, a kind of careful cost-benefit analysis made on the basis of an explicit evaluation of the economic and psychological costs entailed in pursing this strategy in relation to the hoped-for outcome. On the other hand, the causes of the dispute may fade away, and the parties' social relationship is revived in whole or in part, especially where the parties calculate this as being in their self-interest.

Social Complexity and Avoidance

Moreover, in a manner reminiscent of some of the deep contrasts offered in classical sociology and in Auerbach's history of law and non-law in the United States (1983), it is suggested that the greater anonymity and 'moral minimalism' of modern urban cultures (especially 'suburban cultures') makes the costs of avoidance less of a burden (Baumgartner, 1984: 129). Thus, avoidance is likely to increase in importance as a dispute resolution strategy where there is,

- an absence of hierarchical authority,
- easy and frequent entering and leaving relationships,
- a dominance of single-stranded relationships,
- loose-knit social networks, and
- a high degree of functional autonomy and capacity to decide and act alone.

On the other hand, in more traditional rural societies where social relationships are multiplex and enduring and disputes are often polycentric in Fuller's sense, avoidance can entail heavy costs.

Weakness

But deliberative decision-making may not play quite such a pronounced role as this approach suggests, especially in the early stages of disagreement, where 'maximal claims' are being made, or there is growing frustration and hostility – this may be a juncture in the emerging dispute when overly emotionally charged and volatile reactions tend to crowd out cooler, more overtly deliberative, and less instinctive thinking, or such thinking is simply not relevant because not enough is known about the situation. Moreover, rational decision-making may be hindered by a felt need to respond in a manner consistent with wider, entrenched, normative ideas (for example, 'harmony ideology') or a disputant's own engrained experience, or by the encouragement of another person. And it is possible to point to empirical situations in which the model is plainly inapplicable. Take, for example, the case of two African tribal groupings that Gulliver studied, the Arusha and the Ndendeuli,

> In both cases ... the conditions under which dispute avoidance was rare were the converse of the conditions in U.S. suburbia where such avoidance was common: close-knit social networks, multi-stranded relationships and little functional autonomy – in contrast to loose-knit networks and a high degree of autonomy (1996: 140).

So, we may conclude that there is a danger of over-rationalising the bases of decision-making, and seeing avoidance in developmental terms that do not actually assist our understanding.

Violence and Its Forms

At the other end of the spectrum from avoidance in its various forms is self-help. In many societies around the world, the range of processes that can be called into operation when trouble arises also consist of various forms of self-help, including the use of coercion, and in particular, recourse to violence, sometimes with a degree of social acceptance, in response to disagreement or more serious forms of trouble. A common but potentially costly[6] way of dealing with conflict is to make a direct physical attack on the other party in an attempt to respond to a perceived wrong, subdue them into compliance with one's wishes, express frustration, or eliminate competition (especially competition which may be seen as a precursor to violent exchanges).

Violence in Institutionalised Form

While this compulsion is indeed an antithesis of avoidance – as well as of 'talking' – it may be misleading to see the two responses simply in dichotomous terms. As we have noted earlier, in societies where fighting is an institutionalised form of dispute management such hostility may develop into a form that is ritualised, conventionalised and bounded. The European duel, the strongly rule-governed fighting found in some New Guinea societies, and the Eskimos

---

[6] Costs include broken relationships, the risk of retaliation, and harm to people which might be later regretted.

nith song exchanges are important examples of such formalised processes. Some anthropologists have gone further and characterised a whole range of formalised conduct as somehow 'representing' fighting – for example, where ceremonial, competitive presentations of goods such as Potlatch are interpreted as replacements for fighting.[7]

Violence as Closure

Nonetheless, interpersonal violence is a very important form of response to civil trouble and needs to be taken into account in the comparative analysis of dispute resolution. Like the other forms of response, the resort to violent conduct in resolving civil disagreements takes place in a social context and where it occurs, it is one dimension of a social relationship. In this respect at least, it is no different from other modes of response to civil disagreements, including avoidance. It may be thought of, on the other hand, as often constituting a rejection of other modes of response: only coercion is going to be used to resolve the issues between the parties. In this sense, recourse to violence may be part of a process of closure, of socially defining the relationship as finished or non-negotiable and unidimensional in nature except on the terms dictated by the violent partner. In this sense, too, there is some resemblance to avoidance.[8] But, further, resort to coercion may be seen as a rejection in many cases of any sense of procedural fairness and of the need for and value of compromise, two important elements in resolving disagreements by negotiation and mediation.[9]

As we have suggested, coercion, especially violence, is often a type of self-help that itself takes many forms, some more institutionalised than others. A dispute emerges between two or more parties when naming and blaming are followed by a rejected claim. One or more of the parties decides that the use of force is the best, or at least a feasible way of dealing with the trouble that has arisen, or in a spontaneous manner uses violence in an outburst of anger and discontent. Sometimes the more peaceable processes are attempted first and violence follows, sometimes violence may be mixed in with other processes, and in other cases the resort to violence is more direct. The violent conduct may be short-lived, open and emotionally charged, and linked to rage and loss of temper. At the other end of the spectrum, violence may be persistent, secretive, callous and delivered with detachment, as is sometimes the case in sustained domestic violence. And often, there may be a mix of these

---

[7] See, for example, Johnsen (2006).
[8] As Simmel noted, '"force", as usually understood, is used by one party to rob the other of every spontaneity and thereby every true "action" that would be one side of an interaction' ([1908] trans. 2009b: 130).
[9] See Hampshire (1991: 74) on the value of 'compromise'.

types of (mis)conduct. In some societies, more than in others, the circumstances may be such that resort to violence is socially approved, perhaps even seen as noble, even where legally forbidden (Pirie, 2007: 5). On the other hand, it may – as we have noted – be institutionalised in concrete forms of conduct, and we also identify duelling, feuding, honour killings, and even vigilantism as taking on something of an institutionalised form.

Characterising Violence

By violence in the context of dispute resolution, we mean, primarily, the use of, or the threat of the use of, some form of coercion – usually physical – intended to secure a substantive effect that the violent party seeks. That outcome may be one that the violent party considers to be the preferred consequence of such action – this is 'instrumental violence'. In other cases, the coercive, antagonistic, conduct results from a loss of self-control in the course of the disagreement but is not necessarily intended to secure a specific outcome, and in this sense such 'spontaneous' conduct lies on the boundaries of 'self-help'. There may be no intention to benefit oneself with material gain – a situation that may be characterised as 'expressive' violence.

Self-help

Using violence in a civil dispute is a form of self-help, but just as not all forms of violence are clearly identifiable as 'self-help' so not all forms of self-help involve physical violence against the person. In various jurisdictions today, there is still scope for the use of self-help in the assertion of one party's claims, intended to secure rights and interests without necessarily relying on formal legal processes to support this restitutive conduct. Different jurisdictions place differing limitations on the use of self-help, and indeed the legal framework for self-help varies widely among different jurisdictions. In general, self-help is permitted if laws are not broken, and there is no breach of the peace. Thus, for example, a bank or some other financial institution may repossess property such as a house or a car when there has been a default in repayments on a mortgage or some other type of loan. Or one party may simply take possession of an item which is in the possession of another person without permission. But if repossession in some way creates damage, or if force is used, or if certain types of property rights (such as protected tenancies) are infringed then self-help may constitute either a civil wrong or a criminal offence.

Broad Visions

In addition, and although we concentrate on the use of physical force (including sexual violence) in this part of the chapter, there are of course broader understandings of the nature of violence. Thus, the United Nations advises:

> Definition of Domestic Violence
>
> Legislation regarding domestic violence has tended to address physical violence only. However, as a more nuanced understanding of the nature of domestic violence has emerged, a number of countries have enacted and/or amended legislation to adopt definitions which include some or all of the following types of violence: physical, sexual, emotional and/or psychological, and patrimonial, property, and/or economic violence (United Nations [DAW/DESA], 2009: 24-5).[10]

While accepting the value of this characterisation of violence, especially in multiplex, polycentric dispute contexts, the present chapter concentrates on physical violence not only for reasons of space but because it seems to be the morally most gripping concern. Suffice it to say here that the broader vision is nevertheless not only a very appropriate area of analysis, but such analysis may raise many interesting issues. Thus, does violence include threats of violence, an issue we raised by way of introduction when discussing the pressing of the other party into suicide in traditional Chinese society? Or, to take another example, should our understanding of violence encompass 'gossip'? Although ordinarily considered a form of dispute avoidance, it may be plausibly claimed that there is also violence in gossip and the practice of gossiping. Gossip and the untruths it may well contain might undermine the reputation of the other party in a manner that has very serious consequences for that party, including a willingness to resort to violent conduct in the context of the dispute, as in honour crimes for example.

Structural Violence

Johan Galtung has developed several important concepts or characterisations that are seminal in the general literature on violence, and which do help us to some extent at least to understand better the circumstances in which violence is expressed, although the extent to which they may assist in fully understanding instances of interpersonal violence is a matter of some debate (1990). For Galtung, the most pernicious and important form of violence is structural violence, which has more recently been characterised in the following terms:

> Structural violence is the most basic or fundamental form of violence. It is expressive of the conditions of society, the structures of social order, and the institutional arrangements of power that reproduce mass violations of

---

[10] The same UN document also reminds us that laws on domestic violence have often applied only to persons in intimate relationships and, in particular, to married couples. Over time, there has been a welcome expansion of legislation to include other types of survivor of domestic violence, such as persons in same-sex relationships (see, for example, Moscati, Palmer and Roberts (2020)).

personhood 24 hours a day, 7 days a week. Such violence is accomplished in part through 'policies' of informal and formal denial of civil, criminal, and basic human rights for all people ... structural violence refers to the established patterns of organized society that have been institutionalized – rationalized and sanctioned – yet result in systematic harm to millions of victims annually, including, disproportionately, members of the marginal classes of society ... Poverty and homelessness in affluent societies such as the United States, for example, represent a classic form of structural violence.

Structural violence may also be about individuals acting abusively or violently in their private lives, or about individuals acting abusively or violently within the context of their institutionalized roles or public lives. More fundamentally, structural violence reinforces adversarial social organization that incorporates both personal and impersonal ideologies of difference, privilege, and inequality (Barak, 2003).[11]

Cultural Violence: Ideologies of Violence

Galtung also argues that in any society there is likely also to be a system of 'cultural violence'. This we might see as the functional reverse of Greenhouse's 'ethic of avoidance' (1992) or Laura Nader's 'harmony ideology,'[12] in which certain 'aspects of culture – exemplified by religion and ideology, language and art, empirical science and formal science (logic and mathematics) ... can be used to justify or legitimize direct or structural violence' (Galtung, 1990: 291). So, we may say that just as certain societies or social groups within society may propagate what Greenhouse sees as an 'ethic of avoidance' or Nader characterises as 'harmony ideology' – that is, an ideology that promotes the idea that conflict is dysfunctional and that minimising conflict and confrontation is necessary so as to achieve a peaceful and harmonious society – so there are 'ethics' or 'ideologies of violence' in which the use of force is encouraged by social groups as a mode for, inter alia, resolving disputes and other disagreements. In China, when the Cultural Revolution was at its height (1966–1968), disputing parties were encouraged to see their disagreement in 'revolutionary' terms by an ideology of class in which the 'dictatorship of the proletariat' contrasted on the one hand the 'people' to whom the communist revolution belonged (and still belongs), and, on the other, the 'enemy', those who are the former exploiting classes and counter-revolutionaries. From the dichotomy between 'people' and 'enemy' there emerged an approach to the resolution of disputes and other forms of social conflict. Problems within the 'people' – primarily routine civil disputes

---

[11] More generally, some scholars argue that law itself creates violence in legitimating an 'intolerable' economic status quo that is unfair and exploitative, with justifications based on economic doctrines of comparative advantage. See, for example, Cover (1986) and Galtung (1990: 300–1).

[12] See, in particular, Nader (1990).

(such as matrimonial relations, landlord-tenant relations and so on) – were characterised as 'non-antagonistic'; contradictions and to be resolved by methods of 'democracy' (that is, 'persuasion', self-criticism and 'education', primarily delivered though a highly evaluative 'mediation' process). However, similarly routine problems arising between parties who were of the 'people' on the one hand and of the 'enemy' on the other were recharacterised as 'antagonistic contradictions' requiring resolution by methods of dictatorship, including 'punishment' and thought reform, and taking place in an arena that emphasised class conflict, political analysis of correct class position, and the language of class injustice.

More recent work has argued that in many societies around the world today, there has persisted, emerged or re-emerged the phenomenon of 'ideological masculinity', in which men who subscribe to this ideology believe that women's empowerment has left them victimised and discriminated against. The radical revivication of old ideas of male supremacy 'seeks to promote a return to a perceived period of male supremacy, now "lost" to women's rights and self-effacing men (referred to by some members of the alt-right movement as "beta cucks")'.[13]

Domestic Violence: China

In the case of China, such ideas of male supremacy have never gone away, despite many decades of policy and legal emphasis on gender equality. One of us has elsewhere charted attempts since the mid-1990s to introduce national-level anti-domestic violence legislation, and the work of the Supreme People's Court in dealing with domestic violence cases (including management by means of distinctive forms of mediation). In so doing it became clear just how difficult it has been to change thinking so that male on female partner violence in domestic disputes might no longer be seen as 'normal' and requiring at best only mediatory intervention aimed at reconciliation, but rather as a serious matter that may need the intervention of the criminal justice system (Palmer, 2007a; 2014c; 2017). As a result, China's 2015 Anti-Domestic Violence Law was not only introduced after very extensive delays and opposition from 'patriarchal socialist' elements, but also has functioned imperfectly since taking effect in March 2016. Judicial practice, however, still tends to focus on 'saving and repairing marital relationship' and 'maintaining social harmony' and applies a high standard of proof for domestic violence when considering applications for protection orders. Various forms of anti-domestic violence advocacy pursued by civil society groups have been limited in effectiveness by a general tightening of controls on civil society. Thus, the incidence of domestic violence is likely to remain a significant 'structural

---

[13] http://theconversation.com/ideological-masculinity-that-drives-violence-against-women-is-a-form-of-violent-extremism-99603, accessed 2 December 2019.

violence' issue for the women of China for the foreseeable future, despite the belated legislative reform.

Violence and Time

While fully acknowledging that some forms of violence such as domestic violence are notable in no small part because of their persistence over time, it seems likely that we can agree with Randall Collins that resort to violence tends – unlike avoidance – in many cultures to be episodic. In his view, stereotyping images (we might add, as with Hollywood courtroom dramas and their characterisation of the practice of law as litigation theatrics) encourage us to think of violence as endemic. But, he adds:

> if we consider that everyday life unfolds in a chain of situations, minute by minute, most of the time there is very little violence. This is apparent from ethnographic observations, even in statistically very violent neighborhoods. A homicide rate of ten deaths per 100,000 persons (the rate in the United States peaking in 1990) is a fairly high rate, but it means that 99,990 out of 100,000 persons do not get murdered in a year; and 97,000 of them (again, taking the peak rate) are not assaulted even in minor incidents. And these violent incidents are spread out over a year; the chances of murder or assault happening to a particular person at any particular moment on a particular day during that year are very small ... Even the toughest hoodlums are off duty some of the time. Most of the time, the most dangerous, most violent persons are not doing anything violent. Even for these people, the dynamics of situations are crucial in explaining what violence they actually do (Collins, 2008: 14).

'Time' is important in another sense in the context of the interactions between the parties involved in a dispute. The pressure to take immediate, and coercive action, in the exchanges between parties is one that one or both parties may feel keenly as the antagonism between the parties grows. In general, we are socialised into interacting with others in a positive manner, and enjoy such interaction with its conversational exchanges with others. Such interaction comes easily. In contrast, violence is (at least initially) much more problematic. Coercion is not understood to be the norm in ordinary, everyday social interaction. It is an exception to ordinary social interaction, its possible use creates confrontational strain and intensity, and the chances of its actual use are thereby increased. The situation of aggressive encounters only rarely allows us to escape the confrontational tension that is generated by the looming vision of an imposed coercive outcome.

Linking the Macro and the Micro

At the same time, while acknowledging that recourse to violence is reflective of environing structural and cultural (including) ideological factors that encourage its use, such as masculine honour, the opportunity for material benefits, and a social imperative to dominate a person from another ethnic group, it is also the case that violence may also be more or less spontaneous. This is perhaps especially true of the use of interpersonal violence in the course of a dispute between two (or more) parties. Here, broadly speaking and as noted above, a distinction may be drawn between instrumental violence and expressive violence. In looking at violence and other forms of compulsion in a dispute context there does seem to be a large divide between planned, instrumental violence, including the ritualised forms of violence noted earlier, and more ad hoc, random and spontaneous conduct often associated with a violent bout of temper. While some acts of instrumental violence may be explicable in large part as expressions of a wider context of structural violence, and while structural violence may constitute contributory circumstances that are conducive to spontaneous violence, there is a need, in looking at interpersonal disputes, to bring together the macro and the micro in the explanation of spontaneous violence and if possible how specific acts of spontaneous violence come about. The distinguished sociologist, Randall Collins (2008) offers one explanation, as outlined in the next section.

Violence is Unusual

The social reality is that most of the time parties to a quarrel do not use physical violence to fight with each other, a point that we have noted is stressed by Collins. Instead, they may argue, insult, gossip and so on rather than try to make their point by physically aggressive compulsion, or they use forms of pressure against the other party of the kinds identified in the UN definition of domestic violence noted above. In Collins' view, when the parties do resort to physical violence, especially expressive violence, the determining conditions are to be found in the processes of the parties' short-term interaction. Negotiations between the parties in concrete encounters do not follow conventional interaction patterns, but instead for the reasons noted in the preceding paragraph may veer off and degenerate into alternative pathways which lead into a tunnel of violence (see, for example, Collins, 2008: 140). At the entrance of this tunnel is the notion of 'confrontational tension'. As the parties in disagreement continue to disagree, there is a spiralling of the tension and fears in their exchanges. These emotions may, however, drain away, the confrontational tension subsides, and there is an impasse in the parties' relationship.

But there are several avenues to this tunnel, and these may on the other hand create increased tension and open up the tunnel's entrance. One such perilous avenue is 'forward panic' where the confrontational tension builds up and is unconstrained, so that it abruptly degenerates into violence. Because such tensions are experienced far less in everyday life than positive, peaceable and cooperative social interaction, the parties may well be clumsy and unskilled in handling the pressure, and this is an intensifying factor. Other avenues that lead into the tunnel include an impulse to attack the weaker party (for example, as can be the case in domestic violence) precisely because the violent party sees that other party as weak and therefore vulnerable. Also, the inspiration generated by an audience (e.g. drunken bystanders cheering on quarrelling parties in public) may have a significant impact. Clearly, these avenues are processes which may overlap and intertwine; that is, they are not exclusive paths to violence.

The extent to which they are applicable cross-culturally has yet to be determined, as Collins draws primarily on North American data, and gives little attention to anthropological accounts of disputing violence.

Social Complexity and Avoidance

We have noted that in the dispute resolution discourses on avoidance, some attention was given for a period of time to the issue of social and economic complexity and the incidence of avoidance as a dispute resolution strategy. The literature on resort to violence in the context of interpersonal dispute resolution (as opposed to violence more generally) does not seem to have shared such an 'evolutionary' concern. One notable exception is a set of observations by one of the early seminal thinkers on disputes and their resolution, namely Philip Gulliver. He takes the view that – to generalise his comments from observations on 'non-centralised, acephalous' societies – violent self-help, in the form (for example) of feuding may emerge where there are strong, self-organised compartmentalised groups within society that are able to manage, for a period of time, without peaceful cooperation. There are shades of Durkheim's mechanical solidarity here, and indeed of organic solidarity when Gulliver goes on to suggest that where groups are more dependent on each other, resort to violence may be more strategic in nature, and more likely to result in a peaceful outcome in due course. In the latter case:

> individual members have valuable, persisting relationships with each other (e.g., through marriage, kinship, or economic exchange), and especially where members of the groups are residentially intermingled, hostilities cannot long be tolerated. In such situations, the resort to violent self-help may be a regular means not only to express the strength of dissatisfaction and determination but also to precipitate a crisis so that other procedures can be initiated or resumed. Thus there are, for example, the raid on the opponent's home, the seizure or spoliation of property, and the industrial strike. All lead to efforts for peace-making (Gulliver, 1979: 1–2).

There are some similarities here to the avoidance explanations noted earlier. Put together, we see in both approaches the idea that in more 'advanced' or socially complex societies (in the words of one commentator, 'outer suburban communities in the United States') avoidance is a relatively feasible and even attractive course of action. But in such communities too, while resort to violence may still be a practicable course of action, it is likely to be used more strategically and instrumentally, and a settlement achieved in due course.

Conclusions

In this chapter we have given particular attention to aspects of dispute resolution that the conventional dispute resolution literature tends to overlook. As we have explained, there are perfectly good reasons for not giving equal attention to avoidance and self-help than with other responses in which lawyers are much more likely to play a supportive role, namely, negotiation mediation and umpiring. Nevertheless in seeking to understand the way in which people respond to a perceived injurious experience it is important to consider the full range of responses, including avoidance and force. It has been noted that there is cultural variance in the extent to which avoidance or self-help is socially approved, and also that there are recognisable ideologies encouraging avoidance on the one hand and violence on the other. These ideologies, like the culture in which they are embedded, are likely to shape – to some extent at least – the decisions made by individuals who feel that they have suffered an injustice and contemplate some form of response. By giving avoidance and force more attention it may well be the case that the dispute resolution discourse will enable us to influence dispute responses so that the virtues of negotiation, mediation and umpiring are more fully appreciated.

6

Negotiations

The Nature of Negotiation

Negotiation represents the primary, universal route to decision and action in the social world. The core features of negotiation are to be found in widely different contexts, ranging from the unself-conscious routines of everyday life to the formalised, set-piece exchanges of an international conference. These fundamental features remain constant whether the issue is uncontentious or a focus of extreme conflict. Thus, negotiation as a mode of decision-making spans everyday interaction and the more complex, stressful exchanges encountered in the context of disagreement and dispute.

The features of negotiation are revealed most clearly in simple, bilateral exchanges in which information flows in both directions, understanding is achieved and an outcome is reached – the lived counterpart of Habermas' theoretical construct, the 'ideal speech situation' (Habermas, 1979). So, negotiation involves communication, leading to joint decision-making. It is a process over which the parties retain control; exchanges take place within a common universe of meaning; and these determine the outcome in immediate terms. Here the ultimate contrast is with acquiescence in an adjudicatory process in which power over the outcome lies with a third party (Gulliver, 1979: 3–7).

A number of identifiable conditions have to be present if negotiation is to take place. The first involves finding some medium of communication that will allow messages to pass backwards and forwards between the parties; this may, but need not, involve finding a mutually acceptable forum. Second, the parties must formulate and successfully communicate to each other their goals, what they want to achieve in the exchange. Third, in the light of those mutually understood goals, the parties must identify and evaluate the options available to them. It will sometimes be that the greater understanding resulting from an exchange of information will reveal a convergence or compatibility of goals, resulting in an agreed outcome without shifts of position. Otherwise, if an agreed outcome is pursued, this will be an accommodation reached through further exchanges in which the respective bargaining endowments are brought to bear.

In presenting negotiations in their simplest form as a bilateral process of decision-making, achieved through information exchange and learning, we must keep in mind the inevitable embeddedness of negotiation in the surrounding social universe. Negotiation does not take place in a vacuum. Those involved at any moment find themselves as part of a going concern – when they arrive the party or dance is already in progress. Surrounded by other actors, they have been brought up in a universe of understandings, norms and interests that, by and large, they have not themselves constructed. In this context, the norms and institutions of 'law' place explicit, perceived constraints on processes of negotiation. Those involved in negotiation will entertain some picture, however erroneous, of what might happen if they resorted to other modes of decision-making instead – notably lawyer negotiations or adjudication. That picture will necessarily bear significantly on the conduct of negotiations. Mnookin and Kornhauser (1979) memorably describe negotiation as 'bargaining in the shadow of the law'. So, any discussion of the nature of negotiation must show sensitivity to the environment within which negotiation takes place.

Alongside the external environment of negotiation, we need to recognise the internal complexity of many processes of negotiation. People do not necessarily negotiate over a single good with an agreed identity, like a sum of money. Honour, prestige, respect, the recognition of values or some established state of affairs may be at issue in numerous combinations. Here, what Gulliver labels the 'preference set' may differ between parties, and from one phase of negotiation to another (Gulliver, 1979: 88–9).

A picture of negotiation in terms of a simple bilateral exchange between two poles also takes no account of complexity of another kind. While the parties to negotiations may be two 'individuals', they may also be loose groups or corporate bodies, they may be constituted of principals with attached support groups, or they may be champions acting in some representative capacity and there may also be more than two poles with active, party involvement in negotiations (see the sections below dealing with intra- and multi-party negotiations and lawyer negotiations respectively). The structure of negotiations is obviously further complicated by the intervention of third parties in a bridging capacity, from a 'non-aligned' standpoint, with the disputants themselves not always familiar with the meanings that underpin the decision to involve a third party (mediation is considered in Chapter 7).

Negotiation also must be clearly distinguished from adjudication. A picture of the processes of the negotiation and adjudication can be drawn in the following rather oversimplified terms. On the one hand, in the negotiation process, the two disputing parties sit opposite each other. They trade information and views. They have divergent views and perhaps lapse into argument. They may be posturing, not seeking in good faith a mutually agreeable outcome. Or a series of offers and counter-offers may unfold, dealing with the various matters on which the parties disagree, and moving the parties towards an agreed outcome. On the other hand, in the process of adjudication we see a picture of a third figure, perhaps raised physically above the level of the two parties. The latter face the adjudicator, and it is to this judgemental figure that the parties communicate, furnishing information, and offering reasoned arguments. Each party does so in the hope that at the end of this process the adjudicator will decide in their favour. So, a key characteristic of the negotiation process is the absence of a third-party authoritative decision-maker, whereas in the adjudicative process their outcome is to a significant extent the imposed decision by an authoritative third party. In both processes, decision-making is directed towards the creation of an outcome. In both cases the outcome may range from quite specific and enforceable conclusive requirements for the parties, to vague, general and even temporary outcomes that may be with more than a restatement of the status quo. However, as Gulliver emphasises, 'it is not the kind of decision-outcome that is distinctive but rather the process by which the decision is reached' (Gulliver, 1979: 3–4). As a result, 'the crucial distinction ... between adjudication and negotiation is that the former is a process leading to unilateral decision-making by an authoritative third party, whereas the latter is a process leading to joint decision-making by the disputing parties themselves as the culmination of an interactive process of information exchange and learning' (Gulliver, 1979: 7).

And in negotiation, unlike umpiring, the outcome – including a failure to reach agreement – is the creation of the disputing parties. It is their joint decision. Each party needs to secure concessions from the other in pursuit of a favourable outcome. At the start of the decision-making process, the differences between the parties will be at their most pronounced and the purpose of the negotiation is to secure convergence in the parties' positions to the point where there is an outcome agreeable to the parties to the dispute or transaction. In the attempts to secure concessions the parties will likely employ a range of techniques of influence, threats and coercion. They will exchange information and opinions about the facts at issue in the disagreement, argue their case, make promises and point to the relevance of wider norms and values, exchange offers and counter-offers, and through this process of information exchange the negotiation will likely be drawn towards convergence. For the process of information exchange is also one of learning by the parties about each other's understanding of the issue in disagreement – and readjustments in the light of what they have learned in terms of reconsideration, clarification and changed expectations. And these modifications will in turn likely impact on the demands made by each party.

In this process, it may be the case that one party is able to secure an outcome which is nearly all that she or he hoped for at the start of the negotiation. And this successful outcome may reflect unequal powers of coercion, legal and moral strengths, skills of persuasion (including deception) and so on. Nevertheless, four important points stand out even in this extreme case. First, the outcome is determined not by a third party but, rather, by the parties themselves. Secondly, negotiations are rarely one-sided in the full. The weaker party will often find some area of strength in the negotiation process and use it to secure concessions, however minimal, from the stronger party. Thirdly, each party will be subject to the externally received pressures, especially where the negotiation outcome may well impact on these additional actors. Fourthly, how the disputing parties approach the negotiations may well be influenced by whether or not they see their relationship as a single event, or as a long-term tie that needs to be preserved as endured.

An important dimension of the negotiation processes is each party's 'preference set', a term used by Gulliver so as to characterise the developing and unfolding objectives of the negotiating parties. The preference set consists of each party's 'ordered evaluations of issues and conceivable outcome' (Gulliver, 1979: 88). As we have suggested, although parties generally enter into negotiations with certain objectives that they seek to achieve, these aims are likely to undergo transformation during the evolving process of negotiation. The preference set of each party will thus change, as each party refines and adjusts their preference set right through to the end of the negotiation process.

In addition to its changing nature, the preference set has several other important dimensions. One dimension is the preferred order of negotiation goals. This will give the parties to a negotiation a sense of what is an acceptable outcome should they fail to secure complete satisfaction, and therefore also a sense of what is unavoidable and what is unacceptable. Between the best and the worst possible outcome, these will thus be a range of conceivable outcomes that represent acceptable results and as we shall see, subsequent ADR discourse and practice encourages the parties to weigh the minimal satisfaction against the 'best alternative to a negotiated agreement' (BATNA). If there is no agreement, what will the best possible situation be, as each party sees the matter. With a strong BATNA, a party will not lose very much if there is no agreed outcome, but with a weak BATNA a party is not in a strong negotiating position. But, at the same time, each party should also consider the worst outcome that might come to pass if a negotiated agreement is not achieved (WATNA) – that is, what is the worst case scenario for a party if there is failure to conclude an agreement with the other side. It may still be worthwhile for a party to accept an unfavourable agreed outcome if the alternative is even worse: the decision to accept an unattractive offer is based on the realisation that at least it minimises loss or is the best of a bad situation.

As Gulliver stresses, it would be unwise to assure that the negotiating parties are firmly rational in the construction of their preference set. Their evaluations may be imprecise or even very vague, and not necessarily mutually consistent. Negotiation should be seen as an exploratory interaction process between the parties, and it is likely that in the early stages of the process the parties may well be vague and uncertain about their preferred outcomes, but '[a]s [more] information comes from the opponent, the party is able, and also compelled, to gain some better appreciation of what is probable, possible, and impossible and what the opportunity costs might be' (Gulliver, 1979: 103).

Indeed, right through to the end of the negotiation process, the parties are likely to be refining and adjusting their preferences. As they progress through the negotiation process and acquire and absorb new information, the parties come to learn more about each other's substantive position, how they view the negotiation situation and about the issues in dispute. They also come to learn more, and to draw informed conclusions about, each other's conduct. In particular, they understand better the trustworthiness, negotiating style and responsiveness of the other party. This understanding shapes ideas about what is possible and what is not in terms of the outcomes of the negotiation process. And of course the negotiating parties, as we have indicated, are likely to have shifting goals and a change in one goal may have a knock-on effect on awareness of the nature, costs and importance of other goals. Moreover, the negotiating parties may well be influenced by external advice, and this too may be changeable and inconsistent. Moreover, in complex negotiations involving a number of parties, parties on each side will have to try to formulate a common set of negotiating preferences, a process that may encounter significant difficulties.

Intra-party and Multi-party Negotiations

We considered negotiation primarily in terms of a simple bilateral exchange, and much of the existing ADR literature proceeds on the basis of this analytical simplification. However, in real life many negotiations are a good deal more complex than this. Some 'parties' display internal heterogeneity, and negotiations often involve more than two parties. Under these more complex conditions, we argue that the fundamental nature and processual shape of negotiation holds steady. Nonetheless, these complexities may significantly complicate the progress of negotiation. In an intra-party context, complications are likely to arise in terms of both the cyclical and developmental dimensions of the negotiation process. In multi-party exchanges, as more parties are added the complexities progressively increase. The communication arrangements required for multi-party negotiations are necessarily elaborate, and at each of the processual stages identified below (in the section which follows), the presence of more parties, with the concomitant expansion of the universe of meaning, complicates information exchange and decision-making. In this section, we consider the complications inherent in these two types of situation in more detail.

Intra-party Negotiations

In real life, even in two-party situations, each side to a negotiation is often a loose-knit coalition rather than a homogeneous unit. As a result, there is necessarily a good deal of consultation and manoeuvring between the constituent elements within each coalition. We must relax the assumptions ordinarily made that each party is internally united, and able to conduct itself as a cohesive, coherent whole. Each side is often itself an arena within which individuals or constituent groups are intent on securing positions and outcomes that reflect their own interests and interpretations. There is a range of possibilities here: some sides will be almost as monolithic as the normal analytical models presume, but others will be heterogeneous. In some cases, the heterogeneity will be deliberately created, perhaps most obviously in this context by the recruitment of lawyers and other providers of expert knowledge, in an effort to construct what Goffman has called a 'performance team' (Goffman, 1959: 79). These specially recruited partisans are intended to bolster the team's ability to analyse the position and performance of the other side and to improve its own approach to the negotiations – for example, by furnishing informed advice on substantive issues, bringing in procedural expertise, or by enhancing access to relevant sources of power and influence through personal connections. Moreover, even without the assistance of such experts, the divergence of views commonly found within a team may bring with it greater possibility of careful and effective consideration of negotiating options. Nevertheless, such heterogeneity requires some sort of 'negotiation' within or prior to the main negotiations before it can attain such benefits, and may bring with it weaknesses as well as strengths.

Thus, not all team members will have the same degree of commitment to their side's cause. Some may provide only grudging assistance because they have enrolled in or aligned themselves with the team merely because they are beholden to the leader or some other key player in the team. Others may even have chosen to give 'support' because not to do so would leave them open to accusations of disloyalty. Still others may seek to encourage cleavages and to subvert their own side's negotiating position. Their own individual interests will be enhanced, rather than undermined, by the failure of their side to negotiate a satisfactory outcome to the dispute. Such internal weaknesses may become manifest during the course of the main negotiations and be exploited by the other side.

These intra-party exchanges are, in effect, negotiations within negotiations. Perhaps because they do not arise in *direct* response to the main dispute, their precise nature is unclear. Gulliver refers to them as 'negotiations of a kind' (1979: 266) but elsewhere as 'intra-party bargaining' (1979: 267). In our view, they are a form of negotiation. They involve their own dynamic processes of information exchange and, in the case of serious disagreements between team members, they will generate an unfolding process which may lead to an agreed position, along the lines indicated by Gulliver in his developmental model (see the next section). They are constrained by the parameters of the overt party structures and relationships and often will not involve explicit disagreement. However, for those participating in the coalition that is a party to the main dispute, these intra-party negotiations may well be as important, or more significant, than the main, inter-party negotiation. The distinctiveness of this kind of negotiation is alluded to by Goffman when he wrote: 'whether the members of a team stage similar individual performances or stage dissimilar performances which fit together into a whole, an emergent team impression arises which can be conveniently treated as a fact in its own right, as a third level of fact located between the individual performance on the one hand and the total interaction of the participants on the other' (1959: 80).

Gulliver suggests that, in general terms, internal differences and problems within a negotiating party will affect the larger negotiation process in at least three ways.

First, the repetitive exchange of information and the linked process of learning and adjustment that Gulliver characterises as the 'cyclical' model of negotiation will be significantly more complicated as a result of the internal variety in a complex team and the need to present a monolithic front. We may illustrate this by reference to the worker in an organisation who, for example, embarrasses his or her union in negotiations with management by working too hard and thereby undermining the union's definition of a hard day's work. Although such a worker can be subjected to a variety of informal, corrective sanctions, these may not necessarily alter his or her conduct, and this threat to the collective negotiating front that colleagues are attempting to promote cannot be ignored. If the workforce wishes to present a united front, it must secure an agreement with that worker in which he or she modifies his or her conduct at the workplace. Goffman has identified several strategies that a complex negotiating party may have to resort to in order to secure internal unanimity, or at least the appearance of unanimity (1959: 79–105). Thus, there may well be direct pressure placed on members to adhere to a unanimous line, backed by the threat of sanctions, a reduction in the role, or transfer to a primarily ceremonial role, of those who threaten the united front, controlling more effectively the setting in which the negotiations are to take place, or giving one person the right to control and direct the negotiations, and development of a collective sense of secrecy with a rule against disclosure to the other party.

Second, in the broad developmental process, the transition from one phase of the negotiations to the next is likely to be more difficult in situations in which one or both of the main negotiating parties have significant internal differences. Indeed, Raiffa has suggested that such movement may be significantly more problematic when he observes that teams with single players may 'bargain tougher' than do those with multiple players as a result of a 'tendency within teams for the members to compromise [with each other] in the direction of a tougher bargaining stance [toward the other party to the main dispute]' (Raiffa, 1982: 95). Linked to this is the possibility that the real purpose of constructing a negotiating team is not the negotiations per se but, rather, the achievement of a level of cohesion within a group of people that might otherwise be unobtainable, for example, where participation in the team mitigates structural or social cleavages within an organisation. In this fragile situation there is not only greater possibility of defection and disruption but also a need for the persons leading that party to encourage the team to adopt an aggressive stance towards the opposing party in order to promote intra-party cooperation – the possibility of internal dissent is reduced by combative posturing ostensibly adopted in the interests of dealing effectively with the opposition. The position is further complicated by the fact that unanimity is often not the only requirement in the negotiating posture for, as Goffman has indicated, 'there seems to be a general feeling that the most real and solid things in life are ones whose description individuals independently agree upon. We tend to feel that if two participants in an event decide to be as honest as they can in recounting it, then the stands they take will be acceptably similar even though they do not consult one another prior to their presentation' (1959: 88). As a result, it is often important for several members of a negotiating party to agree on the positions they take and be secretive about the fact that these positions were not reached independently. This need may add to the fragile nature of the unity within the negotiating team and thereby foster an even tougher attitude toward the other side.

Third, internal dissension and efforts to cope with such dissension, may well prove singularly distracting and prevent a party from realising its actual strength in the overall negotiations. To some extent this will be because the team's negotiating goal may well be a compromise, with this fact disguised from the other side through the application of some sort of principle of collective responsibility.

The very experienced negotiator, mediator and dispute resolution trainer Tom Colosi stresses that conventional models of negotiation tend to oversimplify the process by means of which the parties attempt to resolve their disagreements. For one thing, the parties are not necessarily monolithic but, rather, are perhaps composed of a variety of members. There is often a real need for the various members of a party to develop some kind of consensus within the side through internal negotiations before discussion and agreement is possible with the other side. In this connection he also notes the importance of 'quasi-mediators' in securing internal consensus within a negotiating team, and the significant complications for internal cohesion that arise as a result of the process of information exchange and learning inherent in negotiating with the other party (Colosi, 1983: 229–30).

The implications of intra-party negotiation for analysis of inter-party negotiation processes has not been given sufficient attention in the relevant literature. Existing analysis, too, has tended to focus primarily on the problems that often arise between the team leader and other members of the party coalition.[1]

---

[1] Some idea of the specific difficulties that can arise in this context is provided by the comparative analysis by Bailey of team co-ordination in political contexts. Briefly stated, he suggests that

Multi-party Negotiations

Multi-party disputes may be found in any context, notably in international disputes, environmental disputes and large-scale commercial litigation. Of course, in many multi-party negotiations coalitions will emerge that reduce the negotiating process de facto to a two-party situation – in effect, some sort of preliminary agreement is reached between several of the parties to stand together against one or more of the other parties. The dividing line between multi-party and intra-party negotiations may be especially difficult to draw in such circumstances. While the basic characteristics of negotiation that we have already identified hold good in multi-party processes, they obviously bring with them greater complexity. First, the networks of communication through which information is exchanged and learning takes place become more elaborate as the parties to the decision become more numerous. Second, as parties increase in number, the goals and interests which have to be identified, communicated and ultimately accommodated become manifold. Correspondingly, the viable options generally constrict and are subject to differential evaluation. Lastly, any bargaining stage in the negotiations becomes more important and protracted as a range of interests needs to be accommodated. The process of alliance formation through negotiations may itself be a somewhat complicated process, and the complications of a multi-party situation will affect the processes of interaction and communication between the various parties in the main negotiations and also impact on the sort of outcome to which they are able to agree.

Some of the distinctive characteristics of multi-party negotiation appear in observations made by Colosi in his account of the aftermath of a 1973 New York school riot. He was part of a team of 'mediator fact-finders' seeking to identify the causes of, and to prevent a reoccurrence of, this serious dispute. An initial problem was to establish which of the many interested parties could participate in the process, a decision that was in due course made not by the mediating fact-finding interveners, but rather by the parties originally and most closely involved in the dispute. There then followed a turbulent period of disagreement over the manner in which decision-making should be carried out, with minority groups holding out for a requirement of full consensus – which had the advantage of making such decisions more authoritative – but others taking the view that a simple majority vote would be more efficient. Only after many complicated exchanges was a decision agreed on how best to make decisions: full consensus decision-making was accepted. Setting an agenda then became a problem, and resolving disagreements on the issue was only possible after internal discussions between various group members, and also direct negotiation between the parties, sometimes with mediators assisting, sometimes

much depends on the nature of the team, and he identifies four types of group, each of which, in his view, requires a different mode of internal co-ordination: unspecialised, transactional, moral and bureaucratic (see Bailey, 1969: 35–57).

without. The protected discussions over the agenda reflected the parties' serious lack of trust in each other. It was only after some six months of regular, well-attended meetings, that the parties could agree common aspirational goals: to have safe schools, and for the parties to learn to trust each. Key to the development of trust was a procedural device that the mediators encouraged – by getting the parties to work together on seemingly unimportant procedural matters, the interveners 'demonstrated how people with different priorities and outlooks could work cooperatively' (Colosi, 1983: 243).

The Processual Shape of Negotiation

We have conceptualised negotiation as a cyclical process of information exchange and learning but have not beyond that identified any processual shape for negotiation. In the North American writing by lawyers, process has tended to be submerged under the examination of bargaining strategies, power and an understandable preoccupation with ethical questions. Thus bargaining, a conceptually identifiable but in many cases small, or even absent, part of the overall process, has assumed a central focus. If negotiation is to be properly theorised, we have to transcend this position; but in what direction?

We have already identified conditions for negotiation, and some of the things that must happen if negotiation is to take place successfully. Negotiation demands the availability of some communication arrangements, ideally a secure forum and some ground rules. The issues need to be formulated and transmitted; differences have to be understood; possible ways forward have to be identified and evaluated; some of these ways forward may contemplate potential changes of position, so 'bargaining' may be required; a solution needs to be found and formulated – and here clarity will often be central. But can we go further than that and argue that negotiation has a conventional, or underlying shape, under which these foci of attention are linked together in any particular way, or even constitute the shape taken by successive, developmental phases in negotiations?

A number of writers have attempted to formulate a developmental process model, identifying the phases through which negotiations must pass if they are to reach an agreed outcome (for example: Douglas, 1957; 1962; Stevens, 1963; Stenelo, 1972; Gulliver, 1979). While these authors come from a variety of disciplines – labour relations, diplomacy, social anthropology – the models of processual shape they have come up with reveal striking similarity.

An early attempt by Ann Douglas, a North American writing about labour negotiations, argued that most negotiations fall into three successive phases:

- an early phase in which disagreement is emphasised and in which the outer limits of what she labels the 'negotiating range' are established;
- a middle phase in which the parties 'reconnoitre the range' and begin to focus on areas which hold some promise of agreement; and

- a final phase in which what she describes as the 'decision-making crisis' is precipitated and agreement is reached or the negotiations break up.

Douglas emphasised that the first phase tends to be characterised by turbulent, conflictual shows of strength, giving way to the calmer and more focused exchanges of the second phase. A further period of potential turbulence may follow before an outcome is reached.

Lars-Göran Stenelo, a Swede writing on international relations, also proposed a three-phase model, suggesting a very similar shape to diplomatic negotiations. He explicitly adopted Douglas' conception of a *negotiation range* in characterising the first phase. This was the phase during which an agenda and 'other procedural questions' had to be arrived at and attempts made 'to define the problem areas and basic issues with which the negotiations are to deal' (1972: 92). In this process, 'areas of disagreement . . . become more clearly delineated' and, once formulated, 'goals must be coordinated' (92, 93). Stenelo also noted, 'search strategies are used in the initial stage in order to reduce the uncertainty concerning the number of possible negotiatory outcomes' (142).

An intermediate stage then follows, labelled the *contract zone*, during which the parties identify those outcomes that they would prefer to no agreement. 'The establishment of a contract zone presupposes that the parties consider a number of alternative ways of reaching agreement' (101). At this stage, 'the parties investigate each other's propensity to make concessions . . . test the stability of each other's positions' and 'search out and identify the main obstacles to agreement' (103). At the same time, search activities 'contribute to the elimination of certain unrealistic alternatives' (143).

In a final phase, the parties use the framework established as the contract zone in trying to reach an agreement. Here the parties 'search for the final conditions required for an acceptance' (143). So, for Stenelo, negotiation is conceptualised as a three-phase *search* process that he summarises as follows (emphasis original):

- 'The initial stage of the negotiation is dominated by the parties' attempts to determine jointly the issues with which the negotiations are to deal, that is the parties attempt to establish *a negotiation range*' (92).
- 'The intermediate stage is dominated by the parties' joint attempt to establish a *contract zone*, . . . the range of outcomes the parties would prefer to no agreement' (101).
- 'In the final stage, the parties attempt to reach an *agreement* within the framework of the established contract zone by uniting on a set of solutions' (106).

A complex feature of Stenelo's formulation is that a number of analytically distinct matters are described as needing attention in the 'initial stage': issues have to be identified, an agenda formulated, areas of disagreement delineated and search activities undertaken to reduce uncertainty as to ultimate outcome. This suggests perhaps that a more elaborate model of process is called for.

In looking for such a model we turn here to the more detailed, eight-phase processual model developed by the British social anthropologist Philip Gulliver (1963; 1971; 1979) on the basis of his field research on negotiations in some small stateless societies in East Africa during the 1950s and later work he did on North American labour disputes. Gulliver expresses substantial agreement with Douglas and Stenelo, and the central phases of his model look very like the three phases they propose.

Gulliver claims that the shapes he identifies are, on an empirical level, widely observable across different cultures in the conduct of negotiations. Gulliver outlines his model briefly in the following terms. Two distinct though interconnected processes going on simultaneously in negotiation. First, there is a cyclical process. This involves a cyclical process of repetitive exchange of information between the parties, the evaluation of such information, and the resultant modifications of hopes and preferences. Secondly, there is also a developmental process at work. This involves the unfolding progression of the process movement from the beginning of the dispute to its conclusion – some outcome – and its implementation.

> The model of the developmental process . . . comprises a series of overlapping sequences or phases, each with its peculiar emphasis and kind of interaction and each opening the way for the succeeding one in a complex progression. Summarily, these phases are (1) the search for an arena for the negotiations; (2) the formulation of an agenda and working definitions of the issues in dispute; (3) preliminary statements of demands and offers and the exploration of the dimensions and limits of the issues, with an emphasis on the differences between the parties; (4) the narrowing of differences, agreements on some issues, and the identification of the more obdurate ones; (5) preliminaries to final bargaining; (6) final bargaining; (7) ritual confirmation of the outcome; and, in many cases, (8) the implementation of the outcome or arrangements for that (Gulliver, 1979: 82).

Something more needs to be said about the successive phases of this developmental model.

An Arena

For the process of information exchange and learning that may culminate in a joint decision to take place at all, the parties need to find sufficient common understandings to enable a conversation to take place and a medium of communication that will enable messages to pass backwards and forwards between them. The 'arena for negotiations' may, but need not, consist of a physical location within which face-to-face meetings take place. For present purposes, an arena is constituted whenever messages pass between the parties, receive attention and elicit response. The necessary arrangements can be provided even while the parties remain at a distance by the traditional 'go-between', the postal services or contemporary modes of electronic communication.

Identifying the Issues and Forming an Agenda

Once communication arrangements are in place, a second phase is reached in which the parties formulate and communicate *the issues* as they respectively see them. Many negotiations conclude at this early stage as assimilation of the respective positions leads to removal of misconceptions, and growth of common definition and understanding. The parties simply come to see that there is no disagreement between them. If issues remain to be resolved, an *agenda* then must be formed in which negotiable issues are identified, ranked and prioritised. Not all the issues initially raised by the two sides will necessarily be susceptible of negotiation. Some of what is raised may simply be to do with expression of hurt and attribution of fault.

Exploring the Limits

There then follows a phase of what Gulliver describes as 'free-roaming, antagonistic and rhetorical behaviour' (1979: 138) in which the parties explore the boundaries of the field within which negotiations may go forward. This can be a phase of open conflict and antagonism in which the sharpest differences are expressed and most extreme demands articulated on both sides. Some of this antagonist expression takes the form of venting or 'letting off steam' so as to relieve negative emotions, though perhaps sometimes with the unintended opposite effect of intensifying parties' negative feelings towards each other.

Narrowing the Differences

Through the previous phase, the parties come to understand the dimensions of the dispute between them, and as they do so the central issues emerge as well as the potential options. Sometimes suddenly, sometimes gradually, the tone of the exchange begins to alter enabling the parties to examine in depth what they conceive as being the main issues between them and the available options. This examination may in itself reveal to the parties an outcome that is acceptable to them, or that further exchanges will be unproductive, in either case bringing the negotiations to a conclusion.

Preliminary Bargaining

If common understanding and agreement still elude the parties once the central issues have been identified, a further phase begins during which an agreed outcome is sought through further exchanges. In the course of these exchanges, adjustments of position may take place as the respective bargaining endowments of the parties are brought to bear. Gulliver suggests that 'final bargaining' is often preceded by a preliminary phase in which the stage is set by preliminaries concerned with 'the search for a viable bargaining range, the refining of persisting differences, the testing of trading possibilities, and the construction of a bargaining formula' (1979: 153). But he makes clear that these are certainly not essential prerequisites of a successful outcome.

Final Bargaining

Gulliver defines bargaining as 'the exchange of more or less specific, substantive proposals' (1979: 160). Ensuing positional change can follow two general routes. Along the first, a 'stronger' party may continue to put his or her demands in an unrelenting and insistent way. In response, the 'weaker' party is forced into a modification of position. Along the second, the parties make linked, reciprocal concessions that enable all to recognise an acceptable outcome.

Ritual Confirmation

Negotiations may well end in impasse or breakdown, leaving the parties pursuing their dispute in other ways. But where an agreed outcome is reached, there is almost invariably a final phase in which agreement is ritually affirmed. The manner in which this is expressed will vary from one culture to another – it may involve writing, a handshake, drinking beer, the taking of oaths or participation in some ceremonial performance.

Implementation

One point widely advanced as a problem with bilateral negotiations as a mode of decision-making is the difficulty of enforcement. Gulliver, in our view rightly, suggests that this difficulty is greatly exaggerated. Consensual agreement, perceived by both parties as a better alternative to anything else available to them, generates commitment that is likely to make it self-enforcing.

Gulliver makes clear that what he is describing represents a model only, with each phase representing an 'analytically distinguishable set of interaction, exchange of information, learning and, in effect, purpose of negotiators' (1979: 172). However, in actual negotiations phases may overlap and not follow each other in a rigid chronology and, given the untidiness of actual social conduct, Gulliver 'cautions against insistence on a too neat and coherent model' (1979: 173).

We would adopt Gulliver's elegant and durable model,[2] subject to two small qualifications. First, we would prefer to treat the initial identification of issues and the subsequent formation of an agenda as analytically distinct, necessarily sequential phases, rather than the single stage he depicts. Each party's initial formulation will have distinctive features and the quality of a performance, requiring to be heard and acknowledged. The reduction of the two or more positions involved into an accepted agenda for discussion involves a significant transformation and represents a watershed that many embryonic negotiations do not manage to traverse. Secondly, in Gulliver's model, the phenomenon of agreement (where that is the outcome) seems to lie uneasily between the phases of *final bargaining* and *ritual affirmation.* In many negotiations, a substantial amount of work lies between the first recognition that an agreement is 'there' and its ultimate formulation. This tricky phase needs explicit acknowledgement. That is not to deny that, in these closing moments, the instrumental and the expressive may be inextricably interwoven with final acts both marking, and conferring validity on, a newly established state of affairs.

More wide-ranging critiques of Gulliver's model question the strength of his claim to its cross-cultural applicability. Moore has questioned the specificity of this processual model to negotiations, noting that in some important respects it replicates the structure of civil litigation, thereby suggesting that Gulliver has perhaps subconsciously adapted his developmental model of negotiations from the processual phases of litigation (Moore, 1995: 16, 18). Moreover, Gulliver is characterised as assuming too easily that negotiations will come to a successful conclusion, having focused his empirical attentions on cases in which the protagonists are interdependent. We find Moore's position here hard to follow. Gulliver outlines the shape of successive phases in a bilateral process of 'information exchange and learning'. In so far as Moore is referring to lawyer negotiations that follow the path of civil process these are *negotiations* and we would have no quarrel with her. However, the processual shape of those phases of litigation which are directed towards the judge, and hence are addressed to a third party, are distinctively different. The finality of agreement that comes from negotiation is founded to a significant degree on consent, whereas the finality in adjudication comes in the form of an authoritatively imposed third-party decision.

A different critique of Gulliver's claim that the nature and processual shape of negotiation holds steady across wide social fields goes to its applicability in different cultural contexts. Sonia Shah-Kazemi (2000) argues that, cultural difference makes it difficult to delineate a universal processual shape for negotiations. There are a number of closely related questions here. First, the profound communication and power complexities in negotiations that cross

[2] We note here that there has been an adoption and vigorous survival of Gulliver's model as the basis of practice in contemporary mediation programmes.

lines of stratification, ethnicity and gender are undeniable. These have particular implications where negotiations are facilitated by a mediator (see Chapter 7). But, Shah-Kazemi goes further, suggesting that Gulliver's process model itself may require significant refinement. In a robust examination of the cultural dimensions of family disputes, Shah-Kazemi argues that, in matrimonial cases, the socio-cultural context may well have a much more profound impact on the negotiations between the parties than Gulliver allows for, and that whether or not the joint decision-making which is central to Gulliver's analysis of the process of negotiation is genuinely 'joint' may be dependent on the 'cultural factors that impose themselves upon relationships' (2000: 303). A close examination of marital disputes is useful because marriage and the values that surround it are often so culturally embedded and socially important. Such an examination shows that there is a great deal of variation in how much choice the individual has in terms of dispute decision-making, and this variation may reflect one or more of a number of cultural dimensions including ethnicity, gender, socio-economic status and religion. Thus, for example, in patriarchal societies, the negotiation process might well take place not between the parties themselves but instead between their male kinsfolk because in such societies the couple are situated in a wider, but tightly-knit framework of kin, that at the very least sees itself an interested party in the dispute and its resolution (Shah-Kazemi, 2000: 309–10).

Whatever view we may take of these debates, the identification of a processual shape for negotiations has two immediate consequences: it removes the exclusive, distorting preoccupation with bargaining; but at the same time identifies in an innovative way the central foci of strategic action – around the problem of 'moving' the negotiations from one phase to the next, the primary task of the mediator. We examine that role in the next chapter, and consider now the strategic aspects of negotiations.

Power in Negotiation

So far we have represented negotiation primarily in terms of agency, or interacting individuals, and have not drawn in structural considerations. One of the central points that Santos is making in arguments considered above in Chapter 3 is that negotiations are not simply interactions between free, interest-pursuing 'individuals'. Participants are necessarily enmeshed in a partially perceived, but largely unexamined framework of constraint over which they have very limited control. This condition is variously represented in different traditions of social theory: in terms of structural constraint (for Marx); in terms of diffuse ('recursive'), multi-faceted networks of power running in different directions and multiple levels (for Foucault); and as 'systems' and 'sub-systems' experiencing 'turbulence' from the environment (for Luhmann). Power in these senses is always 'there'; but we frame the present discussion in straightforward Weberian terms. So 'power' for our immediate purposes is the capability of one human actor, or group of actors, to make others do things they would not otherwise have done.

One of the central implications of a bilateral mode of decision-making is that control over the outcome lies with the parties themselves, and that any outcome will necessarily be informed by the respective resources available to the parties, rather than those available to other people. This feature has encouraged much of the literature on negotiations to present them as 'power' struggles, bargaining processes, and therefore to concentrate on the strategic aspects of negotiation. While it is important to recognise this aspect of negotiations, that they need not be characterised by harmony and consensual decision-making, and that it is inherent in them that in the context of imbalances of power, the 'stronger' may dominate the weaker, two general points need to be emphasised in this context. First, negotiation is not just about 'bargaining'. It is primarily a process of information exchange and learning. Accordingly, an outcome in agreement may well flow simply from better understanding of the respective positions of the parties, as a result of information exchange, without either side's perceived interests being modified at all. The outcome may be that there is no 'issue', whatever perceptions may have been before negotiation commenced. Second, while respective sources of power inform the outcome of negotiations, power sources are multiple and imponderable. Money, love, truth and personality may all be at play. What constitute the power resources in a particular context are unlikely to be straightforward, and these are certainly not limited to material and normative resources.

Despite the complex, multiple nature of power resources in almost all negotiations, we need to distinguish some qualitatively different situations. The power imbalances that characterise differences of rank, and those that arise in the context of stratification, make negotiations across these divides particularly problematic. So, decision-making between sovereign and subject, between employer and employee, or between corporate suppliers of goods and services and individual consumers, present particular difficulty. As a general rule, we would argue that disputes crossing lines of stratification, and more generally those which involve gross imbalances of power, will seldom be well resolved through negotiation.

Strategy in Negotiation

We have noted already the narrowly circumscribed view of negotiation that is taken in much of the ADR literature, where negotiation is largely presented as bargaining. The most important question is identification of the best, that is, the most effective, bargaining strategies. This concern is closely followed by another, related issue – the manner in which various 'distortions' affect the pursuit of 'pure' or 'ideal' strategic conduct, in particular, the impact of power differentials on the bargaining process and the constraints placed on negotiating conduct by ethical considerations. Much of this discussion is informed by neoclassical economics, by the idea of perfect competition, and of distortions to the perfect competition of bargaining. A great deal of this writing also has a narrow focus on the actor, and assumes that those involved in negotiations are rational, calculating beings with clearly defined goals. We would not want to diminish the importance of this attention to strategic questions, so long as such discussion takes place within an overall understanding of the processual shape of negotiations.

Contrasting views of bargaining strategy inform much of existing writing in this area, expressed in terms of 'competitive' and 'cooperative' orientations (Menkel-Meadow, 1993). These are sometimes characterised in other binary terms: distributive–integrative, adversarial–problem-solving, positional–principled, claiming value–creating value, demand–exchange, non-stabilising–stabilising and so on. We consider these two approaches below, relying on the dichotomy most commonly employed, namely, the competitive and cooperative models.

The Competitive Approach

The competitive orientation is usually grounded upon several basic assumptions about what happens in negotiations. First, it assumes that in negotiations most people tend to take a competitive and self-interested view of the proceedings – each side must win as much as it can and, certainly, win more than the other side. Second, it assumes that the negotiating situation propels people towards conduct that is not only competitive but also, potentially at least, antagonistic. Third, it presumes that in most cases, the negotiations will be focused on a limited resource. Accordingly, the negotiation problem is about distribution – what one party gains, the other side loses, because this is a zero-sum game. And, fourth, because people tend to take a narrow view of the negotiation process, the conduct of negotiations today will not materially affect negotiations at some future date. As a result, the competitive orientation encourages strategies that are inherently confrontational.

Typical, recognisable patterns of behaviour of the competitive negotiator are designed to maximise gains in the immediate negotiating situation. The competitive negotiator tends to make high opening demands and to be slow to make concessions. Similarly, this type of negotiator relies on confrontation, threats and forceful arguments, and manipulates both people and process, in particular, trying to uncover as much as possible about the position of the other party and, at the same time, to mislead the other side about that negotiator's own situation. Additionally, the negotiator with a competitive orientation is not open to persuasion on substantive issues. He or she has a fixed goal and that goal is to be achieved. Moreover, the goal is viewed in quantitative and competitive terms; in particular, the concern is to maximise financial rewards. This approach is sometimes seen as *the* paradigm for negotiation, and there is evidence to suggest that in some parts of the world a significant number of parties do approach negotiations in this manner. But, of course, it does not really constitute an analysis of negotiation. Rather, it is essentially a characterisation of one type of tactical approach to negotiation. Even as a 'tactical model', however, there are widely differing views on its efficacy (see, for example, Genn, 1987; Williams, 1983; Lowenthal, 1982).

Problem-solving Orientations

Other writers, notably Fisher and Ury (1981),[3] see the competitive approach as seriously deficient in a number of ways. In their view, it is based on a false set of assumptions about the negotiating world and, as a result, is unnecessarily limiting. The cooperative approach therefore recommends a radically different view of the nature of negotiations or, at least, of what should take place in negotiations. This approach sees people negotiating in terms of self-interest, but this is an enlightened self-interest. People should, and often do, look for a better outcome for both sides by working together on the problems they face.

The cooperative approach stresses that the negotiating parties are likely to share common interests, may well be dependent on each other (especially if they are involved in a long-term relationship in which 'generalised reciprocity' rather than 'immediate returns', or specific reciprocity, is called for)[4] and will often be negotiating about limited resources (and therefore need to be flexible in their goals). Moreover, outcomes that are mutually agreeable, fair to all parties and good for the community, are more likely to be implemented and to endure. As a result, the parties, while trying to maximise their individual returns, should look for joint gains and focus on their common interests. In particular, the negotiators should try to increase the number of issues over which they might reach an agreement – that is, to 'expand the pie', before dividing it. The negotiator, instead of being argumentative, should try to understand the merits of the other party's position as objectively as possible. Accordingly, differences should be explored by non-confrontational debate rather than manipulation and coercion. Moreover, the parties should be willing to be flexible, open to persuasion on substantive issues. They should always be aware of their 'best alternative to a negotiated outcome' (BATNA).[5] For the cooperative approach is, ultimately,

---

[3] See also Carrie Menkel-Meadow's essay, 'Towards Another View of Legal Negotiation' (1984).
[4] See Sahlins (1965).
[5] For further details on the use of BATNA in the negotiation process see, in particular, Fisher, Ury and Patton (1991: 97–106). Briefly stated, the negotiator is advised that BATNA is the most appropriate measure with which to assess settlement offers. An offer should only be accepted if it is better than the negotiator's best alternative to a settlement.

concerned with qualitative goals – the construction, through efficient and rational negotiation, of an agreement that is fair, wise and durable.[6]

Negative characterisations of the collaborative approach outlined above view it as 'naive' and 'romantic' and as therefore dangerously misleading because it encourages parties to be too ready to make concessions. Moreover, empirical research also indicates that even where cooperative solutions are theoretically available, other variables, such as the manner in which legal services are organised, may restrict access to such solutions (Galanter and Cahill, 1994: 1376). Further, the virtues of cooperative or 'win–win' solutions may be complicated by the varied interests of the actors who make up a negotiating team, so that while both sides across a table may appear to win, 'within each team ... there are [those] who may view themselves as definite losers in the process' (Colosi, 1983: 234). As a result, just as the emphasis on competitive bargaining found in the 1970s and early 1980s was supplanted by a late 1980s concern with the virtues of the cooperative and collaborative, so the cooperative model has now been somewhat superseded by empirically more complex understandings of negotiation (see, for example, Kritzer, 1991: 112–29).

Nevertheless, the competitive and cooperative dichotomy continues to define many approaches to negotiating (Menkel-Meadow, 1993: 363–6). The two basic models undoubtedly have their merits. Empirical studies do suggest that many people often approach negotiation in one of these ways, although such work also suggests that parties do not necessarily pursue such strategies once they have become repeat players (Menkel-Meadow, 1993: 376–7). The basic problem with the dichotomy, in our view, is that it is both too general and too specific. It is *too general* because in a sense it is a manifestation in the 'negotiation' context of basic debates about human nature. The *competitive* position takes a Hobbesian, *conservative* view of the social world – only the fittest will survive in our ever-competitive social environment, and the truth about negotiation is that it is the toughest, smartest bargainer who survives. In contrast, the *cooperative* approach is concerned to stress the *social* or communal nature of human life, highlighting the need to stand together, to restrain competitiveness and give full reign to cooperative instincts, in order to survive. Thus, just beneath the surface of the two models are important assumptions about the nature of society. The competitive–cooperative dichotomy is but another variant on this basic theme. On the other hand, these approaches are too narrow because they focus on the conduct of negotiators rather than the process of negotiating. As a result, we often appear to be in the world of cookbooks. These orientations are guides to the construction of a successful negotiation dish. Add a little coercion here (for example, only make one's offer after the other party has made its offer), a dash of 'deceit' there (for example,

---

[6] For an examination of negotiation strategies based on detailed empirical research, see Menkel-Meadow (1993).

by making false statements in regard to one's 'bottom line'), or identify a rich set of agreeable ingredients (thereby expanding the negotiable pie), and a good negotiation outcome is created. But these instrumental approaches ultimately fail because they do not enhance significantly our understanding of the overall shape of the processes of negotiation.

The literature is now increasingly sensitive to the view that the binary characterisations examined above, so long dominant in ADR negotiating theory, are inadequate. Greater explanatory value is to be found in approaches that acknowledge that most negotiators are likely to combine both orientations in their actual bargaining conduct, or that there exists a continuum of negotiating orientations. This 'intermediary' approach can be located in some of the early work of Lowenthal and Gifford, and some key aspects of their findings are still relevant today.

Thus, Lowenthal (1982) stressed that in most negotiations it is necessary to combine competitive and collaborative approaches in the dispute resolving process. An exclusively competitive approach may, for example, undermine trust between the parties to the point where a lasting settlement is not possible. On the other hand, if the parties have deeply entrenched differences of interest, a solely collaborative approach may be an inadequate tool for taking the negotiations forward.

But identifying the most effective mix of strategies may be difficult if such factors as the substantive issues in the dispute, normative constraints, relationship concerns and personality factors point to differing courses of action. In these circumstances it is likely that preliminary communications between the negotiating parties will have a disproportionately significant effect on the process as a whole as one party's initial decision on strategic style will likely influence the other party's choice of strategies. It is also likely that where the parties have found themselves in a competitive bargaining process – even though they may have preferred a more collaborative approach – it will be difficult to break out of the constraints of this approach because a change in orientation by one side will likely be interpreted as a sign of weakness by the other. If there is a transformation to a more collaborative approach by both parties, it will likely be the result of coming together of two factors: a looming deadlock on the one hand and a basic preference of the negotiating parties for a settlement rather than a deadlock. And probably the best method for a party seeking to change the process in the direction of collaboration would be best advised to shift to a more problem-solving approach rather than running the risk of making possibly unreciprocated concessions.[7]

---

[7] As part of his argument that there is a universal principle of reciprocity which shapes our interaction with each other, Lévi-Strauss long ago pointed to the subtleties that may be involved in such exchanges. He uses as a case study the custom in southern France of diners (who may well be strangers) on neighbouring tables in small restaurants pouring into each other's glass the cheap wine that accompanies their meal, so that while each diner eats from herself or himself, the pouring, toasting and drinking of the wine is a form of social interaction. He writes, 'The

In addition to cooperative negotiation and competitive negotiation, there is also 'integrative negotiation'. Whereas Lowenthal saw a combination of cooperative and competitive approaches as a pattern typically found in negotiations, Gifford seeks to supplement this fused approach with an expanded vision that includes 'integrative negotiation' and follows Fisher and Ury's work on *Getting to Yes* (1981) in arguing for the importance of the 'principled negotiator' – that is, someone who attempts to keep the interpersonal relationship between the parties distinct and separate from the merits of the problem or conflict, focuses on interests not positions, generates options and insists on outcomes that are based on some objective standard. This approach is necessary because the 'negotiation dance of concession matching or positioning, which is a part of both competitive and cooperative behavior, often obscures the parties' real interests' (Gifford, 1985: 55). A major dimension of integrative negotiation is a free flow of information between the negotiators so that each party has a firm understanding of the other. The style of integrative negotiation includes 'brainstorming' to develop new options that meet the significant needs of both parties; 'logrolling', in which each party agrees to make concessions on certain issues while the other side concedes on other issues, and as both parties have different priorities so they are better able to reconcile their distinctive priorities; and 'cost-cutting' in which a reduction in the tangible or intangible costs to the other side secures a significant concession in return on some other point at issue. These and other such agreement promoting techniques tend to work best, however, when both the parties share a problem-solving orientation, and there exist multiple issues which are capable of being traded. Often competitive conduct and cooperative conduct alternate within a single negotiation or even occur simultaneously, and agreements that are reached often produce further issues that the parties need to resolve. Shifting between the three styles is not likely to be easy, especially when competitive conduct has undermined the possibility of a good working relationship between the negotiating parties. Gifford concludes:

French custom is to ignore people whose names, occupations and rank are unknown. But in the little restaurant, such people find themselves in a quite close relationship for one to one-and-a-half hours, and temporarily united by a similar preoccupation. A conflict exists . . . sufficient to create a state of tension between the norm of privacy and the fact of community . . . This is the fleeting but difficult situation resolved by the exchanging of wine . . . It substitutes a social relationship for spatial juxtaposition. But it is also more than that. The partner who was entitled to maintain his reserve is persuaded to give it up. Wine offered calls for wine returned, cordiality requires cordiality . . . There is no way of refusing the neighbour's offer of his glass of wine without being insulting. Further, the acceptance of this offer sanctions another offer, for conversation . . . And there is still more. The person beginning the cycle seizes the initiative and the greater social ease which he has displayed puts him at an advantage. For the opening always involves a risk, in that the table companion may respond to the drink offered with a less generous glass, or the contrary risk that he will take the liberty to bid higher, obliging the one who made the first offer (and we must not forget that the bottle is small) either to lose his last trump as his last drop, or to sacrifice another bottle for the sake of his prestige (Lévi-Strauss, 1969: 59–60).

Often, competitive behavior and co-operative behavior alternate within a single negotiation or even occur simultaneously; different issues will be at varying stages of resolution, and agreements resulting from co-operative or integrative bargaining will often produce new issues to be resolved by the parties. Negotiators, however, cannot easily shift between competitive tactics and co-operative or integrative tactics in all instances. Successful competitive tactics, which attack the opponent and his case, jeopardize the positive working relationships necessary for the co-operative and integrative strategies. The combination of competitive strategies and co-operative or integrative strategies will typically occur only at different phases of a negotiation process or on easily separable and distinct issues (1985: 58).

The ideal outcome offered by integrative negotiation (or 'integrative bargaining' as it is more commonly called) of 'win–win', so that the overall value of the deal is expanded to the benefit of all the parties to the dispute or transaction, has become an important part of the claims of the ADR movement to offer a 'better way'. Indeed, as one observer has observed: 'for the past quarter century, the primary normative message of negotiation theory literature has been that negotiators will achieve better outcomes by focusing their attention on the integrative aspects of bargaining rather that its distributive aspect ... I call this the "integrative bargaining supremacy claim"' (Korobkin, 2008: 1324). Indeed, in what is almost a 'civilizing mission, the practitioners of integrative negotiation are characterized in the supportive discourse as worthy of emulation because they are modern, sophisticated, negotiators, who bring a subtle, creative and highly intelligent style to the negotiating table and thereby enhance the possibilities of win-win outcomes. In contrast, the "distributive tactics" of the uncivilized competitive negotiators undermine such possibilities' (Korobkin, 2008: 1324). However, a much more realistic approach to negotiation is to accept that creating value in the negotiation process is much harder than it seems, for 'negotiations generally, and legal negotiations specifically, have more distributive potential than integrative potential. For this reason, lawyer negotiators would be better served ... to think of distributive bargaining as the cake and integrative bargaining as the frosting, rather than reverse' (Korobkin, 2008: 1325).

There are several important reasons that are offered as explanations of the limited effectiveness of integrative negotiations. First, in many cases where there seems to be potential for an integrative approach, the potential is somewhat illusory. Thus, the integrative technique of adding issues so as to increase the size of the cooperative pie has the limitation that it may be more beneficial for one or more of the parties simply to enter into the added proposed part of the transaction with a third party rather than with their immediate negotiating party. So while expanding the pie may well increase the cooperative potential of the agreement, it does not necessarily represent the best outcome for both parties. If one of the parties can negotiate a better outcome on the additional issues with a third party, then they are likely worse off if they deal with their counterpart in the negotiations. Additionally, in fields such as employment negotiations, the deep understanding of the issues and lengthy experience of handling industry specific troubles mean that it is likely that many of the problems and possibilities have already been anticipated and dealt with in the baseline agreement, so that room to manoeuvre for creating a significantly larger pie is less than might be imagined and opportunities for using integrative factors also relatively limited.

Finally, and somewhat paradoxically, clever use of integrative tactics may in fact create opportunities for securing significant gains from competitive distributive tactics. The negotiation surplus generated by integrative tactics still has to be distributed between the parties, and the distribution decisions are more likely to be made on the basis of competitive tactics rather than cooperative tactics, as there is little or no room left for future value creation.

Thus, the win–win claim – while laudable as a spirit with which to approach the task of negotiating – is arguably aspirational rather than a realistic outcome possibility. This is likely to be the case in legal settlement negotiations where – unless, for example, the parties are locked into a long-term relationship and find an add-on such as an apology very meaningful – the scope for adding issues to the baseline agreement is limited and the alternative of an expressive trial is unattractive.

Representative Negotiations

Although traditionally prepared in their legal education for determination of dispute outcomes through knowledge of relevant areas of law, trial and appeal, in reality lawyers in many jurisdictions are involved in dispute resolution primarily as negotiators. They spend much of their time negotiating on behalf of a client with a view to securing a compromise outcome. This process takes place without reference to an umpire responsible for determining whether either the negotiating process, or the compromise outcome, is acceptable in wider terms of legal and moral standards and the public good. It is difficult, however, to generalise about this important activity of lawyer negotiations because even within a particular jurisdiction there is likely to be a wide range of possible processual shapes arising out of variables such as the nature of the dispute, the make-up of the parties, the negotiating 'style' of the lawyers involved, and the type of practice in which the lawyer is normally engaged. These variables have an impact on both the manner in which the lawyer approaches the dispute and its management, and the particular outcomes that he or she finds acceptable. Nevertheless, certain features of lawyer negotiations can be identified.

The first point to note about lawyer negotiations is that they are representative negotiations, in which the parties have delegated the conduct of negotiations to champions. Thus, they are both intra-party negotiations and inter-party negotiations. This necessarily increases the complexity of the processes of negotiation, requiring lines of communication along at least two planes: between each party and his or her professional representative; and between the two representatives themselves.

The picture may be even more complex than this if the principals remain in communication themselves, or if one or both seek to communicate directly with the other's legal representative. Lawyers manage this complexity by insisting that they control communications, generally discouraging direct inter-party contact. They also seek to achieve control by regulating the flow of information to their principals. Their goal is often, in fact, 'total' management of the negotiation process, their assertions regarding the need to have such control normally being buttressed by the claim that lawyers are trustworthy partisans who will promote fully their client's interests. Popular images of lawyers – for example, as untrustworthy, self-interested predators – may not accord with this claim, but the claim is made vigorously nonetheless.

A second general point to make about lawyer negotiations relates to the distinctive way in which lawyers choose to conduct them, utilising the arena of 'litigation'. In the common law world lawyers set out at an early stage along the path towards the court, utilising civil procedure as the framework of their negotiations (see Roberts, Simon, 1997). This strategy, in itself, imposes a distinctive shape on lawyer negotiations and often has very important implications for the progress of the dispute, especially as the emphasis in any trial that might eventually take place will be on evidence and proof, and on a binary win–lose resolution of an essentially financial character, rather than an outcome that suits both parties.

Third, with the transfer of responsibility to the lawyer, a fundamental translation takes place in the course of which the dispute is typically carried over into another universe of meaning constituted by the specialised discourse of the law – like Mnookin and Kornhauser's lawyers bargaining 'in the shadow of the law' (1979). Within this universe, an important element of understanding will be the likely outcome in the event of the dispute proceeding to expert determination by a judge. The recasting of the predominant negotiating language to 'the law' means that the lawyer's control over his or her client is significantly enhanced, for it is the lawyer who is skilled at the legal abstractions and nuances, and the processual formalities that underpin this discourse.[8] Notwithstanding this, empirical research into the realities of lawyer negotiations in the Anglo-American legal world suggests that the deals that are actually cut between the parties' lawyers are not informed by legal principles at all but, rather, are very often simple compromises (see, for example, Menkel-Meadow, 1993; Genn, 1987; Condlin, 1985). Such compromises are sometimes clearly beneficial to the interests of their clients.

---

[8] As Sarat and Felstiner conclude: 'by limiting interpretative activity to their area of expertise, lawyers are able to explain the social world through the lenses of the legal process. They are able to structure conversation to fit their rational-purposive ideology and to limit the impact of their clients' egocentric views of social life' (1988).

In an important essay, Mnookin and Gilson (1994) consider some of the complications that arise through the use of lawyers in negotiations. In their article 'Disputing through Agents', they examine the role of lawyers in matrimonial proceedings, a situation in which negotiations over divorce and associated arrangements can all to easily become a zero-sum game in which the couple's property and children are simply divided, with any gains to the wife coming at the expense of the husband, and vice versa. Lawyers therefore bear a responsibility as the agents of each of the divorcing couples to try to create value and enhance the outcome for each of the parties. Areas in which this might well be possible include the arrangements for the young children of the relationship, as a well-designed and robust co-parenting arrangement is a joint gain for both parents, and also beneficial for the well-being of the child. In addition, by cooperating to reduce the transaction costs of divorce, they may be able to preserve better financial and emotional resources to their mutual benefit, and to distribute their resources more effectively and more in accordance with their personal preferences.

In matrimonial cases, the lawyers may well have a critically important role in helping the parties to overcome some serious obstacles to effective negotiation. The strong emotions that are often generated by matrimonial quarrels may well erect a serious block in the way of rational collaboration. But the lawyer, in contrast to the often emotionally charged parties, is a 'repeat player' whose experience, emotion distance, and perhaps local network of contacts and reputation in local professional circles puts her or him in a position to encourage cooperation without too much risk of exploitation of the client in the divorce negotiation process. Indeed, in some districts a spirit of collaboration may emerge in which local family lawyers voluntarily and informally exchange information and documents. A local reputation for practising law in a cooperative manner may also encourage potential clients with a similar problem-solving, cooperative attitude to dispute resolution methods to seek her or him out for purposes of legal representation. Another factor encouraging cooperative lawyering in matrimonial cases is that a family lawyer is typically much less dependent than (say) a commercial litigator on a small number of wealthy corporate clients, and so is in a position to resist client pressure to change strategy and, indeed, to turn away – as they often do – clients seeking highly competitive representation. Mnookin and Gilson conclude: that their analysis of 'matrimonial practice . . . [shows]. . .that reputational markets may develop that encourage divorcing parties to pursue cooperative strategies in situations where the parties by themselves would feel unable to commit to a cooperative attitude' (Mnookin and Gilson, 1994: 541–6).

Ethical Issues in Negotiation

Negotiations anywhere will be informed by the ethical understandings current in the milieu within which they take place. In many cultures, abstract notions of 'fairness' and 'honesty' take on a different meaning in the context of negotiations. Perhaps because to the onlooker, the wider audience, what often impresses is outcome rather than process, images of the 'good negotiator' seem to stress cleverness, skill and effectiveness rather than probity. It is an expected part of the negotiation process in many cultures that the parties (or their partisan representatives) misrepresent to a greater or lesser degree their real attitudes, their particular circumstances and needs, and their bottom line. Misrepresentation is often built into the negotiation process as a tolerated, perhaps even legitimate, required practice. The line between honesty and dishonesty, between fairness and unfairness, is often difficult to draw. Moreover, drawing that line objectively is also complicated by the likelihood that the parties will view borderline conduct in differing ways – one person's 'puff' is another person's 'misrepresentation'.

On the other hand, trust and credibility are important factors in negotiating relationships, especially continuing relationships, so that a reputation for honesty and fairness is also valuable. An additional complication comes with the use of professional partisans or agents, that is, lawyers, for purposes of negotiation. The professional body – the association or associations of lawyers – then has an interest in the reputation of its members and will construct rules designed to give lawyers' conduct an acceptable face, even while often encouraging lawyers to maximise returns on behalf of their clients.[9] There seem to be many basic issues that face such attempts to impose codes of negotiating conduct by an external authority. A seminal essay in this area is that first published in the *American Bar Foundation Journal* in 1980 by James White, 'Machiavelli and the Bar: Ethical Limitations on Lying in Negotiation'. White highlights very effectively some of the difficulties that surround any attempt to control through rules truthfulness in negotiating. More recently, Clark Freshman (2020) has emphasised that lies, broadly construed, suffuse negotiations (and, indeed, life) so pervasively that we can never escape them but can only learn to negotiate around them, and the imperfect information they present.

Social anthropologists have also enhanced our understanding of the issues. Thus, drawing on Simmel's earlier work on secrecy (1906), Michael Gilsenan explores the problems of truth and falsehood in a Lebanese Muslim village where, beyond a few incontestable objective truths, lying was commonplace in social interaction. He suggests that in this community and elsewhere, lying in the everyday world is not only an expression of self but also a conscious act directed at another; it is always part of social meanings and social reflections. Indeed, the lie is usually accessible to the observer, not in its original form in the actor's intention, but as a judgement made by others (or another) of certain verbal or behavioural signs (Gilsenan, 1976: 191).

---

[9] Thus, for example, the American Bar Association Model Rules of Professional Conduct that a lawyer shall not 'engage in conduct involving dishonesty, fraud, deceit or misrepresentation'. The leading study of ethical issues in negotiation is the very insightful study edited by Menkel-Meadow and Wheeler (2004).

It is . . . in the examination of the lie in action, that we learn the full meaning of the classification 'that is a lie.'

Such judgments may be public and discrediting, or they may be privately made by the other who for some reason has no interest in revealing his judgment and is prepared to go along 'as if' things are as they seem. There may be tacit cooperation and collaboration, or challenge and social compromise. Moreover, all the while others may be unsure, unable to answer the question whether such and such an act or statement is a lie or not, and they may turn to procedures for testing it when it is relevant that they do so. Such 'monitoring' will depend on whether there is information, uniformly or selectively available, for verifying the individual's representation, or whether it is simply unverifiable and a matter of trust. Similarly, the lying subject may have difficulty in discovering if he is believed, and the non-lying subject in realizing that his conduct is labelled by some as a lie. Uncertainty as to the precise degree of lying or truth on both sides will always be present and subject to active assessment in problematic situations. For insofar as falseness undermines our notions of legitimate and right behavior, indeed the certainty of our grasp on the reality of the common-sense world, it constitutes a threat of a serious order to our social reality. The conjunction or disjunction between appearance and reality, shifting and ever critical, is hedged with ambiguity concerning judgment and value, act and intention, what is concealed and what is revealed (Gilsenan, 1976:192).

One problem is that negotiation is typically not a *public* process. As a result, there is often little or no possibility of questioning effectively the truthfulness of assertions made during the course of negotiations. Since there is only a small likelihood of discovery and punishment, ethical norms can perhaps be violated more easily than they would in more public arenas. And once there is a general recognition of this fact in a particular sphere of activity then, and this is a special problem with representative negotiation, in acting truthfully and fairly one may be foregoing advantages that would otherwise be maintained or created by acting in a dishonest (but socially tolerated) fashion. In other words, the dilemma for the representative is, should his or her loyalty be to the wider corpus of ethical norms, which invariably call for honesty and fairness, or to the immediate and particular needs of the party being represented.

An additional difficulty is the need for a professional body to develop a code of conduct that will regulate effectively all types of negotiating. Negotiations cover an almost infinite variety of substantive issues, from war to terrorism to family disputes to contractual disagreements, and so on. In such circumstances, it is necessary to frame rules in very broad language, for example, the American Bar Association requirements that lawyers negotiate honestly and truthfully, and this will inevitably lead to problems of interpretation and enforcement.

A third problematic area, as we have already noted, is constituted by the contradictory pressures apparently inherent in many negotiations. Even if one of the parties wants to be perfectly fair and truthful, if the aim of engaging in the negotiating is to secure a favourable outcome – better than one would have achieved without a negotiated agreement – there is a basic negotiating hope that the other party will over-estimate the strength of one's negotiating position. In negotiating, as a result, concealment and misrepresentation are very often seen as 'natural', and there are many ways in which they may be almost effortlessly effected: for example, the use of silence to create a false impression, verbal diversions to divert attention away from a weak point, and feigned interest in certain items on the agenda in order to increase their trading value.

A further complication arises when continuing professional relationships between negotiating specialists are present. The basic problem here is the tension between the need to represent the interests of the client in the particular case, and the need to adopt strategies that enhance one's overall effectiveness and reputation. Rules of professional conduct usually prescribe the sacrifice of clients' interests for the sake of long-term considerations. But the problem remains, especially in certain kinds of conduct, for example, plea bargaining. Patterns of reciprocity develop between repeat negotiators whose relationship is *inherently* long term and which encourage concessions in the instant case for the sake of the 'generalised reciprocity'.[10]

A fifth difficulty is to be found in the judgements that might have to be made about whether a particular outcome is or is not 'fair'. Of course, it could be argued that outcome is irrelevant – all that a professional body or some other 'significant onlooker' can or should be concerned with is fairness of the negotiating process. But what are called 'distributional issues' lurk in the background, and therefore may pose something of a dilemma for a partisan or some other third party. Indeed, one trenchant criticism of ADR is that it does not achieve its aim to produce fairer outcomes; rather, because negotiations are a social rather than legal process, outcomes inevitably reflect disparities of wealth, status and power. They do so in part because standards of truthfulness and fairness are not so high in negotiations as they are claimed to be for adjudication. An additional complication is that in any social relationship views on fairness are likely to differ, each party will have its own view of what is an equitable outcome, and this may make an objective assessment of a fair result more difficult to assess.

Finally, we should bear in mind the view of Fiss (1984) that private, non-official processes of dispute resolution are not suitable for disputes involving important public concerns. If courts are excluded from the dispute resolution process, how is the public interest to be secured? If the dispute involves matters of substantial public policy – race relations, environmental degradation, and so on – should a body such as the court be required to review thoroughly any settlement worked out privately by the parties?

[10] On generalised reciprocity, see Sahlins (1965).

So what seems to be most at issue is that the promotion of negotiation and settlement as preferred means of dispute resolution in any system necessarily raises questions of quality of process and outcome, and regulation of those who represent others in negotiations. And the imperatives of 'effective negotiation' will continually create tensions in both these areas.

Conclusions

Understanding negotiation requires us to move away from everyday images of the negotiation process. Negotiations are often viewed as involving two competing parties who are very assertive in their approach to each other because they assume the process is a zero-sum game in which the gains of one side are the losses of the other side. In fact, negotiation is not simply a competitive exercise, and there is a real sense in which we negotiate on a daily basis whenever we try to shape the conduct of another person. Negotiation then is the transactional process which can be used for resolving disputes, and in this chapter we have looked at a number of ways in which commentators regard the negotiation process. Our main attention has been an examination of the study of negotiations by Philip Gulliver, who sees the process of negotiation as both linear (more or less) and cyclical. The cyclical process is one of repetitive exchange of information between the parties and deliberations upon the received information. Adjustments are then made in terms of this knowledge and the expectations and preferences of the parties. Thus, the cyclical process drives forward the negotiations so that they also take a developmental shape in which the dispute is handled by the parties. If progress is made, then the parties go through a series of stages of narrowing differences, and perhaps reach a conclusion with an agreement. This is then implemented. We argue that the powerful model offered by Gulliver is also useful for the analysis of mediation in which a third party attempts to assist the disputants in the negotiating parties in their efforts to reach a conclusion. It is to this topic that we now turn.

7

Mediation

Introduction – The Nature of Mediation

With the gradual re-institutionalisation of mediation in the West across the last years of the twentieth century, quite a strong stereotype seems in the process of emerging. This is one of the disinterested professional, deliberately attempting 'to advance the interests of the disputants' (Princen, 1992: 48) by taking responsibility for process, thus assisting embattled parties to reach decisions on the substance of the issues between them. But as we saw in Chapter 4 the image of the professional mediator, self-consciously facilitating other people's decision-making on matters in which she or he has no direct stake, conveys only a partial sense of a very complex constellation of interventions, arguably universally visible in one form or another across the social world.

While the mediator receives quite limited attention in classical social theory, a defining analysis was provided early in the twentieth century by the German sociologist Georg Simmel. In some almost poetic passages of his great *Soziologie* ([1908] trans. 1950), Simmel pointed to the fact that the mediator is always present in the social world even though she may not be named as such and her role may remain unexamined. The constellation yielding the mediator, he argued, is a structural feature, generally observable across cultures in all groups of more than two elements. Reflecting upon the nature of bilateral relations and upon the fundamental ways in which these are transformed by the presence of a third party, he noted: 'dyads . . . have very specific features . . . the addition of a third person completely changes them' ([1908] trans. 1950: 138). He went on, in a few deft paragraphs, which are provided below, to delineate the mediator as non-aligned facilitator, distinguished from the partisan supporter on the one hand and the arbitrator with determinative authority on the other,

> For the analysis of community life it is important to make it clear that the constellation heretofore identified in all groups that count more than two elements occurs continually even where the mediator is not specifically selected, is even not particularly known or identified as such. The group of three is here only a type and schema; all cases of mediation reduce in the end to its form. There is absolutely no community of three, from the hour-long conversation to the life of a family, in which now these, now those two do not get into a

disagreement of a harmless or pointed, momentary or long-lasting, theoretical or practical nature – and in which the third would not function mediatively. This happens countless times in quite rudimentary form, only hinted at, mixed with other actions and interactions from which the mediative function is never purely absent. Such mediations need not even take place in words: a gesture, a kind of listening, the mood that comes from a person, suffices for giving a misunderstanding between two others a direction toward unity, to make the essential commonality perceptible underneath a sharp difference of opinion, to put this in a form in which it is most easily discharged. It is not at all necessarily a matter of actual conflict or strife; rather there are a thousand entirely minor differences of opinion, the hint of an antagonism between personalities, the emergence of wholly momentarily opposed interests or feelings – which colors the fluctuating forms of every enduring collective life and is determined by the presence of a third continually and almost unavoidably performing the mediating function. This function rotates, so to speak, among the three elements, because the ebb and flow of shared life tends to realize that form in every possible combination of members (Simmel, [1908] trans. 2009a: 104).[1]

Although Simmel thus firmly fixes 'the third' in a non-aligned, non-determinative role, mediation still represents an elusive, fugitive label, presently resorted to all too easily and with little precision in the context of contemporary transformations in the management of disputing. While a contrast with the partisan supporter, on the one hand, and the arbitrator, on the other, helps to provide an identity for the mediator in rough and ready terms, 'mediation' is a label claimed by interveners of widely different rank and ambition. Mediation may be attempted by anyone from the hesitant neighbour to an authoritative professional, and, as Simmel's primary analytic distinction indicates, 'help' may range from minimal assistance with communications to an extensive and expert advisory role.

Three general dimensions need to be explored here. First, the idea of the disinterested intermediary: mediators often – perhaps typically – have their own interests, even in the substance of a dispute. Second, wide areas of apparently mediatory intervention go far beyond the parsimonious role of facilitating decision-making by taking care of process. Third, professional qualification as an intervener covers a small area, capturing only a little about the provenance and standing of the mediator.

The Idea of a Non-aligned Intermediary

The image of the 'neutral' third party, purposively intervening in the affairs of others – whether out of altruistic goodwill, social responsibility or professional calling – is a very powerful one. Yet almost any third-party intermediary has

---

[1] See also Simmel ([1908] trans. 1950: 148–9).

some interest in a matter in which he or she intervenes. The bystander, the neighbour, the kinsman, the co-worker, the employer and the political leader all have a stake in things 'getting back to normal', even if this is no more than an interest in everyday life 'going on' without the dislocation of a quarrel among some of those adjacent to them.

Simmel approaches this problem of what is involved in non-alignment by contrasting the position of the mediator with that of the partisan ([1908] trans. 1950: 149–50). For him, a defining characteristic of the mediator is that he or she is not a partisan: either because the mediator stands outside the interests of the parties; or because, although engaged, he or she stands in a structurally intermediate position. As an example of the latter situation, he offers the situation of the bishop acting as an intermediary between the secular government of the state within which his diocese is situated and the Pope in Rome:

> The non-partisanship that is required for mediation has one of two presuppositions. The [mediator] is non-partisan either if he stands above the contrasting interests and opinions and is actually not concerned with them, or if he is equally concerned with both. The first case is the simpler of the two and involves fewest complications. In conflicts between English laborers and entrepreneurs, for instance, the non-partisan called in could be neither a laborer nor an entrepreneur. It is notable how decisively the separation of objective from personal elements in the conflict . . . is realized here. The idea is that the non-partisan is not attached by personal interest to the objective aspects of either party position. Rather, both come to be weighed by him as by a pure, impersonal intellect; without touching the subjective sphere. But the mediator must be subjectively interested in the persons or groups themselves who exemplify the contents of the quarrel which to him are merely theoretical, since otherwise he would not take over his function. It is, therefore, as if subjective interest set in motion a purely objective mechanism. It is the fusion of personal distance from the objective significance of the quarrel with personal interest in its subjective significance which characterises the non-partisan position.

However, he continues:

> The situation becomes more complicated when the non-partisan owes his position, not to his neutrality, but to his equal participation in the interests in conflict. This case is frequent when a given individual belongs to two different interest groups, one local, and the other objective, especially occupational. In earlier times, bishops could sometimes intervene between the secular ruler of their diocese and the pope. The administrator who is thoroughly familiar with the special interests of his district, will be the most suitable mediator in the case of a collision between these special interests and the general interests of the state which employs him. The measure of the combination between impartiality and interest which is favorable to the mediation between two locally separate groups, is often found in persons that come from one of these groups but live with the other. The difficulty of positions of this kind in which the mediator may

find himself, usually derives from the fact that his equal interests in both parties, that is, his inner equilibrium, cannot be definitely ascertained and is, in fact, doubted often enough by both parties (Simmel, [1908] trans. 1950: 149–50).

Gulliver sets any claim to 'neutrality' in perspective. He shows that mediators often lean towards one or other of the parties, or may have a significant interest in the resolution of a dispute, so that the 'truly disinterested, impartial mediator is rather rare' (Gulliver, 1979: 214). The manner in which a mediator came out with her or his intervention will likely be affected by the particular context and the reasons for the mediatory intervention. The mediator's ties with the parties, understanding of the issues in dispute and her or his wider social status in the community may significantly impact on the mediator's role in the resolution process.

Thus, one important variable in the nature of the mediator is the extent to which she or he has an 'interest' in the dispute and its parties. In many societies there is a strong preference for an intervener who has a clearly superior status – a Nuer leopard-skin chief, a Pathan saint, or a professional mediator of a well-known dispute resolution agency – and with this status comes a duty to resolve disputes.

Local leadership roles are seen in many societies as bearing a responsibility to resolve disputes and to expound the moral norms of the community and its common interests and needs. But, of course, it is always possible that in carrying out this obligation she or he is actually pursuing self-interest, such as skilfully preventing a clear resolution of the dispute in order to further a hidden strategy of 'divide and rule'. Secondly, visibility is reassuring for the parties when the mediatory intervention is by a person well known for her or his wisdom, fairness or social prestige. Thirdly, it may be that the mediator is seen as being disinterested because she or he is quite external to the disputants' local community – a stranger with little concern for the social situation within which the dispute has arisen. A final type of mediator often seen as 'disinterested' is an expert figure – perhaps a lawyer, perhaps a priest, perhaps some other type of professional specialist – whose special knowledge and training is accompanied by a concern with how best to resolve the issues rather than to seek any immediate personal gain.

But in other circumstances, mediators may be directly concerned with either the specific issues in dispute or the disputing parties themselves, or both. For example, the leaders of a state that might be affected if neighbouring counties decided to wage war on each other might well volunteer to mediate in order to avoid the conflict and the potentially harmful consequences for that state. Or, in some circumstances, partiality has to be accepted because there is no alternative – someone is better than nobody at all. In other cases, the mediator may have divided loyalties, enjoying close links with both disputing parties, and seeks to encourage a negotiated outcome to protect her or his ties with both disputants (or transacting parties).

Gulliver takes the view, however, that impartiality is often more apparent than real. He advises that it is always wise to pose the question 'what is in it for the [person] in the middle' (1979: 217). This is a concern even in the case of a reputable, professional mediator whose claim to impartiality has to be balanced by a need to gain and retain a reputation for dispute resolution ability and success. Moreover, in circumstances in which the process of mediation is intended to play a wider, socially transformative role, there may be a strong expectation that the mediator place communal interests before the parties' needs, as has clearly been and still is the case in Chinese society.

Throughout the nearly four decades of economic reform following the death of Mao Zedong in 1976, mediators in China have been expected to deliver party-state policies goals of social stability and unity. All three main official types of mediator – community or 'people's' mediators, judges and arbitrators who mediate, and administrative officials with mediation responsibilities – are expected to resolve and if necessary suppress disputes after they have arisen, and even to be proactive where appropriate in order to prevent disputes arising in the first place. In the first two decades of reform, mediators were tasked in particular with protecting the interest of and promoting acceptance of recently wealthy households emerging as a result of the economic reform away from a socialist state-planned economic system to a more market-oriented economy. But as political and social instability has grown since the late 1990s, the official focus increasingly has been upon maintaining social order through mediation. Mediation in the local community, mediation in the courts, and in disputes to be resolved through administrative mediatory intervention (such as in environmental cases), have all adopted this approach and its general quest for creating a 'harmonious' Chinese society.

The general policy reprioritising mediation arose after 2000, in the wake of the Chinese leadership's perception that the more formal adjudicative justice experiment in responding to civil disputes in the 1990s was failing to deliver necessary levels of political stability and social harmony. But this revivication of mediation cannot simply be a return to old-style Maoist mediation policies and practices (very directive and evaluative) because of the many changes that have taken place in China in recent years, largely as a result of rapid economic change – the loss of relatively discrete residential and work communities, more sophisticated and diverse personal values, a greater range of sources of knowledge and so on (Fu and Palmer, 2015: 11). Hence, the ideological development of the official goal of creating a 'harmonious society' within China.[2]

With a specific focus on international disputes, Thomas Princen draws a distinction between what he labels the 'principal mediator' and the 'neutral mediator' (1992: 19 et seq.). The former may well have indirect interests in the issue in dispute, such as securing peace in the region where the dispute in

---

[2] See also, Palmer (1988) and (2014b).

question arises; whereas the latter have no interests in the issues between the parties. That does not mean that they have no interest in the dispute. 'They may want to see agreement reached, peace realised, efficiencies gained. They may want to improve their self-images or burnish their reputations as peace-makers or elder statesmen. They may have religious or philosophical reasons for involving themselves. They may be just looking for something to do. Whatever the case, neutral mediators have interests, but they lie outside the issues in dispute and, therefore, are not subject to bargaining with the disputants' (1992: 49–50). Princen also suggests that this opposition suggests two fundamentally different kinds of intervention (1992: 29).

The Ambition and Scope of the Mediator's Intervention

Mediators vary very greatly in the planned scope and ambition of their interventions. So mediation may range from a minimal intervention that aspires to do no more than set in place or improve the quality of communications between the parties – passing messages between the parties; facilitating information exchange – to an active, direct intervention encompassing the provision of specialist evaluation and advice. Here Simmel argues that the mediator functions in one of two analytically distinctive ways: either by simply providing the linkage through which negotiation may take place; or by actively seeking to eliminate differences ([1908] trans. 1950: 146–7). An extensive role may involve the mediator in seeking to inform the way in which the parties see their relations, feeding in advice and information from outside, evaluating options, proposing and pressing for favoured outcomes. In these respects, the nature of the mediator's role and the range of her interventions will closely depend both on the mediator's rank and upon the stage of the negotiations at which a particular intervention takes place. With such variations will shift the degree to which the mediator comes to share control/power over the outcome with the parties. In some cases, the mediators may act as a 'go-between', with the parties physically apart and not directly communicating with each other. Although such a mediating go-between may function as a simple message carrier, the situation may provide opportunities to shape the exchanges of information between the parties. The parties' dependence on the mediator in this situation, and distance from each other, mean that they may have limited ability to assess if information is being re-worked and the information flow reshaped. The go-between is likely to be all the more effective if the negotiations are going poorly and the go-between wishes to create a particular outcome.[3]

Gulliver also provides a useful characterisation of the different types of mediator as identified by degree of intervention. He offers a continuum

---

[3] See Gulliver (1979: 227).

running from virtual passivity at one end to virtual arbitrator at the other, with 'chairman', 'enunciator', 'prompter' and 'leader' as progressively more inter- ventionist intermediary positions. Even mediators who use a passive style will nevertheless have an impact on the negotiation process between the parties simply by virtue of her or his presence. Just by keeping order and facilitating procedure the passive mediator may be shaping the resolution process in significant ways, and deliberate passivity may even sometimes be used as a way of provoking the parties into a more positive and meaningful interaction.

A more interventionist style is that of 'enunciator' of rules and norms relevant to the issues to be resolved, although some issues – the level of wages for example – may not be open to normative assessment in many other instances. The mediator will be able to emphasise certain directions and ignore others by 'the choice of norms, the particular juncture when they are expressed, the way this is done, and the kind of emphasis given' (Gulliver, 1979: 223). A more interventionist approach is to be found in the mediator who sees her or his role as that of 'chairperson'. Such a mediator takes a more active part in promoting co-ordination between the parties, emphasising spe- cific points of agreement, offering procedural suggestions, initiating separate meetings with the parties – 'caucusing' – or even emphasising the importance of certain kinds of evidence. Again, these skills may be used primarily for the good of the parties and their goal of agreement but they may also be employed so as to get the parties to move forward in a manner that the mediator considers to be desirable or even beneficial to her or his interests. From the overall perspective of the negotiation process, the promoter mediator is probably most effective towards the end of the process, when the parties' differences are being narrowed and co-ordination is emerging. The role of 'leader' involves the mediator more directly injecting her or his own opinions and recommendations, including evaluations of information, offers and demands from the parties. Such a leader-mediator may even directly offer suggestions to the parties on the terms of an agreement – in some cases, the parties may welcome this, as the mediator may be stating what they feel unable to state themselves.[4]

A number of now classical accounts present mediation as an intervention auxiliary to decision-making processes in which the parties themselves are engaged, and so link mediation definitively to negotiations. Under such analyses the mediator's primary role involves facilitating other people's nego- tiations; the mediator initiates, sustains or revives negotiation. Without first imagining negotiations, it is difficult to imagine the mediator; and any under- standing of the mediator's role is dependent on a primary understanding of negotiations (Stevens, 1963: 123; Gulliver, 1979: 213).

---

[4] Gulliver (1979: 200–25).

While we agree with this position, it is possible to delineate mediation much more expansively than this. But we argue that in doing so two analytically distinct forms of intervention, with quite different processual shapes, become concealed beneath the conventional label of mediation. One involves a primarily facilitatory role, setting in place the communications arrangements between parties that will enable them to negotiate; the other contemplates a role of expert consultancy, familiar across a wide range of professions that prioritises skills in information retrieval, expert diagnosis and prescription.

Our preference would be to confine the label mediation to interventions corresponding broadly to the first of these models, contrasting those with the primarily 'advisory' interventions contemplated under the second. To be sure, modes of practice corresponding to both these processual models are already clearly visible within the emergent 'mediation' profession. On the whole they are treated lightly as embodying variant 'facilitatory' and 'evaluative' strands of a process that embraces all forms of intervention falling short of a decision being made for the parties. But this inclusive approach papers over an important analytic distinction between what we would label 'advisory' and 'facilitatory' interventions. This apparent community also conceals a huge philosophic divide between those who see mediation as fundamentally an intervention supportive of party negotiation and those who see it as another expert intervention akin to those which have long developed within, say, engineering, law and medicine.

If mediation is conceptualised as a matter of facilitating joint decision-making, the appearance of the mediator nonetheless transforms the simple bilateral process of negotiation. The presence of the mediator, however sensitive and unobtrusive, must necessarily extend the universe of meaning within which negotiation goes forward. The mediator's understandings must inevitably inform the subsequent course of negotiations, and some degree of control passes to the mediator, whether we describe this in terms of control over 'process' or over 'outcome'. Inevitably too, power relations between the parties may be subtly, even grossly, transformed by the arrival of the mediator. So while negotiations may be realised by the mediator, they are also changed.

In the context of the re-institutionalisation of mediation in the West during the latter part of the twentieth century, emphasis was initially placed on the relatively modest objective of repair, facilitating joint decision-making in the turbulent context generated by a dispute. But more ambitious, even grandiose, objectives subsequently began to emerge. First, as a logical extension of the dispute resolution role, the potential of the non-aligned facilitator in assisting with the construction and management of transactions is being developed. This form of intervention now extends to the continuous monitoring of complex transactions with a view to pre-empting the cost and delay of disputes had these been allowed to arise. Most ambitious, perhaps, has been the strand of theory and practice represented by 'transformative' mediation. Here conflicts are not viewed as problems to be resolved but rather as opportunities for personal, moral growth and transformation – occasions on which mediators can 'change people' (Bush and Folger, 1994: 81).

The Provenance and Legitimacy of the Mediator

When we begin to think about 'mediation', we identify a relation that is always there in the social world whenever more than two people are involved. As Simmel carefully insisted, 'the triad' is almost invariably present in some form: 'the constellation thus characterized constantly emerges in all groups of more than two elements' ([1908] trans. 1950: 148). But when we speak of 'the mediator', we are probably thinking of someone who self-consciously assumes this relation towards others, deliberately putting its elements to use, whether in everyday life or in forwarding the business of rule.

When we ask where mediators come from, and start to inquire about the attributes that give them the standing to intervene, the answers are extremely varied and closely dependent on socio-cultural context. Ethnographic accounts vividly reveal this diverse provenance for the mediator. While the non-aligned 'third' may often be a kinsman or neighbour, the mediator may equally well appear as a transitory 'big man' (such as the Ndendeuli 'notables' reported by Gulliver, 1971; see Chapter 4), or as religious or political superiors, holders of rank and office. In other societies mediators are drawn from among 'outsiders', marginal figures like holy men and women who live on the edge of a community (such as the Pathan 'saints' described by Barth, 1959). Under mediation's contemporary re-institutionalisation in the West, of course, mediators appear as specialists, authoritative professionals who have been taught how to do it, have certificates of competence and subscribe to codes of practice.

A rough typology of mediator provenance might begin in the following terms:

- The 'superior' in terms of kinship, economics or politics.
- 'Being there': the adjacent friend, neighbour or workmate.
- The 'outsider': whose very 'distance' and transparent lack of any 'stake' gives legitimacy to her interventions.
- The 'professional' mediator.

Mediation and its Neighbours

Delineating mediation as we have in this introduction draws a clear analytic line between mediation and three immediate neighbours: the partisan; the adviser; and the arbitrator. Clearly, in real life, these interventions may shade into one another. Particularly in multi-party negotiations, parties may move in and out of an intermediary role as they try to move negotiations forward; and as the Arusha example (see Chapter 4) vividly illustrates, partisans on either side may nudge their principals towards agreement. In the same way, a line between the active, directive mediator and the adviser/consultant may in practice be difficult to draw. The purpose for which an intervener activates the flow of information provides a key here. Where information is elicited primarily as the basis for expert diagnosis and prescription, this is no longer mediation. Two abstract 'models' can be used to mark out the difference involved here.

Under the first model, the intervener:

- establishes communication between the parties;
- ensures that the issues are identified and communicated;
- sees to it that options are identified and evaluated;
- encourages any necessary positional change; and
- helps with the formulation of any ensuing agreement.

Under the second model, the intervener:

- establishes communication with each of the parties;
- obtains information about the nature of the dispute;
- evaluates this information to reach a diagnosis;
- issues a prescription on the basis of expert knowledge; and
- attempts to persuade the parties to accept this solution.

Again, the line between the mediator and the arbitrator is equally clear-cut in analytic terms, as Simmel insists. Whereas the arbitrator assumes power to make decisions for the parties to a dispute, no such power is surrendered to the mediator; ultimate control over the outcome remains with the parties themselves. But this line may be obscured in real-life processes, particularly where the rank or posture of the intervener may make the nature of the intervention, and hence the location of power over an outcome, appear uncertain.

> When the mediator is chosen, one will prefer, in otherwise similar circumstances, the equally disinterested over the equally interested; so, for example, the Italian cities in the middle ages would often obtain their judges from other cities to be sure of their impartiality with regard to the internal party feuds.

> With this, there is the transition to the second form of reconciliation by the impartial: that of arbitration. As long as the third element functions as a genuine mediator, the cessation of the conflict still remains exclusively in the hands of the parties themselves. By the selection of an arbitrator, however, they have handed over the final decision; they have, if you will, outsourced their drive for reconciliation; it has come to be in the person of the arbitrator, whereby it gains particular clarity and power vis-à-vis the antagonistic parties. The voluntary appeal to an arbitrator, to whom one submits a priori, presupposes a greater subjective trust in the objectivity of the judgment than does any other form of adjudication. Since even before the state court only the action of the plaintiffs, in fact, arise from confidence in a fair-minded decision (because they view it in their case as beneficial for the just); the defendants must enter into the process, irrespective of whether or not they believe in the impartiality of judge.

Arbitration, however, as mentioned, comes about only through such trust on the part of both sides. In principle mediation is sharply differentiated from arbitration by the indicated difference, and the more official the action of reconciliation is, the more it adheres to this distinction (Simmel, [1908] trans. 2009a: 106).

This passage also maps out the essential difference between the arbitrator and the judge, namely, that in arbitration both must agree the principle of resort to an umpire. This and other differences are dealt with in greater detail in Chapter 7.

The Mediator in the Negotiation Process: The Processual Shape of Mediation

What an intervener should be doing will depend on how her or his role is conceptualised. Clearly, the polar models we outlined specify quite different tasks for the mediator – one prioritises the role of facilitator of communications; the other requires skills in information retrieval, and requires expert diagnosis and prescription. Henderson (1996) and Boulle (1996) propose classification of the mediator's task under three broad heads, going to communications (assisting in the conveyance of messages), procedure (structuring the session and providing norms of procedure) and substance (providing specialised information and advice). But even if we confine mediation to facilitating communication, we can see a spectrum of interventions, depending upon how active a role is attempted. Our sense is that most mediators would give some help in identifying the issues and making sure these were communicated effectively and assimilated. But there would be differences of view as to what involvement might be appropriate in identifying and reviewing options, let alone pressurising parties towards what the mediator might see as an appropriate outcome.

Beyond these generalisations, if mediation is identified as a process auxiliary to negotiation, identification of the different things the mediator may aspire to do is best examined by thinking about the processual shape of negotiations. Throughout the process of negotiation, the primary and undisputed role must be in providing help with communications, enabling the parties to engage in the process of information exchange and learning that lies at the heart of decision-making by negotiation (see Chapter 5). Here, the mediator is especially important in facilitating the potentially difficult transition from one phase of negotiations to another, however those phases might be conceptualised. Beyond those generalisations, the nature of the mediator's intervention may best be understood in the context of different phases in the negotiation process.

The Arena

For negotiations to take place, messages must be exchanged by the parties. The mediator may facilitate this communication, even make it possible, by acting as a go-between, providing a conduit for the information exchanged. In circumstances where the parties are distant from each other, or seriously at odds, there may be no face-to-face meeting at all, and communication may be achieved exclusively through the mediator. But in most cases the ambition of the mediator will be to establish a secure arena in which the parties can communicate directly with each other. In schematic terms, even where the parties are present together with the mediator, two modes of communication must be distinguished, direct and through the intervening third party:

(1)   Direct communications

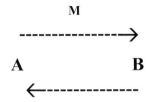

(2)   Indirect communications through the intervening third party

Obviously, these differences have implications both for the quality of the communication between the parties, and for the degree of control that the mediator exercises over the negotiations.

While part of the mediator's role at this preliminary stage will be to provide an arena in the physical sense, the role extends indispensably to creating a general climate conducive to, and supportive of, negotiations. One practical way to achieve this is by making sure some basic ground rules are acknowledged and followed. The most rudimentary negotiations require some normative understandings about the conditions of exchange. In many cases these will be shared, even taken for granted by the parties, and require no restatement by the mediator. But in others, a central part of the mediator's role will be the provision and guarantee of the normative framework relating to such fundamental matters as turn-taking in communication and physical restraint.

This dimension of mediation is captured by Fuller (1971: 325) when he identifies 'the central quality of mediation' as lying in 'its capacity to reorientate the parties toward each other, not by imposing rules on them, but by helping them to achieve a new and shared perception of their relationship, a perception that will redirect their attitudes toward one another'. In bringing this about 'the primary quality of the mediator . . . is not to propose rules to the parties and to secure their acceptance of them, but to induce the mutual trust and understanding that will enable the parties to work out their own rules' (1971: 326).

The Issues as Perceived by the Parties

Once the parties are in communication, the primary task of the mediator must be to make sure that the issues as they respectively see them are both clearly articulated and heard by the other side. Many mediated negotiations will not proceed beyond this stage, either because this primary exchange reveals that the 'issues' involved are no more than misunderstandings as to respective positions, or because one or other of the parties concludes on the basis of the information made available that no basis for negotiation is present. But until the positions and goals of the parties are articulated and communicated, subsequent stages in the process cannot move forward; so it is an uncontested part of the mediator's role to facilitate this.

Forming an Agenda

Once the positions and goals of the respective parties have been identified and put on the table, they have to decide which of these can be the subject of joint decision-making and then order the chosen issues into an agenda. The mediator may play a central role in this process of selection, sorting and prioritisation.

Identification and Evaluation of Options

It appears common ground among commentators on mediation (for example, Douglas, 1957; 1962; Stenelo, 1972; Gulliver, 1979) that the ensuing stage, during which the boundaries of the field are explored and central issues brought into focus, is often one of turbulence. Here the mediator plays a critical role managing this turbulence and in assisting the transition from a mood of antagonism to one in which cooperative decision-making can take place. At the same time any mediator will need to ensure that the options as the parties see them are identified and explored. At the stage where options come to be identified and evaluated, the opportunity arises for the mediator to intervene in a manner that goes beyond facilitating communication, making professional judgements and tendering advice on the substance of the dispute. Opinions will differ as to whether this more extensive role is appropriate, as to how far mediatory and advisory roles may safely be combined.

Bargaining

In the bargaining phase of negotiations, two fundamental issues as to the scope of the mediator's intervention arise. First, as in the preceding phase, there must be the question of whether it is part of the mediator's role to identify and evaluate potential components of exchange, bringing to bear outside professional expertise. Second is the question of how far it is appropriate for the mediator to go in attempting to off-set imbalances of power resources enjoyed by the respective disputants.

Towards Settlement

In moving towards the stage of settlement, the question is again posed as to the extent to which an active advisory role is compatible with mediation. Is it a proper part of the mediator's role to identify the settlement that seems, in his or her professional judgement, the most appropriate to the parties' case; or should the mediator allow the parties to construct their own solution, unassisted as to what the substance of that solution should be?

Formulating Agreement

A further opportunity arises for an active role on the part of the mediator in formulating and arranging ritual affirmation of the outcome reached by the parties. In many instances a central element in this phase will be the skilled achievement of reducing the agreement reached to written form.

Implementation

As we noted in Chapter 5, freely agreed solutions almost by definition have something in them for all negotiating parties and should therefore be self-enforcing. But there may in some cases be a continuing role for the mediator in helping to arrange implementation, and in facilitating further negotiation where implementation proves problematic. Some contemporary mediation schemes build this element of 'monitoring' into the service that is provided.

In formulating an overall processual shape for mediation in this way, we adhere primarily to Gulliver's elegant model of negotiation introduced in Chapter 6, modified in the ways discussed there. This shape emphasises both the continuing and the changing roles of the mediator as negotiations proceed. A continuing element lies in maintaining secure communications; new roles emerge with the arrival of successive phases of the negotiations. This processual shape also emphasises another primary challenge in any successful mediation: the skilled task of moving the parties across the often difficult terrain between one processual phase and the next. For Bush, indeed, it is important for us to understand the value added of mediation – what are the positive qualities that it offers which are not found to the same degree in other processes of dispute resolution. And we are able to identify at least two such core dimensions. First, mediation allows the substantive solutions to the dispute to remain within the control of the disputing parties, rather than determined by a 'higher authority'. Parties therefore have to agree the standard for an acceptable outcome, and also to look for solutions for which they have the ability to implement. Thus, he argues, we can speak of an 'empowerment function' of mediation. It enables the self-determination, and thereby to create imaginative solutions that reflect the parties' needs. Secondly, and following Fuller, by recognising and acknowledging the position of the other party in a dispute through mediation, we 'humanise' each other, and 'help us to recognize each other as fellows even when we are in conflict ... [this is] ... the recognition function of mediation' (Bush, 1989: 270).

The Late Twentieth-century Re-institutionalisation of Mediation

Introduction

The revival of institutionalised mediation as a widely approved route to decision-making – in many respects an extraordinary and unexpected turn of events – is in an immediate sense realised through three closely linked developments. The first of these can be loosely described as the arrival of the 'new professionals' in dispute resolution. These new specialist groups have emerged over the last two decades, offering services which compete – even if only indirectly – with those provided by lawyers. The new professionals have presented mediation as promising a 'third way' between external, hierarchically imposed decision and representation by legal specialists. But the contemporary prominence of mediation – and the wider ADR movement of which the revival of mediation forms a part – is as much attributable to concurrent, independent initiatives within the courts and on the part of lawyers.

As mediators have consolidated their position as an autonomous professional group, judges in common law jurisdictions have at the same time re-presented themselves in a new primary role as sponsors of settlement, directly encouraging facilitative interventions in the vicinity of their courts and themselves acting in mediatory roles. The arrival of 'the new professionals', and the concurrent transformations in civil justice, predictably led to defensive movements of recovery on the part of the lawyers that have included laying claim to mediation as part of legal practice. These two latter strands are examined further in Chapters 8 and 9.

Under the contemporary re-institutionalisation of mediation, emphasis has primarily been placed on the objective of dispute resolution, facilitating joint decision-making in the turbulent context generated by a dispute. But more ambitious objectives have subsequently begun to emerge. First, as a logical extension of the dispute resolution role, the potential of the non-aligned facilitator in assisting with the construction and management of transactions is being developed. This form of intervention now extends to the continuous monitoring of complex transactions with a view to pre-empting the cost and delay of disputes had these been allowed to arise.

More ambitious, even grandiose, has been a strand of theory and practice represented by 'transformative' mediation that claims to lead mediation beyond its primary dispute resolution role. Adherents of transformative mediation distance themselves from what they diminishingly refer to as 'the problem-solving' tradition in mediation, claiming to help bring about a paradigmatic shift from an 'individualist' to a 'relational' world-view. For the transformative mediator, 'disputes can be viewed not as problems at all but as opportunities for moral growth and transformation' (Bush and Folger, 1994: 81–5). In the transformative orientation, the dispute offers two kinds of possible moral growth. The first is the self-strengthening of a party's capacity for dealing with difficulties. The second is enhancement of a party's capacity to relate to and understand others, to acknowledge the perspectives of others. Through mediation carried out in this transformative spirit the focus is less on 'solving the problem' and rather more on helping the parties to be transformed in both aspects of this moral growth: this means striving to bring to the surface in handling the dispute the 'intrinsic goodness that lies within the parties as human beings' (Bush and Folger, 1994: 84). Success is therefore to be defined as securing through mediation a change in the parties for the better, so that the parties achieve both kinds of moral development: strength of self and capacity for relating to others. In this approach, 'empowerment' thus refers to the parties' achievement of a strengthened awareness of their self-worth and ability to deal with various kinds of trouble, and 'recognition' is the expanded willingness of disputing parties to acknowledge and respond to the problems and humanity of others (Bush and Folger, 1994: 85).

Practice Models

Evolving practice models in common law jurisdictions vary substantially as to methods of communication employed, the structure of the sessions and as to the scope of the mediator's intervention. One primary variable hinges on whether the mediator plans to bring the parties together in face-to-face negotiations or simply provide communication arrangements while they remain apart. We can imagine instances in which the parties stay at a distance throughout, with the mediator moving backwards and forwards between them: the 'shuttle' mediation associated with some forms of international diplomacy here represents the paradigm case. But this approach can be found in other contexts where space or extreme hostility make direct contact problematic. While this form of mediation may be confined to a 'go-between' role, it is by no means necessarily limited to such minimal intervention, as the potential power of the mediator is greatly enhanced while he or she remains the only means of communication between the parties.

Even where the mediator brings the parties physically together, practice models differ sharply as to the proportion of work done in direct communication. For some mediators it is an article of faith never to see the parties outside a joint session (for example, this was the practice of the North American mediator, John Haynes: see Haynes, 1993). In other models of mediation, notably in commercial disputes, most of the work is done through separate meetings, with the parties coming together only at the beginning of the process and for affirming an outcome at the end.

Some models involve resort to separate meetings at particular stages in the process. Marian Roberts, writing about family mediation, explains the value of separate meetings at an early stage, immediately following a joint introductory session:

> The purpose of these interviews is to give each party an opportunity to state their views, objectives and any fears to the mediator on their own. This means that they can have their say free from fear of interruption or contradiction. It gives the mediator an opportunity to gain a clearer understanding of existing or future fears about safety issues and the issues in dispute. It is the common experience of mediators that a version of the dispute with which both parties apparently agree in the introductory joint session often turns out to be perceived quite differently by one party when interviewed alone (Roberts, Marian, 1997: 110–11).

Simmel points to a further advantage of separate early stage meetings following which the positions of the respective parties are fed back in a joint session by the mediator. Where the mediator reveals to the parties their respective claims and arguments, there may be a sobering effect and the parties modify their tone and reduce their assertiveness. Positions reported by the mediator may be heard and recognised in a way that would have been inconceivable if directly articulated by the parties. Separate meetings, sometimes described as 'caucasing', in which the parties communicate only through the mediator, rather than directly in his or her presence, necessarily increase opportunities for the mediator to extend control over the process.

> The very great opportunity that non-partisan mediation has to produce this belief lies not only in the obvious elimination of misunderstandings or in appeals to good will, etc. It may also be analyzed as follows. The non-partisan shows each party the claims and arguments of the other; they thus lose the tone of subjective passion which usually provokes the same tone on the part of the adversary. What is so often regrettable here appears as something wholesome, namely, that the feeling which accompanies a psychological content when one individual has it, usually weakens greatly when it is transferred to a second. This fact explains why recommendations and testimonies that have to pass several mediating persons before reaching the deciding individual, are so often ineffective, even if their objective content arrives at its destination without any change. In the course of these transfers, affective imponderables get lost; and these not

only supplement insufficient objective qualifications, but, in practice, they alone cause sufficient ones to be acted upon ([1908] trans. 1950: 146–7).

At a later stage, separate meetings can be used by the mediator in efforts to break a deadlock.[5]

Contemporary professional mediators are quite sharply divided as to the appropriate ambition and scope of their role. Proponents of the more minimalist approach to mediation are increasingly characterised in the literature and practice of ADR as providing a 'facilitative' form of mediatory intervention. They strongly resist the idea that the mediator might provide an informed prediction of the likely outcome if the dispute is adjudicated, or even an informed evaluation of the relative merits of the parties' positions. We have seen, however, the possibility that even a minimalist mediator may influence the process of dispute resolution by characterising the issues in a certain manner, clarifying factual difficulties, encouraging the parties to consider various options and so on. Such a 'minimalist' position may be contrasted with what lawyer mediators in particular now label 'evaluative mediation'. In this evolving form of mediation, the mediator advises on the respective strengths and weaknesses of each side's position and proposes solutions including the terms of a possible agreement. In order to analyse differing style of mediation more effectively, Leonard Riskin has explored some key features of facilitative and evaluative approaches to mediatory intervention.

Riskin (1994) draws our attention, first, to the important distinction that has emerged over the part thirty years or so between facilitative and evaluative mediation. In the facilitative orientation, the mediator proceeds to assist in the dispute resolution process primarily by enhancing and clarifying communications between the parties so that they themselves might better decide the outcome. The mediator refrains from offering a personal opinion, inter alia, to avoid an impression of favouring one party or position and because she or he feels insufficiently expert in (say) the technical aspects of the dispute.

This distinction is then coupled with the question of degree of intervention: does the mediator approach her or his mediatory intervention in a robust and expansive fashion, or is the mediator's definition of the problem and therefore strategy more restricted and less intrusive in its focus. The first approach Riskin characterised as 'broad', the second as 'narrow'. In the narrow approach, the strategy is to try to resolve the dispute more or less as a court would decide the matters at issue. The broad approach is more likely to search for the various interests underlying the dispute, and such interests will likely go beyond legal matters. Although at first glance we might assume that mediators would tend to fall into one of two main styles – that is, either 'facilitative-narrow' or 'evaluative-broad' in Riskin's analysis – the picture is in reality more complex and there are four main styles of mediation practice. Working from a basic

[5] See also Gulliver (1979: 227).

assumption that the parties have the capacity within themselves to develop good solutions, the facilitative mediator shapes her or his intervention to assist the parties to create their outcomes. The 'facilitative-narrow' mediator will likely approach the mediation in the spirit of, where necessary, helping the parties to be more realistic about their position, to do some reality testing including perhaps an assessment of likely court outcomes and the strengths and weaknesses of the parties' legal claim. The 'facilitative-broad' mediator, on the other hand, is likely to go beyond such legal analysis and assist the parties in their understanding and discussion of a range of issues that affect their interests. The focus, then, is on encouraging the parties to create and offer proposals that reflect these understanding interests. In contrast, as we have seen, the evaluative mediator intervenes in a style that assumes that the parties seek steering and guidance from the mediator. The parties, in their perspective, seek the mediator's direct assistance so as to reach an appropriate outcome. In the 'evaluative-narrow' style, the mediator is likely to assess the merits of the parties' claims, to indicate likely court outcomes, to suggest settlement terms, to direct the parties towards settlement and so on. The broader evaluative approach, however, typically involves the mediator proposing imaginative outcomes that reflect a wide range of party interests, and advising on the likely effect on the parties of failure to settle (Riskin, 1994: 111–13).

The drift towards evaluative mediation experienced in the United States – and, to a lesser extent, in other parts of the Anglo-American common law world – over the past two decades, finds parallels elsewhere in the world. The didactic style of mediation found, for example, in the PRC is also highly evaluative, but the evaluation covers not only the legal position of the parties but also the moral and political correctness of the parties' conduct, as well as perceived societal needs (Palmer, 1988). Although that broad authority to evaluate is not matched in the mediation as it has developed within the context of the Anglo-American common law world, the rise of evaluative mediation has nevertheless attracted some trenchant criticism. Thus, for example, Lela Love and Kimberlee Kovach argue, in effect that evaluative mediation is something of an oxymoron, and that an unhappy consequence of 'Riskin's Grid' is that it appears to have encouraged mediators to play a more actively judgmental role (1998). Instead, they argue, there should be clarity of purpose in mediation, and no confusion of roles.

> Recently, Riskin published a map of the mediation universe – the Riskin Grid. The Grid divides mediation into four quadrants, each defined by a mediator's orientation with respect to two continuums: evaluative-facilitative role and narrow-broad problem definition. The Grid has made a substantial contribution both by clarifying the state of mediation practice today and by sparking a vigorous debate about the direction the practice should take in the future. The question remains, however, whether users should rely on a map that characterizes one-half of the mediation universe as evaluative, whether the boundaries of mediation practice should include the option of an evaluative orientation.

Since its introduction, the Grid has tended to legitimize evaluative activities conducted under the banner of mediation ... This trend should stop.

An evaluative role fits a neutral serving in dispute resolution processes where the neutral assists by deciding or opining. That orientation comports with a philosophical map that instigates adversarial advocacy before a decision-maker who applies rules to 'facts' and offers an opinion either to influence or spur party decision-making and settlement (e.g., summary jury trials, early neutral evaluation, and non-binding arbitration) or to generate 'win-lose' outcomes (e.g., arbitration, private judging, and traditional litigation). However, if mediation is to remain a unique alternative to these processes, one that fosters party autonomy and decision-making, a mediator with an evaluative role could undermine those goals and align mediation with the evaluative-adjudicative processes. Consequently, we contend that the Riskin Grid, if used as a guide to what mediation should and can be and what mediators should and can do, will lead its users astray.

To some extent, of course, 'evaluation' inheres in every aspect of human conduct, as well as many mediator tactics [but] mediator should not 'answer' the question posed by the dispute (i.e., what is a fair, just, or likely court outcome). That job belongs to the parties.

As Riskin's Grid indicates, many mediators in practice evaluate the fair or likely court outcome when necessary to move forward on a particular issue or on the entire dispute ... [and] ... in certain instances 'mixed' evaluative and facilitative processes nonetheless can prove useful. Some mediators who mix mediation and case evaluation effectively help disputing parties. While functionalists would dismiss the importance of naming the process so long as it works, accurate labels, maps, and guides have significance (Kovach and Love, 1998: 71–5).

Elsewhere, Lela Love explains at some length why mediators should resist the temptation to evaluate. Love argues that the debate over whether mediators should 'evaluate' revolves around confusion over the nature of the evaluation that should take place in mediation (1997: 937). An 'evaluative' mediator does not, in her view, deliver the kind of evaluation that the parties really need. Love briefly defines an 'evaluative' mediator as one who 'gives advice, makes assessments, states opinions – including opinions on the likely court outcome, proposes a fair or workable resolution to an issue or the dispute, or presses the parties to accept a particular resolution' (1997: 938). The evaluative mediator, in evaluating, assessing and deciding for the parties, is therefore not so different from other types of 'evaluators' – judges, arbitrators and other neutral third-party decision-makers (1997: 939, 940). The role of the mediator is fundamentally different, and has at its heart the crucial task of facilitating evaluation, assessment and decision-making by the parties themselves. The good mediator should:

facilitate communications, promote understanding, focus the parties on their interests, and seek creative problem solving to enable the parties to reach their own agreement. Mediators push disputing parties to question their assumptions, reconsider their positions, and listen to each other's perspectives, stories, and arguments. They urge the parties to consider relevant law, weigh their own values, principles, and priorities, and develop an optimal outcome. In so doing, mediators facilitate evaluation by the parties (Love, 1997: 939).

More specifically, there are a number of identifiable complications that the evaluative mediator brings to the mediation process. First, and perhaps foremost, the role and role requirements of evaluators and facilitators are fundamentally incompatible. When a mediator engages in evaluative tasks, she or he is diverted from the clear and simple goal of facilitation:

> These differences between evaluators and facilitators mean that each uses different skills and techniques, and each requires different competences, training norms and ethical qualities to perform their respective functions. Further, the evaluative tasks in determining facts, applying law or custom and delivering an opinion, not only divert the mediator away from facilitation, but also can compromise the mediator's neutrality – both in actuality and in the eyes of the parties – because the mediator will be favouring one side or the other in his or her judgment ... Mediators cannot effectively facilitate when they are evaluating (1997: 939).

Where evaluative mediation is successful, in the sense of producing a 'result', the success is in reality the result of use of a clearly identified 'mixed process' – which we discuss in Chapter 8 – rather than the assumption of different roles by the mediator in a process of 'evaluative mediation'.

An additional complication is that evaluation by the mediator tends to encourage the parties to be competitive and adversarial. Trying to do their best to secure a result from the evaluating mediator, the parties feel the need to secure a 'result' from the evaluation, and thereby fail to develop the 'respectful collaboration' necessary for the creative problem-solving dimensions of the mediatory process. Where a mediator provides an opinion which can seriously disadvantage one of the parties, that party may choose to disagree with the unfavourable opinion, and believe that the mediator has 'sided' with the opponent, perhaps even withdrawing from the mediation. Moreover, codes of conduct such as the Model Standards for Mediators produced by the American Arbitration Association, caution neutrals against assuming additional roles. Their thrust is that the process should be kept pure. If the neutral takes on an additional role, so that the decision-making processes become 'mixed,' as when an arbitrator mediates or a mediator evaluates, then this should only be done at the request and with the informed consent of the parties. A further problem is that by making it acceptable or customary for mediators to give opinions on likely court outcomes or merits of legal claims, a restriction is in effect placed on the types of individual who may join the ranks of mediator. In some cases, only lawyers will have the necessary competence, so weakening the field of mediators. And mediation itself may be thereby dragged into the adversarial paradigm, undermining the practice of 'good mediation'. An added complication is that incorrect mediator evaluations are difficult to undo, so that there are real concerns regarding due process and the quality of justice that disputants receive when they are diverted from courts into the private, alternative mechanism of evaluative mediation. Mediators may well be shielded by a quasi-judicial immunity from the consequences of any careless evaluative opinions – in contrast, appellate processes are in place for reversing a court's erroneous decisions, and participants in arbitration consciously waive any rights of appeal as they have chosen arbitrators on the basis of their track records or expertise in a given area. In addition, ADR already provides parties with evaluative alternatives to litigation in the form of arbitration, rent-a-judge, early neutral evaluation and the summary jury trial. Accordingly, a genuinely collaborative mediation paradigm, which in Love's view excludes 'mediator evaluation', satisfies the need for a genuine alternative to the adversarial disputing paradigm where parties fight and the neutral acts as assessor. Mediators must avoid the 'trash and bash' approach – evaluative mediators are tempted to 'trash' the parties' cases, predicting loss and risk if litigation is pursued, and to 'bash' settlement proposals that the other side will not accept, so that mediation becomes 'a mere adjunct of the adversarial norm' (Love, 1997: 944). Finally, evaluative mediation blurs the lines of demarcation between mediation and other processes, so that the 'disputant consumer' does not always understand what it is that she or he has opted for – if the process is to be mixed, then better to label it so, in order to enhance integrity of process, disputant satisfaction and uniformity of practice.

The Regulation of Mediation

The contemporary institutionalisation of mediation and its incorporation in civil justice arrangements underline the need for a well-defined regulatory framework. As Marian Roberts argues, 'the very advantages of mediation over the adversarial system can also create potential risks. Conducted privately and informally, necessarily without the safeguards of due process, there exist opportunities for manipulative and oppressive behaviour, not only between the parties themselves but also by the mediator' (Roberts, Marian, 2005: 511). Safeguarding a fair process has to go beyond the trust that creates the relationship between mediator and the parties, as Marian Roberts has emphasised (2005).

The National Institute for Dispute Resolution's (NIDR) Interim Guidelines for Selecting Mediators, published in 1993, represent an early attempt at specifying required qualities of the mediator. In England, the first serious work on the quality assurance of mediation was carried out in the not-for-profit sector by National Family Mediation during the 1990s. This covered selection, training, accreditation, supervision of practice and performance evaluation, as well as drafting policies and standards for mediation practice (see, for example, National Family Mediation, 1998). Subsequently, a single regulatory body for family mediators, the UK College of Family Mediators was formed in 1996 by the main family mediation providers. The College's main objectives are: 'to set, promote, improve and maintain the highest standards of professional conduct and training for all those practising in the field of family mediation; to advance the education of the public in the skills and practice of family mediation; and to make available the details of registered mediators qualified to provide family mediation' (Roberts, Marian, 2005: 515).

Concurrently, a statutory basis for public funding of family mediation was enacted, introducing quality assurance requirements for those providing publicly funded mediation. This legislative framework required publicly funded mediators to comply with a Code of Practice and be audited by a government body, the Legal Services Commission. This body published a Quality Mark Standard for Mediation (MQM), introducing quality assurance standards for both family and community mediators. One consequence of the introduction of government funding for mediation was to encourage family lawyers, mainly solicitors, to train as mediators in very large numbers, leading the Law Society to establish its own code of practice for 'solicitor mediators' (Roberts, Marian, 2005: 520).

Two linked initiatives have brought further consolidation of the regulatory framework for mediators in England. First, mediators in the community, civil, commercial, family and industrial relations fields participated with the Law Society during the 1990s in a government-sponsored project to create 'occupational standards' for mediation, leading to a mediation qualification. This took place under a larger government project to devise National Vocational Qualifications (NVQs). Shortly after this project had been completed, mediation organisations in the commercial, community and family fields came together in a Joint Mediation Forum to draft a common Model Code of Conduct for mediators (Roberts, Marian, 2005: 521).

As Marian Roberts has shown, for a number of important reasons there are particular difficulties in resolving family disputes through the mediation process. In addition to basic questions of fairness and power inequalities (which might include a history of domestic violence), there are susceptibilities to emotional distress and dangers of coercion that potentially come from the private and informal nature of the process, confidentiality, and more often than not a range of interests (including in particular those of any children to the relationship) that need to be taken into account. Given these dangers, there is a particular need to create and implement uniform standards for professional competence and conduct for family mediators and to protect fair process and solutions:

> Safeguarding a fair process requires mediators to bear constantly in mind, and to address in training and practice, the vital questions raised about their authority, power and potential to exercise influence. First, how can the authority of the

mediator be exercised in ways that serve the essential objectives of the process and protect its fundamental characteristics and principles? Second, when does the exercise of that authority cease to serve those objectives, becoming instead an abuse of power with the mediator exerting unacceptable pressures upon one or both of the parties who then act (or fail to act) in ways that they would not otherwise have done? That is why trust, although still remaining the cornerstone of the relationship between the mediator and the parties, is insufficient, needing to be buttressed by the objective safeguards of professional regulation (Roberts, Marian, 2005: 511–12).

In the case of the United Kingdom, even before the establishment in 1996 of the UK College of Family Mediators, providers of family mediation put in place a range of rigorous standards for practitioners and for evaluating mediator performance in terms of these standards. In particular, the not-for-profit provider of family mediation known as 'National Family Mediation' created a national framework that included a code for promoting ethical and professional practice standards, a commitment to equal opportunities and uniform procedures governing selection, training, supervision of practice and accreditation of mediators (Roberts, Marian, 2008: 236–7).

In 1996, the Family Law Act that provided the possibility of public funding for mediation of family disputes, and largely in response to this development the National Family Mediation was consolidated with two other providers to become the UK College of Family Mediators. This 'marked the formal arrival in the use of family mediation as a new profession' (Roberts, Marian, 2008: 238), and one of the main tasks of the College is to provide mechanisms for self-regulation, evaluation and accountability and it therefore created specialist complaint and discipline committees.

> The UK College also approves independent provider bodies, 'Approved Bodies' to carry out the functions of recruitment, selection, training (including continuing professional development courses) and ppc/supervision,[6] according to its standards. In this way, the requisite separation of standard-seeing and monitoring on the one hand, and the provision of functions such as training and service delivery, has been secured. However, structural tensions arising from these conflicts of function, have always posed a threat to the stability of the UK College as a regulatory body of individual members (the provider bodies having nominated representatives with voting powers on the governing board of the UK College). This threat, exacerbated by competition for membership in a small field, risks damaging the fruits of ten years of collaboration and professional achievement and a return to the destructive proliferation of bodies that brought about the need for the UK College in the first place.

---

[6] The term 'ppc/supervision' refers to the system of 'professional practice consultant'. Such figures have responsibilities for 'supporting and supervising' mediators. See 'Code of Practice for Professional Practice Consultants (PPCs)', available at www.collegeofmediators.co.uk/sites/default/files/CoM%20PPC%20Code%20of%20Practice%201.2_0.pdf, accessed 6 January 2020.

While publicly funded family mediation provision is, properly, to be subject to stringent quality assurance standards, difficult questions arise and need to be addressed: to what extent will the security of external funding, inevitably bringing with it demands of accountability and quantifiable measures of effectiveness, lead to a stifling, or even loss, of autonomy, flexibility and creativity and peer professional control of family mediation? How can the benefits of a variety of models and individual practice styles, and of consistency and uniformity of high standards, be balanced? How can a proper balance be achieved too, between external regulation by government and the law (Roberts, Marian, 2008: 239).

The need for an adequate regulatory framework was underlined in the Council of Europe's Recommendation to the Governments of Member States on family mediation of 1998. Section 11 states unequivocally that mediation should not in principle be compulsory. More generally, 'irrespective of how mediation is organized and delivered, States should see to it that there are appropriate mechanisms to ensure the existence of procedures for the selection, training and qualification of mediators, standards to be achieved and maintained by mediators' (s 11(c)). Following a subsequent Commission of the European Communities Green Paper on Alternative Dispute Resolution in 2002, stakeholders prepared a draft Code of Conduct for Mediators.

The determination of the Law Society in England to control the activities of solicitors practising as mediators and a growing insistence that mediation is 'part of legal practice', raise important issues of regulation across professional boundaries. In a succinct but important essay, Carrie Menkel-Meadow examines the problem of professional responsibility. As she observes, one of the most important issues in the regulation of ethical standards for ADR is whether or not mediation is seen as a form of practising law. Given that the most fundamental model of mediation practice is facilitative, with non-legal interests being very relevant to the resolution outcome, it is tempting to see mediation as being quite separate from legal practice. But if indeed there is a positive answer to this question, and mediation is seen as being at least in some respects the practice of law, a related question also has to be addressed: should we then require mediators to be lawyers? In the early days of mediation, this question was not taken seriously. Once attitudes began to change, and the feeling developed that mediation might indeed be one form of legal practice,[7] so the issue then arose: should the ethics codes of lawyers apply when lawyers mediate? However, any such application faced the difficulty that many key issues in mediation could not be dealt with adequately in any such code – confidentiality as between parties and with mediators, conflicts of

---

[7] As she points out 'to the extent that mediators, especially those who work within court programs or by court referral, "predict" court results or "evaluate" the merits of the case (on either factual or legal grounds), they are giving legal advice' (Menkel-Meadow, 1996: 57). Other aspects of mediation that have a particularly legal dimension are the drafting of agreements intended to be legally binding, but in the absence of the parties' own lawyers. The study by Menkel-Meadow and Wheeler (2004) remains the leading study of ethics in negotiation.

interest, fees, co-mediating with a non-lawyer and so on. Moreover, to apply the norms of lawyers' codes of ethics to a form of neutral third-party intervention would possibly have a restricting effect on the work of mediators, limiting the willingness of capable persons committed (say) to a firmly facilitative style of mediation from offering such services.

It would seem that there is no easy answer to the question. As Menkel-Meadow suggested, there will be some mediatory conduct that clearly does not amount to the practice of law, but in other circumstances, the position is less certain:

> When mediators engage in some prediction or application of legal standards to concrete facts – and especially when they draft settlement agreements, I think they are 'practicing' law. That means neutrals who are not trained as lawyers need to be wary of evaluative mediation. They still have other options as mediators: they can limit their role to facilitation, co-mediate with lawyers, or ask the parties to release them from liability for bad legal advice. Non-lawyer mediators might still be subject to the (seldom enforced) regulations against unauthorized practice of law. Lawyers can't get such a sweeping release from their malpractice liability (Menkel-Meadow, 1996: 61).

Professional accountability, however, is just one part of the broader questions of the nature of ethical conduct in mediation work, and in the Anglo-American common law world this is a particularly problematic issue in an increasingly multi-cultural society. A further complication is one where it is increasingly recognised that in a multi-cultural society mediation needs to be practised in a culturally sensitive manner. But we may no longer assume that there are 'homogeneous ethical values among either disputants or mediators. Many societies are affected by increasing cultural diversity as a result of immigration as well as social change. This creates challenges for mediators in particular cases, as well as for mediation organizations creating codes of ethics' (Morris, 1997: 307).

The Issue of Impartiality

There is quite a strong Western stereotype of the mediator as impartial, even 'neutral'; an intervener carefully distanced from the interests of either party (Gulliver, 1979: 212). In the United States, the Standards of Conduct (1994) approved by the American Arbitration Association, the Society of Professionals in Dispute Resolution and the American Bar Association Section on Dispute Resolution require the mediator to 'conduct mediation in an impartial manner', and in this country, the Law Society's Code of Conduct for Mediators defines the role as one of a 'neutral facilitator of negotiations'. But such a claim is rarely advanced without qualification by mediators themselves, and in some contexts appears as a construct set up by researchers intent on knocking it down (see, for example, Dingwall and Greatbach, 1993).

The Implication of Rank and Office in Mediation

Questions of rank and tenure of office are as important as the claimed ambition of the intervener in determining the location of control over process and outcome. The intervention of an unobtrusive neighbour will inevitably be received differently from that of the authoritative professional or holder of some identified office. However modest their respective objectives may be, parties will experience a neighbour who mediates differently from a professional intervener, however tactful and unobtrusive the latter may attempt to be. There are separate, related problems here:

- Can members of other professional groups mediate safely given the public perceptions that have been generated by the exercise of their primary roles?
- Can mediation be safely combined with the delivery of other forms of specialised help?

The predicament of the lawyer or judge who attempts to mediate provides the obvious example of the first problem. Given the long-standing familiarity of the public with the partisan advisory and representative roles of the lawyer, and with the authoritative decision-making of the judge, can either avoid bringing that primary persona into the very different role of the mediator? The second problem is equally exemplified by the lawyer. Parties experiencing difficulty with joint decision-making may require both help with communications and some expert advice or information. Can these different forms of help be safely delivered by the same person?

As we have seen, the traditional involvement of lawyers, judges and other legal specialists in dispute resolution has raised important ethical and regulatory issues when such figures act as mediators. Their specialist training in, and expert knowledge of, the law does not, however, necessarily assist in the mediation process, and raises the question of the appropriateness of legal experts as mediators (and indeed, as party representatives). Thus, the lawyers' background in adversarial litigation and the judges' familiarity with handing down an imposed decision that is legally binding on the parties as well as the authority their roles carry within them 'is going to color the way in which mediatory intervention by registrars and judges is perceived by disputants, whether the [legal] specialists themselves want this or not' (Roberts, Simon, 1983: 555). And, of course, in more objective terms, legal specialists are not necessarily trained for, nor expert in, the essential dimensions of mediation, and therefore may not be at all suited to mediation where 'the beauty of mediation is … that it leaves responsibility for decision-making in the hands of the parties themselves … [and] … this feature is inevitably diluted or lost altogether as the process is moved in ideological terms, in terms of the intrusion of specialist personnel, even in terms of space, "nearer to the law"' (Roberts, Simon, 1983: 555). So there is a strong case for maintaining a barrier between the mediation process and the places and personnel of law. The primary aims of mediation are modest ones, to enhance the flows of information exchanged between the parties and to encourage them to create an outcome that is their own solution to the issues that divide them. This aim may be thwarted when a legal expert third-party intervention seeks to offer a legally authoritative or informed re-definition of their situation.

A further difficulty arises with the attempts to combine the roles of therapist and mediator. The arguments are laid out clearly in the exchange between Marian Roberts and John Haynes examined in some detail in Chapter 9.

The Management of Power Imbalances in Mediation

Whatever the complexities of 'power' in negotiation processes, outcomes of bilateral exchanges will inevitably reflect to some extent the bargaining endowments of the different parties. So, even if we conclude that mediatory intervention is generally inappropriate where significant imbalances of power exist between the parties, occasions will arise in mediation where one party appears significantly 'weaker' than the other, and the question is thus posed as to the extent to which the mediator can or should attempt to redress this imbalance. In some cultures the answer to this question is taken for granted; in others it may assume considerable importance. Mediators themselves differ as to the extent to which such intervention is an appropriate part of their work. In North America, a variety of mediatory techniques and strategies have been evolved in order to deal with inequalities of power. Bush, with his concept of 'active impartiality', advocates a distinctive means of dealing with this problem:

> the obligation of impartiality ... is necessary to fulfill both aspects of the empowerment-and-recognition role. What I mean by impartiality, however, goes beyond the usual connotation of disclosure of conflicts and neutrality regarding outcome ... one might ask how mediators can do so much pushing without alienating one or both parties ... the answer lies in an expanded conception of the obligation of impartiality.

> Mediators should be visibly even-handed ... in their pushing ... they should direct their invitations, support, encouragements, challenges and urgings toward each party in turn, and each should see clearly that the other is receiving similar treatment. If necessary, mediators should explicitly assure the parties that they intend to behave identically toward each side, and of course they should always fulfill this assurance. Mediators whose pushing is positive in character, and who adhere to the requirement of active impartiality, can serve for each side as translator to the other and also serve each side as devil's advocate for the other. And they can do so without ever losing the trust and confidence of both sides that is necessary to fulfilling both aspects of the mediator's role. I should note, however, that this may be much easier to do if the mediator does at least some of this pushing while meeting separately with each side ...

> One other aspect of the obligation of active impartiality is also quite important in fulfilling both aspects of the empowerment-and-recognition role. The

impartiality of mediators means not only that they are allied with neither side, but that because of a lack of personal investment, they have more distance and perspective on the parties' discussions. This position 'above the fray' should not be a passive listening post. Rather, it should be the basis for what I call the mediator's job of narration. The mediator can impartially hear, and impartially report to the parties, many crucial parts of their own dialogue that they themselves may not have grasped fully or even heard because of their closeness to the situation. Offers, counteroffers, new options for resolution, actual agreements on issues, and statements of acknowledgment and recognition all are presented frequently in mediation sessions without one or both parties even realizing what has occurred. To fulfill both the empowerment and recognition functions, the mediator can and should be an actively impartial narrator who lets no relevant exchange between the parties go unheard or ignored (Bush, 1989: 281–2).

While many commentators subscribe to the view that mediation is inappropriate in disputes in which there are significant power imbalances between the parties, this is not a universal view. Genevieve Chornenki argues that excessive concentration on power imbalances between the parties may well detract from mediation as an aid to joint problem-solving. She takes the view that mediators frequently write and talk of 'balancing' power, and the mediator is encouraged to reduce the power of the dominant party or to empower the weaker party. But this preoccupation with power as the control or influence of one party over the other creates the unhelpful feeling that if the troublesome power imbalances could somehow be eliminated or reduced 'then the benefits of mediation could be enjoyed by all' (Chornenki, 1997: 163). The focus should instead be on transcending this issue by focusing on the idea of mediation as a joint problem-solving exercise so that while the parties do exercise power they do not do so as influence or control but rather as a kind of collective force or 'power-with'.

The possibility of creating this 'power-with' is enhanced when the mediator is able to get the parties to:

- Focus individual energies on a collective problem, not an individual one. The problem may be no more elegant than 'on what basis can the plaintiff give and the defendant receive a release?' Or, it can be more complex, 'how can we foster respect and human dignity in the workplace?'
- Form a genuine commitment to examine whether and to what extent the collective problem can be solved. This need not be commitment to definitely achieve a result, but commitment to the effort entailed in constructing an outcome.
- Accept mutual influence in the sense of willingness to try and persuade others, and openness to being persuaded by others. This relates to being understood and to understanding, rather than to convincing and converting.
- Engage in overt behaviour, but not necessarily private belief, that is respectful and non-obstructionist in the sense that it does not detract from the focused energy of the group.
- Maintain a willingness to foster or at least tolerate a level of capability on the part of each individual participant in the mediation process. This involves

their ability to identify and actualise goals, options, skills, resources and decision-making. While there is no requirement that the parties be equal in their abilities here, rough parity of capability is a necessary prerequisite to the kind of negotiating undertaken at an interest-based mediation.

- Sustain an ability to recognise other points of view, other interpretations, other inferences, other versions of the controversy; the ability to paddle around in the other party's canoe. Known as recognition, this is an important condition.
- From the starting point of relative self-absorption, parties achieve recognition in mediation when they voluntarily choose to become more open, attentive, sympathetic, and responsive to the situation of the other party, thereby expanding their perspective to include an appreciation for another's situation.
- The hallmark of recognition is letting go – however briefly or partially – of one's focus on self and becoming interested in the perspective of the other party as such, concerned about the situation of the other as a fellow human being, not as an instrument of fulfilling one's own need.
- As a condition of power-with in a commercial mediation, however, recognition need not take the form of true compassion and connection. It could merely be an expression of enlightened self-interest. What does matter is that recognition is expressed overtly in words or actions. Mere alterations in belief, while valuable, are insufficient to bring about the active, kinetic phenomenon of power-with described here.
- Honesty. Engage in honest, authentic communication. If a commercial party tells the mediator that something is important to it when it is not, or advances an interest as a foil to hide what is truly important, this is counterproductive. It will busy the mediator in trying to achieve what has been stated as being important, for no useful end (Chornenki, 1997: 167–8).

These are the positive attitudes that parties should bring to the mediation process.

Gender, Culture and Ethnicity

In the family law field, from the early 1980s, there has been a persistent feminist critique of mediation, suggesting that private, consensual processes of decision-making mask, and so perpetuate, the power inequalities suffered in particular by women in the family (Crouch, 1982; Bottomley, 1984; 1985). Under this view, women in mediation both face their former partners at a disadvantage and are subjected to the male-oriented preconceptions of the mediator. In England this critique was renewed in the context of the passage of the Family Law Act 1996. Important North American studies indicate a number of process dangers in mediation which are faced by women unless essential safeguards are maintained (Grillo, 1991). In her seminal essay on the process dangers for women of mediation – especially mandatory mediation – Grillo argues that this mode of dispute resolution disempowers women relative to men. Differences in financial resources, access to legal advice, experience necessary to evaluate effectively possible outcomes, and attitudes to compromise do, it is argued, tend to favour the interests of men and to work against the interest of women,

> Men do not experience [the] same fear of sexual domination ... they do not live in constant fear of having the very integrity of their lives intruded upon ... Because the existential and subjective experience of the world differs for men and women, it is sometimes difficult to explain, in legal language, the basis for attention to areas of law that are of particular interest to women such as rape, sexual harassment, and reproductive freedom. For example, rape might be characterized and treated as any other crime of violence if the underlying sexual domination of women by men is not taken into account. Once institutionalized sexual domination is seen as something the law should address, however, rape becomes a very particular harm unlike any other, a combination of violence and sexual domination ... Men may not comprehend their role in this system of sexual domination any more than women may be able to articulate the source of their feeling of disempowerment. Yet both of these dynamics are at work in the mediation setting. It may seem a large leap, from acts of physical violence and invasion to the apparently simple requirement that a woman sit in a room with her spouse working toward the resolution of an issue of mutual concern. But that which may be at stake in a court-ordered custody mediation – access to one's children – may be the main reason one has for living, as well as all one's hope for the future. And because mandatory mediation is a forced engagement, ordinarily without attorneys or even friends or supporters present, it may amount to a form of 'psychic breaking and entering' or, put another way, psychic rape ...

> Although mediation can be useful and empowering, it presents some serious process dangers that need to be addressed ... When mediation is imposed rather than voluntarily engaged in, its virtues are lost. More than lost: mediation becomes a wolf in sheep's clothing. It relies on force and disregards the context of the dispute, while masquerading as a gentler, more empowering alternative to adversarial litigation. Sadly, when mediation is mandatory it becomes like the patriarchal paradigm of law it is supposed to supplant ... mandatory mediation is especially harmful: its messages disproportionately affect those who are already subordinated in our society, those to whom society has already given the message, in far too many ways, that they are not leading proper lives (Grillo, 1991: 1605–10).

However, North American and Australian research studies argue that there are few differences between the ways in which women and men experience the process of mediation and its outcomes, Thus, Kelly and Duyree look at gender issues in a study of several different Northern California settings where mediation services are offered for the resolution of custody and divorce disputes and issues. They concluded:

> there were no gender differences with respect to perceptions of the mediator along a number of dimensions. Both men and women rated their mediators fairly highly on the mediators' warmth and on sensitivity to client feelings, with

no significant sex difference on either measure. Further, men and women were just as likely to report that their mediators were mostly helpful in proposing options for resolving disputes and in identifying useful ways to arrange custody and visitation.

With respect to respondents' views of the impartiality and/or neutrality of the mediator, neither the women or men believed that the mediators had imposed their own viewpoints on them. Nor was there a gender difference with respect to whether men and women perceived that the mediators favored their spouse: The majority of men and women disagreed with the statement that the mediators favored their spouses in the mediation process.

There were two mediator dimensions along which there were significant gender differences. While both men and women rated fairly positively the mediators' skill, women were significantly more likely to agree that the mediators were skilful. Similarly, women rated the mediators' ability to keep the mediation focused on important issues in the session significantly more highly than did the men . . .

The findings of research in two different settings addressing custody and divorce disputes and issues indicated that there were few significant differences between the men and women in their perceptions of the mediators' functioning, the process of mediation, and the outcomes of the mediation process. Where significant gender differences appeared, the women rated the mediation experience more favorably than did the men (Kelly and Duyree, 1995: 37).

Kelley and Duyree go on to suggest that there are several factors at work which, in their view, help to explain why women find the mediation process satisfactory:

First, an important element of the mediation process is the opportunity to express one's views – a place in which women have a voice. Critics of mediation have condemned the process because they believe that women's voices are not heard and integrated into the final resolutions. However, empirical data obtained from women in two very different mediation settings contradict that theoretical position.

It would appear as well that the mediation process may have benefit for women beyond being given the opportunity to have a voice. Women in both settings reported that they gained confidence in their ability to stand up to their spouse as a result of the mediation. Women not only found a voice but appeared to feel that their voices were heard and legitimated enough to provide them with greater strength or resolve in relation to their former spouse. This greater sense of empowerment may be related to the structure of mediation, which insists that the interests and views of each disputant be articulated and treated with respect. Given the concerns raised that mandatory mediation inherently disempowers people, it was an important finding that women in both voluntary and mandatory mediation settings reported this increased confidence.

Further, women appeared to place value on the opportunity that mediation provided for them to set aside (even if temporarily) some of their anger at their spouse and focus on their children's needs. This experience in mediation is in contrast to the experience of litigating custody and visiting issues, which encourages and consolidates angry parental perceptions and positions, even those which may not be reality-based nor in the children's best interests. In other ways as well, the data do not support the notion that women feel disadvantaged in the mediation process. Women, including those who did not reach full agreement, still believe in the process and would recommend it to their friends. They prefer it to litigation (Kelly and Duyree, 1995: 41–2, 45).

A parallel and related critique raises questions about the conditions under which it can be safe for a member of one cultural or ethnic group to mediate in a dispute involving members of another, given the potentially diverging cultural understandings involved. In England, National Family Mediation's practice guidelines recognise this problem and propose explicit safeguards. Sonia Shah-Kazemi questions the safety of such a route:

> It is possible to perceive the benefits of exploring the different models of mediation where, for example, community members approve the third party as authorized to perform the tasks of mediation. However, if minority community members are deemed not to have the requisite neutrality required and neutral professionals are chosen instead, the principle of autonomy that community or cross-cultural mediation is predicated upon is then compromised. The initiative to mediate comes then from a source that does not really 'belong'. Contrary to the more commonly held view that it is the mediator who needs to identify with their client, advice and involvement can only be efficacious and acceptable when there is that 'identification' with the mediator by the client. Where a community is a minority, an outsider remains just that, no matter how sympathetic, so much so that even a member of the community who has rejected some of its normative ethics is considered an outsider. All of this follows as a consequence of the heightened salience accorded to the normative framework in any minority community, whose abiding identity as such is founded in large part on this framework.

In her view, it is simply not realistic to expect minority persons to use mediation services that fail to understand the needs, the language and the cultural themes, dynamics and nuances of that minority grouping. As a result:

> the ideal, then, is for mediators to be of the same cultural background as the parties, since no form of training can, a priori, impart a fully comprehensive understanding of the 'universe of meaning' that shapes our responses to the whole gamut of situations that arise in the course of life. However, this does not absolve all mediators from the need to acquire training into the dynamics of culture, because to be effective mediators it is necessary to recognize problems involved in bridging the gaps – often unconscious – between the psychological responses differentiated, precisely, by divergent cultural attitudes. Only in light of this awareness can there be any question of appreciating the impact that cultural values have upon the dynamics of a dispute and its resolution (Shah-Kazemi, 2000: 319–20).

Confidentiality in Mediation

The fact that mediation typically takes place in the context of other decision-making processes, as is the case in mediation that occurs in the context of legal proceedings, raises issues relating to the use of information disclosed and knowledge acquired in the course of mediation. Unless the substance of discussions taking place in mediation is protected against subsequent revelations, the process of mediation is likely to be affected. In particular, the exchange of information between the parties will be influenced, the independent position of the mediator may be undermined (especially if he or she is later required to report on the mediation), and third parties may be left in an exposed position. Moreover, in some systems, one of the perceived advantages of mediation is that it is often a private process, and this privacy needs to be protected. As a result, in certain parts of the United States, there are now very rigorous confidentiality rules governing information disclosed in the course of mediations.

Marian Roberts considers the need for confidentiality in the context of mediation in matrimonial disputes, stressing that the relationship between the mediator and the disputing parties is grounded in the principle of confidentiality. It is the basis of the trust which necessarily informs the relations between the mediator and the parties, and may significantly affect the parties' willingness to participate in the mediation, in the sense that the parties need to feel that they will not suffer damage by failure to keep the process fully private.

Thus, it should be the firm duty of a mediator to make clear to the parties at the beginning of the process that all information exchanged between them is confidential. Discovery of such information to parties outside the process should only take place as a result of their joint and express consent or by an authoritative demand such as a court order – that is to say, the promise of confidentiality is not absolute and in exceptional circumstances posing, for example, serious dangers to the safety of the parties or their children, or both, the welfare of children and factual information about property and financial issues are among the mostly important exceptional circumstances. In general, however, when the mediator makes a promise of confidentiality, that confidentiality should then belong to the parties, and it is their decision as to what may be disclosed externally. Another difficulty that may arise is that information given in confidence by one party – in say a caucus – might be very important to later discussion of the issues. If that party will not agree to disclose this information to the other party, then the obstacle thus created to further meaningful consideration of the issues may be sufficiently damaging to the negotiations that the mediation session will need to be brought to a close. In general, however, mediation serves an important public interest in promoting cooperative decision-making and the reduction of conflict, and immunity from disclosure is essential to the effectiveness of the process (Roberts, Marian, 2008: 190).

Mediation Agreements

In many legal systems one of the virtues claimed for mediation is that agreements that are successfully concluded through this process are likely to be stable and to reduce problems of enforcement. Where the outcome has been reached through a consensual process, and the parties have themselves constructed the agreement with the assistance of the good services of a mediator, they are likely to comply with the terms of the deal that they have struck. However, mediation agreements are not always the conclusive stage in the dispute resolution process, and where execution of agreements becomes problematic this may have an adverse impact on the mediation process itself. The parties are not confident that any agreement reached will be final and effective.

The argument that mediation agreements are likely to secure greater compliance than adjudicated outcomes was significantly advanced in seminal essays by McEwen and Maiman on empirical analysis of the work of small claims courts. They report:

> Our data strongly support the hypothesis that mediation is more likely than adjudication to lead to compliance with the resolution ... 70.6% of the mediation agreements with a monetary settlement were reported to be paid in full, compared to 33.8% of the adjudications ...

> The ... data [does] support the inference that there is something about the mediation process itself – as distinguished from the sort of agreements and arrangements for implementation that it tends to produce – that leads mediation defendants to be more likely than adjudication defendants to pay their debts. Some mediation advocates would attribute this to the responses which the process elicits from those who take part in it. In this regard, our data show that mediation leads more often than adjudication to settlements that litigants, defendants especially, perceive to be fair ...

> [But] while the greater sense of fairness in mediation than in adjudication accounts for some of the difference in compliance rates, it alone cannot explain the disparity. One must look more closely then at the feelings and perceptions of participants in mediation and adjudication to explain the differences between payment rates in the two kinds of cases ...

> [Our] data [does also] suggest that the higher compliance rates found in mediated cases probably result in large part from the experience of entering into – literally, signing – an agreement to end the dispute on certain specified terms. This appears to affect both plaintiffs' and defendants' perceptions of the debt. People are more likely to feel bound by an obligation they have undertaken voluntarily and more or less publicly than one imposed upon them in a court of law. It also seems highly likely that the mediator contributes to the disputant's sense that this obligation should be taken seriously – a marked contrast to the message of pessimism or, perhaps even worse, indifference about collection of the debt which was communicated by some of the judges. Finally, the fact that defendants who took part in unsuccessful mediations had a substantially better compliance record than those who had not participated in mediation at all

suggests that the negotiation process itself – independent of its outcome – helps to inculcate a sense of responsibility about payment. Perhaps merely facing one's opponent for a time, having the opportunity to speak with and to hear him or her, humanizes and personalizes the process enough to affect the defendant's attitude toward payment (McEwen and Maiman, 1981: 260–4).

Of course, in many circumstances party dissatisfaction with a mediation agreement may lead to further negotiation and mediation of the dispute. Nevertheless, a key question is the extent to which a legal system or society should allow the parties to resort to the courts in their efforts to secure enforcement. The need for mediation agreements to be legally enforceable, and the ways in which this might be done, are discussed below in the context of contemporary China, where mediation – especially extra-judicial mediation – continues to be a central feature of the civil justice system,

> An important aspect of the status of people's mediator concerns the efficacy of the agreements which they persuade the disputants to conclude. A corollary of the emphasis on the voluntary character of people's mediation and the 'mass' nature of mediation committees is the rule that – in contrast to 'in-court mediation agreements', arbitration, and adjudication – people's mediation agreements are not legally binding on the parties. The difficulty which this may create for people's mediators is illustrated by a letter to the legal press from a mediation committee in Shaanxi, central China, in which the writer observes that many local people are bypassing the committee and taking their cases straight to court. It is unlikely that such a letter would have been written had not the committee been faced with a substantial number of such cases.

> In order to counteract difficulties of this nature both academic writers and the authorities have highlighted important aspects of this area of mediation work that enhance the status accorded to people's mediation agreements. Ordinarily the agreements give rise only to contractual relations between the parties, and in this connection their limited efficacy is sometimes used to illustrate the differences between extra-judicial mediation and court hearings. Nevertheless, Chinese sources stress that extra-judicial mediation agreements do have a 'constraining force' on the parties, which would seem to imply that the parties are generally expected to honor the obligations assumed in the agreement. Moreover, if the parties affirm their consent to the written instrument by having the document stamped by a 'responsible government department' within one year from the date on which the disputant's rights were infringed, then the agreement does have legal effect. In addition, it is stressed that the parties may benefit from 'administrative' implementation of their agreement in certain circumstances, such as those in which the chairman of a local village committee also serves as chairman of the mediation committee – presumably various kinds of informal sanctions would be applied if one of the parties renounced the mediated agreement (Palmer, 1988: 270–1).

The status of the people's mediation agreement as a civil contract was later confirmed by the Chinese Ministry of Justice in Article 5 of its 'Several Rules for the Work of People's Mediation Committees' 2002,

Article 5

According to the 'Several Rules of the Supreme People's Court on Hearing Civil Cases Involving a People's Mediation Agreement', there is nature of civil contract in mediation agreements reached by means of mediation by a people's mediation committee with civil rights and obligations and signed or sealed by both parties to the dispute. All parties shall perform their obligations according to the agreement and shall not alter or dissolve the agreement without the other party's consent.

Other articles in the same set of Rules attempt to strengthen the status of the agreement. Thus, Article 36 authorizes the mediation committee to conduct checks in order to ascertain if the obligations entered into in the agreement are being met. Article 37 allows a people's mediation committee to call on governmental or judicial assistance implementing an agreement in which one party (or both parties) is failing to fulfil her or his obligations, and Article 38 requires the committee to assist the court in the matter if judicial proceedings are relied on:

Article 38

For a civil case in which any party refuses to fulfil the agreement or goes back on her or his word after the execution of the mediation agreement is filed with the people's court, the people's mediation committee in charge of the dispute case shall assist the people's court in a trial.

These provisions were further strengthened in 2010 when China's first full Law of People's Mediation was promulgated and put into effect (1 January 2011). Articles 31–3 provide:

Article 31

Mediation agreement concluded upon mediation by the people's mediation committee shall be legally binding and the parties shall fulfill according to the agreement.

The people's mediation committee shall carry out supervision of the fulfillment of mediation agreement and urge the parties to fulfill the agreed obligations.

Article 32

After mediation agreement has been concluded upon mediation by the people's mediation committee, should dispute arise between the parties in respect of fulfillment of mediation agreement or the content of the mediation agreement, one party may file a lawsuit with the People's Court.

Article 33

After mediation agreement has been concluded upon mediation by the people's mediation committee, where both parties deem necessary, they may apply to the People's Court jointly for judicial confirmation within thirty days from the day the mediation agreement takes effect. The People's Court shall conduct a review of the mediation agreement promptly and confirm the validity of the mediation agreement according to law.

Where the People's Court confirms that the mediation agreement is valid, one party refuses to fulfill or has not completely fulfilled, the other party may apply to the People's Court for mandatory execution.

Where the People's Court confirms that the mediation agreement is invalid, the parties may alter the original mediation agreement or conclude a new mediation agreement through the people's mediation approach. It may also file a lawsuit with the People's Court.

Conclusions

Thus, a range of questions surrounds the scope and ambition of mediatory intervention:

- Should the mediator's role be confined to improving the communication arrangements between the parties, or should a more extensive role be attempted?
- Beyond providing a structural framework for the process of negotiation, how far should the mediator seek to inform, or further to control, the outcome?
- Has the mediator responsibility for the nature and quality of the outcome? Is the outcome simply a matter for the parties; or can we see the mediator as accountable?
- If the mediator is seen as responsible for the outcome, does this extend to:
  (a) handling imbalances of power in support of the weaker party?
  (b) seeking to ensure the protection of third parties who may be affected by the outcome?
- To what extent and in what ways should a mediation agreement be made enforceable in law.

A number of these concerns manifest themselves in the question of the provision of legal advice in the course of mediation.

8

Umpiring: Courts and Tribunals

Introduction

Once we start to imagine the range of third-party interventions in dispute processes – forms of 'the triad' – the line between 'mediation', considered in Chapter 6, and 'umpiring' marks the essential internal boundary in analytic terms. It is a move from *facilitation*, on the one hand, to *determination*, on the other; the power of decision is surrendered to a third party.

The simplest case we might imagine is that where two parties in dispute agree to approach a non-aligned third – the 'neutral stranger' – and ask her to make a determination for them. A whole range of attributes might give the decision-maker legitimacy in a particular case. The parties might trust her: because she has no stake in the issue; because of her reputation as a wise and fair decision-maker; because of her professional background and training. Simmel underlined the defining quality of this simple case: it lies in the consensual nature of the reference – the disputing parties *agree* to the determination of their issues by someone else. As he observed: 'the voluntary appeal to an arbitrator . . . presupposes a greater subjective confidence in the objectivity of judgement than does any other form of decision' ([1908] trans. 1950: 151).

Another instance of third-party determination arises where the *rank* of the third party approached – a parent, employer, religious or political superior – gives that person authority to decide the matter on request of one disputing party alone, irrespective of the wishes of the other. Such situations of institutionalised hierarchy/seniority obviously involve quite different kinds of legitimacy claims to those applicable in the earlier case.

The native categories of Western legal theory broadly recognise this difference in drawing a primary distinction between agents providing private *arbitration* and state-sponsored *courts*. A defining characteristic of the court is its link to the state. Courts, in exercising their powers of adjudication, have almost invariably been seen as part of government, sponsored by those at the centre who claim to exercise a steering rule. This association with government distinguishes the court from umpiring processes in which the choice of intervener is left to the parties themselves. The latter processes have been conceptualised in native legal theory under the broad heading of *arbitration*.

While arbitration shares the basic procedural features of adjudication, namely the submission of proofs and arguments to a third party with authority to impose a binding outcome. However, the basis of the arbitrator's intervention is different, lying in the joint invitation of the parties.

In this chapter, we begin by considering the relationship between government and dispute institutions, examining the implications for disputing of the processes of centralisation historically associated with state formation. We then look at the ways in which different forms of umpire acquire legitimacy. Turning specifically to state-sponsored 'courts', we consider the range of roles these can be seen as performing. While it may be a defining characteristic of a court that, by virtue of state sponsorship, it has the *capacity* to make a third-party determination, delivery of judgment is not necessarily its primary responsibility or the reason for parties to resort to it. We conclude by looking at arbitration in its principal institutional contexts.

Government and Dispute Institutions

We can never hope to chart the historical emergence of umpiring institutions in more than a conjectural way; and anyway this trajectory may well have followed a different sequence from one culture to another. While anthropologists have rarely reported institutions of third-party decision-making in acephalous societies, leading texts on arbitration conventionally claim that state-sponsored adjudication developed historically out of arbitral proceedings (Mustill, 1989; Redfern and Hunter, 2004). But whether we imagine the origin in private institutions under which disputants agreed to place their differences before a trusted third party, or in the co-option of mediatory arrangements by those in power as centralisation developed, is ultimately neither here nor there. Whatever view we take of the general origins of umpiring institutions – as being present before centralised government developed and then co-opted, or as evolving with government – those in power seem invariably to have provided dispute institutions for their subjects. Further, 'courts' have historically played a central part in projects of colonial expansion. As Shapiro notes, 'the origin of judicial systems in many parts of the world is to be found in conquest' (1981: 220).

Historically, wherever we find processes of centralisation taking place, courts seem to have appeared and come to represent a central means through which 'government' has revealed itself. This was recognised long ago by Maine in his *Dissertations on Early Law and Custom* (1883: 160) where he noted the intimate link between rulership and adjudication. Subsequently, others have underlined this connection (see, for example, Fuller, 1978). We can find examples of this conjunction as far apart as Imperial China (Bodde and Morris, 1967) and (much later) in the Tswana kingdoms of the Kalahari (Schapera, 1956). The extract from Shapiro's study of courts emphasises the generality of the close relationship between government and the courts:

The congruence of administering and judging must be specially noted. Indeed, the observer who did not so firmly believe in the independence of judging might take judging for a special facet of administering. Both the judge and adminis-trator apply general rules to particular situations on a case-by-case basis. Both tend to rely heavily on precedent, fixed decisional procedures, written records, and legalized defense of their decisions. Both are supplementary lawmakers engaged in filling in the details of more general rules. Both are front-line social controllers for more distant governing authorities. And in a startling number of instances both are the same person, and a person who draws little or no distinction between administering and judging . . .

Perhaps the most important factor in explaining the historical congruence of judging and administering is to be found in a far broader aspect of the adminis-trator's responsibility for social control. The origin of judicial systems in many parts of the world is to be found in conquest. This is obviously true for imperial judicial systems such as those of Rome, China, and the . . . empires of central Africa such as the Barotse . . . and it is also clearly true for the common law courts imposed over the old moot and hundred folk courts by the Norman conquerors. Conquest created the British courts of colonial India and Africa as well as many other colonial court systems. The Supreme Court of the United States and the lower federal courts insofar as they operate on the old Confeder-acy are courts of conquerors. Even where courts are not directly imposed by force of arms, they will often be identified with the political regime or with distant rather than local authority.

Conquerors use courts as one of their many instruments for holding and controlling conquered territories. And more generally, governing authorities seek to maintain or increase their legitimacy through the courts. Thus a major function of courts in many societies is a particular form of social control, the recruiting of support for the regime (Shapiro, 1981: 20, 22–4).

In Europe, since medieval times, we can say for certain that courts, as final authoritative agencies of third-party decision-making, have played a central role in government. This close link between the development of courts and the extension of central government power in the common law world is firmly characterised in the account by Van Caenegem who describes it as a key feature in the emergence of the common law:

the rise to absolute predominance of the central royal courts under Henry II, as the free man's courts of first instance for all the more important and frequent complaints connected with land-holding throughout the country. There was a dual phenomenon here, centralization and specialization. Centralization meant that an enormous amount of litigation, that would in earlier times have origin-ated in the local courts and stayed there, now came up before a central body of royal judges. The transfer of pleas from local courts through writs of *pone* and *tolt* was easily obtained and local courts were under constant central supervision through the rule *nemo tenetur respondere*, the writ of prohibition and the *writ de falso judicio*. Under Henry I the enforcement of new royal enactments was left to the local courts. Henry II entrusted this to his own justices in eyre. For a man who had unjustly lost his free tenement to appear in the *curia regis* was exceptional in AD 1100, but common by AD 1200. With centralization came professional specialization. The common nucleus of the central courts, i.e. of the justices in eyre, the Common Bench at Westminster, the Exchequer and the Bench *coram rege*, was the old feudal *curia regis*, something like the primeval amoeba in biology. In this undifferentiated body business of all sorts, political, fiscal and judicial, was transacted on non-professional, casual lines. Under pressure of work a division of labour developed. The barons of the Exchequer formed an institution, distinct, if not always separated from the king's justices; among the latter some were justices itinerant, on eyre in the counties, others, of higher rank, resided at Westminster, still others, the Bench *coram rege* travelled with the king and could consult him if necessary. Initially these men had been temporarily borrowed from their other occupations. Later their work as royal justices became their main task. Their professional outlook and expertise improved correspondingly. They all formed one cohesive group, applied one common law and one set of procedures which was so conveniently expounded in Glanvill ... (Van Caenegem, 1988: 18–20)

This truth that courts are ultimately creatures of government has important implications. However plausibly in a modern polity they may present them- selves as dispassionate neutrals – there to 'help' people by arriving at disinter- ested decisions in accordance with general, known criteria – they also exercise a steering role. Historically, rulers never established and underwrote judicial institutions simply for the purpose of settling disputes among their subjects. Central was the ambition to remain in power; and certainly in much of the medieval European world, for example, the principal means available to monarchs for controlling their subjects was the judge.

The Legitimation of Third-party Decision-making

In the simple case where two parties agree to put their dispute to a 'neutral stranger' for decision, the problem of legitimation does not really arise. Their very agreement confers legitimacy on the chosen process. So the primary legitimacy claim of the arbitrator lies simply in consent, the fact that the parties have chosen her or him to decide.[1]

In the first instance, a court's claim to legitimacy lies in its link to govern- ment. The authority of the courts to intervene is founded in their incorpor- ation in the official hierarchy. That said, there is at first sight a paradox in the fact that courts in some cultures make a feature of their independence from the legislature and the executive. The native claim to the 'independence of the judiciary' and the doctrine of 'separation of powers' is a central part of legal ideology in the common law world. But this self-conscious claim to autonomy

---

[1] Even so, the progressive steps taken in modernity to tie the enforcement of arbitral proceedings to courts at national level in itself underwrites the legitimacy of international arbitration.

from other branches of government does not in any sense represent a repudi-
ation of the courts' status as part of the apparatus of the nation state.

Concurrent claims to legitimacy are sustained by long-established processual conventions, associated with the general rubric of the 'rule of law'. The
publicity of court processes, their explicit commitment to a common repertoire of rules, and the established procedural understandings determining
access to them, all go to build up authority, as well as helping to engender a
consistent approach to decision-making.

Another means of providing legitimacy for the outcomes of state-sponsored
adjudication lies in the hierarchical appellate structure of most judicial systems.
Perhaps more commonly, provision may be made for appellate and similar
processes that give the losing party access to an alternative outcome. Of course,
an unfavourable conclusion may be anticipated by one of the parties and efforts
may be made to select a particular arena likely to confer a better result – a
strategy often referred to as 'forum shopping', but it is primarily through
appellate processes that the parties seek to alter a concrete outcome. The right
to appeal is acknowledged in most legal systems and plays an important role
not only in encouraging losing parties to accept unfavourable adjudicatory
outcomes, but also in facilitating governmental control of the judicial system
and, more generally, in promoting the political interests of the ruler.

At the same time, when courts are seen as part of or close to the administrative system, an appeals mechanism also serves as a check on the performance of administrative subordinates as it provides an independent source of
information to those at the top about local level performance. In order to make
the ordinary upward flow of information more manageable, administrative
systems necessarily keep reports to superiors brief and focused, but an appeal
case may well provide many details of a particular case which by its very
natures is likely to point to a specific incident of administrative failure. For this
reason, local level decision-makers may press parties into mediation in the
name of harmony but, in reality, their motive is the expectation that from
mediation there is unlikely to be an appeal. When there is a separate judicial
hierarchy, appeals retain this supervisory function, so that the appellate system
serves as a mechanism by means of which higher courts are able to check and
criticise the work of lower tribunals, and by revising appealed decisions to not
only 'correct an injustice' but to remind the lower courts of the superiority of
the higher judicial body. The latter function also helps us to understand
why the claim of appeal often stops only at the highest level of centralised
political control. Lower appeal courts could most likely correct an injustice,
but the appellate system needs to have at its apex a supreme authority because
the system is ultimately intended to serve the control purposes of that supreme
authority rather than provide an avenue to justice for a losing party: Accordingly, 'appellate institutions are more fundamentally related to the political
purposes of central regimes than to the doing of individual justice' (Shapiro,
1981: 52).

The manner in which this legitimating element of hierarchical review is built into a judicial process varies from one culture to another. Common law jurisdictions are characterised by an appellate structure primarily activated by an aggrieved disputant, whereas in civilian jurisdictions this element is subordinated to an automatic revision process under which an outcome passes for review before successively senior figures in the judicial hierarchy. This striking contrast between common law and civilian traditions is examined in the work of comparative proceduralist, Mirjan Damaška. In civilian jurisdictions and other systems with a 'well-integrated judicial hierarchy' the initial trial outcome is not seen as final but, rather, as being subject to review by a superior body. In a number of classical East Asian jurisdictions, indeed, original decisions were regarded more as provisional drafts that only became final after official review and endorsement by a superior official. In addition, hierarchical review was comprehensive, so that facts, law and reasoning were all reconsidered. And if new evidence is discovered post-trial, then typically it is to be submitted to the reviewing authority rather than the original adjudicator. Moreover 'perfunctory and conclusory statements of grounds, so prevalent among trial judges in common-law jurisdictions, invite rebuke and reversal in a hierarchical judicial system' (Damaška, 1986: 49). We should therefore not assume that the meaning of trials is the same in hierarchical systems as it is in the more 'coordinate' systems found in the common law tradition (Damaska 1986: 23–8; 38–46).

The role of lawyers also provides an important element in promoting acceptance of courts as authoritative third-party decision-makers. The close link that exists in the Anglo-American common law world between courts and lawyers underlines this significance. The role of the lawyer in the adjudication process has been viewed as an indispensable feature of that process, and one that promotes the legitimacy of the adversarial system itself. Fuller, for example, has argued that the involvement of the lawyer as an advocate is necessary for the good functioning of adjudication on two principal grounds. First, the slow unfolding of a case and, in particular, the presentation of evidence and arguments and challenges made by the advocate lawyer on behalf of his or her client encourages the judge to reach his or her decision in a reasoned and deliberate manner, avoiding in particular the pitfall of forming too hasty a view of the needs of each party's case. Second, the use of the lawyer as a representative enables the judge to maintain the role of neutral umpire, thereby concentrating on making a 'wise and informed decision of the case' (Fuller and Randall, 1958: 1159–61; see also Fuller, 1978).

In most common law jurisdictions, the element of 'distance' from government is also underlined in the provenance of the higher judiciary, recruited as they are from the legal profession. The judiciary in common law countries has never been a career path within the civil service, as it has been in the civilian world; rather judicial appointment represents the ultimate career stage of the successful barrister. Judges remain on as Benchers of their Inns, and their names remain associated with the Chambers they belonged to before appointment.

In the evolving civilian tradition, however, the concern from very early on was to develop the judicial role as a professional career. And this career was located in an increasingly rigid and hierarchical bureaucracy, with the judges accorded only limited discretionary powers of decision-making. In the extract that follows, Damaška characterises this development in succinct terms:

> [With] the strengthening of princely absolutism in the sixteenth and seventeenth centuries ... centralized bureaucracies started to dominate the governmental apparatus in the influential Continental countries. Even language was now affected by pressures toward regimentation. Official discourse was to be conducted in rigidly structured speech forms, dry, Latinate, and 'abstract' in comparison with the colloquial private idiom. The idea of impersonal office was extended to the very heart of government. Despite the famous later dictum of Louis XIV, '*l'état c'est moi*,' it is in this period that the idea of the state became detachable from the personal status of the ruler and converted into an institutionalized (impersonal) locus of allegiance.
>
> In the great majority of Continental countries judicial officials became career professionals. Lay participation in the legal process, where it survived at all, was reduced to insignificance or to a ritual. No longer were judicial functionaries, now organized into a hierarchy, perceived as unrelated to the center of state power. And unlike the judges of the church, secular adjudicators were no longer permitted to mould ordinances and other legal sources to conform to their conscience. The integrity of a powerful central authority was thought to require strict governance by rules. Highly placed judges found the resulting shrinkage of discretionary space quite acceptable: they became accustomed to deciding on the basis of orderly documents that screened out 'messy' situational and personal nuances likely to exert pressure toward leeway in decision making. As a bureaucratic maxim of the period asserted, *quod non est in actis non est in mundo* ('what is not in the file does not exist') (Damaška, 1986: 32–8).

The Role of Courts

Courts can be seen as fulfilling a number of analytically distinct roles, beyond being a decision-making branch of government concerned primarily with public order and helping citizens to resolve their disputes. As one of the public faces of government, the courts have primary, exemplary roles in the cognitive and normative domains, constituting, keeping in place and justifying a particular view of how the social world is, and ought to be. Powerful ideological and ritual resources are often harnessed for these purposes. In England, the gothic splendour of the Royal Courts of Justice symbolises the historical continuity of government, representing order and continuity in the social world as the long-standing, skilled achievement of those in power. In the same way, government has blatantly co-opted the potent image of the blind goddess with her scales in presenting itself as the purveyor of 'justice'. Within the building, the authority and hierarchies of government are emphasised through formality, of space, dress and language. Dickens captured the impression that this could make on an unsympathetic onlooker in a famous passage from his account of London's renowned heavy smog and legal fog infusing nineteenth-century Chancery proceedings:

> And hard by Temple Bar, in Lincoln's Inn Hall, at the very heart of the fog, sits the Lord High Chancellor in his High Court of Chancery.
>
> On such an afternoon, if ever, the Lord High Chancellor ought to be sitting here – as here he is – with a foggy glory round his head, softly fenced in with crimson cloth and curtains, addressed by a large advocate with great whiskers, a little voice, and an interminable brief, and outwardly directing his contemplation to the lantern in the roof, where he can see nothing but fog. On such an afternoon, some score of members of the High Court of Chancery bar ought to be – as here they are – mistily engaged in one of the ten thousand stages of an endless cause, tripping one another up on slippery precedents, groping knee-deep in technicalities, running their goat-hair and horse-hair warded heads against walls of words, and making a pretence of equity with serious faces, as players might. On such an afternoon, the various solicitors in the cause, some two or three of whom have inherited it from their fathers, who made a fortune by it, ought to be – as are they not? – ranged in a line, in a long matted well (but you might look in vain for Truth at the bottom of it), between the registrar's red table and the silk gowns, with bills, cross-bills, answers, rejoinders, injunctions, affidavits, issues, references to masters, masters' reports, mountains of costly nonsense, piled before them. Well may the court be dim, with wasting candles here and there; well may the fog hang heavy in it, as if it would never get out; well may the stained glass windows lose their colour, and admit no light of day into the place; well may the uninitiated from the streets, who peep in through the glass panes in the door, be deterred from entrance by its owlish aspect, and by the drawl languidly echoing to the roof from the padded dais where the Lord High Chancellor looks into the lantern that has no light in it, and where the attendant wigs are all stuck in a fog-bank! This is the Court of Chancery . . . that there is not an honourable man among its practitioners who would not give – who does not often give – the warning, 'Suffer any wrong that can be done you, rather than come here!' (Dickens, [1852–3]1994: 2–3).

In the period of late nineteenth-century European colonial expansion, courts played both a symbolic and a substantive role as expressions of the metropolitan power. In the former British African territories, for example, one early jural act under Order in Council was the establishment of a High Court. A dual system was then perfected with the subsequent recognition of 'native courts' administering 'native' (later, 'customary') law. This led in jural terms to the marginalisation of indigenous agencies, whatever the realities on the ground might have been (Abel, 1979: 168, 195–7).[2] As we saw in Chapter 2,

---

[2] It also often led to quite informal procedures in the conduct of civil trials in the colonial courts – see, for example, Johnston's account of civil proceedings in Weihaiwei, northern China (1910: 104–8).

Richard Abel considers that the imposition of Western courts in the developing world, and the resulting relegation of local systems of justice to a secondary position, is a phenomenon that finds a modern-day equivalent in jurisdictions experiencing moves towards ADR in the late twentieth century, in which community justice, consumer dispute agencies and so on are best seen as second-class justice for second-class citizens.

The decision-making practices of the courts have a further role, beyond the simple resolution of disputes. In making decisions in accordance with 'rules', the courts keep the normative repertoire under constant review and revision. We have noted earlier how Fiss, in a fundamental apology for adjudication, goes so far as to argue that the role of judges in resolving disputes is secondary to their function of restating important public values: 'adjudication is the social process by which judges give meaning to our public values' (Fiss, 1979: 2). The centrality of adjudication is reasserted by presenting judgment as the means through which the core repertoire of norms in society is publicised and refurbished. In some legal cultures this represents another primary role played by an appellate structure, as Shapiro emphasises:

> In this context social control and lawmaking are usually intimately connected. Appeal is not simply a device for ensuring a certain uniformity in the operations of rank-and-file social controllers. It also ensures that they are following rules or laws or policies of social control acceptable to the regime. Indeed, appeal is a key mechanism in injecting centralized social control into the conflict resolution activities of courts. For appeal is the channel through which the central political authority assures itself that its rank-and-file conflict resolvers are applying legal rules that resolve conflicts in the desired directions. Earlier we noted that the substitution of legislated law for rules created by the mutual consent of the parties introduced a third set of interests into two-party litigation, whatever interests were embodied in the legislation. At least in large and complex societies, trial courts are too many and too localized to articulate this third set satisfactorily. Appellate courts are more suitable (1981: 54).

The story of courts as public decision-making bodies takes a new turn with the increasingly important place that is accorded to adjudication and courts in a wide range of international legal assistance programmes. Worries about the quality of governance in Africa, Latin America and Eastern Europe in particular have encouraged many donor agencies – but perhaps most strikingly the World Bank[3] – and governments to emphasise the importance of formal legal frameworks and institutions. Accordingly, the notion has gained ground that perhaps the most important responsibility of governments in developing countries is to provide a meaningful 'rule of law', and that efforts to implement this goal should give central place to an independent judiciary in which accessible and efficient courts apply the law in an even-handed, fair-minded,

---

[3] See, for example, Shihata (1995).

and predictable fashion. It is the view of Santos that the project to promote rule of law ideals, democracy and judicial reform in the developing world is ineluctably doomed to fail. Historical experience shows us that the globalising forces of capitalism 'make it very difficult' for the rule of law and its courts to sustain national democracies. Rising social injustice and inequality and the ability of powerful corporation and others to circumvent the laws which regulate their operation undermine the legitimacy and effectiveness of 'rule of law' reform (Santos, 2000: 279–81). To these factors might be added issues of cultural identity, sometimes expressly stated as 'resisting western values'.

Courts are also used by litigants in a range of ways that go beyond the simple request for delivery of judgment. We may go to court to publicise an already existing state of affairs, or simply to waste the resources of an enemy.[4] Perhaps most notably, litigation has come to be used in the common law world as lawyers' principal vehicle for their settlement strategies. So settlement, rather than being a 'private' process, has merged procedurally with the 'public' pursuit of judgment. Conceptualising their handling of disputes from the outset as 'litigation', and setting out on the path towards the court at an early stage, lawyers aim to 'settle' disputes, typically a very long way down the avenue to trial, rather than allow them to go all the way to judgment. We noted in an earlier chapter how a particular syndrome has developed under which late settlement is achieved by using the procedural framework prescribed for bringing a dispute to trial and judgment.

The Heterogeneity of Court Practice

While courts generally present themselves first and foremost as agencies of authoritative third-party decision-making, they vary markedly in the way preparation for decisions is arranged. Within continental Europe we find an active, inquisitorial role under which much of the burden of preparation and inquiry falls upon the court. In England, as in North America, the courts historically remain a potent but immobile backdrop while the parties prepare for an adversarial trial at their own pace. More recently – in England only in the last two decades – the common law picture has begun to change, as the judiciary has shown a growing determination to assume control over preparations for trial and overall to adopt a more active, 'managerial', role.

Heterogeneity of court practice goes considerably beyond these narrow procedural questions; it is even an over-simplification to suggest that delivery of judgment represents the only, even the primary, aim of court-like institutions. As Martin Shapiro argues below, in some cultures courts assume openly mediatory functions. In this respect, what appear to be large-scale changes in state management of civil disputes have become visible over at

---

[4] For a case study of the cultural embeddedness of the various social and legal factors that may influence the decision to go to court, see Lowy (1978).

least two decades right across the common law world. At the heart of these changes lies a growing recognition of 'settlement' as an approved, privileged objective of civil justice. The courts have come to present themselves not just as agencies offering judgment but also as sponsors of negotiated agreement.

Shapiro offers us an explanation for the persisting, conventional view that courts are solely places of umpiring. He suggests that popular images of courts have stressed the coercive aspects of court work. The effect of this is to over-emphasise the umpiring functions of courts and to underplay other processes of dispute resolution that the courts in reality have often used. Thus, for example, mediation is often a component in judging because courts also need to secure consent, and this encourages judges to limit the coercive dimension in their dispute resolution functions: 'mediation and arbitration in the context of the opportunity to go into court if the parties cannot come to agreement is a typical pattern encountered in both communist and capitalist states' (Shapiro, 1981: 9).

And, Shapiro continues, the fact is that courts in common law jurisdictions have traditionally converted what he calls 'indivisible disputes' – such as disputes over injury to person and property – into disputes over sums of money, so that 'even a judge who must declare that one party is legally right and the other legally wrong need not resort to winner-take-all solutions' (Shapiro, 1981: 10). The style of decision-making is often to impose a com-promise in which the money-damages awarded is more than the loser would like, but also less than the winner feels is justified. Moreover, the doctrine of 'balancing of equities' has long required courts of equity to fashion remedies that do not impose costs on one party that significantly outweigh benefits to the other (Shapiro, 1981: 10).

Contemporary Transformations in the Common Law World

A very general shift in terms of both what courts 'are' and how they do their work became visible in the last years of the twentieth century right across the common law world. In the most general terms, there has been a move to include sponsorship of *settlement* as a primary objective, to be attempted first before trial and judgment. When the role of the courts was being re-examined in the United States in the mid-1970s, Frank Sander proposed the realisation of a hypothetical, ideal court as 'a flexible and diverse panoply of dispute resolution processes' and introduced the terms 'multi-door courthouse' and 'alternative dispute resolution'.[5] In the United States and Canada – right across North America as a whole – this vision has been vigorously realised. There is a general recognition that sponsorship of settlement is a primary responsibility – and this is explicitly inscribed in the procedural rules. In

---

[5] See also comments by Sander in Chapter 3.

many United States jurisdictions, mandated mediation is one of the engines driving this process. The result in processual terms has been a progressive hybridisation of the courts.

Reflecting on his characterisation of the civil justice system in the United States in the mid-1970s, Sander advised, that the system offered:

> a hierarchy and structure within many disputes presented to court are not appropriate for court adjudication and could be better handled by some other mechanism.

> This situation led me to suggest ... a more comprehensive and diverse mechanism known as a Dispute Resolution Centre. This Centre would provide a variety of dispute resolution processes, according to the needs of the particular dispute. This concept was later termed the 'multi-door courthouse' (MDC).

> What would such an institution look like? A provisional first-step type of MDC could consist essentially of a screening and referral clerk who would seek to diagnose incoming cases and refer them to the most suitable ADRMs [Alternative Dispute Resolution Mechanisms]. Depending on the available mechanisms in the particular community, referral might be made to mediation, arbitration, court adjudication, fact-finding, malpractice screening, media actions lines or an ombudsman. Such a model would be subject to all the familiar deficiencies of a referral scheme. For example, slippage often occurs between the act of referral and the receiving agency's actual handling of the case.

> A more ideal model would contain all the 'doors' under one roof, as part of an integrated dispute resolution centre. Such a mansion might feature the following doors:

> (1) effective and accessible small claims adjudication;
> (2) services for family, landlord/tenant, and other continuing relations cases;
> (3) ombudsmen for the processing of disputes between citizens and large bureaucracies;
> (4) social service agencies providing mental health counselling and treatment of alcohol and drug related problems;
> (5) trial court of general jurisdiction for novelty statutory and constitutional claims, as well as major criminal cases; and
> (6) compulsory arbitration for small monetary claims.

> Additional dispute processing forums might include those mediating or arbitrating juvenile matters and those handling ordinance violations such as bad checks and health code and building code violations. . . .

> An integrated multi-door courthouse would have a number of benefits as well as potential pitfalls. First, such a full-service MDC would provide an efficient way of availing a wide range of dispute processes. It could also serve as a major source of information and referral, transcending the particular 'doors' that are available. Secondly, bringing such diverse ADRMs under the court umbrella would solve the increasingly difficult question of how to fund alternative mechanisms. Likewise it would avoid the pro-court adjudication bias inherent

in the present system where the state pays the costs of court adjudication but not those of other, more suitable, mechanisms.

Third, because of the predominant emphasis on courts in our society, most alternatives are seldom used ... A major difficulty appears to be popular unfamiliarity with these mechanisms. This requires additional public education, but it also argues for building ADRMs into an expanded court system (Sander, 1985a: 11–13).

Elsewhere Sander raised a series of questions:

If the alternatives to adjudication have all the advantages claimed for them why are they not more widely used? Are there aspects of the legal system that deter the use of alternatives? Or does the lack of demand for alternatives reflect the fact that the alternatives movement is primarily a product of the self-interest of the alternatives providers, rather than an expression of the needs of alternatives consumers?

Is there an adequate empirical basis for the claimed advantages of the alternatives? How, for example, can one adequately measure the asserted advantages of mediation over adjudications? Is it possible to develop a sophisticated cost-benefit analysis of alternative processes?

Is there a risk that the availability of alternatives will shunt low and middle-income disputants to a form of second-class justice, consisting primarily of semi-coerced compromise settlements, while the so-called first-class justice offered by the courts becomes available only to the rich and powerful? In thinking about this question, the reader should be aware that the neighborhood justice center clientele consists primarily of low-income disputants referred by courts and prosecutors as an alternative to criminal proceedings.

Is there a danger that mediation, with its emphasis on accommodation and compromise, will deter large-scale structural changes in political and societal institutions that only court adjudication can accomplish, and that it will thus serve the interests of the powerful against the disadvantaged?

To the extent that new modes of dispute resolution call for new practitioners, with skills different from those who practise in the judicial system, what steps should be taken to ensure that these practitioners have the requisite skills? Should there be regulation of the practice of dispute resolution similar to that of the practice of law?

Can the alternatives movement survive success? If alternative dispute resolution processes become widely used, will they suffer from the woes common to other heavily-used institutions – increasing costs and delay, bureaucratization, and perfunctory performance?

One solution is,

public institutionalization of alternative dispute resolution [in the form] of the Multidoor Courthouse. This concept calls for a multi-faceted intake center where disputes are analyzed according to their salient characteristics and referred to that process, or sequence of processes, most appropriate for their resolution. This proposal is now being tested under ABA auspices in Houston, Tulsa, and Washington, DC. The results of that experiment should help to tell us whether this idea is indeed a promising herald for more effective dispute resolution (Sander, 1985b: 260–1).

An early realisation of Sander's idea was the Middlesex Multi-Door Courthouse (MMDC) in Massachusetts, which Stedman describes as a court-annexed ADR programme:

> which provides a comprehensive approach to dispute resolution within the administrative structure of a trial court. It was established in 1989 with the overall goal of improving the administration of justice through more timely resolution of disputes, greater cost-effectiveness for the courts and the con-sumers, and increased public satisfaction with process and outcome. The pro-gramme delivers a wide variety of dispute resolution services through a single coordinating entity ... The original planning for the multi-door courthouse was initiated outside the court system by a small group of private citizens who developed a demonstration project and raised most of the money for its implementation. Although the impetus did not originally come from the judi-ciary, court leaders were encouraging and supportive. From the beginning, the multi-door courthouse was planned as a court-annexed programme and organ-ised on the understanding that, if successful, it would be formally integrated within the Massachusetts Trial Court.

> The multi-door courthouse opened its doors to cases in 1990 in the Middlesex (Cambridge) Superior Court, situated just outside Boston. The Middlesex court was selected because of its demographics and the fact that it has the most active civil case load in Massachusetts. Cases are randomly selected for screening from the court's civil case list. In addition, they can be referred by the judiciary or the parties. The programme has now provided services to more than 6,000 cases. In 1994, 1,200 cases went through individual case-screening conferences. Four per cent settled at the screening or before a follow-up. Forty per cent opted out of a referral to one of the multi-door courthouse's doors. Some of these elected to go to a private ADR provider, some that the case could be settled without add-itional intervention, and others that judicial intervention was unnecessary (a few of these cases also will re-enter the programme at a later date). Altogether, approximately 56 per cent of the screened cases elected to go forward with one of the multi-door courthouse's dispute resolution options. Of these, 71 per cent settled at or within 60 days. Many of the rest had partial settlements or would otherwise settle before the trial date. Follow-up reports on the cases indicate that almost all participants felt that the process had been highly beneficial, even if it did not result in immediate settlement.

Stedman advises that the experimental MDC used an initial screening system to classify and commence the processing of cases. Although standard tort and contract disputes were a predominant part of the MDC's workload, virtually all types of civil case came to the MDC, including commercial, property, construction, consumer, employment and business partnership dis-putes. She further notes that:

Cases are still randomly selected from the court docket. However, increasingly cases are referred by the judge or lawyers involved. This reflects the increased acceptance of ADR in general and the multi-door courthouse concept in particular. Judicial referrals generally arise from status conferences, pre-trial hearings or attempts by the parties to seek equitable relief by way of injunctions or temporary restraining orders. A few cases have been sent in the middle of trial for the purpose of resolving a discrete issue or, occasionally, the entire case. In such circumstances and if a screener is available, the case is handled on a walk-in basis. Otherwise, referral occurs by way of a mandatory screening order sent out by the court. Although cases are taken randomly off the docket, they are reviewed to determine their suitability before the actual order is sent. (1996: 119–27, 133–5, 137–40).

A similar picture developed in the Australian courts. Commercial court judges, notably, have developed strict and sophisticated regimes of 'case management'. These include:

- a move to the 'individual docket system' under which a single judge is responsible for managing a case throughout its trajectory;
- rigid timetabling after an early stage planning appointment; and
- the power to order mediation, irrespective of the wishes of the parties.[6]

In England and Wales too there was a gradual but accelerating departure from the historical position under which English judges have allowed the parties to prepare for adversarial trial very much in their own way and at their own pace, dealing with 'interlocutory' matters only where the parties bring them to their attention. Moves in this direction first appeared as spontaneous initiatives within the judiciary in a regime of early stage meetings in divorce county courts. A Commercial Court Practice Statement of 10 December 1993 and the general Practice Direction of 24 January 1995 followed, representing an enormous shift when thought about in the context of older understandings of what courts are and what they do. Reaching out into the period before the trial, they considerably extended the involvement of the court in a domain that was never 'private', because it lay along the route to the court, but which had hitherto been occupied by the parties and their professional representatives alone. Early indications that the sponsorship of settlement would become an explicit, official objective appeared first in the Heilbron/Hodge Report (1993) and then in the Interim version of the 'Woolf' Report, *Access to Justice* (1995). In the latter, judicial 'case management' is prescribed and its overall purpose identified as:

> to encourage settlement of disputes at the earliest appropriate stage; and, where trial is unavoidable, to ensure that cases proceed as quickly as possible to a final hearing which is itself of strictly limited duration (II.5.16).

---

[6] See, for example, arrangements in the Victorian courts. There, Order 50.07 of the Supreme Court Rules provides that: 'at any stage of a proceeding the Court may with or without the consent of any party order that the proceeding or any part of the proceeding be referred to a mediator'.

In his interim report, Lord Woolf, argued that there were problems of cost, delay and complexity in the English civil justice system, that adversarial-minded lawyers in particular were responsible for much of this state of affairs, and that in the interest of access to justice the courts needed to assume a more proactive role.[7]

This would mean that the handling of civil cases would henceforth need much greater judicial and court control. The Woolf proposals were operationalised in the form of new Civil Procedure Rules (1998), which provided for judicial case management; differing procedural tracks each reflecting the size and complexity of the case; the earlier exchange of information between the parties as well as a generally more cooperative approach including consideration of early settlement; a robust timetable of steps to be taken in the litigation process; and encouragement of mediation – in the sense, at least, of making a costs order against a party who did not show willingness to attempt mediation despite court encouragement. Thus, mediation comes close to being mandatory even though in the interim report Lord Woolf had declared 'I do not propose that ADR should be compulsory either as an alternative or as a preliminary to litigation ... I do, however, believe that the courts can and should play an important part ... in providing information about the availability of ADR and encouraging its use in appropriate cases' (Woolf, 1995: Chapter 18 paras. 3–4).

So common law courts were henceforth to be seen as *managers of negotiated settlement*, with their ultimate determinative powers in a last-resort, fall-back role. These courts can no longer be characterised as a largely immobile backdrop in the pre-trial period, awaiting a central role in trial and judgment. We discuss some features of this transformation in the direction of hybridisation further in Chapter 10.

Nevertheless, while the passage from Shapiro above is an invaluable reminder that courts are not exclusively devoted to the decision-making process of adjudication, and often in effect assume mediatory functions, and despite these changes in the direction of a more managerial role for judges, it should also be borne in mind that judges may in effect impose an outcome to the dispute on the parties by virtue of some preliminary judicial ruling. Thus, for example, in an essay analysing the changing relationship between adjudication and settlement in the United States, Kritzer observes that a significant number of cases are determined by authoritative decisions other than judgment. The claim often made that 'most civil cases settle' needs to be qualified because the decision to settle may, in fact, be a direct response to a significant

---

[7] The reader is, however, reminded that Genn's perceptive analysis of the situation was that cutting legal aid was a fundamentally important reason: 'in my view, the sense of urgency about a review of the civil courts came less from any new problems in civil justice and more from concern about expenditure on legal aid, and, paradoxically, the rising cost of criminal justice' (2012: 399).

umpiring decision imposed on the parties prior to the definitive judicial ruling on the principal issues in dispute.[8] This 'judicial shadow', which should also be seen as one from adjudication, hangs over and influences settlement processes in a variety of ways, as Kritzer points out:

> It is well known to those involved in the courts, either as practitioners or as researchers, that very few cases get the full adjudicatory treatment ending with a verdict ... and a judgment. The figures commonly cited range from 5 per cent to 10 per cent of cases filed ever getting to trial ... A typical assumption is that cases that are not resolved by trial are not adjudicated, and are not influenced by adjudication. In fact, ... adjudication is an explicit factor in the outcome of many cases [and] this is only the tip of the judicial 'shadow' because ... [there are difficulties in] assessing the role of adjudication as an implicit factor in the settlement process.

Detailed empirical analysis of court records shows that while the most commonly-held vision of adjudication is one of a trial before a judge or a jury, this is not an accurate description of what goes on in ordinary civil litigation.

> There are a variety of ways between trial and settlement by which a case can be resolved ... cases [may be] terminated through arbitration, decisions, or dismissal for cause; thus almost a quarter of the cases terminated through a decision of an adjudicator (and this excludes default judgments).

> But this is not the end of adjudicatory involvement. Many cases may be settled because of an adverse decision on the part of a judge ... the clearly looming visage of the judge was important in [a] substantial proportion of cases; and, it is equally likely that the potential of adjudication was at the least a dim specter for yet more cases.

> While the argument that the law or the coercive influence of potential adjudication plays an important part in the settlement of cases in our civil courts is not new, it is important to try to grasp the breadth of this influence. Much of the rhetoric surrounding the alternative dispute resolution movement ... seems to presume that it would be fairly easy to simply move cases out of the courts, and one item of evidence that seems to support this argument is the small percentage of cases that actually go to trial. Yet, focusing on the trial rate misses much of the role of adjudication in the resolution of cases brought to the civil justice system. Very simply put, the settlement of many (if not most) cases relies upon the adjudication of others; to decouple those that settle from those that are adjudicated misses the fundamental reality underlying the workings of the system ...

> In a sense, much of the discussion of alternative dispute resolution may have the world upside down. It may not be that we need to find alternatives to litigation or adjudication, but rather that we need to understand the impact of adjudication as the alternative to settlement, whether that settlement is reached

---

[8] See also Galanter and Cahill (1994).

through simple negotiations, mediation, or what might be called 'pseudo-adjudication' (mini-trials, summary trials, etc.).

For the judge interested in facilitating the disposition of cases, the message of this analysis is that a lot can be accomplished by adjudicating, and particularly if that adjudication is carried out in a manner that is predictable so that, where possible, parties are able to anticipate what the decision is likely to be.

Moreover, Kritzer suggests, our understanding of the term 'settlement' is too broad-brush, for there may be an important distinction between settlement for the right reasons and settlement for the wrong reasons.

Cases that leave the courts through settlement may exit because adjudication has resolved some or all of the key questions in dispute, even if the case did not go all the way to trial. Even where no adjudication takes place, settlement may occur for the 'right' reasons (e.g., the parties are able to agree upon the valuation appropriate for the case when there is no real dispute over damages). This is not to suggest that some settlements occur for the 'wrong' reasons (e.g., one party can no longer afford the costs of litigation, or the delay until the trial forces a party to take a lower settlement now than could be achieved through a jury trial). Rather, one cannot presume that all settlements are wrong or that all adjudicated outcomes are wrong (i.e., the world is not black and white). Thus, in . . . the discussion of adjudication, settlement, and alternative dispute resolution, researchers and reformers must come to grips with the problem of assessing when particular modes of resolution are good and bad, and when one mode of resolution is *better* than another (Kritzer, 1986: 161–5).

Of course, even within the same legal system judges may themselves adopt quite varying approaches to the judicial role, especially where they operate in courts in which they are allowed a good deal of discretion in their formulation and expression of the judicial role. This is demonstrated by Conley and O'Barr (1990: 106–11) in their analysis of the operation of small claims courts in various parts of the United States. The authors characterise *five* different judicial approaches to decision-making that are identified by their research findings – differing approaches that undermine the stereotype of the common law judge as an impassive umpire, at least in the context of the small claims court.

The courts of the state, in which civil judgments are rendered on behalf of the government, do not necessarily monopolise third-party decision-making in civil cases. Indeed, as with the development in the common law world of the system of Chancery courts applying rules of equity, and relying more on written procedures, as supplementary to the common law, alternative forms of adjudication may develop even within the state judicial system. This internal differentiation is today reflected in a wide range of specialised courts and tribunals, offering styles of umpiring and specialist knowledge that are claimed to be particularly suitable for the resolution of family, commercial, labour, immigration and other issues.

The Popular Element in Courts

The stereotype of the court is that of a dispute resolution mechanism whose powers of adjudication are exercised by professional, specialist and know-ledgeable decision-makers who are also members of the ruling elite. While this characterisation widely mirrors actual practice, explicit attempts have often been made for a variety of reasons to inject lay or populist elements into this state-sponsored umpiring process. In many such cases, however, it is clear that the popular element has been inserted not as a means of making the courts more accessible to the people but, rather, as a mechanism for enhancing central, state control. Thus, although the English jury may have come to represent by the nineteenth century a form of protection against a coercive judiciary, it has been asserted that it began life as 'an oppressive exercise of the highest powers of government. The jurors were compelled to answer under oath and became subject to penalties for perjury. No preordained rules set limits to the kinds of questions that might be asked' (Dawson, 1960: 119). The equivalent of the jury in the courts of the civilian tradition is the lay assessor whose significance often lies as much in the specialised, expert knowledge that he or she brings to the court as it does to the addition of a lay element. In many other situations, a system of lay judges is relied on to supplement a centralised system of professional judiciary and administration. Perhaps the best-known example of this is the development in England of the role and status of the justice of the peace. The system, however, was in reality much less an arrangement for promoting popular participation than it was a structure for enhancing the interests of central government.[9]

The emphasis on popular participation often appears in particularly dramatic form during the establishment and institutionalisation of socialist regimes. In the course of the revolution, the 'people's court' or 'tribunal' provides a popular forum in which 'people's justice' is imposed on class enemies (see, for example, Leng, 1967: 14–19). In the early years of a communist regime, too, these institutions may continue to be used as revolutionary instruments for assisting in the task of undermining the old order. These courts often have jurisdiction not only over criminal cases but also over problems relating to marriage, family and property. In the extract that follows, Sachs outlines the key features of the system of 'popular justice' that developed in Mozambique (1984: 101–4). Popular justice, he writes, was an essential part of a much wider process of social transformation, in which alternatives had to be found after the collapse of traditional power because it had become too closely identified with colonial power, so that when the latter was destroyed the former also collapsed with it.

> The nature of Portuguese colonialism forced it to adopt a high degree of direct state compulsion in its quest for labour, and the chiefs and indunas were given

---

[9] See, for example, Dawson (1960: 136–44).

important though junior tasks in the structure of compulsion so created . . . [and] . . . to the extent that the chiefs exercised power in colonial times they lost their popular authority; even the judicial power they exercised became tainted, since it came to be regarded as a perk for the services rendered to the colonial state, handsomely rewarded in terms of the gifts necessary to 'open' the court . . . in interviews with the new judges, a strongly expressed theme that emerges is the contrast they seek to establish between their work and the venality of the justice administered in the past by the regulos (chiefs) . . . the only custom that really counted in the courts of the chiefs in the late colonial period was the custom of visiting the chief's house the night before the hearing with a gift more extravagant than that given by the opponent.

The destruction of the institution of traditional power was accompanied in the post-colonial period by the creation of new organs of local power, in which active parts were played by women from the Women's Organisation and by young people from the Youth Organisation. The courts were accordingly not the first institutions to break away from the gerontocratic and sexist assumptions of traditional society, imposing as it were, new values from the top . . .

[But] if aspects of traditional law are rejected, that will be because they are regarded as feudal, as impediments to the creative capacity of the Mozambican people, and not because they are African or customary. Similarly, if the objective is eventually to eliminate completely the Portuguese legal codes, this is not because they were imposed by outsiders, but because their language, content and assumptions are inconsistent with the concrete legal needs of the Mozambican people . . . These are the fundamental questions: not 'African' versus 'Western'; 'customary' versus 'modern'.

[T]he central question [is one of] finding the correct strategies in order to relate what might be called a vast sector of informal popular justice, with all its improvisations, heterogeneity and conservatism, to the more dynamic, coherent and progressive Popular Justice system of the courts (Kritzer, 1986: 161–5).

The history of popular courts has, however, often been one of incorporation into a more regular system of socialist legality as administered by an authoritarian communist regime. They are frequently no more courts of the 'people' than the regime is a government for the 'people' – in reality, both are dominated by the Communist Party, and operate under close Party control and scrutiny. Hayden has explored the manner in which Yugoslav labour courts functioned in the late 1960s, and shown that in reality the apparent success of these 'social courts' in providing enhanced access to justice lies in their development of some of the characteristic features of regular rather than popular courts (1984: 235–43).

Tribunals

In England and Wales, one of the most important mechanisms for providing greater access to formal adjudicatory justice is the tribunal. This institution, which can be traced back to the earliest years of the last century, is now found in a wide variety of settings and varies considerably in its structure and processes. The principal function of the tribunal is as an administrative appeal body, hearing cases brought by citizens against decisions made on behalf of the state by civil servants and others, although some forms deal with private sector issues as, for example, in the case of industrial tribunals. The particular origins of the tribunal in this country would appear to lie in a felt need to provide an accessible, specialised forum for resolving disputes that arose as a result of reforming social welfare legislation introduced at the end of the first decade of the last century:

> in devising the national insurance scheme ... the Liberal Government of Lloyd George ... drew extensively on the social insurance policies of Bismark in Germany. Still convinced that the courts were inappropriate for hearing appeals of this kind, the British Government also adopted the Bismarkian idea of the tribunal. Hence, dissatisfied unemployment insurance claimants could appeal against the decision of an insurance officer to a 'court of referees'. Although labelled 'courts', courts of referees were nothing of the sort. They comprised three members, one appointed by the Board of Trade, one member from a panel representing local employers, and the final member from a workman's panel (Sainsbury and Genn, 1995: 417).

From this small beginning the idea of the tribunal has evolved significantly and come to enjoy widespread acceptance in this country, so that there are now well over sixty different tribunals operating currently. Sainsbury and Genn (1995) have argued that the civil justice reforms inspired by Lord Woolf missed an opportunity to enhance access to civil justice by failing to give sufficient regard to the potential role of tribunals.

Conclusions

Over the past half century and more, the role of courts and litigation has generally expanded. The courts in many parts of the world have become important fora for challenging legislative supremacy, governmental miscon-duct, securing human rights, and so on, often in the spirit of promoting the rule of law. But at the same time, the ADR movement has drawn attention strongly to the limitations of courts in providing access to justice and so there has been procedural experimentation and efforts to avoid recourse to the courts as a form for decision-making in civil justice. As we shall see in a later chapter, it may well be the case that we are now at a turning point where courts are coming back into fashion because they are incorporating elements of ODR which enables them to deliver civil justice with a significantly enhanced degree of efficiency, although doubts persist about the quality of justice delivered through online processes.

9

Umpiring: Arbitration

Introduction

In conceptual terms arbitration realises the foundational idea of the 'neutral stranger', standing ready to decide a question which the parties have brought before him or her. So here the umpire is privately chosen, and makes a decision within a procedural environment of the parties' choosing. But the contrast with state-sponsored adjudication is no longer so crisp as this ideal picture might imply. Arbitration, as an escape from the perceived problems of adjudication, has long been institutionalised within a number of locations, most notably in the commercial sphere, to the extent that notions of privacy and procedural informality have become much less significant. In its traditional 'pure' form arbitration is essentially private and voluntary, and is dependent on the parties' agreement to be bound by the decision of the arbitration panel – a creature of contractual agreement between the parties. However, arbitration is now sometimes also a compulsory, non-consensual, form of dispute settlement – it is used by the courts in a number of jurisdictions either to assist in especially troublesome types of cases, or to manage better the flow of routine cases.

However, it is important to bear in mind that even private arbitration typically involves the central elements of a court adjudication. That is, evidence and arguments are submitted to a neutral third party. That third party has the authority to issue a binding decision based on objective standards. Of course, there are important differences between the two processes, in particular, in private umpiring the parties typically attempt to resolve their disputes by recourse to procedures much less formal than those employed by the courts. In addition, the parties have both chosen to arbitrate, and selected the arbitrator themselves, or at least specified the arbitration panel from which the arbitrator will be drawn. But, in essence, arbitration is a private form of 'adjudication', with the third party intervening to control exchanges between both sides and to impose a decision. It is a form of private umpiring, however, which brings with it flexibility, simplified procedures and other advantages that have endeared it, in particular, to the commercial world.

It is possible to identify a number of key features of 'arbitration' of the private, voluntary kind, that is, the 'pure' or 'ideal' type of arbitration.

First, in its purer forms the parties either agree in advance that specified types of dispute will be arbitrated, or after a dispute has arisen they enter into an ad hoc agreement to arbitrate. The parties also agree that the arbitrator's decision will be binding on them. In many jurisdictions, courts will recognise and enforce agreements to arbitrate, and very often they will not provide any extended review of the merits of an arbitrator's decision. They will only consider setting aside the arbitration award on grounds of public policy or procedural irregularity. Indeed, looked at from the point of the state, arbitration has many advantages as a form of umpiring – it provides important interest groups with a certain and contextualised form of dispute resolution that has little or no draining effect on the resources of the state. However, as an institutionalised form of private umpiring it must be subjected to two particular kinds of limitation or control. First, it must not produce substantive outcomes that are unacceptable to the state – hence the public policy requirement that is found on a fairly widespread basis. Second, the state must continue to be able to make the claim that, in some respects at least, adjudication, that is, state umpiring, is fundamentally superior simply because it is state sponsored. Accordingly, the state retains the right to resist arbitration outcomes that result from the 'inferior' procedures on which arbitration relies.

Second, the usual practice is for arbitration to be carried out as a private process, and this approach to dispute settlement can take many forms because the parties have considerable freedom to choose the particular rules by which the arbitration will be conducted. They may, and often do, design the process to be employed, and provide the substantive standards to be used by the arbitrator in making a decision, these standards often being specified in the form of a contract.

Third, even in common law systems, the arbitrators do not consider themselves bound by any doctrine of precedent. Of course, in a number of fields, such as labour or industrial relations, arbitration awards are published, and arbitrators will look to such awards for guidance. But the arbitrator generally is free to decide the outcome on the merits of each party's position in the instant case.

Fourth, in arbitration the parties themselves are able to select the umpire who will decide the outcome. Typically, they use this freedom to select a decision-maker with expert knowledge of the substantive facts of the dispute because he or she has personal experience of the same sort of business and therefore a good grasp of the working norms and shared understandings of the trade. Thus, there is no need to attempt to educate a judge and, where employed, a jury in the specifics of the business activities involved. This need to educate is a hurdle that may, in some circumstances, be well nigh insurmountable and, in any event, will cost time and therefore money to deal with in a court case. Indeed, we might emphasise at this point that the origins of 'modern arbitration' appear to lie in the preference of eighteenth-century English merchants to resolve their disputes in accordance with trade customs rather than by 'the laws of the state', and to rely upon their own kind rather than the state for decision-making. To this day, this aspect of arbitration remains very important. The trade-specialist arbitrator's expertise may be crucial when the dispute is founded on a problem of contract interpretation that, in turn, is based on some disagreement over the nature of the trading customers' understanding of the nature of the commodities being traded; or when the dispute concerns the belief by one party that the other party has supplied goods that fail to meet certain 'expected' standards.

Of course, over the years, and in various jurisdictions, arbitration has increasingly come to be used in a wide variety of disputing contexts. Four areas of economic activity where arbitration has for some time often been very commonly used are: labour relations, construction work, manufacturer-consumer relations and insurance. Its perceived successes in these fields have further encouraged reliance on arbitration in such areas as medical malpractice, prisoner grievances, environmental disputes, and so on. Lon Fuller examines two of the fundamental problems that can arise in one of the most significant of these specialised fields, namely labour relations.

He points to the existence of two principal conceptions of the arbitration process. In one understanding, the arbitrator is seen primarily as a judge, whose task is to 'do justice according to the rules imposed by the parties' contract, leaving the chips to fall where they may' (Fuller, 1963: 3). In the other view, the arbitrator adapts her or his procedures according to the nature of the case being handled, exercising 'a roving commission to straighten things out, the immediate controversy marking the occasion for, but not the limits of, his intervention' (Fuller, 1963: 4). Similarly, the first perspective sees the collective bargaining agreement or labour contract as a firmly legal document and to be interpreted as such. The other is that the collective bargaining agreement is a uniquely constituted document which serves as 'a charter of the parties' rights and a set of resolutions never really expected to be fully realised in practice' (Fuller, 1963: 5). However, in the realities of arbitration practice, the approach taken by arbitrator is not always as consistent as this picture suggests so that, for example, a strict constructionist may be able to coax an agreement by skilful and subtle use of her or his reputation for strict interpretation, hinting at outcomes, and gently threatening a decision.

Another important feature of the arbitration process is that its ideology and reality may come to be quite divergent. The 'perceived' benefits of private arbitration are often claimed to be: privacy of the proceedings – if the parties wish their dispute resolution to be shielded from public scrutiny, arbitration, a private forum, is preferable to the courts, which rarely deny public access; procedural informality; expertise of the decision-maker; finality of the decision – no appeal; low cost, especially if lawyers are not used; and speed – the parties do not have to wait for a trial date to be set, but can proceed to arbitration as soon as they are ready. These successes have become something of an 'ideology' of arbitration. However, in well-developed systems of arbitration this ideology may have little to do with the reality. Costs can escalate quickly. Established arbitrators with good reputations may charge highly for travel time and study time. There are also sometimes substantial costs for mundane matters such as hire of the meeting place or providing a transcription of the hearing and of course, in large commercial cases the parties may feel impelled to employ legal representation. A 'queue' may well develop – the arbitrator with a high reputation may take a very long time to resolve the dispute, because he or she has a heavy case load. Moreover, the parties to such disputes may themselves take a very long time to agree on the arbitrator and a hearing date.

One reason for such developments is that a process of 'institutionalisation' almost inevitably takes place even in the face of efforts to keep arbitration pure, flexible and simple – new 'procedural norms' are almost necessarily developed to deal with perceived problems, so that with the passage of time the hearings become legalistic and inflexible. In other words, arbitration has an inherent tendency to become counterproductive in terms of time, costs and formality. To this difficulty may be added the criticism that arbitration often suffers from a number of interrelated difficulties that may be thought of as reflecting the practice as opposed to the rhetoric or ideology of arbitration. These include: low quality of arbitrators, who are often perceived as being 'unsuccessful professionals'; a tendency on the part of arbitrators not to adjudicate properly but rather to try to compromise – in particular, in order to maintain good relations with an otherwise 'losing party'; linked to this tendency is the problem that anticipation of an imposed 'compromise' solution may encourage inflexibility in the disputing parties' 'negotiating' positions, and this necessitates reliance on special forms of arbitration (such as final offer arbitration) to deal with the problem.

In other words, as a result of pressures of institutionalisation and imperfect control of practice, there may be an inherent tendency for arbitration to lapse into a very second-rate version of court adjudication. This, in turn, may help to turn a particular area of arbitration into a battleground between legal specialists – the lawyers, who want greater and tighter legal control of arbitration, and the trade specialists, that is, experts in the practice and customary norms and expectations of a field of economic activity who try to resist the intrusion of lawyers.[1]

Arbitration – Court-linked

In recent years, there have been developments, especially in the United States, in the direction of so-called 'compulsory arbitration'. For example, the parties may be required to use a system annexed to state or federal trial courts if the case involves claims for money damages below a certain amount, and the

[1] On the 'juridification' of arbitration, see Flood and Caiger (1993).

case does not fall within certain specified exceptional situations. Because the decisions made by arbitrators in these court-annexed systems are not binding – the parties have a right to trial *de novo* – such systems are perhaps better characterised as a mixed process. Thus, one of the main goals of court-annexed arbitration is to use non-binding arbitration to promote early settlement. However, this use does not constitute traditional arbitration; the decisions of the arbitrators are not binding. Nor does it merely constitute a form of negotiation because an adjudicative process is actively used to promote settlement. As a result, we consider this and other forms of arbitration which are used in close conjunction with other primary processes in Chapter 8.

Arbitration – International

Over the past few decades, an important area of development in arbitration has been the increasing tendency for international business disputes to be resolved through the process of private arbitration. The emergence of international commercial arbitration has clearly been stimulated in part by the growing processes of globalisation of economic activity. In their impressive study, Yves Dezalay and Bryant Garth describe the emergence of the system of private international justice, and some of the current lines of development in the world of international commercial arbitration.

By the mid-1990s they could reliably report that 'international commercial arbitration is now flourishing; it is the accepted method for resolving transnational commercial disputes' (Dezalay and Garth, 1996: 311). Its rapid development in the second half of the twentieth century is attributed to a number of factors including: the cold war, the interventionism of the welfare state, and the state interventionism. In seeking to understand the nature of international commercial arbitration we should recall, for example, that in the first half of the twentieth century arbitration declined rather than expanded as a result in part of the development of the New Deal in the United States and welfare states elsewhere, so that new regulatory systems became more powerful and important at the expense of arbitration.

More generally, we can see that arbitration is constantly pulled towards two contradictory roles, business interests at one end of the spectrum, and the law and its application at the other. A key institutional factor in the development of international commercial arbitration was therefore to be found in the role of the International Chamber of Commerce (ICC). This body initially looked for arbitrators drawn from academic circles so that 'the ICC represented . . . an alliance between the European grand professors and their disciples from countries at the periphery. It was organized around institutions like the Hague Academy of International Law and doctrines that reflect a typical academic neutrality – exemplified by the lex mercatoria. This learned investment served to break the stigma associated with business justice as a second-class justice' (Dezalay and Garth, 1996: 313).

But in addition to this academic influence, a core feature of the ICC approach was that it served as a private institutional platform that did not draw upon the rules and regulations of the nation state. The ICC was and still is an organisation of private business so that, for example, 'the ICC could persuasively argue that the arbitration of disputes with third-world or Communist states was simply a matter of private, commercial arbitration' (Dezalay and Garth, 1996: 313). The ICC was able to claim that it was not beholden to Western states, but also the international commercial arbitration was entirely neutral. 'The academic world of learned law was able to provide the neutral authority through the *lex mercatoria*, and this learned doctrine was validated by the authority of the European grand professors over their disciples in the third world. This authority facilitated the putting aside of potentially threatening third-worldist legal claims' (ibid.). The ICC prospered on the basis of their structural foundation, though in recent years there have been changes resulting from the growing involvement of US-style legal practice, different ideas between Asia and the West about the issues such as human rights and democratic governance, state involvement in the expanding world of multilateral and bilateral investment treaties, and the growth of supranational agencies, such as GATT, the EU, NAFTA, the WTO and ICSID. In this increasingly complex environment, future developments will very much depend on the responses of various national based groupings, 'who fight ... on the terrain of the international' (Dezalay and Garth, 1996: 317).

Dezalay and Garth also encourage us to understand that 'international commercial arbitration' is not one entity but, rather, many:

> despite the networks and relationships associated with international commercial arbitration ... there is no objective thing called 'international commercial arbitration'.

> It is important not to reproduce uncritically, the discourse of those who proclaim that transnational business disputing or international commercial arbitration by definition refers to the particular representation that supports their position. Success in international commercial arbitration, indeed, comes in part by persuading others that the position of particular groups and individuals does represent international commercial arbitration. There is, therefore, an incentive – not unusual in law or, for that matter, in any marketing exercise – to try to 'make it by faking it', exaggerating the experience of individuals and institutions in order to allow them to gain acceptance as successful: Contests about definitions and details of practice, in short, must be part of the object of study (Dezalay and Garth, 1996: 31–2).[2]

---

[2] We should also note development of international investment arbitration, with its dispute resolution system, the International Centre for Settlement of Investment Disputes (ICSID). See for example, Nottage (2014).

Processual Styles in International Arbitration from a Comparative Perspective

Another factor encouraging growth of international commercial arbitration around the world over the past few decades has been its 'transplantability'. In addition to the 1958 New York Convention (the Convention on the Recognition and Enforcement of Foreign Arbitral Awards), the foundational instrument for international arbitration, which has assisted by requiring courts of contracting states to recognise private agreements to arbitrate and to recognise and enforce arbitration awards made in other contracting states, the 1985 UNCITRAL Model Law on International Commercial Arbitration was specifically drafted to encourage 'borrowing' by providing harmonised norms and principles for national legislation to regulate the private processes of arbitration. There are more than 100 jurisdictions around the world who have adopted, or enacted legislation, based on the Model Law.[3] Elsewhere there are plenty of examples of more ad hoc approaches to borrowing. For example, in Hong Kong, now a highly important centre for international commercial arbitration, the embrace of modern arbitration began in 1982, when a modified form of the 1979 Arbitration Act of England and Wales was adopted in Hong Kong. That formed the basis for the subsequent creation of a Hong Kong Arbitration Centre which has played an important role in arbitration in East Asia. That centre, too, has adopted the UNCITRAL Model Law, as well as elements of ADR in its services.

An obvious and crucially important aspect of the localisation of the standards and norms of international commercial arbitration is the extent to which a local jurisdiction is prepared to adopt the UNCITRAL Model Law on International Commercial Arbitration. Not all jurisdictions do adopt the Model Law, and often it is adopted with some local adaptations. As we have seen, some observers and practitioners see the spread of international commercial arbitration as a site of conflict and competition, with differences in legal culture and professional rivalry causing friction. And this competition and variation makes it difficult to see in international commercial arbitration a unified identity. However, other commentators see international commercial arbitration as a creature of convergence and exchange, with a fusion of common law and civil law procedural traditions creating a new phenomenon of an 'international commercial arbitration culture' . In an interesting analysis, Tom Ginsberg argues that the concept of legal culture can be used to highlight one very important aspect of the development of international commercial arbitration. That is, the development of international commercial arbitration – fuelled by economic pressures – is a process which has led to the creation of a

---

[3] See UNCITRAL Model Law on International Commercial Arbitration (1985), with amendments as adopted in 2006, available at www.uncitral.org/uncitral/en/uncitral_texts/arbitration/ 1985Model_arbitration_status.html, accessed 2 December 2019.

distinctive culture of arbitration, and this international culture of arbitration supplants older models of international commercial arbitration as well as local legal cultures of arbitration (Ginsberg, 2003).

The issue of the relationship between culture and arbitration is also taken up in an essay by Laura Pair in which she acknowledges that institutional arbitrations, because they tend to take place with clearer, more well-defined rules of procedure, tend to be less susceptible to cultural influences than ad hoc arbitral proceedings (Pair, 2002–3: 58). Nevertheless, she argues cogently that even in institutional arbitrations differences in legal tradition may well influence the arbitral process significantly, especially as it is an alternative form of dispute resolution and therefore arguably more susceptible to cultural reshaping than (say) trial proceedings. We can also see that differing kinds of cultural influence can affect the lawyers' and parties' expectations of the procedure used in arbitrations so that, it could be argued, 'a common law, Anglo-American Lawyer will more likely expect a highly adversarial approach, while a civil law East Asian will expect that an inquisitorial and conciliatory approach be taken by the arbitral panel and all parties involved' (Pair, 2002–3: 60).

In drawing the broad contrast between common law and civilian practitioners, she suggests that the common law practitioner involved in an arbitration is more used to and more comfortable with an adversarial approach in which the arbitrator, like the judge, has a relatively limited role. This will affect the approach of the practitioner. The adversarial approach may affect matters at all stages of the proceedings including notification, identification of facts, responsibilities of the parties, and so on. The civil law practitioner expects a more active decision-maker, and in particular one who is familiar with inquisitorial ways of proceeding with responsibility for ensuring that she or he has all the evidence to make a good decision. As a result, even if proceedings are based on the UNCITRAL Model Law on Commercial Arbitration, there will likely be some significantly different expectations of proceedings in four or more ways: the orality of proceedings, discovery and pre-hearing procedure, treatment of witnesses – especially the parties and the use of cross-examination – and style of record keeping.

Thus, The UNCITRAL Model Law Rule 24(1) allows the arbitral tribunal to make the decision on whether or not there will be an oral hearing for the presentation of evidence and arguments. A hearing is to be held if a party so requests. However, Rule 24 does not indicate how much weight will be given to the oral hearing, and how much detail will be covered in the oral hearing if there is one. Clearly, the arbitrator's view of the necessity and conduct of the hearing will be important. Lawyers who practise in common law jurisdictions would likely tend to prefer the oral hearing over pleadings, and expect weight to be attached to her or his advocacy. But the civilian system practitioner will tend to want all the relevant information identified and provided in detail and in writing as soon as possible.

The UNCITRAL Model Law has only limited provisions on pre-hearing procedures. Rule 23(1) stipulates that parties should support their claims and defences with all the relevant documents. The Rule does, however, also permit references to materials to be used as a basis for evidence to be submitted later, unless otherwise agreed. In addition, The UNCITRAL Model Law Rule 24(3) requires all the material submitted to the arbitration panel also to be submitted to the other party. This leaves a lot of space for culture to create divergent expectations. The common law advocate expects rigorous pre-hearing discovery, and also expects to use it strategically – to delay rendering information in order to make a strategic gain. The civilian advocate on the other hand expects disclosure of all relative information as soon as possible, and over a longer period of time, to be reviewed by the decision-maker regardless of when it became known. Clearly, there is potential here for conflicting expectations in the conduct of an arbitration.

The manner in which witnesses are to be handled is another aspect of this problem. Thus, a third area of difference is to be found in the treatment of witnesses – especially the parties and cross-examination. The UNCITRAL Model Law has very little to say about this aspect of proceedings. So, there may be issues over: whether or not a party may be a witness, whether or not the witness statements may be written, whether written statements take precedence over the evidence of witnesses who have been directly examined, and whether cross-examinations should take place. Thus, a practitioner from a common law jurisdiction, would expect to be able to call a party as a witness, whereas in civilian jurisdictions the tendency is not to allow this – mainly because the expectation is that the position of the parties will be revealed through other documents. The practice in international commercial arbitration has moved to the common law approach, but in other aspects of this issue the matter is less settled. For example, the common law advocate will feel comfortable with cross-examination, seeing this as a crucial tool for testing witness credibility, and for bringing out facts that may not otherwise be presentable. In civilian legal culture it is the decision-maker – the judge – who takes on the role of assessing witness credibility and seeing the relative importance of witness statements.

Moreover, the UNCITRAL Model Law also has little to say about record keeping. In major proceedings in common law systems, there is usually a system in which the proceedings are recorded word for word. In civilian systems, the approach to recording the proceedings is less stringent, with the decision-maker taking notes of a witnesses as she or he sees fit. In an arbitral proceeding, this might then be followed by the parties discussing the notes and supplementing them to prepare a written summary. This will often refer to documentary evidence as well, and thus may well reduce the impact of cross-examination.

These differences, clearly, are important for looking at culture and international commercial arbitration in different parts of the world, including Asia and Africa. This is because, of course, the common law and civilian traditions, through colonialism, are entrenched in specific legal systems of former colonial territories, and even where they are not the direct relate of colonisation, they are transplants from European systems that have been chosen as templates for legal modernisation. China, Japan and Thailand are obvious examples in the East Asia region.

Although it is difficult to make broad generalisations about regional cultural influences without slipping into stereotypes, it is worthwhile trying to identify some broad areas of cultural influences on local expectations of international commercial arbitration. When we look at non-Islamic Africa, we can see that there is probably little that we may identify as an 'African' distinctiveness in procedural rules, Indeed, in a continent with such diverse cultures, we would not expect much procedural uniformity. But there still may well be important culturally influenced expectations. Arguably there is a dislike for arbitration based on a fear that the proceeding may favour the stronger party. More conciliation-focused processes are favoured over especially adversarial arbitration processes. And if adversarial proceedings are contemplated, then the parties and their lawyers seem to turn to the courts for their forum. In francophone areas of Africa, it seems that international commercial arbitration was suppressed to a significant degree, and this too may help to explain why there are relatively few African arbitrators involved in international commercial arbitration.

We can identify two broad areas of cultural influence in East Asia. First, as a legacy of legal modernisation programmes of the twentieth century, there is a significant division between civilian and common-law jurisdictions. Secondly, in those areas of East Asia strongly influenced by Confucian values, there may be said to be an entrenched preference for non-confrontational methods of dispute resolution. We have seen above that this amounts to a 'harmony ideology' – that is, a concern with harmonious social relations in the community rather than a culture of rights assertiveness. Thus, dispute-resolvers have been expected to act out of a sense of public duty. Judges are expected to bring about a good settlement through mediation rather than give judgment. In addition, confidentiality tends to be viewed distinctively, in the sense that it is seen as less important than it is in 'the West'. East Asian parties, more than their Western counterparts, want to maintain 'face' by keeping proceedings and the information they reveal as confidential as possible. We can see some of the cultural distinctiveness when we look at the rules for international commercial arbitration of CIETAC (the China International Economic and Trade Arbitration Commission), and in particular the emphasis in those rules on mediation as preceding arbitration in the dispute resolution process.

In the Islamic Middle East a principal influencing factor is the Sharia. Although not the case everywhere in the Middle East, the tendency has been to see international commercial arbitration in terms of 'conciliation'. A central concept is that of *sulh*, or a religious and social duty to reconcile. The Koran encourages parties to use *sulh* in order to resolve their disputes and to promote 'reconciliation' between them. An arbitrator (or judge) may not turn the parties away if they cannot be reconciled. There is a duty on any person who umpires a case and apportions blame between parties to do so with fairness and justice, and if necessary impose *sulh* between conflicting parties. The main aim of arbitration is to ensure that disputes between Muslims are resolved amicably and justly.

Conclusions

Arbitration is, like adjudication, a form of umpiring in which a third party imposes a decision on the disputing parties. Arbitration has a long history and is found in a wide range of legal cultures around the world, as well as manifesting differences that relate to the broad distinction between arbitration in the common law and civil law traditions. It is also increasingly the case that many business parties prefer to use arbitration to resolve international commercial and investment disputes, finding that recourse to the courts is unsatisfactory in several respects. There is an immense range of arbitration processes that can be applied to deal with a dispute, and also divergent cultural values have an influence. The recourse to arbitration especially by business parties has been very important in promoting acceptance of alternative dispute resolution. But at the same time we have to bear in mind that it is a form of imposed decision-making and therefore fundamentally a type of umpiring. In that sense arbitration should not be seen as part of ADR (Al-Ramahi, 2008).

Hybrid Forms and Processual Experimentation

Introduction

In examining in detail three of the primary processes of decision-making – negotiation, mediation and umpiring – we have tried to give these modes an analytical clarity that is not necessarily revealed so sharply in real-life forms. At the same time, we have left largely unexamined the relationships prevailing between these different processes, and the relative value attached to them, where they are found together in a particular culture. But we have already noted, in our chapter analysing processes of negotiation (Chapter 6), the manner in which negotiations are routinely pursued through litigation in the common law world, as a result of the unwillingness of lawyers to contemplate the construction of an agreed resolution to a dispute without mobilisation of the court process. So bilateral processes may take place along the route towards the court. We also saw how in many legal cultures judges may depart from an adjudicatory procedure, abandoning a binary, win-or-lose approach to decision-making in favour of encouraging the parties to construct their own solutions. In some jurisdictions, the role of the judge may be seen as one in which mediation is stressed, and adjudication to be relied on to secure an outcome only as a final and unwelcome last resort (see, for example, the case of contemporary China: Fu and Palmer, 2017; Palmer, 1989). Moreover, as Gulliver has observed, the role of mediator in some cultures is conceptualised and practised in directive, almost 'umpire-like terms' (Gulliver, 1979: 225–6). In any event, the accumulation of experience by a mediator may tend to encourage an active, intrusive, manipulative approach, resulting in an imposed solution that, in reality, crosses the line into adjudication.

Examples from the Borderlands

So it is not always easy in the real world to draw a clear line between umpiring, negotiating and mediating processes. The extent to which such departures from the primary processual forms is officially accepted, or even encouraged, varies considerably from one culture to another, as Gulliver has emphasised. His work offers analysis of a number of ethnographic examples of practices that lie in the borderlands between umpiring, negotiating and mediating processes – but argues that these do not invalidate the basic analytical value of the distinction.

One important example to which Gulliver points, is the account by Laura Nader (based on her field research in the late 1950s in rural Mexico) of the decision-making style of local judges (*presidente*) in a village known as Ralu'a. This 'umpire' carefully shaped his umpiring duties in order to take into account local culture and its social realities, so that – as Nader expresses the matter in one of her early essays – the 'judgement that the *presidente* gives on a matter is always a compromise ... The *presidente*'s understanding of what is best for "making the balance" – which as often or not means the restoration of relations to a former condition ... in which conflict was absent' (Nader, 1969: 84–5). In handling cases, the *presidente* is at once a mediator, adjudicator and group therapist.

In a case carefully analysed by Nader, the *presidente* dealt with a complaint made by a woman who alleged that when she and her small son were working in a field, a young man had assaulted her son, who then required medical treatment. The assailant complained that the son has consistently bad-mouthed him but the mother did little to stop the verbal abuse and, indeed, defended the son against the allegations of troublemaking made against him. The assailant's grandmother owned the field in which the mother and son had been working, and so the *presidente* sought to understand better the dynamics of the dispute by determining that the complainant and her son had been working in the field not at the suggestion of the assailant but, rather, at the request of the defendant's grandmother. Given this situation, clearly the assailant was unlikely to have made the decision to allow the mother and son to work the fields, and the grandmother's decision may have been an aggravating factor. The *presidente* then sought to bring an end to the dispute not by detailed examination of the facts and determination of fault but, rather, by focusing on the specific issue of compensation. He asked the plaintive how much she expected to receive from the defendant in order to pay for her son's treatment. The mother demanded 30 pesos, whereas the defendant counter-offered only 20 pesos. The mother was then asked by the *presidente* if she would accept the counter-offer, and the case was quickly concluded when she accepted. The *presidente* was central to this process, handling the mother's complaint and imposing himself on the defendant. The mother looked to him for some sort of decision in her favour, and the *presidente* clearly acted with authority in summoning the defendant and controlling the hearings. So, in several respects, he conducted himself as an umpire. However, he did not expressly make a judgment of guilt in terms of the defendant's conduct, only implying such a judgment by asking the plaintive what payment she wanted in order to correct the problem. However, the defendant did not challenge that implication, instead focusing on the specific question of the amount of the compensation. In handling the case in this way, the *presidente* was seeking to achieve a result agreeable to both parties – in effect, he was encouraging the parties themselves to negotiate a facilitated agreement which then became an outcome of which he approved. So while the *presidente* was very much administering the proceedings and exercising the authority of an umpire, the reality was that the process was shaped in such a way that the umpire merely confirmed the party's own agreement. It seems clear that the *presidente* could have imposed a decision – and, indeed, did indirectly make a decision – but in the context of a small village characterised by multiplex face-to-face relations he preferred the parties to themselves arrive at a consensual outcome. And in handling the case, 'what is important . . . is not what is "objectively so" but rather the parties' perception of what is so [and] fault-finding and fact-finding [are] in general played down considerably' (Nader, 1969: 86).[1]

Another example highlighted by Gulliver (1979: 30–3) is drawn from the writings of Barton on the Malay people known as the Ifugao, where the mediators or '*monkalun*' play multiple roles. In Barton's account, the *monkalun* combines the role of mediator and umpire:

> From the time at which a controversy is formally entered into, the principals and their kin are on a basis of theoretical . . . enmity. A great number of taboos keep them apart. Diplomatic relations between the two parties have been broken off and all business pertaining to the case is transacted through the third party, the *monkalun*. He hears the testimony that each side brings forward to support its contention. Through him each controversant is confronted with the testimony of the other. It is greatly to the interest of the *monkalun* to arrange a peaceful settlement, not only because he usually receives a somewhat larger fee in such case, but because the peaceful settlement of cases in which he is mediator builds up a reputation for him, so that he is frequently called and so can earn many fees. To the end of arranging this peaceful settlement, the *monkalun* reports to each party to the controversy the strong points of the testimony in favor of the other party, and oftentimes neglects the weaknesses. (Barton, 1919: 95–6).

Gulliver concludes that in:

> the decision-making process among the Ifugao . . . the disputants retained the ability to define the issues, reach a verdict, make offers, and reject or accept the offers. They were affected by the influence, persuasion, and pressures of the go-between acting as facilitating mediator. Although the go-between backed his varied suggestions by reference to allegedly accepted norms, he shifted his emphasis and reference according to his audience and the desired responses he sought. Both in the particular case and from Barton's other accounts, it seems clear that for the Ifugao people there was no question that a go-between himself should, or in fact did, make the decision . . . The disputants retained that ability, in practice as in normative expectation, so that the outcome came from their interdependent decisions (Gulliver, 1979: 33).

---

[1] Gulliver's account is at 1979: 29–30.

And indeed, according to Barton, in some cases the decision-making authority was very explicitly in the hands of the go-between:

> The *monkalun* [becomes an] umpire in trials by ordeal. He interprets undue haste or a faulty performance as a confession of guilt. On the day following the trial by fire or hot water he goes to the house of the accused and examines the hand and forearm. If he finds white inflamed blisters, he pronounces him guilty. In the case of a duel, he pronounces the one struck by the missile guilty. The Ifugaos believe that the gods of war and justice turn missiles aside from the innocent in these duels. For the umpire to be manifestly unfair, would be for him seriously to imperil his own life (Barton, 1919: 99).

In reflecting on these 'marginal case' examples, drawn from studies of rural Mexico and northern Luzon in the Philippines, Gulliver concludes that while adjudication, mediation and negotiation are useful analytical constructs:

> Purely within the context of an ethnographic analysis of these particular cases it may not much matter what we call the processes of the treatment of disputes. It might be sufficient to understand them as well as possible and to discover their significance in the ongoing life of the local community and the wider society (Gulliver, 1979: 33).

Even under conditions where the primary processes remain distinct, they may still be found closely linked together in processual terms. Perhaps, for example, there are strong cultural imperatives requiring that negotiation, mediation and adjudication be resorted to in sequence, with parties moving on from one process to another only where attempts to achieve an outcome through one 'stage' have been exhausted. We may see this serial application of differing decision-making processes through examination of the procedural values prevailing in the Southern African Tswana kingdoms of the Kalahari during the nineteenth century, retained at local level under the Bechuanaland Protectorate and surviving on under the Republic of Botswana. There the parties are required to attempt negotiation first, resort to mediatory help where that fails and to seek an adjudicated solution only in the last resort (Comaroff and Roberts, 1986: 108–10).

Towards Conscious Creation of Hybrid Processes

Historically, however, it is also clear that such orderly understandings have not generally characterised the arrangements of the common law world. We have already stressed, at several points in this study, the entangled relationship of lawyer negotiations and the pursuit of adjudication in contemporary common law jurisdictions. But this 'processual anarchy' went much further than this. While judgment – subject to appeal – remained final and authoritative, there were no clear understandings as to the relative beauty of different modes of resolution or as to a fixed processual trajectory.

In many societies in the West, widely shared folk assumptions about the handling of conflict attach a high value *both* to decision-making through consensual agreement and to justice (especially as achieved by court-based adjudication). So, in this culture, common understandings seem to point us in two rather different directions, evoking separate images of apparently equal purity and allure. Yet the relationship and relative value of these two approaches to handling trouble has never been entirely clear. Parties could, until recently, resort to trial and judgment without trying any other process first.

However, in many parts of the common law world, the past three decades have seen significant moves away from entrenched, historic understandings about process. In broad, schematic terms three important changes are increasingly visible. First, the old processual anarchy is under challenge from a growing perception that a negotiated solution should always be sought initially. Secondly, the courts are increasingly seen as having a primary responsibility to sponsor settlement. They can no longer wait impassively to fulfil a final role in litigation, trial and judgment. Thirdly, a welter of hybrid forms has grown up around each of the primary processes. Legal professionals – especially judges and lawyers – have played a key role in the evolution of these hybrid forms, which now represent the vanguard of ADR development. Indeed, the emergence of these new forms may be viewed as something of a co-option of the ADR movement by specialists trained in legal rules and procedures. These developments have in many cases been given official blessing.

Many observers now see such experimentation as having attained sufficient maturity and sophistication that we can speak of it as a form of 'systems design'. From this perspective, when a lawyer or some other dispute resolution specialist creates a new method that fits more closely with the perceived needs of the parties, using a combination of several forms of intervention in a new processual mix to meet this goal, she or he is often designing a new system such that it (hopefully) constitutes a better 'forum for the fuss' at hand. Thus, for example, Greenberg argues for a new, more reconciliation-focused, approach to dealing with discrimination at the work place – one in which employees and employers are encouraged to work together to create a discrimination-free work environment, rather than see them pitted against each other in court, or failing to secure a mutually satisfactory outcome through more conventional negotiation and mediation processes. She argues for a three dimensional 'system': education about implicit bias in workplace conduct; a transformative mediation process; and an assessment system that provides for public accountability and recognition for affirmative actions taken by employers and employees to address work place discrimination caused by implicit bias. In such a system, the three components encourage in employees and employers 'the cognitive and psychological shifts that are essential predicates for true reconciliation to take place' (Greenberg, 2015: 78). Many other examples of processual innovation, however, are directly linked to the umpiring processes of adjudication and arbitration, and are also – as we have suggested – an important aspect of the institutionalisation of ADR, redefining 'alternative' processes of mediation and negotiation so that they become part of a more formal, mainstream, approach to dispute resolution.

This general tendency towards the emergence of hybrid forms over the past four decades or so has a number of overlapping strands, but these may be essentially characterised in terms of modifications to each of the three primary processes already discussed. First, there have been attempts to enhance lawyer negotiations through the injection of facilitatory forms that mimic adjudication so that, somewhat paradoxically, ADR in this context means some sort of re-imposition of adjudicatory elements and values. Examples of these initiatives are discussed later in this chapter. In many of them, specialised forecasting procedures are inserted in the process of negotiation, and the parties are themselves drawn back into the process with the support of additional lawyers in non-aligned, advisory or consultancy roles. Alongside resort to these specialised devices for forecasting outcomes and sponsoring settlement, there have been a number of developments in the manner in which mediation is practised including, in particular, its linkage to arbitration to produce so-called 'med-arb', the annexing of mediation to the court and, in family disputes, the combination of therapy and mediation. At the same time there have been a number of attempts to refurbish adjudication by modifying or supplementing the trial process with further devices – a number of these refurbishment efforts being closely related to those developed by lawyers in support of their negotiations. These court-based initiatives include judicial settlement, early neutral evaluation, court-annexed arbitration and the summary jury trial. There have also been important developments in the field of arbitration.

Settlement as Civil Justice

In looking at these still evolving processes of hybridisation, the place to begin is with the contemporary representation and practice of civil justice itself. Right across the common law world, large-scale changes in governmental understanding and management of civil disputes have become visible over three decades or more, as we have indicated in earlier chapters. At the heart of these changes lies a growing identification of 'settlement' as an approved, privileged objective of civil justice. The courts present themselves not just as agencies offering judgment but also as sponsors of negotiated agreement.

In England the transformation to settlement first appeared as spontaneous, piecemeal initiatives within the judiciary, and are now drawn together and given official blessing through entirely re-cast Civil Procedure Rules (CPR) which came into force in April 1999.[2] On one level this apparently striking

---

[2] The CPR are available through the Ministry of Justice web pages, available at www.justice.gov.uk/courts/procedure-rules/civil, accessed 17 December 2019.

break with the past did no more than endorse what had been long established practice – the use of 'litigation' as the vehicle for lawyer negotiations. What was different was the idea of active judicial commitment to this process. The revisionist approach to civil procedure was expressed in the Civil Procedure Rules, which introduced two radical and novel features:

- First, an explicit attempt is made to construct a pre-litigation phase in which the conduct of the respective legal teams is prescribed and potentially enforced through cost sanctions. The shape of the pre-litigation phase is laid down in *Pre-Action Protocols*.
- Secondly, in providing *a strict regime of case management* once litigation is initiated, 'settlement' is explicitly prioritised as the primary objective of civil justice.

The Rules begin with a broad programmatic statement. This identifies an 'overriding objective' which is 'to enable the court to deal with cases justly' (Rule 1.1(1)). The Rules go on to provide that 'the court must further the overriding objective by actively managing cases' (Rule 1.1(4)). This requirement (note the imperative tone: 'the court must . . .') signals the government's determination to adopt and consolidate the intention of the senior judiciary 'to change the whole culture, the ethos, applying in the field of civil litigation'.[3] This procedural regime thus departs from the historical position under which English judges have allowed the parties to prepare for adversarial trial very much in their own way and at their own pace, dealing with 'interlocutory' matters only where the parties bring them to their attention. The court is no longer a potent but immobile backdrop in the pre-trial period, awaiting its central role in trial and judgment.

Let us now look at the core features of the system put in place by the Civil Procedure Rules.

The Pre-litigation Phase

Looking first at the attempt to police the pre-litigation phase, we see on the part of government a bold, unprecedented ambition to police an area of activity formerly treated unambiguously as in the 'private' sphere. In all types of civil dispute, parties are now expected to follow *pre-action protocols* that set out the steps parties are expected to take before issuing court proceedings. For some types of dispute, specific pre-action protocols exist; in all other cases the parties are expected to follow the general *Practice Direction for Pre-action Conduct and Protocols*.[4] The Direction provides specific guidance: 'the court

[3] The Lord Chief Justice, announcing the general Practice Direction of 24 January 1995: [1995] 1 WLR 262.
[4] Available at www.justice.gov.uk/courts/procedure-rules/civil/rules/pd_pre-action_conduct, accessed 2 December 2019.

will expect the parties, in accordance with the overriding objective ... to act reasonably in exchanging information ... and generally in trying to avoid the necessity for the start of proceedings' (Rule 4.1). Claims have to be made in writing and such claims have to be answered promptly. Normally, this pre-action phase will include 'the parties conducting genuine and reasonable negotiations with a view to settling the claim economically and without court proceedings' (Rule 4.2).

If, when litigation is subsequently commenced, these procedures have *not* first been followed, the court has power to impose cost sanctions on the parties. The Court of Appeal, in *Halsey v Milton Keynes General NHS Trust*,[5] decided that the court does not have the power to order the parties to attempt mediation; and that the court's proper role is to encourage rather than to compel settlement. But if a party is found to act unreasonably in refusing mediation, the court has power to displace the normal rules as to the allocation of costs against a successful litigant.

Dyson LJ set out some grounds on which it would be reasonable to decline mediation:

- reasonable belief in a watertight case;
- other settlement efforts already made;
- costs of entering mediation unacceptably high; and
- damaging delay.

Prior to *Halsey*, there had been some suggestion in the courts that they had power to mandate mediation.[6] *Halsey* seems to represent the better view, endorsing the value of mediation while recognising the essential element of voluntariness that must underlie fair negotiation.

The Conduct of the Litigation Process

Once litigation is commenced, the Rules spell out in general terms what 'active case management' involves. This emerges as a dual process under which the court is at once required to do everything it can to facilitate settlement, and where that is not possible, to clear the route towards judgment. The first of these contrasting imperatives is expressed as a triple mandate to the judges. First, it is a matter of 'encouraging the parties to co-operate with each other in the conduct of the proceedings' (Rule 1.4(2)(a)). Secondly, active case management includes 'encouraging the parties to use an alternative dispute resolution procedure if the court considers that appropriate and facilitating their use of

---

[5] [2004] EWCA (Civ) 576.
[6] See *Dunnett v Railtrack plc (Practice Note)* [2002] EWCA Civ 303; [2002] 1 WLR 2434; [2002] 2 All ER 850, CA; *Cowl v Plymouth City Council (Practice Note)* [2001] EWCA Civ 1935; [2002] 1 WLR 803, CA; *Shirayama Shokusan Co. Ltd v Danovo Ltd* [2003] EWHC 390 (Ch); [2004] 1 WLR 2985.

such procedure' (Rule 1.4(2)(e)). Thirdly, case management also includes 'helping the parties to settle the whole or part of the case' (Rule 1.4(2)(f)).

The primary injunction to 'cooperate' may seem to be no more than ordinary common sense: but its full implications are not at all clear. A minimal understanding requires the judge to prevent those analogues of warfare, delay and ambush, which have historically been normal means of wasting an adversary by postponing trial. But perhaps the requirement goes far beyond that, making the judge responsible for seeing that legal teams come clean about the negotiatory character of litigation, treating it as a process of information exchange and learning, directed towards joint decision-making. However we read it, this injunction requires a sea change in the traditional approach of lawyers to litigation, in its very essence an antagonistic, adversarial and secretive process under which actual combat ('fighting') is simply represented in an externally monitored, heavily ritualised textual and verbal exchange.

The second part of the mandate, which gives the courts a general responsibility to encourage settlement by proposing ADR and providing a necessary space in the litigation process while this is attempted, is equally remarkable. It reveals the astonishing speed with which a rather disparate bundle of foreign novelties is now confidently identified and officially adopted as part of the English local scene. Thirty years ago, it would hardly have been possible to find the phrase 'alternative dispute resolution' in the index of a major United States law journal. Yet by 1991, even in London, the Beldam Committee on Alternative Dispute Resolution established by the General Council of the Bar was 'convinced that the case was made out for the courts themselves to embrace the systems of alternative dispute resolution ... We believe that ADR has much to offer in support of the judicial process'.[7]

In following Beldam and embracing 'alternative dispute resolution procedures', the Civil Procedure Rules sanction the use of quite a disparate collection of practices. But these are essentially of two types: forecasting devices that enable the parties and their legal teams to examine their positions against a predicted judicial determination; and interventions that directly facilitate negotiations. Among the forecasting devices are technical procedures like the 'mini-trial' or 'executive tribunal' and 'Early Neutral Evaluation' (see section below). The latter comprises mediation in its manifold forms. These categories are by no means discrete, as within the former various hybrids may be found under which forecasting procedures are directly linked to facilitatory interventions. In all this, the essential point is that through writing this array of devices into the Civil Procedure Rules, the supervisory reach and technical repertoire of the civil courts are enormously extended.

---

[7] *Report of the Committee on Alternative Dispute Resolution*, General Council of the Bar, October 1991, p. 1.

The final part of the mandate, 'helping the parties to settle', most probably represents the most fundamental change of all. Beneath the simplicity and apparent good sense of this last injunction lies a shift that is qualitatively different from anything else the new Rules involve. Going beyond the management of litigation – in the sense of making sure opportunities to settle are taken where this is appropriate and speeding the parties to trial where it is not – it offers an active engagement on the part of the judge in the settlement process itself. In short, the Rules encourage the judge to become something of a mediator. All this is pretty much uncharted territory in this jurisdiction, although in North America active judicial involvement in settlement has a much longer history.

Looking at this programme as a whole, it is worth emphasising an obvious point about the strategic choice which government took. The 'dual' nature that lawyers have fashioned over the years for civil litigation receives endorsement. Litigation remains the approved vehicle for lawyer negotiations. Yet an alternative route lay available. Government *could* have devised a procedural framework with the objective of prising settlement and litigation apart. The first step towards such a goal is actually made with the pre-action protocols; but this separation is not carried through as the dual objectives still continue in the litigation phase. While settlement no longer remains invisible and submerged, lawyers are still largely free to approach practice in a distinctive way that inevitably involves progressive entanglement of settlement and trial. The essential point here is that, as lawyers have come to use litigation in pursuit of settlement, negotiatory and adjudicatory resolution are inevitably entwined.

Negotiation-related Innovations

Some of the most important innovations that have evolved in the post-Pound Conference world of civil justice are to be found in the area of negotiation, and are essentially – although not exclusively – efforts to press the parties into a more realistic assessment of the dispute and their positions so as to encourage settlement.

The Mini-trial

One 'alternative' device invoked in aid of settlement in the course of lawyer negotiations is the 'mini-trial' (sometimes labelled the 'modified settlement conference' or 'executive tribunal') first developed in North America in the context of commercial disputes.[8] The mini-trial is essentially a predictive, forecasting device conceived by its sponsors as a means of informing clients

---

[8] Specifically, it was first used in 1977 to resolve a dispute concerning a patent infringement.

about the strengths and weaknesses of their respective cases and providing an indication of the likely outcome of adjudication, thus prompting them to agree to settle. This is achieved through the respective legal teams presenting their cases to the parties themselves – senior executives in commercial cases – who are assisted in evaluating their positions by a 'neutral adviser'. The neutral adviser may feed information and advice about the law into the process and, if requested to do so, offer an opinion about the likely outcome of litigation if the matter comes to trial.

This procedure has two distinctive features when compared with conventional lawyer negotiations. First, the parties themselves are drawn back into a primary role, listening to the presentation of the respective arguments, evaluating these and then, ideally, moving on to direct, bilateral negotiations. Secondly, there is the introduction of an independent third party, the neutral expert, in both an advisory and a forecasting capacity. In a useful statement of key aspects of the process, Leiberman and Henry emphasise that 'the mini-trial is not in fact a trial at all but a highly-structured settlement process' (1986: 427). In addition, the mini-trial is intended to be a flexible process and therefore there is no one sole procedural model. Nevertheless, it seems clear that many of the key features are directed at generating or indirectly promoting trust between the disputing parties. Trust-building elements include the parties' initial negotiation of the procedural ground rules; restricted scope for discovery and 'pre-trial' preparation; a two-day limit on the length of the hearing so that each side has to present its best case and focus on central concerns rather than digress into more marginal issues; the pressure on the lawyers to address representatives of the parties – who have authority to settle, but who are primarily concerned with business interests rather than legal technicalities; the conduct of the hearing by the third-party neutral whose role is to encourage settlement and only secondarily to offer an advisory opinion on likely trial outcome; and confidentiality of proceedings – the parties in committing themselves to such confidentiality are, it is hoped, likely to trust each other more. Immediately after the hearing the parties' representatives meet privately in order to negotiate a settlement – only if these exchanges fail will the neutral adviser offer an advisory opinion.

Early Neutral Evaluation

A related device, 'early neutral evaluation' (ENE) involves the respective legal teams in putting a case, at a relatively early point, to a neutral or group of neutrals (sometimes in the United States a mock jury) to obtain for the client a forecast of the possible judicial outcome, again with a view to encouraging settlement. We further discuss this innovation in the context of its use by the court.

Lawyers who advocate and use these devices say that one of the greatest obstacles to settlement is the stressed, impassioned corporate executive who will not listen to sensible professional advice in cases where a negotiated outcome is in the client's best interests. They claim that these procedures are often successful in bringing clients 'back to reality', making them agree to settle.

It is hard to know what to make of these procedures, or of the justification for them offered by those who use them. They seem to imply a huge lack of confidence in traditional lawyering practices, and necessarily involve a loss of control that is often uncomfortable for lawyers, especially those well-grounded in traditional approaches to litigation. One of us has argued before (Roberts, Simon, 1993) that these devices have their most immediate application as means of damping down unrealistic expectations which the legal teams may themselves have recklessly nourished, even created, at an earlier stage in the dispute process. They are, in effect, crisis management techniques made necessary in a culture where the habit of late settlement, advantageous only to the profession, has left the client with insufficient information and advice in the early phases of a dispute.

The mini-trial and ENE were initially developed by ADR specialists to be used in support of negotiations by the parties' legal teams. They have subsequently come to be used by the courts as well, introduced at early stage meetings, in the course of efforts to generate settlement discussions.

Alongside resort to these specialised devices for forecasting outcomes and sponsoring settlement, there have been general moves by lawyers to present themselves in neutral advisory and consultancy roles. While in North America lawyers have for some time acted in neutral capacities alongside the traditional partisan roles, in many common law jurisdictions this pretension to neutrality is a considerable departure from established practice, and again represents a response to perceived threats represented by developments outside the legal profession. The role of the 'neutral adviser' in the 'mini-trial', typically a lawyer, is one example of this.

In England and Wales, both the Bar and the Law Society have sanctioned experiments under which lawyers may fulfil joint consultancy roles in some categories of family dispute. Under the scheme sanctioned by the Law Society, and operated by the Family Mediators' Association (FMA), a solicitor may cooperate with another professional 'with experience in marital or family work' in helping 'couples cope with the legal, financial and emotional problems of separation and divorce, as well as arrangements for children'. This includes assisting parties 'to work out proposals for settlement' and reach joint decisions in the context of family breakdown. While the FMA has given the label of 'mediation' to this innovatory form of lawyer intervention, it does not appear to be by any means limited to facilitating the communication between parties necessary to joint decision-making. Rather, at the core is a matter of providing expert consultancy to the parties jointly upon the arrangements regarding children, finance and property necessitated by family breakdown, and providing the parties with the framework within which to put these arrangements in place.[9]

Negotiating in the Shadow of Arbitration

A further form of hybrid process involves the linked, sequential use of different forms of intervention by neutral third parties. One example is in collective negotiations over labour issues. Arbitration has long been used to assist in collective bargaining for employment terms and conditions. The public interest in ensuring continuity of public services may result in arbitration being mandated by law should the collective negotiation fail to secure agreement.[10] It seems to be more attractive in forward-looking contract negotiation where the focus is perhaps more firmly on the parties' interests rather than rights standards. This possibility of resort to arbitration may, however, have a chilling impact on the unfolding negotiations. The parties worry that in making early concessions they may be disadvantaging themselves, as the arbitrator may impose on the parties an outcome that simply splits the difference between them.

One solution to this problem is final-offer arbitration in which the arbitrator is not allowed to make a compromise outcome but, rather, must choose between the final offers of each party. This encourages, it is believed, the parties to make more reasonable final offers, and this in turn also encourages the parties to negotiate more realistically themselves without resort to arbitration. The parties are in effect drawn towards each other and away from unrealistic positioning and so avoid any need for arbitration and its win–lose outcome (Goldberg et al., 2012: 418–20).

The problem of a win–lose outcome and its risks of financially unmanageable damage to the party who loses is also one of the factors which have encouraged the development of 'High-Low' agreements in the arbitration process. In this development, the parties agree in advance the winning party's damages will not exceed a certain amount, but that if the same party loses rather than wins then the other party will nevertheless recover a certain – albeit much lower – amount. This approach also reduces the incidence of compromise arbitral verdicts and itself may be thought of as a form with advance compromise, helping to generate a more amicable feel to the negotiation and encouragement to settle without any need for arbitration.

The procedure known in North America as 'med-arb' is another such process. Under this procedure a neutral is called in by the parties and authorised to mediate and then move into the role of arbitrator where mediation fails to promote settlement. We take up this process later in this chapter.

---

[9] The Family Law Bar Association's 'conciliation board' procedure provides another example.
[10] For an interesting account of the issues involved see Kersey and Sherk (2007).

Mediation-related Innovations

Another broad area of innovation has developed around attempts to reinforce mediation by infusing or joining it with other forms of dispute management. As we have just noted, one major form of development has been 'med-arb'. Another has been court-annexed mediation. A third important hybridisation has arisen where mediation is combined with another form of professional intervention. An example is provided by the attempted combination of mediation and family therapy.

Med-arb

In the process characterised as 'med-arb', the third-party intervener is expected to attempt a mediation of the differences between the parties. In the event of failure to achieve a mediated outcome acceptable to both parties, the same third party assumes the role of arbitrator and makes a binding and final award. Although ordinarily found in the institutional context of arbitration, most schemes in effect give primacy to the mediation phase of the proceedings, and in practice are attempts to enhance the efficacy of mediation by reinforcing mediation with the threat of umpiring – indeed, they are sometimes referred to as 'mediating with a club' (Fuller, 1963). In the common law world, the origins of this approach appear to lie in the contrasting views of the most appropriate role for the arbitrator found in the United States earlier in the last century:

> In the 1930s and 1940s two views of the arbitrator's role existed. One view was that the arbitrator served primarily to further the relationship of the parties. The proponents of this view thought of the arbitrator as the impartial chairman of a joint committee and believed that he should seek through mediation to assist the parties in resolving their grievances. To the extent that the parties could resolve their disputes, it was thought that their relationship and their capacity to resolve future disputes would be strengthened. Only if the parties could not resolve a dispute through mediation would the impartial chairman impose a decision. Furthermore, when required to decide a grievance, the impartial chairman, while remaining loyal to the contract, would attempt to do so in a fashion that was guided primarily by a desire to further the parties' relationship.
>
> The opposing view saw the arbitrator not as an impartial chairman but as an umpire who should concern himself solely with deciding the grievance. In reaching a decision, the umpire should not consider which result would benefit the relationship of the parties, but instead should limit himself to interpreting and applying the contract in the manner that would best express the parties' intent as articulated in the contract (Goldberg, 1982: 272–3).

The author of this extract, Stephen Goldberg, concludes with the observation that, in the subsequent evolution of arbitration, the impartial chairman approach declined in favour of the umpiring view.

The case against the fusion of roles that the 'impartial chairman' approach envisaged was built up most forcefully by Fuller (1963) in his analysis of the place of the arbitrator in collective bargaining. Briefly stated, he argues that mediation and arbitration are essentially different in their purpose and morality – the morality of mediation is optimum settlement, with the parties giving up what they value less in return for what they value more, whereas the morality of arbitration is to be found in the contractual agreement to enter into arbitration. The two methods also differ, in his view, in their processual essentials in that mediation seeks to secure adjustment to the position of the parties so that an outcome is achieved that most nearly meets their interests, whereas arbitration enables each party to present arguments and evidence in her or his favour. In particular, 'private consultations with the parties, generally wholly improper on the part of an arbitrator, are an indispensable role of mediation' (Fuller, 1963: 24). In addition, for Fuller the essential facts of a dispute differ, or, if the same, are viewed differently, in the two processes. A further difficulty may well be that a mediator-turned-arbitrator will find it difficult to hear proofs and arguments with an open mind, undermining the integrity of the umpiring decision. Indeed, Fuller maintains that even in polycentric disputes in which the parties have agreed to arbitration, the roles of mediation and arbitration must be kept firmly apart so that the 'integrity of the adjudicative process' can be preserved (1963: 38–9). Moreover, it is not only occasional arbitrators that will find it difficult to cope: even very skilled and experienced arbitrators are often unable to overcome the inherent limitations in the fused role of mediator and arbitrator. And where the arbitrator takes over both mediation and umpiring functions, the repeated intervention of the arbitrator is likely to create a sense of dependence in the parties which, in turn, will discourage them from making their own decision (Fuller, 1963: 39–42).

Nevertheless, the perceived advantages of combining mediation with arbitration have steadily led to a revival of this approach, and various procedural innovations have been designed to overcome some of the difficulties involved. From the 1970s onwards, arguments were put forward in support of the use of mediation-arbitration in a variety of dispute contexts. Thus, for example, Spencer and Zammit made proposals in the mid-1970s, very early on in the ADR movement, which highlighted the benefits that might accrue from the linked, sequential use of mediation and arbitration in disputes over child-related matters – even an unsuccessful mediation may have nevertheless narrowed and more precisely defined the issues involved in the matrimonial dispute. But, at the same time, they cautioned that:

> in no event should the mediator ever serve as arbitrator, even if requested to by the parties. The possibility that the mediator might later become the arbitrator would tend to make the parties less open and candid during mediation. In addition, the arbitrator must be impartial. His activities as a mediator in the same dispute may easily have an adverse effect on this necessary characteristic of

the arbitration. For the same reasons, a mediator should never be callable as a witness, expert or otherwise, during an arbitration, nor should he submit a report of any kind to the arbitrator (Spencer and Zammit, 1976: 934, n. 92).

Other proposals and experiments have been less concerned to keep the role of mediator and arbitrator apart in the med-arb process. Indeed, in the area of family law, the state of California introduced a form of med-arb in contested child custody cases in which the mediator has the authority to make a recommendation to the court should the mediation fail to produce an agreement (see Folberg and Taylor, 1984: 277–80). A very rigorous characterisation of the benefits of fusing mediatory and arbitral roles was put forward in the early 1980s by Goldberg in proposals which provided for the issuing of an advisory (non-binding) opinion by the mediator in which the latter predicts the likely outcome if the dispute proceeds to arbitration. He argued that in offering the parties an initial option of mediation rather than going directly to arbitration in collective labour disputes, the mediator might not only be able to resolve the dispute but also if the mediator's intervention did not secure an agreement then the mediator might still be able to assist the parties by offering an oral advisory opinion that encourages settlement. Should these efforts fail to get the parties to reach an agreement, then an arbitrator would intervene in order to impose a decision, with strict confidentiality maintained in respect of the information exchanged during the mediation process. Even if it did not lead to an agreement, the mediation phase offered the prospect of eliminating:

> the concept of 'winning' a grievance, substituting the concept of negotiations leading to a mutually satisfactory resolution. To the extent that the parties focus on seeking a mutually satisfactory outcome through negotiations, they should develop a mutual understanding of each other's concerns. This mutual understanding, in turn, should lead not only to the resolution of more grievances without resort to mediation or arbitration, but also to the improvement of their entire relationship (Goldberg, 1982: 283).

On the other hand, the arbitration phase offered finality of decision-making and, in addition, would sometimes clarify issues that the collective bargaining contract did not address clearly by examining:

> the language of the contract, its bargaining history, prior practice, and various canons of construction, and conclude that, if the negotiators had foreseen the particular problem and been able to resolve it, it is more likely that they would have resolved it in one way rather than another (Goldberg, 1982: 284).

The apparent success of med-arb and its variants in the United States then encouraged its adoption in the United Kingdom, and in several important essays, arbitrators sought to assess and advise on the merits and the problems that an embrace of med-arb might entail. Thus, Newman neatly summed up ambiguity in attitudes when he wrote:

One method of addressing concerns about the non-binding nature of mediation is the hybrid technique of MedArb. Its purpose is to commit the parties, usually through a clause in their contractual agreement, to continue the ADR processes in a manner that will ensure resolution of the dispute. Assume the disputants will first attempt to negotiate a settlement. If that fails, they will embark upon mediation and if no agreement is reached the mediator will change roles and become an arbitrator empowered to impose a binding solution on the parties. Many doubts have been expressed, particularly by lawyers, whether MedArb inevitably compromises the neutral's capacity legally to act in an adjudicative capacity while at the same time undermining the efficacy of the initial mediation where the mediator should seek to create an atmosphere of trust and a willingness to impart confidences to him in the caucus sessions. There are other extremely practical considerations. If the parties agree, during the original contract negotiations, that they will use a form of MedArb in the resolution of any disputes that arise it is difficult to assess when the mediation phase should give way to the arbitral. Simply to place the responsibility on the mediator to advise the parties when mediation should give way to arbitration is an inadequate response (Newman, 1994: 174).

He also gave particular attention to the problem of role conflict in the relationship between the mediator and arbitrator in the hybrid process. On the one hand, if the mediation fails and that same mediator is subsequently appointed as arbitrator of the same dispute, there are clear advantages in terms of costs, time and understanding of the case – it may be the case, for example, that the mediation resolves nearly all the issues but a small number of differences remain unbridged, and the mediator turned arbitrator is particularly suited to render a binding decision on the outstanding problems. And the parties' realisation that the mediator is authorised subsequently to umpire if necessary may well make the mediation process more effective in producing a settlement than would mediation alone. On the other hand, mediation is based on principles of voluntariness and permits the parties to agree without an imposed decision, and when the mediator-arbitrator mediates then there may be issues of coercion, or of failure of the parties to disclose information that would help the mediation because it might count against them in the imposed decision because the parties' confidential compromised positions for settlement expressed during the mediation stage might well influence the arbitrator's decision (Newman, 1994: 174–6).

A more forceful critique is offered by Elliott when he wrote that '[t]he thought of mixing mediation and arbitration, with one person playing the role of both mediator and arbitrator, sends a shudder though many lawyers' (Elliott, 1996: 175). He advises that, especially in jurisdictions where mediation tends to use private caucusing extensively, and the parties expect the mediator to advise, formally or informally, on the merits of each party's case, dangers lurked:

What causes lawyers most concern is a mediator privately caucusing with each side. Fundamental to our notion of justice is the right to know and be able to answer an opponent's case. How can this be done if one side or the other has no way of knowing what the other party is saying? It is unsettling to think of what the other side might have said, and what influence that might have on the mediator-turned-arbitrator.

> While private caucus meetings are problematic for lawyers, they can also pose a dilemma for the mediator-turned-arbitrator. How much reliance, if any, can be placed on what is said in caucus meetings (when some very frank comments might be made and when the other side may have no opportunity to rebut what is said, or to shed other light on them, or put them in a different context)? (Elliott, 1996: 176).

Another problematic area is the issue of bias:

> A med/arb process may raise questions of bias, real or perceived, in the minds of the parties. This issue is most likely to arise if the mediator is particularly assertive, or provides an advisory opinion in the course of the mediation (an 'advisory opinion' is a non-binding expression of the mediator's opinion of the most likely outcome if the case goes to arbitration, based on what the mediator has heard in mediation). Equally, as a result of private caucus sessions, the mediator may feel biased to one side or other on the basis of what he or she hears in confidence (Elliott, 1996: 176).

And the fundamental characteristics of the two processes made closely connecting them inappropriate:

> The questions asked by the mediator will seek to bring out the interests of the parties in order to expand the settlement possibilities. The very issues that can play a vital role in mediation may be precisely the things counsel may not want canvassed in an arbitration hearing. Once underlying interests have surfaced during a mediation, it may be unrealistic to expect a mediator-turned-arbitrator to put them aside when making an arbitration award. In fact, to put aside what is said in mediation may well lessen the quality of the decision, even if it is theoretically and practically possible to do so (Elliott, 1996: 177).

In Asia, the use of med-arb for commercial dispute resolution is gaining popularity. Jurisdictions such as Japan, Hong Kong and Singapore encourage its use, and in one legal culture – namely, the PRC – the hybrid process of med-arb has become an entrenched preference in resolving commercial dispute. In China's leading arbitration institution, the China International Economic and Trade Arbitration Commission (CIETAC) and other local arbitration commissions, it is the dominant form of decision-making. The Chinese approach sees med-arb in broad terms, and any hybrid process of mediation and arbitration is thus labelled regardless of whether, for example, the arbitral tribunal or an arbitrator takes over the mediation itself, or if an arbitrator plays the dual role of mediator or the roles are kept separate. But here too reliance on med-arb is being challenged. One major question that has been raised is whether the Chinese practice of med-arb is compatible with due process values – it is argued that med-arb proceedings in China fail to deal with issues of actual and apparent bias, and are undermined by failure to ensure confidentiality. According to Gu Weixia:

> One of the core issues in the med-arb process in China is the dual capacity of arbitrators and mediators. In order to enhance efficiency, mediation process in China is often conducted by the very same arbitrator(s) of the case. This is, according to official discourse, because the arbitrator who participated in the mediation will become familiar with the details of the case in the course of mediation. Even if mediation fails, the decision-making process will be speeded up and the dispute can thereby be resolved within a shorter timeframe. In the absence of proper procedural safeguards, however, the impartiality of the arbitrator may be affected by reason of having participated in the mediation process (Gu Weixia, 2015: 85).[11]

The dual mediator-arbitration role is, in fact, justified also by cultural arguments. Within Chinese legal culture, and especially today when official policies promote a 'harmonious society'; the ideal outcome is one achieved by mediation, so that even within the context of large-scale commercial disputes, the real function of arbitration is to strengthen the chances of securing a mediated settlement.

Mediation and Therapy

There have also been efforts to combine mediation with family therapy at various points of time within the development of ADR over the past forty years. In some ways that should not be a surprise, as there are factors which do encourage us to see a fusing of mediatory and psychotherapeutic intervention as both natural and sensible. Thus, as Gibbs pointed out in his seminal analysis of the Kpelle Moot style of mediation, the mediation procedures amongst the Kpelle are 'therapeutic in that, like psychotherapy, they re-educate the parties through a type of social learning brought about in a specifically structured interpersonal setting' (Gibbs, 1963: 6). The mediation process in these circumstances has features suggestive of the strategies and techniques of many psychotherapists, providing as it does an environment of emotional support for the parties that is infused with concern to understand the parties' issues, a venting phase in which the parties unburden themselves and explain in their own words the problems as they see them, a restrained reaction on the part of the listeners to the emotional turmoil of the preceding venting phase, and then an encouragement of the parties to see the issues from the perspective of the audience, much as an analyst seeks the parties' acceptance of her or his definition of the situation as part of the process of reintegration.[12] Further,

---

[11] See also De Vera (2004).

[12] As Marian Roberts has pointed out, 'whatever the therapeutic framework, the therapeutic process covers recognisable stages – a critical assessment stage (whether formal or informal,

one particular form of therapy, namely family systems therapy seems to offer a particularly attractive toolbox of techniques and strategies for dealing with the often emotionally fraught difficulties in family relationships, as it stresses the interdependence of members of the family and the ways in which the difficulties affecting individual family members are likely to impact on and to affect other members. Although subject to rigorous criticism, as we shall see later, the idea and practice of fusing psychotherapy and mediation processes continues so that, for example, in London some mediation training providers – such as Regent's University – continue to stress the value of courses that meld the two approaches:

Mediation and Alternative Dispute Resolution (ADR) – Course

This course will enable you to develop the particular skills and methods required for successful mediation and conflict management, including both conflict resolution and conflict avoidance.

The skills for effective mediation are similar to those required for successful counselling. The course therefore employs well-proven psychotherapy and counselling techniques as part of the training programme.[13]

In a series of insightful commentaries, however, Marian Roberts has argued that not only are there fundamental contradictions in the two approaches but also there are likely to be serious process dangers if there is a fusion of the roles. Despite some surface similarities between the two approaches, there are also profound contradictions which undermine the argument for efforts aimed at combining the two processes. Perhaps most importantly, the domain assumptions of the two modes of intervention are contradictory:

The primary objective of family therapy is to modify 'dysfunctional' behaviour. It does this by challenging and changing the organization of the family in such a way that the perceptions and experiences of the family members change . . . The basic assumption of family therapy therefore is of dysfunction, possibly psychiatric, in the family that requires treatment.

As far as mediation is concerned, marital breakdown and the disputes that arise from it are not regarded as symptoms of psychopathology, nor are the parties regarded as suffering from incapacities that render therapeutic intervention necessary. Nor is it the object of mediation to challenge the perceptions of the parties. On the contrary, the parties are regarded as competent both to define the issues for themselves and to come to their own decisions. Their meanings are seen as essential to an accurate understanding of their dispute and its context. The focus of mediation is a modest one, limited in most cases to the purpose of

---

comprehensive or minimal) and a diagnosis stage (incorporating history-taking) leading to the choice of the most effective therapeutic intervention' (2014a: 24).

[13] See, www.regents.ac.uk/study/short-courses/professional-development/adr.aspx, accessed 9 August 2016. One mediation practice in London that expressly offers both mediation and therapy is Family Law in Partnership (see: http://flip.co.uk/area/family-support-services/, accessed 2 December 2019).

negotiated joint decision-making on the specific substantive issues in dispute. If the process and outcomes of mediation lead to a reduction of bitterness and conflict in the relationship between the parties, then the process can be therapeutic in the widest sense. That quality of improved understanding is one of the most distinctive benefits of the process but it need not be its primary object (Roberts, Marian, 2014a: 25).

The differences in approach also mean that in the mediation process the therapist necessarily plays a managerial role, with a therapist deriving much power in the process from her or his claim to have a monopoly of meaning and to be the knowing expert – that is to say, it is the therapist's concepts and analysis that dominate, informing and governing diagnosis and treatment (Roberts, Marian, 2014a: 25–6).[14] In contrast, the mediator:

> affirms the supremacy of the parties' meanings and decision-making authority. The parties' control over the definition of the issues is fundamental to their control over the decision-making process and its outcome. One of the first tasks of the mediator is to gain an understanding of the issues as they are perceived by the parties themselves. This means giving paramount worth to the perceptions, feelings and meanings of the parties. The mediator can have no privileged perspective on how to view and interpret experience. The skill of the mediator must lie in facilitating the crucial exchanges of accurate and constructive information that lead, through adjustments of expectations and preferences, to greater understanding, co-ordination and order, and eventually to a settlement of the dispute ... The mediator's expertise lies, therefore, in ensuring that the capacity of the parties to take responsibility for their own affairs is recognized and protected (Roberts, Marian, 2008: 23).

A further important contrast lies in the significance attached to history and evaluation. Therapy, like the law, involves making judgements about the past. Mediation, in contrast, is concerned primarily with enhancing communication so as to create a better future.

The contradictory nature of the two modes of intervention in addition may well create hazards if the two modes are brought together in a single mixed process:

- the negotiation and decision-making process of mediation could become tainted with the stigma of family dysfunction and treatment associated with family therapy and boundaries could become blurred;
- family disputes could be perceived as pathological or dysfunctional;

---

[14] In this context we might note Rosen's perceptive suggestion that the Kpelle Moot might not be a particularly useful good comparator. He writes, 'the particular form this process takes ... is distinctive to the Kpelle ... it is interesting to ask whether its effectiveness depends on the general style of psychological coercion and how such a process might transfer into other cultures' (Rosen, 2006: 44–5).

- the focus on the underlying dynamics of relationships and their interpretation – regarding the parties' definitions of the issues as 'presenting' problems – privileges the meanings of the intervener rather than those of the parties. This claim to a monopoly of meaning increases the power of the therapist as knowing expert and affirms their leadership role in contrast to that of the mediator;
- the family systems view is that it is by challenging and changing behaviour that changes of perception and experience will occur. This is the reverse of the process by means of which change is perceived to be brought about in mediation – by exchanges of information leading to learning and therefore an improvement of understanding;
- family therapy from its earliest development in the 1950s until the 1990s has been acknowledged to be a manipulative approach using covert techniques (such as hypothesising; circular questioning; reframing techniques such as positive connotation designed to achieve systemic levelling, etc.) to manipulate the perceptions and preferences of the parties; and
- the loose and liberal adoption in mediation of the language, typologies and the manipulative techniques of family therapy could be viewed as the attempt by one group of professionals to appropriate mediation as an extension of their activities by means of the transforming influence of their specialist discourse (Roberts, Marian, 2014b: 113).

If, however, the two processes are to be used together, then the practitioners involved must be aware of the lurking danger identified by John Haynes – a pioneering family mediator with a background in family therapy – namely, the unreflective use of therapy by a mediator unable to make progress in the mediation of a difficult dispute. For example, if there is an underlying problem that seems to be the cause of impasse, the question may arise:

> how can the mediator surface the issue without performing therapy? The answer to this question lies in the focus of the mediator. The mediator's task is to manage the negotiations between the parties required to resolve the conflict. The task is not to transform the clients or to resolve their individual problems. The only work the mediator engages in to resolve interpersonal problems is the least amount of change required to facilitate the negotiations. As long as the mediator views himself as the manager of the negotiations, he will not engage in a therapeutic relationship with the clients (Haynes, 2004: 203).

Refurbishing Umpiring

Paradoxically, dispute processes once characterised as alternatives to adjudication have in the last two decades or so been increasingly co-opted by the courts. The simple opposition of the mainstream and the 'alternative' has accordingly become less clear as a result of the incorporation of 'ADR' techniques into the process of adjudication and arbitration.

Judicial Promotion of Settlement

Notwithstanding criticisms of the kind expressed by Fiss in 'Against Settlement' (see Chapter 3), judges themselves have become actively involved in the promotion of settlement and this objective is increasingly endorsed in statutes and rules of court. In the section on Settlement as Civil Justice above we looked at the broad shift that has taken place in England and Wales over the past four decades such that civil courts now have as one of their most important civil justice goals the creation of a context within which the parties are very much encouraged to settle rather than go to trial. We now look more closely at judicial involvement in settlement.

Ordinarily, in the United States such involvement takes place in the context of a judicial settlement conference consisting of an informal exchange of views guided by the trial judge, although it may also be combined with a pre-trial conference. This involvement may be one of mediation, as one judge has acknowledged: 'we are catalysts in settlement. Our role is not that of a traditional judge. Our role at that stage is that of mediator' (quoted in Galanter, 1985: 4). This approach marks the emergence of the common law judge as an active manager of the process of litigation, even ready to assist the parties to reach settlement through mediatory intervention. The latter approach has been greatly strengthened by several amendments to Rule 16 of the Federal Rules of Civil Procedure,[15] so that where authorised by local rules and relevant statutes, judges are expected to promote settlement activity. Although some states do thus empower judges to engage in settlement discussion with the disputing parties, in others, as well as in the federal courts, judges have from time to time been regarded as having promoted settlement too rigorously.

Galanter provides an examination of the development of this judicial involvement in the settlement of civil cases in the United States, taking as his starting point the fact while settlement had long been a common outcome of litigation it was only from the early 1970s onwards that settlement per se acquired legitimacy and was explicitly valued in judicial circles. Prior to this, settlement had been encouraged primarily as a matter of administrative convenience and officially characterised in the politically safe language of 'adjustment', 'compromise' and 'conciliation'. But through the rigours of judicial experience and the impact of new ideals of civil justice promoted in the emerging ADR movement, settlement came to be regarded instead as a process that often produced outcomes superior to those of adjudicative decision-making, in large part precisely because settlement facilitated compromise solutions that were now regarded by civil court judges as superior

---

[15] Federal Rule of Civil Procedure 16 regulates judicial supervision of litigation in pre-trial conferences. First adopted in 1938, it has been amended several times over the years in order to facilitate promotion of settlement during pre-trial conferences. See, www.law.cornell.edu/rules/frcp/rule_16, accessed 2 December 2019.

expressions of justice. And, added Galanter, 'if settlements are good, it is also good that the judge actively participates in bringing them about. He should do this not only by his management of the court … but also by acting as a mediator' (Galanter, 1986: 261). In 1983, this transformation to active involvement by the judge was – as we have just noted – formally endorsed when the Federal Rules of Civil Procedure at Rule 16 were revised so as to facilitate active judicial involvement during pre-trial in settlement discussions and other 'extra-judicial processes' leading to non-adjudicative outcomes. As a result, 'cases that once might have been settled by negotiation between opposing counsel are now settled with the participation of the judge. We have moved from dyadic to mediated bargaining' (Galanter, 1986: 262).

The settlement conference as managed by the judge has been succinctly characterised by one experienced judge in the following terms:

> A settlement conference can be divided into three distinct phases: (1) joint initial session, (2) separate caucus with each party, and (3) joint concluding phase. The caucus phase is the most challenging and the most important. This is when the judge meets separately with each party to explore its underlying concerns, discuss the merits of the dispute, develop settlement options, and obtain the next settlement proposal for presentation to the other side. During the caucus, the judge must exercise judgment and develop strategies to move the case toward settlement. In the caucus, the judge engages each party in confidential discussions to determine its settlement goals and evaluate whether and how those goals can be achieved. Oftentimes, the merits of the case recede into the background while other concerns, such as the emotional and financial stress of the litigation process, come to the forefront (Denlow, 2010: 21).

The authority which the judge brings to the negotiations is clearly an important factor in securing settlement, as Judge Denlow reports:

> Whether the judge views a settlement proposal as fair is important to many parties. For example, when the judge discusses recent settlements in similar cases or simply sets out why he believes a particular amount is within the range of reasonable settlements, the parties often view such feedback as paramount (Denlow, 2010: 24).

Empirical research similarly reports:

> In a majority of settlement conferences, when a judge recommends particular terms of settlement, the recommendation is based on the pragmatic belief of what will be acceptable to all the parties (Robinson, 2009: 154).

And while many judges look primarily to the parties' legal positions when handling the settlement conference process, they are also able to take a wider view of the matters before them:

> [Our] expectation [is] that settlement judges primarily focus on the law. Enough judges conform to this expectation to explain the stereotype, but significant percentages of judges report primarily focusing on satisfying underlying needs, goals, fears, or feelings [of the parties] (Robinson, 2009: 155).

Nevertheless, this concern does not mean that the judicial settlement confer-ence is explicitly a form of mediation, suggesting that Galanter is perhaps overstating the case when he characterises the process of judge-assisted settle-ment as one of 'mediation':

> It is important for the parties to leave a Settlement Conference feeling that they have achieved an agreement that is at least reasonably justified under the law. While there may sometimes be a derivative benefit of improving the relationship between the parties, this is not the focus of the Settlement Conference process. In contrast, while resolving the underlying ... dispute is certainly one of the major goals of mediation, it is usually not the only goal, and 'success' in mediation is not necessarily defined by reference to the law or legal concepts (Erlichman, Gregory and St. Florian, 2014: 433).

In England and Wales, as we saw in Chapter 8, a parallel growth in the acceptance of the role of the courts as sponsors of settlement took place from the early 1970s onwards. The key points in this evolution were a 1971 Practice Direction that encouraged family courts to promote 'conciliation' in the early stages of the divorce process, then a Commercial Court practice statement in 1993 and a practice direction issued by the Lord Chief Justice and the Vice Chancellor in 1995 (both of which also encouraged parties to settle wherever possible), Lord Woolf's subsequent reports on the need for radical civil justice reform (1995; 1996) and the culmination of these developments in the 1999 Civil Procedure Rules. The 'overriding objective' of this refurbished civil procedure system is for 'the court to deal with cases justly' (Rule 1.1(1)). The new system offers several important innovations which, however, offer a rather nuanced understanding of what is 'just'. First, it gives particular atten-tion to the manner in which the parties and their legal representatives carry out the preparatory steps for bringing suit, these rules on the preliminary exchanges being characterised as 'Pre-Action Protocols'. If a case subsequently proceeds to litigation, costs sanctions will be imposed on the parties should they have failed to conduct genuine and reasonable negotiations at an early stage. Secondly, and perhaps more importantly, once litigation has been initiated a vigorous system of judicial case management applies as 'the court must further the overriding objective by actively managing cases' (Rule 1.1.(4)). Thirdly, settlement is characterised as a central goal of civil justice and courts should therefore actively promote attempts at settlement. This requires the judges to encourage or help the parties to 'co-operate with each other in the conduct of proceedings' (Rule 1.4(2)(a)), 'use an alternative dispute resolution procedure if the court considers that appropriate and facilitating their use of such procedure (Rule 1.4(2)(e)), and 'settle the whole or part of a case' (Rule 1.4(2)(f)). Thus, the court's role now includes an explicit facilitation of negoti-ation and encouragement of the use of mediation and ADR processes, and in meeting these role requirements the supervisory reach and processual options of the civil courts are also extended, perhaps even to the point of implicitly encouraging the judge to act as a mediator rather than just as an enabler of negotiation. In this way, the court's role is in effect replacing the older process of lawyer-controlled negotiation conducted within the track of litigation – that is, within the process of 'litigotiation' in Galanter's terms. Indeed, lawyers should now be seen as instead bearing a professional duty to assist the courts in achieving the declared overriding objective of the civil procedure rules to deal with cases 'justly' (Rule 1.3). It has become a responsibility of the parties' lawyers to cooperate in good faith with each other and with the court in such matters as reducing expense, handling the case so that it proceeds in a manner that is efficient, fair, and proportionate to the issues, size, and importance of the case and so on, and to try to ensure that the parties cooperate with each other and give proper consideration to ADR possibilities.

The Judge as Mediator

In a number of jurisdictions in the Anglo-American common law world over the past three decades or so judge facilitated negotiation and mediation have been incorporated into the judicial process, either directly or indirectly. There is a wide range of innovations here. When we look at those developments in which the judge is explicitly cast as a mediator, we see a range from mediation conducted by a judge who will try the case if no settlement is reached – a process which raises a number of the issues noted by Fuller in his critique of med-arb outlined above – to court-appointed mediators who conduct compulsory mediation prior to any trial that might eventually take place. In the case of direct judicial mediation, the activities of the judge in promoting an agreement between the parties through judicial settlement conferences and the like are in reality one dimension of a growing embrace of judicial managerialism.

The direct involvement of the judge in mediation efforts has, somewhat paradoxically, been formally accepted much longer in many jurisdictions within the civilian tradition. Writing in the early 1980s, Röhl observed that:

> The courts in West Germany are bound by the code of Civil Procedure (Sect. 279 ZPO) to endeavor at every stage of the legal procedure to promote a consensual settlement. German lawyers go so far as to suggest that the statute expresses a preference for settlement over judgment. There are, however, no further instructions telling the judge, when, how, by which means and how intensively he should try to move the parties toward a settlement (1983: 2).

In judicial practice, informal norms of intervention nevertheless had emerged,

> In the *Judges Journal* (Deutsche Richterzeitung) and similar practice-related writings, authors speak [...] in favor of settlement. They talk about the peacemaking function of the judge and give practical advice on how to lead parties to a settlement ... they claim that successful mediation requires especially thorough preparation and an extended public hearing. On the other hand, nobody really doubts that judges expect, and to some extent actually get, relief in their workload from settlements in court. A settlement not only eliminates the time-consuming

process of taking evidence, but it also does away with the need to write opinions
for adjudicated decisions, the task most judges like least (1983: 3–4).

The broad discretion traditionally allowed judges in Germany and other
continental systems to intervene in this manner is perhaps best explained by
Damaška's pithy observation that in procedural systems, 'how far the combat
motif can be carried out in the legal process depends [to a large extent] on the
degree to which intervention by a third side – the state adjudicator – is
permitted. The more limited the opportunity for intervention, the more pronounced the combat motif' (Damaška, 1986: 79). In continental systems, where
there is generally speaking a bureaucratic, hierarchical, system of authority
(including broad possibilities of appeal), a managerial style of government and
a strong inquisitorial concern with policy implementation, there is a non-
combative and fertile context within which judicial intervention in the spirit
of encouraging settlement and often taking the form of mediation by the trial
judge might well thrive. Empirical research suggested that this context was
sufficiently comfortable for a range of case-handling styles to emerge (Röhl,
1983: 5), but in any event 'the judge himself addresses the parties and gives
advice if their case is not well-prepared . . . the judge asks the parties to offer
evidence . . . and summons the witnesses and the experts and questions them'
(Röhl, 1983: 7). Indeed, a common strategy was for the judges to preserve the
parties' expectation of their day in court through to judgment but use an
unanticipated move to mediation as a means for securing an agreed settlement,
and another was for the judge herself or himself to give the parties a specific
proposal for a settlement, and 'from the parties' perspective such a proposal can
be understood as a prediction of a decision the judge would probably enter if
[she or] he had to decide the case' (Röhl, 1983: 23–4).

But it seems that much like the earlier experience in the United States as
observed by Galanter, judges' widespread promotion of settlement through
direct intervention under the then civil procedure rules was more a matter of
practice than explicitly approved doctrine. Indeed, it was not until the ideas
and ideals of the ADR movement were diffused into Germany in the 1990s
that the term 'mediation' gained formal recognition, primarily as a transplanted concept from the United States, and then through local level judicial
experimentation (Tochtermann, 2013: 523, 528). The concept of 'mediation'
was explicitly incorporated into German law in the 2012 Mediation Law
(*Mediationsgesetz*), although some space for this development had also been
created by reforms in 2002 to the civil procedure law that provided for the
introduction of a 'special, rather formalized, conciliation hearing which pre-
cedes any Court proceeding' (Kunze, 2002: 3), and earlier encouragement by
state Ministers of Justice for courts to promote 'in-court conciliation'
(Gottwald, 1997: 758). Regional courts played an important role by initiating
numerous pilot projects, so much so that how mediation is seen is now very
much dependent on 'whether the mediation takes place under the aegis of the

judiciary or whether the parties opt for mediation without judicial influence'
(Tochtermann, 2013: 524).

Following the introduction of the 2012 Mediation Law and the preceding
general debate about its possible enactment, many courts initiated pilot
mediation projects at the regional level, sometimes with considerable support
from state Ministries of Justice. The parties were not obligated to participate
in mediation and in many of these experimental systems the trial judge and
mediating judge were different (Tochtermann, 2013: 530),

> For example, in the pilot project at the regional court of Göttingen, Lower
> Saxony, the competent judge reviews the case and decides whether mediation
> could lead to a resolution of the conflict. If the judge deems mediation appro-
> priate, [she or] he refers the case to a colleague who is a trained mediator and
> who is not entitled to render a decision on the case if the mediation proves
> unsuccessful. The reviewing procedure was later abolished ... so that every case
> is now referred to the mediator-judges if the parties consent. If the parties
> are willing to participate in mediation the trial judge then suspends the pro-
> ceedings by means of a court order.

> If the parties do mediate a settlement, the mediating judge may record the
> settlement as an enforceable court settlement ... however, if the parties break off
> their negotiations, the case is adjudicated by the trial judge.

> This procedure has since served as a model for many subsequent pilot projects
> throughout Germany.

> As a consequence of the pilot project's structure, the cases involved reach the
> courts before being diverted to the mediator-judges, and thus the legal aspects
> of the dispute typically play a major role in the mediation session, resulting in
> the mediator's role usually being of a highly evaluative nature (Tochtermann,
> 2013: 531).

However, it is not clear that the mediator-judges' role is so very different
from the pre-reform judicial encouragement of settlement by the trial judge,
with both approaches infused with a very directive and evaluative ethos.
Moreover, this aspect of the development of ADR in Germany has meant that
the courts, rather than decreasing their involvement in civil disputes, have
maintained or even extended their reach. The judges involved in this project
qua mediator-judges apparently found the experience very rewarding and
participated in the pilot reforms enthusiastically. But lawyers, anxious to
develop a new field of professional practice, severely criticised the free provision of mediation through the courts introduced by the reforms. Further, the
legislatures were unhappy to see an expansion of the reach of the courts when
their hope had been that ADR would reduce the burdens of state funding
of the courts. As a result, the pilot projects apparently came to an end in
2013. However, there was sufficient success in the projects for the system to
re-appear in another form. In one variant system, a case is referred to another
judge (a *Güterichter*), who is not officially characterised as a mediator but who

may well 'make use of mediation techniques, evaluate the legal position of the parties … make … proposals for a settlement and … suggest other processes such as early neutral evaluation' (Tochtermann, 2013: 533).

Elsewhere, as we indicated in the introductory section to this chapter, we find examples in which the role of the judge is one in which mediation is stressed, and adjudication relied on to secure an outcome only as a final and unwelcome last resort (Palmer, 1988; Fu and Palmer, 2017). In the PRC, the highly evaluative and directive style of mediation[16] used by the judges of the civil chambers in the People's Courts[17] and encouraged by successive versions of the civil procedure law first introduced in 1981[18] has been given even greater emphasis in the past decade or so.

This enhanced emphasis reflects the Chinese leadership's worries about growing social unrest, which it sees in part as a failure of the more rights-based litigation and adjudication-orientated civil justice policies and practices which prevailed in the 1990s to contain social discontent, as well as new policy goals laid down by the Chinese leadership aimed at fostering in China a 'harmonious society' (*hexie shehui*).

In the pre-trial stage, at any point during the trial itself, and in appellate proceedings, the judge is encouraged to attempt mediation, and to liaise with local community organisations and enterprise leaders so as to secure their help to get the parties to consent to and participate in mediation, and to settle the dispute through a mediation agreement.[19]

In these circumstances, there is not necessarily a clear line that can be drawn between judicial and extra-judicial processes within the court. Nor is there a firm separation of trial judge and mediator judge – indeed, the deliberate fusion of umpiring and mediation responsibilities is seen to be a strength (as we noted above in the parallel case of Chinese med-arb). The view is that such role-fusion offers virtues of flexibility of process, more muscle to the judge's mediation efforts, greater knowledge of the facts of the case for the mediator-judge should she or he subsequently have to impose an adjudicated outcome, as well as a greater certainty of implementation of the agreed outcome in a rapidly changing socio-economic environment in which enforcement of civil law is often difficult (Chen, 2015). As a result of the policy emphasis on securing mediated outcomes, by 2012 two out of every five first instance cases handled by the civil chambers in the people's courts were disposed of by means of judicial mediation (Fu and Palmer, 2015: 5).

---

[16] Zhou (2015: 269).
[17] Palmer (1989: 2007a).
[18] 1981 Civil Procedure Law of the People's Republic of China (for trial implementation); this was superseded in 1991 by a full Code of Civil Procedure, and then further revised in 2007 and 2012. Throughout the various revisions of the law there has been a continuity of emphasis on mediation as the preferred form of decision-making in the civil chambers of the people's courts.
[19] See Zhang Xianchu (2015) for a general account of the pervasive nature of mediation in mainland China over the past fifteen years.

Such a system, however, also has severe weaknesses, especially when viewed from a comparative perspective. Although it is characterised within China as a more 'natural way' of resolving disputes – a distinctive feature of Chinese and other East Asian legal cultures – the fused roles approach fails to address such issues as confidentiality, the authoritative and directive influence of the mediating judge in the mediation process, an over-emphasis of the value of mediated outcomes in a very bureaucratised system of annual appraisal of judicial performance and the uncertain relationship of mediation to efforts to promote the rule of law as encouraged by constitutional reform in 1999 (Chen, 2015). Moreover, the system often creates a difficult role conflict for the judge: 'should I adjudicate, or should I reconcile?' (Xian, 2015).

Annexing Mediation to the Court

In the common law world, however, one rapid development has been the growing use of court-annexed or court-referred mediation. The preference has been for the judge in civil proceedings to refer cases to mediation rather than to mediate herself or himself the dispute before the court. Sometimes, the procedural system that has been put in place mandates the parties to mediate, sometimes it places an obligation on the parties in good faith to consider mediation, and sometimes it may use quasi-compulsion by, for example, imposing costs on a party that fails to take up opportunities for mediation or at the very least to consider mediation.

Court-ordered Mediation

Graham provides an interesting examination of an early example of compulsory court-annexed mediation in family disputes in one county in California. He observes: 'mediation is mandatory in that parties to a contested custody case must participate in an initial referral to mediation, unless the requirement is weighed by the court upon a showing of good cause . . . in the determination of good cause, the presence of domestic violence is the only definitive criterion' (1993: 1113). However, it is recognised that keeping the parties in mediation against their will beyond a certain point is counterproductive and so the court rules provide that while all parents must comply with a referral to mediation, and are encouraged by the court to give mediation an opportunity to work, nevertheless 'compulsion to attend beyond the initial stage would appear to be futile' (1993: 1124). Graham concludes, nevertheless, that:

> Even if mediation were slightly more costly and slower than litigation, there might be reasons to expose parents to that option. The adversarial process of divorce takes a particular toll on the children who are involved. The ability of mediation to eliminate much of the anger and anxiety involved in adversarial proceedings could make it preferable for disputes involving children . . . [so] . . . comparison of mediated outcomes with litigated outcomes must await long-term use of such programs (1993: 1123–4).

Court-referred Mediation: The Mayor's and City of London Court Mediation Scheme

In England and Wales under the civil procedural rules noted earlier, the Mayor's and City of London Court offers a voluntary mediation scheme for dealing with, in particular, contract, tort, property and commercial cases:

> Mediation under the Scheme is a selective process, taking place at the discretion of a District Judge. A referral may originate either in a request from one of the parties, or in a suggestion from a Judge made on reading the papers or at a Case Management Conference; but in the great majority of cases under the Pilot, the initial suggestion has come from a Judge. Mediation is then only ordered with the agreement of all parties to the dispute. In referring to mediation, the District Judges do not operate a formal 'intake procedure', explaining to parties the nature and goals of mediation or giving directions as to information to be assembled and exchanged prior to mediation. But a *Guide for Parties Preparing for Mediation* [Form: M&C Med 13] is forwarded to parties at a later date (Roberts, Simon, 2013: 126).

Most of the cases referred to mediation are made early on in the court proceedings as illustrated in the following case dealing with a problem of the quality of some laundry baskets:

> A claim was filed on 16th June 2006 in respect of an unpaid invoice relating to the sale of laundry baskets. A defence was entered on 27th denying agreement to buy in the numbers supplied and counter claiming in respect of poor quality. Judge Trent considered the papers on 28th July on return of the Allocation Questionnaires and arranged a Case Management Conference to be held on the telephone on 22nd August. On that occasion, the parties accepted the judge's suggestion that mediation should be attempted. A letter of request was sent to the City Disputes Panel on 5th September and a mediation was set up to take place on 26th September. Agreement was reached at a mediation conducted on that occasion (Roberts, Simon, 2013: 126–7).

But the judge may also sometimes merely encourage settlement between the parties, only referring them to a mediator when bilateral attempts at settlement have proven unsuccessful (Roberts, Simon, 2013: 127).

The referral is conducted in very formal terms, commencing when a judge authorises the dispatch of an initial letter proposing mediation from the Court Mediation Officer to both parties commending 'mediation to the parties as a "cost-effective flexible process that offers a wider range of settlement outcomes than the court can offer at trial"' (Roberts, Simon, 2013: 127–8). In addition, the letter advises the parties of the nature and the availability of the Court Scheme:

- The readiness of the court to grant a stay of proceeding to enable mediation to take place;
- The responsibility of legal advisers to advise their clients of the advantages of mediation;

- The potential cost consequences of an unjustified refusal to mediate;
- The importance of referring the letter's contents immediately to a legal adviser.

Attached to the letter are:

- A leaflet, prepared by the Court, explaining the advantages of mediation and the details of the Mediation Scheme.
- A form of response [Form: M&C Med 3] through which parties confirm their willingness or unwillingness to enter mediation and inform the Court of any dates on which they will be unable to attend mediation (Roberts, Simon, 2013: 128).

We should note the letter's identification of two vital points of information to be conveyed to the parties, first, the duty of the parties' legal advisers to explain the benefits of mediation to the parties and, secondly, the potential costs of any unjustified refusal to mediate. In addition, there are two attachments to the Court Mediation Officer's letter, the first being a court leaflet explaining the details of the mediation scheme and pointing to the advantages of mediation and the second a response form in which the parties inter alia confirm willingness (or not) to mediate. Where the parties affirm their willingness to mediate, the action is stayed and the parties are put in touch with the mediation provider – in this case, the City Disputes Panel – who contacts the parties, makes the arrangements necessary for the mediation, appoints a mediator and advises on the mediation fees (which must be paid before the mediation takes place). The procedure to be used in the mediation is not specified by the court itself but, rather, is contained in the mediation provider's guidelines and code of practice on mediation:

> Mediators under the Scheme differ as to whether it is appropriate to make contact with the parties prior to mediation. Those who do so, use these prior contacts to explain the procedure and acquire a preliminary understanding of the respective negotiating positions, moving directly into a plenary session when the parties meet at the IDRC. Others have short introductory meetings with each party at the beginning of the session.
>
> Mediators observed under the Scheme differ as to whether they communicate primarily with the parties or their legal representatives (if present). Some mediators communicate directly with the parties, placing the parties immediately on either side of them at the table to underline this priority. Others ask at the beginning who they should communicate with primarily; yet others speak directly to the legal representatives as a matter of course.
>
> In all cases observed, the mediator stressed that his or her role was to facilitate negotiations by helping with communication and the exchange of information rather than advising on or encouraging any particular outcome. However, interventions by the mediator invariably went beyond those of a 'go-between'. All mediators drew the parties' attention at an early stage, and at subsequent

moments during the mediation, to the economic consequences of continued litigation. This was done in a variety of ways. One mediator simply asked the respective legal teams to provide him with a 'schedule of costs incurred so far and an estimate of those involved in proceeding to trial'. Another approach was for the mediator to conduct a 'risk assessment' with each party in which the costs and prospects of continued litigation were explicitly examined. Here one strategy was to focus attention on the figures recorded in the Allocation Questionnaire, which appear often to underestimate the true cost of proceeding to trial. One mediator read out to those present a newspaper report of a Court of Appeal case in which the overall costs had very far exceeded the relatively small sum originally claimed.

All the mediators observed used a system of 'shuttle' mediation. After an initial joint session, they invariably separated the parties and subsequently conducted the greater part of the process alone with each side, moving backwards and forwards between their respective rooms. Some mediators encouraged the parties to remain in joint session for a short time after a preliminary exchange of positions; but none let the joint session continue when contentious issues started to be addressed. Once separated, parties were not brought together again until a final joint meeting at which any understanding reached was confirmed, formalized and recorded in writing.

This structural arrangement has important consequences for the mediator and for the parties. For mediators, this arrangement makes them do more of the work; but gives them greater power. However limited the role that mediators outlined for themselves at the outset of mediation, as the shuttled [process] developed, a strong tendency was observed for the role to expand to include active engagement in producing an agreed result. Typically, the later stages involved progressively energetic attempts to narrow the gap between the sum tendered by one and the amount demanded by the other.

This procedure, under which 'mediation' is constituted of a succession of bilateral negotiations between the mediator and a party, can be regarded as a very impoverished form of intervention, despite its virtually universal use in London commercial mediations. The 'process benefits' of mediation are lost – the parties get little sense that any agreement reached is their joint achievement, and the process is of no help in enabling them to communicate with each other better in the future (Roberts, Simon, 2013: 128–31).

Within this dispute resolution system, the views of the participants – mediators, parties and legal representatives – are considered to be important, and the court invites some of these participants to complete a short questionnaire so as to give the court their views on their involvement in the process:

Responses indicate that the Scheme has been well received by parties and their representatives, as well as by the mediators. Mediation, introduced into what is already a 'culture of settlement', is widely represented as having the central advantage of enabling negotiation to continue where bilateral exchanges have been interrupted by conflict that the dispute itself has generated. Even where a mediated outcome is perceived as far from ideal, parties value the early 'closure' that mediation brings, enabling them to 'get on' with their lives.

Those answering the questionnaire have been unanimous that the cases in which they participated were suitable for referral to mediation and that the reference came at an appropriate moment in the litigation process. Respondents have also generally agreed that the information supplied by the Court before mediation was adequate for the purposes of mediation. However, some lawyers have requested that in future a formal 'bundle' – going beyond the Statement of Claim and the Defence – should be provided. It has also been suggested that parties should be encouraged to supply the mediator with short synopses of their respective positions prior to mediation.

Respondents who took the opportunity to comment on the administration of the Scheme have generally been very complimentary about its organisation.

Parties and their representatives have almost all been of the view that mediators showed a good understanding of the important issues in dispute and exercised satisfactory skill in seeking to facilitate settlement.

Despite this general satisfaction with the process, parties do not invariably feel happy about diversion to mediation, or with the ensuing result ... Even where further litigation would be prohibitively costly, some lay parties prove very hard to distract from their day in court ...

As monitor of the Mediation Scheme at the Mayor's and City of London Court, I received three complaints during the first five years of the Scheme's operation. In the first of these a lay party had been coerced into mediation on an inconvenient day by the mediator; and that the mediator [a solicitor] had then shown partiality towards the other party's representative solicitor. The second involved a lay party's complaint that he had been disadvantaged by the settlement effectively reached by the insurance companies concerned. The third was a complaint by a solicitor that his client had been put under unacceptable pressure to go to mediation by the judge (he made no complaint about the subsequent mediation or the settlement reached) (Roberts, Simon, 2013: 137–9).

Simon Roberts' empirical study of this scheme shows that one problem that can arise is where a party fails to send along to the mediation a sufficiently senior member of the organisation involved in the dispute and who lacks the authority to settle. In these circumstances, the overly junior participant may cause considerable delay in the resolution process by frequently seeking instructions and guidance from absentee seniors. Another problem that may arise is where the legal representative of a party is a barrister specialising in court work, and inclined to treat the mediation as if it was an exercise in litigation rather than a negotiation process leading to a joint decision. More generally, the mediation process could be undermined by the asymmetries created where one side of the dispute is a lay party, and the other side is represented by a (partisan lawyer). In addition, achieving a settlement through mediation proves more difficult where the principal parties did not attend mediation in person, so that their legal representatives needed to break off the process in order to consult the principals (Roberts, Simon, 2013: 141–2).

The Mayor's and City of London Scheme for mediation is clearly voluntary – but not entirely so given the cost sanctions that can be imposed on a party that is successful (winning the case, that is, if the dispute goes to trial). When the court explicitly requires the parties to attend mediation before allowing a trial to take place, however, there is clearly a problem of voluntariness in the participation in mediation and a persisting doubt that Hazel Genn and colleagues have characterised as 'twisting arms' or 'quasi-compulsory mediation' (Genn et al., 2007).

Genn also notes elsewhere, however, that the empirical evidence is that in court-based mediation schemes in England and Wales the lawyers play a critical gatekeeping role: the pilot scheme (which she and colleagues examined) was not interpreted by most solicitors as compulsory in any sense and many regarded opting out as a mere bureaucratic move. Considered justification for opting out included the timing of the referral, the anticipated cost of mediation in low value claims, the intransigence of the opponent, the subject matter of the dispute and a firm belief that the case would likely settle in any event and mediation was therefore unnecessary (Genn et al., 2007: 198).

Nevertheless, there remain powerful criticisms of the annexation or incorporation of mediation into the judicial process and of the drive to make it compulsory. There is rigorous debate about the appropriateness of court-linked mediation, raising as it does important issues relating to consent, choice of mediator, remuneration, and court accountability for the manner in which the mediation is carried out. The reader is referred to Thornquist (1989) and Ingleby (1993) for early and perceptive critiques.

The Special or Settlement Master

A further novel procedure, now commonly followed in North American jurisdictions, is the appointment of a 'special master' (sometimes referred to also as a 'settlement master') by the court at early stage appointments. The special master will be an experienced neutral, familiar with the area of dispute concerned. Such an appointment will likely be made where the court considers that the possibilities of settlement have not been exhaustively explored by the parties themselves, especially in particularly complex civil cases. As Judge Jack B. Weinstein, who has influenced important substantive and procedural aspect of mass tort litigation, observes, in handling of cases that are complex and large, 'Special Masters ... might well be needed to supplement the judge and to act as brokers among the various interested groups ... to serve as a bridge and buffer to the many communities, individuals, and government officials affected' (1995: 49, 95). The role of the special master is to orchestrate the exploration of possibilities for settlement, reporting back to the court with a draft agreement or a recommendation that the case proceeds on to adjudication. The Federal Rule of

Civil Procedure, Rule 53, defining the role of the special master is, however, couched in very broad terms:

(a) *APPOINTMENT.*
  (1) Scope. Unless a statute provides otherwise, a court may appoint a master only to:
  (A) perform duties consented to by the parties;
  (B) hold trial proceedings and make or recommend findings of fact on issues to be decided without a jury if appointment is warranted by:
    (i) some exceptional condition; or
    (ii) the need to perform an accounting or resolve a difficult computation of damages; or
  (C) address pretrial and post-trial matters that cannot be effectively and timely addressed by an available district judge or magistrate judge of the district.

Special masters are typically private lawyers, retired judges or law professors. The history of the special master goes back to early English Chancery practice, and was formally adopted by the Federal Rules of Civil Procedure in the United States in 1938. They are appointed by a judge in an individual case when there is a 'special condition' or need, and the system in effect involves a delegation of judicial case management functions. Although emerging to play an important role in a number of very important mass tort cases, the special masters are in fact brought in to assist the court and the parties in quite a wide range of cases, including those for child custody, construction, natural resources allocation, land use planning boundary disputes between states, and even sometimes just to help a court deal with an extremely heavy case load. A 'special master' was also appointed by the US Congress to administer compensation for victims of the 9/11 2001 attacks (Feinberg et al., 2011).[20]

A particularly important development, however, has been the accretion of mediation functions by the special masters. Courts in the United States came increasingly to appoint special masters with a view to handling a number of

---

[20] But see also Berkowitz who argues that the special master was given unacceptably robust decision-making powers in administering compensation for the 9/11 victims:

> 'Special Master is a powerful decision maker vested with unfettered discretion to craft and run the Fund. All of our traditions, constitutional, doctrinal, and otherwise, militate against such authority being concentrated in a single individual. Moreover, previous congressional experience with national compensation schemes warns against the vesting of such [unreviewable] discretion in a single individual' (2006: 2–3).

This critique notwithstanding, Herszenhorn (2016) notes the appointment of a special master to oversee a new fund to compensate victims of state-sponsored terrorism:

> The fund, created by Congress late last year, will provide compensation to victims of attacks like the bombings of American embassies in East Africa in 1998 and the bombings of the American Embassy and Marine Corps barracks in Lebanon in the early 1980s. It is also intended to compensate the Americans taken hostage at the United States Embassy in Tehran in 1979.

the preparatory tasks in civil suits and to assist the parties to reach their own settlement, and in carrying out these tasks found themselves supporting negotiations between the parties, sometimes to the point where they were in effect acting more as mediators. Indeed, in the famous *Agent Orange* case, Judge Weinstein specifically appointed several lawyers as special 'settlement masters', with mediation and settlement functions (Silberman, 1989: 2130).

In the early 1980s case, *United States v Michigan*, a complex litigation over many issues involving management of one of the largest lakes in the world, with the five named parties representing virtually all Michigan citizens, the court found the issues to be so complex, and umpiring solutions seemingly so inappropriate given this complexity, that:

> The court . . . assigned the special master to mediate among the named parties and the litigating amici. Because the case would eventually [go for trial before] the judge, his ability to facilitate negotiation was limited by his strong ethical constraints against prejudging the outcome of the case. Therefore, the master performed this role while insulating the judge from the details of any bargaining. As a part of the mediation role, the master also kept the parties' critical decision-makers aware of the progress of the litigation and the negotiations. He met with the leaders and sometimes virtually all the members of the tribes, officials of the U.S. Department of the Interior, and Michigan's Governor, Attorney General, and the Director of its Department of Natural Resources (McGovern, 1986: 463).

The special master has thus become an important procedural innovation, offering among other services, a form of pre-trial facilitated negotiation and mediatory intervention. Doubts have been expressed, however, about certain procedural aspects of the role, including the relationship and communications between the trial judge and the special master (especially if the master feels the need to secure 'leverage' by behind the scenes contact with the judge) and over-reliance on a limited number of social masters capable of handling the complex issues often involved and leading to 'potential conflicts of interest' (Weinstein, 1995: 108; Silberman, 1989: 2015).

In addition, one of the special master mediators appointed by Judge Weinstein in the *Agent Orange* case has described his approach in that case in terms that suggest that the mediation process itself can sometimes be very robust in the special master context:

> Backed by Weinstein, we mediators played each side against the other.

> For hours each day, Shapiro and I met privately with the lawyers representing the veterans. A dark, empty Brooklyn courtroom with no windows was our venue of choice. We warned them that their case was woefully weak and depended on the court's willingness to let the jury hear medical testimony about the link between Agent Orange and the alleged injuries; were the lawyers willing to take the risk that Weinstein would summarily dismiss their claims? Shapiro and I took turns playing 'good cop, bad cop.' First Shapiro would argue that the case was weak, that even a sympathetic judge such as Weinstein would not let

the jury hear it. Then I would interrupt; even if the case was heard by the jury, the appellate court likely would reject any verdict, Weinstein notwithstanding. At best, the Vietnam veterans' victory would be Pyrrhic.

We made the opposite arguments to the eight defendant chemical companies. We warned them that the court was sympathetic to the plight of Vietnam veterans and would be disinclined to deny them their day in court before a Brooklyn jury. Besides, we reminded the companies, they benefited from plenty of insurance to pay for a comprehensive settlement. Why not settle now and avoid protracted litigation with an uncertain outcome? We argued that practical business realities pointed toward a settlement.

We hammered away, day after day, week after week, trying to get the veterans and the chemical companies to agree to a comprehensive deal and avoid a trial.

In the early morning hours of May 7, 1984, just as potential jurors were ordered to court to be interviewed for the trial, and after a final all-night mediation effort, Judge Weinstein announced a comprehensive settlement. The court, the mediators, and the lawyers had not left the courthouse until after midnight the previous evening, exhausted but satisfied that a complex, uncertain trial had been avoided (Feinberg, 2012: 27–8).

The Summary Jury Trial

The summary jury trial is a court-based development of the mini-trial. Emerging around 1980, it is a method intended to afford the disputants some insight into the most probable jury reaction to their cases. It is thought to be especially useful when settlement discussions have seemingly reached an impasse:

> The summary jury trial is not intended to supplant the traditional jury trial. Instead, judges should employ the device when conventional lawyer-judge negotiations fail to produce settlement. This effective judicial procedure fosters meaningful settlement discussions between parties whose uncompromising bargaining positions require a deliberate and controlled context to move toward agreement (Lambros, 1989: 798–9).

The process is in effect a truncated version of a trial in which concise presentations are made by the parties' lawyers before an advisory jury, with a judge or magistrate presiding. Attendance by the parties and their lawyers is compulsory. The jurors, who are unaware that their verdict is non-binding and advisory, are questioned about the verdict that they have reached, and about the parties' summary presentations. In the light of the verdict and the questions and answers that follow, settlement negotiations and perhaps mediation take place. The verdict of the jury is not, however, admissible at the trial that follows from failed settlement negotiations (Lambros, 1993).

The aim of this procedural innovation is to afford each disputant the opportunity to predict more accurately the outcome of the trial, and to encourage the disputants and their lawyers to reach a settlement and avoid the costs of a full trial. Nevertheless, the extent to which parties are in fact encouraged to settle by this novel procedure is unclear, and it is a process that does entail significant costs. It is therefore probably most effective in cases where a lengthy trial is in prospect or particularly difficult issues of fact or law are involved.[21] It is not clear, however, that the federal courts in the United States actually do have the authority to make participation in the summary jury trial mandatory (see Woodley, 1995). Other criticisms of this innovation argue that the summary jury trial amounts to little more than a rather costly method of pushing the parties into settlement, adding another layer of procedural complexity and not necessarily giving an accurate prediction of full trial outcomes because the evidence presented in the summary jury trial may be incomplete and therefore unreliable (Posner, 1986: 387–9).

Perhaps because of such negative views, the summary jury trial has not gained widespread acceptance in the civil courts (Croley, 2008: 1586). However, some observers now take the view that the public-private mix which the summary jury trial offers – of a public hearing of the parties' cases and the private processes of settlement negotiation and mediation – may have much greater potential for enhancing access to justice than has hitherto been recognised.[22] Thus, Welsh encourages the courts to 'take a second look at the summary jury trial, a dispute resolution process that has fallen into some disuse' (2010: 1158). The summary jury trial and its contextualising negotiation and mediation stages – in which the language of discussion may well be more readily understood by marginalised individuals – have the potential to deliver prompt resolution, justice and dialogue:

> Pre-trial and pre-litigation consensual procedures that offer real voice and opportunity for effective dialogue and resolution to marginalized individuals should be lauded, not undermined. Surely our courts, as part of a democratic justice system, want to continue to encourage individuals and institutions to listen to each other and work together toward solutions, before accessing expensive and precious public resources. Assuring access to the courts helps to achieve this goal . . . [and] . . . a summary jury trial would provide a marginalized plaintiff with the opportunity to tell her story to a judge, jury and decision-makers for the defendant (Welsh, 2010: 1185).

Early Neutral Evaluation

As noted above in our discussion of 'negotiation-related innovations' an additional area in which courts have attempted to innovate by reliance on neutral intermediaries who promote settlement between the disputing parties

---

[21] This process also, however, offers the possibility of its strategic use in pre-trial proceedings so that it becomes a complicating element in the negotiations between the parties rather than an effective aid to settlement.

[22] There are clear parallels here with the arguments of Luban (1995), in his partial defence of Fiss, as discussed in Chapter 3.

is early neutral evaluation (ENE). This procedure, which originated in the United States District Court for the Northern District of California (San Francisco), evolved out of the role of special master, and is intended to encourage each party to understand better its own legal position in the case by providing a forum in which the parties present their respective cases and receive an independent, neutral assessment of the likely outcome. Briefly stated, the process involves a meeting between the parties and their lawyers (ideally within 150 days of filing suit), chaired by a neutral evaluator, in which points of agreement and the strengths and weaknesses of each party are considered. The neutral, who is typically in the Californian scheme a respected lawyer who is expert in the subject matter of the case, prepares a written case evaluation that, if the parties do not settle with his or her encouragement, provides guidance in the development of a plan for subsequent management of the case.

On the basis of presentations by both sides and evaluator questioning of the parties, the neutral evaluator offers an objective assessment of the evidence and arguments and likely outcome. This hopefully will form the basis of settlement negotiation, but if an agreement between the parties does not result, then the evaluator will help the parties to plan for information sharing and discovery in respect of key issues. The process is confidential, and the evaluator barred from sharing information with the judge assigned for the trial. The intention is that ENE will enhance communication, make discovery cheaper and easier and encourage the parties to be more realistic about their respective positions (Brazil, 1990: 407–9). There are clear parallels here with the evaluative mediation process, although with less involvement in, and responsibility for, negotiations between the parties. In reality, the overall shape of the ENE process is subject to considerable variation:

> The ENE process was intended to lie somewhere between mediation, in which a third party with substantial procedural expertise facilitates communication among the parties in the interest of settling some or all of the issues in dispute, and nonbinding arbitration, in which a third party with substantial subject matter expertise reviews the case presented by the litigants and determines an appropriate outcome. As conducted, ENE ran the gamut from one extreme to the other, and sometimes bore little resemblance to any other process. Most evaluators appraised their cases in some respects, but the specificity and directness of these appraisals varied tremendously from actual predictions of jury verdicts to subtle hints about possible weaknesses of a claim or defense ... As a result of the variation in the timing and conduct of ENE sessions, we cannot easily generalize about the process. All we can say that is universally true of ENE is that it is a confidential meeting of the parties, their attorneys, and a neutral third party who is an experienced and respected trial attorney (Rosenberg and Folger, 1994: 1495).

Nevertheless, it seems that there is a high level of party satisfaction with the process, especially in regard to early disposition of cases, parties' enhanced understanding of cases, and substantial costs savings (Rosenberg and Folger, 1994: 1496).

In England and Wales, the ENE process has been specifically encouraged by the Commercial Court, especially in its important 1996 Practice Statement (Commercial Cases: Alternative Dispute Resolution [No. 2]):

> If, after discussion with those representing the parties, it appears to the judge that an early neutral evaluation is likely to assist in the resolution of the matters in dispute, he may offer to provide that evaluation himself or to arrange for another judge to do so. If that course is accepted by the parties, the judge may thereupon give directions as to such preparatory steps for that evaluation and the form which it is to take and he considers appropriate. The parties will in that event be required to arrange for the Commercial Court Listing Office the time for the evaluation hearing having regard to the availability of the judge concerned.

> Where neutral evaluation is provided by a judge, that judge will, unless the parties otherwise agree, take no further part in the proceedings either for the purpose of the hearing of summons or as trial judge.

> Except where an early neutral evaluation is to be provided by judge, the parties will be responsible for agreeing up on a neutral for the purposes of ADR and will be responsible for his fees and expenses . . . the Commercial Court keeps a list of individuals from bodies that offer mediation, conciliation and other ADR services. If, after ADR has been recommended to them by the judge, the parties are unable to agree upon a neutral for ADR they may by consent refer to the judge for assistance in reaching such an agreement.

> On the hearing of any summons in the course of which the judge invites the parties to take steps to resolve the differences by ADR he may on that occasion order as to costs that the parties may incur by reason of the using, or attempting to use, ADR as may in all the circumstances seem appropriate.

The use of early neutral evaluation by the courts is now governed by CPR Rule 3.1(2)(m):

The court's general powers of management
3.1

(1) The list of powers in this rule is in addition to any powers given to the court by any other rule or practice direction or by any other enactment or any powers it may otherwise have.
(2) Except where these Rules provide otherwise, the court may –

. . .

(m) take any other step or make any other order for the purpose of managing the case and furthering the overriding objective, including hearing an Early Neutral Evaluation with the aim of helping the parties settle the case.

The evaluating judge examines the applicable law and relevant facts of the case, considers the parties' submissions, and provides the parties with a non-binding evaluation. The Commercial Court continues to encourage early neutral evaluation, but it does require the parties to secure approval of the evaluator from the Commercial Court List, and the neutral evaluating judge is not allowed then to continue to be involved in the case if there is no settlement, unless the supporters request such continued involvement. The official guide provided for intending litigants on the procedures of the Commercial Court characterises the system in the following terms:

G.2: Early neutral evaluation

G2.1
In appropriate cases and with the agreement of all parties the court will provide a without-prejudice, non-binding, early neutral evaluation ('ENE') of a dispute or of particular issues.

G2.2
The approval of the Judge in Charge of the List must be obtained before any ENE is undertaken.

G2.3
If, after discussion with the advocates representing the parties, it appears to a judge that an ENE is likely to assist in the resolution of the dispute or of particular issues, he will, with the agreement of the parties, refer the matter to the Judge in Charge of the List.

G2.4
(a) The Judge in Charge of the List will nominate a judge to conduct the ENE.
(b) The judge who is to conduct the ENE will give such directions for its preparation and conduct as he considers appropriate (HM Courts and Tribunals Service, 2014: 55–6).

Although thus encouraged by the courts and with the judge as the evaluator, ENE may also take place extra-judicially, before or during the litigation process. The choice of evaluator is then a matter for the parties who may agree an evaluator or be guided by a recognised institutional provider.

Court-annexed Arbitration

In addition to these processes of settlement discussions involving the judge, and court-related mediation programmes, procedural innovations have been introduced in which the court encourages or even exercises an authority to order arbitration before the case is allowed to proceed to trial. In the United States, court-annexed arbitration is ordinarily used by trial courts in order to deal with cases of relatively low monetary value which raise particularly complex or novel legal issues or where the legal issues are clearly much more important than the factual dimensions of the case. The system is mandatory but non-binding, with the parties presenting their cases in an informal, simplified hearing to a court-approved arbitrator (or arbitrators) who renders an award. This award may be rejected by either party by opting for a trial *de novo* – otherwise, the award becomes final after a time limit has been reached. The basic features of this system, and arguments for its wider mandatory use, are clearly identified in an analysis by Broderick (1989) of the first programme of court-annexed compulsory arbitration to be introduced into the federal court system. In the United States, experiments began in the US District Court in the eastern district of Pennsylvania in the late 1970s, after the Follow-Up Task Force of the Pound Conference had encouraged experimentation with court-annexed arbitration in the federal courts, in the hope that this might broaden access to the justice system by encouraging the efficient and cost-effective resolution of civil disputes.

Experience with the scheme suggested a need to limit the scheme to cases below a certain amount – that is, for a scheme of financial capping – so that the scheme was then limited to cases where the amount in dispute was $75,000 or less. A more generous capping might encourage losing parties in higher value cases to demand a trial *de novo*, thereby reducing the arbitration programme to just one more step in the litigation process. Moreover, parties had to deposit arbitration fees in advance of the hearing. Broderick continues: 'For the most part, the program is administered by the clerk of the court. When the plaintiff files his or her complaint, the local rule provides that damages are presumed to be not in excess of $75,000 unless counsel certifies otherwise'. In order to assist the parties, moreover, and to avoid unnecessary arbitration: 'The local arbitration rule specifically provides that in the event a party files a motion for judgment on the pleadings, summary judgment or similar relief, the case may not be arbitrated until the court has ruled on the motion' (1989: 220).

The court appoints three arbitrators – typically, these are randomly selected from a large pool of experienced lawyers who have been certified to arbitrate. Federal Rules of Evidence are used as guidelines for admissibility of evidence, with some local modifications. The arbitration takes place in the federal courthouse itself, but if the case proceeds to a court trial, neither the fact that the case was arbitrated nor the arbitrator's award are admissible, save in exceptional circumstances. If the arbitration is concluded successfully, the arbitration clerk prepares a judgment for the judge to sign, attaching to that judgment the arbitral award. The award records only the outcome of the arbitration, and does not offer findings of fact, conclusions of law, arbitrators' opinions or whether or not the panel's decision is unanimous. The award becomes a final judgment within thirty days and unless one or both parties demand a trial *de novo*, no appeal against the arbitral award is allowed. But if the case goes to trial, it will do so quickly, as if it had never been before the arbitration panel. Arbitration fees are only returnable to a party if it wins the case and the court's judgment is more favourable than the arbitrator's award.

A general problem in mixed processes where the processes are staged is that the initial stage is often in danger of being used by the parties for discovery purposes. In order to prevent this court-ordered arbitration scheme from degenerating into a fishing expedition, a good faith requirement was introduced so that:

> After a decision of the court denying a defendant's demand for trial de novo on the ground that the defendant failed to participate in good faith at the arbitration trial, the court amended its local rule to specifically provide that if a party fails to participate in the arbitration process in a meaningful manner, the court may deny that party's demand for trial de novo. Since this amendment to the local rule, there has been no indication that the parties are using the arbitration trial as a discovery device (Broderick, 1989: 222).

These court-annexed arbitration programmes have, however, been subject to weighty criticism. Thus, Eisele (1991) has argued that such programmes contain an inherent contradiction that is, in effect, a barrier to justice. He argues that 'if the decision is to file suit and go to trial, it is my view that the parties should not be forced to go through one of these procedures as a condition precedent to their right to trial before a . . . judge . . . the people of this nation [should have] their day in court . . . unencumbered by costly non-judicial diversions' (1991: 35–6). Doubtful claims of enhancing efficiency and facilitating party interests should not therefore be used to justify the use of inferior processes of arbitration that in reality are aimed at coercing settlement. Moreover, the use of court-ordered arbitration in relatively small cases – 'small' as defined by arbitrarily determined case-value capping – may make the process more, rather than less, expensive for the economically weak parties, because it requires in effect funding for what becomes a two-stage decision-making process. And the more relaxed rules on evidence gathering, together with an absence of cross-examination, are also likely to disadvantage the weaker party. Thus, compulsory arbitration schemes should be resisted by the court: 'Principle should be vindicated; rights established; extortion resisted; and justice – pure justice – done at least occasionally' (1991: 37). Posner, too, constructs broadly similar criticisms, arguing that court-ordered arbitration may be less expensive than a civil trial but it is likely to be more expensive than settlement negotiations per se, as it requires the parties to pay for compulsory arbitration proceedings before being allowed to proceed to trial. This is in effect an unconstitutional financial barrier to justice and inappropriately removes many smaller cases from federal court jurisdiction (Posner, 1986: 387–9).

Rent-a-Judge

The process of rent-a-judge for private umpiring is another Californian innovation and like ENE it is also one that emerged out of the use of special masters. It bears some similarities to arbitration, especially ad hoc arbitration in as much as in both processes the third-party decision-maker and the dispute resolution process are chosen after the problem between the parties has emerged, and it is the parties themselves who pay the fees for the service of private judging. So, in a real sense, parties choose between rent-a-judge and arbitration. However, unlike arbitration, rent-a-judge is an official element of the state court system and a judgment arrived at through the rent-a-judge process has the same legal effect as a judgment from other state courts.

After its introduction in the mid-1970s, the growth of private judging was an important stimulus to the creation and subsequent expansion of the important ADR services provider called 'Judicial Arbitration and Mediation Services', or JAMS as it later became known.[23] According to JAMS, the rent-a-judge system typically takes the form of a private trial that is held before a retired judge, but the judgment may be appealed on grounds of errors of law or weaknesses in evidence.[24] The system has been diffused from California to many other states in the USA. Although there are considerable local variations, a set of core features may be identified. First, it is the parties who choose the judge, and the consent of both parties is an essential precondition to the process. Secondly, it is usually a retired judge or former senior lawyer who acts as a third-party decision-maker. Thirdly, both parties present their evidence and arguments to the private judge who then delivers a reasoned judgment on the basis of factual evidence and the applicable law. As noted above, while the decision of the private judge is binding, it may be appealed against in a regular state court, unlike in an arbitration. In California, the parties select the judge and agree the basic processual features, including when and where to have the trial.

This process is, superficially at least, attractive: 'In some ways, the rent-a-judge system seems to be an ideal hybrid of public and private justice. It offers the speed, efficiency and convenience of arbitration and mediation along with an enforceable appealable state Court decision . . . [and] . . . individual litigants have undoubtedly benefited from rent-a-judge' (Kim, 1994: 189). It has been suggested that three types of case are especially appropriate for private judging,

---

[23] JAMS characterises its development in the following terms: 'The Hon. H. Warren Knight (Ret.) founded J A M S in 1979. During that time our panel included retired judges and JAMS was an acronym for, Inc. (J•A•M•S). Since then, we have grown to welcome members of ENDISPUTE, Bates/Edwards, ADR Associates, and a diverse group of neutrals and associates. Through a combination of the expertise of our associates and distinguished neutrals and effective business practices, we have set the standard for ADR providers nationwide. Now we are JAMS, a distinguished global panel of retired judges and attorneys with uncompromising objectivity who are capable of resolving the most complex disputes where the parties appear to be unyielding (www.jamsadr.com/about-the-jams-name/, accessed 2 December 2019).

[24] 'Private Judging – A private trial conducted by a former judge and is most similar to a conventional trial in that judgment may be appealed for errors of law or as against the weight of the evidence' (www.jamsadr.com/adr-glossary/, accessed 2 December 2019).

- *Family disputes* – Divorces are especially suitable rent-a-judge cases. Few parties are involved, and the issues at stake are very rarely of public significance.
- *Torts* – Garden-variety, single-plaintiff cases that require only the application of existing standards are most appropriate for rent-a-judges to hear. In these cases, the rent-a-judge's function would be mostly fact-finding. As discussed above, however, mass tort and products liability cases may be less suited for rent-a-judge courts.
- *Complex commercial litigation* – Although large sums of money are usually at stake, these cases also involve few interests, and the issues are rarely of significant public importance. Rent-a-judges may even be better suited than public court judges to hear these cases if they have expertise in a particular area (Kim, 1994: 195).

Despite its increased popularity and diffusion over the past few decades, there are persistent critiques of the place of the rent-a-judge process in a civil justice system. One very strong reservation is that the process is essentially a form of private dispute resolution which is too closely associated with the public power of the courts. There are serious worries that since judges are creatures of public law with authority to impose a binding decision that is appealable to the state courts, it is not appropriate for them to be chosen by private agreement between the parties. The main external check on their conduct is the 'market' – thus, despite their public or 'quasi-public' role, rent-a-judges lack public accountability, carrying out their business with the authority of the state but in truth lacking a public mandate.

Secondly, this dispute resolution process often results in the judge imposing an adjudicative outcome, even though the parties' main concern in fact may be to secure a favourable settlement – and if she or he is not careful then parties will be drawn into trying to select a private judge whose past decisions are strongly indicative of how she or he will read the case to which she or he might be invited to sit. Thus, there is a real danger of private interest 'judge-shopping' that has to be guarded against. And, because the parties choose the judge to rent, the reputation of the judge will be important to her or him if she or he wishes to develop a successful practice in private judging.

Thirdly, to be able to rent a judge is essentially a privilege for those who are able to afford the services of private judges, and so this hybrid process might be considered to be an unfair privilege of the wealthy, denying the socio-economically disadvantaged.

Conclusions

The development of ADR since the 1970s in many parts of the world has seen within it innovative modifications of the primary processes of negotiation mediation and umpiring, often in an imaginative and useful way, and also in the spirit of fitting the forum to the fuss. In many ways the inventiveness is admirable and indeed mixed processes have come to be at the forefront of developments in the dispute resolution movement. But, at the same time, the hybridisation that has taken place has done so largely in the hands of legal professionals. The shortcoming of this is that it takes the dispute resolution process further away from one of the original values of the ADR movement, namely, allowing parties to retain control over the process of resolving their dispute, and to relate to each other – in some cases at least – in a way that would facilitate good relations in the future.

11

The Ombuds and its Diffusion: From Public to Private

Introduction

This chapter looks at the rapidly growing dispute resolution institution of the 'ombudsman', for which the now preferred terms are 'ombuds' or 'ombudsperson'. The term ombuds is ordinarily used to characterise an official appointed by government to receive and examine complaints made by citizens against the administration. The ombuds is an independent agency, whose investigative findings are in many jurisdictions not binding in law, but which are nevertheless binding in practice. It is an example of a 'mixed process' institution, but one that is not only unique but also rapidly growing in importance in the Anglo-American common law world. In looking at the ombuds we are considering a dispute resolution system in which primary processes of dispute resolution are combined by the mixing creatively of two or more forms so as to create a more effective 'hybrid', but the ombudsman has never fitted neatly into the typology of responses to disputes that we have identified in this book. It is in many cases a form of umpiring that is modified in several important ways by adding elements of negotiation and mediation. When people around the world learn about civil justice reform in the United Kingdom, they often think about important reforms to civil procedure law – the Civil Procedure Rules introduced by Lord Woolf in the late 1990s. But the truth is that in the United Kingdom, the ombuds is by far the fastest growing form of ADR. Initially the ombuds dealt with public law disputes, but in the past twenty years it has become even more important in the private sector. Here we look at some examples of how the ombuds system works, and also consider why some jurisdictions resist its introduction.

The work of the ombudsperson involves umpiring – making judgments about claimed abuses of public administrative conduct – but it also encompasses a concern to enhance standards of government and may involve extensive use of negotiation with the parties in dispute and mediation. The French institution of 'Médiateur' referred to in Chapter 1 conveys the essentially hybrid nature of the ombudsperson's approach to dispute resolution, indicating something of a concern to promote conciliation as well as to deal with maladministration.

In the common law world, the ombudsperson has been in effect a transplant from the civilian tradition (Verkuil, 1975: 851–6). During the past four decades, the ombudsperson has been established in a wide variety of jurisdictions (Wiegand, 1996). The perceived effectiveness of the ombudsperson has in the United Kingdom encouraged its use in the private as well as the public sectors. The influence of the United States' experience has also been important in this regard, for in that country the idea of the ombudsperson has primarily been applied as part of the management of large organisations, both public and private. The ombudsperson serves as a neutral member of the organisation, reporting directly to the most senior executive and ordinarily positioned outside the established hierarchy of management. The ombudsperson attempts through such processes as counselling, mediation, fact-finding and making recommendations to overcome disputes in the workplace (Singer, 1990: 102). In the United Kingdom, however, the ombudsperson in the private sector has come to serve primarily as an institution for investigating and dealing with complaints made by members of the public against individuals or bodies in particular areas of commercial and professional activity – insurance, banking, conveyancing, lawyers, the media, and so on.

The Growing Importance of the Ombuds

Public and Private Sector Roles

The ombuds initially had an important public law role, and served for many years mainly as a means of dealing with citizen complaints about the state. That is served as an alternative to judicial review. But in the past three decades in the West the ombuds has spread into the private sector. Large private sector institutions such as banks have been criticised for using their strong market powers to treat consumers unfairly, and are in many ways rather like governments – they are large bureaucracies in which it is often difficult to get a quick response if a customer has a problem. So, the ombuds system has rapidly been adopted by these large institutions in an effort to retain customer confidence in the goods and services they offer the public. As a result, although we often think of the ombuds as a way of handling public disputes, in fact the ombuds in many jurisdictions today is mainly concerned with private sector disputes, such as consumer complaints.

Distinctiveness of the Ombuds

The ombuds system of dispute resolution has some very distinctive features. As we have pointed out, it is a mixed process which often combines in innovative ways the three primary processes of dispute resolution – negotiation, mediation and adjudication. For example, making a complaint to an ombuds is ordinarily without cost – it is free of charge. Also, the decision of an ombuds in a case is not necessarily binding – the force of the ombuds decision is his moral rather than legal authority.

Historical Development – Rome and Scandinavia

This ombuds role is sometimes traced back to the ancient Roman 'tribunes of the plebeians' whose role was to intervene in the political process on behalf of ordinary citizens. The concept of the 'ombudsman' or 'ombuds' thus has a very long history, but its modern development took place in Scandinavia. We find in the Danish Law of Jutland, from the middle of the thirteenth century onwards, the term 'umbozman' was used to refer to a royal civil servant in a region of the country, though we know the term was used even before this in Sweden. From the sixteenth century onwards, it is also used in the other Scandinavian languages such as the Icelandic 'umboðsmaður', the Norwegian 'ombudsn' and the Danish 'ombudsd'. The term 'ombuds' is thus first found in early Scandinavian languages – where it carried the meanings of first, 'to accuse' and, secondly, 'to represent' – thus, in terms of its etymology, the word umbud/ombud basically means a substitute or surrogate, that is somebody who is authorised to act for somebody else (and this is a meaning the ombud still carries today in Scandinavian languages) in expressing a grievance.

Historical Development: Islamic Influences?

The more modern understanding of the term may be found initially at the beginning of the eighteenth century, when an 'Office of Supreme Ombuds' (later to be called the 'Chancellor of Justice'), was established in 1713 by the then Swedish King, Charles XII. King Charles XII at that time was in fact in exile in Turkey. And so he needed a representative in Sweden who would in his absence ensure that judges and civil servants acted in accordance with the laws and with their administrative duties. Interestingly, the inspiration for the creation of this Swedish Supreme Ombuds may have been the Turkish institution of the Diwan-al-Mazalim or 'Board of Grievances'. In Arabic, the term Diwan refers to a tribunal, and Mazalim is a concept meaning 'a person who complains of being seriously wronged'. It has been revived as a kind of 'ombudsman' system in a number of contemporary Islamic States, in particular in Saudi Arabia, as David Long (1973) has pointed out. The Diwan-al-Mazalim in classical Islamic governance was a role that acted as a check on governmental performance. It was found in the area that is now Turkey from the seventh century onwards. So there is a very good chance the exiled Swedish King learned of its usefulness as a complaints mechanism from his time as an exile in Turkey. Under the system King Charles introduced in Sweden, if his judges and civil servants did not act lawfully or administer correctly, the Supreme Ombuds had the right to prosecute them for negligence. We should note, in passing, that the ombuds is not the only possible example of early

Islamic influence on the development of the law in Europe through the process
of transplantation. Thus, some scholars today argue that the famous 'Inns of
Court' in London's historic legal district, with its professional class of independent lawyers, have their origins in the Islamic world. In these Inns, English
Barristers used to be trained in law, live together as a community, and dine
each day in the Hall of their Inn. It is argued that the Inn is in reality not an
indigenous invention but, rather, a transplantation of the Sunni Islam schools
of legal theory, which were often housed in 'Madrassas' around mosques.
Scholar-jurists in these 'Madrassas' debated each other on unclear points
of law, in much the same way as English barristers do. How might London
lawyers have learned about these 'Madrassas' ? The answer, most probably, is
through the Crusades, in which Christians went to the Middle East to fight
against Muslim armies.

Historical Development – Separation of Powers Ideal

From these traditional bases, at the beginning of the nineteenth century the
idea of the ombuds as a representative who would 'accuse' was further
developed. An especially important factor in this advance was the ideal of
separation of powers as developed by Montesquieu in the late eighteenth
century. Montesquieu argued that the best government would be one in which
power was balanced among three groups of officials. First, the executive
who enforced laws, parliament (which made laws), and the judges of the courts
(who interpreted laws). Montesquieu thought it most important to create
separate branches of the state with equal but different powers. That way, the
state would avoid placing too much power with one individual or group of
individuals. This idea of dividing government power into three branches
we know, of course, as the 'separation of powers'. And this also encouraged
the idea that there should be an independent figure who would make sure these
various branches of the state – especially the government – did not abuse
the power given to them. Thus, in Sweden, the Swedish Parliamentary Ombuds
was set up by the Government in 1809, as a supervisory agency, independent of
the executive branch, which would safeguard the rights of citizens by establishing a process of independent inquiry into alleged governmental misconduct.
This Parliamentary Ombuds was established by the Swedish Parliament, as a
parallel institution to the then still-operating Chancellor of Justice. And it is
this Parliamentary Ombuds – rather than the Chancellor of Justice – that is the
key institution that the Scandinavian countries subsequently shaped into its
present-day form of ombuds, and which has been adopted in many other legal
systems. So, it is the predecessor of current ombuds institutions. In a sense, all
today's ombudsmen are a result of the transplantation of this idea – perhaps a
fusion of Scandinavian and Islamic ideas of good governance.

So, in many parts of the world today, the ombuds has been, or is being
introduced. And although the classic model is the public law model – citizen

complaints of maladministration by state officials – it has for several reasons become even more important in the private sector. Often, the ombuds is designed to be a very special form of dispute resolution, and these special features help us to understand its migration to the private sector and more general diffusion. Its distinctive features include: (1) it does not easily 'fit in' with existing institutions – the ombuds is not intended to be part of the executive, or the judiciary or the legislature (although, as we shall see, it may have links with the legislature in some cases); (2) it is thus often planned to be 'free floating', working at a level above existing institutions; (3) the ombuds' basic procedure is something like a 'judicial inquiry', in which a judge independently decides on the correctness of a citizen complaint, but in the process of decision-making, may find negotiation and mediation produce results that mean that no adjudicative type decision is needed; (4) the ombuds tries to be small scale, so that it does not become a 'self-interested' institution looking for ways of generating revenue so that it can survive; (5) the ombuds tries to create a level playing field – the ombuds is not a citizen champion per se – instead, the role of the ombuds is to make sure that if a complaint of maladministration is made, the accusation is investigated properly and fairly, regardless of the power and authority of the respective parties; and (6) the ombuds is designed to be a prestigious, independent, influential and well-respected institution – sometimes, even more so than the courts.

Two Kinds of Ombuds

Broadly speaking, the ADR literature now identifies two kinds of ombudsperson, one operating in the public sector, the other in the private sector.

Public Law (Scandinavian) Model

First, there is the public law type, and this is the basic model. The public law type ombuds developed out of a need to ensure good governance and a route to justice for those whose rights had been infringed by poor governance. Nowadays, the basic understanding of this type of ombuds office is one of a public official who is appointed, (a) to hear citizen complaints about maladministration; (b) to conduct independent fact-finding investigations; and (c) then to correct any maladministration that the ombuds concludes has occurred. Clearly, this role is one of a kind of 'umpire', but it is also sometimes one with important mediatory and negotiation functions. This is because in the course of investigation, the ombuds may be able to get the parties to talk to each other more effectively – that is, the ombuds facilitates negotiations – or can act as a communication bridge between the parties as a kind of mediator, so that the problem is resolved before a report needs to be made. In some jurisdictions, especially in the common law world, an ombuds responsible for the handling of concerns about national government is more formally referred to as the 'Parliamentary Commissioner' (for example, the United Kingdom Parliamentary Commissioner for Administration). In a number of states nowadays, this type of ombuds' duties extends beyond dealing with alleged maladministration. Such an ombuds is also expected to promote and protect human rights. In such instances, then, the ombuds is seen not just as a dispute resolver, but also as a national human rights institution.

The Basic Process in Current Systems

In the public ombuds systems as we find them today, we can see a number of common features. The ombuds investigates complaints. The ombuds is inquisitorial in approach, rather than adversarial, in that this is not a process in which lawyers argue the case in front of an umpire, but their ombuds may also facilitate negotiation and carry out mediation. The ombuds tries to be accessible, as part of a modern system of access to justice, but sometimes not too accessible lest the case load becomes too large to handle. The ombuds does not charge any fees for handling the complaint – it is a free service, in that making a complaint to an ombuds is ordinarily without cost, and this is very different from litigation or even professional mediation. The ombuds process is expected to provide just, fair outcomes, but in addition to assist government agencies to be proactive in offering better governance by giving the defendant agency feedback on the lessons learned through the handling of the complaint.

Private Ombudspersons: Organisational Ombuds and 'Sectoral' Ombuds

The public model, although not without problems, has stimulated the thinking of many people about how to handle better disputes outside the public sector. Increasingly, use is made of a person who is a neutral member within a particular organisation, or regulatory body, who is given the responsibility for helping to resolve disputes relating to a particular kind of activity (for example, banking) through investigation and recommendations, but also – much more than in the public sector ombuds – by negotiation and mediation. In fact, this private sector development has spread so far and wide that we can now identify two sub-types of the private sector ombuds: (1) within a single organisation; and (2) within a sector or sphere of activity – a 'sectoral ombuds'. In England and Wales, for example, one type of sectoral ombuds – the Insurance Ombuds – seems to have been a particularly effective mechanism. First set up in 1981, it then grew steadily in importance. Insurance companies in an increasingly competitive market were very worried about the impact of any adverse report on their commercial reputation and therefore willing to consider settlement of claims in circumstances where they ordinarily would not. It was then followed by the creation of other ombuds systems dealing with financial and related matters: Banking (1985), Building Societies (1986),

Estate Agents (1990), Pensions (1991), Legal Services (1991), Housing (1996), Telecommunications (2003), and so on.

In the text which follows we look at these different types in a little more detail.

Public Law Ombuds

In general, as noted above, an 'ombuds' refers to a state official appointed to provide a check on government activity in the interests of the citizen. In particular, it handles and investigates complaints of improper government conduct which has infringed the rights of a citizen. If the 'ombuds' investigation shows a complaint to be substantiated, the problem may be rectified by the governmental agency concerned. Alternatively, an ombuds' report is published, containing findings and making recommendations for change. Resulting remedies may include financial compensation. Ombuds in most jurisdictions do not have the authority to initiate legal proceedings – nor to bring a prosecution on the grounds of a complaint. The major advantage of an ombuds is that he or she examines complaints from outside the offending state institution, thus avoiding the conflicts of interest inherent in self-policing. Outside Scandinavia, however, the introduction of ombuds has sometimes been difficult and controversial. The reasons for these difficulties are not clear, but may reflect the fact that any public law ombuds system that is good requires: (1) an appropriate, highly trained and honest individual for the office; and (2) the cooperation of relevant officials from within the state bureaucracy.

United Kingdom

In the United Kingdom, the office of the Parliamentary Commissioner for Administration was created in 1967, covering the activities of central government departments. A separate (National) Health Service ombuds was subsequently created, but this has to date always been the same person and the two offices are combined. The Local Government Ombuds (formally the Commission for Local Government Administration for England and Wales) was created in 1973, and for Scotland in 1974. In the case of the Parliamentary Ombuds, in order to avoid worthless or mischievous complaints being taken up, complainants must first contact their local Member of Parliament (MP). The MP acts like a filter – if she or he is satisfied that a complaint is well-founded, then she or he asks the Parliamentary Ombuds to take up the case against a public authority. So the grievance handling process is 'indirect'. This is also, however, one ground for criticising the UK system – there is no direct access to the ombuds. UK critics also claim that the Ombuds appears to be independent but, in reality, since the appointees are very often recruited from the ranks of officials there is a danger that the real role of the ombuds recruited in this way is merely to rubber stamp controversial official decisions. Nevertheless, there is much public confidence in the system, and since the early 1970s, a whole range of other public and private sector-specific ombudsmen have been created, in large part stimulated by the success of this model.

Organisational Ombuds

Nowadays, there are many private companies, universities, non-profit organisations and so on that have also introduced an ombuds to deal with complaints by their own employees, or other relevant persons. These ombuds roles are meant to function independently, and often operate according to International Ombuds Association (IOA) Standards of Practice. Although they may well be required to submit annual reports to the CEO or board of directors, they typically do not serve any other role in the organisation. They are beginning to appear around the world within organisations of various sorts. They may be seen as avenues of complaint and sometimes act as alternatives to anonymous hot lines, especially in states where hot lines are considered inappropriate or are illegal. Sometimes they function in addition to hot lines, and where they do ombuds offices usually receive many more calls than do hot lines, and so a hot line may show the need for an ombuds or ombuds office. Our understanding is that in the PRC today, the preference is to stick to 'hot lines'. Since the 1960s, the ombuds profession has grown in the West, but especially in the United States, and Canada. It is found, as we have indicated, in corporations, non-governmental organisations, universities and some government agencies. This organisational ombuds is high-ranking in an organisation, but not part of executive management, at least not in the sense of being able to make management decisions. Using ADR approach, the ombuds provides avenues of access to justice to whistleblowers or employees and managers with ethical concerns and so on. It can provide both specific and generic solutions (that is, an outcome which protects and applies to a class of people, rather than just a single individual). It may use negotiation, and mediation, track problem areas, and make recommendations for changes to policies or procedures in support of systems change.

One particularly important function is to monitor and pick up 'new things' – that is, issues that have not hitherto been faced in the organisation. This is particularly important if the 'new thing' is 'disruptive' in the sense of requiring the organisation to review and possibly improve its policies, procedures and/or structures. In recent years there has been growing interest in the organisational ombuds and about how the office of ombuds relates to other internal conflict management systems.

An organisational ombuds may sign up to IOA 'standards of practice', and will try to be neutral and visibly outside ordinary line and staff command structures. It does not possess any management decision-making powers, and does not see itself as a representative of the organisation within which it operates. The ombuds office typically maintains no case records for an employer and keeps its work and findings as confidential as possible, with the possible exception of where there appears to be a looming danger of severe harm. However, even here, there may be other solutions than breaking confidentiality – organisational ombuds programmes can almost always find 'options', such as helping a visitor to make an anonymous report about the issue.

Sectoral Ombuds

But in addition, we have noted that the ombuds has come to be used for dispute resolution in a wide variety of fields. In the United Kingdom, these extended uses include banking, insurance, building societies (institutions which lend money to people who wish to buy a house), the London stock exchange, pensions and the Legal Services Ombuds as established by sections 21–6 of the Courts and Legal Services Act 1990. The latter is, of course, of special interest to legal practitioners. The purpose of the Legal Services Ombuds is to assist those persons who feel that they wish to make a complaint against a member of the legal profession and whose initial protest to the Law Society or the Bar Council has not met with a satisfactory response. The ombudsperson will investigate the case and recommend financial compensation and other remedies. The Legal Services Ombuds makes annual reports to Parliament and the Lord Chancellor/Ministry of Justice.

Financial Ombuds Service

However, a much more striking area of growth in ombuds services over the past ten years has been in the financial services sector. The traditional route for pursuing a grievance against an organisation providing financial services was the civil court, but with the growth of ADR in the past two decades and with considerable governmental encouragement, the Financial Ombudsman Service (FOS)[1] now offers a highly successful process by means of which disputes can be resolved extra-judicially and, in many cases, the parties encouraged to settle. One strength of the FOS is that it offers a variety of ADR options including early neutral evaluation (or 'ENE'), negotiation, mediation, as well as a form of adjudication and even intervention by the ombuds herself or himself. Broadly speaking, these processes operate sequentially, so that if one method fails to resolve the disputed issues the next is attempted. The FOS, like other ombuds, is regarded as both independent and influential, so that the scheme is to a significant extent intended to offer a form of protection and reassurance

[1] Financial Ombudsman Service, available at www.financial-ombudsman.org.uk/, accessed 3 December 2019.

for the consumer in a situation in which there are often significant imbalances of power and knowledge.

Legal representation in the ombuds processes is discouraged, and the ombuds services are given free. In the FOS and other private sector ombuds systems, funding is provided by member firms against which complaints might be brought. For these firms, the FOS is a system worth supporting because it provides a second level response when their own in-house complaints mechanisms fail, and also because it is fully confidential – the names of the parties involved in a dispute in which the FOS intervenes are not further disclosed.

The early history of the FOS begins in 1997, when the government noted that there were eight separate complaints schemes in operation in the financial services and banking sectors, and proposed a rationalisation that was implemented through the 2000 Financial Services and Markets Act. A single statutory system was established, subsequently joined also by mortgage brokers, insurance brokers and National Savings and Investments, in which the FOS offers an independent investigatory mechanism that also attempts to provide solutions – amicable or, if necessary, imposed – for the alleged misconduct of organisations offering financial products and services. In exercising its functions, the FOS attempts to be fair, informal, reasonable and quick. It has jurisdiction in cases up to the value of £100,000. A consumer dissatisfied with the manner in which the FOS has handled her or his case may still bring suit in court, but a FOS decision is binding on the member firm against whom a complaint has been brought, just as it is on a consumer once she or he accepts a decision. In the year ending 31 March 2008, the FOS received nearly 800,000 initial inquiries and complaints from consumers, and in fact dealt with nearly 125,000 complaints and disputes, many within one month of the initial contact by using its ADR-type processes. More than one half of the cases were about bank credit, insurance and investment (including certain special types of mortgage). There has thus been a spectacular rise in the FOS caseload from the 50,000 complaints and disputes handled in the first year of the operations of the FOS after its establishment in 2001. There seems to be an important contrast here with the dramatically diminished case load of the Queen's Bench Division of the High Court, reflecting a significant shift in civil justice from courts to the alternatives, especially that of the ombuds. The case load of the Queen's Bench Division of the High Court reflects this transformation, for in 1997 on the eve of the Woolf reforms, the Division handled some 120,000 civil cases, but some ten years later this figure was down to 12,000, reflecting a significant shift in civil justice from courts to the alternative process of the ombuds.

Offers finality and consistency

Few if any claims are litigated after FOS intervention. Both rejected consumers and losing firms accept authority and impartiality of the ombuds. For one thing, many cases are settled quickly through the negotiation and mediation functions of the FOS. And even when there has to be an imposed decision, it seems that both rejected consumers and losing firms accept the outcome as determined by the authority and impartiality of the ombuds when a decision goes against them. Also, the FOS offers sometimes very detailed reasoning in complaint rejection, and this helps the losing party to understand why they have lost. Consistency of decision-making is important – in effect there is a system of precedent, and many important decisions are published on the website of the FOS.

Process

One strength of the FOS is that it offers – usually in a sequence – a variety of ADR options including early neutral evaluation (or 'ENE'), negotiation, mediation, as well as a form of adjudication. Much of the complaint handling is dealt with by trained staff, many of whom are legally qualified. These ombuds staffers initially receive and consider the facts of the case, advise the parties on what they see to be the problem – that is, they offer 'early neutral evaluation' – and encourage the parties to resolve their differences through telephone calls. If this type of negotiation does not succeed then mediation may then be used, with the same staff member or perhaps a higher level member of staff. Only if that fails will a senior staff member – even the ombuds him- or herself in very difficult cases at the final stage – intervene as a final mediator or otherwise she or he will make 'determination'. Broadly speaking, these processes operate sequentially, so that if one method fails to resolve the disputed issues the next is attempted. The FOS, like other ombuds, is regarded as both independent and influential, so that the scheme is to a significant extent intended to offer a form of protection and reassurance for the consumer in a situation in which there are often significant imbalances of power and knowledge.

Accountability

This system has also proved itself to be fully accountable – which is very important for everybody. Two very important avenues of accountability are, first, the funding system and, secondly, access to the courts. Thus, first, although it is an industry funded body, in no way is the FOS answerable to the funders. Instead, it is legally established through Parliament as an independent statutory body – this means it has a Governing Board, the members of which are unpaid volunteers with relevant experience but no personal interest in the work of the FOS – to which FOS must present an annual report for approval. The Board appoints – and can remove an unsatisfactory office holder – the Financial Ombudsperson. Secondly, for the industry defendant in a case before the FOS, there is a real finality in the decision-making, in that the industry defendant has to accept any decision of the ombuds as being binding and final. Losing consumers, as we have noted, on the other hand can still take case to court. This is a very powerful right for the person who brings a grievance. The court will look at the decision of the ombuds, and if it feels there is a problem, then it will accept the case. In these ways, the system has quickly proved itself to offer finality in decision-making, which is very import-ant for everybody involved in a dispute.

Transplanting the Ombuds to China?

Despite the rapid growth of the ombuds form of dispute resolution, some jurisdictions refuse to allow it to be introduced. Thus, for example, China is unwilling to allow the development of an ombuds system within the mainland. The basic reason is that in a 'one-party state', which does not practice 'separation of powers', the ombuds is thought to be 'too independent' and 'too Western' in origin. The evidence from Hong Kong, however, is that this institution, although as we have seen largely European in provenance, can work quite easily and well in a Chinese cultural context. The Hong Kong Ombuds Service is a public-type ombuds, and has been in existence for more than twenty years.[2] On average it handles about 5,000 complaints a year. Only 120 or so of these complaints each year require full investigation and deter-mination, and of these two out of every five complaints are substantiated. Groups as well as individuals can bring complaints. Complaints can be lodged by email or telephone or by a standard form for bringing complaints. As with ombuds in many other parts of the world, many complaints are cleared up by investigation and explanation, by negotiation or by mediation. It is only some 2 per cent of all complaints that require a final decision. In 2009–10, the Ombuds made more than 140 recommendations for improvement in adminis-tration on the basis of the experience it had gained in handling complaints. This reflects the fact that one of the most important functions of such an ombuds is to improve administrative performance.

Maladministration and Supervision in China

China has various systems for dealing with problems of poor government, and these have many strengths. There is supervision by people's congresses, but this could perhaps be more effective than it is. There are also systems of administrative remedies, such as Xingzheng Fuyi or administrative review, and Xinfang or letters and visits – these are popular, but often overwhelmed by demand. And there is administrative litigation (Xingzheng Susong) – but this will only examine the lawfulness of administrative conduct, not reasonableness

---

[2] Office of the Ombudsman, Hong Kong, available at www.ombudsman.hk/en-us/, accessed 3 December 2019.

of administrative conduct. In addition, in reality, many administrative suits are dealt with informally, before trial, by mediation, even though the Administrative Litigation Law for many years provided that mediation may not be used.

Transplantation: An Ombuds System for China?

Nevertheless, there is a good argument for introducing an ombuds system in China. Hong Kong is an excellent example of how well the ombuds can work in a Chinese cultural context. By introducing first a public law type ombuds, the existing system of dealing with administrative complaints would be strengthened. The ombuds would not replace the other way of dealing with administrative disputes. Instead, it would provide another way of handling problems – not administrative, not judicial and not legislative. And, as in many other parts of the world, its likely success would encourage the growth of private sector ombuds. Of course, there would be problems, as there have been in the West. It is not easy to secure very high quality personnel to work as ombudspersons, or in the office of the ombuds. In addition it is not always easy to secure cooperation from defendant state agencies, and ensuring that the ombuds is fully independent is also in many places a hurdle that needs to be overcome. But if these problems could be resolved, then as elsewhere in the world, the ombuds might serve as a responsive link between ordinary people and the government.

Conclusions

The ombuds, especially the public law type ombuds, is a very interesting development. It is an important step on the road to good government – there is a growing sense around the world that we have a right not only to lawful government but also to good government. From the point of view of the judicial system it may also have the function of encouraging overall confidence in the ideal of the rule of law. At the same time, as processual innovation in dispute resolution becomes more institutionalised and professional as a result of the development of the ADR movement in the Anglo-American common law world, so the boundaries between different kinds of process become blurred. So the reality of much of the work of an ombuds such as the UK's FOS is a mix of investigation and mediation, and often produces an outcome that so many parties want from a dispute resolution process, namely an agreement out-of-court that resolves their differences. Over the past thirty years or so, its success has encouraged no less than three different types of transplantation: from public sector to private sector, from Europe to many other parts of the world, and from the domestic to the international sphere. The experience of the United Kingdom is that while detractors still tend to question the extent to which the ombuds is genuinely independent, the absence of direct financial costs in bringing a complaint and of any need for legal representation, the expert knowledge that the ombuds offers in her or his specialised field, and the relatively simple procedures that have to be followed are all factors which make the ombuds a growing and important avenue for resolving disputes and accessing justice.

12

Online Dispute Resolution and its Diffusion: From Private to Public

Introduction

The ever-growing use of the Internet and increasing reliance on electronic commerce in recent times has created the need for new and more innovative approaches to handling disputes.[1] One particular problem with the rapidly expanding use of the Web for many types of transaction is that the parties involved may be located in quite different parts of the world. Moreover, there is always the worry that while the use of the Internet for resolving disputes might be efficient and cost-effective, the lack of familiarity on the part of some parties with using the Web – especially the 'digital divide'[2] – gives rise to issues of fairness and access to justice. In general, the literature assumes that online dispute resolution or 'ODR' is the expected and almost always appropriate process for handling disputes that arise through use of the Internet, especially in the area of e-commerce. ODR, however, can also be used alongside other forms of dispute resolution, and may be characterised broadly as the use of information and communications technology in the processing of disputes, including their prevention. And ODR is not necessarily limited to use of the Internet, as 'other, less sexy technologies also fall into this definition of ODR: telephones (both wired and unwired), LCD projectors, spreadsheets and word processors all fit as well ... That many mediators and arbitrators use these technologies every day goes unmentioned because technology has become the new normal' (Rule, 2016: 8).

---

[1] Thanks to Zhao Yun (2020), whose article in press on ODR we have found most helpful, and Lin Yang, Maria Moscati, and Zhou Ling for kind comments on this chapter. We have also found useful the recent study by Ethan Katsh and Orna Rabinovich-Einy (2017) and the monograph by Zhou Ling (2020).

[2] The notion of 'digital divide' refers to the significant gap that has emerged in many parts of the world in relation to use of the Internet and information technology. On the one hand there are disadvantaged members of society, including for example, the impoverished, elderly, countryside dwellers, and persons with disability. These do not have convenient access to computers or the Internet, or are unable to use the e-technology effectively because of a disability. On the other hand, there are the wealthier, more middle-class, and younger urban dwellers for whom going online is their first rather than their last thought when dealing with issues.

Over the past decade or so, the use of ODR – which emerged in the 1990s alongside the growth of e-commerce as an innovative set of dispute resolution processes[3] – has seen in many parts of the world, an expansion to the public sector, including courts.[4] So, ODR is an area of processual innovation that has expanded from use in the private sector to the public domain especially court systems, either as an enhancement to more conventional judicial procedures or as an alternative. In this sense we see a contrast in the pattern of innovative diffusion. While the ombuds has spread from the private to the public sector, propelled by the perceived advantages of independence and so on that it offers, ODR has expanded in the opposite direction. It has been drawn into the public sphere and formal institutions of dispute resolution, largely because of the apparent advantages of efficiency that handling disputes over the Internet brings. The public sector use of ODR includes the development of 'virtual courts', in which online communication and digital storage is used to deliver case management, file storing and access, and decisions by the court.

This chapter explores the significance of the rise of ODR and considers the processes of ODR, as well as the regulatory issues surrounding its use. We note that a number of commentators point to problems of regulation, arising in part because of the ever-changing nature of the ODR field. Some conclude that self-regulating ODR has problems, and call for reforms. The chapter also explores the use of ODR in China, most probably the world's heaviest and most innovative user of ODR, before looking at the growing phenomena of e-courts.

ODR and ADR

At first, ODR methods mostly imitated offline ADR processes. As a result, initial attempts to use online processes to resolve disputes tended to be characterised as 'Online ADR' or 'E-ADR'. Thus, in the first significant ODR pilot project, with eBay in the late 1990s, an experienced human mediator used email to interact with the disputants using the same strategies with which he engaged disputants offline (Wolf, 2012).

---

[3] See for example, Menkel-Meadow (2016). At the same time, e-commerce sites such as Amazon and eBay provided online processes for quickly resolving purchase disputes, assisting strongly the emergence of online dispute resolution, or 'ODR'. The approach to ODR includes computerised decision-making, and online negotiation, mediation, arbitration, community courts and adjudication.

[4] Thus, while it is true that the early development of ODR reflected the approaches of ADR and it is also accurate to say that there are processes in ODR that are parallel to those found in ADR – such as online negotiation, mediation and arbitration – it is not the case that it is only ODR processes that can utilise online methodologies. Indeed, in recent years, ODR has spread into litigation and umpiring.

Some of the most influential ADR specialists remain seriously sceptical of the virtues of ODR:

> What I wonder about is what drove me to ADR in the first place – where in the tick boxes and the email communications will there be room to brainstorm and create a different solution, give an apology, come to understand someone else's perspective and improve, rather than just 'resolve', relations and disputes. For me Online Dispute Resolution may be one tool for some 'access' to dispute resolution of some kind, but I would not over-claim the 'justice' part. I recently resolved an ongoing dispute with one of my airlines online – what I felt was relief it was over and done, not any sense that 'justice' had been served, and it was very clear that at the other end of my computer was not someone with the power or discretion of a mediator or judge to consider a more creative and tailored solution. I got what the tick boxes or company policy allowed. Will we be getting small claims or civil justice in a programmed set of legally required tick boxes? I thought the common law allowed more flexible rulings and mediators and negotiators working in the 'shadow of the law' could still fashion new and creative remedies that looked to the parties' futures, as well as past conflicts. I remain intrigued by what ODR might be able to do in some cases, but remain a bigger fan of old-fashioned in-person ADR, because for me, one size will not fit all – I remain a process pluralist – ODR will work in some matters for some people, but let us not yet throw out the baby (ADR) with the bathwater (the old and rigid legal system) (Menkel-Meadow, 2016: 7).

Other dispute resolution specialists see ODR in a different light, as an evolving set of processes that will, in due course, come to infuse many, if not all areas, of dispute resolution:

> The goals of the ODR field mirror the goals of ADR ... they include access to justice, efficiency and transparency[5] of dispute resolution, quality of solutions, satisfaction and justice ... When Frank Sander introduced the concept of the Multi-Door Courthouse at the Pound Conference in 1976 he gave the example of a courthouse with different doors, each providing a customized resolution process to meet the needs of particular kinds of disputes. With ODR we now have the potential to offer an online Multi-Door Courthouse with not just a couple dozen doors, but potentially hundreds or thousands of doors, each enabling us to 'fit the forum to the fuss' by providing a process customized to meet the specific needs of parties. In fact, we can even build new doors 'on the fly', assembling appropriate resolution flows even as the parties are explaining the specifics of their situation. The promise of ODR in improving the quality of resolutions is enormous, and we are just getting started in exploring its full potential (Rule, 2016: 9).

These contrasting views – in which one approach stresses the virtues of personal contact that ADR brings, and the other the benefits that the

---

[5] Thus, for example, ODR offers records that enhance traceability.

application of ODR's new online technologies offer – will doubtless persist for a long time to come. But, the development of e-commerce continues to fuel the growth of ODR in many parts of the world.

The forces of globalisation, especially the growth of international trade are pushing ODR into an ever more important position. Technological innovation has encouraged changes in the manner in which trade is conducted, in particular with a shift in transaction methods from direct contact to the impersonal trading of e-commerce and the electronic contract. In this new world, however, it is still necessary for the parties to agree on the transaction and for them to fulfil their contractual obligations. Sometimes this does not occur and therefore a way of resolving the party's differences has to be created and, increasingly, ODR is seen as the best way of handling online transactional disputes. This is both because the parties are already in an online relationship and because dispute resolution awards are located in cyberspace. E-commerce offers consumers and other buyers a very wide choice of available products. For the seller e-commerce opens up the possibility of offering products and securing customers in a new world of borderless trade (Wahab, 2004; Katsh and Rabinovich-Einy, 2015).

Prior to the mid-1990s, there were only a small number of ODR methodologies in existence and these were largely experimental in nature. In large part, this was because the Internet was initially a network based in the United States, and the US National Science Foundation's acceptable use policy excluded commercial use of the Internet. It was only when commercial activity on the Internet was permitted in the mid-1990s that disputes related to commerce came to the fore. Once the Internet became an important forum for commercial activities, the idea of using ODR processes quickly emerged, as many users saw that the growth of online transactions would likely mean that more online disputes would occur.

Moreover, the idea developed that more familiar offline dispute resolution processes were cumbersome in the online environment, and so:

> its developers soon realized that new processes and systems had to be designed, ones that fit the nature, values, and culture of the online environment. As a result, ODR systems became the preferred (and in some cases, the only) avenue for addressing disputes between sellers and buyers on eBay, between registered domain name holders and trademark owners, and between Wikipedia editors with widely diverging world views and ideologies (Katsh and Rabinovich-Einy, 2015: 8).

So, with the growth of ODR, it was perceived that the introduction of digital technology would likely trigger innovative thinking. And from this, the idea of dedicated online institutions specialising in dispute resolution arose. But as commercial use of the Internet was still relatively limited, the initial projects were primarily supported by academics and non-profit institutions. Their work included not only dispute resolution per se but also advice, for example, to website owners on how they might best approach the problem of a complaint or similar issue that was directly against them. The success of these schemes encouraged commercial agencies to move to ODR, and as a result the number of ODR systems emerged which are essentially commercial in nature. Despite the significant financial burdens involved in constructing and applying ODR systems, the number of firms offering some form of ODR has steadily expanded. Then, in something of a snowballing fashion, commercial success in using ODR processes has encouraged governmental and international organisations to concern themselves with, or to go ahead and adopt ODR processes. Thus, the influential United Nations Conference on Trade and Development (UNCTAD) E-Commerce and Development Report (2003) concluded there has been growing recognition by not only commercial interests but also governmental agencies that online resources can be used to handle many of the problems that are created in the online environment. However, because commercial interests now dominated the emerging field of ODR the tendency was to allow self-regulation of the ODR processes. The need to retain consumer confidence in the process of ODR subsequently led to an acceptance of the idea that some degree of government regulation would be helpful in assuring quality of the ODR processes (Zhao, 2020).

Given the very significant role that e-technology and online services can play in ODR, so that use of this novel form of handling disputes developed and became institutionalised, the idea emerged that online facilities and relevant online software constituted a 'fourth' party in the dispute handling process. ODR came to be regarded as seen as helping the endeavour by assisting not only the disputing parties but also, where involved, a third-party intervener.[6]

ODR Systems

The processes of ODR cover an extensive collection of schemes, platforms and programs. These extend from education, advice and so on at one end, through to negotiation and mediation, and on to umpiring at the other. Moreover, like 'ADR', there is not a fully agreed understanding of the nature and content of 'ODR'. Nevertheless, we can usefully point to several characteristic methods and styles.

Cybersettle

Many of these emerged in order to deal with disagreements between parties involved in Internet dealings in the area of relatively low value, large volume and broadly uniform sales transactions. ODR platforms functioning to handle such disagreements have not needed to be complex. Good examples

---

[6] See for example, Rainey (2014).

may be found in platforms such as Cybersettle and Smartsettle which use blind-bidding systems of resolution:

> In Blind Bidding, parties submit offers for settlement to a central computer and do not reveal the offers to one another. The system's computer software determines if the offers are within a proximity range set ahead of time by the software or the parties, and if they are, the dispute is resolved by splitting the difference between the offers. If the offers are not within the specified range, they are not disclosed and the offer-making process continues, either for a set number of rounds or indefinitely, depending upon the system. In effect, the system collapses the advocacy and inquiry dimensions of bargaining into offer making, and reduces negotiation to the exchange of proposals. It is a system adapted to resolving disputes about damages more than liability, and cases that involve single, uncomplicated, standardized issues that are not cost effective to litigate. Claims under insurance policies of various types are the most common examples (Condlin, 2017: 275–6).

It should be added that when a party inputs a demand, the system will create a settlement range by automatically adding 20 per cent to the demand. And ordinarily the parties can input three rounds of bidding. If no settlement is reached by the end of the three rounds, then the parties are then free to start a new resolution attempt, using the same portal.

In general, Cybersettle seems most relied on for dealing with disputes about damages (rather than liability), and most of the cases handled are single-standard, relatively routine, and low value disputes. Smartsettle is another platform in this style. But while offering broadly similar services to Cybersettle, it is a little more elaborate, with additional features that serve to make clear parties' interests, detect potential compromises, secure party satisfaction, and generate optimal solutions.

Thus the blind-bidding process primarily has elements of an online negotiation system, but it can also be seen as an online mediation system. Since only two parties are involved in the dispute resolution process, it is clearly an online negotiation system. But at the same time, in some respects the technology intervenes as a mediatory third party, helping as it does the two parties to achieve a settlement. More advanced ODR models also emerged:

> Square Trade, for example, offered a platform for resolving delivery, warranty, billing, and misrepresentation disputes between one-time actors in online, commercial transactions. A party filed a claim by choosing from a set of pull-down menus, filled in open-text boxes, and ranked solutions from a set of choices suggested by the Square Trade software. Square Trade would email the party's responses to the other party in the dispute and ask her to fill in the same boxes and make the same selections. If the dispute was not resolved through this automated process, it would be referred to an online mediator who, communicating privately with both sides through asynchronous email, would help the parties identify common ground using strategies and practices similar to those used in face-to-face mediation. In effect, Square Trade combined features of

blind bidding with those of in-person mediation to offer an online version of facilitated mediation (Condlin, 2017: 726).

Online Jury Proceedings

At the other end of the spectrum are to be found online jury processes. These were developed initially in order to provide predictive forecasts of likely jury verdicts, as well as to anticipate other issues relating to the handling of the trial such as the best lines of argument to be used in a trial jury selection and so on. Like the mini-trial and the summary jury trial, the online jury procedure is only an approximation of an actual trial jury, and is essentially a predictive device. The 'members' of the jury do not actually see the parties in dispute. In effect what the jury trial does is provide a venue in which the public can offer to the dispute forum their online opinions about the disputants' cases.

One of the best-known forms of the online jury process is iCourthouse. This is a site in which the parties in dispute may submit their case and supportive evidence in a 'trial book' and seek the thoughts of the public in regard to their case. The forum provided by iCourthouse provides the opportunity for users to vote on what they see as the best way of resolving the dispute. The users may choose the disputes in the system in which they can make comments and may choose for which party they may vote. Jurors may extend the invitation to others so that there is no limit on the number of invitations issued. Users may communicate directly with and ask questions of the parties. Voting outcomes are not binding but are intended to serve as guidelines for the parties on how best to resolve the disagreement. One of the main problems of the system, however, is quality control: for example, users can log in using different names and give their comments many times, and it seems a disproportionate influence is exerted by those who make initial voting and comments, so there are questions about the representativeness and impartiality of the votes cast. Moreover, there are difficulties in checking the validity of information provided by the parties for public judgement through the system.

Domain Name Dispute Resolution

As the Internet grew in importance so there developed a number of difficulties, including disputes between parties. One particular problem was (and still is) characterised as 'cybersquatting'.[7] The latter term refers to registration in bad faith of domain names. In order to deal with this problem ICANN, the Internet Corporation for Assigned Names and Numbers, established in 1999 the Uniform Domain Name Dispute Resolution Policy (UDRP). In due course, a number of dispute resolution service providers came to deal with this problem,

---

[7] See, Harvard Law Review, 1999.

in association with ICANN, and there is a general recognition that these have been successful in their dispute resolving services. These providers now include WIPO (the World Intellectual Property Organisation), NAF (the National Arbitration Forum, ADNDRC (Asian Domain Name Dispute Resolution Centre), the Czech Arbitration Court Arbitration Centre for Internet Disputes, and ACDR (Arab Centre for Domain Name Dispute Resolution).

The UDRP process of dispute resolution uses an online platform for receiving both the complaint and the response provided by the defending party. The domain name holder is bound by UDRP rules in the dispute resolution process – which has to be completed online, and within a period not exceeding 60 days. Decisions once reached are made publicly available online, and include reasons in support of the position taken by the panel. One of the perceived strengths of the system is that an outcome is usually enforced, as those who are authorised to act as registrars in the system will lose their accreditation if they fail to ensure that an outcome is fully implemented. The decision made by panellists, however, may only be implemented after ten days, during which time neither party has decided to take their case to court. The possible outcomes under the system are that the complaint is rejected or, secondly, that the domain name should be awarded to the person bringing the complaint, or the domain name is so problematic that it has to be cancelled. Complaints are made on the basis of three possible issues – an existing name is very similar to a name in which the complainant holds the rights, the respondent does not hold legitimate rights or interests in that domain name, and, thirdly, although the domain name has been correctly registered it is being used in bad faith.

Regulation

With the development of ODR systems, the question emerged of how they might be best regulated. Initially the new dispute resolvers involved in the emerging systems of ODR took the view that because the Internet had no physical borders and few boundaries, so ODR should not be subject to national laws and government regulation. These arguments were reinforced by the sheer pace of change, so that innovative developments in information technology carried alongside them the idea that technology related laws would have typically a very short shelf life. Accordingly, attempts to deal with this problem by generalised drafting would not create effective governance because the wording is too broad and precise.

However, increasing difficulties with the Internet and its misuse in various ways have encouraged governments to try to impose regulatory control of some parts of the Internet in order to uphold national interests. Of particular concern has been constructing a proper legal framework for online arbitration, especially as international commercial arbitration is already a very heavily regulated field, including especially the New York Convention on the

Recognition and Enforcement of Judgments of Foreign Arbitral Awards 1958. More generally, it is only recently that various jurisdictions and international institutions have attempted to develop legislative instruments relating to ODR and e-commerce, and an important difficulty remains that jurisdictions are shaped by state boundaries and it may be difficult to determine in cross-border transactions exactly what law should be applied.

Alternatively, recourse to self-regulation as a principal regulatory mechanism for ODR has been favoured by a number of commentators. Here, the idea is that it is the Internet agencies that are the most likely to understand which regulatory regime is likely to be the most effective, and therefore government intervention should be limited to providing a legal framework for electronic commerce. It is also based on the idea that competition between different ODR providers would encourage use of the best dispute handling processes available, and the best regulations in which they operate, in order to be commercially successful. Users dissatisfied with one provider would look to other providers for dispute resolution services.

There are, however, some difficulties with self-regulation. It is not always clear how providers' compliance with the relevant standards is assured under a self-regulating system. It also remains the case that consumers in general take the view that self-regulation tends to serve the interests of the sellers rather than dissatisfied buyers. In order to assist in promoting public confidence in the system, a 'Trustmark' programme has been established in which an external body satisfies itself that an ODR service provider has properly enforced or implemented its ODR standards and provides services of sufficient quality. The Trustmark appears on the website of an ODR provider as a confidence promoting symbol. An e-commerce seller's failure to post this symbol would indicate to the outside world that the seller is unable or unwilling to meet relevant standards.

In order to provide better regulation of ODR, UNCITRAL has taken a steadily increasing interest in procedural aspects of ODR since the turn of the century. These include UNCITRAL technical notes on ODR adopted in 2016. Although not intended to be legally binding, the suggested rules in the notes are intended to apply to cross-border, low value, e-commerce transactions and to encourage ODR systems to abide by principles of fairness, transparency, due process and accountability. They offer a model of the resolution process from commencement of proceedings to negotiation and into facilitated settlement, so the notes are an important attempt – albeit non-binding – to provide guidelines and standards for ODR systems.

ODR: The Flourishing in China

Hitherto the research that has been carried out into ODR has been relatively limited in part because service providers are not keen to be researched (Kasch and Rule, 2016), and also because traditional socio-legal research methods are not especially suited to research into online phenomena. It is also the case that a great deal of the research that has appeared concerns the growth in ODR in the United States, Europe and other parts of the developed world. However, the programmes of economic reform pursued in China in recent years have resulted in extensive use of the Internet especially for purposes of e-commerce.[8] Companies such as e-commerce leader Alibaba have in a very innovative way developed internal ODR systems. These have not only been successful in themselves but also encouraged other developments including e-courts – in particular China's new e-commerce court in Hangzhou, Zhejiang Province, established in partnership with China Telecom, and other corporations. The Hangzhou e-court incorporates online filing and case management, online transmissions and adjudication of cases, online mediation and payments. The court's jurisdiction focuses on Internet-related disputes, typically small commercial transactions. The location in Hangzhou is significant: this city is also the place of business of the Alibaba group (Lin Yang, manuscript).

Until recently, the entrenched usage of mediation in Chinese legal culture has tended to resist efforts at meaningful and innovative dispute resolution. But the pace of social and generational change and technical development taking place in China are creating a new world of dispute resolution. In particular, the e-commerce leader, the Alibaba Group, runs the Taobao Marketplace, a very large consumer-to-consumer website. It hosts a Taobao Users Dispute Resolution Center in which Taobao customers can volunteer to be a Taobao 'dispute assessor'.[9] These unpaid volunteer assessors review evidence and make rulings – on average on several thousand cases a day – on disagreements between consumers and merchants in online purchasing disputes (the typical consumer complaints concern items received that fail to match website descriptions).[10] There are more than half a million such volunteers, and some of them often serve several times a day in the crowdsourcing system of justice. The volunteers sit on thirty-one-member panels that review evidence submitted by buyers and sellers in dispute; outcomes are decided by a simple majority vote. Assessors choose cases according to their interests, and may participate in up to twenty cases per day. The Center also deals with differences between Taobao merchants and Taobao itself – indeed, it was initially created for this purpose – in cases where the merchants felt

[8] China's Standing Committee of the National People's Congress passed the new e-commerce law on 31 August 2018, and it took effect on 1 January 2019 as the E-Commerce Law of the People's Republic of China 2018.
[9] See the protocol of Taobao Crowd Adjudication (for trial implementation), available at http://pan.taobao.com/jury/help.htm?spm=a310u.3042613.0.0.07nHZ9&type=standard, accessed 16 April 2017. Note, at present this website appears to have been closed down, and to have been replaced by a mobile phone version (requiring users to install its APP).
[10] Those assessors who make significant contributions to the system may, however, make charitable donations to several designated non-profit organisations from Taobao.

aggrieved by penalties imposed on them by the company for violating website rules. Although Taobao has extensive administrative staff to support the ODR system, it faces a vast case load which necessitates the volunteer assessor system. Approximately one-third of all complaints against Taobao and its online sellers are handled by the Center, and clearly one of the functions of the dispute resolution is enhancing the commercial profile of Taobao so that it has more online sales.

Both buyers and sellers can volunteer to be dispute assessors, but Taobao will then verify volunteers' identities, and prior use of Taobao services, which must include at least one year's membership. The resolution process is initiated when the aggrieved buyer seeks a refund. If the merchant disputes the claim, the customer is given the option of having the case settled by Taobao's customer service or by the dispute resolution centre. Aggrieved buyers then submit a formal complaint online with supporting evidence, the disputing parties plead their case in an online forum, and after assessing the claims and evidence, the assessment panel members cast their voting. The popular view is that decisions tend to be made in favour of the buyer.[11] The jurors are anonymous, and no communication is allowed between the disputing parties. A Taobao seller is required to participate in the dispute resolution process as a condition for selling on the platform. A seller who loses a dispute and then refuses to give the aggrieved buyer the refund due risks expulsion. In such a case, Taobao refunds the consumer, while subtracting the same amount from the deposit that all sellers have to make when they join the Taobao system. Assessors are ranked on the basis of the number and complexity of cases they have resolved, and complicated disputes are handled by higher-ranked assessors. Assessors are also expected to give feedback to Taobao on how the online stores at Taobao might improve their selling (Erickson, 2017; Ye Jian, 2016; Fang Xuhui, 2014; Wang Yueying, 2017).

The Emergence of E-courts

As suggested above, as a result of the success of ODR in the private sector – especially in dealing with small-scale consumer disputes – the public sector, including in particular, the courts, has increasingly been prepared to incorporate elements of ODR as well as digital technology more generally. Courts are not the only governmental agency using ODR progressively more, but they are clearly one of the most important. The attraction for the absorption of ODR processes into judicial work is not so very different from the early arguments in favour of court embrace of ADR, namely that there are important case-handling efficiencies to be gained by using digital technology. In some cases, the courts link up with online private providers and in other cases the court uses

---

[11] It is also the case that some commentators feel that buyers do bring false complaints, and the system does not regulate effectively against this misconduct.

ODR technology as one part of the dispute handling process only. Increasingly disputants look not only to conducting a transaction online but also resolving a dispute online, primarily because it too saves them time and financial costs.

Despite these advantages, the public sector has in general been slow to take up ODR possibilities. This is in part because of worries about equality of access to justice of the parties in view of the digital divide, and partly also because in the public sector there is more limited competition of the kind that has helped to push ODR into the forefront in the handling of, for example, consumer disputes. So, courts have been slow to embrace the innovation of ODR. But in China as disputants got used to Alibaba, eBay and other ODR processes so their willingness to use e-courts has increased. In China today, not only do we now see an electronic court but also through the assistance of Internet communication companies such as Ten Cent there are specific linkages that enable an aggrieved person, for example, to register a claim with a court by using a smartphone facility such as WeChat. In addition, the development of digital technology in the work of lawyers and courts has changed styles of professional legal work so that it is easier to accommodate ODR processes. As might be expected, however, much of the technology that has been adopted by courts looks mainly still to enhance efficiency and reduce budgets. It is only recently that there has been a concern with developing really innovative ways of providing online access to justice in the courts.

Katsh and Rabinovich-Einy identify three general phases in the adoption of ODR-type technology by the courts. The initial phase was based on concerns with efficiency and case management. This was followed by a phase in which there was impact from the growth of the government which, because it made governmental information and new tools available to the public encouraged ODR initiatives. And then a third phase surfaced in a number of jurisdictions in which the courts have been rethinking in innovative ways the manner in which legal processes may be conducted online. Although Katsh and Rabinovich-Einy conclude that the full potential of digital technology and enhancing access to justice by delivering digital justice has yet to be fully realised, nevertheless positive changes are taking place:

> Over time, court websites have improved dramatically, as website design advanced, interactivity increased, and software began to be used more often to tailor legal information to meet individual needs and circumstances. Courts in Illinois, California, and New York partnered with legal aid organizations to provide large and resource-rich self-help sites. Courts have redesigned their sites to allow for search engine optimization, videos, podcasts, and interactive questionnaires that help litigants navigate the system. These changes have dramatically sped up the time it takes courts to process self-represented litigants' applications.

> Legal aid organizations have developed a variety of tools to assist self-represented parties. Some sites now allow for remote guidance using various software programs, relying on multilingual staff and even, in some cases,

volunteer attorneys. Software has the potential to improve access to justice not only by offering legal aid staff to remote rural areas or to individuals unable to reach legal aid organizations but also by offering assistance on an anonymous basis – a feature that can rarely be ensured when providing aid in person. Technology also lowers training and collaboration costs for legal aid staff with the assistance of new training software, technology for virtual meetings, and free online courses. Some have suggested developing technology that would better allocate much-needed legal services to those most in need of legal services.

One particularly impressive tool for self-represented litigants is A2J Author, designed by the Chicago-Kent College of Law. After many hours of observation, the college created a web-based product that could assist self-represented litigants in divorce proceedings and simplify court procedures. Through a series of plain language questions, the software is able to assess the needs of the party and refer him or her to the appropriate body/process/form. A virtual guide welcomes the litigant and walks him or her toward a graphical virtual courtroom. As the party answers questions, he or she progresses and can always see what stage he or she is at in the process. The prototype was later expanded to include additional guided interviews in a collaboration between the Chicago-Kent College of Law and the Center for Computer-Assisted Legal Instruction. There are now over 1,200 guided interviews available, which have been used over 75,000 times ... the product is a model for how answering simple questions can make it unnecessary to understand legal intricacies. (Katsh and Rabinovich-Einy, 2017: 157).

Thus, we may say that the courts' approach to ODR in many parts of the world is now changing. Technology is increasingly appreciated as an opportunity to rethink the manner in which courts can handle disputes as well as making the courts more efficient. A recent initiative that is still taking shape is to be found in England and Wales, with a projected shift to online courts on a grand scale (Susskind, 2015). In this proposed system the court would deal with civil disputes up to the value of £25,000 primarily through ODR. There will be an online initial phase, followed by what is termed 'online facilitation' and then online judgment. Particularly interesting is the second stage where the parties are assisted on the one hand by accomplished facilitators and on the other by computerised negotiation tools so that, hopefully, the parties reach a settlement without the need to move on to a third stage – online judgment.

These ideas have been incorporated into the very important Lord Justice Briggs' report on civil court reform, in which the idea of the ODR is characterised as an Online Solutions Court (Briggs, LJ, 2016). The hope is that the system will function from start to finish without the support of lawyers, although lawyers would not necessarily be excluded from the process because it is still accepted that legal advice can assist the parties in seeking a resolution to their differences. Also, in some cases evidence may need to be tested by lawyerly cross-examination. In order to make the system more workable for non-lawyers, simplified procedure rules will be relied on rather than the Lord Woolf-inspired Civil Procedure Rules. The system will add to the efficiency of the courts because case management will be primarily conducted by case officers rather than judges, supplemented by legally qualified and judicially trained case officers for more complex cases. Litigants could appeal a decision internally, or in the County Court and ultimately at the Court of Appeal, assuming these proposed reforms are fully implemented.

Conclusions

On the face of it at least, it does seem to be the case that in relatively small and simple disputes there is a great deal of practical advantage for both the parties and the dispute resolver to use ODR methods. There are a number of factors which seem to affect the ability of ODR providers to construct a successful dispute resolution scheme online. These include the participatory experience of the disputing parties, the ODR providers' capacity to resolve disputes swiftly and cheaply, and the perceived neutrality of the process and compliance with final outcomes. ODR also offers possibilities of technical innovation that may be game-changing in years to come.

There remains an important question, however, of whether the system is better at delivering efficiency than it is at the delivery of justice. So, certainly, while ODR is a growth industry and offers the prospects of considerable innovation, there are difficulties and limitations in its application. In addition, it is the fact that in most systems – especially those used in the court – there is a mixed reliance on soft web programs for handling disputes and the use of ordinary human intervention, often intervention with great skills. That is to say, the ODR systems are probably better at dealing with small-scale financially based disputes, but where larger questions involve moral judgement or the emotional engagement of the parties then ODR will not necessarily be the best approach, or will need to be mixed in with more established ADR and adjudicatory processes.

13

Institutionalisation of ADR

Introduction

This chapter explores the nature and consequences of greater acceptance in legal practice and discourse of ADR values and processes, and their attendant incorporation in the formal civil justice systems in many jurisdictions around the world. Over the past four decades, there has been widespread diffusion of ADR, primarily from the United States, not only to many legal systems in the common law world, but also to states with civilian traditions. In addition, societies with strong cultures of dispute resolution outside the courts – such as China – have also refurbished their approaches in the past decade or so. ADR is at once a social movement, a value system and ideology, discourse, social and legal practice, and a source of inspiration for technical refurbishment of civil justice. The chapter explores key aspects of the formalisation ADR and related features of the processes of institutionalisation, and argues that the symbolic representation of ADR as offering a 'multi'-door courthouse provides a restricted view of the possibilities that the advance of ADR might bring. The present chapter also points to uncertainties about the fate of ADR and reflects on the continuously evolving relationship between ADR and formal legal institutions and processes. We suggest that while formalisation is a very likely outcome of many of the initiatives that we may characterise as 'ADR', and this outcome may bring with it positive features, one of the problems that formalisation creates is that the fundamental values of ADR may become obscured from vision, in particular the idea that there is a social need to get the parties to a dispute to learn how best themselves to resolve their differences.

Subsequent to the seminal Pound Conference in 1976, for nearly four decades there have been wide-ranging transformations taking place in the practice and the theorising of access to civil justice. In many parts of the common law world, and in many civilian jurisdictions too, a diffusion of the values of 'informalism' and a willingness to transplant and develop procedural innovations, often incorporating informal dimensions of processes of dispute resolution, have helped to alter profoundly the face of civil justice. As a result, processes of dispute resolution, and indeed many of the values infusing civil justice systems, that were once peripheral (at least, in theory) have now become central features of many contemporary civil justice systems. Indeed, we now find that reliance on these processes has become so prevalent that the 'alternative' in 'alternative dispute resolution' or 'ADR' is now often cast aside in favour of such terms as 'complementary', 'additional', 'appropriate', or simply abandoned to give us 'dispute resolution'.

This movement for reform in the direction of ADR, was – or so Cappelletti argued – a 'third wave' of the 'Access to Justice Movement', and it followed on from civil procedure reforms such as small claims courts, class actions and so on, and from enhanced legal aid provision. But unlike these earlier changes, ADR does not necessarily offer the parties enhanced access to adjudicative justice but, rather, primarily proffers 'settlement' as the likely outcome through private processes such as mediation and negotiation. And in many ways its heroic figure is not the authoritative (Herculean) judge, but rather the problem-solving, facilitative dispenser of 'mediation'. Not surprisingly, this development was not universally welcomed by those committed through legal practice or by intellectual preference to litigation and the role of courts as rule-focused institutions of justice and definers of core values. Truth rather than reconciliation is needed, and the growth of informal processes represents a danger to this core value.

At the same time, the systems of civil justice, in incorporating ADR processes, have indulged in what might be characterised as a 'new formalism'. One important general justification for the embrace of the greater diversity in accessible dispute resolution for a dispute in civil justice systems is that ADR expands the choices available to disputing parties. But this claim is not always realised in practice, and it was fears of such failures that fostered some of the early criticism of ADR. Moreover, with the introduction of ADR processes, often in the name of offering greater consumer choice, somewhat paradoxic-ally, because the introduction of ADR processes has very often been accompanied by other shifts, such as judicial case management, so the parties have less room to manoeuvre. With the incorporation of aspects of ADR into refurbished formal justice systems, a degree of freedom has in many respects been lost. Thus, for example, the ADR processes of mediation may be mandated by the court, either directly or less directly by, for example, costs awards against parties who fail to consider mediation to the satisfaction of the court. In the PRC, where legal culture has long emphasised the value of mediated processes, a resurgent use of mediation has been officially promoted over the past decade in the name of promoting a 'harmonious society'. This has not only pushed many disputants into mediations that they do not seek, but even troubled the trial judges (who in China both mediate and adjudicate the dispute if mediation fails), who find themselves more answerable to court leaders for outcomes: when an outcome is perceived by leaders as unsatis-factory, the judge's mediatory efforts can be scrutinised much more closely than an adjudicated outcome in which the judge can plausibly claim to have merely 'applied the law'. At the same time, local level official insistence on mediation as the only appropriate way for dealing with domestic violence has sometimes had tragic consequences.

Alongside the mandating of mediation, judicial case management has often been strengthened in other ways, so that, for example, in the post-Woolf Report reforms in England and Wales, trials are characterised as deserving specific tracks of complexity and duration. They are branded in terms of complexity in a threefold scheme that enables the managerial judge to select what is seen as the appropriate level of processual formality for the case. Thus, many cases are pushed into the 'Small Claims track', others into the 'Fast track', and still others into the 'Multi-track' (including ADR). In addition, pre-trial negotiation processes have been formalised; as Pre-Action Protocols mean that the parties are encouraged to attempt negotiation first on pain of potential costs penalties. These Protocols have had a profound impact on the manner in which negotiation is conducted, and in truth have been very effective in encouraging early settlement. However, if litigation is pursued, there is court referral to appropriate ADR procedures as a precondition to trial.

Another way of saying this is that even while ADR is being incorporated into the formal civil justice system in order to inject virtues of informality, ADR has, through its absorption into the formal civil justice system, and also from self-generated, ineluctable pressures, become more formal. It has at the same time also, paradoxically, generated in some ways greater formalisation of the civil justice system as a whole, while at the same time claiming, at the ideological level at least, to offer release from such processes. It has also enabled the state to redefine the goals of the civil justice system, so that the principal objective has often become settlement and one of its principal processual manifestations – 'mediation' – is now an effectively commonplace feature of disputing resolution processes in many places. But this is a complicated outcome, and one in which informalism has to a significant extent been formalised. And although promotion of ADR processes such as mediation is, it is often claimed, a way of enhancing 'access to justice' in reality the motives are reduction of case load, reduced costs and so on.[1]

Informal and Formal Justice Reconsidered

Of course, as we suggested in Chapter 2, understandings of the formal and the informal vary between legal cultures (and between differing legal communities within those cultures), though clearly the values that we characterise in general as formal are more likely than not to be associated with the involvement of the state and its authoritative institutions. A 'model' of informal justice contains

---

[1] Earlier analyses of the formalisation of ADR processes include, for example, Monroe (1987), Menkel-Meadow (1991), Press (1997), Langer (1998), Roberts, Simon (2002) and Mosten (2004). An earlier version of the present chapter on formalisation was published as Palmer (2014a).

a number of identifiable core elements that are seen as superior to orthodox, formal justice and in a number of respects are an explicit reaction to state provision of civil justice. In specific social situations at specific points of time a number of these values will be present, but not necessarily all will be manifested at one and the same time. These core features of 'informalism' include the development of processes and associated institutions that are non-bureaucratic in structure and relatively undifferentiated from society, relying on small, local fora which – unlike large legal bureaucracies – can get to grips with the social relationships of the parties. They are often private, though this may depend on cultural values regarding privacy, and so in China, for example, they very often are not: instead, mediatory proceedings may be a matter of public concern for the local community. In informal processes, there may also be a reluctance to use professional or official language. They aspire to be accessible to ordinary people, and not to rely on the services of ('expensive') professionals. Third-party interveners are often valued as lay people with mediatory skills and perhaps with some – but not a great deal – of training, who are not necessarily paid for their services. Their responsibilities may include a significant concern to facilitate transactional negotiations so as to prevent future disputes. There may well be a concern to rely on local standards of conduct and common-sense thinking, rather than making decisions in terms of official law. Often there is reliance instead on substantive and procedural 'rules' that are vague, unwritten, flexible, and reflective of good common sense – so that 'the law' does not stand in the way of achieving substantive justice in the 'instant' case. There may also be an intention to resolve disputes in such a manner as to promoting harmony between the parties and within local communities, in part because this approach will get to the 'real' underlying cause of the problem(s), in part because the search is for outcomes mutually acceptable to the parties rather than achieved through the strict application of legal rules, and in part because this approach carries an ethic of treatment. It is likely that in all legal cultures there is some line of thinking which manifests these principles of informalism to a certain extent, even in the ways in which they structure and administer their courts. Even within our current legal practice, professional jokes may reflect such values, albeit in a negative manner – for example 'any lawyer can achieve justice; it takes a really good litigator to achieve an injustice'.

In contrast, in many legal systems a dominant ideological strand typically stresses perceived values of formal justice for dispute resolution through law and legal institutions. The values or elements that are, to a greater or lesser degree, given emphasis include the provision of specialised bureaucratic mechanisms that are differentiated from society so that such mechanisms are able to make good, independent and technically correct decisions. There is a reliance on legal professionals with relevant expert knowledge and the capacity to articulate and to enforce the law – an impartial, publicly available official law (typically, that of the state) that may be imposed on the parties, which is interpreted in terms of the bounded discourses of law, and to which the executive is itself subject. There is a felt need for clear, fair procedures, open hearings, and present also is a strong concern with both procedural and substantive justice, because due process is a key element in the rule of law. The authority of the state, with courts able to compel the parties to accept that authority, underpins and infuses the dispute resolution process. But, argue proponents of informalism, these ideals of formal justice may well come to act as a barrier to the provision of substantive justice. For example, with reference to adversarial proceedings, Pound himself advised that one of the dangers of formal procedure is that it opens the system to a 'sporting' approach to justice – one in which civil justice becomes a game, with a concern on the part of the parties and their legal representatives to win at all costs and in which 'the courts, instituted to administer justice according to the law, are made agents or abettors of lawlessness'.

In this chapter, by formalisation we mean no more than a shift in values, rules and practice from informal to formal. With the development and increasing acceptance of ADR processes, initially grounded in and expressing informalism, by many formal legal systems over the past four decades there is not one but, rather, several transformations taking place. That is, in the spread of ADR and as ADR and its values of informal justice becomes a more important element in the overall civil justice system – something of a 'delega-lisation process' of the system as a whole, so the innovative processes of ADR tend to become more formalised as a result of various pressures, both external and internal.

The growth of the modern ADR 'movement' by no means exhausts the history of the search for alternatives, and this growth is itself understood better in a broader historical context of what Laura Nader has described as the 'recurrent dialectic' between informal and formal justice (1986). Both Nader and Abel (1982b) were quick to stress at the start of the ADR movement, in the early 1980s, that there is a cyclical dimension often to be found, in which a legal system oscillates between positions somewhere close to the informal and formal ends of the spectrum. And a more comparative perspective suggests that it is state-organised adjudication that is the real novelty – in England, for example, the Royal Courts only began functioning in the twelfth century. In the early history of the United States, as Auerbach (1983) has examined so elegantly, certain communities within American society resolved disputes without recourse to court-centred dispute resolution processes, preferring to resolve trouble situations themselves and to avoid using the expertise of lawyers and the procedural track of litigation. It was only subsequently that economic change, social and geographical mobility and so on, brought formal umpiring processes such as adjudication and arbitration to the fore. Moreover, any historical understanding should surely also encompass the experiences of dispute resolution mechanisms of more than northern Europe and North America.

In this book we have focused primarily on civil justice, for that is where 'informalism' in the shape of the ADR movement has had most impact over the past three to four decades. But, we should note that the spread of informalism has some important potential linkages with other areas of the justice system. Thus, with regard to administrative cases, it should be pointed out that in a number of jurisdictions, whether in theory and/or in practice, the question has arisen should the processing of disputes between citizen and state include the use of mediation and other ADR techniques as dispute resolution techniques?[2] And with respect to criminal justice, developments such as Victim Offender Mediation have, it seems, had some success in dealing with issues such as juvenile delinquency. At the same time, we must also remember that there may be a deeper connection between civil justice and penal policy. There seems to be a curious parallel to be found in a number of jurisdictions in which the emphasis (say) on mediation in civil justice is matched by an emphasis on draconian formal punishments in the criminal justice system.

The Mixed Message of the 'Multi-door Courthouse'

Sander and Fuller: Fitting the Forum to the Fuss

Frank Sander's 1976 speech at the Pound Conference on 'The Causes of Popular Dissatisfaction with the Administration of Justice' is widely seen, particularly in legal academic circles, as the defining event – the 'light-bulb moment' – in the development of 'modern' ADR.[3] At the Pound Conference, Sander argued that the formal processes of traditional litigation systems deal effectively with only certain kinds of dispute. He suggested that the remaining types of disputes might better be addressed through other mechanisms. In this thinking, he was of course paralleled by Lon Fuller's more general reflections on the 'processual integrity' of differing forms of dispute resolution – in particular, the relative suitability of mediation for dealing with many kinds of 'complex', multi-stranded disputes. Sander further suggested that the courts of the future might help parties access justice better by, first, screening incoming complaints, then categorising them according to principles which hopefully matched the case with the most suitable form of resolution, and then offering the parties the best matched process. In this model of the multi-door courthouse, of course, some disputes would still go to trial. But others would go to arbitration, or to mediation, or to fact-finding, or to some other mechanism well-tailored for the particulars of the dispute in question. This has helped to establish the important ADR principle that we should seek to 'fit the forum to the fuss'. There is little doubt that Sander's inspirational work has had a seminal influence in breaking down proceduralist resistance to ADR

---

[2] See, for example, Bondy, Doyle and Reid (2005), Bondy (2004) and Supperstone (2006).
[3] Sander (1979); Sander and Goldberg (1994); Sander and Rozdeicer (2006).

innovations, and encouraging much more widespread use of ADR processes in many civil justice systems.

Symbolic Legacy

But at the same time, it created an enduring symbolic legacy: it suggests that civil justice is still primarily a matter for court decision-making, with ADR processes to be brought within the sphere of an institution hitherto dedicated primarily to dispensing formal justice, namely, the court. And since governments would be reluctant – except perhaps in the case of China today where very palatial courthouses are once more built to reflect the power and glory of the paternalistic state prospering under successful Communist Party rule – to invest in new plant, so the old architecture of the court building would sometimes continue to impose itself on the thinking of judges and the parties and their representatives. So, the multi-door courthouse ideal not only encourages processual pluralism but in some ways casts ADR in the shadow of the court, and therefore also constitutes an unfortunate trap, continuing to suggest as it does that the natural place for resolving disputes is the formal institution of the court.

Sander's Original Idea: The Comprehensive Justice Centre

Indeed, in this connection it is important to note that Frank Sander did in fact initially prefer another name for his new invention: his personal choice was the rather more neutral-sounding 'comprehensive justice centre'. He confesses that it was the ABA – the lawyers no less – that encouraged him to give it the grander and more judicially orientated name. He explained fairly recently, in sharing some reflections on the fate of his idea with Professor Mariana Hernandez Crespo, his thinking about the relationship between ADR and the court system.

> FRANK SANDER: Well, there is no inherent relationship. I think, on the other hand, it is a pretty natural relationship because courts are our main, perhaps our most important, dispute-resolution place. So, one can make a strong argument that the multi-door courthouse ought to be connected with the courts, but technically the comprehensive justice center [or multi-door courthouse] that I mentioned could be quite separate from the courts. It is a little bit like the story about Willie Sutton, the bank robber, who, when asked why he robbed banks, said, 'That's where the money is.' The court is where the cases are, so it is natural to have the court as one door of the multi-door courthouse – that is the idea. But, it could be that the court could be over here and the other processes [arbitration, mediation, etc.] could be over there; there is nothing inherent [in the scheme] that prevents this.

Nevertheless, Professor Crespo in reply seems to confirm this court-centric view of the role of ADR when she elaborates, 'Yes, but the main point is that citizens need to know where to go when they have conflicts . . . this is all about the idea of the multi-door courthouse being an alternative for litigation in the courts.'[4]

It seems likely that this court-centric approach has significantly affected the thinking of many people involved in ADR – even while advocating change, the emphasis has remained focused on the courts. That is, the court has retained prominence in substantial part because the early and very potent symbol of a new approach to civil justice has been no more than a refurbished court. And therefore, also, the place to which aggrieved citizens are in fact encouraged to go in the refurbished civil justice system is to the lawyer's office, not the neighbourhood justice centre – that is, if there is one.

Woolf's Doors

Indeed, in England and Wales this has been the foundation of a major criticism of Lord Woolf's late 1990s civil justice reforms. With his encouragement, especially as contained in his two major Reports on civil justice reform (1995; 1996), the government made a crucial tactical decision. The track of civil litigation received continuing ratification as the main avenue for accessing civil justice. Litigation would remain the approved vehicle for civil justice, including lawyer negotiations. And cases that go for trial are, as we have noted, characterised as being suitable for specific procedural 'tracks'. Yet, an alternative route was available. The government could, for example, have devised a procedural framework with the objective of separating settlement and litigation more clearly. And as Sainsbury and Genn have complained, even the development of 'informal courts' such as tribunals was not encouraged (1995). Nowhere in the vast corpus of the Woolf Reports, nor in the government's subsequent presentation of the ensuing procedural regime, are wider potential choices explored. Was the availability of another way of doing things even considered by the architects of the refurbished civil justice regime? It seems not, and it is our suspicion that the template of the 'multi-door courthouse' has to bear some responsibility for the narrowness of vision.

What Happened to Naming, Blaming and Claiming?

In fact, the sociology of law has long offered ADR and access to civil justice a more powerful approach. This is the 'Naming, Blaming and Claiming' paradigm first developed by Felstiner, Abel and Sarat (1980–1). The paradigm of dispute development is often given a short nod in standard ADR textbooks, but the primarily law student audience for whom such texts are prepared has perhaps unwittingly discouraged wider interest in exploring the potential of

---

[4] Sander and Hernandez Crespo (2008: 671).

this type of analysis. In a powerful and more recent exploration using this analytical paradigm, one of these authors first explains the origins of the approach adopted and then shows its value for our better understanding of the dispute development process. He writes that the showing of a particularly moving film,

> prompted me to revisit an article I co-authored almost twenty years ago that urged scholars to explore the hidden domains of civil justice and to examine processes that we labeled 'naming, blaming, and claiming'. In that article, my co-authors and I argued that 'trouble, problems, [and] personal and social disloca-tion are everyday occurrences. Yet, social scientists have rarely studied the capacity of people to tolerate substantial distress and injustice.' We suggested that responses to those events could be understood as occurring in three stages. The first stage, defining a particular experience as injurious, we called naming. The next step in the life cycle of a dispute 'is the transformation of a perceived injurious experience into a grievance. This occurs when a person attributes an injury to the fault of another individual or social entity.' This stage we called blaming. The third step occurs 'when someone with a grievance voices it to the person or entity believed to be responsible and asks for some remedy'. This final stage is called claiming. We contended that 'only a small fraction of injurious experiences ever mature into disputes. Furthermore, we know that most of the attrition occurs in the early stages: experiences are not perceived as injurious; perceptions do not ripen into grievances; grievances are voiced to intimates but not to the person deemed responsible.' Paying attention to the process of dispute transformation and the high rate of attrition in, or resistance to, the emergence of disputes was, we contended, a way of putting the burgeon-ing argument about the litigation explosion in context. We argued that the processes through which disputes emerge, or through which people decide to lump it 'are subjective, unstable, reactive, complicated, and incomplete.' Most of what occurs in this domain of civil justice is cultural, not legal. These events occur in the everyday lives of ordinary citizens who struggle to make sense of who they are and who they want to be in a world of risk, danger, and injury. Yet, it should not be a surprise that lawyers play key roles as agents and audiences in the complex cultural processes of naming, blaming, and claiming, sometimes assisting to calm people down, thereby discouraging the blaming or claiming, while at other times, amplifying grievances and encouraging disputing.

He continues,

> The paradigm of 'Naming, Blaming and Claiming' offers students of ADR so many valuable insights. It helps us to understand better that one of the most fundamental problems we face in ensuring equality between citizens in securing access to justice is in fact to enable poorer and more disadvantaged members of society to realise that their rights have been infringed, and encouraging them not to be held back by 'grievance apathy' and an oppressive sense of the inevitability of injustice. With better legal consciousness, the disadvantaged should be able to turn a 'named' grievance into a claim against the cause of their distress – who is it who is to be blamed. It pushes us also into understanding better that early

responses from the party blamed, by way of acknowledgement of wrongdoing, including an apology, can prevent a dispute from developing in the first place. It encourages us to recognize the importance of the fact that if and when a grievance finally arrives in a lawyer's office, the lawyer reshapes the situation, perhaps offering a different and more legally informed view of the nature of the wrong that is the grievance, the most appropriate party to blame, and how best (with a view to going possibly to trial) to frame the claim. But, of course, most grievances do not reach that stage, but, rather are dealt with by 'lumping' or by negotiations between the parties. Despite these and other strengths, Sarat noted in his re-engagement with the model that for the United States at least, 'the conviction that we are a distinctively, if not uniquely, litigious society, and that the legal profession bears a large share of the blame for this condition, persists'.[5]

So, much of what takes place in dispute emergence is not legal but rather cultural in nature. The context of the emerging dispute is everyday social life in which the participants are trying to survive in an uncertain world. When the dispute reaches the lawyers office, however, it is often transformed by its redefinition in legal terms and loss of control to the lawyer handling the issue. But this transformation has perhaps too easily drawn attention away from the importance of the processes of dispute emergence. Thus, the Naming, Blaming and Claiming paradigm did not succeed – as we think it should have – in relocating our civil justice gaze away from the courts and from lawyers. We may perhaps take the liberty of requoting Frank Sander's comments when he says, as noted above: 'Willie Sutton, the bank robber, who, when asked why he robbed banks, said, "That's where the money is." The court is where the cases are' and reply in a somewhat contrary spirit: 'but the court is not where most of our disputes are'. Disputes are found everywhere as part of our everyday life, and the real promise of ADR remains lost if ADR processes are merely used to enhance the flexibility and speed of formal civil justice systems. For one of the real strengths of ADR is to encourage us and show us how to avoid recourse to lawyers and courts, to avoid dependency on others for resolving our disputes, and to regain control of how we relate to each other when there are trouble situations.

An excellent case study of access to housing entitlements in London shows us the value of the 'Naming, Blaming and Claiming' paradigm. Many homeless

---

[5] Sarat (2000: 426–7). Recent reflections by Galanter on our expanded perception of injustice have drawn attention again to the importance of this paradigm. Our greater knowledge of the world, and our enhanced social capabilities, tend to result in a greater sense of injustice – as the scope of possible interventions increases so more and more unfortunate events become defined by the possibilities of intervention. Thus, famine or social subordination, or a flawed appearance is no longer necessarily characterised as an unalterable fate. Instead, it is a chance of possible intervention. So, what was once regarded as a matter of fate may come to be seen as (say) the product of inappropriate policy, and thereby generating a sense of injustice (Galanter, 2010: 125).

applicants who fail in their attempt to seek assistance from a public authority in London for their urgent housing needs, do not perceive that they have an injurious experience (or 'unperceived injurious experience' – unPIE). The homeless applicant is simply unaware of an entitlement to make an application in the first place: some of the homeless are not able to articulate their problems, while some have difficulty understanding the system for assisting people who are homeless or in housing need. Nuances of language (where English is not the client's first language) are not taken into account, and there is misunderstanding on the client's side, particularly where local authorities set traps through their gatekeeping role. This also means that interpreters are not always used. As a result, many homeless applicants remain at the unPIE stage, unless their experience is transformed and they move on to the 'naming' stage, as a result of assistance by friends, relatives or a housing law practitioner, and are made aware of their entitlement (Ng, 2009).

It may also be that the continuing focus on ADR innovations in and around the court has prevented us from fully recognising the importance of the growth of the ombuds (or ombudsman, or ombudsperson) in the civil justice system in many parts of the world over the past thirty years or so. Although this institution, originally found in Sweden, was introduced in the late 1960s as a mechanism for dealing with complaints made by citizens against maladministration by the government it is now also used for dispute resolution in a wide variety of fields. In the United Kingdom, for example, these extended uses include banking, insurance, building societies (institutions which lend money to people who wish to buy a house), the London stock exchange, pensions and even lawyers' services.

As noted in an earlier chapter, in the United Kingdom the development of the ombuds of the past two decades and more has included an important response to issues in financial services namely, the creation of FOS or the Financial Ombudsman Service. This form of handling financial consumer grievances has, in effect, successfully replaced civil litigation for handling grievances in the field of financial services, especially for problems such as the mis-selling of mortgages and payday lending. The FOS is a statutory body established under the Financial Services and Markets Act 2000, and is intended to provide a dispute resolution system that is quick, informal and independent. It also seeks to establish benchmarks of good practice within the financial sector and this is important in a sector in which disparity in resources between the parties may be very considerable. The processual approach of a FOS ombudsperson is inquisitorial in the sense that as the decision maker she or he has responsibility to initiate action by means of an inquiry or an investigation once a complaint has been received and accepted. Legal representation is not encouraged and cases rarely go to court. Most complaints are resolved by the ombuds by what is, in effect, early neutral evaluation of the case. If the complainant accepts the decision then the determination is final and binding on the parties. A complainant who rejects the finding may bring a civil suit, but this is a right denied the defendant institution. The high degree of specialisation, confidentiality, procedural flexibility and experience that the ombudsman service develops in handling what are often quite similar cases are important strengths. As a result, the FOS caseload has expanded considerably over the past twenty years, not only replacing civil litigation but also reflecting an enhanced access to justice that the system delivers.

Formalisation and its Contexts

The Contexts of Formalisation

Now, exploring in a little more depth the evolving scene of ADR, we may characterise the changes that have and are still taking place as involving several differing but interrelated movements and pressures. But these are not simply to be characterised as processes of 'formalisation' or 'deformalisation' (that is, a movement away from formal values, norms and processes). On the face of it, the growth of ADR seems to reflect a growing role for informalism in the civil justice system. But, as we have already indicated, there is plenty of evidence available to suggest that in addition, as informal values and processes are diffused and incorporated into the formal justice system, they have often been injected with formalist ideals, and as a result, may lead somewhat paradoxically to even greater formalism. So, there is in truth often a rather complicated situation – in many jurisdictions, there is now a quite varied complex of processes, institutions and practices that have come to share the 'super-absorbent, mopping-up brand' of 'ADR'. In this sense, the label 'ADR' is not necessarily very helpful, suggesting as it does a unity that often is illusory. Nevertheless, some patterns emerge when we stand back a little from the immediate picture.

As we have already observed, one area of change has been the formalisation of some aspects of negotiation. Thus, 'Pre-action Protocols' were established in the United Kingdom in 1999, following Lord Woolf's Access to Justice reports of the mid-1990s, in which he identified a need to enable, 'parties to a dispute to embark on meaningful negotiations as soon as the possibility of litigation is identified, and ensure that as early as possible they have the relevant information to define their claims and to make realistic offers to settle'. It was recommended that pre-action protocols should set out codes of workable practice which parties should follow when faced with the prospect of civil litigation, and the protocols outline the steps that parties should take in seeking information from, and to provide information to, each other before making a legal claim. The prime intention is to set out the claim in full to the defendant in an attempt to negotiate a settlement. Unreasonable failure by either party to comply with the relevant protocols should be taken into account by the court, for example in the allocation of costs or in considering any application for extra time; and the operation of protocols should be monitored and their detailed provisions modified where necessary. These measures have been implemented through the Civil Procedure Rules 1999, and since then pre-action protocols relating to specific types of claims have been adopted by way of practice directions. This approach, giving greater formality to negotiation, has been adopted or is under active consideration, by a number of other common law jurisdictions since then – for example, Hong Kong.

Earlier on in the development of ADR, other modifications to the negotiation processes were introduced, primarily as forecasting devices intended to give parties who were negotiating a commercial dispute a clearer idea of the likely outcome if the case went to trial. One such early development was the 'mini-trial', a private presentation of each side's arguments and supporting evidence to senior management. The latter, having formed their own view of the issues and likely outcome, are then in a position to negotiate more effectively. This innovation spread, and one variant that emerged was the summary jury trial in civil cases likely to go before a jury: short versions of each side's case are put to a mock jury, which then gives an advisory verdict. This likely outcome is then communicated to the parties in order to facilitate more effective negotiations.

Professionalisation of Mediation

One of the most significant of the contemporary transformations in the culture of disputing is the emergence of new professionals specialising in dispute resolution, especially mediation. And when the relevant actors talk of 'ADR' they often in truth just mean mediation. Over the past thirty years or so a new profession – that of the 'mediator' – has emerged. Alongside this development there have been responsive, in some ways defensive, changes on the part of the legal profession. In England and Wales, the barristers of Garden Court Chambers for example, were among the first to hold themselves out as offering not only litigation but also mediation services. Many of the early initiatives in favour of ADR did in fact come from solicitors involved in matrimonial work. Nowadays, many large law firms have re-modelled their 'litigation' departments so that they are now presented as offering 'dispute resolution' service. Bridging the first and the second type of professional are often those 'retired' from the judiciary, who now see themselves in a new role as facilitators and conciliators rather than as adjudicators.

As just noted, over the past three decades or so, there is the embryonic growth of new specialised groups – 'the new professionals in dispute resolution', especially 'the mediators'. In many jurisdictions, this is perhaps a really radical change, representing a major stride towards the institutionalisation of 'mediation' through the creation and consolidation of a new professional grouping. New institutions have come to offer themselves as service providers, threatening to undermine the monopoly hitherto enjoyed by the legal professions. But as numerous studies have shown, there is often a lack of public confidence in or at least awareness of what the mediators can offer, and this has had at least three effects. First, it has strengthened the case for mandating mediation: if parties won't try mediation how can they come to learn of its benefits? Secondly, it has pushed service providers into training and regulation functions. The new profession of mediator is trained in a variety of ways by a variety of bodies. And in a way that many find uncomfortable, outside of the United States at least, the trainers are also often the regulators. Thirdly, it has encouraged the globalisation of service providers. As they search for new markets, so the ADR providers such as CEDR and JAMS look to greener pastures overseas. CEDR has cooperated with the CCPIT Mediation Centre to offer mediation training in the PRC with generous support from the Foreign and Commonwealth Office Global Opportunities Fund.

Complications

In addition, as we have also noted, this process of 'professionalisation' is a complicated one. First, a significant number of the new mediators are also lawyers, many of them concurrent professional practitioners but others simply offering negotiation and mediation services. Still others – as we have noted – are retired judges, some perhaps simply looking for work after stepping down from the bench, but other perhaps naturally drawn to the new profession: the kind of judge that Conley and O'Barr refer to as the 'mediator judge' whose inclination even when adjudicating has invariably been – 'through the manipulation of procedure' to promote mediated settlements (1990). Secondly, while in some respects mediators appear to be competing with lawyers, they may also assist rather than compete: that is, they may work in a cooperative relationship with lawyers and other experts (such as accountants) to facilitate communication and secure settlement. This style of cooperation may become especially important in jurisdictions in which voluntary party negotiations are once more a very significant means of managing disputes. As we have seen, one effect of the Woolf reforms in England and Wales has indeed been to give party negotiations much greater prominence in the early stages of the litigation process. In addition, while some of the new mediators offer their services as a matter of public service, or at least on a not-for-profit basis, others are firmly commercial in their approach.

At the same time as a new profession of the 'mediator' has emerged, there have been responsive, defensive adjustments on the part of the legal profession – including, as just noted, those in practice as lawyers and others who have 'retired' from the judiciary. In England and Wales, this development has included the Bar, that is, the branch of the legal profession most wedded to advocacy and litigation. Now there is a further marriage, between the lawyer and ADR, and with it the creation of a new offspring in the form of the 'mediator advocate'. It has encouraged more imaginative understandings of what lawyers should do – for example, engage in 'collaborative lawyering'. Processually, another important, professional response has been mediation in 'bad faith', albeit disguised. Solicitors managing litigation in large London law firms do allow their clients and themselves to indulge in mediation, largely out of fear of an adverse costs award if they do not, but also then use the mediation to try to gain insights into the position, legal and factual, of the other party.

On the other hand, the involvement of professional lawyers in ADR seems to have been an important factor in promoting greater 'formalisation' in the mediation process. Despite Lela Love's observation (1997) that there are as many as ten good reasons why a mediator should not evaluate, lawyers involved in mediation often come almost willy-nilly to play an evaluative role, with their predictive skills high on the list of evaluative strengths. And indeed this has been paralleled by the development of ENE, or early neutral evaluation. One of us has been employed as an 'ADR expert' by parties on how best to approach court-referred mediation – for example, advising a European family locked in battle with a newly discovered Chinese side of a testator's family on how best to mediate with a mainland Chinese party in a court-referred mediation. One of the problems here, however, is the state of dependence that is encouraged. The involvement of professionals, offering expert advice and services, in mediation, necessarily reduces the informalist value of mediation as an autonomous, self-governing process.

Education and Regulation

As we have suggested, as a newly emerging profession, in many parts of the world mediators struggle to make a good living. In our experience, a number of mediators turn to part-time teaching not only to supplement their income, but also to advertise their services. But the major development that is important from the perspective of the issues addressed in this chapter are the parallel development of institutions offering not only mediation services but also formal training and regulation. Institutions offering mediation services, if only by means of a list of recommended mediators, find that they can survive better financially if they also offer training. And then, having trained mediators, and added their graduates' names to the list, they provide a regulatory framework to promote and ensure good conduct. But clearly there are problems here, in that there is much potential conflict of interest in an institution which is indeed wearing all three mediation hats at once. In this respect, the 2008 European Directive on Mediation has not been very helpful, indicating that a high degree of local autonomy in regulation is acceptable:

Article 4
Ensuring the quality of mediation

1. Member States shall encourage, by any means which they consider appropriate, the development of, and adherence to, voluntary codes of conduct by

mediators and organizations providing mediation services, as well as other effective quality control mechanisms concerning the provision of mediation services.

2. Member States shall encourage the initial and further training of mediators in order to ensure that the mediation is conducted in an effective, impartial and competent way in relation to the parties.

Processual Innovation

There has been, as we have seen, the development of novel threshold procedures – often called 'hybrid processes' – in front of the courts, and also in some cases, within the courts. These are perhaps the most important part of the developments in civil justice across a whole range of jurisdictions over the past twenty years or so in the direction of the creation of a wide range of hybrid forms. These have grown up around each of the primary processes of negotiation, mediation and umpiring, but many of them, if not a majority, are court centred. Legal professionals have played a key role in the evolution of these hybrids forms, which now in many respects represent the frontline of ADR development. Indeed, the emergence of these new forms may be viewed as something of a co-option of the ADR movement by specialists trained in legal rules and procedures. These have in many cases been given official blessing. We have also noted attempts to enhance lawyer negotiations through greater use of umpiring type techniques such as the mini-trial, and the summary jury trial that are intended to forecast likely court outcomes if the dispute goes to trial.

In addition, there is the mixing of processes that often involves the incorporation of mediation into other more formal processes – for example, the injection of mediation into arbitration to produce so-called 'med-arb', the appropriating of mediation by the court as a preliminary to full trial, and, in family troubles, the fusing of therapy and mediation. Moreover, there have been a number of attempts to refurbish adjudication by modifying or supplementing the trial process with further devices – a number of these refurbishment efforts being closely related to those developed by lawyers in support of their negotiations. These court-based initiatives include judicial settlement, early neutral evaluation and court-annexed arbitration. There have also been important and somewhat similar developments in the field of arbitration. It should be added here that the ombuds, noted earlier, often use mediation alongside other methods in their approach to handling complaints.

Compulsion

One of the key issues to emerge from the innovations around adjudication is the question of the extent to which, if at all, the court should mandate parties to participate in such processes – such as mediation – and if there is such mandating, who should bear responsibility for the process. It is not the only difficult issue – other concerns include how to assess whether mediation has been entered in good faith, the status of mediation agreements, breaches of confidentiality of the mediation process, and the legal responsibility of the mediator for the outcome agreed by the parties. On the face of it, court mandating of mediation is rather like imposing democracy on a polity by force of arms, and an obvious contradiction in terms. But the counter-argument is that mediation is advantageous to the parties and for society as a whole, and for the court it has obvious benefits: reducing trial caseloads, encouraging wider recognition of the virtues of mediation, and so on. Many parties still want their day in court, this old-style adversarial approach needs to be met head-on in order to overcome resistance to mediation. As a result, it is now common in many jurisdictions for mediation to be a full or fairly strict pre-trial requirement, despite the fact that some of the earliest and powerful critiques of ADR have come in this area. And even today, there must be severe worries about mandated mediation as creating, rather than removing, barriers to justice.

Formalisation and the Routinisation of Charisma?

Routinisation

We have so far characterised the developments in the greater formalisation of ADR mainly in terms of professional and judicial interests. But there are other, some would argue ineluctable, processes at work – and these are also pressures which promote formalisation. As we have noted, the nature of ADR processes is changed as they become more closely associated with the formal justice system, or in response to internal pressures. These raise the issue of the sustainability of ADR initiatives, and the easiest way of approaching this issue is perhaps to remind us all of the essential features of the arguments of Peter Fitzpatrick (1993), Sally Engle Merry (1993) and others. That is, once the new message of the value of ADR has been received and ADR is put into practice, there are pressures of institutionalisation at work that may result in changes that fundamentally transform the meaning of the institution. The revolutionary 'charisma' of ADR necessarily, and somewhat paradoxically, becomes 'routin-ised'.[6] In particular, alongside a tendency for ADR to become incorporated in the state system, there is often – despite its basic impulse to stand in formal opposition to state law – a 'replication and strengthening of the language and cultural forms of popular justice so that it comes to mirror in many ways the very system of formal justice that it in theory opposes' (Merry, 1993: 60). In his important jurisprudential examination of the notion of 'popular justice', Peter

---

[6] See Weber (1964).

Fitzpatrick similarly argues that the ideals of informal justice are rarely capable of being sustained, in large part because they are put into effect in a process which mirrors the ideology and practice of formal justice, so that the ambitions of informalism – expressed in its 'origin myth' – are only achieved with great difficulty. Nevertheless, it is important also to bear in mind that many of the ineluctable changes that take place are done in a spirit of strengthening the process, and trying to ensure fairer outcomes (1993).

Knights of Labour

In the development of modern ADR discourse, and as we have noted above, Jonathan Garlock (1982) in the early 1980s documented this process in an important case study: the experience of the initially Philadelphian working-class organisation that emerged in the late 1860s under the title 'Knights of Labour'. This was a kind of general trade union, and in the eyes of the leaders and many of the members of this organisation, the conventional court structure seemed weighted against working people, dealing out overly severe punishment in criminal cases and proving inaccessible in civil cases in which a working-class person was the plaintiff. An 'alternative' system of dispute resolution was established for members, but one that, as the movement became more firmly institutionalised, came to model itself on the official court system. As a result, it both lost the advantages of informalism, and incurred the wrath of the authorities who viewed it as a threat to state power.

Juridification

One of the pressures at work in the institutionalisation process is characterised by Flood and Caiger as 'juridification'. In their seminal essay (1993) on construction arbitration they describe how the highly specialised and dispute-ridden field of construction arbitration is a competitive arena between construction experts and lawyers, with lawyers slowly gaining the ascendancy despite lack of technical knowledge. The lawyers have been able to 'juridify' the arbitration process so that the experts – socially in the role of arbitrator – are marginalised. The emphasis that Flood and Caiger place on the role of professional 'competition and rivalry' does, however, in our view only partly explain what has been at work. Another reason for such developments is a process of 'repetitive' decision-making at work, creating complexity even in the face of efforts to keep arbitration pure, flexible and simple. New 'procedural norms' are almost necessarily developed to deal with perceived problems, so that with the passage of time and greater experience the hearings become legalistic and less flexible. In other words, arbitration has an inherent tendency to become more technical and therefore also time-consuming, costly and formal.

Harmony and Deformalisation in China?

Let us now look at some key aspects of civil justice change currently taking place in the world's most populous jurisdiction, and one which it seems encouraged Chief Justice Warren to issue a clarion call for us in the West to search for a 'better way', namely, the PRC. Despite its obvious importance, the experience of China tends not to be drawn on in debates about ADR and its role in civil justice systems.

In China, for much of the late 1990s there was a period of sustained emphasis on the need for greater reliance on the civil chambers in the people's courts and the process of adjudication for resolving civil disputes, an emphasis strongly advocated by the then President of the Supreme People's Court, in an effort to more firmly institutionalise the ideal of the 'rule of law'. Such efforts may be seen as culminating in 1999 with an amendment to that Constitution (1982) at Article 5 calling on China henceforth to be governed in accordance with (the rule of) law. But over the past decade China's leadership has explicitly argued that the main role of the civil justice system should be to promote a 'harmonious society' (*hexie shehui*). Perhaps, had the relevant Chinese leaders such as President Hu Jintao been students of Laura Nader, a different term might have been used. The effect of this promotion of 'harmony ideology' in China has been to promote much greater use of mediation, both outside and inside the courts, for resolving civil disputes.

One of us has elsewhere examined how – despite an explicit ban on the use of mediation in administrative cases handled by the people's courts – pre-trial judicial mediation has come to be the dominant mode for resolving public law cases that come before the courts, and how the Supreme People's Court has been forced to recognise this 'bottom-up' pressure by characterising resulting mediation agreements in formal terms as 'negotiated settlements' (*hejie*) (Palmer, 2014b). But even in civil justice, the re-advance of mediation is paralleled by a significant degree of formalisation. Thus, in respect of rules: although the new People's Mediation Law 2010 is rather general and non-specific on many issues, different government ministries have issued notices, interim measures and rules which offer detailed specification of mediation (and to a lesser extent arbitration) procedures and processual ethics across a range of different fields. For example, rural land disputes, labour disputes, electricity supply disputes, maritime disputes and hydroelectric project disputes. These rules aim to systemise and formalise the processes of mediation, arbitration and even negotiation.

In respect of practice, in empirical studies of Chinese grass-roots dispute resolution, some commentators argue that the state built hierarchy and net-worked relations between mediation organs and the state – part of a new system of what is called 'Grand Mediation' (*Da Tiaojie*) has turned mediation organs – especially the local community mediation bodies or 'people's mediation committees' – into quasi-bureaucratic organisations. There is an element of hierarchy here, as well, as the new system gives superior level mediation organs significant indirect controls over lower-level mediation organs through budget control, evaluation and guidance. So, in China too, we see that the advance of informalism is also closely associated with a formalisation of ADR-type processes, the more so the more they are co-opted into the final justice system.

Conclusions

We have noted that the growing use of 'ADR' may result in a greater degree of formalisation in hitherto informal justice processes, creating problems of inflexibility, rigidity and so on from which ADR is meant to offer release. This is the contradiction of formalisation. External pressures such as professional rivalry, the state as representative of the public interest, the location of much of ADR discourse in law schools and legal practice, and the determination on the part of even ADR 'experts' to continue to see the court as the most natural forum for the resolution of civil disputes, all encourage this development. Internal pressures of institutionalisation are also at work, as we have seen: for the revolutionary message of ADR to be put into practice, problems are encountered and compromises have to be made that may well come to undermine the 'origin myth' as Fitzpatrick calls it. As a result, there has in many ways been a co-option of the ADR movement by specialists trained in legal rules and procedures.

To this worry – the apparent impossibility of sustaining the values of informal justice in an institutional setting over time – we should remind ourselves of the reservations about greater reliance on informal justice expressed in the early 1980s. Some of the changes we have noted seem to resonate with the pessimistic forecasts of the early 1980s, which saw the development of informal justice as often constituting an unwarranted extension of state power, and a form of second-class justice reserved for the poor and other disadvantaged persons. In addition, in a manner that has not been fully considered, a transformation has taken place in the meaning of civil justice. The traditional identity of civil justice systems as offering independent and fair third-party determination of outcomes, has been replaced with a concern with settlement. In England, for example, Lord Woolf in his seminal reports on Access to Justice (1995; 1996) characterised the primary objective of civil justice as the sponsorship of settlement, with judgment reduced to the solution of last resort. The Civil Procedure Rules of 1999 implemented this novel vision, so that settlement is now the orthodox civil justice. But this is still not the understanding of many ordinary people. And for this reason, the incorporation of ADR processes carries the danger of restricting rather than enhancing access to justice.

We have argued above, that from early on the ADR movement has developed within the parameters of a vision shaped by the ideal of a multi-door courthouse. And ADR might have taken a different, less formal turn, had it chosen to focus instead on (say) issues of dispute transformation highlighted by the 'Naming, Blaming and Claiming' paradigm, and ways in which the understandings this paradigm brings might enhance access to justice for ordinary people. Nevertheless, the embrace of ADR processes by the formal civil justice system is not necessarily to be fully resisted. First, we continue to overlook the important defence of the Fiss (1984; 1985) critique of ADR as made by David Luban (1995) in the mid-1990s. No civil justice system can operate purely on the basis of court-based adjudication because among other things the courts will be blocked and trials delayed. Nor can it be based purely on settlement – there will always be cases in which an authoritative body will need to apply the law to resolve the differences between the parties. To that observation we might add one made by Galanter and Cahill in their essay 'Most Cases Settle' (1994): yes, cases often settle, but that does not necessarily mean that adjudication has not had a role to play, because it may be as a result of a preliminary court ruling that the parties chose to settle. So, the question is not all or nothing, but rather, how much settlement and how much adjudication; how best to carefully balance the two. And where settlement is used to resolve differences, then the Fiss objections can be met by requiring out-of-court settlements to be filed with a public authority and with suitable safeguards made available to the public. Many of the decisions – though not mediated outcomes – of the FOS in the United Kingdom are published in something like this manner.

In addition, the advance of ADR has included the development of novel institutions or refurbishment of established bodies – such as the modern ombuds – which are providing much better access to justice and offering specialist dispute resolution. With greater awareness, some of the process dangers of informalism have been effectively responded to – for example, the place of mediation in matrimonial disputes in which there has been domestic violence has been more properly thought through and safeguards introduced. The spread of the ADR message has democratised to a significant extent the dispute resolution process, and promoted more responsive and collaborative lawyering – for example 'therapeutic jurisprudence and preventive law', or TJPL. Of course, dispute resolution behind closed doors does limit the extent to which civil justice can through public adjudication encourage social change, and also enhance access to justice for the poor and otherwise disadvantaged. Compromise, lumping of grievances and acceptance of injustice is not always desirable. But at the same time we should bear in mind that compromise is often a virtue and indeed, as Stuart Hampshire has emphasised, without it social life is not possible (1991; 1999). ADR therefore needs to be more socio-legal in approach than it is at present. The issue is not whether and how ADR processes should be incorporated into litigation and court procedures, but, rather, how best to get people to learn how to resolve their differences. This may seem an unrealistic perspective, but surely it is nevertheless the fundamental advantage that the truly 'alternative' processes of dispute resolution offer.

14

Reflections

Introduction

In earlier chapters we have charted the progress of what can only be described as a sea change in civil justice arrangements. Visible right across the common law world, there have been corresponding – if less fundamental – reverberations in civilian jurisdictions too. Over three or so short decades, what appeared in the 1980s as marginal novelties have become established features of the disputing scene. ADR, with its objective in 'settlement' and its principal institutional realisation in 'mediation', is now a virtually unremarkable feature of disputing cultures almost anywhere we look.

Looking at these transformations in the most general terms, two preliminary points might be made about them. First, they appear to realise some of the almost apocalyptic forecasts of the early 1980s concerning 'the changing nature of state power in late capitalism' (Santos, 1980), the shifting balance between understandings of 'lifeworld' and 'system' (Habermas, 1981) and the increasing dominance of 'reflexive law' (Teubner, 1983). While civil justice has historically presented itself as being fundamentally about the availability of third-party determination, an important ideological shift away from that position has taken place. Here in England, for example, Lord Woolf in his seminal reports on Access to Justice (1995; 1996) characterised the primary objective of civil justice as the sponsorship of settlement, with judgment reduced to the solution of last resort. Introducing the cultural change he wanted to bring about, he spoke entirely unselfconsciously of settlement as justice, leaving behind foundational images formed in the classical world and subsequently sustained over millennia in the Judaeo-Christian-Islamic traditions. Virtually without fuss or protest, the Civil Procedure Rules 1999 now achieve his novel vision. So settlement is now civil justice, just as 'command' has retreated behind 'inducement'.

A second aspect of this transformation in the common law world can perhaps be best described as the replacement of an historic procedural anarchy by a new formalism. For many generations it had been up to the disputing parties which route to resolution they took, what mode of achieving an outcome they tried first. There was no need to negotiate directly or resort to the 'good offices' of a non-aligned third party before issuing a writ; but that is now no longer the case. In England, for example, the proper procedural path is now marked with absolute clarity. The three primary processes around which this book is organised now represent a virtually obligatory sequence. Pre-Action Protocols warn potential litigants to attempt negotiation first on pain of potential costs penalties; once litigation is initiated, reference out to appropriate ADR procedures as a precondition to trial is built into the early stages of civil process (see Chapters 7 and 8).

The Contemporary Scene

In looking at this still evolving scene in more detail, we have characterised contemporary transformations in the culture of disputing as representing three diverging but interconnected movements: the embryonic growth of new specialised groups – 'the new professionals in dispute resolution', 'the mediators'; responsive, defensive adjustments on the part of the legal profession; and the development of novel threshold procedures in front of the courts. Thus, as we have noted, a quite disparate complex of institutions and practices has come to share the fugitive label of 'ADR'.

The 'New Professionals'

The first of these three movements seems the most radical, involving as it does substantial steps towards the institutionalisation of 'mediation' and the consolidation of new professional groupings. But the emergent shapes are not entirely clear-cut. First, a significant number of mediators are also lawyers, many of them in concurrent professional practice. Second, while in some respects mediators appear in more or less direct competition with lawyers, they offer to help in an entirely different way – by supporting party negotiations, rather than competing with lawyers in offering advisory and representative services.

This points to a key feature of contemporary change: the extent to which party negotiations are achieving greater prominence and becoming subject to the attention of supporting professionals. This shift raises difficult questions:

- First, what (if any) limitation would we want to see on the development of a culture in which voluntary party negotiations are seen as a primary, preferred means of managing disputes?
- Secondly, what forms of professional support would institutionalised party negotiations ideally receive?

On one level, reservations about the institutionalisation of party negotiations seem unnecessary, even absurd. What we are seeing is no more than open recognition of an existing state of things – consensual settlement has always been the first option, and any movement to reclaim back further control and responsibility previously lost to lawyers and the public justice system must be a good thing. But, as we saw in Chapter 3, there have been strong currents of argument against extending the ambit of 'settlement'; and the real worry that bilateral negotiations may operate to the disadvantage of weaker parties in the numerous circumstances where significant imbalances of power may be present. So the growing fashion for party negotiations raises again the important issues around which the 1980s debate about 'informalism' developed.

A number of points can be made about the growing institutionalisation of ADR processes, reflected in the panoply of agencies now developing in support of both party and representative negotiations. First, there are diverging views among mediators about professionalisation. Family mediators have from an early stage aspired to professional status, through for example the UK College of Family Mediators. On the other hand community and neighbourhood mediators have, on the whole, taken another direction, preferring the image of the caring bystander to that of the skilled professional.

At the same time, institutionalisation within these various fields has taken different forms. While core strands of community and family mediation have developed through service-based provision in the not-for-profit sector, commercial mediation has predictably developed primarily in the private sector. Here, alongside the pioneering provider, CEDR, small specialist groups have become important in the development and provision of ADR.

Lawyers and ADR

These developments appear to represent an open challenge to the monopoly over dispute management hitherto claimed by lawyers acting in a representative capacity, placing direct pressure upon some deeply entrenched practices. Certainly, the arrival of the new professionals in dispute resolution has prompted some reaction from the legal profession. But, in general terms, moves on the part of the courts to assume closer control over litigation have been much more influential on lawyers, forcing them to give much more attention to their practices in pursuit of settlement. These moves, threatening the lawyer's control over client and settlement process, have prompted a re-assessment of settlement practices including the now notorious culture of late-stage negotiations.

We have also noted how one specific response on the part of lawyers has been to re-model some areas of legal practice, introducing the label of 'alternative dispute resolution' as the trademark of these innovations. Some of these initiatives involve the development of specific technical procedures with the ostensible objective of drawing the client back into the decision-making process and accelerating settlement: the 'mini-trial', 'early neutral evaluation' (ENE), and 'the modified settlement conference' are some examples which we considered in Chapter 8. We posed the question there whether these are 'real' aids to settlement or simply crisis management measures, designed to allay mounting consumer anxiety and dissatisfaction.

At the same time we noted that lawyers are moving to act as mediators, even claiming mediation as an established part of legal practice. So far this development has been primarily in the family and commercial spheres but there is every sign that it will become more widespread. These developments underline the importance of some of the general questions that we posed in Chapter 6:

- First, how far can the mediator appropriately go beyond providing a structural framework for negotiations?
- Secondly, can an advisory role be safely combined with impartial facilitation of negotiations?
- Thirdly, should the mediator assume responsibility for the nature and quality of the outcome of mediated negotiations?
- Finally, can mediation safely be offered as an element of legal practice, or should it develop exclusively as an independent professional intervention with its own regulatory framework?

The Changing Nature of the Court

Parallel to the emergence of the new professionals, and the responsive action of lawyers in re-modelling certain areas of professional practice, has been the progressive involvement of the judiciary in the sponsorship of settlement. While this form of judicial activity has an ancient pedigree in the civilian world, and goes back some decades in North America, it has been received and become entrenched in the rest of the common law world with astonishing speed and assurance over the last decade. As we have already noted, the cultural changes involved go beyond the process of litigation. In England, for example, the Pre-Action Protocols purport to reach out into, reshape and regulate conduct that had hitherto been seen as securely in the 'private' sphere. In the context of litigation itself, the new, concurrent aspirations to management and the sponsorship of settlement require us to understand the 'court' in entirely new terms. Historically, foundational responsibilities for conduct of the trial and delivery of judgment have now receded into the background, postponed to the primary task of sponsoring and managing negotiations. We should not disguise the magnitude of the shift involved as we struggle to represent, for both ourselves and others, what a court 'is'.

- How should we respond to this growing readiness on the part of the courts to reach out into, and assume management of, what was formerly securely in the 'private' sphere?
- What has 'the court' become with this assumption of a diagnostic and managerial role, and its engagement in the active sponsorship of settlement?
- How do these new ambitions accord with sustaining the capacity to deliver authoritative third-party determinations?

The Future

This overall picture is presently changing too fast for any accurate forecast of what the civil justice system will look like a decade from now, but some suggestive markers have already been laid down. While one strand of ADR represents a movement of escape and of resistance to lawyer domination, the historic resilience of lawyers is already revealed in the speed with which they have represented ADR as part of their own repertoire. ADR is already firmly recognised as something which lawyers do, a change reflected in the way 'ADR units' have been established in many large commercial law firms, in the widespread rebranding of litigation departments in the promotional literature, and in the numbers of big city lawyers now claiming to be 'trained mediators'. Just as significant has been the welcome extended to ADR by the courts across the common law world.

While ADR's fugitive and polymorphous qualities may have ensured its ready adoption by the legal establishment, from the point of view of the commentator all of this presents a formidable task of reorientation. First, with the rediscovery of institutionalised mediation there is now a new domain clearly visible on the map of dispute processes. This field needs to be marked out and carefully explored. We have only begun to ask what kind of intervention mediation is. How is it different in its reach and ambition from established professional roles? What is going to be the relationship of this precariously established terrain occupied by the 'new professionals' to the adjacent areas of civil justice and legal representation? Second, the very identity of the lawyer is placed in question by the novel pretension to occupy non-aligned roles and to claim mediation as part of legal practice. Can those we have trusted as fierce partisans readily sustain this new hybrid persona? Beyond these reorientations, the most pressing requirement is to rethink what a court 'is'. The regime of intervention prescribed in the Civil Procedure Rules clearly endorses and consolidates an already established trend towards court sponsorship of settlement. In encouraging judges to act as mediators, the Rules also signal a profound change in the mode of intervention historically practised by the English judiciary.

As noted above, the determination of lawyers that they are going to be mediators, and that mediation should become an established part of legal practice, has implications both for the nature of mediation and for the regulatory framework within which it develops. Here a dual future seems already foretold. The new professionals in dispute resolution seem broadly set upon developing mediation as a narrow, facilitative intervention, supportive of party decision-making. But insofar as mediation so conceived develops within the context of established legal practice, it is hard to see it retaining such confined objectives, concentrated around the support of communications between the parties. It is likely to evolve, rather, as an 'evaluative' intervention (lawyers are already using this term), more akin to specialist advisory and consultative processes.

A parallel dualism is threatened in the sphere of regulation. The Law Society and the Bar are already seeking detailed control over their members in the exercise of mediatory roles, rather than seeing this activity as something outside legal practice. This determination is already establishing a parallel regime of regulation alongside those evolving among the new professionals. This could threaten the healthy development of mediation understood as a distinctive response to dispute management. It will only be through the survival of the 'mediator' as an independent professional that distinctive practice standards and institutions of quality assurance will crystallise. The development and refinement of mediation-specific standards is important to the practice of dispute resolution as a whole. Dispute resolution is bettered by the presence of a variety of options for response – each with their own distinctive and possibly incommensurable advantages.

We have already argued that the novel determination of common law courts to act as sponsors of settlement represents an enormous shift when thought about in the context of existing understandings of what courts are and what they do. Reaching out as some of them do into the period before the trial, they considerably extend the involvement of the court into a domain hitherto occupied by the parties and their professional representatives alone. Old understandings about what is 'private' and what is 'public' in the sphere of dispute management have already become blurred with these developments, but the likely future evolution of processes around the courts remains uncertain. One possibility might be the gradual evolution of a new, relatively discrete phase of institutionalised settlement seeking, interposed between private negotiations and the commencement of litigation, with litigation itself becoming more narrowly focused on moving to trial and judgment. The sharp reduction in the number of starts in the civil courts since the new procedural regime was introduced perhaps in itself forecasts this outcome. Certainly, most lawyers are not comfortable for a court to be supervising their negotiations. This in itself suggests that the alternative possibility of the present hybrid process continuing in the long term is improbable. So, with the identity of the mediator, the lawyer and the court uncertain, further changes of a fundamental kind must, at least potentially, remain in prospect.

All of this is going on at a moment when the centrality of state law is itself under challenge on the wider scene. The now centuries-old dominance of the nation state is in the process of being displaced from 'above', both through the progressive entrenchment of larger political groupings (the European Union, etc.) and through the overarching activities of multinational corporations, despite 'populist' resistance. It is widely argued that 'globalisation' brings with it the formation of new legal orders at a supra-national level; and there is certainly a plethora of new court-like institutions appearing on the international scene, uncoupled from the state and national laws. Will these new institutions mimic those at national level in their lately assumed identity as sponsors of settlement, or revert to the older tradition of authoritative determination? Or is a still more revised understanding of the court needed? Consider technological growth. Will the rapid growth of emergent technologies (giving rise to, for example, the use of 'big data') outstrip the degree to which courts, however they are conceived, function as institutional instruments of dispute resolution? Or might there be a radical reconceptualisation in the offing of the court's functions that accommodates these trends and others? Whatever the case is, the development of online services and the digitalisation of communication further blur the distinction between public and private spheres in society. And 'courts' continue to be constituted in this negotiated space at transnational level can be read either as a grand, imaginative leap of faith or as a sad failure of institutional design.

Appendix A

Some Role Plays

Role-playing exercises offer students an opportunity to explore the issues raised in a dispute processes course in a practical, experiential manner, and to apply theory and newly developing skills to simulated real world situations. Students who take the role plays seriously (not all do!) will hopefully find such exercises helpful in understanding better the complexity of some of the issues with which they are presented in their course. They should hopefully develop a firmer grasp of the idea that there is much to be gained from attempting to solve problems jointly in a manner that realises the interests of the parties – even though there may be much difficulty before an acceptable outcome is secured. Students may also find role playing helps them to see better the points of view of the people around them, and to understand how to relate to others more effectively. Among the likely benefits of an effective role play exercise for an individual student are enhanced self-awareness, greater problem-solving capacity, more effective communication, improved creativity and better collaboration skills.[1]

However, we also offer two cautionary notes.

First, while many students enjoy role plays, some may find them disturbing, especially if they experience the process as being akin to real life. As we stress in this book, negotiation and other dispute resolution processes may be full of tension, anxiety and struggle. They are generally not 'enjoyable events'. So, in using the role plays in this Appendix, or other exercises, please bear in mind that while – for all the reasons given above – the role play is meant to simulate real life in order to enhance students dispute resolution skills and understanding, there is a need to avoid the exercises being experienced as real life itself. This means making sure the simulations remain as role plays, and that students have a firm understanding that this is so. There are various techniques that may be used to help maintain the boundary between fiction and fact. First, a teacher may advise students that participation in a proposed role

---

[1] A strong case for using role simulation exercises is the Harvard University Program on Negotiations' Teaching Negotiation Resource Center, *Understanding the Impact of Role-Play Simulations*, available at www.pon.harvard.edu/free-reports/thank-you/?freemium_id=59733&n=1, accessed 3 December 2019.

play is voluntary and if anybody feels uncomfortable then an alternative activity, such as writing an essay or a report on a relevant issue, is possible. Secondly, each exercise can have an observer present for each of the parties, and these observers give feedback on the exercise when it has finished, so that it will be certain that unacceptable conduct, such as excessive aggression in the role play, will be reported on. More generally, observers can report back on what impressed them the most in the exercise, what else was done well, and what she or he would do differently. It may also be useful, thirdly, to walk around the classroom, listening to the unfolding resolution process, clarifying where necessary aspects of the exercise, giving advice on and controlling unacceptable conduct, or responding to any signs of distress. Fourthly, after an exercise is completed, there should of course be a debriefing, with parties and observers reporting back to the class as a whole. The participants should be asked to, for example, recount parts of the resolution process where things went best for them or the mistakes from which they barely recovered, their 'skill' in creating a good outcome. The teacher will be especially useful in identifying and explaining the relationship between issues encountered in the exercise and the relevant areas of dispute resolution discourse, and usually this is best done as the final part of a debriefing. Finally, the teacher should be willing to discuss with the student why it is she or he feels at risk if participating in the role play, and explore together the ways in which the student might still be involved in the exercise (or other exercises).

Secondly, in the dispute resolution field, the role play has been extended to include experiences based, for example, on dance. This development reflects another area of concern regarding role plays, namely their inappropriateness and ineffectiveness, as argued by Alexander and LeBaron (2013):

> In [our article] Death of Role-play (2009) we critiqued the use of role-play in negotiation training, from a number of perspectives. We questioned its cultural appropriateness as a methodology, illustrating how participants from some ethno-cultural groups are uncomfortable with pretending to impersonate others. Drawing upon relational-identity theory . . . which highlights the variability of human behavior according to context and roles, we examined the utility and resonance of prescribed, standardized scripts with which participants may have limited experience or connection. Our discussion also probed pre- and post-work, exploring the adequacy of preparation and advance briefing when role-plays are used. Finally, we questioned whether the dramatic adventure of playing a role actually results in durable and reproducible new behaviors in post-course interventions . . . we suggested that continuing the current over-reliance on culturally-encapsulated, standardized scenarios and character roles could prove to be the death of the popular pedagogical vehicle known as the role-play. Christopher Honeyman and James Coben . . . picked up on this theme when, drawing upon feedback from an international group of negotiation teachers, they wrote that . . . negotiation teachers:
>
> 1) over-rely on 'canned' material of little relevance to students;

and

2) share an unsubstantiated belief that role-plays are the one best way to teach . . .

However, in our experience, teaching ADR with an often culturally diverse postgraduate student audience on London University LLM programmes for more than two decades, role plays have often proved to be an experience enjoyed and appreciated by our students. In addition, one of us used Chinese-English bilingual versions of such material to teach Chinese undergraduates in mainland China for many years, and found that students participated often with even greater enthusiasm, seizing the chance to participate in an 'edu-entertainment experience' in which they often with gusto drew behavioural inspiration from TV dramas to act out disputes and their resolution (or unresolved outcome). Indeed, Chinese television itself has gone one step further and sought to educate Chinese citizens in mediation as a dispute resolution process through reality television programmes such as 'Gold Medal Mediation' (Zhao, 2015). The extent to which this has made them better as dispute resolvers is not known, however. It is also very unclear where the line is to be drawn between reality and fiction in these circumstances.

Teachers are encouraged to adapt the role plays offered below to suit the particular circumstances of their course. The exercises offered below are non-jurisdiction specific, and are intended to be that way in order to encourage attention to process rather than the application of legal rules. But of course it is open to a course teacher to add rules from her or his own jurisdiction to enhance the legal relevance of the exercise. The exercises may also be varied by adjusting the number and nature of the parties and other actors (we find in more public law focused disputes, for example, the addition of journalists to the simulation sometimes helpful), the extent to which Internet facilities are available to the parties, the degree of authority enjoyed by agents or subordinate members of an organisation who have been asked to represent the company in a negotiation or mediation, specification of particular cultural values and norms that may affect process and outcomes, and so on.

Role simulation exercises may also be found at: www.pon.harvard.edu/shop/category/role-simulations/, accessed 3 December 2019.

Sample Exercises

Since these exercises are open to be read by anybody perusing the book, it is suggested that if they are used in class then they be modified not only to suit the needs of the particular class but also so as to maintain the confidentiality of the material given separately to each party.

Instructors are encouraged to develop their own exercises in the light of what they perceive to be the needs and interests of their students. Source materials can be found in newspaper accounts, court judgments, and so on.

Exercise 1: The Incinerator Plant

This role play is designed primarily as a negotiation exercise, but it may also be organised as mediation (by adding a mediator) into the role play. In various guises, it is an introductory exercise often used in dispute process courses to illustrate some of the basic features of negotiation and also to introduce class members to each other. It is best done as a negotiations exercise between two persons, or between two teams of two persons. The fact sheets should if possible be kept confidential to the respective parties.

Fact Sheet for BUYERS (Yuedong Rubbish Disposal Company)

Background Note

Increasingly, many governments are turning to the burning of waste in order to deal with their growing mountains of rubbish, and the toxic leaching from landfill sites.

However, incineration plants must be designed to ensure that the flue gases reach a temperature of at least 850 °C (1,560 °F) for two seconds in order to ensure proper breakdown of toxic organic substances. In order to comply with this at all times, it is required to install backup auxiliary burners (often fuelled by oil), which are fired into the boiler in case the heating value of the waste becomes too low to reach this temperature alone.

Your Role

You are a negotiator hired to solve a problem by the Yuedong Rubbish Disposal Company.

The Facts

In the market town of Tuopu, in the fictional country of Arcadia, the local government has a serious waste management problem. It has decided to contract out collection of rubbish to the private sector, and the Yuedong Rubbish Disposal Company has won the contract for local waste management for the next three years.

But the company also has a problem. After winning the contract, it found that so much rubbish was produced locally that it needed to purchase a new waste incineration plant with a very high operating temperature – at least 850 degrees centigrade for at least two seconds – in order to ensure proper breakdown of toxic organic substances in Tuopu's local waste. This type of plant is called the L-850.

The company that the Yuedong Rubbish Disposal Company normally buys incineration plants from is currently on strike, as there is a long-term dispute over wage demands by the workers, and so the Yuedong Company is worried that it won't be able to purchase the necessary incineration plant until well after the contract with the Tuopu local government commences. As a result, the Yuedong Company will not be able to dispose of rubbish properly once the contract has started. Under the terms of the contract, there are very heavy penalties which may be imposed on the Yuedong Company if its rubbish collection and treatment work falls below a certain standard.

It should be added that because this supply problem has so shocked the Yuedong Company, it is now thinking of building its own manufacturing plant so as to ensure such a problem does not happen again in the future.

But at this point of time, a new supplier of a suitable high temperature incineration plant has to be found promptly.

However, most incineration plant manufacturers do not produce a high temperature burning plant of the type that the Yuedong Company needs, and in fact most other companies could not even tool up in time to produce the plant needed by the Tuopu Company until at least six months after the contract commences.

Only one company may be able to help your client in time.

The company is Snoopy Supercharged Incinerator Plant Manufacturers, a new operation engaged in the business of producing waste disposal plants and their components for local governments and waste disposal companies. Snoopy is the newest and most modern incinerator plant manufacturing operation in Arcadia, and your client thinks Snoopy may be able to serve the Tuopu Company's needs.

Your Instructions

You have been requested to determine whether Snoopy can produce (on rush order) the necessary incinerator plant for the Yuedong Company and, if so, to negotiate a deal with them. The following facts may be helpful to you:

- Snoopy is a new company in the business and there is a good chance that they would like to cultivate a business relationship with them. Although there are no definite plans, Yuedong will probably need to buy (or itself manufacture) several additional plants in the coming few years.
- Normally it would cost Yuedong 230 million RMB per unit to buy this type of plant from its normal supplier.
- In order to make a profit on its Tuopu operations, the Yuedong Company must keep the cost of any disposal plant it purchases below 310 million RMB.

Yuedong hopes that Snoopy can deliver such a plant in time, on rush order with delivery to be made no later than about five months from today (31 July, to be precise). Otherwise, it is very likely the Yuedong Company will be in breach of contract with the Tuopu authorities, and suffer very heavy financial penalties.

Accordingly, you have been authorised to spend any amount up to 430 million RMB to secure the necessary incineration plant in time.

You have been retained by Yuedong to purchase such a waste incineration unit, to be delivered not later than 31 July this year.

Fact Sheet for SELLERS (Snoopy Supercharged Incineration Plants)

Background Note

Increasingly, many governments are turning to the burning of waste in order to deal with their growing mountains of rubbish, and the toxic leaching from landfill sites.

However, incineration plants must be designed to ensure that the flue gases reach a temperature of at least 850 °C (1,560 °F) for two seconds in order to ensure proper breakdown of toxic organic substances. In order to comply with this at all times, it is required to install backup auxiliary burners (often fuelled by oil), which are fired into the boiler in case the heating value of the waste becomes too low to reach this temperature alone.

Your Role

You are a specialist negotiator recently retained by the Snoopy Supercharged Incineration Plant Manufacturing Company to assist with a sales problem.

The Facts

Your client, Snoopy, is a new Guangdong-based operation engaged in the business of producing waste treatment incineration plants and spare-parts (including backup auxiliary burners) for such plants. Snoopy is the newest and most modern waste incineration manufacturing operation in the (fictional country) of Arcadia. However, as a new company it has been beset by teething problems.

The most disastrous of these problems occurred in the autumn of last year. Snoopy had received an order from a large overseas company for four special 500 degrees centigrade waste incineration plants (the S-500 plants). Snoopy agreed to fill the order on a 'rush' basis within two months after the deal had been negotiated. Under normal circumstances, Snoopy could have easily delivered on time (because of its new, high-speed production equipment). However, due to a production blunder, Snoopy erroneously produced four 1,000 centigrade incineration plants. These super-hot waste treatment plants are called the 'XL-1000'. When the mistake was realised, it was too late to correct the order and deliver on time. The account was lost and Snoopy was thus stuck with four units of the 1,000 centigrade waste incineration plants.

Unfortunately for Snoopy, the XL-1000 is an incineration plant rarely used in the waste treatment industry; it may be best described as a very new, powerful, and 'peculiar' design plant that would be used for especially hazardous waste. As a result, it is virtually impossible to sell in normal market channels.

Last week, Snoopy received an inquiry from Cathay Waste Treatment Company for an extra-large and powerful incineration plant. Snoopy tried to sell the XL-1000 incineration plants to Cathay, but the incineration plants were apparently too small for Cathay's needs. Cathay is reluctant to change its operations at this late date, but the Cathay management has indicated to

Snoopy as a last resort they might be willing to buy two of the XL-1000 model incineration plants at a knockdown price.

Unless Snoopy can unload the XL-1000 incineration plants, it stands to lose a substantial amount of money.

The following facts may be helpful to you:

- Under normal circumstances, your client would sell this type of incineration plant for about 270 million RMB per unit for regular orders and 320 million RMB per unit for 'rush orders'. A rush order in the trade is generally considered to be any order calling for delivery in five months or less from the date of contracting.
- In order to make a profit on this type of incineration plant, Snoopy would have to sell at 240 million RMB per unit or more.
- Cathay has indicated that – if pressed – they might be willing to buy the XL-1000 incineration plant at 125 RMB per unit.
- If the incineration plants have to be scrapped, your client could get about 100 million RMB per unit.
- Now desperate, Snoopy is willing to sell at any price above the scrap price.

Yuedong Rubbish Disposal Company, a major waste collection and treatment enterprise in Guangdong, has just called Snoopy and inquired about an order for high temperature incineration plants. As with Cathay, Snoopy would like to sell the XL-1000 incineration plants to the Yuedong Company. At the same time, your client has advised you that Yuedong has itself started to build or is thinking of building a small incineration plant manufacturing operation of its own in a neighbouring province, which it could presumably expand to compete with Snoopy, and you have therefore been instructed to handle the Yuedong Company with kid gloves.

Your Instructions

Given these facts, you have now arranged to meet with a representative from the Yuedong Company to attempt to work out a deal. You have been retained by Snoopy to:

- sell as many of the XL-1000 incineration plants as you can to the Yuedong Company,
- for the best possible price per unit.

Thus, Snoopy expect you to maximise the gross sum that it will receive if a sales agreement is reached.

Exercise 2: Matrimonial Problems

This is a mediation exercise, designed to illustrate some of the difficulties a mediator faces when dealing with issues of children in matrimonial disputes. The exercise may be reconfigured to offer a dispute between a same-sex couple.

Instructions for Mother (who is called: Betty)

You are the mother of a seven-year-old girl called Amy. You married Amy's father, who is called Charlie, shortly before her birth and lived with him in an apartment in Silver City (in the fictional jurisdiction of Never-never-land) until six months ago when you discovered he was having an affair. When you confronted him about the affair, he left to live with his girlfriend. You remained living with daughter Amy in the former matrimonial home. No divorce proceedings have been issued and nothing has been agreed regarding the division of the matrimonial assets, or custody of Amy.

Amy's father is now seeking contact with Amy – he wishes to have rights of visitation to Amy – and has issued an application in the local court. You have not yet been given a date for the first court hearing. You went to a lawyer for advice and she advised you to try mediation as a way of dealing with the father's request. Amy's father agreed to mediation and you are today attending your first session of mediation. Under the very restrictive rules on legal aid in Never-never-land, you are unable to obtain legal aid because of your apparently high level of income. In reality, you have substantial debts and are even a little worried about how you will pay your lawyer if you do not come to an agreement today.

You do not want Amy's father to have contact (that is, visitation rights, in which Amy would stay with the father for some of the time) for the following reasons:

- You feel Charlie is only making the application to upset you because you will not agree to sell the former matrimonial home in Silver City and split the proceeds of sale equally with him.
- When you lived together he was always too busy to bother to spend any time with Amy.
- He will not do anything with Amy if he does see her. He will either leave her with his parents or just sit and watch television with her.
- He obviously does not care about Amy because he has not paid any child maintenance since he left.
- It was his choice to leave – it is not your fault he is no longer living at home and seeing Amy every day.
- You do not like his girlfriend and do not want Amy to see her. You particularly dislike the idea of Amy seeing Charlie hold his girlfriend's hand or even giving his girlfriend a kiss.
- You do not like his parents. Charlie's father drinks too much and gets angry too easily, and Amy is apparently frightened of going to their house.

Instructions for Father (who is called: Charlie)

You are the father of a seven-year-old girl called Amy. You are called Charlie. You married Amy's mother, who is called Betty, shortly before the birth of

Amy and lived with her until six months ago. You only married Betty because she was pregnant. You were never happy in the marriage and about one year ago you met someone else and fell in love with her. You feel this happened mainly because Amy's mother did not take any interest in you, as she was only interested in Amy and her own friends and family. You left Amy's mother, Betty, six months ago and moved in with your girlfriend. Amy's mother and Amy remained living in the former matrimonial home. No divorce proceedings have been issued and nothing has been agreed regarding the division of the matrimonial assets, or custody of Amy.

Since you left you have been asking to see Amy and you really miss her. You feel you were a good father but were never allowed to have any views on how Amy should be brought up – her mother Betty made all the decisions. When you were allowed to spend time with Amy she always had lots of fun. You also feel it is important for Amy to see your parents as they are her family too. When you used to take Amy to their house she always enjoyed spending time with your parents. You want her to get used to your girlfriend as the girlfriend is part of your life now and you think she would be very good in dealing with Amy once they have got to know each other better.

You want to get on with your life. You feel it would be fair to sell the former matrimonial home and divide the money equally with Amy's mother. You have not paid any child maintenance for Amy since you left because her mother Betty will not let you see her.

You feel it would be fair for you to have Amy for half the time and for her to stay with her mother for the other half. You work, however, and therefore only seek for Amy to stay with you every weekend and at least half of all school holidays.

You also want Amy to have a good education, especially as you feel that your parents did not support your education enough.

You have issued an application in the local court for contact with Amy (that is, visitation rights, in which Amy would come and stay with you for some of the time). You have not yet been given a date for the first court hearing. You went to a lawyer for advice and he advised you to try mediation. Amy's mother agreed and you are today attending your first session of mediation.

Instructions for Mediator

You are mediating a dispute between the parents of a seven-year-old girl called Amy. Amy's parents separated about six months ago and Amy lives with her mother, Betty.

Amy's father, Charlie, has issued an application to the local court for contact with Amy (that is, visitation rights, in which Amy would stay with the father some of the time) but no court date for the hearing has yet been fixed.

Betty and Charlie (and Amy) lived together in an apartment in Silver City (in the fictional jurisdiction of Never-never-land) until six months ago when Charlie left the matrimonial home.

On the whole, courts in Never-never-land favour children having contact (visitation) with their father so long as it is in the child's best interest to do so.

It is usual in Never-never-land for children of separated parents who live with their mother to spend every second weekend and up to half of each school holiday with their father.

You have not been provided with any details as to why the parties are in dispute over the contact (visitation).

The mother and father of Amy have invited you to mediate their dispute, today.

Exercise 3: Benny and Yolanda's Dispute Needs Mediation

This is a mediation exercise, designed to illustrate the difficulties that can arise when neighbours have a 'misunderstanding'.

Facts

In leafy Urbania, a suburb of one of the largest towns in the state of Treeland, two neighbours are in dispute. They are Benny Boon and Yolanda Young.

Causes of the Dispute

Their disagreement arose when one of the disputants, Benny Boon, chopped down a beautiful Japanese cherry tree situated in the next-door garden of Yolanda Young. Benny had the tree cut down in the erroneous belief that it was situated on his land, close to the eastern edge of his front garden. In fact, however, the tree was located on Yolanda's land, close to the western edge of her front garden. There are no boundary markers separating the two gardens. Benny had assumed, incorrectly, that the two front gardens are square-shaped and equal in size. In reality the two plots are irregular in shape and Yolanda's garden is slightly wider than Benny's.

Benny had the tree removed because he wishes to create a new garden path running along the eastern edge of his front garden. This path will, he hopes, save him several precious minutes in his early morning dash to catch the fast commuter train into town. Benny is a busy business executive and his offices are situated in the town centre. The tree was in the line of his proposed path, and even if left standing the fallen leaves and blossoms would make the path slippery and dangerous.

But, What Is the Tree Worth, and What Would It Cost to Replace?

Benny paid a tree surgeon €100 to remove the tree and to chop it into logs. As firewood these logs are worth €75 (Note: in Treeland, the currency is the euro).

The cherry tree was planted as a seedling forty years ago. It is seemingly very healthy, and producing excellent blossoms and fruit. However, in recent years a mysterious disease has been attacking such trees. As a result, local nurseries have stopped selling them, although they continue to stock other kinds of fruit tree. These other kinds of fruit tree are much smaller than the one removed because such trees cannot be transplanted when more than ten years old. The largest trees in stock sell for approximately €500, the precise cost depending on the quality of the tree being purchased.

Yolanda's Grievance and Claim

Yolanda, upset at the tree's removal without her notice, seeks compensation from Benny. She believes that the tree was worth €1,500 because of its beautiful shape, splendid blossoms and fine fruit.

Benny and Yolanda moved into the area at approximately the same time four years ago. They had been friends at college.

As Yolanda has several young children to raise and runs a business from home she has little time for gardening. As a result, when Benny told the gardener he regularly employs to maintain the land on which the tree stood, Yolanda kept silent – even when Benny had the tree chemically sprayed to protect it against disease. Benny also maintains a small area of Yolanda's back garden. The two neighbours had never discussed the question of the tree and its maintenance. Both had taken fruit from the tree.

However, neither had spoken to the other for several years following an incident in which Benny very nearly reversed his car by mistake over one of Yolanda's children.

Yolanda is upset at the loss of the tree. If necessary, she will take her case to court, seeking €1,500 to compensate for loss of the tree, and has told a friend that she will not accept an out-of-court settlement for less than €900.

Benny's Response

Benny believes that Yolanda is behaving very badly, and that Yolanda's willingness to allow him to maintain the property is the root cause of the dispute. Benny had used the land for four years and Yolanda's failure to object to this use prevented him from discovering his error.

It is Benny's view that Yolanda has not suffered any real damage because despite his efforts to protect the tree there was a very high probability that within several years disease would have destroyed the tree. It would have had to have been removed at Yolanda's expense.

He has therefore suggested to Yolanda that she pay him €25, this sum being the difference in value between the value of the firewood now neatly placed in one corner of his garden and the costs which he paid to the tree surgeon for removing the tree.

They Agree to Attempt Mediation

As a last chance to avoid going to court, Benny and Yolanda have agreed to have their dispute mediated by Leslie, who is an experienced mediator serving at the Urbania Community Mediation Centre. This offers a free mediation to local customers as it is supported financially by the local government.

It has also been agreed that Benny and Yolanda can bring one friend to the mediation with them.

NOTE: participants will divide into groups of three, and

- Leslie will attempt to mediate the dispute between
- Benny (with friend) and
- Yolanda (with friend).

Note: If the mediation fails . . .

Yolanda is thinking of hiring Walter Williams to serve as her counsel. Walter tells her that his charge is €40 per hour and that if the case goes to trial he will need to spend at least twenty hours on the case. There is no contingency fee system in Treeland. Benny is thinking of asking Carol Candy to serve as his counsel. She has told him that her charge is €40 per hour, and then if the case goes to trial, she will need to spend at least twenty hours on the case.

Exercise 4: Not in My Backyard?

This is a group negotiation exercise, which can also be organised as a mediation exercise.[2]

Participants should divide themselves into (approximate) groups of six persons (three will be Atlas, three will be Neighbourhood Association). The two parties need to negotiate a mutually acceptable outcome.

And if run as a mediation exercise then for each cluster of the two parties there should be a single mediator, or two mediators who will attempt a joint mediation. The mediator's role is to assist the two parties to negotiate a mutually acceptable outcome.

The Location of the Problem

About a year ago the Atlas Cement Company, a large national company producing cement, purchased some vacant land at the end of Marshall Road on the outskirts of the City of Warrington.

Since this area is outside the city limits of the City of Warrington, it is not subject to the city's urban planning restrictions.

---

[2] This is based on an exercise that we both took part in when it was organised by Professor Edward Sherman (Tulane University Law School) in the late 1980s while teaching a dispute resolution course as a distinguished visitor at the Institute of Advanced Legal Studies, University of London.

However, a community of migrant workers living in about 200 houses already existed along and close to Marshall Road. This community has called itself Sleepy Hollow and it has formed a resident's (or neighbourhood) association.

However, neither 'Sleepy Hollow' nor the resident's association has been officially recognised by the authorities.

The Atlas property is less than one hundred yards from the community calling itself 'Sleepy Hollow'.

And the only road to the Atlas property passes through the neighbourhood on Marshall Road.

The Origins of the Problem

Atlas has now constructed a truck depot and a truck washing facility on its property, and has plans to expand it further in the next year to include a warehouse and supply facility for its operations in the entire region.

The local community has watched the development with great concern.

Casual inquiries made by the local residents to the personnel at the depot about what was planned have not yielded any information.

The Nature of the Problem

The opening of depot operations three months ago has resulted in multiple complaints by the local residents, including:

- Noise from loading the cement trucks for the day's work beginning at 5 a.m. and from unloading and washing down the trucks at the end of the day at about 9 p.m. The noise from these operations is increased by the blast from the backup horns that are standard and legally-required safety equipment on the trucks.
- Dropping of cement on Marshall Road from trucks coming from the depot when their containers are filled or from cement allowed to accumulate outside the containers. The cement is then run over by other cars, spattering the cars and making the road dangerous to navigate.
- Parking of Atlas trucks at various times during the day on the shoulders of Marshall Road in front of the depot and sometimes up the road and into the neighbourhood area. This is done because there is insufficient space within the depot area, as presently constructed, when a large number of trucks are waiting to be filled.
- Pollution of a stream that flows through the depot property and then through the back of community of Sleepy Hollow, caused by the run-off from the lorry washing area in the depot. Fish in the stream have been killed, and neighbourhood children can no longer swim there.

- Ugliness in the depot buildings and grounds, including a good deal of littered equipment and raw materials on the ground, a high barbed wire fence around the perimeter of the property, a rusted hut which was brought in to serve as the depot building, and plans for a three-storey high warehouse building to be constructed next to the property line on the road for the sake of convenience.

Local Reaction to the Environmental and Related Problems

Over the past three months, the neighbourhood association has held many meetings, resulting in the following actions:

- Complaints to Atlas concerning the matters listed above. Association members had difficulty in finding who was in charge at the Atlas depot and, on finally being directed to the depot manager, found that he would rarely return their phone calls. When they did reach him, he was defensive and said Atlas was doing the best it could and 'you can't run a cement company without some noise and some mess'. Calls to the regional office of the company were not returned.
- The filing of an environmental grievance against Atlas concerning the pollution of the stream with the government's environmental agency. The complaint has been assigned a number, and an inspection by an environmental officer has been scheduled at the end of this month. The agency is badly overworked and understaffed and even if it finds a violation of the environmental laws, it may choose not to seek court enforcement or court enforcement might be denied.
- The filing of a complaint with the relevant local government department concerning the dropping of cement on Marshall Road. The department wrote Atlas a letter informing it of the complaint, and Atlas wrote back stating that it would see that any cement dropped is cleaned up. Atlas sent out clean-up teams for the first couple of weeks thereafter, but neighbourhood members say they are now infrequent and the dropping continues. The government department could take legal action, but it is badly understaffed, and so somewhat reluctant to commit resources to this problem.
- The hiring of a legal representative by the residents' association to look into possible legal remedies. The lawyer has advised them that they may have a nuisance cause of action for an injunction and/or damages against Atlas based on the excessive noise, dropping of cement, off-road parking, and stream pollution. This lawyer estimates that even if they seek an injunction, Atlas could delay the proceedings so that it might take a year. The expected attorney fees, if Atlas fights the suit strenuously, might be as much as US$20,000. The lawyer estimates their chance of winning at about 60 per cent. So far, the lawyer's fees have already reached US$2,000.

- The Sleepy Hollow residents intend to file an objection to any further building permits sought by Atlas, such as for the construction of a warehouse. The neighbourhood association very much regrets not having objected to earlier building permits, which resulted from it not being aware of what was happening. Aesthetic grounds are not normally sufficient objections to building permits.

Growing Hostility

In the past few weeks, the hostility between the neighbourhood and Atlas has escalated.

- There have been several arguments between Atlas lorry drivers and other motorists involving shouting and, in two cases, the stopping of vehicles and physical confrontations.
- A march by some members of the community to the depot gates was met by armed guards hired by Atlas who were accompanied by a local policeman who told local residents not to cause trouble and to disperse.
- Atlas has experienced a number of acts of vandalism, ranging from rock throwing that has broken windows and damaged property, to cutting of openings in its cyclone fence and the theft of property.
- Last week several of its trucks had punctured tyres , which were discovered to have been caused by large nail-type tacks spread on the road and entrance areas near the depot. Atlas cleaned them up, but they have reappeared several times since.

Atlas has consulted with its staff counsel at regional headquarters and has retained local counsel concerning the various complaints filed against it. Its legal fees to date are estimated at US$3,500.

Current Situation

- There are two parties – Atlas and local residents – and they have agreed to try to meet to discuss the situation.
- Each party should hold a preliminary meeting to decide upon its composition and strategy.
- The two parties should then meet to discuss their differences and to explore the possibility of a negotiated outcome.

References

Abel, Richard L. 1973. 'A Comparative Theory of Dispute Institutions in Society', *Law and Society Review* 8(2): 217–347.

    1979. 'Western Courts in Non-western Settings: Patterns of Court Use in Colonial and Neo-colonial Africa', in Barbara E. Harrell-Bond and Sandra B. Burman (eds.) *The Imposition of Law*. New York: Academic Press, 167–200.

    1980. 'Delegalization: A Critical Review of its Ideology, Manifestations and Social Consequences', in Erhard Blankenburg et al. (eds.) *Alternative Rechtsformen und Alternativen zum Recht* 27. Paper delivered at the Second National Conference on Critical Legal Studies, Madison, Wisconsin (1978).

    1982a. 'Introduction', in Richard L. Abel (ed.) *The Politics of Informal Justice, Volume 1: The American Experience*. New York and London: Academic Press, 1–13.

    1982b. 'The Contradictions of Informal Justice', in R. L. Abel (ed.) *The Politics of Informal Justice, Volume 1: The American Experience*. New York and London: Academic Press, 267–320.

    (ed.) 1982c. *The Politics of Informal Justice, Volume 1: The American Experience*. New York and London: Academic Press.

    (ed.) 1982d. *The Politics of Informal Justice, Volume 2: Comparative Studies*. New York and London: Academic Press.

Abel-Smith, Brian and Robert Stevens 1967. *Lawyers and the Courts: A Sociological Study of the English Legal System 1750–1965*. London: Heinemann.

Alexander, Nadja 2002. 'From Common Law to Civil Law Jurisdictions: Court ADR on the Move in Germany', *ADR Bulletin* 4(8): 110–13.

Alexander, Nadja and Michelle LeBaron 2013. 'Embodied Conflict Resolution: Resurrecting Roleplay-based Curricula through Dance', in Christopher Honeyman, James R. Coben, Andrew Wei-Min Lee (eds.) *Educating Negotiators for a Connected World*. St Paul, MN: DRI Press, 539–67.

Al-Ramahi, Aseel 2008. 'Sulh: A Crucial Part of Islamic Arbitration'. LSE Law, Society and Economy Working Papers 12/2008, available at www.lse.ac.uk/law/working-paper-series/2007-08/WPS2008-12-Al-Ramahi.pdf, accessed 3 December 2019.

Astor, Hilary and Christine Chinkin 2002. *Dispute Resolution in Australia*. 2nd ed. Chatswood, NSW: Butterworths.

Auerbach, Jerold S. 1983. *Justice Without Law? Resolving Disputes Without Lawyers*. Oxford and New York: Oxford University Press.

Austin, J. 1955 [orig. 1832]. *The Province of Jurisprudence Determined*. London: Weidenfeld and Nicolson.

Bailey, Frederick G. 1969. *Stratagems and Spoils*. Oxford: Basil Blackwell.

Barak, Gregg 2003. *Violence and Nonviolence: Pathways to Understanding*. (Electronic resource, Chapter 4 'Structural Violence'). Thousand Oaks, CA: SAGE Publishers; London: Corwin.

Barth, Frederick 1959. *Political Leadership among the Swat Pathans*. London: Athlone Press.

Barton, Roy F. 1919. 'Ifugao Law', *American Archaeology and Ethnology* 15(1): 1–186.

Baumgartner, Mary P. 1984. 'Social Control in Suburbia', in Donald Black (ed.) *Towards a General Theory of Social Control, Volume 2: Selected Issues*. Orlando, FL: Academic Press, 79–103.

Beldam, Lord Justice (Sir Roy) 1991. *Report of the Committee on Alternative Dispute Resolution*. October 1991, London: General Council of the Bar.

Berkowitz, Elizabeth 2006. 'The Problematic Role of the Special Master: Undermining the Legitimacy of the September 11th Victim Compensation Fund', *Yale Law and Policy Review* 24(1): 1–42.

Black, Julia 1966. 'Constitutionalising Self-regulation', *Modern Law Review* 59(1): 24–55.

Bloch, Maurice 1971. 'Decision-making in Councils among the Merina of Madagascar', in Audrey Richards and Adam Kuper (eds.) *Councils in Action*. Cambridge: Cambridge University Press, 29–62.

Bodde, Derk and Clarence Morris 1967. *Law in Imperial China*. Cambridge, MA: Harvard University Press.

Bohannan, Paul 1957. *Justice and Judgment among the Tiv*. London: Oxford University Press for the International African Institute.

Bok, Derek 1983. 'A Flawed System of Law and Practice Training', *Journal of Legal Education* 33: 570–85.

  2013. *Higher Education in America*. Princeton, NJ and Oxford: Princeton University Press.

Bondy, Valerie 2004. 'Who Needs ADR?' *Judicial Review* 9: 306–11.

Bondy, Valerie, Margaret Doyle and Val Reid 2005. 'Mediation and Judicial Review – Mind the Research Gap', *Judicial Review* 10: 220–28.

Bottomley, Anne 1984. 'Resolving Family Disputes: A Critical Review', in M. D. A. Freeman (ed.) *State, Law and the Family: Critical Perspectives*. London and New York: Tavistock Publications and Sweet and Maxwell, 13–22.

  1985. 'What is Happening in Family Law? A Feminist Critique of Conciliation', in J. Brophy and C. Smart (eds.) *Women in Law*. London: Routledge and Kegan Paul, 167–87.

Boulle, Laurence 1996. *Mediation: Principles, Process, Practice*. Sydney: Butterworths.

Boyd, Marion 2004. 'Dispute Resolution in Family Law: Protecting Choice, Promoting Inclusion' (December 2004) at, Ontario Ministry of The Attorney General www.attorneygeneral.jus.gov.on.ca/english/about/pubs/boyd/fullreport.pdf, accessed 7 January 2020.

Brandt, Paul 1997. 'The Formation of the English Legal System, 1150–1400', in Antonia Padoa-Schioppa (ed.) *Legalisation and Justice*. European Science Foundation. Oxford: Clarendon Press, 103–21.

Brazil, Wayne D. 1990. 'A Close Look at Three Court-sponsored ADR Programs: Why They Exist, How They Operate, What They Deliver, and Whether They Threaten Important Values', *University of Chicago Legal Forum* 1990: 303–98.

Briggs, Lord Justice 2016. *Civil Courts Structure Review: Final Report.* Judiciary of England and Wales, available at www.judiciary.uk/publications/civil-courts-structure-review-final-report/, accessed 3 December 2019.

Brockman, R. H. 1980. 'Commercial Contract Law in late Nineteenth Century Taiwan', in Jerome Alan Cohen, Fu-mei Chang Chen and R. Randle Edwards (eds.) *Essays on China's Legal Tradition.* Princeton, NJ: Princeton University Press, 76–136.

Broderick, R. J. 1989. 'Court-annexed Compulsory Arbitration: It Works', *Judicature* 72(4): 219–22.

Burger, Warren E. 1976. 'Agenda for 2000 AD – Need for Systematic Anticipation', *Federal Rules Decisions* 70: 92–94.

  1982. 'Isn't There a Better Way', *American Bar Association Journal* 68: 274–7.

Bush, R. A. Baruch 1989. 'Efficiency and Protection, or Empowerment and Recognition?: The Mediator's Role and Ethical Standards in Mediation', *Florida Law Review* 41: 253–86.

Bush, R. A. Baruch and J. P. Folger 1994. *The Promise of Mediation: Responding to Conflict through Empowerment and Recognition.* San Francisco, CA: Jossey-Bass Publishers.

Cappelletti, Mauro 1993. 'Alternative Dispute Resolution Processes within the Framework of the World-wide Access-to-Justice Movement', *Modern Law Review* 56(3): 282–96.

Cappelletti, Mauro and Bryant Garth 1978a. *Access to Justice, Volume I: A World Survey.* Alphen aan den Rijn: Sijthoff and Noordhoff.

  1978b. 'Access to Justice: The Newest Wave in the Worldwide Movement to Make Rights Effective', *Buffalo Law Review* 27: 181–292.

Castan, Nicole 1983. 'The Arbitration of Disputes under the Ancient Regime', in J. Bossy (ed.) *Disputes and Settlements.* Cambridge: Cambridge University Press, 219–60.

Chen Yongzhu 2015. 'The Judge as Mediator in China and its Alternatives: A Problem in Chinese Civil Justice', in Fu Hualing and Michael Palmer (eds.) 'Mediation in Contemporary China: Continuity and Change', Special Issue, *Journal of Comparative Law*, 10(2): 106–25. Republished in Fu Hualing and Michael Palmer (eds.) 2017. *Mediation in Contemporary China: Continuity and Change.* London: Wildy, Simmonds and Hill, 140–66.

Chief Justice's Working Party on Civil Justice Reform 2001. *Civil Justice Reform: Interim Report and Consultative Paper.* Hong Kong: Hong Kong Special Administrative Region Government.

Chornenki, G. 1997. 'Mediating Commercial Disputes: Exchanging "Power Over" for "Power With"', in Jule Macfarlane (ed.) *Rethinking Disputes: The Mediation Alternative.* London: Cavendish Publishing, 163–8.

Chotalia, Shirish P. 2006. 'Arbitration Using Sharia Law in Canada: A Constitutional and Human Rights Perspective', *Constitutional Forum Constitutionnel* 15: 63–78.

Clastres, Pierre 1977. *Society Against the State: Essays in Political Anthropology.* Translated by Robert Hurley. Oxford: Blackwell.

Cohen, Amy J. 2009. 'Revisiting Against Settlement: Some Reflections on Dispute Resolution and Public Values', *Fordham Law Review* 78: 1143–78.

Cole, Sanford D. 1905. 'The Ancient Tolzey and Pie Poudre Courts of Bristol', *Transactions of the Bristol and Gloucestershire Archaeological Society* 28: 111–23.

Collins, Randall 2008. *Violence: A Micro-sociological Theory*. Princeton, NJ: Princeton University Press.

Colosi, Thomas R. 1983. 'Negotiation in the Public and Private Sectors', *American Behavioural Scientist* 27(2): 229–53.

Comaroff, John and Simon Roberts 1977. 'The Invocation of Norms in Dispute Settlement: The Tswana Case', in Ian Hamnett (ed.) *Social Anthropology and Law*. London, San Francisco and New York: Academic Press, 77–112.

Comaroff, John L. and Simon Roberts 1986. *Rules and Processes: The Cultural Logic of Dispute in an African Context*. Chicago, IL: University of Chicago Press.

Condlin, Robert J. 1985. '"Cases on Both Sides": Patterns of Argument in Legal-dispute Negotiation', *Maryland Law Review* 44: 65–136.

    2017. 'Online Dispute Resolution: Stinky, Repugnant, or Drab', *Cardozo Journal of Conflict Resolution* 18: 717–58.

Conley, John M. and William M. O'Barr 1990. *Rules Versus Relationships: The Ethnography of Legal Discourse*. Chicago, IL and London: University of Chicago Press.

Cover, Robert 1986. 'Violence and the Word', *Yale Law Journal* 95(8): 1601–29.

Cownie, Fiona and Anthony Bradney 2020. 'Dispute Avoidance', in Maria Federica Moscati, Michael Palmer and Marian Roberts (eds.) *Comparative Dispute Resolution: A Research Handbook*. Cheltenham, UK and Northampton, MA: Edward Elgar Publishing.

Croley, Steven 2008. 'Summary Jury Trials in Charleston County, South Carolina', *Loyola of Los Angeles Law Review* 41(4): 1585–624.

Crouch, Richard E. 1982. 'The Dark Side of Mediation Still Unexplored', *Family Advocate* 4(3): 27–35.

Damaška, Mirjan R. 1986. *The Faces of Justice and State Authority*. New Haven, CT and London: Yale University Press.

Danzig, Richard 1973. 'Towards the Creation of a Complementary, Decentralised System of Criminal Justice', *Stanford Law Review* 26: 1–26.

Dawson, John P. 1960. *A History of Lay Judges*. Cambridge, MA: Harvard University Press.

De Vera, Carlos 2004. 'Arbitrating Harmony: "Med Arb" and the Confluence of Culture and Rule of Law in the Resolution of International Commercial Disputes in China', *Columbia Journal of Asian Law* 18(1): 149–94.

Deckert, Katrin 2013. 'Mediation in France: Legal Framework and Practical Experiences', in Klaus J. Hopt and Felix Steffek (eds.) *Mediation: Principles and Regulation in Comparative Perspective*. Oxford: Oxford University Press, 455–519.

Denlow, Morton 2010. 'Settlement Conference Techniques – Caucus Dos and Don'ts', *Judges' Journal* 49(2): 21–8.

Denti, Olga and Michela Giordano 2010. 'Till Money (and Divorce) Do Us Part: Premarital Agreements in the American and Spanish Legal Discourse', in Vijay K. Bhatia, Christopher N. Candlin and Maurizio Gotti (eds.) *The Discourses of Dispute Resolution*. Peter Lang: Berne, 101–25.

Department for Constitutional Affairs 2004. *Judicial Statistics: Annual Report, 2003*. London: Department for Constitutional Affairs.

Dezalay, Yves and Bryant Garth 1996. *Dealing in Virtue: International Commercial Arbitration and the Construction of a Transnational Legal Order*. Chicago, IL and London: The University of Chicago Press.

Dickens, Charles [1852–3]1994. *Bleak House*. Harmondsworth, Middlesex: Penguin Books.

Dingwall, R. and David Greatbach 1993. 'Who is in Charge? Rhetoric and Evidence in the Study of Mediation', *Journal of Social Welfare and Family Law* 15: 367–87.

Doo Leigh-wai 1973. 'Dispute Settlement in Chinese-American Communities', *American Journal of Comparative Law* 21: 627–53.

Douglas, Ann 1957. 'The Peaceful Settlement of Industrial and Inter-group Disputes', *Journal of Conflict Resolution* 1: 69–81.

  1962. *Industrial Peacemaking*. New York: Columbia University Press.

Dworkin, Ronald 1986. *Law's Empire*. London: Fontana.

Edwards, Barry 2013. 'Renovating the Multi-Door Courthouse: Designing Trial Court Dispute Resolution Systems to Improve Results and Control Cost', *Harvard Negotiation Law Review* 18: 281–347.

Eidmann, Dorothee and Konstanze Plett 1991. 'Non-judicial Dispute Processing in West Germany: The Schiedsstellen Contribution to the Resolution of Social Conflicts and Their Interaction with the Official Legal System', in Karl J. Mackie (ed.) *A Handbook of Dispute Resolution*. London and New York: Routledge and Sweet and Maxwell, 171–200.

Eisele, Thomas G. 1991. 'The Case Against Court-annexed ADR Programs', *Judicature* 75(1): 34–40.

Elliott, David C. 1996. 'Med/arb: Fraught with Danger or Ripe with Opportunity', *Arbitration* 62(3):175–83. Originally published as David C. Elliott 1995. 'Med/Arb: Fraught with Danger or Ripe with Opportunity?', *Alberta Law Review* 34(1): 163–75.

Erickson, J. 2017. 'How Taobao is Crowdsourcing Justice in Online Shopping Disputes', 17 July 2014, available at www.alizila.com/how-taobao-is-crowdsourcing-justice-in-online-shopping-disputes/, accessed 3 December 2019.

Erlichman, Reece, Michael Gregory and Alisia St. Florian 2014. 'The Settlement Conference as a Dispute Resolution Option in Special Education', *Ohio State Journal on Dispute Resolution* 29(3): 407–60.

Evans-Pritchard, E. 1940. *The Nuer*. Oxford: Oxford University Press.

Fang Xuhui 2014. 'Wangshang Jiufen Jiejue Jizhi de Xin Fazhan – Cong Wangluo Peishentuan dao Dazhong Pingshen Zhidu' ['The New Developments of Online Dispute Resolution: From Crowdsourced Online Dispute Resolution to Crowd Assessors System'], 11 *Jiangxi Shehui Kexue* [Jiangxi Social Science] No. 11 for 2014: 124–29.

Feinberg, Kenneth R. 2012. *Who Gets What: Fair Compensation after Tragedy and Financial Upheaval*. New York: New York Public Affairs.

Feinberg, Kenneth R., Camille S. Biros, Jordana Harris Feldman, Deborah E. Greenspan and Jacqueline E. Zins 2011. *Final Report of the Special Master for the September 11th Victim Compensation Fund of 2001, Volume I*. Washington DC: US Department of Justice.

Felstiner, William L. F. 1974. 'Influences of Social Organization on Dispute Processing', *Law and Society Review* 9(1): 63–94. Reprinted in L. Friedman and S. Macaulay 1977. *Law and the Behavioral Sciences* (2nd ed.) New York: Bobbs-Merrill; in R. Cover and O. Fiss 1979. *The Structure of Procedure*. Mineola, NY: The Foundation Press; in R. Tomasic and M. Feeley 1982. *Neighborhood Justice*.

New York: Longman; and in R. Cover, O. Fiss and J. Resnick 1988. *Procedure*. Mineola, NY: The Foundation Press.

1975. 'Avoidance as Dispute Processing: An Elaboration', *Law and Society Review* 9(4): 695–706.

Felstiner, W. L., R. L. Abel and A. Sarat 1980–1. 'The Emergence and Transformation of Disputes: Naming, Blaming, Claiming ...', *Law and Society Review* , Special Issue on Dispute Processing and Civil Litigation, 15(3/4): 631–54.

Fisher, Roger and William Ury 1981. *Getting to Yes*. Boston, MA: Houghton Mifflin.

Fisher, Roger, William Ury and Bruce Patten 1991. *Getting to Yes*. 2nd ed. New York: Penguin Books.

Fisher, Talia and Leora Bilsky 2014. 'Rethinking Settlement', *Theoretical Inquiries in Law* 15(1): 77–124.

Fiss, Owen M. 1979. 'Forms of Justice: Forward, the Supreme Court 1978 Term', *Harvard Law Review* 92(1): 1–58.

1984. 'Against Settlement', *Yale Law Journal* 93: 1073–90.

1985. 'Out of Eden', *Yale Law Journal* 94: 1669–73.

Fitzpatrick, Peter 1993. 'The Impossibility of Popular Justice', in Sally Engle Merry and Neal Milner (eds.) *The Possibility of Popular Justice*. Ann Arbor MI: University of Michigan Press, 453–74.

Flood, John and Andrew Caiger 1993. 'Lawyers and Arbitration: The Juridification of Construction Disputes', *Modern Law Review* 56: 412–40.

Folberg, Jay and Alison Taylor 1984. *Mediation*. San Francisco: Jossey-Bass.

Freeman, Michael D. A. 1984. 'Questioning the Delegalization Movement in Family Law: Do We Really Want a Family Court?', in J. M. Eekelaar and S. N. Katz (eds.) *The Resolution of Family Conflict*. Toronto: Butterworths, 7–25.

Freshman, Clark 2020. '(Mindfully) Negotiating around "Lies": The Science of Non-verbal Communication for the "Soft" and "Hard"', in Maria-Federica Moscati, Michael Palmer and Marian Roberts (eds.) *Comparative Dispute Resolution: A Research Handbook*. Cheltenham, UK and Northampton, MA: Edward Elgar Publishing.

Fried, Morton H. 1967. *The Evolution of Political Society*. New York: Random House.

Fu Hualing and Michael Palmer 2015. 'Introduction', in Fu Hualing and Michael Palmer (eds.) 'Mediation in Contemporary China: Continuity and Change', Special Issue, *Journal of Comparative Law*, 10(2): 1–24. Republished in extended form in Fu Hualing and Michael Palmer (eds.) 2017. *Mediation in Contemporary China: Continuity and Change*. London: Wildy Simmonds and Hill, 1–33.

Fu Hualing and Michael Palmer (eds.) 2017. *Mediation in Contemporary China: Continuity and Change*. London: Wildy, Simmonds and Hill.

Fuller, Lon L. 1963. 'Collective Bargaining and the Arbitration', *Wisconsin Law Review* 18(3): 39–42.

1971. 'Mediation: its Forms and Functions', *Southern California Law Review*, 44: 305–39.

1978. 'The Forms and Limits of Adjudication', *Harvard Law Review* 92: 353–409.

Fuller, Lon L. and J. D. Randall 1958. 'Professional Responsibility: Report of the Joint Conference of the ABA-AALS', *American Bar Association Journal* 44: 1159–62.

Galanter, Marc 1974. 'Why the "Haves" Come Out Ahead: Speculations on the Limits of Legal Change', *Law and Society Review* 9: 95–160.

1984. 'World of Deals: Using Negotiation to Teach About Legal Process', *Journal of Legal Education* 34: 268–76.

1985. 'A Settlement Judge, Not a Trial Judge: Judicial Mediation in the United States', *Journal of Law and Society* 12: 1–18.

1986. 'The Emergence of the Judge as a Mediator in Civil Cases', *Judicature* 69(5): 257–62.

1994. 'Predators and Parasites: Lawyer-Bashing and Civil Justice', *Georgia Law Review* 28(3): 633–82.

2010. 'Access to Justice in a World of Expanding Social Capability', *Fordham Urban Law Journal* 37: 115–28.

Galanter, Marc and Mia Cahill 1994. 'Most Cases Settle: Judicial Promotion and Regulation of Settlements', *Stanford Law Review* 46: 1339–91.

Galtung, Johan 1990. 'Cultural Violence'. *Journal of Peace Research* 27(3): 291–305.

Garlock, Jonathan 1982. 'The Knights of Labor Courts: A Case Study of Popular Justice', in Richard L. Abel (ed.) *The Politics of Informal Justice, Volume 1: The American Experience*. New York: Academic Press, 17–34.

Ge Jun 1996. 'Mediation, Arbitration and Litigation: Dispute Resolution in the People's Republic of China'. *UCLA Pacific Basin Law Journal* 15: 122–37.

Geertz, Clifford 1982. *Negara: The Theater State in Nineteenth-century Bali*. Princeton, NJ: Princeton University Press.

Genn, Hazel G. 1987. *Hard Bargaining: Out of Court Settlement in Personal Injury Actions*. Oxford: Clarendon Press.

1998. *The Central London County Court Pilot Mediation Scheme: Evaluation Report*. London: Department for Constitutional Affairs.

2012. 'What is Civil Justice For? Reform, ADR, and Access to Justice', *Yale Journal of Law and the Humanities* 24(1): 398–417.

et al. 2007. *Twisting Arms: Court Referred and Court Linked Mediation under Judicial Pressure*. London: Ministry of Justice.

Gibbs, James L. 1963. 'The Kpelle Moot', *Africa* 33: 1–10.

Gifford, Donald G. 1985. 'A Context-based Theory of Selection Strategy in Legal Negotiations', *Ohio State Law Journal* 46: 41–95.

Gilsenan, Michael 1976. 'Lying, Honor, and Contradiction', in Bruce Kapferer (ed.) *Transaction and Meaning: Directions in the Anthropology of Exchange and Symbolic Behavior*. Philadelphia, PA: Institute for the Study of Human Issues, 191–219.

Ginsberg, Tom 2003. 'The Culture of Arbitration', *Vanderbilt Journal of International Law* 36: 1335–45.

Gluckman, Max 1955. *The Judicial Process among the Barotse of Northern Rhodesia*. Manchester: Manchester University Press.

Goffman, Erving 1959. *The Presentation of Self in Everyday Life*. New York: Doubleday Anchor Books.

Goldberg, Stephen B. 1982. 'The Mediation of Grievances under a Collective Bargaining Contract: An Alternative to Arbitration', *Northwestern University Law Review* 77: 270–315.

Goldberg, Stephen B., Frank E. A. Sander, Nancy H. Rogers and Sarah Rudolph Cole 2012. *Dispute Resolution: Negotiation Mediation, Arbitration and Other Processes*, 6th ed. New York: Wolters Kluwer.

Gottwald, Peter 1997. 'Civil Procedure Reform in Germany', *American Journal of Comparative Law* 45(4): 753–66.

Gould, Nicholas 2019. 'Conflict Avoidance and Dispute Resolution', available at www .fenwickelliott.com/sites/default/files/nick_gould_-_conflict_avoidance_and_dispute_resolution.indd_.pdf, accessed 3 December 2019.

Graham, L. E. 1992–3. 'Implementing Custody Mediation in Family Courts: Some Comments on the Jefferson County Family Court Experience', *Kentucky Law Journal* 81: 1107–32.

Greenberg, Elayne E. 2015. 'Fitting the Forum to the Pernicious Fuss: A Dispute System Design to Address Implicit Bias and 'Isms in the Workplace', *Cardozo Journal of Conflict Resolution* 17(1): 75–114.

Greenhouse, Carol 1989. *Praying for Justice: Faith, Order, and Community in an American Town*. Ithaca, NY: Cornell University Press.

1992. 'Signs of Quality: Individualism and Hierarchy in American Culture', *American Ethnologist* 19: 233–54.

Greenidge, A. H. J. 1971. *The Legal Procedure of Cicero's Time*. New Jersey: Rothman Reprints (orig. 1901, New York: Augustus M. Kelley).

Griffith, J. A. G. 1997. *The Politics of the Judiciary*. 5th ed. London: Fontana Press.

Grillo, T. 1991. 'The Mediation Alternative – Process Dangers for Woman', *Yale Law Journal* 100: 1547–620.

Gu Weixia 2015. 'When Local Meets International: Mediation Combined with Arbitration in China and Its Prospective Reform in a Comparative Context', in Fu Hualing and Michael Palmer (eds.) 'Mediation in Contemporary China: Continuity and Change', Special Issue, *Journal of Comparative Law* 10(2): 84–105. Republished in Fu Hualing and Michael Palmer (eds.) 2017. *Mediation in Contemporary China: Continuity and Change*. London: Wildy Simmonds and Hill, 112–39.

Gulliver, P. H. 1963. *Social Control in an African Society. A Study of the Arusha: Agricultural Masai of Northern Tanganyika*. London: Routledge and Kegan Paul.

1971. *Neighbours and Networks: The Idiom of Kinship in Social Action among the Ndendeuli of Tanzania*. Berkeley, CA: University of California Press.

1979. *Disputes and Negotiations: A Cross Cultural Perspective*. New York and London: Academic Press.

1988. 'Anthropological Contributions to the Study of Negotiations', *Negotiation Journal* 4(3): 247–55.

1996. 'On Avoidance', in David J. Parkin, Lionel Caplan and Humphrey J. Fisher (eds.) *The Politics of Cultural Performance*. Providence, RI: Berghahn Books.

Habermas, Jürgen 1979. *Communication and the Evolution of Society*. Translated by T. McCarthy. Boston, MA: Beacon Press.

1981. *Theorie des kommunikativen Handelns, Volume 1: Handlungsrationalität und gesellschaftliche Rationalisierung; Volume 2: Zur Kritik der funktionalistischen Vernunft*. Suhrkamp. [English, 1984. *The Theory of Communicative Action. Volume I: Reason and the Rationalization of Society*. Translated by T. McCarthy; 1987. *The Theory of Communicative Action. Volume II: Lifeworld and System*. Translated by T. McCarthy. Boston, MA: Beacon Press].

Hampshire, Stuart 1991. *Innocence and Experience*. Cambridge, MA: Harvard University Press.

1999. *Justice is Conflict*. London: Duckworth.

Hanson, Mark J. 2006. 'Moving Forward Together: The LGBT Community and the Family Mediation Field', *Pepperdine Dispute Resolution Journal* 6(2) 295–311.

Harrington, Christine B. 1982. 'Delegalisation Reform Movements: A Historical Analysis', in Richard Abel (ed.) *The Politics of Informal Justice, Volume 1: The American Experience.* New York: Academic Press, 48–63.

Hart, H. L. A. 1961. *The Concept of Law.* Oxford: Clarendon Press.

Harvard Law Review 1999. 'Developments in the Law: The Law of Cyberspace', *Harvard Law Review* 112(7): 1574–704.

Hayden, Robert M. 1984. 'Popular Use of Yugoslav Labor Courts and the Contradiction of Social Courts', *Law and Society Review* 22: 709–37.

Haynes, John 1993. *The Fundamentals of Family Mediation.* London: Old Bailey Press.
  2004. 'Teacher-parent Conflict: A Dispute Over the Classroom', in John M. Haynes, Gretchen L. Haynes and Larry Sun Fong (eds.) *Mediation: Positive Conflict Management*, Albany: State University of New York Press, 201–48.

Heilbron, H. and H. Hodge 1993. *Civil Justice on Trial: The Case for Change.* London: Joint Report of the Bar Council and Law Society, United Kingdom.

Henderson, Douglas 1996. 'Mediation Success: An Empirical Analysis', *Ohio State Journal of Dispute Resolution* 11: 105–48.

Her Majesty's Courts and Tribunal Services 2014. (updated March 2016). *The Admiralty and Commercial Courts Guide*, available at www.gov.uk/government/publications/admiralty-and-commercial-courts-guide, accessed 3 December 2019.

Herszenhorn, David M. 2016. 'Kenneth Feinberg Named to Lead Terrorism Compensation Fund', *New York Times*, 30 March 2016, available at www.nytimes.com/2016/03/31/us/politics/kenneth-feinberg-terrorism-fund.html, accessed 18 December 2019.

Hobbes, Thomas 1651. *Leviathan: or, The Matter, forme and power of a commonwealth ecclesiasticall and civill.* London: for Andrew Crooke at the Green Dragon in St Paul's Church-Yard.

Hopt, Klaus J., and Felix Steffek (eds.) 2013. *Mediation: Principles and Regulation in Comparative Perspective.* Oxford: Oxford University Press.

Huang, Philip C. C. 1996. *Civil Justice in China: Representation and Practice in the Qing.* Stanford, CA: Stanford University Press.

iCourthouse, available at www.icourthouse.com/main.taf, accessed 19 December 2019.

Ingleby, Richard 1993. 'Court-Sponsored Mediation: The Case Against Mandatory Participation', *Modern Law Review* 56(3): 441–51.

Irvine, Lord 1999. 'Paper given by Rt Hon Lord Irvine of Lairg at the Inaugural Lecture of the Faculty of Mediation and ADR', available at streithilfe.org/downloads/lord_irving_of_lairg270199.pdf, accessed 3 December 2019.

Jiang Shigong 2000. 'Quanli de zuzhi wangluo yu falü de zhilihua – Ma Xiwu Shenpan fangshi yu zhongguo falü de xin chuantong' ['Organizational Nexus of Power and Governmentality of Law: Ma Xiwu's Judicial Mode and the Formation of New Legal Tradition in China']. *Beida Falü Pinglun* [Peking University Law Review] 3(2): 1–61.

Johnsen, D. Bruce 2006. 'A Modern Potlatch?' *PERC* (Property and Environment Research Center) 24(2) (1 June 2006), available at www.perc.org/2006/06/01/a-modern-potlatch/, accessed 3 December 2019.

Johnston, Sir Reginald Fleming 1910. *Lion and Dragon in Northern China*. London: J. Murray.

Johnstone, Quentin 1967. *Lawyers and Their Work: An Analysis of the Legal Profession in the United States and England*. New York: Bobbs-Merrill.

Jones, William C. 1994. *The Great Qing Code*. Oxford: Oxford University Press.

Katsh, Ethan and Orna Rabinovich-Einy 2015. 'Technology and Dispute Systems Design: Lessons from the Sharing Economy', *Dispute Resolution Magazine* 21: 8–14.

  2017. *Digital Justice: Technology and the Internet of Disputes*. New York: Oxford University Press.

Katsh, Ethan and Colin Rule 2016. 'What We Know and Need to Know About Online Dispute Resolution', *Southern Carolina Law Review* 67: 329–44.

Kelly, J. B. and M. A. Duyree 1995. 'Women's and Men's Views of Mediation in Voluntary and Mandatory Mediation Settings', *Family and Conciliation Courts Review* 30(1): 35–49.

Kelly, J. M. 1966. *Roman Litigation*. Oxford: Clarendon Press.

Kersey, Paul and James Sherk 2007. 'Interest Arbitration: Risky for Unions and Employers'. Published on 1 March 2007, available at https://www.heritage.org/jobs-and-labor/report/interest-arbitration-risky-unions-and-employers, accessed 16 March 2020.

Kim, Anne S. 1994. 'Rent-a-Judge and the Cost of Selling Justice', *Duke Law Journal* 44: 166–99.

Koch, Klaus-Friedrich 1974. *War and Peace in Jalemo*. Cambridge, MA: Harvard University Press.

Korobkin, Russell 2008. 'Against Integrative Bargaining', *Case Western Reserve Law Review* 58: 1323–42.

Kovach, Kimberlee K. and Lela P. Love 1998. 'Mapping Mediation: The Risks of Riskin's Grid', *Harvard Negotiation Law Review* 3: 71–5.

Kritzer, Herbert M. 1986. Adjudication to Settlement: Shading in the Grey', *Judicature* 70(3): 161–5.

  1991. *Let's Make a Deal: Understanding the Negotiation Process in Ordinary Litigation*. Madison, WI: University of Wisconsin Press.

Kunze, Axel 2002. 'Major Changes in the German Civil Procedure Code', *International Legal Practitioner*, 27(1): 3–7.

Lambros, Thomas D. 1989. 'The Federal Rules of Civil Procedure: A New Adversarial Model for a New Era', *University of Pittsburgh Law Review* 50 (3): 789–808.

  1993. 'The Summary Trial: An Effective Aid to Settlement', *Judicature* 77(1): 6–8.

Langer, Rosanna 1998. 'The Juridification and Technicisation of Alternative Dispute Resolution Practices', *Canadian Journal of Law and Society* 13(1): 169–86.

Leacock, E. B. and R. B. Lee (eds.) 1982. *Politics and History in Band Societies*. Cambridge: Cambridge University Press.

Leng, S. C. 1967. *Justice in Communist China: A Survey of the Judicial System in Communist China*. Dobbs Ferry, NY: Oceana Publications.

Lévi-Strauss, Claude 1969. *The Elementary Structures of Kinship*. London: Eyre and Spottiswoode. Originally 1949. *Les Structures élémentaires de la Parenté*. Paris: Presses Universitaires de France.

Lieberman, Jethro and James F. Henry 1986. 'Lessons from the Alternative Dispute Resolution Movement', *University of Chicago Law Review* 53: 424–39.

Lin Yang (manuscript). On file with authors.

Llewellyn, K. and E. A. Hoebel 1941. *The Cheyenne Way: Conflict and Case Law: Conflict and Case Law in Primitive Jurisprudence*. Norman, OK. University of Oklahoma Press.

Locke, John [1690] trans. 1924. *Two Treatises of Government*. London: Dent, Everyman's Library.

Long, D. E. 1973. 'The Board of Grievances in Saudi Arabia', *Middle East Journal* 27(1) 71–5.

Lord Chancellor's Department 1999. *Judicial Statistics: Annual Report, 1998*. London: Lord Chancellor's Department.

Loughlin, Martin 2003. *The Idea of Public Law*. Oxford: Oxford University Press.

Love, Lela P. 1997. 'The Top Ten Reasons Why Mediators Should Not Evaluate', *Florida State University Law Review* 24: 937–48.

Lowenthal, Gary T. 1982. 'A General Theory of Negotiation Process, Strategy, and Behavior', *University of Kansas Law Review* 31: 69–114.

Lowy, Michael J. 1978. 'A Good Name is Worth More than the Money: Strategies of Court Use in Urban Ghana', in Laura Nader and Harry F. Todd (eds.) *The Disputing Process–Law in Ten Societies*, New York: Columbia University Press, 181–208.

Luban, David 1995. 'Settlements and the Erosion of the Public Realm', *Georgetown Law Journal* 83: 2619–62.

Lubman, S. 1967. 'Mao and Mediation: Politics and Dispute Resolution in Communist China', *California Law Review* 55: 1284–359.

Ma Xiwu 1955. 'Xin minzhu zhuyi geming jieduan zhong Shan-Gan-Ning bianqu de renmin sifa gongzuo' ['People's Judicial Work in the Shan-Gan-Ning Border Region during the Stage of the New Democratic Revolution']. Zhengfa Yanjiu (Political and Legal Research) 7–27. Reprinted in Zhang Xipo (ed.) 1983. *Ma Xiwu Shenpan Fangshi* [Ma Xiwu's Adjudicatory Style]. Beijing: Falü Chubanshe [Law Press], 80–100.

MacCormack, Geoffrey 2018. 'Coercion and Suicide in Traditional Chinese Law: Evolution of the Statutory Rules', *Journal of Comparative Law* 13(2): 217–60.

MacCormick, Neil 1981. *H.L.A. Hart*. Stanford, CA: Stanford University Press (2nd ed. 2008).

Mackie, Karl J. (ed.) 1991. *A Handbook of Dispute Resolution*. London and New York: Routledge and Sweet and Maxwell.

Maine, Henry 1861. *Ancient Law, Its Connection with the Early History of Society, and Its Relation to Modern Ideas*. London: John Murray.
    1883. *Dissertations on Early Law and Custom*. London: John Murray.

Malinowski, B. 1926. *Crime and Custom in Savage Society*. London: Kegan Paul, Trench, Trubner and Co.

Markesinis, Basil 1990. 'Litigation-Mania in England, Germany and the USA: Are We So Very Different?', *Cambridge Law Journal* 49(2): 233–76.

McEwen C. A. and R. J. Maiman 1981. 'Small Claims Mediation in Maine: An Empirical Assessment', *Maine Law Review* 33: 237–68.

McGovern, Francis E. 1986. 'Toward a Functional Approach for Managing Complex Litigation', *University of Chicago Law Review* 53: 440–93.

McThenia, Andrew W. and Thomas L. Shaffer 1985. 'For Reconciliation', *Yale Law Journal* 94: 1660–8.

Menkel-Meadow, Carrie J. 1984. 'Towards Another View of Legal Negotiation. The Structure of Problem Solving', *UCLA Law Review*, 31: 754–842.

1985. 'For and Against settlement: Uses and Abuses of the Mandatory Settlement Conference', *UCLA Law Review* 33: 485–516.

1991. 'Pursuing Settlement in an Adversary Culture: A Tale of Innovation Co-opted or "the Law of ADR"', *Florida State University Law Review* 19: 1–46.

1993. 'Lawyer Negotiations: Theories and Realities – What We Learn from Mediation', Special Issue, Dispute Resolution: Civil Justice and its Alternatives, *Modern Law Review*, 56(3): 361–79.

1995. 'Whose Dispute is it Anyway? A Philosophical and Democratic Defense of Settlement (in some cases)', *Georgetown Law Journal* 83: 2663–96.

1996. 'Is Mediation the Practice of Law?', *Alternatives to the High Cost of Litigation* 14: 57–61.

1997. 'Ethics in Alternative Dispute Resolution: New Issues, No Answers from the Adversary Conception of Lawyers' Responsibilities', *Southern Texas Law Review* 38: 407–54.

1999. 'Ethics and Professionalism in Non-Adversarial Lawyering', *Florida State University Law Review* 27: 153–88.

2002. 'Ethics in ADR: The Many "Cs" of Professional Responsibility and Dispute Resolution', *Fordham Urban Law Journal* 28: 979–90.

2003. *Dispute Processing and Conflict Resolution: Theory, Practice, and Policy.* Aldershot and Burlington, VT: Ashgate and Dartmouth.

2016. 'Is ODR ADR? Reflections of an ADR Founder from 15th ODR Conference', The Hague, 22–3 May 2016, *International Journal of Online Dispute Resolution* 3: 4–7.

Menkel-Meadow, Carrie J. and Michael Wheeler 2004. *What's Fair?: Ethics for Negotiators.* San Francisco, CA: Jossey Bass-Wiley.

Menkel-Meadow, Carrie J., Lela Porter Love, Andrea Kupfer Schneider, and Michael Moffitt 2020. *Dispute Resolution: Beyond the Adversarial Model.* 3rd ed. New York: Wolters Kluwer.

Merry, Sally Engle 1993. 'Sorting Out Popular Justice', in Sally Engle Merry and Neal Milner (eds.) *The Possibility of Popular Justice.* Ann Arbor, MI: University of Michigan Press, 31–66.

Merry, Sally Engle and Neal A. Milner (eds.) 1993. *The Possibility of Popular Justice: A Case Study of Community Mediation in the United States.* Ann Arbor, MI: University of Michigan Press.

Mnookin, Robert H. and Ronald J. Gilson 1994. 'Disputing through Agents: Cooperation and Conflict between Lawyers in Litigation', *Columbia Law Review* 94: 509–49.

Mnookin, Robert, and Lewis Kornhauser 1979. 'Bargaining in the Shadow of the Law: The Case of Divorce', *Yale Law Journal* 88: 950–97.

Monroe, Bruce 1987. 'Institutionalization of Alternative Dispute Resolution by the State of California', *Pepperdine Law Review* 14: 944–98.

Moore, Sally Falk 1973. 'Law and Social Change: The Semi-Autonomous Field as an Appropriate Subject of Study', *Law and Society Review* 7: 719–46.

1995. 'Imperfect Communications', in Pat Caplan (ed.) *Understanding Disputes: The Politics of Argument.* Oxford and Providence, RI: Berg Publishers, 11–38.

Morris, Catherine 1997. 'The Trusted Mediator: Ethics and Interaction in Mediation', in Julie Macfarlane (ed.) *Rethinking Disputes: The Mediation Alternative.* London: Cavendish Publishing.

Moscati, Maria Federica 2014. *Pasolini's Italian Premonitions: Same-sex Unions and the Law in Comparative Perspective.* London: Wildy, Simmonds and Hill.

2015. 'Same-sex Couples and Mediation: An Overview', in Maria Federica Moscati (ed.) *Same-sex Couples and Mediation in the EU*, for EU Commission – DG Civil Justice – Project: Litigious Love: Same-sex Couples and Mediation in the EU, London: Wildy, Simmonds and Hill, 1–13.

2017. 'Together Forever: Are you Kidding Me? Catholicism, Same-sex Couples, Disputes and Dispute Resolution in Italy', in Samia Bano (ed.) *Gender and Justice in Family Law Disputes: Women, Mediation, and Religious Arbitration*, Waltham, MA: Brandeis University Press, 292–317.

2020. 'Dispute Resolution, Domestic Violence and Abuse between Lesbian Partners', in C. Ashford and A. Maine (eds.) *Research Handbook on Gender, Sexuality and the Law*, Cheltenham: Edward Elgar.

Mosten, F. S. 2004. 'Institutionalization of Mediation', *Family Court Review* 42(2): 292–303.

Murphy, W. T. and Simon Roberts 1987. 'Introduction' to Special Issue of The Modern Law Review, 'Legal Scholarship in the Common Law World', *Modern Law Review* 50: 677–87.

Murray, Daniel E. 1961. 'Genesis and Development of Equitable Procedures and Remedies in the Anglo-Saxon Laws and in the English Local and Fair Courts and Borough Customs', *Sydney Law Review* 3: 451–62.

Mustill, Lord 1989. 'Arbitration: History and Background', *Journal of International Arbitration* 6: 43–56.

Nader, Laura 1965. 'The Anthropological Study of Law', *American Anthropologist*, Special Issue, *The Ethnology of Law*, Laura Nader (ed.) *American Anthropologist* 67(6): 3–32.

1969. 'Styles of Court Procedure: To Make the Balance', in Laura Nader (ed.) *Law in Culture and Society*. Chicago: Aldine, 69–91.

1986. 'The Recurrent Dialectic between Legality and its Alternatives: The Limits of Binary Thinking', *University of Pennsylvania Law Review* 136: 621–45.

1990. *Harmony Ideology: Justice and Control in a Zapotec Mountain Village.* Stanford, CA: Stanford University Press.

2002. *The Life of the Law: Anthropological Projects*, Berkeley, CA: University of California Press.

National Family Mediation 1998. *Cross-Cultural Mediation Policy and Practice Guidelines.* London: NFM.

Newman, P. 1994. 'Mediation-Arbitration (MedArb): Can it Work Legally?', *Arbitration* 60(3): 173–83.

Ng, Patricia 2009. *Down and Out and Denied in London: Appropriate and Inappropriate Dispute Processes for Homeless Applicants*; Unpublished PhD thesis, School of Law, SOAS, University of London.

Nottage, Luke 2014. 'In/Formalisation and Glocalisation of International Commercial Arbitration and Investment Treaty Arbitration in Asia', in Iwo Amelung, Moritz Bälz, and Joachim Zekoll (eds.) *Dispute Resolution: Alternatives to Formalization – Formalization of Alternatives?* Leiden: Brill, 211–49.

Pair, Lara M. 2002-3. 'Cross-Cultural Arbitration: Do the Differences between Cultures Still Influence International Commercial Arbitration Despite Harmonisation?', *ISLA Journal of International and Comparative Law* 9: 57–74.

Palmer, Michael 1987. 'The Surface-Subsoil Form of Divided Ownership in Late Imperial China: Some Examples from the New Territories of Hong Kong', *Modern Asian Studies* 21(1): 1–119.

   1988. 'The Revival of Mediation in the People's Republic of China: (1) Extra-Judicial Mediation', in W. E. Butler (ed.) *Yearbook on Socialist Legal Systems 1987*. New York: Transnational Books, 219–77.

   1989. 'The Revival of Mediation in the People's Republic of China: (2) Judicial Mediation', in W. E. Butler (ed.) *Yearbook on Socialist Legal Systems 1988*, New York, Dobbs Ferry: Transnational Books, 143–69.

   2007a. 'Controlling the State?: Mediation in Administrative Litigation in the People's Republic of China', in Larry Backer (ed.) 'China: Law, Finance and Security', Special Issue, *Transnational Law and Contemporary Problems* 2007: 165–87.

   2007b. 'On China's Slow Boat to Women's Rights: Revisions to the Women's Protection Law, 2005', *The International Journal of Human Rights* 11(1-2): 151–77.

   2009. 'The Development of the Legal System of the People's Republic of China', in Stanley N. Katz (ed.) *Oxford Encyclopaedia of Legal History*, New York: Oxford University Press.

   2014a. 'Formalisation of Alternative Dispute Resolution Processes: Some Socio-legal Thoughts', in Iwo Amelung, Moritz Bälz, and Joachim Zekoll (eds.) *Dispute Resolution: Alternatives to Formalization – Formalization of Alternatives?* Leiden: Brill-Nijhoff, 17–44.

   2014b. 'Mediating State and Society: Social Stability and Administrative Suits', in Sue Trevaskas, Flora Sapio, Elisa Nesossi and Sarah Biddulph (eds.) *The Politics of Law and Stability in China*. Cheltenham: Edward Elgar, 107–26.

   2014c. 'Men are Superior to Women' (*nan zun nü bei*)? Slowly Healing the Harm of Domestic Violence in Contemporary Chinese Law', in Natalia Iu Erpyleva and Maryann E. Gashi-Butler (eds.) *Liber Amicorum in Honour of Professor William Butler*. London: Wildy, Simmonds and Hill, 277–97.

Parmiter, Geoffrey M. 1981. 'Bristol In-Court Conciliation Procedure', *Law Society Gazette*, 25 February 1981.

Pirie, Fernanda 2007. *Peace and Conflict in Ladakh: The Construction of a Fragile Web of Order*. Leiden: Brill.

Posner, R. 1986. 'The Summary Jury Trial and Other Methods of Alternative Dispute Resolution: Some Cautionary Observations', *University of Chicago Law Review* 53(2): 366–93.

Pospisil, Leopold J. 1958. *Kapauku Papuans and Their Law*. New Haven, CT: Yale University Publications in Anthropology.

Pound, Roscoe 1906. 'The Causes of Popular Dissatisfaction with the Administration of Justice', *American Bar Association Report* 29(1): 395–417.

Press, Sharon 1997. 'Institutionalization: Savior or Saboteur of Mediation?' *Florida State University Law Review* 24: 903–17.

Princen, Thomas 1992. *Intermediaries in International Conflict*. Princeton, NJ: Princeton University Press.

Rabinovich-Einy, Orna and Ethan M. Katsh 2012. 'Digital Justice: Reshaping Boundaries in an Online Dispute Resolution Environment', *International Journal of Online Dispute Resolution* 1: 5–36.

Raiffa, Howard 1982. *The Art and Science of Negotiation*. Cambridge, MA: Harvard University Press.

Rainey, Daniel 2014. 'Third-party Ethics in the Age of the Fourth Party', *International Journal of Online Dispute Resolution* 1: 37–56.

Rappaport, R. A. 1967. *Pigs for the Ancestors: Ritual in the Ecology of a New Guinea People*. New Haven, CT: Yale University Press.

Rawlings, Richard 2010. 'Changed Conditions, Old Truths: Judicial Review in a Regulatory Laboratory', in Dawn Oliver, Tony Prosser and Richard Rawlings (eds.) *Regulation after the Regulatory State*. Oxford: Oxford University Press.

Read, James S. and H. F. Morris 1972. *Indirect Rule and the Search for Justice: Essays in East African Legal History*. Oxford: Oxford University Press.

Redfern, Alan and Martin Hunter 2004. *Law and Practice of International Commercial Arbitration*. 4th ed. London: Sweet and Maxwell.

Rhode, Deborah L. 2004. *Access to Justice*. Oxford and New York: Oxford University Press.

Riskin, L. L. 1994. 'Mediator Orientations, Strategies and Techniques', *Alternatives* 12(9): 111–14.

Roberts, Marian 1997. *Mediation in Family Disputes: Principles of Practice*. 2nd ed. Aldershot: Arena.

    2005. 'Family Mediation: The Development of the Regulatory Framework in the United Kingdom', *Conflict Resolution Quarterly* 22(4): 509–26.

    2008. *Mediation in Family Disputes: Principles of Practice*. 3rd ed. Hampshire and Burlington, VT: Ashgate.

    2014a. *Mediation in Family Disputes: Principles of Practice*. 4th ed. Hampshire and Burlington, VT: Ashgate.

    2014b. 'A View from the Coal Face: Interdisciplinary Influences on Family Mediation in the United Kingdom', Special Issue (Dedicated to the memory of Professor Simon Roberts, 1941–2014), on Interdisciplinary Study and Comparative Law, *Journal of Comparative Law* 9(2): 108–18. Republished in Nicholas H. Foster, Maria Federica Moscati and M. Palmer (eds.) 2016. *Interdisciplinary Study and Comparative Law*. London: Wildy, Simmonds and Hill, 139–53.

Roberts, Simon 1979. *Order and Dispute*. Harmondsworth and New York: Penguin. (2nd ed. 2013: New Orleans, LA: Quid Pro Books.)

    1983. 'Mediation in Family Disputes', *Modern Law Review* 46(5): 537–57.

    1993. 'Alternative Dispute Resolution and Civil Justice: An Unresolved Relationship', *Modern Law Review*, 56: 452–70.

    1997. 'The Path of Negotiations', in M. Freeman (ed.) *Current Legal Problems 1996*. Oxford: Oxford University Press, 97–109.

    2002. 'Institutionalized Settlement in England: A Contemporary Panorama', *Willamette Journal of International Law and Dispute Resolution* 10: 17–35.

    2013. *A Court in the City of London: Civil and Commercial Litigation in London at the Beginning of the 21st Century*. London: Wildy, Simmonds and Hill.

Robinson, Peter 2009. 'Settlement Conference Judge – Legal Lion or Problem Solving Lamb: An Empirical Documentation of Judicial Settlement Conference Practices and Techniques', *American Journal of Trial Advocacy* 33(1): 113–66.

Röhl, Klaus F. 1983 'The Judge as Mediator', Dispute Processing Research Program, Working Paper 1983–89. Madison, WI: University of Wisconsin, Madison Law School.

Rosen, Lawrence 2006. *Law as Culture*, Princeton, NJ: Princeton University Press.

Rosenberg, Joshua D. and H. Jay Folger 1994. 'Alternative Dispute Resolution: An Empirical Analysis', *Stanford Law Review* 46: 1487–551.

Rosenberry, Katharine 2005. 'Organizational Barriers to Creativity in Law Schools and the Legal Profession', *California Western Law Review* 41(2): 423–57.

Rule, Colin 2016. 'Is ODR ADR: A Response to Carrie Menkel-Meadow', *International Journal of Online Dispute Resolution*, 3: 8–11.

Sachs, Albie 1984. 'Changing the Terms of the Debate: A Visit to a Popular Tribunal in Mozambique', *Journal of African Law* 28(1 and 2): 99–106.

Sahlins, Marshall 1965. 'On the Sociology of Primitive Exchange', in Michael Banton (ed.) *The Relevance of Models for Social Anthropology*. Association of Social Anthropologists Monograph No. 1. London: Tavistock, 139–238.

Sainsbury, Roy and Hazel G. Genn 1995. 'Access to Justice; Lessons from Tribunals', in A. A. S. Zuckerman and Ross Cranston (eds.) *Reform of Civil Procedure: Essays on 'Access to Justice'*. Oxford: Clarendon Press, 413–29.

Sander, Frank E. A. 1976. 'Varieties of Dispute Processing', *Federal Rules Decisions* 70: 111–34.

   1979. 'Varieties of Dispute Processing', in A. Leo Levin and Russell R. Wheeler (eds.) *The Pound Conference: Perspectives on Justice in the Future*, St Paul, MN: West Publishing Co., 65–81.

   1985a. 'Alternative Methods of Dispute Resolution: An Overview', *University of Florida Law Review* 37(1): 1–18.

   1985b. 'Alternative Dispute Resolution in the United States: An Overview', in American Bar Association (ed.) *Justice for a Generation*. St Paul, MN: West Publishing Company, 253–61.

Sander, Frank E. A. and Stephen B. Goldberg 1994. 'Fitting the Forum to the Fuss: A User-friendly Guide to Selecting an ADR Procedure', *Negotiation Journal* 10(1): 49–68.

Sander, Frank E. A. and Lukasz Rozdeiczer 2006. 'Matching Cases and Dispute Resolution Procedures: Detailed Analysis Leading to a Mediation-centered Approach', *Harvard Negotiation Law Review* 11: 1–41.

Sander, Frank and Mariana Hernandez Crespo 2008. 'A Dialogue Between Professors Frank Sander and Mariana Hernandez Crespo: Exploring the Evolution of the Multi-Door Courthouse', *University of St. Thomas Law Journal* 5: 665–71.

Santos, Boaventura de Sousa 1980. 'Law and Community: The Changing Nature of State Power in Late Capitalism', *International Journal of the Sociology of Law* 8: 379–97.

   1982. 'Law and Community: the Changing Nature of State Power in Late Capitalism', in R. Abel (ed.) *The Politics of Informal Justice, Volume 1: The American Experience*. New York: Academic Press.

   2000. 'Law and Democracy: (Mis)trusting the Global Reform of Courts', in Jane Jenson and Boaventura de Sousa Santos (eds.) *Globalizing Institutions: Case Studies in Regulation and Innovation*. Aldershot: Ashgate.

Sarat, Austin 2000. 'Exploring the Hidden Domains of Civil Justice: "Naming, Blaming and Claiming" in Popular Culture', *DePaul Law Review* 50: 425–52.

Sarat, Austin and William L. F. Felstiner 1988. 'Law and Social Relations: Vocabularies of Motive in Lawyer/Client Interaction', *Law and Society Review* 22: 737–69.

Sarkin, Jeremy 2001. 'The Tension between Justice and Reconciliation in Rwanda: Politics, Human Rights, Due Process and the Role of the Gacaca Courts in Dealing with Genocide', *Journal of African Law* 45(2): 143–59.

Schapera, Isaac 1943. *Land Tenure in the Bechuanaland Protectorate*. Botswana: Lovedale Press.

  1956. *Government and Politics in Tribal Societies*. London: C. A. Watts.

Scott, Colin 2010. 'Regulatory Governance and the Challenge of Constitutionalism', in Dawn Oliver, Tony Prosser and Richard Rawlings (eds.) *Regulation After the Regulatory State*, Oxford: Oxford University Press.

Shah-Kazemi, Sonia Nourin 2000. 'Cross-Cultural Mediation: A Critical View of the Dynamics of Culture in Family Disputes', *International Journal of Law Policy and the Family* 14: 302–25.

Shapiro, Martin 1981. *Courts: A Comparative and Political Analysis*. Chicago, IL: University of Chicago Press.

Shihata, Ibrahim F. J. 1995. 'Legal Framework for Development: The World Bank's Role in Legal and Judicial Reform', in Malcolm D. Rowat, Waleed Malik and Maria Dakolias (eds.) *Judicial Reform in Latin America and the Caribbean*. World Bank Technical Note 280. Washington, DC: World Bank, 13–14.

Silberman, Linda 1989. 'Judicial Adjuncts Revisited: The Proliferation of Ad Hoc Procedure', *University of Pennsylvania Law Review* 137: 2131–78.

Simmel, Georg 1906. 'The Sociology of Secrecy and of Secret Societies', *American Journal of Sociology* 11(4): 441–98.

  [1908] trans. 1950. 'The Triad', in *The Sociology of Georg Simmel*. Translated by Kurt H. Wolff. New York and London: The Free Press, 145–69.

Simmel, Georg [1923] trans. 1955 by Kurt H. Wolff, *Conflict and the Web of Group Affiliation* (trans. Reinhard Bendix). Glencoe, IL: The Free Press.

  [1908] trans. 2009a. 'The Quantitative Conditioning of the Group', in Georg Simmel, *Sociology: Inquiries into the Construction of Social Forms*, Volume 1. Translated and edited by Anthony J. Blasi, Anton K. Jacobs and Mathew Kanjirathinkal, with an introduction by Horst J. Helle, Leiden and Boston, MA: Brill, 53–128.

  [1908] trans. 2009b. 'Domination and Subordination', in Georg Simmel, *Sociology: Inquiries into the Construction of Social Forms*, Volume 1. Translated and edited by Anthony J. Blasi, Anton K. Jacobs and Mathew Kanjirathinkal, with an introduction by Horst J. Helle, Leiden and Boston, MA: Brill, 129–26.

  [1908] trans. 2009c. 'Conflict', in Georg Simmel, *Sociology: Inquiries into the Construction of Social Forms*, Volume 1. Translated and edited by Anthony J. Blasi, Anton K. Jacobs and Mathew Kanjirathinkal, with an introduction by Horst J. Helle, Leiden and Boston, MA: Brill, 227–305.

  [1908] trans. 2009d. *Sociology: Inquiries into the Construction of Social Forms*. Volume 1. Translated and edited by Anthony J. Blasi, Anton K. Jacobs and Mathew Kanjirathinkal, with an introduction by Horst J. Helle, Leiden and Boston, MA: Brill. Originally published in 1908 in Leipzig under the title *Soziologie: Untersuchungen über die Formen der Vergesellschaftung*, by Verlag von Duncker and Humblot.

Singer, Linda 1990. *Settling Disputes: Conflict Resolution in Business, Families, and the Legal System*. Boulder, CO: Westview Press.

Spencer, Janet M. and Joseph P. Zammit 1976. 'Mediation-arbitration: A Proposal for Private Resolution of Disputes between Divorced or Separated Parents', *Duke Law Journal* 25(5): 911–39.

Stedman, Barbara Epstein 1996. 'Multi-option Justice at the Middlesex Multi-Door Courthouse', in Roger Smith (ed.) *Achieving Civil Justice: Appropriate Dispute Resolution for the 1990s*, London: Legal Action Group, 119–41.

Stein, Peter 1984. *Legal Institutions: The Development of Dispute Settlement*. London: Butterworths.

  1999. *Roman Law in European History*. Cambridge: Cambridge University Press.

Stenelo, Lars-Göran 1972. *Mediation in International Negotiations*. Lund: Studentlitteratur.

Stevens, C. M. 1963. *Strategy and Collective Bargaining Negotiation*. New York: McGraw-Hill.

Supperstone, Michael et al. 2006. 'ADR and Public Law', *Public Law* 2006: 299–319.

Susskind, Richard 2015. 'Online Dispute Resolution: For Low Value Civil Claims', Online Dispute Resolution Advisory Group, Civ. Just. Council (February 2015), available at www.judiciary.uk/wp-content/uploads/2015/02/Online-Dispute-Resolution-Final-Web-Version1.pdf, accessed 3 December 2019.

Tamanaha, Brian Z. 2008. 'Understanding Legal Pluralism: Past to Present, Local to Global', *Sydney Law Review* 30: 375–411.

Teubner, Gunther 1983. 'Substantive and Reflexive Elements in Modern Law', *Law and Society Review* 17: 239–85.

Thornquist, Leroy J. 1989. 'The Active Judge in Pretrial Settlement: Inherent Authority Gone Awry', *Willamette Law Review* 25: 743–75.

Tochtermann, Peter 2013. 'Mediation in Germany: The German Mediation Act 2011: Dispute Resolution at the Crossroads', in Klaus J. Hopt and Felix Steffek (eds.) *Mediation: Principles and Regulation in Comparative Perspective*. Oxford: Oxford University Press, 521–84.

Tully, James 1993. *An Approach to Political Philosophy: Locke in Contexts*. Cambridge: Cambridge University Press.

Turnbull, Colin M. 1966. *Wayward Servants*. London: Eyre and Spottiswoode.

Turner, Victor 1957. *Schism and Continuity in an African Society: A Study of Ndembu Village Life*. Manchester: Manchester University Press.

UNCITRAL Model Law on International Commercial Arbitration 1985, with amendments as adopted in 2006, available at www.uncitral.org/uncitral/en/uncitral_texts/arbitration/1985Model_arbitration_status.html, accessed 3 December 2019.

United Nations Commission on International Trade Law (UNCITRAL) 2016. *Technical Notes on Online Dispute Resolution*, available at www.uncitral.org/pdf/english/texts/odr/V1700382_English_Technical_Notes_on_ODR.pdf, accessed 3 December 2019.

United Nations Conference on Trade and Development (UNCTAD) 2003. *E-Commerce and Development Report*, available at https://unctad.org/en/Docs/ecdr2003_en.pdf, accessed 3 December 2019.

United Nations (DAW/DESA – Division for the Advancement of Women, Department of Economic and Social Affairs) 2009. *Handbook for Legislation on Violence against Women*. New York: United Nations Publications.

Van Caenegem, R. C. 1988. *The Birth of the English Common Law.* Cambridge: Cambridge University Press.

Van der Sprenkel, Sybille 1962. *Legal Institutions in Manchu China.* London: Athlone Press.

Van Wezel Stone, Katherine 2001. 'Dispute Resolution in the Boundaryless Workplace', *Ohio State Journal of Dispute Resolution* 16: 427–89.

Verkuil, P. R. 1975. 'The Ombudsman and the Limits of the Adversary System', *Columbia Law Review* 75: 845–56.

Wahab, Mohamed 2004. 'Globalization and ODR: Dynamics of Change in E-commerce Dispute Settlement', *International Journal of Law and Information Technology* 12: 123–52.

Wang Liu Huichen 1959. *The Traditional Chinese Clan Rules.* (Monograph VII of the Association for Asian Studies). Locust Valley, NY: J. J. Augustin.

Wang Yueying 2017. 'Taobao Wangdian Yunying Jiaoyi Jiufen Jiejue Jizhi Cunzai de Wenti ji Duice' ['The Existing Problems and the Solutions for the Dispute Settlement Mechanisms of Taobao Shop Operation'], *Chuanbo Zhiye Jiaoyu* [Shipbuilding Vocational Education] No. 5 for 2017: 74–7.

Weber, Max 1964. *Theory of Social and Economic Organization.* Translated by A. M. Henderson and Talcott Parsons. New York: Free Press.

  [1917] 1978. *Economy and Society.* Edited by Gunther Roth and Claus Wittich. Translated by Ephraim Fischoff et al. New York: Bedminster Press.

Weinstein, Jack B. 1995. *Individual Justice in Mass Tort Litigation: The Effect of Class Actions, Consolidations, and other Multiparty Devices.* Evanston, IL: Northwestern University Press.

Welsh, Nancy A. 2010. 'I Could Have Been a Contender: Summary Jury Trial as a Means to Overcome Iqbal's Negative Effects upon Pre-Litigation Communication, Negotiation and Early, Consensual Dispute Resolution', *Penn State Law Review* 114: 1149–90.

White, J. J. 1980. 'Machiavelli and the Bar: Ethical Limitations on Lying in Negotiation', *American Bar Foundation Research Journal* 5(4): 926–38.

Wiegand, Shirley 1996. 'A Just and Lasting Peace: Supplanting Mediation with the Ombuds Model', *The Ohio State Journal on Dispute Resolution* 12(1): 95–144.

Williams, Gerald R. 1983. *Legal Negotiation and Settlement.* St Paul, MN: West Publishing.

Wolf, Michael J. 2012. 'Collaborative Technology Improves Access to Justice', *New York University Journal of Legislation and Public Policy* 15: 777–89.

Wolski, B. 2017. 'Collaborative Law: An (Un)Ethical Process for Lawyers?', *Legal Ethics* 20(2): 224–41.

Woodburn, James 1972. 'Ecology, Nomadic Movement and the Composition of the Local Group Among Hunters and Gatherers: An East African Example and Its Implications', in Peter J. Uko, Ruth Tringham and G. W. Dimbleby (eds.) *Man, Settlement and Urbanism.* London: Duckworth, 193–206.

Woodley, Ann E. 1995. 'Saving the Summary Jury Trial: A Proposal to Halt the Flow of Litigation and End the Uncertainties', *Journal of Dispute Resolution* 1995: 213–98.

Woolf, Lord 1995. *Access to Justice: Interim Report to the Lord Chancellor on the Civil Justice System of England and Wales*, London: HMSO.

1996. *Access to Justice: Final Report to the Lord Chancellor on the Civil Justice System of England and Wales.* London: HMSO.

Wu Yuning 2017. 'People's Mediation Enters the 21st Century', in Fu Hualing and Michael Palmer (eds.) *Mediation in Contemporary China: Continuity and Change,* London: Wildy, Simmonds and Hill, 34–58.

Xian Yifan 2015. 'Grassroots Judges of China in the Resurgence from Adjudicatory to Mediatory Justice: Transformation of Roles and Inherent Conflict of Identities', in Fu Hualing and Michael Palmer (eds.) 'Mediation in Contemporary China: Continuity and Change', Special Issue, *Journal of Comparative Law,* 10(2): 126–41. Republished in Fu Hualing and Michael Palmer (eds.) 2017. *Mediation in Contemporary China: Continuity and Change.* London: Wildy Simmonds and Hill, 167–87.

Ye Jian 2016. 'Xinxing wangluo jiufen jiejue ji zhi: dazong pingshen zhi: yi guonei mou daxing wanggou wangzhan wei li' ['New network dispute resolution mechanisms: the public evaluation system – taking a large online shopping website in China as an example'] *Fazhi Bolan* [Legal Perspective] 12: 18–20.

Yilmaz, Ihsan 2002. 'The Challenge of Post-modern Legality and Muslim Legal Pluralism in England', *Journal of Ethnic and Migration Studies,* 28(2) 343–54.

Zhang Xianchu 2015. 'Rethinking the Mediation Campaign', in Fu Hualing and Michael Palmer (eds.) 'Mediation in Contemporary China: Continuity and Change', Special Issue, *Journal of Comparative Law* 10(2): 44–64. Republished in extended form in Fu Hualing and Michael Palmer (eds.) 2017. *Mediation in Contemporary China: Continuity and Change.* London: Wildy, Simmonds and Hill, 59–86.

Zhang Xipo (ed.) 1983. *Ma Xiwu Shenpan Fangshi* [Ma Xiwu's Adjudicatory Style]. Beijing: Falü Chubanshe [Law Press].

Zhao Yixian 2015. 'Divorce Disputes and Popular Legal Culture of the Weak: A Case Study of Chinese Reality TV Mediation', in Fu Hualing and Michael Palmer (eds.) 'Mediation in Contemporary China: Continuity and Change', Special Issue, *Journal of Comparative Law 10(2): 218–36.* Republished in Fu Hualing and Michael Palmer (eds.) 2017. *Mediation in Contemporary China: Continuity and Change.* London: Wildy, Simmonds and Hill, 319–41.

Zhao Yun 2020. 'Regulatory Regime for Online Dispute Resolution (ODR): Current Forms and Future Development', in Maria Federica Moscati, Michael Palmer and Marian Roberts (eds.) *Comparative Dispute Resolution: A Research Handbook.* Cheltenham, UK and Northampton, MA: Edward Elgar Publishing.

Zhou Ling 2015. 'Consumer Council Dispute Resolution: A Case Study', in Fu Hualing and Michael Palmer (eds.) 'Mediation in Contemporary China: Continuity and Change', Special Issue, *Journal of Comparative Law,* 10(2): 254–75. Republished in Fu Hualing and Michael Palmer (eds.) 2017. *Mediation in Contemporary China: Continuity and Change.* London: Wildy Simmonds and Hill, 364–91.

2020. *Access to Justice for the Chinese Consumer: Handling Consumer Disputes in Contemporary China* (Civil Justice Systems Series). Oxford: Hart Publishing.

Further Reading

[All web addresses given in this section and 'Recommended Viewing' were operational 1 October 2019.]

The literature on dispute processing is vast, and its relationship to law and other disciplines wide ranging, often crossing disciplinary boundaries. Its scope ranges from 'cook-book' characterisations of 'how to do it better', to abstract accounts offering universalising claims, to comparative studies, to proposals for law reform, and to system designs intended to provide sophisticated procedural solutions to commercial, environmental and other complex quarrels. Much of this immense literature is generally supportive of the idea of enhancing access to justice, empowering the parties and securing the interests of the parties. Sadly, however, the studies are themselves not always readily accessible to interested readers, either because, for example, they are most easily located in electronic databases for which institutional subscriptions are (in effect) required or are to be found in relatively expensive books. The readings suggested below, especially those for specific chapters, therefore include entries that are free, open access, online, follow-up sources that speak to issues noted in the text. Many, however, will also be available to students and other readers with access to university supported databases, and will hopefully also facilitate the writing of their research essays. A number of the sources referred to in the text of the book may also be located in pdf form on the Internet, and can often be located by providing the author(s) name, short title and adding 'pdf' in the search. Many other items are likely to be available in second-hand bookshops at (hopefully) very reasonable prices.

Every effort has been made to trace all the copyright holders, but if any have been inadvertently overlooked we will be pleased to make the necessary arrangement at the first opportunity.

SOME FOUNDATIONAL AND CENTRAL TEXTS

Abel, Richard L. (ed.) 1982. *The Politics of Informal Justice, Volume 1: The American Experience*, New York and London: Academic Press.

1982. *The Politics of Informal Justice, Volume 2: Comparative Studies*, New York and London: Academic Press.

Allport, Leslie 2005. *Supervision in Mediation: Linking Practice and Quality*. Sion: Institut Universitaire Kurt Bosch.

Andrews, Neil H. 2018. *The Three Paths of Justice: Court Proceedings, Arbitration and Mediation in England*. Dordrecht, Heidelberg, London and New York: Springer.

Astor, Hilary and Christine Chinkin 2002. *Dispute Resolution in Australia*. 2nd ed. Chatswood, Australia: Butterworth.

Aubert, Vilhelm (ed.) 1977. *Sociology of Law*. Harmondsworth: Penguin.

Auerbach, Jerold S. 1983. *Justice without Law? Resolving Disputes without Lawyers*. Oxford and New York: Oxford University Press.

Baldwin, Robert, Colin Scott and Christopher Hood (eds.) 1998. *A Reader in Regulation*. Oxford: Oxford University Press.

Banakas, Efstathios K. (ed.) 2011. *Global Wrongs and Private Law Remedies and Procedures*. London: Wildy, Simmonds and Hill.

Barton, Roy F. 1919. *The Kalingas: Their Institutions and Customary Law*. Chicago, IL: University of Chicago Press.

Beldam, Lord Justice (Sir Roy) 1991. *Report of the Committee on Alternative Dispute Resolution*. October 1991, London: General Council of the Bar.

Bercovitch, Jacob 1984. *Social Conflicts and 3rd Parties: Strategies of Conflict Resolution*. Boulder, CO: Westview.

Binnendijk, Hans 1987. *National Negotiating Styles*. Washington, DC: Foreign Service Institute, US Dept of State.

Bisno, Herb 1988. *Managing Conflict*. Newbury Park, CA: Sage Publications.

Blake, Robert 1984. *Solving Costly Organizational Conflicts*. San Francisco, CA: Jossey-Bass.

Blake, Susan, Julie Browne and Stuart Sime 2016. *The Jackson ADR Handbook*. 2nd ed. Oxford: Oxford University Press.

  2016. *A Practical Approach to Alternative Dispute Resolution*. 4th ed. Oxford: Oxford University Press.

Bondy, Varda and Margaret Doyle 2011. *Mediation in Judicial Review: A Practical Handbook for Lawyers*. London: The Public Law Project.

Bondy, Varda, Linda Mulcahy, with Margaret Doyle and Val Reid 2009. *Mediation and Judicial Review: An Empirical Research Study*. London: The Public Law Project, Nuffield Foundation.

Bossy, John A. (ed.) 1983. *Disputes and Settlements: Law and Human Relations in the West*. Cambridge: Cambridge University Press.

Boule, Laurence and Miryana Nesic 1996. *Mediation Principles, Process, Practice*. Sydney: Butterworths.

Bradney, Anthony and Fiona Cownie 2000. *Living without Law: An Ethnography of Quaker Decision-making, Dispute Avoidance, and Dispute Resolution*. Aldershot: Dartmouth Publishing Company.

Brown, David L. 1983. *Managing Conflict at Organizational Interfaces*. Reading, MA: Addison-Wesley.

Brown, Henry J. 1991. *Alternative Dispute Resolution: Report, Courts and Legal Services Committee*. London: Law Society, Legal Practice Directorate.

Brown, Henry J., Shirley Shipman, Ben Waters and William Wood 2018. *Brown and Marriott's ADR Principles and Practice*. 4th ed. London: Sweet and Maxwell.

Bush, R. A. B. and J. P. Folger 1994. *The Promise of Mediation: Responding to Conflict through Empowerment and Recognition*. San Francisco, CA: Jossey-Bass.

Caplan, Pat (ed.) 1995. *Understanding Disputes: The Politics of Argument*. Oxford and Providence, RI: Berg.

Cappelletti, M. (General Editor) 1978–9. *Access to Justice*. Alphen aan den Rijn: Sijthoff and Noordhoff, and Milan: Giuffrè Dott. Four volumes in six binders. Vol. I, Bks. 1 and 2: *A World Survey* (Mauro Cappelletti and Bryant Garth, eds.), Vol. II, Bks. 1 and 2: *Promising Situations* (Mauro Cappelletti and John Weisner, eds.), Vol. III: *Emerging Issues and Perspectives* (M. Cappelletti and B. Garth, eds.), Vol. IV: *The Anthropological Perspective* (Klaus-Friedrich Koch, ed.).

Carter, Jimmy 1984. *Negotiation: The Alternative to Hostility*. Macon, GA: Mercer University Press.

Coffin, Royce A. 1973. *The Negotiator: A Manual for Winners*. New York: AMA Publishing.

Comaroff, John L. and Simon A. Roberts 1986. *Rules and Processes*. Chicago, IL: University of Chicago Press.

Damaška, Mirjan R. 1986. *The Faces of Justice and State Authority: A Comparative Approach to the Legal Process*. New Haven, CT: Yale University Press.

Davis, Gwynn 1988. *Partisans and Mediators: The Resolution of Divorce Disputes*. Oxford: Oxford University Press.

Davis, Gwynn and Marian Roberts 1988. *Access to Agreement: A Consumer Study of Mediation in Family Disputes*. Milton Keynes: Open University Press.

Davis, Gwynn, Stephen Cretney and Jean Collins 1994. *Simple Quarrels*. Oxford: Clarendon Press.

De Girolamo, Debbie 2013. *The Fugitive Identity of Mediation: Negotiations, Shift Changes and Allusionary Action*. London: Routledge.

Deutsch, Morton. 1973. *The Resolution of Conflict: Constructive and Destructive Processes*. New Haven, CT: Yale University Press.

Dingwall, Robert and John Eekelaar (eds.) 1988. *Divorce Mediation and the Legal Process*. Oxford: Clarendon Press.

Douglas, Ann 1962. *Industrial Peacemaking*. New York: Columbia University Press.

Dyson, Lord 2018. *Justice: Continuity and Change*. Oxford: Oxford University Press.

Eckhoff, Torstein 1969. 'The Mediator and the Judge', in V. Aubert (ed.) *Sociology of Law*. Harmondsworth: Penguin Books.

European Parliament and the Council of the European Union 2008. *Directive 2008 on Certain Aspects of Mediation in Civil and Commercial Matters*.

Fisher, Roger 1994. *Beyond Machiavelli: Tools for Coping with Conflict*. Cambridge, MA: Harvard University Press.

Fisher, Roger and William Ury 1981. *Getting to Yes*. Boston, MA: Houghton Mifflin.

Folberg, Jay 1984. 'Divorce Mediation – The Emerging American Model', in J. M. Eekelaar and S. N. Katz (eds.) *The Resolution of Family Conflict, Comparative Legal Perspectives*. Toronto: Butterworths.

Folberg, Jay and Anne Milne (eds.) 1988. *Divorce Mediation: Theory and Practice*. New York: Guilford Press.

Folberg, Jay and Alison Taylor 1984. *Mediation: A Comprehensive Guide to Resolving Conflicts without Litigation*. San Francisco, CA: Jossey-Bass.

Fu Hualing and Michael Palmer (eds.) 2017. *Mediation in Contemporary China: Continuity and Change*. London: Wildy, Simmonds and Hill.

Genn, Hazel G. 1987. *Hard Bargaining: Out of Court Settlement in Personal Injury Actions*. Oxford: Clarendon Press.

2009. *Judging Civil Justice.* Cambridge: Cambridge University Press.

et al. 2007. 'Twisting Arms: Court Referred and Court Linked Mediation under Judicial Pressure', Ministry of Justice Research Series 1/07, May.

Gulliver, Philip H. 1979. *Disputes and Negotiations: A Cross-cultural Perspective.* New York and London: Academic Press.

Hamnett, Ian (ed.) 1977. *Social Anthropology and Law.* London: Academic Press.

Hampshire, Stuart 1989. *Innocence and Experience.* Harmondsworth: Penguin.

2000. *Justice is Conflict.* Princeton, NJ: Princeton University Press.

Haynes, John M. 1993. *The Fundamentals of Family Mediation.* London: Old Bailey Press.

Hopt, Klaus J. and Felix Steffek (eds.) 2012. *Mediation: Principles and Regulation in Comparative Perspective.* Oxford: Oxford University Press.

Illich, John 1973. *The Art and Skill of Successful Negotiation.* Englewood Cliffs, NJ: Prentice Hall.

1992. *Dealbreakers and Breakthroughs.* New York: Wiley.

Ingleby, Richard 1992. *Solicitors and Divorce.* Oxford: Clarendon Press.

Kennedy, Gavin 1993. *Pocket Negotiator.* London: The Economist Bookshop.

Keshavjee, Mohamed M. 2013. *Islam, Sharia and Alternative Dispute Resolution: Mechanisms for Legal Redress in the Muslim Community.* London: I. B. Tauris.

Knapp, Mark L. 1972. *Nonverbal Communication in Human Interaction.* New York: Holt, Rinehart and Winston.

Knox, Colin and Rachel Monaghan 2014. *Informal Justice in Divided Societies: Northern Ireland and South Africa.* New York: Palgrave Macmillan.

Kolb, Deborah M. (ed.) 1985. *The Mediators.* Cambridge, MA: MIT Press.

(ed.) 1986. *Her Place at the Table: Gender Negotiation.* San Francisco, CA: Sage Publishing.

(ed.) 1994. *When Talk Works: Profiles of Mediators.* San Francisco, CA: Jossey-Bass.

Kreisberg, Louis 1989. *Intractable Conflicts and their Transformation.* Syracuse, NY: Syracuse University Press.

Kressel, Kenneth 1985. *The Process of Divorce.* New York: Basic Books.

Lang, Michael D. and Alison Taylor 2000. *The Making of a Mediator: Developing Artistry in Practice.* San Francisco, CA: Jossey-Bass.

Levin, A. Leo and Russell R. Wheeler 1979. *The Pound Conference: Perspectives on Justice in the Future.* Proceedings of the National Conference on the Causes of Popular Dissatisfaction with the Administration of Justice. St. Paul, MN: West Publishing Co.

Levine, Donald N. (ed.) 1971. *Simmel on Individuality and Social Forms.* Chicago, IL: University of Chicago Press.

Lewicki, Roy J. 1993. *Negotiation – Readings, Exercises and Cases.* 2nd ed. Homewood, IL: Irwin.

Liddell Hart, Basil H. 1974. *Strategy.* New York: Signet Books.

Lockhart, Charles 1979. *Bargaining in International Conflicts.* New York: Columbia University Press.

Lubman, S. 1967. 'Mao and Mediation: Politics and Dispute Resolution in Communist China', *California Law Review* 55: 1284–359.

Maccoby, Eleanor A. and Robert H. Mnookin 1992. *Dividing the Child: Social and Legal Dilemmas of Custody.* Cambridge, MA: Harvard University Press.

Madigan, Josepha 2012. *Appropriate Dispute Resolution (ADR) in Ireland: A Handbook for Family Lawyers and Their Clients*. United Kingdom: Lexisnexis.

Matthews, Roger (ed.) 1988. *Informal Justice?* London: Sage.

Menkel-Meadow, Carrie J. 1996. 'Is mediation the practice of law?', *Alternatives to the High Cost of Litigation* 14: 57–61.

2003. *Dispute Processing and Conflict Resolution: Theory. Practice, and Policy*. Farnham: Ashgate Press.

Menkel-Meadow, Carrie J. (ed.) 2012. *Complex Dispute Resolution*. Vols. 1–3. Farnham: Ashgate Press.

(ed.) 2016. *Mediation and Its Applications for Good Decision Making and Dispute Resolution*. Cambridge: Intersentia.

Menkel-Meadow, Carrie J., L. P. Love, A. K. Schneider and J. R. Sternlight 2005. *Dispute Resolution: Beyond the Adversarial Model*. 2nd ed. New York: Aspen Publishers.

Menkel-Meadow, Carrie J., L. P. Love, A. K. Schneider and M. Moffit 2019. *Dispute Resolution: Beyond the Adversarial Model*. 3rd ed. New York: Wolters Kluwer.

Mnookin, Robert, Scott Peppett and Andrew Tulemello 2000. *Beyond Winning: Negotiating to Create Value in Deals and Disputes*. Cambridge, MA: Belknap Press.

Moore, Charles 1996. *The Mediation Process: Practical Strategies for Resolving Conflict*. 2nd ed. San Francisco, CA: Jossey-Bass.

Moscati, Maria Federica 2014. *Pasolini's Italian Premonitions: Same-sex Unions and the Law in Comparative Perspective*. London: Wildy, Simmonds and Hill.

Moscati, Maria Federica, Michael Palmer and Marian Roberts (eds.) 2020. *Comparative Dispute Resolution: A Research Handbook*. Cheltenham, UK and Northampton, MA: Edward Elgar Publishing.

Mulcahy, Linda and Emma Rowden 2019. *The Democratic Courthouse: A Modern History of Design, Due Process and Dignity*. London: Routledge.

Nelken, David (ed.) 2012. *Using Legal Culture*. London: Wildy, Simmonds and Hill.

Nierenberg, Gerard I. 1973. *Fundamentals of Negotiating*. New York: Hawthorne Books.

1981. *The Art of Negotiating*. New York: Simon and Schuster.

Parkinson, Lisa 2014. *Family Mediation: Appropriate Dispute Resolution in a New Family Justice System*. 3rd ed. Bristol: Family Law.

Permanent Bureau of the Hague Conference of Private International Law 2011. *Draft Guide to Good Practice under the Hague Convention of 25 October 1980 on the Civil Aspects of International Child Abduction Mediation Part V: Mediation*. The Hague: HccH.

Pinter, Frances 1984. 'Questioning the Delegalization Movement in Family Law: Do We Really Want a Family Court?', in J. M. Eekelaar and S. N. Katz (eds.) *The Resolution of Family Conflict: Comparative Legal Perspectives*. Toronto: Butterworths.

Piper, Christine 1993. *The Responsible Parent: A Study in Divorce Mediation*. London: Harvester Wheatsheaf.

Pruitt, Dean 1981. *Negotiation Behavior*. New York: Academic Press.

Raiffa, Howard 1982. *The Art and Science of Negotiation*. Cambridge, MA: Harvard University Press.

Rangarajan, L. N. 1985. *The Limitation of Conflict: A Theory of Bargaining and Negotiation*. New York: St. Martin's.

Roberts, Marian 1988. *Mediation in Family Disputes: A Guide to Practice*. 1st ed. Aldershot: Wildwood House.

1997. *Mediation in Family Disputes: Principles of Practice.* 2nd ed. Aldershot: Ashgate.

2007. *Developing the Craft of Mediation: Reflections on Theory and Practice.* London: Jessica Kingsley Publishers.

2014. *A–Z of Mediation.* London: Palgrave Macmillan.

2014. *Mediation in Family Disputes: Principles of Practice.* 4th ed. London: Ashgate Publishing.

Roberts, Simon 1979. *Order and Dispute: An Introduction to Legal Anthropology.* Harmondsworth: Penguin.

2002. 'Institutionalized Settlement in England: A Contemporary Panorama', *Willamette Journal of International Law and Dispute Resolution* 10: 17–35.

2013. *A Court in the City: Civil and Commercial Litigation in London at the Beginning of the 21st Century.* London: Wildy, Simmonds and Hill.

2013. *Order and Dispute: An Introduction to Legal Anthropology,* 2nd ed. New Orleans, LA: Quid Pro Books.

Rogers, Nancy H., R. C. Bordone, F. E. A. Sander and C. A. McEwen 2014. *Designing Systems and Processes for Managing Disputes.* Aspen, CO: Aspen Publishers.

Rosen, Lawrence 1989. *The Anthropology of Justice: Law as Culture in Islamic Society.* Cambridge: Cambridge University Press.

2006. *Law as Culture: An Invitation.* Princeton, NJ: Princeton University Press.

Rubin, Jeffrey Z. and Bert R. Brown 1975. *The Social Psychology of Bargaining and Negotiation.* New York: Academic Press.

Saaty, Thomas 1989. *Conflict Resolution: The Analytical Hierarchy Approach.* New York: Praeger.

Santos, Boaventura de Sousa 1982. 'Law and Community: The Changing Nature of State Power in Late Capitalism', in Richard Abel (ed.) *The Politics of Informal Justice, Volume 1: The American Experience.* London and New York: Academic Press, 24–266.

Schlegel, Stuart A. 1970. *Tiruray Justice: Traditional Tiruray Law and Morality.* Berkeley, CA: University of California Press.

Shapiro, Martin 1981. *Courts: A Comparative and Political Analysis.* Chicago, IL: University of Chicago Press.

Simmel, Georg 1950 [1908]. *The Sociology of Georg Simmel.* Wolff, K. (ed.). Glencoe, IL: Free Press.

2009 [1908]. *Sociology: Inquiries into the Construction of Social Forms.* (Vol. 1), Translated and edited by Anthony J. Blasi, Anton K. Jacobs and Mathew Kanjirathinkal, with an introduction by Horst J. Helle. Leiden and Boston: Brill. (*Soziologie: Untersuchungen über die Formen der Vergesellschaftung,* was originally published in 1908 in Leipzig by Verlag von Duncker and Humblot).

Steffek, Felix, Hannes Unberath, Hazel G. Genn, Reinhard Greger and Carrie J. Menkel-Meadow (eds.) 2013. *Regulating Dispute Resolution – ADR and Access to Justice at the Crossroads.* Oxford and Portland, OR: Hart Publishing.

Stenelo, Lars-Göran 1972. *Mediation in International Negotiations.* Malmo: Nordens boktryckeri.

Stevens, Carl M. 1963. *Strategy and Collective Bargaining Negotiation.* New York: McGraw-Hill.

Strauss, Anselm 1978. *Negotiations: Varieties, Contexts, Processes and Social Order.* San Francisco, CA: Jossey-Bass.

Stroebe, Wolfgang 1988. *The Social Psychology of Intergroup Conflict: Theory, Research and Applications*. New York: Springer-Verlag.

Stulberg, Joseph B. 1987. *Taking Charge/Managing Conflict*. Lexington, MA: Lexington Books.

Susskind, Lawrence and Jeffrey Cruikshank 1987. *Breaking the Impasse: Consensual Approaches to Resolving Public Disputes*. New York: Basic Books.

Ury, William 1988. *Getting Disputes Resolved: Designing Systems to Cut the Costs of Conflict*. San Francisco, CA: Jossey-Bass.

Walton, Dick and Robert McKersie 1965. *A Behavioral Theory of Labor Negotiation*. New York: McGraw-Hill.

Wheeler, Hoyt N. 1985. *Industrial Conflict: An Integrative Theory*. Columbia, SC: University of South Carolina Press.

Winston, Kenneth I. 1981. *The Principles of Social Order: Selected Essays of Lon L. Fuller*. Durham, NC: Duke University Press.

Woolf, Lord 1995. *Access to Justice: Interim Report to the Lord Chancellor on the Civil Justice System in England and Wales*. London: HMSO.

1996. *Access to Justice: Final Report to the Lord Chancellor on the Civil Justice System of England and Wales*. London: HMSO.

2008. *The Pursuit of Justice*. Oxford: Oxford University Press.

Yates, Douglas 1985. *The Politics of Management*. San Francisco, CA: Jossey-Bass.

Zartman, William I. 1978. *The Negotiation Process: Theories and Applications*. Beverly Hills, CA: Sage Publications.

1982. *The Practical Negotiator*. New Haven, CT: Yale University Press.

Also see a number of the official reports cited below in the further reading for specific chapters.

IMPORTANT JOURNALS, OTHER THAN LEADING LAW JOURNALS

In suggesting journals that focus on dispute resolution, accessibility of websites has been an important consideration, and limiting concern to journals dedicated to the study of arbitration and commercial dispute resolution has also been an important factor shaping the titles recommended below.

African Journal of Conflict Resolution
Armed Forces and Society
Australasian Dispute Resolution Journal
Cardozo Journal of Conflict Resolution
CDR Magazine
Conflict Management and Peace Science
Conflict Resolution Quarterly
Conflict Trends
Cooperation and Conflict
Dispute Resolution International
Dispute Resolution Magazine
East African Journal of Peace and Human Rights
Ethnic Conflict Research Digest

Family Mediation Quarterly
Global Change, Peace and Security Journal
Harvard Negotiation Law Review
International Journal of Conflict Management
International Journal of Humanities and Peace
International Journal of Peace Studies
International Journal on World Peace
International Negotiation: A Journal of Theory and Practice
Journal for Peace and Justice Studies
Journal for the Study of Peace and Conflict
Journal of Comparative Law
Journal of Conflict and Security Law
Journal of Conflict Resolution
Journal of Conflict Studies
Journal of Dispute Resolution
Journal of Peace Education
Journal of Peace Research
Law and Society Review
Mediation Quarterly
Ohio State Journal on Dispute Resolution
Online Journal of Peace and Conflict Resolution
Peace and Conflict Studies
Peace and Conflict: Journal of Peace Psychology
Peace Research: The Canadian Journal of Peace and Conflict Studies
Pepperdine Dispute Resolution Law Journal
Research in Social Movements, Conflict and Change
Studies in Conflict and Terrorism
Willamette Journal of International Law and Dispute Resolution
World Arbitration and Mediation Review

USEFUL WEBSITES

In addition to the above journals, some of which have interesting and sometimes useful webpages of their own, the following sites may serve as helpful starting points for those readers seeking more information about dispute processes and related activities. (Like the citations given in the references offered in specific chapters, these were all in operation at 1 October 2019.) Commercial dispute resolution providers or law firms that provide ADR services, and governmental websites, are generally not included in the list. The list is not intended to be fully inclusive: entries reflect to a significant extent the personal preferences of the authors. The selection below has a predominance of north American sites, reflecting the strong interest in ADR and online access found there. A number of important essays on disputes and their resolution are made available without charge at Dispute Resolution and Arbitration Commons (http://network.bepress.com/law/dispute-resolution-and-arbitration/). This is also the case for SSRN (Social Science Research Network) (www.ssrn.com/index.cfm/en/). Guidance on a number of Online Dispute Resolution (ODR) services may be found at Mediate.com (www.mediate.com/).

ADR on the Web – Links and Resources:

Federal ADR Program Manager's Resource Manual, www.adr.gov/manual/

ADR Resources, http://adrr.com/.

American Bar Association, Section of Dispute Resolution, www.americanbar.org/groups/dispute_resolution/.

Better Business Bureau Dispute Resolution Services, www.bbb.org/consumer-complaints/file-a-complaint/get-started.

Center for the Study of Dispute Resolution, https://law.missouri.edu/csdr/.

Centre for Effective Dispute Resolution (CEDR), www.cedr.com/.

Conflict Net (closed 2017) but still see, www.igc.org/.

Conflict Resolution Education Connection, https://creducation.net.

Conflict Resolution – University of Colorado Boulder, www.colorado.edu/sccr/conflict-management.

CPR Institute for Dispute Resolution, www.cpradr.org/resource-center, or www.cpradr.org/.

Dispute Resolution and Arbitration Commons, http://network.bepress.com/law/dispute-resolution-and-arbitration/.

Family Mediators Association, https://thefma.co.uk/.

Federal ADR Program Manager's Resource Manual, www.adr.gov/manual/.

Financial Ombudsman Service (FOS), www.financial-ombudsman.org.uk.

Forum, www.adr-forum.com/.

Fresno Pacific University – Center for Peacemaking and Conflict Studies, www.fresno.edu/visitors/center-peacemaking.

Georgetown University, E. B. Williams Law Library, www.law.georgetown.edu/library/.

HG Legal Resources, http://hg.org/adr.html.

IALS (SAS) Alternative Dispute Resolution and Commercial Arbitration, https://libguides.ials.sas.ac.uk/ADRandcommercialarbitration.

Mediate. Com, www.mediate.com/.

Mediation Information and Resource Center, www.mediate.com/.

Mediation Works, Inc., www.mwi.org/.

National Center for Information Technology and Dispute Resolution, http://odr.info.

Program on Negotiation, Harvard Law School, www.pon.harvard.edu/.

Rand Institute for Civil Justice, www.rand.org/well-being/justice-policy/centers/civil-justice.html.

Scheinman Institute of Conflict Resolution, Cornell University, www.ilr.cornell.edu/scheinman-institute.

Social Science Research Network (SSRN), www.ssrn.com/index.cfm/en/.

Straus Institute for Dispute Resolution, https://law.pepperdine.edu/straus/.

The Justice Center of Atlanta, www.justicecenter.org/.

VA Mediation Program Design, www.va.gov/adr/.

World Intellectual Property Organisation (WIPO) – ADR, www.wipo.int/amc/en/.

CHAPTER 1 INTRODUCTION

Alexander, Nadja 2001. 'From Common Law to Civil Law Jurisdictions: Court ADR on the Move in Germany', *ADR Bulletin: The Monthly Newsletter on Dispute Resolution* 4(8): 110–13, available at https://ink.library.smu.edu.sg/sol_research/1892.

Bachar, Gilat J. and Deborah R. Hensler 2017. 'Does Alternative Dispute Resolution Facilitate Prejudice and Bias? We Still Don't Know', *Southern Methodist University Law Review* 70: 817–36, available at https://pdfs.semanticscholar.org/e8c9/d4fe82170173fdf42f893ab4bdcf7166b109.pdf.

Briggs, Lord Justice 2013. *Chancery Modernisation Review: Final Report.* available at www.judiciary.gov.uk/announcements/chancery-modernisationreview-final-report/.

 2015. *Civil Courts Structure Review: Interim Report.* (December 2015), available at www.judiciary.gov.uk/wp-content/uploads/2016/ 01/ccsr-interim-report-dec-15-final1.pdf.

 2016. *Civil Courts Structure Review: Final Report. Judiciary of England and Wales.* available at www.judiciary.uk/publications/civil-courts-structure-review-final-report/.

Busby, Nicole and Morag McDermont 2016. 'Access to Justice in Employment Disputes: Private Disputes or Public Concerns', in E. Palmer, T. Cornford, Y. Marique and A. Guinchard (eds.) *Access to Justice: Beyond the Policies and Politics of Austerity.* Oxford: Hart Publishing, 175–96 (pre-print version available at https://research-information.bristol.ac.uk/files/65136609/10._Busby_and_McDermont_for_website.pdf).

Dispute Resolution Magazine 2012. 'Appreciating Frank Sander', *Dispute Resolution Magazine* 19(1): 4–22, available at http://franksander.com/wp-content/uploads/2018/10/DRM_Fall12_Sander_Final.pdf.

Douglas, Katherine 2012. *The Teaching of Alternative Dispute Resolution in Selected Australian Law Schools: Towards Second Generation Practice and Pedagogy,* doctoral dissertation RMIT University, available at https://pdfs.semanticscholar.org/c08a/81dab7efacb845e5c216adbae8a4a04ff688.pdf.

Galanter, Marc 2010. 'Access to Justice in a World of Expanding Social Capability', *Fordham Urban Law Journal* 37(1): 115–28, available at https://ir.lawnet.fordham.edu/cgi/viewcontent.cgi?article=2324&context=ulj.

Genn, Hazel G. 2013. 'What Is Civil Justice For? Reform, ADR, and Access to Justice', *Yale Journal of Law and the Humanities* 24(1): 397–417, available at https://pdfs.semanticscholar.org/a4f3/ab49ea04101aac07dd6577a34482165718f1.pdf.

Gulliver, Philip H. 2004. Interview with Philip Gulliver [Video file and text], available at www.dspace.cam.ac.uk/handle/1810/448.

Jackson, Sir Rupert 2010. *Review of Civil Litigation Costs: Final Report,* available at www.judiciary.gov.uk/wp-content/uploads/JCO/Documents/Reports/jackson-final-report-140110.pdf.

 2017. *Review of Civil Litigation Costs: Supplemental Report Fixed Recoverable Costs* (July 2017), available at www.judiciary.gov.uk/wp-content/uploads/2017/07/fixed-recoverable-costs-supplementalreport-online-2-1.pdf.

 2018. *The Reform of Civil Justice.* 2nd ed. London: Sweet and Maxwell.

Lande, John 2018. 'For Pragmatic Romanticism in Law and Dispute Resolution: Reflections on Galanter's Remarkably Realistic Analysis of Why the Have-Nots Come Out Behind' *University of Missouri School of Law Legal Studies Research Paper* No. 2018-04, available at https://papers.ssrn.com/sol3/papers.cfm?abstract_id=3097140.

Legg, Michael 2016. 'A Comparison of Regulatory Enforcement, Class Actions and Alternative Dispute Resolution in Compensating Financial Consumers', *Sydney Law Review* 3: 311–38, available at http://classic.austlii.edu.au/au/journals/SydLawRw/2016/15.html.

Love, Lena and Kimberlee K. Kovach 2000. 'ADR: An Eclectic Array of processes Rather than One Eclectic Process', *Journal of Dispute Resolution* 2000(2): 295–307, available at https://larc.cardozo.yu.edu/cgi/viewcontent.cgi?article=1364&context=faculty-articles.

Menashe, Doron 2018. 'A Critical Analysis of the Online Court', *University of Pennsylvania International Law Journal* 39(4): 921–53, available at https://scholarship.law.upenn.edu/cgi/viewcontent.cgi?article=1967&context=jil.

Menkel-Meadow, Carrie J. 2017. 'Conflict Resolution by the Numbers', *Negotiation Journal* 33(4) 317–22, UC Irvine School of Law Research Paper No. 2017-58, available at SSRN: https://ssrn.com/abstract=3072564.

    2019. 'Mediation 3.0: Merging the Old and the New' (9 January 2019); 2018. *Asian Journal on Mediation* 1–20, UC Irvine School of Law Research Paper No. 2019-01, available at SSRN: https://ssrn.com/abstract=3312971.

Morris, Catherine (ed.) *Conflict Transformation and Peacebuilding: A Selected Bibliography*, available at www.peacemakers.ca/bibliography/.

Moscati, Maria Federica 2015. *Same-sex Couples and Mediation: A Practical Handbook.* Manual. DG Justice, Specific Programme Civil Justice 2007–2013, available at http://sro.sussex.ac.uk/id/eprint/54466/1/2015_MOSCATI_SS_COUPLES_MEDIATION.pdf.

    2017. 'Together Forever: Are You Kidding Me? Catholicism, Same-sex Couples, Disputes and Dispute Resolution in Italy', in Samia Bano (ed.) *Gender and Justice in Family Law Disputes: Women, Mediation, and Religious Arbitration.* Waltham, MA: Brandeis University Press, 292–318.

Palmer, Michael and Simon Roberts 2007. 'ADR', in David S. Clarke (ed.) *Encyclopedia of Law and Society: American and Global Experiences*, Thousand Oaks, CA: Sage Publications, 421–6.

Program on Negotiation 2018. 'What is the Multidoor Courthouse Concept?', available at www.pon.harvard.edu/daily/international-negotiation-daily/a-discussion-with-frank-sander-about-the-multi-door-courthouse/.

Sander, Frank E. A. 1979. 'Varieties of Dispute Processing', in A. Leo Levin and Russell R. Wheeler (eds.) *The Pound Conference: Perspectives on Justice in the Future*, St Paul, MN: West Publishing.

Sander, Frank and Mariana Hernandez Crespo 2008. 'A Dialogue between Professors Frank Sander and Mariana Hernandez Crespo: Exploring the Evolution of the Multi-Door Courthouse', *University of St. Thomas Law Journal* 5(3): 665–74, available at https://ir.stthomas.edu/ustlj/vol5/iss3/4/.

Smith, Roger 2016. *Civil Courts Structure Review: Legal Education Foundation Comment on the Interim Report by Lord Justice Briggs*, available at www.thelegaleducationfoundation.org/wp-content/uploads/2016/02/Briggs-Response.pdf.

Sternlight, Jean R. 2007–8. 'Dispute Resolution and the Quest for Justice', *Dispute Resolution Magazine* 1(1): 14–19, available at https://scholars.law.unlv.edu/facpub/261/.

Woolf, Lord 1996. *Access to Justice: Final Report to the Lord Chancellor on the Civil Justice System of England and Wales*. London: HMSO, available at https://webarchive.nationalarchives.gov.uk/20060213223540/http://www.dca.gov.uk/civil/final/contents.htm; the interim report (1995) appears to be unavailable online.

CHAPTER 2 CULTURES OF DECISION-MAKING: PRECURSORS TO THE EMERGENCE OF ADR

Bakht, Natasha 2004. 'Family Arbitration Using Sharia Law: Examining Ontario's Arbitration Act and Its Impact on Women', *Muslim World Journal of Human Rights* 1(1): 1–24, available at www.researchgate.net/publication/40824050_Family_Arbitration_Using_Sharia_Law_Examining_Ontario's_Arbitration_Act_and_its_Impact_on_Women/link/00463516e93c0d8718000000/download.

Bradney, Anthony and Fiona Cownie 2000. *Living without Law: An Ethnography of Quaker Decision-making, Dispute Avoidance, and Dispute Resolution*. Aldershot: Dartmouth Publishing Company.

Burton, Nicholas and Jonathan Bainbridge 2019. 'Spiritual Discernment, the Incorporated Organization, and Corporate Law: The Case of Quaker Business Method', *Religions* 10(1): 35, available at www.mdpi.com › pdf.

Chotalia, Shirish P. 2006. 'Arbitration Using Sharia Law in Canada: A Constitutional and Human Rights Perspective', *Constitutional Forum Constitutionnel* 15(2): 63–78, available at https://journals.library.ualberta.ca/constitutional_forum/index.php/constitutional_forum/article/view/11058/8499.

Fitzpatrick, Peter 1993. 'The Impossibility of Popular Justice', in Sally Engle Merry and Neal Milner (eds.) *The Possibility of Popular Justice*. Ann Arbor, MI: University of Michigan Press. Also at 1992. *Social and Legal Studies* 1(2): 199–215.

Fu Hualing and Michael Palmer 2017. 'Introduction', in Fu Hualing and Michael Palmer (eds.) *Mediation in Contemporary China: Continuity and Change*. London: Wildy, Simmonds and Hill, available at https://papers.ssrn.com/sol3/papers.cfm?abstract_id=2943961.

Greenhouse, Carol 1989. *Praying for Justice: Faith, order, and community in an American Town*. Ithaca: Cornell University Press.

1992. 'Revisiting Hopewell: A Reply to Neal Milner: [Commentary]', *Law and Social Inquiry* 17(2): 335–50 (also available upon request at www.researchgate.net/publication/230242804_Revisiting_Hopewell_A_Reply_to_Neal_Milner). The Southern Baptists Convention's website is at www.sbc.net.

Hanycz, Colleen M. 2007. 'Whither Community Justice?: The Rise of Court-connected Mediation in the United States', *Windsor Yearbook of Access to Justice* 25(1): 159–210, available at https://digitalcommons.osgoode.yorku.ca/cgi/viewcontent.cgi?referer=https://www.google.com.hk/&httpsredir=1&article=3524&context=scholarly_works.

Merry, Sally Engle 1993. 'Sorting Out Popular Justice', in Sally Engle Merry and Neal Milner (eds.) *The Possibility of Popular Justice*. Ann Arbor, MI: University of Michigan Press, 31–66.

Milner, Neal 1992. 'The Intrigues of Rights, Resistance, and Accommodation', *Law and Social Inquiry* 17(2): 313–33 (this may be requested from the author at

www.researchgate.net/publication/264469270_The_Intrigues_of_Rights_Resistance_
and_Accommodation.)

Moscati, Maria Federica 2015. *Litigious Love – Same-sex Couples and Mediation in the
European Union*, available at http://sro.sussex.ac.uk/id/eprint/54467/1/2015_MOS
CATI_%28ED%29_Same-Sex_Couples_and_Mediation_in_the_EU.pdf.

    2015. *Same-sex Couples and Mediation: A Practical Handbook*. Manual. DG Justice,
Specific Programme Civil Justice 2007–2013, available at http://sro.sussex.ac.uk/
id/eprint/54466/1/2015_MOSCATI_SS_COUPLES_MEDIATION.pdf.

Nader, Laura 1984. 'The Recurrent Dialect between Legality and its Alternatives: The
Limits of Binary Thinking', *University of Pennsylvania Law Review* 136: 621–45,
available at https://scholarship.law.upenn.edu/cgi/viewcontent.cgi?article=4624&
context=penn_law_review.

Parfitt, Steven 2019. 'Why the Knights of Labour Still Matter', *Discover Society* , available
at https://discoversociety.org/2019/01/02/focus-remembering-the-knights-of-labor/.

CHAPTER 3 THE DEBATES AROUND CIVIL JUSTICE AND THE MOVEMENT
TOWARDS PROCEDURAL INNOVATION

Fordham Law Review 2009. 'Against Settlement: Twenty-Five Years Later', Special Issue
Fordham Law Review 78(3), available at https://ir.lawnet.fordham.edu/flr/vol78/
iss3/. See essays by Howard M. Erichson, 'Reflections on the Adjudication-
Settlement Divide'; John Bronsteen, 'Some Thoughts about the Economics of
Settlement'; Amy J. Cohen, 'Revisiting against Settlement: Some Reflections on
Dispute Resolution and Public Values'; Kenneth R. Feinberg, 'Reexamining the
Arguments in Owen M. Fiss, Against Settlement'; Samuel Issacharoff and Robert
H. Klonoff, 'The Public Value of Settlement'; Michael Moffit, 'Three Things To Be
against ("Settlement" Not Included)'; Jacqueline Nolan-Haley, 'Mediation Excep-
tionality'; Hon. Jack B. Weinstein 'Comments on Owen M. Fiss, Against Settlement
(1984)'; Owen M. Fiss 'The History of an Idea'; Bethany R. Berger, 'What Owners
Want and Government Do: Evidence From the Oregon Experiment'; Rachel
M. Birnbach, 'Love Thy Neighbor: Should Religious Accommodations that Nega-
tively Affect Coworkers' Shift Preferences Constitute an Undue Hardship on the
Employer Under Title VII?'; Kathryn J. Harvey, 'The Rights of Divorced Lesbians:
Interstate Recognition of Child Custody Judgments in the Context of Same-sex
Divorce; Denise Mazzeo, 'Securities Class Actions, CAFA and a Countrywide
Crisis: A Call for Clarity and Consistency'; Daniel Northrop, 'The Attorney-Client
Privilege and Information Disclosed to an Attorney with the Intention that the
Attorney Draft a Document To Be Released to Third Parties: Public Policy Calls for
at Least the Strictest Application of the Attorney-Client Privilege'; Uriel Rabinov,
'Toward Effective Implementation of 11 U.S.C. § 522(d)(11)(E): Invigorating a
Powerful Bankruptcy Exemption'.

Genn, Hazel G. 2009. *Judging Civil Justice* (The Hamlyn Lectures). Cambridge:
Cambridge University Press, available at https://socialsciences.exeter.ac.uk/
media/universityofexeter/collegeofsocialsciencesandinternationalstudies/lawimages/
hamlyntrust/Genn_judging_civil_justice.pdf.

2012. 'What Is Civil Justice For? Reform, ADR, and Access to Justice', *Yale Journal of Law and the Humanities* 24(1): 397–417 (Article 18) available at http://digitalcommons.law.yale.edu/yjlh/vol24/iss1/18.

2012. 'Why the Privatisation of Civil Justice is a Rule of Law Issue', (36th F. A. Mann Lecture, Lincoln's Inn, 19 November 2012), available at www.ucl.ac.uk/laws/sites/laws/files/36th-f-a-mann-lecture-19.11.12-professor-hazel-genn.pdf.

Luban, David 1995. 'Settlements and the Erosion of the Public Realm', *Georgetown Law Journal* 83: 2619–62.

Menkel-Meadow, Carrie J. 1995. 'Whose Dispute Is It Anyway? A Philosophical and Democratic Defense of Settlement (In Some Cases)', *Georgetown Law Journal* 83: 2663–96, available at https://scholarship.law.georgetown.edu/cgi/viewcontent.cgi?referer=https://www.google.com/&httpsredir=1&article=2771&context=facpub.

2013. 'The Historical Contingencies of Conflict Resolution', *International Journal of Conflict Engagement and Resolution* 1: 32–55, UC Irvine School of Law Research Paper, No. 2013-155, available at SSRN: https://ssrn.com/abstract=2337189.

CHAPTER 4 DISPUTES AND DISPUTE PROCESSES

Barton, Roy F. 1919. 'Ifugao Law', *American Archaeology and Ethnology* 15(1): 1–186, available at http://digitalassets.lib.berkeley.edu/anthpubs/ucb/text/ucp015–003.pdf.

Bloch, Maurice 1992. *Prey into Hunter: The Politics of Religious Experience*. Cambridge: Cambridge University Press, available at http://voidnetwork.gr/wp-content/uploads/2016/09/Prey-into-Hunter-by-Maurice-Bloch.pdf.

Hall, Margaret C. 1989. 'Triadic Analysis: A Conceptual Tool for Clinical Sociologists', *Clinical Sociology Review* 7(1): 97–110 (Article 12), available at http://digitalcommons.wayne.edu/csr/vol7/iss1/12.

Lidvinka, Thomas 2016. 'Bronislaw Malinowski and the Anthropology of Law', in Mateusz Stępień (ed.) *Bronislaw Malinowski's Concept of Law* . Cham: Springer International, 55–81, available at www.academia.edu/17468023/Bronislaw_Mali nowski_and_the_Anthropology_of_Law._In_Bronislaw_Malinowskis_Concept_of_Law_edited_by_Mateusz_St%C4%99pie%C5%84.

MacRae, Graeme 2005. 'Negara Ubud: The Theatre-state in Twenty-first-century Bali', *History and Anthropology* 16(40): 393–413. This may be read online at www.researchgate.net/publication/263677565_Negara_Ubud_The_Theatre-state_in_Twenty-first-century_Bali.

Resnick, Judith 1995. 'Many Doors? Closing Doors? Alternative Dispute Resolution and Adjudication', *Faculty Scholarship Series*, available at https://digitalcommons.law.yale.edu/fss_papers/894.

Sourdin, Tania 2015. 'The Role of the Courts in the New Justice System', *Yearbook of Arbitration and Mediation* 7: 95–116, available at https://elibrary.law.psu.edu/cgi/viewcontent.cgi?article=1033&context=arbitrationlawreview.

Strathern, Andrew 1993. 'Great-men, Leaders, Big-men : The Link of Ritual Power', *Journal de la Société des Océanistes Année* 97: 145–58, available at www.persee.fr/doc/jso_0300-953x_1993_num_97_2_2929.

Zumeta, Zena n.d. 'Styles of Mediation: Facilitative, Evaluative, and Transformative Mediation', available at www.mediate.com/articles/zumeta.cfm.

CHAPTER 5 DEVELOPMENT OF DISPUTES, AVOIDANCE AND SELF-HELP

Bohmer, Carol 1994. 'Victims Who Fight Back: Claiming in Cases of Professional Sexual Exploitation', *Justice System Journal* (1994): 73–92 (not available online).

Brake, Deborah L. and Joanna L. Grossman 2008. 'The Failure of Title VII as a Rights-claiming System', *North Carolina Law Review* 86: 859–935, available at https://scholarlycommons.law.hofstra.edu/cgi/viewcontent.cgi?article=1165&context=faculty_scholarship.

Calvita, Kitty and Valerie Jenness 2013. 'Inside the Pyramid of Disputes: Naming Problems and Filing Grievances in California Prisons', *Social Problems* 60(1): 50–80, available at www.prisonlegalnews.org/news/publications/naming-prob lems-filing-grievances-ca-prisons-calavita-jenness-2013/.

Carlson, Kirsten M. 2013. 'Priceless Property', *Georgia State University Law Review* 29(3): 685–730, available at https://papers.ssrn.com/sol3/papers.cfm?abstract_id=2030248.

Charlesworth, Sara et al. 2011. 'Naming and Claiming Workplace Sexual Harassment in Australia', *Australian Journal of Social Issues* 46(2): 141–61, available at www.researchgate.net/publication/266081314_Charlesworth_S_McDonald_P_and_Cerise_S2011_'Naming_and_Claiming_Sexual_Harassment_in_Australia'_Australian_Journal_of_Social_Issues_462_141-161/link/5866daad08aebf17d39aeba9/download.

DeVille, Kenneth A. and Mark E. Steiner 1997. 'The New Jersey Radium Dial Workers and the Dynamics of Occupational Disease Litigation in the Early Twentieth Century', *Missouri Law Review* 62(2): 281–314, available at https://scholarship.law.missouri.edu/mlr/vol62/iss2/2.

Felstiner, William L. F., Richard L. Abel and Austin Sarat 1980–1. 'The Emergence and Transformation of Disputes: Naming, Blaming, Claiming . . .' *Law and Society Review* Special Issue on Dispute Processing and Civil Litigation 15 (3/4): 631–54, available at https://pdfs.semanticscholar.org/03ed/dd4b19d00a2d9bff2e700bae97a45942aa18.pdf.

Laniya, Olatokunbo O. 2005. 'Street Smut: Gender, Media, and the Legal Power Dynamics of Street Harassment, or Hey Sexy and Other Verbal Ejaculations', *Columbia Journal of Gender and Law* 14(1): 91–130, available at http://brooklynmovementcenter.org/wp-content/uploads/2013/04/streetsmut.pdf.

Meyersfeld, Bonita 2016. 'A Theory of Domestic Violence in International Law', Yale Law School Dissertations 3, available at http://digitalcommons.law.yale.edu/ylsd/3, and at https://digitalcommons.law.yale.edu/cgi/viewcontent.cgi?article=1002&context=ylsd.

Palmer, Michael 2014. 'The Formalization of Alternative Dispute Resolution Processes: Some Socio-legal Thoughts', in Iwo Amelung, Moritz Bälz and Joachim Zekoll (eds.) *Formalisation and Flexibilisation in Dispute Resolution*. Leiden: Brill.

Sarat, Austin 2000. 'Exploring the Hidden Domains of Civil Justice: "Naming, Blaming, and Claiming" in Popular Culture', *DePaul Law Review* 50: 425–52, available at https://via.library.depaul.edu/law-review/vol50/iss2/3.

van der Zeeuw, Alex Laura Keesman and Don Weenink 2017. 'Sociologizing with Randall Collins: An interview about Emotions, Violence, Attention Space and Sociology', *European Journal of Social Theory* 1–15, available at www.researchgate.net/publication/317710444_Sociologizing_with_Randall_Collins_An_interview_about_emotions_violence_attention_space_and_sociology.

Worsely, Dareen 2012. *Conflict Avoidance and Dispute Resolution in Construction*, RICS Guidance Note, 1st ed. (GN 91/2012), available at www.academia.edu/28526735/Conflict_avoidance_and_dispute_resolution_in_construction.

CHAPTER 6 NEGOTIATIONS

Bear, Julia B. and Linda Babcock 2012. 'Negotiation Topic as a Moderator of Gender Differences in Negotiation', *Psychological Science* 23(7): 743–4, available at www.researchgate.net/publication/225375121_Negotiation_Topic_as_a_Moderator_of_Gender_Differences_in_Negotiation/link/58c300d1aca272e36dd0421f/download.

Bowles, H. R. and F. Flynn 2010. 'Gender and Persistence in Negotiation: A Dyadic Perspective', *Academy of Management Journal* 53(4): 769–87, available at https://projects.iq.harvard.edu/files/hbowles/files/gender_persistence.pdf.

Brunner, J. 2014. 'Patent Prosecution as Dispute Resolution: A Negotiation between Applicant and Examiner', *Journal of Dispute Resolution* 2014(1): 1–15, available at https://scholarship.law.missouri.edu/cgi/viewcontent.cgi?referer=https://www.google.com/&httpsredir=1&article=1691&context=jdr.

Craver, Charles B. 2017. 'Do Alternative Dispute Resolution Procedures Disadvantage Women and Minorities?', *Southern Methodist University Law Review* 70: 891–912, available at https://scholar.smu.edu/smulr/vol70/iss4/6.

Curhan, Jared R., Hillary A. Elfenbein and Noah Eisenkraft 2010. 'The Objective Value of Subjective Value: A Multi-round Negotiation Study', *Journal of Applied Social Psychology* 40(3): 690–709, available at www.eza.org/fileadmin/system/pdf/Online-Kurs_2012/FLC/Curhan_Objective_Value_of_Subjective_Value.pdf.

De Dreu, Carsten 2008. 'The Virtue and Vice of Workplace Conflict: Food for (Pessimistic) Thought', *Journal of Organizational Behavior* 29: 5–18, available at www.researchgate.net/publication/227663423_The_Virtue_and_Vice_of_Workplace_Conflict_Food_for_Pessimistic_Thought.

De Girolamo, Debbie 2013. 'The Negotiation Process: Exploring Negotiator Moves through a Processual Framework', *Ohio State Journal on Dispute Resolution* 28: 353–86, available at https://pdfs.semanticscholar.org/c75c/3b6bf370b844809fe772d76cb945d34fb8bb.pdf.

Hollander-Blumoff, Rebecca 2010. 'Just Negotiation', *Washington University Law Review* 88: 381–432, available at https://openscholarship.wustl.edu/law_lawreview/vol88/iss2/2/.

Imai, L. and M. J. Gelfand 2010. 'The Culturally Intelligent Negotiator: The Impact of Cultural Intelligence (CQ) on Negotiation Sequences and Outcomes', *Organizational Behavior and Human Decision Processes* 112(2): 83–98, available at https://culturalq.com/wp-content/uploads/2016/06/OBHDP-2010-Imai-Gelfand.pdf.

Kelly, E. J. and N. Kaminskienė 2016. 'Importance of Emotional Intelligence in Negotiation and Mediation', *International Comparative Jurisprudence* 2(1): 55–60, available at https://repository.mruni.eu/bitstream/handle/007/14771/4453-9870-1-SM.pdf?sequence=1.

Menkel-Meadow, Carrie J. 1993. 'Lawyer Negotiations: Theories and Realities. *What We Learn from Mediation*', *Modern Law Review* 56(3): 361–79.

2015. 'Alternative and Appropriate Dispute Resolution in Context Formal, Informal, and Semiformal Legal Processes', available at https://papers.ssrn.com/sol3/papers.cfm?abstract_id=2584188.

2015. 'Mediation, Arbitration, and Alternative Dispute Resolution (ADR)', in *International Encyclopedia of the Social and Behavioral Sciences*, Elsevier, UC Irvine School of Law Research Paper No. 2015-59, available at SSRN: https://ssrn.com/abstract=2608140.

Sinaceur, M., G. A. Van Kleef, M. A. Neale, H. Adam and C. Haag 2011. 'Hot or Cold: Is Communicating Anger or Threats More Effective in Negotiation?' *Journal of Applied Psychology* 96(5): 1018–32, available at www.researchgate.net/publication/51234251_Hot_or_Cold_Is_Communicating_Anger_or_Threats_More_Effective_in_Negotiation.

Susskind, Lawrence 2010. 'Looking at Negotiation and Dispute Resolution through a CA/DA Lens', *Negotiation Journal* 26(2): 163–6, available at www.researchgate.net/publication/230468267_Looking_at_Negotiation_and_Dispute_Resolution_through_a_CADA_Lens.

CHAPTER 7 MEDIATION

Allport, Lesley 2016. 'Exploring the Common Ground in Mediation', PhD dissertation, University of Birmingham, available at http://etheses.bham.ac.uk/6746/1/Allport16PhD.pdf.

Bernard, Phyllis E. 2008. 'Minorities, Mediation, and Method: The View from One Court-connected Mediation Program', *Fordham University Urban Law Journal* 35: 1–37, available at https://ir.lawnet.fordham.edu/ulj/vol35/iss1/1.

Chan, Chris King-Chi and Elaine Sio-Ieng Hui Chan 2014. 'The Development of Collective Bargaining in China: From "collective bargaining by riot" to "party state-led wage bargaining"', *The China Quarterly* 217: 221–42.

Craver, Charles B. 2017. 'Do Alternative Dispute Resolution Procedures Disadvantage Women and Minorities?', *Southern Methodist University Law Review* 70: 891–912, available at https://scholar.smu.edu/smulr/vol70/iss4/6.

Fu Hualing and Michael Palmer (eds.) 2017. *Mediation in Contemporary China: Continuity and Change*. London: Wildy, Simmonds and Hill.

Genn, Hazel G. 2012. 'Why the Privatisation of Civil Justice is a Rule of Law Issue', 36th F. A. Mann Lecture, Lincoln's Inn, 19 November 2012, available at www.ucl.ac.uk/laws/sites/laws/files/36th-f-a-mann-lecture-19.11.12-professor-hazel-genn.pdf.

Halegua, Aaron (2018). 'Legal Preemption in China: How Government Legal Aid Squeezed Out Barefoot Lawyers and Labor Non-governmental Organizations', available at https://economics.harvard.edu/files/economics/files/halegua-aaron_legal_preemption_in_china_ec2342_25oct2017.pdf.

Keshavjee, Mohamed M. 2016. 'Alternative Dispute Resolution (ADR) and Its Potential for Helping Muslims Reclaim the Higher Ethical Values (Maqasid) Underpinning the Sharia', in Habib Tiliouine and Richard J. Estes (eds.) *The State of Social Progress of Islamic Societies*, 607–21. Cham: Springer, available at www.researchgate.net/profile/Asharaf_Salam/publication/300077335_Demographic_Challenges_of_the_Rapidly_Growing_Societies_of_the_Arab_World/

links/5bc33c78299bf1004c5f2fa0/Demographic-Challenges-of-the-Rapidly-Growing-Societies-of-the-Arab-World.pdf#page=635.

Maliepaard, Marie Irene 1982. *Religious Trends and Social Integration: Moslem Minorities in the Netherlands*, available at https://lirias.kuleuven.be/retrieve/522012.

Matari, Sarah S. 2010. 'Mediation to Resolve the Bedouin-Israeli Government Dispute for the Negev Desert', *Fordham International Law Journal* 34(4): 1089–130, available at https://ir.lawnet.fordham.edu/cgi/viewcontent.cgi?referer=https://www.google.com/&httpsredir=1&article=2297&context=ilj.

Menkel-Meadow, Carrie J. 2013. 'Regulation of Dispute Resolution in the United States of America: From the Formal to the Informal to the "Semi-formal"', in Felix Steffek, Hannes Unberath, Hazel Genn, Reinhard Greger and Carrie J. Menkel-Meadow (eds.) *Regulating Dispute Resolution: ADR and Access to Justice at the Crossroads*. Oxford: Hart, available at https://scholarship.law.georgetown.edu/facpub/1291.

_____ 2016. *Mediation and Its Applications for Good Decision Making and Dispute Resolution*. Cambridge: Intersentia, available at www.law.uci.edu/faculty/full-time/menkel-meadow/mediation-applications-for-good-decisionmaking-Acta-KULeuven.pdf.

Michel, James 2011. 'Alternative Dispute Resolution and the Rule of Law in International Development Cooperation', *Journal of Dispute Resolution* (2011): 21–45, available at https://scholarship.law.missouri.edu/jdr/vol2011/iss1/3.

Nolan-Haley, Jacqueline 2014. 'Mediation: The Best and Worst of Times', *Cardozo Journal of Conflict Resolution* 16: 731–40, available at http://ir.lawnet.fordham.edu/faculty_scholarship/652.

Quek Anderson, Dorcas 2013. 'Facilitative Versus Evaluative Mediation: Is There Necessarily a Dichotomy?', (1 December 2013) *Asian Journal on Mediation* 66–75, available at SSRN: https://ssrn.com/abstract=2889142.

Ridley-Duff, R. and A. Bennett 2011. 'Towards Mediation: Developing a Theoretical Framework to Understand Alternative Dispute Resolution', *Industrial Relations Journal* 42(2): 106–23. http://shura.shu.ac.uk/6446/1/28_-_Towards_Mediation_-_Development_a_Theoretical_Framework.pdf, and at, http://citeseerx.ist.psu.edu/viewdoc/download?doi=10.1.1.695.6865&rep=rep1&type=pdf.

Roberts, Marian 2015. 'Hearing Both Sides: Structural Safeguards for Protecting Fairness in Family Mediation', *Family Law Journal* 45(6): 718–26, available at www.selfmb.org.uk/wp-content/uploads/2017/04/FamilyLawProofs2015HearingBothSides.pdf.

Zhuang, W. and F. Chen 2015. '"Mediate First": The Revival of Mediation in Labour Dispute Resolution in China', *The China Quarterly* 222: 380–402.

CHAPTER 8 UMPIRING: COURTS AND TRIBUNALS

Alter, K. J. 2013. 'The Multiple Roles of International Courts and Tribunals: Enforcement, Dispute Settlement, Constitutional and Administrative Review', in Jeffrey L. Dunoff and Mark A. Pollack (eds.) *International Law and International Relations: Synthesizing Insights from Interdisciplinary Scholarship*, available at http://scholarlycommons.law.northwestern.edu/facultyworkingpapers/212.

Aronson, O. 2010. 'Out of Many: Military Commissions, Religious Tribunals, and the Democratic Virtues of Court Specialization', *Virginia Journal of International Law* 51(2): 231–98, available at www.researchgate.net/publication/228128294_Out_of_Many_Military_Commissions_Religious_Tribunals_and_the_Democratic_Virtues_of_Court_Specialization.

Busby, Nicole and Morag McDermont 2012. 'Workers, Marginalised Voices and the Employment Tribunal System: Some Preliminary Findings', *Industrial Law Journal* 41(2): 166–83, available at www.bristol.ac.uk/media-library/sites/law/migrated/documents/marginalisedvoices.pdf.

Elliott, Mark and Robert Thomas 2012. 'Tribunal Justice and Proportionate Dispute Resolution', *Cambridge Law Journal* 71(2): 297–324, available at www.research.manchester.ac.uk/portal/files/27079090/POST-PEER-REVIEW-PUBLISHERS.PDF.

Finder, Susan 2018. 'China's Translucent Judicial Transparency', Peking University School of Transnational Law Research Paper, available at https://ssrn.com/abstract=3344466. (Now published in Fu Hualing, Michael Palmer and Zhang Xianchu (eds.) 2019. *Transparency Challenges Facing China.* London: Wildy, Simmonds and Hill.)

Fleming, Joseph Z. 2012. 'Just Like Umpires: Why Chief Justice Roberts Correctly Relied on Baseball to Describe the Supreme Court of the United States', *Alberta Government Law Review* 5: 286–331, available at www.albanygovernmentlawreview.org/Articles/Vol05_1/5.1.286-Fleming.pdf.

Fu Hualing 2016. 'Building Judicial Integrity in China', *Hastings International and Comparative Law Review* 39(1): 167–81, University of Hong Kong Faculty of Law Research Paper No. 2015/048, available at SSRN: https://ssrn.com/abstract=2684603.

He Xin 2007. 'Why Did They Not Take on the Disputes? Law, Power and Politics in the Decision-making of Chinese Courts', *International Journal of Law in Context* 3(3): 203–25, available at www.cityu.edu.hk/slw/lib/doc/Frank_pub/6.pdf.

    2012. 'A Tale of Two Chinese Courts: Economic Development and Contract Enforcement', *Journal of Law and Society*, available at SSRN: https://ssrn.com/abstract=2026306.

Kritzer, Herbert 2003. 'Martin Shapiro: Anticipating the New Intuitionalism', in Nancy Maveety (ed.) *The Pioneers of Judicial Behavior.* Ann Arbor, MI: University of Michigan Press, available at https://faculty.polisci.wisc.edu/kritzer/research/supcourt/shapiro.pdf.

Lande, John 2011. 'The Revolution in Family Law Dispute Resolution', *Journal of the American Academy Matrimonial Law* 24: 411–49.

Mangan, D. 2013. 'Employment Tribunal Reforms to Boost the Economy', *Industrial Law Journal* 42(4): 409–21, available at https://pdfs.semanticscholar.org/484d/a00bb27d28456a12bf924d9fe214a1799f52.pdf.

McKee, Theodore A. 2007. 'Judges as Umpires', *Hofstra Law Review* 35: 1709–24, available at https://law.hofstra.edu/pdf/academics/journals/lawreview/lrv_issues_v35n04_cc1.mckee.35.4.final.pdf.

Preston, B. J. 2014. 'Characteristics of Successful Environmental Courts and Tribunals', *Journal of Environmental Law* 26(3): 365–93, available at https://pdfs.semanticscholar.org/30be/33607bbbe3efac91e746d8f0bcc79f99b7f8.pdf.

Pring, George and Catherine Pring 2010. 'Increase in Environmental Courts and Tribunals Prompts New Global Institute', *Journal of Court Innovation* 3(1):11–21, available at www.nycourts.gov/court-innovation/Winter-2010/jciPring.pdf.

Roberts, Anthea 2011. 'Comparative International Law? The Role of National Courts in Creating and Enforcing International Law', *International and Comparative Law Quarterly* 60(1): 57–92, available at https://documents.law.yale.edu/sites/default/files/Roberts%20-%20Comp_Intl_Law.pdf.

Tamir, Moustafa 2014. 'Law and Courts in Authoritarian Regimes', *Annual Review of Law and Social Science* 10: 281–99, available at https://ssrn.com/abstract=2498774.

Zhang Taisu 2012. 'The Pragmatic Court: Reinterpreting the Supreme People's Court of China', *Columbia Journal of Asian Law* 25: 1–61.

Zhou Ling 2017. 'Consumer Council Dispute Resolution: A Case Study', (31 March 2017). UCD Working Papers in Law, Criminology and Socio-legal Studies Research Paper No. 03/2017, available at SSRN: https://ssrn.com/abstract=2943962 or http://dx.doi.org/10.2139/ssrn.2943962.

CHAPTER 9 UMPIRING: ARBITRATION

Ali, Shahla F. and Odysseas G. Repousis 2018. 'Investor-State Mediation and the Rise of Transparency in International Investment Law: Opportunity or Threat?' (18 March 2018), *Denver Journal of International Law and Policy* 45(2): 225–50, available at SSRN: https://ssrn.com/abstract=3216254.

Brekoulakis, S. and M. B. Devaney 2016. 'Public-private Arbitration and the Public Interest under English Law' (11 November 2016), Queen Mary School of Law Legal Studies Research Paper No. 248/2016, available at https://ssrn.com/abstract=2868024.

Demaine, Linda J. and Deborah R. Hensler 2004. '"Volunteering" to Arbitrate through Predispute Arbitration Clauses: The Average Consumer's Experience', Santa Monica, CA: RAND Corporation, available at www.rand.org/pubs/reprints/RP1156.html.

Dempsey, P. S. 2004. 'Flights of Fancy and Fights of Fury: Arbitration and Adjudication of Commercial and Political Disputes in International Aviation', *Georgia Journal of International and Comparative Law* 32(2): 231–305, available at https://digitalcommons.law.uga.edu/gjicl/vol32/iss2/2.

Giorgetti, Chiara 2017. 'International Adjudicative Bodies', in J. Katz Cogan et al. (eds.) *The Oxford Handbook on International Organizations*. Oxford: Oxford University Press, 881–902, available at https://scholarship.richmond.edu/law-faculty-publications/1407/.

Gu Weixia 2017. 'The Developing Nature of Arbitration in Mainland China and Its Correlation with the Market: Institutional, Ad Hoc, and Foreign Institutions Seated in Mainland China', *Contemporary Asia Arbitration Journal* 10(2): 257–91, November 2017, University of Hong Kong Faculty of Law Research Paper No. 2017/037, available at SSRN: https://ssrn.com/abstract=30855682014.

Karamanian, Susan L. 2017. 'Courts and Arbitration: Reconciling the Public with the Private', *Arbitration Law Review* [electronic version] 9: 1–15, available at https://elibrary.law.psu.edu/arbitrationlawreview/vol9/iss1/20/.

Ku, Julian G., Roger Alford and Xiao Bei 2015. 'Perceptions and Reality: The Enforce-
    ment of Foreign Arbitral Awards in China', *ExpressO* 1–29, available at http://
    works.bepress.com/julian_ku/2/.

Lipsky, David B., J. Ryan Lamare and Michael D. Maffie 2014. 'Mandatory Employ-
    ment Arbitration: Dispelling the Myths', *Alternatives to the High Cost of Litigation*
    32(9): 133–9, available at https://digitalcommons.ilr.cornell.edu/articles/1274.

Park, William 2017. 'Soft Law and Transnational Standards in Arbitration: The Chal-
    lenge of res judicata', Boston University School of Law, Public Law Research Paper
    No. 17-26, 1–21, available at https://scholarship.law.bu.edu/faculty_scholarship/
    370.

Shapiro, Matthew A. 2019. 'Delegating Procedure', *Columbia Law Review* 118: 983–1065,
    available at https://scholarlycommons.law.hofstra.edu/faculty_scholarship/1226.

Sovern, Jeff, Elayne E. Greenberg, Paul F. Kirgis and Liu Yuxiang 2015. '"Whimsy little
    contracts" with Unexpected Consequences: An Empirical Analysis of Consumer
    Understanding of Arbitration Agreements', *Maryland Law Review* 75(1): 1–134,
    available at https://digitalcommons.law.umaryland.edu/mlr/vol75/iss1/2/.

Stipanowich, Thomas J. 2013. 'Living with ADR: Evolving Perceptions and Use of
    Mediation, Arbitration and Conflict Management in Fortune 1,000 Corporations',
    available at http://works.bepress.com/thomas_stipanowich/23/.

Thomas, Lord 2016. 'Developing Commercial Law through the Courts: Rebalancing the
    Relationship between the Courts and Arbitration', *The Bailii Lecture* given on
    9 March 2016, available at www.bailii.org/bailii/lecture/04.pdf.

Welsh, Nancy A., Andrea K. Schneider and Kathryn Rimpfe 2014. 'Using the Theories
    of Exit, Voice, Loyalty, and Procedural Justice to Reconceptualize Brazil's Rejec-
    tion of Bilateral Investment Treaties', *Washington University Journal of Law and
    Policy* 45: 105–43, available at https://works.bepress.com/nancy-welsh/7/.

CHAPTER 10 HYBRID FORMS AND PROCESSUAL EXPERIMENTATION

Chua, Eunice 2018. 'A Contribution to the Conversation on Mixing the Modes of
    Mediation and Arbitration: Of Definitional Consistency and Process Structure',
    Transnational Dispute Management 1–15, available at https://ink.library.smu.edu
    .sg/sol_research/2771.

Deason, Ellen E. 2013. 'Combinations of Mediation and Arbitration with the Same
    Neutral: A Framework for Judicial Review', *Yearbook of Arbitration and Medi-
    ation* 1: 219–42, available at https://elibrary.law.psu.edu/arbitrationlawreview/
    vol5/iss1/12/.

Gu Weixia 2014. 'The Delicate Art of Med-Arb and Its Future Institutionalisation in
    China', *Pacific Basin Law Journal* 31(2): 97–216, available at https://escholarship
    .org/uc/item/5911549r.

Hussin, A., C. Kuck and N. Alexander 2018. 'SIAC-SIMC's Arb-Med-Arb Protocol',
    New York Dispute Resolution Lawyer 11(2): 85–7, available at https://ink.library
    .smu.edu.sg/sol_research/2832.

Hyung Kyun Kwon 2017. 'Med-Arb Adoption in Securities Law Disputes: Advantages
    and Costs', *Concordia Law Review* 2(1): Article 3, available at https://commons.cu-
    portland.edu/clr/vol2/iss1/3.

Menkel-Meadow, Carrie J. 2015. 'Mediation, Arbitration, and Alternative Dispute Resolution (ADR)', *International Encyclopedia of the Social and Behavioral Sciences*, UC Irvine School of Law Research Paper No. 2015-59, available at https://ssrn.com/abstract=2608140.

—— 2020. 'Hybrid and Mixed Dispute Resolution Processes: Integrities of Process Pluralism', in Maria Federica Moscati, Michael Palmer and Marian Roberts (eds.) *Comparative Dispute Resolution: A Research Handbook*. Cheltenham, UK and Northampton, MA: Edward Elgar Publishing.

CHAPTER 11 THE OMBUDS AND ITS DIFFUSION: FROM PUBLIC TO PRIVATE

Clark, D. P. 2013. 'The Role of the Ombuds in a Knowledge-Intensive Corporation: A Partner for Conflict Prevention and Mitigation', Washington College of Law Working Papers No. 40, 1–9, available at https://digitalcommons.wcl.american.edu/fac_works_papers/40.

Hedeen, Timothy 2017. 'Ombuds as Nomads?: The Intersections of Dispute System Design and Identity', *University of St. Thomas Law Journal* 13: 233–47, available at https://ir.stthomas.edu/ustlj/vol13/iss2/5/.

Menkel-Meadow, Carrie J. 2015. 'Mediation, Arbitration, and Alternative Dispute Resolution (ADR)', *International Encyclopedia of the Social and Behavioral Sciences*, UC Irvine School of Law Research Paper No. 2015-59, available at https://ssrn.com/abstract=2608140.

—— 2015. 'Process Pluralism in Transitional/Restorative Justice – Lessons from Dispute Resolution for Cultural Variations in Goals beyond Rule of Law and Democracy Development' (Argentina and Chile) *International Journal of Conflict Engagement and Resolution* 3(1): 3–32, UC Irvine School of Law Research Paper No. 2015-86, available at, https://papers.ssrn.com/sol3/papers.cfm?abstract_id=2683501.

Stewart, Daxtron R. 2012. 'Evaluating Public Access Ombuds Programs: An Analysis of the Experiences of Virginia, Iowa and Arizona in creating and Implementing Ombuds Offices to Handle Disputes Arising under Open Government Laws', *Journal of Dispute Resolution* 2012(2): 437–505, available at https://scholarship.law.missouri.edu/jdr/vol2012/iss2/4.

Thomson, Stephen 2017. 'The Public Sector Ombudsman in Greater China: Four "Chinese" Models of Administrative Supervision' *University of Pennsylvania Journal of International Law* 39(2): 435–90, available at https://scholarship.law.upenn.edu/cgi/viewcontent.cgi?article=1958&context=jil.

Van Soye, Scott C. 2007. 'Illusory Ethics: Legal Barriers to an Ombudsman's Compliance with Accepted Ethical Standards', *Pepperdine Dispute Resolution Law Journal* 8(1): 117–46, available at https://digitalcommons.pepperdine.edu/drlj/vol8/iss1/4.

CHAPTER 12 ONLINE DISPUTE RESOLUTION AND ITS DIFFUSION: FROM PRIVATE TO PUBLIC

Brand, Ronald A. 2012. 'Party Autonomy and Access to Justice in the UNCITRAL Online Dispute Resolution Project', (August 2012). University of Pittsburgh Legal Studies Research Paper No. 2012-20, available at SSRN: https://ssrn.com/abstract=2125214.

Civil Justice Council 2015. *Online Dispute Resolution for Low Value Civil Claims* (Online Dispute Resolution Advisory Group) available at www.judiciary.uk/wp-content/uploads/2015/02/Online-Dispute-Resolution-Final-Web-Version1.pdf.

Cortés, Pablo 2010. 'Developing Online Dispute Resolution for Consumers in the EU: A Proposal for the Regulation of Accredited Providers' (1 January 2010), *International Journal of Law and Information Technology* 19(1): 1–28, available at https://papers.ssrn.com/sol3/papers.cfm?abstract_id=1819086, for a discussion on the need for better regulatory standards for mandatory ODR.

  2010. *Online Dispute Resolution for Consumers in the European Union*. Abingdon and New York: Routledge, available at www.oapen.org/download?type=document&docid=391038.

Ebner, Noam 2012. 'E-Mediation', in M. S. Abdel Wahab, E. Katsh and D. Rainey (eds.) *Online Dispute Resolution: Theory and Practice*. The Hague: Eleven International Publishing, 357–82, available at https://ssrn.com/abstract=2161451.

Harkens, Adam 2019. 'Fairness in Algorithmic Decision-making: Trade-offs, Policy Choices, and Procedural Protections', *Amicus Curiae (New Series)* 1(1): 84–96.

Hörnle, Julia 2012. 'Encouraging Online Dispute Resolution in the EU and Beyond – Keeping Costs Low or Standards High?' (29 September 2012), Queen Mary School of Law Legal Studies Research Paper No. 122/2012, available at https://ssrn.com/abstract=2154214 or http://dx.doi.org/10.2139/ssrn.2154214.

Kim Woojong 2016. 'Critical Evaluation of the Online Dispute Resolution for Cross-border Consumer Transaction Under E-commerce' (27 May 2016), available at https://ssrn.com/abstract=2853303 or http://dx.doi.org/10.2139/ssrn.2853303.

Laidlaw, Emily 2019. 'Re-imagining Resolution of Online Defamation Disputes', *Osgoode Hall Law Journal* 56(1): 162–202, available at https://digitalcommons.osgoode.yorku.ca/ohlj/vol56/iss1/8https://digitalcommons.osgoode.yorku.ca/cgi/viewcontent.cgi?article=3390&context=ohlj.

Larson, David A. 2019. 'Designing and Implementing a State Court ODR System: From Disappointment to Celebration', *Journal of Dispute Resolution* 2019(2): 77–102, available at https://scholarship.law.missouri.edu/jdr/vol2019/iss2/7.

Lodder, Arno R. and John Zeleznikow 2005. 'Developing an Online Dispute Resolution Environment: Dialogue Tools and Negotiation Support Systems in a Three-step Model', *Harvard Negotiation Law Review* 10: 287–337, available at https://ssrn.com/abstract=1008802.

Negi, Chitranjali 2015. 'Concept Online Dispute Resolution in India' (19 April 2015), available at https://ssrn.com/abstract=2596267 or http://dx.doi.org/10.2139/ssrn.2596267.

Quek Anderson, Dorcas 2018. 'Ethical Concerns in Court-Connected Online Dispute Resolution', *International Journal of Online Dispute Resolution* 5(1-2): 1–19, Singapore Management University School of Law Research Paper No. 40/2019, available at https://ink.library.smu.edu.sg/cgi/viewcontent.cgi?article=4860&context=sol_research.

Roberge, Jean-François and Veronique Fraser 2018. 'Access to Commercial Justice: A Roadmap for Online Dispute Resolution (ODR) Design for Small and Medium-sized Businesses (SMEs) Disputes', (9 December 2018), *Ohio State Journal on Dispute Resolution*, available at SSRN: https://ssrn.com/abstract=3299246.

Rule, Colin 2017. 'Designing a Global Online Dispute Resolution System: Lessons Learned From Ebay', *University of St. Thomas Law Journal* 13: 354–69, available at https://ir.stthomas.edu/ustlj/vol13/iss2/10/.

Salter, Shannon 2017. 'Online Dispute Resolution and Justice System Integration: British Columbia's Civil Resolution', *Windsor Yearbook of Access to Justice* 34: 112–29, available at SSRN: https://ssrn.com/abstract=2965745 or http://dx.doi.org/10.2139/ssrn.2965745.

Schmitz, Amy J. and Colin Rule 2019. 'Online Dispute Resolution for Smart Contracts', *Journal of Dispute Resolution* 2019: 103–25, University of Missouri School of Law Legal Studies Research Paper No. 2019-11, available at SSRN: https://ssrn.com/abstract=3410450.

Sela, Ayelet 2016. 'Can Computers Be Fair? How Automated and Human-powered Online Dispute Resolution Affect Procedural Justice in Mediation and Arbitration', (20 December 2016), *Ohio State Journal on Dispute Resolution* 33: 91–148, available at https://ssrn.com/abstract=3074311.

UNCITRAL 'UNCITRAL Technical Notes on Online Dispute Resolution', available at www.uncitral.org/pdf/english/texts/odr/V1700382_English_Technical_Notes_on_ODR.pdf.

van den Heuvel, Esther 2000. 'Online Dispute Resolution as a Solution to Cross-Border E-Disputes: An Introduction to ODR', available at www.oecd.org/internet/consumer/1878940.pdf.

Wing, Leah 2016. 'Ethical Principles for Online Dispute Resolution: A GPS Device for the Field', *International Journal of Online Dispute Resolution* 3(1): 12–29, available at SSRN: https://ssrn.com/abstract=2973278.

Xu Alison (Lu) 2017. 'Chinese Judicial Justice on the Cloud: A Future Call or a Pandora's Box? An Analysis of the "Intelligent Court System" of China', *Information and Communications Technology Law* 26(1): 59–71, available at http://eprints.whiterose.ac.uk/119304/1/13600834.2017.pdf.

CHAPTER 13 INSTITUTIONALISATION OF ADR

Ahmed, M. and Dorcas Quek Anderson 2019. 'Expanding the Scope of Dispute Resolution and Access to Justice', *Civil Justice Quarterly* 38(1): 1–8, available at https://ink.library.smu.edu.sg/sol_research/2838.

Blomgren, Lisa, Susan Raines, Timothy Hedeen and Lisa-Marie Napoli 2010. 'Mediation in Employment and Creeping Legalism: Implications for Dispute Systems Design', *Journal of Dispute Resolution* 2010(1): 129–50, available at https://scholarship.law.missouri.edu/jdr/vol2010/iss1/7.

Dingwall, Robert and Emilie Cloatre 2006. 'Vanishing Trials: An English Perspective', *Journal of Dispute Resolution* 2006(1): 51–70, available at https://scholarship.law.missouri.edu/jdr/vol2006/iss1/7.

Feeley, Malcolm M. 2019. 'Private Alternatives to Criminal Courts: The Future is All Around Us', *Columbia Law Review Online* 119: 38–84, available at https://works.bepress.com/malcolm_feeley/254/.

Flood, John A. and Andrew G. Caiger 1993. 'Lawyers and Arbitration: The Juridification of Construction Disputes', *The Modern Law Review* 56(3): 412–40, available

at www.academia.edu/1404731/Lawyers_and_arbitration_the_juridification_of_
construction_disputes.

Koch, Michael 2019. 'Problem with your Bank Account? Tell It to the . . . Arbitrator?',
Boston College Law Review 60: 1605–40, available at https://lawdigitalcommons.bc
.edu/bclr/vol60/iss6/4.

Levinson, Marsha 2019. 'Mandatory Arbitration: How the current System Perpetuates
Sexual Harassment Cultures in the Workplace', *Santa Clara Law Review* 59(2):
485–524, available at https://digitalcommons.law.scu.edu/lawreview/vol59/iss2/6.

Menkel-Meadow, Carrie J. 2010. 'Maintaining ADR Integrity' (19 August 2010), *Alternatives to the High Cost of Litigation* 27(1): 7–9, January 2009, UC Irvine School of
Law Research Paper No. 2009-6, available at https://ssrn.com/abstract=1340185.

  2013. 'Regulation of Dispute Resolution in the United States of America: From the
Formal to the Informal to the "Semi-formal"', Georgetown Law Faculty Publications and Other Works 1291, 419–54, available at https://scholarship.law
.georgetown.edu/facpub/1291.

Minzner, Carl F. 2011. 'China's Turn against Law', *American Journal of Comparative
Law* 59: 935–84, available at https://ir.lawnet.fordham.edu/faculty_scholarship/4.

Nolan-Haley, J. 2018. 'Mediation, Self-represented Parties, and Access to Justice:
Getting There From Here', *Fordham Law Review Online* 87(1), available at
https://ir.lawnet.fordham.edu/flro/vol87/iss1/15.

Palmer, Michael 2014. 'Formalisation of Alternative Dispute Resolution Processes:
Some Socio-legal Thoughts', in Joachim Zekoll, Moritz Bälz and Iwo Amelung
(eds.) *Formalisation and Flexibilisation in Dispute Resolution*. Leiden: Brill, 15–44.

Pappas, Brian A. 2015. 'Med-Arb and the Legalization of Alternative Dispute Resolution', *Harvard Negotiation Law Review* 20: 157–203, available at https://works
.bepress.com/brian-pappas/1/.

Press, Sharon 1997. 'Institutionalization: Savior or Saboteur of Mediation?', Faculty
Scholarship. Paper No. 316, available at http://open.mitchellhamline.edu/facsch/
316.

Quek Anderson, Dorcas 2019. 'The Convergence of ADR and ODR within the Courts:
The Impact on Access to Justice', *Civil Justice Quarterly* 38(1): 126–43, available
at https://ink.library.smu.edu.sg/cgi/viewcontent.cgi?article=4800&context=sol_
research.

  2019. 'Ethical Concerns in Court-connected Online Dispute Resolution', *International Journal of Online Dispute Resolution* 5(1-2): 20–38, available at https://
ink.library.smu.edu.sg/sol_research/2902.

Quek Anderson, Dorcas, E. Chua and T. M. Ngo 2018. 'How Should the Courts Know
Whether a Dispute Is Ready and Suitable for Mediation? An Empirical Analysis of
the Singapore Courts' Referral of Civil Disputes to Mediation', *Harvard Negotiation Law Review* 23(2): 101–43, available at https://ink.library.smu.edu.sg/sol_
research/2791.

CHAPTER 14 REFLECTIONS

Menkel-Meadow, Carrie J. 2009. 'Maintaining ADR Integrity', *Alternatives to the High
Cost of Litigation* 27(1): 7–9, UC Irvine School of Law Research Paper No. 2009-6,
available at SSRN: https://ssrn.com/abstract=1340185.

Recommended Viewing

Chapter 1 Introduction

Little Injustices (1981)

This is a film created by one of the fiercest critics of the ADR movement, anthropologist Laura Nader, sister of consumer advocate Ralph Nader. It is in large part a study of problem-solving in the local courts of a Zapotec Indian village in Oaxaca, Mexico, in the late 1950s. As Nader observed during her fieldwork there, in dealing with the disputes of everyday life, the court's approach was to look for balanced outcomes rather than to apportion blame to the parties. This is nicely illustrated in the court's handling of a case in which a truck driver damages a basket of chillies. Insights from this fieldwork experience are then used to explore issues of access to justice in the United States.

Background Readings

Denvir, John 2004. 'What Movies Can Teach Law Students', in Michael Freeman (ed.) *Law and Popular Culture* [Current Legal Issues 2004, Vol. 7] Oxford: Oxford University Press, 183–93.

Nader, L. 2002. 'Moving On – Comprehending Anthropologies of Law', in J. Starr and M. Goodale (eds.) *Practicing Ethnography in Law: New Dialogues, Enduring Methods*. New York: Palgrave Macmillan, 190–201.

Interview with Philip Gulliver

Gulliver, P. 2004. Interview with Philip Gulliver [Video file], available at www.dspace.cam.ac.uk/handle/1810/448.

Chapter 2 Cultures of Decision-making: Precursors to the Emergence of ADR

Little Injustices (1981)

This is a film created by one of the fiercest critics of the ADR movement, anthropologist Laura Nader, sister of consumer advocate Ralph Nader. It is in large part a study of problem-solving in the local courts of a Zapotec Indian village in Oaxaca, Mexico, in the late 1950s. As Nader observed during her fieldwork there, in dealing with the disputes of everyday life, the court's approach was to look for balanced outcomes rather than to apportion blame to the parties. This is nicely illustrated in the court's handling of a case in which a track driver damages a basket of chillies. Insights from this fieldwork experience are then used to explore issue of access to justice in the United States.

Background Reading

Nader, L. 2002. 'Moving On – Comprehending Anthropologies of Law', in J. Starr and M. Goodale (eds.) *Practicing Ethnography in Law: New Dialogues, Enduring Methods*. New York: Palgrave Macmillan, 190–201.

Chapter 3 The Debates around Civil Justice and the Movement towards Procedural Innovation

Intolerable Cruelty (2003)

This is a popular film which tells the tale of a Beverly Hills divorce lawyer – a key member of a professional association called the National Organization of Matrimonial Attorneys – with a fearsome hardball status as the litigator who always wins very favourable settlements for female parties, and super-effective in shielding the personal fortunes of male parties. He is practising in present-day Los Angeles, but encounters difficulties of various kinds in a case involving Mrs Marylin Rexroth, a very experienced party to matrimonial proceedings. The divorce lawyer sees premarital and matrimonial processes almost exclusively through the lens of tense negotiation and elaborate court-room antics.

Wedding Crashers (2005)

This movie opens with a scene in which the male stars (Owen Wilson and Vince Vaughn) co-mediated a divorce dispute between two polarised parties. Although there is much slapstick in the film, it does provide an interesting example of divorce mediation, and of the growing impact of ADR even in cinema representations of justice, which tend to be predominantly court room dramas or litigation of the kind characterised in *Intolerable Cruelty*.

Background Reading

Farkas, Brian and Lara Traum 2017. 'The History and Legacy of the Pound Conferences' (15 May 2017), *Cardozo Journal of Conflict Resolution* 18: 67, available at SSRN: https://ssrn.com/abstract=2968653.

Chapter 4 Disputes and Dispute Processes

Charisma (1999)

This Japanese film is a drama about a dispute between a number of people about an exceptional but possibly toxic tree growing in a local forest. The film mainly focuses on a police negotiator who, having failed to prevent the death of an important hostage, has been relieved of his official duties. He is surrounded by many divergent views about the future of the tree, and has to decide which best to help promote. The movie brings out the tension between individual and collective interest in Japanese society, offers an ecological message, but, most importantly, portrays the manner in which a dispute can get out of hand and turn into violence.

Background Reading

Mes, T. 2001. 'Charisma', available at www.midnighteye.com/reviews/charisma/.

Chapter 5 Development of Disputes, Avoidance and Self-help

Karaoke Court

This is an arbitration process and live performance where participants select, prepare and perform songs as a way of resolving their disputes with each other. The performance is overseen by the Karaoke Court judge, who invites the audience as 'jury' to decide who should win each case. The processes and decision of the Karaoke Court are made legally binding via the participants' signing of an arbitration contract. The work is inspired by Eskimo and Inuit tradition of Song Duels, where litigants presented grievances to the entire community for judgment in the form of humorous and satirical song. Available at http://lawsimagination.weebly.com/karaoke-court.html.

See also: www.youtube.com/watch?v=4s1yYLFPfkM; www.theguardian.com/artanddesign/2016/jun/22/karaoke-court-jack-tan-artist-yard-theatre.

North Country (2005)

This is a disturbing story of gender inequality at the workplace, and how women had to practise avoidance in various ways to survive at the workplace despite constant sexual harassment.

Prisoners (2013)

This is a moving and dark film about a man whose daughter and friend's daughter go missing – they slip out from a Thanksgiving dinner and fail to return. The father, Keller Dover, becomes very violent towards a troubled loner – a young man with likely mental disabilities – who the father believes has abducted them, when the police fail to charge him on grounds of insufficient evidence. The futility of the violent response to the troubled situation is carefully characterised in the film.

Background Readings

Cadagan, Maria F. 2009. 'Section One: International Parental Abduction: New York Law and the Convention on the Rights of the Child', *New York City Law Review* 12(2): 474–87.

Mnookin, Jennifer L. 2005. 'Reproducing a Trial: Evidence and Its Assessment in Paradise Lost', in Austin Sarat, Lawrence Douglas and Martha Merrill Umphrey (eds.) *Law on the Screen*. Stanford CA: Stanford University Press, 153–200.

Shalev, Karen, Martin Schaefer, Alex Morgan 2009. 'Investigating Missing Person Cases: How Can We Learn Where They Go or How Far They Travel?' *International Journal of Police Science and Management* 11(2): 123–9.

Smolin, David M. 2011. 'The Missing Girls of China: Population, Policy, Culture, Gender, Abortion, Abandonment, and Adoption in East-Asian Perspective', *Cumberland Law Review* 41(1): 1–66.

Stefan, Cristian-Eduard 2013. 'Management of Crime Scene Investigation in the Case of Missing Children', *Public Security Studies/Studii de Securitate Publica* 2(4): 144–50.

Chapter 6 Negotiations

Draft Day (2013)

This is a US football movie. However, no football is really played in the film. Indeed, the film does not even focus on an athlete or a coach but, rather, explores the work of a team's general manager. This is Sonny Weaver Jr, who takes over management of the struggling Cleveland Browns. In an effort to improve the team's fortunes, Sonny makes several unorthodox moves on the league's draft day, when each team picks new prospects to join its roster. Essentially this is a study in sports business negotiation, and office politics, and particularly when the negotiations are finally being concluded in the movie's last fifteen minutes or so, *Draft Day* offers interesting insights into the management of the negotiation process.

Background Reading

Ruud, J. K., W. N. Ruud and F. Moussavi 2017. 'You've Got A Deal! Using the Film Draft Day to Teach Fundamental Contract Law and Analytical Skills', *Journal of Legal Studies Education* 34(1): 41–61.

Lost in Beijing (Pingguo) (2007)

'Apple' Li and her husband are migrant workers in Beijing. Apple works in a foot-massage parlour owned by Lin Dong (he and his wife, Wang Mei, are wealthy but childless and approaching middle age). Lin owns a massage business. One afternoon he rapes one of his workers, Apple, while she is drunk. But Apple's husband, An Kun, a window washer, witnesses the assault. He is angry not only with Lin but also with his wife, and he seeks compensation. Apple discovers that she is pregnant and is not sure whether it is her husband or her boss who is the father. And this complicates the 'compensation' negotiations. Lin wants to buy the child; Wang agrees but has conditions; An Kun goes back and forth and barely contains his anger; Li gives birth. Among other things, a useful study of gender inequalities in negotiation, as the two men negotiate and argue over how to tie up a deal, but the assaulted woman, Apple, is not considered an important part of the negotiation process.

Background Readings

Chan Kam Wing and Will Buckingham 2008. 'Is China Abolishing the Hukou System', *China Quarterly* 2008(195): 582–606.

Sherwin, Richard K. 2005. 'Anti-Oedipus, Lynch: Initiatory Rites and the Ordeal of Justice', in Austin Sarat, Lawrence Douglas and Martha Merrill Umphrey (eds.) *Law on the Screen*. Stanford: Stanford University Press, 106–53.

Yang Xiushi and Xia Guomei 2008. 'Temporary Migration and STD/HIV Risky Sexual Behavior: A Population-based Analysis of Gender Differences in China', *Social Problems* 55(3): 322–46.

Chapter 7 Mediation

The Story of Qiu (Qiu Ju Da Guansi) (1992)

This movie explores one Chinese woman's effort to obtain justice against the headman of her village, who is part bully and part hero, in the face of a system that through mediation repeatedly creates barriers for her. The film asks fundamental, eternal questions about dispute resolution. Her quest – from village, to township, to county seat, to city – leads to unexpected consequences, especially when she hands over control of her case to a lawyer, so that the outcome is far from the result that she wished for, and in so doing the film also portrays the disadvantages of adjudication. Running through the film is a series of issues. How is mediation carried out in China, and what does it achieve? What roles do social institutions play, as compared with official, legal institutions? And what is the relationship between mediation, law and justice in China's political-legal culture? The answers are especially complex in traditional settings that are in the midst of rapid modernisation.

Background Reading

Cohen, J. A. and J. L. Cohen 2007. 'Did Qiu Ju Get Good Legal Advice?', in
     C. K. Creekmur and M. Sidel (eds.) *Cinema, Law, and the State in Asia*. Gordons-
     ville, USA: Palgrave Macmillan, 161–74.

Chapter 8 Umpiring: Courts and Tribunals

Erin Brockovitch (2000)

This is a drama based on a real case about class-action litigation concerning
the quest for redress in a major environmental pollution case in which the
heroic figure is a resolute filing clerk working for a minor law firm. She is an
unemployed single mother, desperate to find a job, but down on luck in her
life. She pushes the law firm who lost her road accident case in court into
giving her a temporary job, but then looking through materials on a pro-bono
case in which her firm has responsibility but little confidence or money with
which to handle the case, she realises that strange-looking real estate transactions disguise a local problem of serious pollution from the plant of a public
utilities company. This problem is one of deadly toxic waste that the company
has been illegally discarding and which has seriously harmed local residents.
Through Erin's determination to see justice done, a series of events – naming,
blaming and claiming – unfolds. With some help from external expert litigators, her law firm successfully brings class-action lawsuits against a powerful
and wealthy corporation that had been determined not to admit any liability
for the grievous harm done to local people.

Background Readings

Asimow, M. and S. Mader (eds.) *Law and Popular Culture: A Course Book*. 2nd ed.
     New York: Peter Lang, especially Chapters 14 ('Family Law. Assigned Film: Kra-
     mer vs. Kramer 1979', 302–20) 12 ('The Civil Justice System. Assigned Film:
     A Civil Action 1998', 241–70) and 13 ('Civil Rights. Assigned Film: Philadelphia
     1993', 271–301).
Greenfield, S., G. Osborn and P. Robson 2010. 'Fact, Fiction and the Cinema of Justice
     (II): Specificities', in S. Greenfield, G. Osborn and P. Robson (eds.) *Film and the
     Law: The Cinema of Justice*. Oxford: Hart Publishers, 177–96.
Johnson, R. and R. Buchanan 2001. 'Getting the Insider's Story Out: What Popular Film
     Can Tell Us about Legal Method's Dirty Secrets', *Windsor Yearbook of Access to
     Justice* 20: 87–110.
Nockleby, John T. 2007. 'Introduction: Law and Popular Culture', Symposium Intro-
     duction, *Loyola Law Review* 40: 859–68.
Waldman, D. 2005. 'A Case for Corrective Criticism: A Civil Action', in A. Sarat,
     L. Douglas and M. M. Umphrey, *Law on the Screen*. Stanford, CA: Stanford
     University Press, 201–30.

Courthouse on the Horseback (*Mabei shang de fating*) (2006)

This is an extremely moving film about a circuit court and its judges in rural and mountainous southwest China (Yunnan Province) populated by ethnic minorities. Judge Feng, the main character, is a wise and humane judge, resolving minor disputes in the remote minority villages of the Yunnan mountains with compassion and skill. Although he is travelling in the area, aided by an old horse carrying all the court facilities, including a round-sized national emblem, the symbol of the state authority, as the representative of the Chinese socialist state, and indeed is very concerned with upholding the dignity of the court as a state institution in the remote countryside, he is respected and admired by the inhabitants of the mountain hamlets. A crisis occurs when the national emblem is lost, Judge Feng characterising the emblem as being just as 'holy' as the image of Buddha worshipped by local people. Much of the depiction of cases is centred on attempts at reconciling state sponsored justice and local norms and processes.

Background Readings

Berry, C. 2004. 'Introduction: Towards a Post Socialist Cinema', in C. Berry, *Postsocialist Cinema in Post-Mao China: The Cultural Revolution after the Cultural Revolution*. New York and London: Routledge, 1–21.

Black, D. A. 2004. 'Narrative Determination and the Figure of the Judge', in M. Freeman (ed.) *Law and Popular Culture* [Current Legal Issues 2004, Vol. 7] Oxford: Oxford University Press, 677–86.

'Chinese mayor: Judges Should Watch More American Courtroom Dramas, Action Films', available at www.hollywoodreporter.com/news/chinese-mayor-judges-should-watch-428280.

Greenfield, S., G. Osborn and P. Robson 2010. 'Missing (in) Action (I): Judges', in S. Greenfield, G. Osborn and P. Robson (eds.) *Film and the Law: The Cinema of Justice*. Oxford: Hart Publishers, 124–43.

My Cousin Vinny (1992)

Bill Gambini and Stanley Rothenstein are two friends from New York who are driving through the southern United States. They stop at a local convenience store to pick up a few snacks, but to their surprise they are then arrested. Under the impression that they have been wrongly arrested for shoplifting, they discover to their horror that they have in fact been arrested for murder and robbery offences and face the death penalty. In the need to find a lawyer who will represent them they turn to a cousin of one of the detainees. However, cousin Vinny (Vincent Laguardia Gambini) is newly qualified and has no trial experience. So, inexperienced Vinny has to defend his clients in an unfriendly courtroom, with a crusty judge, local interests and prejudice against big-city residents to battle against. Just when all seems lost, Vinny's fiancée,

Mona Lisa Vito, is able to use her expert knowledge as a former mechanic to show that the two young men on trial were not driving the real thieves' getaway, and so helps to show the defendants' innocence. Although a film about a criminal trial, it is an illuminating 'tongue-in-cheek' account of how experienced litigators can run rings around an inexperienced party through their better understanding of the 'real' rules of the litigation process.

Background Readings

Asimow, Michael 2004. 'Popular Culture and the American Adversarial Ideology', in Michael Freeman (ed.) *Law and Popular Culture* [Current Legal Issues 2004, Vol. 7] Oxford: Oxford University Press, 606–37.

Asimow, Michael and Shannon Mader 2013. *Law and Popular Culture: A Course Book*, 2nd ed. New York: Peter Lang, especially Chapters 2 ('The Adversary System and the Trial Genre. Assigned Film: *Anatomy of a Murder* (1959)', 23–43) 8 ('The Criminal Justice System. Assigned Television Show: *Law and Order* (Season 5, episodes 1–4)', 153–80) and 9 ('The Jury. Assigned Film: *12 Angry Men* (1957)', 181–200).

Greenfield, Steve, Guy Osborn and Peter Robson 2010. *Film and the Law: The Cinema of Justice*. 2nd ed. Oxford: Hart Publishing, especially Chapters 4 ('Strictly Court-room? Law Film and Genre', 51–67) and 5 ('The British Law Film: From Genre to Iconography', 68–79) and 6 ('Military Justice on Screen', 80–93).

Mnookin, Jennifer L. 2005. 'Reproducing a Trial: Evidence and Its Assessment in Paradise Lost', in A. Sarat, L. Douglas and M. M. Umphrey, *Law on the Screen*. Stanford, CA: Stanford University Press, 153–200.

Nead, Lynda 2004. 'Courtroom Sketching: Reflections on History, Law and the Image', in Michael Freeman (ed.) *Law and Popular Culture* [Current Legal Issues 2004, Vol. 7] Oxford: Oxford University Press, 173–82.

Philadelphia (1993)

A gay lawyer infected with AIDS, is fired from his law firm in fear that they might contract AIDS from him. He sues his former law firm with the help of a homophobic lawyer, Joe Miller. During the court battle, Miller sees that Beckett is no different than any human being, overcomes his homophobia and helps to win the case before AIDS overcomes the plaintiff. The film shows, inter alia, that stubbornness on the part of the law firm's senior partners meant that a negotiated settlement could not be reached, and for the law firm that litigation was not a good alternative to a negotiated outcome.

Background Readings

Asimow, Michael and Shannon Mader 2013. 'Civil Rights. Assigned Film: Philadelphia (1993)', in Michael Asimow and Shannon Mader, *Law and Popular Culture: A Course Book*, 2nd ed. New York: Peter Lang, 271–301.

Boso, Luke A. 2013. 'Urban Bias, Rural Sexual Minorities, and the Courts', *UCLA Law Review* 60(3): 562–637.

Gilden, Andrew 2013. 'Cyberbullying and the Innocence Narrative', *Harvard Civil Rights-Civil Liberties Law Review* 48(2): 357–408.

Shapiro, Michael J. 2005. 'The Racial-Spatial Order and the Law: Devil in a Blue Dress', in A. Sarat, L. Douglas and M. M. Umphrey, *Law on the Screen*. Stanford, CA: Stanford University Press, 82–105.

Chapter 9 Umpiring: Arbitration

The Arbitration (2016)

An Arbitration panel is constituted to find out the truth when the CEO of a company who has an affair with his employee is sued for sexually harassing her.

Chapter 10 Hybrid Forms and Processual Experimentation

I Am Sam (2001)

A moving account of a child custody dispute involving a caring father, who is a person with mental disability. His seven-year-old daughter, for whom he has much love and a great sense of responsibility, is taken away from him by child welfare authorities. The film shows the difficulties in using adjudication by itself as a mode for assessing evidence and resolving complex family disputes, the value of negotiated outcomes, and the flexibility that willingness to negotiate in good faith can bring to the resolution of a dispute so as to create 'win–win' outcomes. Learning from each other through the negotiation process and the importance of inclusiveness are also important themes.

Background Readings

Menkel-Meadow, Carrie J. 2005. 'Legal Negotiation in Popular Culture: What Are We Bargaining For?', in M. D. A. Freeman (ed.) *Law and Popular Culture*. Oxford: Oxford University Press.

Murdach, Allison D. 2006. 'Social Work in the Movies: Another Look', *Social Work* 51(3): 269–72.

Chapter 11 The Ombuds and its Diffusion: From Public to Private

The Movie about the Ombudsman for Children in Norway

This is a short movie about the Ombudsman for Children in Norway, which is intended to assist protection of the rights of children, and how those with worries about a child's family or school position can look for assistance from the Ombudsman (www.youtube.com/watch?v=dLa9rvPxEk4).

The Insider (1999)

The Insider tells the true story of a man who decided to tell the world about what major tobacco companies in the United States knew about and held from the public – the truth about the dangers of smoking cigarettes. A research scientist in one of the major tobacco firms is fired but tells his story to a producer for the CBS TV documentary programme '60 Minutes', looking to expose the dishonesty of the cigarette industry. But external pressure kills the story. The scientist is sued and subjected to a smear campaign so as to stop the full story reaching the public. The film shows the importance of having safe channels of complaint within and outside organisations so that complaints about misconduct by a company or other organisation, which it is in the public interest to bring to light, can be made and the complainant not victimised.

Background Readings

Beller, Rachel 2011. 'Whistleblower Protection Legislation of the East and West: Can It Really Reduce Corporate Fraud and Improve Corporate Governance – A Study of the Successes and Failures of Whistleblower Protection Legislation in the US and China', *NYU Journal of Law and Business* 7(2): 873–930.

Haigh, Richard and Peter Bowal 2012. 'Whistleblowing and Freedom of Conscience: Towards a New Legal Analysis', *Dalhousie Law Journal* 35(1): 89–126.

Pascoe, Janine and Michelle Welsh 2011. 'Whistleblowing, Ethics and Corporate Culture: Theory and Practice in Australia', *Common Law World Review* 40(2):144–73.

Robertson, Michael 2004. 'Seeing Blind Spots: Corporate Misconduct in Film and Law', in Michael Freeman (ed.) *Law and Popular Culture*. [Current Legal Issues 2004, Vol. 7] Oxford: Oxford University Press, 385–403.

Chapter 12 Online Dispute Resolution and its Diffusion: From Private to Public

Professor Richard Susskind OBE, 'The Case for Online Courts', chaired by Professor Dame Hazel Genn, UCL LAWS, Published 20 February 2017, UCL Judicial Institute Lecture and Panel Discussion, at www.youtube.com/watch?v= VEItwvisanQ.

The Social Network (2010)

Harvard student Mark Zuckerberg creates the social networking site that would become known as Facebook. However, he is subsequently sued by two brothers who claimed he stole their idea, and the co-founder who was later pushed out of the business. Not a film about ODR, but a film showing disputes about online innovations.

The Girl with the Dragon Tattoo (2011)

This English-language version (there is a Swedish-language version that predates it) is the story of a disgraced journalist, Mikael Blomkvist (Daniel Craig), as he investigates the long-term disappearance of a wealthy patriarch's niece. He is aided by a computer hacker named Lisbeth Salander, who uses her e-skills to help uncover corruption, torture and murder.

Background Readings

Gilden, Andrew 2013. 'Cyberbullying and the Innocence Narrative', *Harvard Civil Rights-Civil Liberties Law Review* 48(2): 357–408.

Heo Soong Wook 2101. 'The Protection of Private Information in the Internet under Tort Law in Korea: From the Perspectives of Three Major Legal Conceptions of Law', *Journal of Korean Law* 1: 109–24.

Poblet, M., P. Casanovas, J. López-Cobo, A. Cabrerizo and J. Prieto 2010. 'Mediation, ODR, and the web 2.0: A Case for Relational Justice', *AI Approaches to the Complexity of Legal Systems. Complex Systems, the Semantic Web, Ontologies, Argumentation, and Dialogue*, 205–16.

Tripathi, S. M. and Ors 2009. 'Internet Governance: A Developing Nation's Call for Administrative Legal Reform', *International Journal of Legal Information* (formerly *International Journal of Law Libraries*) 37: 368–84.

Chapter 13 Institutionalisation of ADR

The Sweet Hereafter (1997)

Austin Sarat writes that this film about a small town and a tragic accident that befell many of its families reminded him that the 'naming, blaming and claiming' paradigm is a powerful but neglected analytical tool:

> *The Sweet Hereafter* provides a vehicle for understanding the manner in which civil justice is mythologized in that world of images. The *Sweet Hereafter* tells a story in words and pictures of the seldom seen processes of naming, blaming, and claiming. The film positions law against fate, thereby exposing the fragility and the power of law, as well as the avoidance and allure of litigation. At this point, I am particularly interested in highlighting the exploration of the contingency and variability in the reception of law's appeals that are presented in *The Sweet Hereafter*. Through such an exploration, this film provides one counterweight against media portraits of the much ballyhooed litigation explosion (Sarat 2000: 429).

Background Reading

Sarat, A. 2000. 'Exploring the Hidden Domains of Civil Justice: Naming, Blaming, and Claiming in Popular Culture', *DePaul Law Review* 50: 425–52.

Index

A2J Author, 299
Abel, Richard, 17, 37, 56–7, 73, 102, 199, 305, 308
Academy of Family Mediators, 62
access to justice, 51
  alternative outcomes, 195
  human right, 52–3
  legal aid, 53
  legal education, 54
  legal poverty, 52
  litigation and judicial reforms, 53
  ombuds, 278–80
  Online Dispute Resolution (ODR), 289, 298
  tribunals, 210–11
active impartiality, 180
adjudication, 124
  critique of, 52
  heterogeneous practice, 200–1
Agent Orange case, 261
Al-Ramahi, Aseel, 223
alternative dispute resolution
  and lawyers, 325–6
  contemporary scene, 70–2
  critiques, 67–70
  new professionals, 61–2
  re-modelling legal practice, 63–5
  routinisation, 317–18
  United States, 36
  Woolf Report, 38
Althusser, Louis, 56, 61
American Arbitration Association, 34, 173, 178
American Bar Association, 150, 178
Amerindians, 78
Arab Centre for Domain Name Dispute Resolution (ACDR), 294
arbitration, 237
  commercial
    development of, 217–18

UNCITRAL Model Law on International Commercial Arbitration, 219–21
  compulsory, 216, 267–8
  court-annexed systems, 216, 254
    case against, 268
    case for, 267–8
    Middlesex Multi-Door Courthouse (MMDC), 204–5
  final-offer, 237
  High-Low agreements, 237
  ideology and reality diverging, 215
  imperfect control of practice, 216
  institutionalisation, 216
  juridification, 318
  labour relations, 215, 237
  neutral stranger, 191, 213
  private, 213, 215
  pure form, 213–15
  rent-a-judge, 268–70
  special masters, 259–62
  United States, 36
arbitrators
  court-annexed arbitration, 267
  med-arb, 240
  not bound by precedent, 214
  quality of, 216
arena councils, 80
Arusha people, 84, 89, 96, 113
Asian Domain Name Dispute Resolution Centre (ADNDRC), 294
Auerbach, Jerold, 17, 25–6, 36–7, 39–40, 44–5, 52, 112, 305
Australia, 62, 183, 205
avoidance approach, 75–6, 106–8
  and social context, 121–2
  avoidance ethic, 111
  basis of decision-making, 112

avoidance approach (cont.)
  changing legal practice, 108
  grievance apathy, 110
  harmony ideology, 111–12
  lumping grievances, 110
  protracted, 110
  social complexity, 112
  temporary, 109

Bailey, Frederick, 80
balancing of equities, 201
Bar Council, 64, 281
Barak, Gregg, 117
bargaining
  divorce, 148
  mediation, 166
barristers, England, 63, 258, 276, 313
Barth, F., 161
Barton, R. F., 43, 86, 227
Baumgartner, Mary P., 112
Bechuanaland, 91, 228
Beldam Committee, 233
best alternative to a negotiated agreement
    (BATNA), 126, 141
big men, 89–91
blaming, 73, 102–3, 105, 114, 307–12
Blind Bidding, ODR, 292
Bodde, Derk, 192
Bohannan, Paul, 10, 75
Bok, Derek, 52, 54
borough courts, 23
Botswana, 228
Bottomley, A., 182
Boulle, Laurence, 163
Brandt, Paul, 23
Brazil, Wayne D., 264
Briggs, Lord Justice, 6, 299
British Association of Lawyer Mediators
    (BALM), 65
Broderick, Raymond, 267–8
Brown, Henry, 64
Burger, Warren, 11, 17, 52
Bush, R. A., Baruch, 153, 161, 168, 181

Cahill, M., 142, 321
Caiger, Andrew, 318
Canada, 47, 62, 201, 280
Cappelletti, Mauro, 52, 54, 302
case management
  Australia, 205
  English procedure, 5, 65–6, 205, 232–4, 303
  special masters, 259–62

centralisation, 46
Centre for Dispute Resolution (CEDR),
    62, 64
Chancery, 198, 208, 260
Charles XII, 275
Chen Yongzhu, 253–4
China
  Communist justice, 28–33, 40–1, 48–9
  Cultural Revolution, 117
  domestic violence, 118
  evaluative mediation, 171
  formal justice, 19–20
  guilds, 36
  harmony ideology, 111–12, 117, 222, 319
  judge-mediation, 250–4
  litigation, 111
  med-arb, 242
  mediation
    agreements, 188–90
    Communist regime, 40–1
    post-Mao, 157
  neutral third parties, 157
  ombuds, transplanting to, 284–5
  Online Dispute Resolution (ODR), 295–7
  popular justice, 28
China International Economic and Trade
    Arbitration Commission (CIETAC),
    222, 242
Chinatowns, 33
Chornenki, Genevieve, 181–2
Chotalia, Shirish P., 12
civil justice
  and state power, 56
  Canada, 47
  formal. See formal justice
  informal. See informal justice
  private justice, 268–70
  settlement objective, 230–4
  Woolf Report, 67
civil law courts
  lay assessors, 209
civil law systems
  Civil Procedure Rules. See Civil
    Procedure Rules
Civil Procedure Rules, 5, 65, 206, 230,
    249–50
  broad opening statement, 231
  conduct of litigation process, 232–4
  pre-litigation phase, 231–2
civil society, vs. state power, 46
claiming, 102, 105, 308–12
Clastres, Pierre, 79

coercion. *See* self-help
Cohen, Amy, 69–70
Collins, Randall, 119–21
colonialism, 24–5, 57, 209, 222
Colosi, Tom, 130–2, 142
Comaroff, John L., 228
command
   institutionalised, 91–9
   third-party interventions, 89–91
commercial arbitration
   development of, 217–18
   UNCITRAL Model Law on International
      Commercial Arbitration, 219–21
common law jurisdictions
   arbitrators not bound by precedent, 214
   lawyers' role, 220–2
   neutrality, 236
   ombuds, 274, 277
communist systems, 28–33, 40–1, 48–9
competitive strategies, 145
complementary justice, 52
comprehensive justice centre, 307–8
compulsory arbitration, 216, 267–8
compulsory mediation, 254, 259
Condlin, Robert J., 147, 292–3
confidentiality, mediation, 186, 240, 243
conflict
   disputes, distinguished, 104
Confucianism, 19, 111
Conley, John M., 208, 314
consumer protection, 54
cooperative approach, negotiations, 141–3
cost-cutting strategies, 70
Council of Europe, 177
court-annexed arbitration, 216, 254,
    266–8
court-ordered mediation, 254
court-referred mediation, 255–9
courts
   appellate structures, 195–6
   borough courts, 23
   centralisation, 46
   Chancery, 198, 208
   colonial, 24–5, 193, 198
   English history, 22–4
   forum shopping, 195
   heterogeneous practice, 200–1
   landlord tenant, 57
   link to state, 191
   Middlesex Multi-Door Courthouse
      (MMDC). *See* Middlesex Multi-Door
      Courthouse (MMDC)

Piepowder courts, 23–4
   popular elements, 209–10
   role, 197–200
   sponsoring settlements, 65–7, 326
   Tolzey courts, 24
CPR Institute of Dispute Resolution,
    63–4
Croley, Steven, 263
Crouch, Richard E., 182
Cybersettle, ODR, 292
cybersquatting, 293–4
Czech Arbitration Court Arbitration Centre for
    Internet Disputes, 294

Damaška, Mirjan, 8, 196–7, 251
Danzig, Richard, 10, 52
Dawson, John P., 209
decisions
   command attributes, 89–91
   dyads, 81
   institutionalised command, 89–99
   legacy of command, 77–9
   mediatory interventions, 86–9
   negotiations
      bilateral exchange, 82
      partisans, 82, 128
      third-party interventions, 82–3
   public decision-making, 76–7
   revision of public decision-making, 79
   third-party interventions, 84–5
   triads, 81
Denlow, Morton, 248
Denti, Olga, 108
Dezalay, Yves, 217–18
Dickens, Charles, 198
Dingwall, Robert, 178
dispute processes
   and social context, 121–2
   avoidance. *See* avoidance approach
   categories of responses, 104–6
   concept, 73–5, 101–2
   creative lawyering, 109
   decision-making. *See* decisions
   hybrid forms. *See* hybrid forms
   perceived injurious experience (PIE),
      103
   typologies of response, 75
      avoidance approach, 75–6
      public decision-making, 76
      self-help, 76
   unperceived injurious experience
      (unPIE), 103

disputes
   conflict, distinguished, 103
   pre-emption, 106–8
Doo Leigh-wai, 34
Douglas, Ann, 132–4, 165
duels, 3, 76, 111, 228
Durkheim, Émile, 61, 74, 121
Duyree, M. A., 184
Dworkin, Ronald, 77
dyads, 81, 153

early neutral evaluation (ENE), 235–7, 263–6
e-courts, 297–300
Edward I, 22
Eisele, Thomas G., 268
Elliott, David C., 236, 241
England
   early neutral evaluation (ENE), 265–6
   Mayor's and City of London court-referred
      mediation scheme, 255–9
   Solicitors in Mediation, 63
   sponsored settlements, 249–50
environmental welfare, 54
Erickson, J., 297
Erlichman, Reece, 249
ethics
   negotiations, 148–52, 177–8
ethnicity
   and informal justice, 33–4
   and mediation, 185
European Union, 1, 9, 328
evaluative mediation, 170–4
Evans-Pritchard, E., 86
evasive conduct. See avoidance approach
Exchequer, 194
expert evidence, 66
eyres, 22, 193

family disputes, rent-a-judge, 270
Family Law Bar Association, 63
family mediation
   gender, and, 182–5
Family Mediators Association (FMA), 62–3,
   236
family systems therapy, 244
Fang Xuhui, 297
Felstiner, William L., 73, 75, 102–3, 105–7, 308
feuding, 115, 121
final-offer arbitration, 237
Financial Ombuds Service (FOS), 281–2
   accountability, 283

   offer finality and consistency, 282
   process, 283
Fisher, Roger, 70, 141, 144
Fiss, Owen, 56, 58–61, 68–70, 151, 199, 247,
   321
Fitzpatrick, Peter, 48, 317, 320
flagitatio, 21
Flood, John, 48, 318
Folberg, Jay, 240
Folger, J. P., 161, 168, 264
formal justice
   China, 19–20
   Roman law, 20–2
formal law
   justice, tension between, 17
forum shopping, 195
Foucault, Michel, 56, 61, 138
Freedmen's Bureau, 36
Freeman, Michael, 37
Fried, Morton H., 91
Fu Hualing, 48, 157, 253
Fuller, Lon, 164, 167, 192, 196, 215, 238–9, 250,
   306

gacaca courts, 24
Galanter, Marc, 53, 75, 142, 247–51, 321
Galtung, Johan, 116–17
Garth, Bryant, 217–18
GATT, 218
Geertz, Clifford, 80–1
gender, and mediation, 182–5
General Council of the Bar, 233
Genn, Hazel, 67, 141, 147, 211, 259, 308
genocide, Rwanda, 24
Germany, 251–2
Gibbs, James, 10, 243
Gibson, Ronald J., 148
Gifford, Donald G., 143–4
Gilsenan, Michael, 149
Ginsberg, Tom, 219
Giordano, Michela, 108
Glanvill, Ranulf de, 194
Gluckman, Max, 10, 75
Goffman, Erving, 128–30
Goldberg, Stephen, 237–8, 240
Gottwald, Peter, 251
government. See state power
Graham, L. E., 254
Greatbatch, D., 178
Greenberg, Elayne E., 229
Greenhouse, Carol, 26–7, 111, 117

Greenidge, A. H. J., 20
Gregory, Michael, 249
grievance apathy, 105, 110
Grillo, T., 182–3
Gu Weixia, 243
guilds, 34–6
Gulliver, Philip, 13, 74–5, 84, 86, 88–9, 106–7,
    110–11, 113, 121, 123–9, 132, 134–7,
    152, 156–9, 161, 165–6, 178, 226–7, 236

Habermas, Jürgen, 58, 123, 323
Hadza people, 79
Halsey v Milton Keynes General NHS Trust
    case, 232
harmony ideology, 117, 222, 270, 319
Harrington, Christine B., 45–6, 48
Hayden, R. M., 210
Haynes, John, 246
Heilbron/Hodge Report, 5, 205
Henderson, Douglas, 163
Henry I, 193
Henry II, 22, 193
High-Low agreements, 237
Hobbes, Thomas, 77
Hoebel, E. A., 75
Hong Kong, 219, 242, 284–5
honour killings, 115
Huang, Philip, 98
Hunter, Martin, 192
hybrid forms, 225
    arbitration, 237
    Civil Procedure Rules. *See* Civil
        Procedure Rules
    court-annexed arbitration, 266–8
    court-ordered mediation, 254
    court-referred mediation, 255–9
    early neutral evaluation (ENE), 235–7,
        263–6
    judge as mediator, 250–4
    judicial promotion of settlement, 247–50
    med-arb, 238–43
    mediation, 316
    mediation and therapy, 243–6
    Mexico, 226–7
    mini-trials, 234–5
    modifications to primary processes, 230
    Philippines, 227–8
    rent-a-judge, 268–70
    settlement as civil justice, 230–4
    special masters, 259–62
    summary jury trials, 262–3

systems design, 229
Tswana people, 228

iCourthouse, ODR, 293
IDR (Europe) Ltd, 62, 64
Ifugao people, 42, 227–8
impartiality, mediators, 157, 178
In Place of Strife, 4, 65
informal justice, 48
    and ethnicity, 33–4
    changes over time, 48–9
    critiques, 56
        against settlement, 58–61
        politics, 56–8
    family relations, 43–4
    guilds, 34–6
    ideals of, 18–19
    kinship, and kingship, 42–3
    politics, 27–33
    religious motivations, 25–7
    San Francisco Community Boards, 38–40
    self-regulation, 46–8
    specialised courts, 45–6
    territorialism, 37–42
    United States, 44–6
informalism. *See* informal justice
innovations
    arbitration, 237
    court-annexed arbitration, 266–8
    early neutral evaluation (ENE), 235–7,
        263–6
    legal aid, 53
    med-arb, 238–43
    mediation and family therapy, 243–6
    mini-trials, 234–5
    rent-a-judge, 268–70
    sponsored settlements, 249–50
    summary jury trials, 262–3
Inns of Court, 276
International Centre for the Settlement of
    Investment Disputes (ICSID), 218
International Chamber of Commerce (ICC),
    217
International Dispute Resolution Centre
    (IDRC), 65
International Ombuds Association (IOA)
    Standards of Practice, 280
Internet Corporation for Assigned Names and
    Numbers (ICANN), 293
intra-party negotiations, 127–30
Ireland, 107

Jale people, 78
JAMS Endispute Inc., 63–4
Japan, 242
Jiang Shigong, 32
Joint Mediation Forum, 175
judge-shopping, 270
Judicial Arbitration and Mediation
    Services (JAMS), 269
judiciary
  as mediators, 250–4
  common law systems, 8
  democratic selection, 28
  judge-shopping, 270
  rent-a-judge, 268–70
  sponsored settlements, 326
  third-party interveners, 238
juridification, 318
juries
  mock, 235, 313
  summary jury trials, 262–3
justices of the peace, 209
Justinian, 22

Kalinga people, 86
Katsh, Ethan, 71, 290, 298
Kelly, J. B., 184–5
Kelly, J. M., 21
Kgatla people, 91–6
Kim, Anne S., 269
kinship, and kingship, 42–3
Knights of Labour, 27, 318
Koch, Klaus, 78
Kornhauser, L., 124, 147
Korobkin, Russell, 145
Kovach, Kimberlee, 171
Kritzer, Herbert, 142, 206–7
Kung San people, 79
Kunze, Axel, 251

Lambros, Thomas D., 262
landlord tenant courts, 57
Law Society, 63–4, 175, 177–8, 236, 281,
    328
lawyers
  and alternative dispute resolution,
    325–6
  litigation, 200
  professional ethics, 148–52, 177
  re-modelling legal practice, 63–5
lay assessors, 209
Leacock, E. B., 79

leaders and followers, 77
LeBaron, Michelle, 332
Lee, R. B., 79
legal aid, 53
legal poverty, 52
Leng, S. C., 209
Lévi-Strauss, Claude, 144
lex mercatoria, 217–18
litigation, 51, 73
  affordability, 53
  China, 111
  civil, 69
  commercial, 270
  conduct of process, 232–4
  English history, 22
  lawyers, 200
  pre-action protocols, 231, 234, 249, 303, 312,
    324, 326
  pre-litigation phase, 231–2
  procedural reforms, 53
litigotiation, 4, 250
Llewellyn, K., 75
Lloyd George, David, 211
Locke, John, 77
logrolling, 144
Loughlin, Martin, 76
Louis XIV, 197
Love, Lela, 171–2, 315
Lowenthal, Gary T., 141, 143–4
Lubman, S., 40
Luhmann, Richard de, 56, 138
lumping grievances, 97, 101, 107, 110, 310, 321
lying, negotiations, 149–50

Ma Xiwu Shenpan Fangshi, 28–33
MacCormack, Geoffrey, 106
Maiman, R. J., 187
Maine, Henry, 77
Malinowski, Bronislaw, 79
Markesinis, Basil, 8
Mayor's and City of London court-referred
    mediation scheme, 255–9
Mbuti people, 79
McEwen, C. A., 187
McGovern, Francis, 261
McThenia, Andrew W., 59
med-arb, 237–43
  China, 242
  confidentiality, 243
mediation
  agenda setting, 165

agreements, 69, 187–90, 319
and ethnicity, 185–6
and family therapy, 243–6
arenas, 163–5
bargaining, 166
caucasing, 169
communal interests, 157
compulsion, 316
compulsory, 254, 259
confidentiality, 186, 240
education, 315
European Directive, 2008, 315
evaluative, 170–4
feminist critique, 182
formulating agreement, 166
gender, and, 182–5
Germany, 251
hybrid forms, 316
identification of options, 165
implementation of solutions, 166–7
interventions, distinguishing, 161–3
nature, 153–4
neutral mediator, 157
neutral third party, 154–8
new professionals, 6, 167, 313, 324–5, 327
power imbalances, 180–2
power-with, 181–2
practice models, 168–74
premarital agreements, 108
principal mediator, 157
professionalisation, 313–15
Quality Mark Standard for Mediation
    (MQM), 175
rank and office of mediators, 179–80
regulation, 315
towards settlement, 166
transformative, 168
UK community, 38
US community, 39
mediators
China, 157
codes of conduct, 173
evaluative-broad, 171
evaluative-narrow, 171
facilitative-broad, 171
facilitative-narrow, 171
immunity, 174, 186
impartiality, 154–8, 178–9
Law Society Code of Conduct, 178
legitimacy, 161
Newman model, 240

non-aligned intermediaries, 64
professional ethics, 148–52
quasi-mediators, 130
rank and office, 179–80
regulation, 174–8
scope of interventions, 158–61
trash and bash approach, 174
Melanesia, 89–90
Menkel-Meadow, Carrie J., 69, 140, 142, 147,
    177–8, 289
Merry, Sally Engle, 38–9, 48, 317
Mexico, 226–7
Middlesex Multi-Door Courthouse (MMDC),
    204–5
Milner, Neal, 38
mini-trials, 233–5, 313
Mnookin, Robert H., 124, 147–8
Moore, Sally Falk, 47, 137
Morris, Clarence, 192
Mozambique, 209–10
multi-party negotiations, 131–2
Murray, Daniel E., 23
Mustill, Lord, 192

Nader, Laura, 226–7, 305, 319
NAFTA, 218
naming, 102–3, 105, 308–12
National Arbitration Forum (NAF), 294
National Conference on the Causes of Popular
    Dissatisfaction with the Administration
    of Justice. See Pound Conference
National Family Mediation (NFM), 62, 174,
    176, 185
National Institute for Dispute Resolution
    (NIDR), 62, 174
National Vocational Qualifications (NVQs),
    175
Ndembu communities, 74
Ndendeuli people, 86–9, 113
negotiations
adjudication, distinguishing, 124
agenda setting, 135
arenas, 134
Arusha people, 84
best alternative to a negotiated agreement
    (BATNA), 126, 141
bilateral, 82
conditions required, 123, 132
diplomatic, 133
ethical issues, 148–52, 177–8
external environment, and, 124

negotiations (cont.)
  features, 123
  final bargaining, 136
  implementation, 136–8
  internal complexities, 124
  intra-party, 127–30
  labour, 132–4
  limits, exploring, 135
  lying, 148–52
  multi-party, 131–2
  narrowing differences, 135
  outcome creation, 125–6
  partisans, 82, 128, 149
  performance teams, 128
  phases, 132–4
  power imbalances, 138–9
  preference sets, 126–7
  preliminary bargaining, 135
  principled negotiators, 144
  representative, 146–8
  ritual confirmation, 136
  strategies, 139
    competitive, 145
    competitive approach, 140–1
    cooperative approach, 141–3
    cost-cutting, 70
    integrative, 145–6
    logrolling, 144
  third parties, and, 124
  third-party interventions, 82–3
neighbourhood justice centres, 46
neoliberalism, 69
neutral mediator, 157, 178
neutral stranger, arbitration, 191, 213
neutral third parties, mediation, 154–8
New Guinea, 76, 78, 113
new professionals
  alternative dispute resolution, 61–3
  mediation, 6, 167, 313, 324–5, 327
New York Convention on the Recognition and
    Enforcement of Judgments of Foreign
    Arbitral Awards 1958, 219, 295
Newman, P., 240–1
North America
  colonial institutions, 25
  informal justice, 40
  med-arb, 237
  mediation and gender, 182
  mini-trials, 234–5
  special masters, 259–62
Nuer people, 86, 156

O'Barr, William M., 208, 314
ombuds
  China, transplanting to, 284–5
  definition, 273
  distinctive features, 274
  Financial Ombuds Service (FOS), 281–2
    accountability, 283
    offer finality and consistency, 282
    process, 283
  France, 9, 273
  Islamic influence, 275
  organisational, 278, 280–1
  public and private sector roles, 274
  public law model, 277–8
  Scandinavia, 275
  sectoral, 278, 281
  separation of powers, 276–7
  United Kingdom, 279–80
Online Dispute Resolution (ODR), 71, 287
  Blind Bidding, 292–3
  China, 295–7
  commercial systems, 291
  Cybersettle, 292
  cybersquatting, 293
  e-courts, 297–300
  globalisation, and, 290
  growth, 71
  initial attempts, 288
  Internet, and, 290
  online jury proceedings, 293
  regulation, 294–5
  scepticism towards, 289
  Smartsettle, 292
  Square Trade, 292
online jury proceedings, 293
ordeals, 3

Pair, Laura, 220
Palmer, Michael, 10, 48–9, 98, 118, 157, 171,
    188, 225, 253, 319
Panel of Independent Mediators, 64
partisans
  negotiations, 82, 128, 149
  non-aligned mediators, 155
Pathans, 156, 161
perceived injurious experience (PIE), 103
performance teams, negotiations, 128
Philippines, 42
Piepowder courts, 23–4
Pirie, Fernanda, 115
plea bargaining, 151

Plett, Konstanze, 8
politics, and informal justice, 27–33
popular justice, 21
    China, 28
    Mozambique, 209–10
Portugal, 27, 209
Posner, R., 263, 268
Pospisil, Leopold J., 90
Pound Conference, 39, 267, 301, 306
Pound, Roscoe, 19, 44, 305
power
    mediation
        feminist critique, 182
        power imbalances, 180–2
        rank and office of mediators, 179–80
    state. *See* state power
power-with, 181–2
pre-action protocols, 231, 234, 249, 303, 312,
    324
preference sets, 126–7
Princen, Thomas, 153, 157
principal mediator, 157
principled negotiators, 144
private arbitration, 213, 215
private judging. *See* rent-a-judge
private spheres, 42
professional ethics, lawyers, 177
public spheres
    court dominance, 3
    decision-making, 76
    Online Dispute Resolution (ODR), 288
    social world, 80

Quality Mark Standard for Mediation
    (MQM), 175
quasi-mediators, 130

Rabinovich-Einy, Orna, 71, 290, 298–9
Raiffa, Howard, 129
Randall, J. D., 196
rape, 183
Redfern, Alan, 192
reflexive law, 56, 323
religion, 25–7
rent-a-judge, 268–70
ResoLex, 65
Riskin, Leonard, 170–2
Roberts, Marian, 174–7, 186, 244–6
Roberts, Simon, 179, 255–8
Robinson, Peter, 248
Röhl, K. F., 250–1

role-playing exercises, 333–45
Roman law
    formal justice, 20–2
Rosenberg, Joshua D., 264
rule of law
    developing countries, 199
    rent-a-judge, 269
Rwanda, 24

Sachs, Albie, 209
Sainsbury, Roy, 211, 308
Sander, Frank, 7, 10, 52, 55, 63, 201, 203–4,
    237, 289, 306–7, 310
Santos, Boaventura de Sousa, 18, 28, 56, 61,
    138, 200, 323
Sarat, Austin, 73, 102, 309, 321
Sarkin, Jeremy, 25
self-help, 76, 96, 101, 113–14
    as closure, 114–15
    broad nature, 115
    characterising, 115
    confrontational tension, 120
    cultural violence, 117–18
    domestic violence, China, 118–19
    forward panic, 120
    institutionalised, 113
    instrumental and spontaneous violence, 119
    non-violent, 115
    structural violence, 116–17
    violence and time, 119
separation of powers, 194, 276–7
settlement masters. *See* special masters
settlements
    as civil justice, 230–4
    court-sponsored, 65–7, 326
    judicial promotion, 247–50
Shah-Kazemi, Sonia, 137–8, 185
Shapiro, Martin, 192–3, 195, 199–200, 206
Silberman, Linda, 261
Simmel, Georg, 74, 81, 149, 153–6, 158, 161–3,
    169, 191
Singapore, 242
Smartsettle, ODR, 292
social context
    and dispute processing, 121–2
socialism, 27
Society of Professionals in Dispute Resolution
    (SPIDR), 62
Solicitors Family Law Association (SFLA), 65
Solicitors in Mediation, 63
sorcery, 74

special masters, 259–62
Spencer, Janet M., 239
Sprenkel, Sybille van der, 20, 36
Square Trade, ODR, 292
St. Florian, Alisia, 249
state power
  and civil justice, 56
  changing nature, 56
  kinship, and kingship, 42–3
Stedman, Barbara Epstein, 204
Stein, Peter, 20–1
Stenelo, Lars-Göran, 133, 165
Stevens, Carl M., 132, 159
strategies
  lawyers use of litigation, 200
  negotiations, 139
    competitive approach, 140–1
    cost-cutting, 70
    integrative, 145–6
    logrolling, 144
summary jury trials, 262–3
Susskind, Richard, 299
Sweden, 275–6, 311

Tamanaha, Brian Z., 47
Tanzania, 79, 83–4, 86
Taobao Users Dispute Resolution Center,
  296
Taylor, Alison, 240
Territorialism, 37–41
Teubner, Gunther, 56, 323
third-party intervention
  command attributes, 89–91
  decision-making, 84–5
  go-betweens, 158
  institutionalised command, 91–9
  umpiring. See umpiring
Tochtermann, Peter, 251–2
Tolzey courts, 24
torts, rent-a-judge, 270
transformative mediation, 168
triads, 81, 85, 161
trial book, 293
tribunals, 210–11
Tswana people, 91–7, 192, 228
Turnbull, Colin, 79
Turner, Victor, 10, 74–5

UK College of Family Mediators, 175–6, 325
umpiring
  adjudication. See adjudication

arbitration. See arbitration
courts. See courts
legitimation, 194–7
UNCITRAL Model Law on International
  Commercial Arbitration, 219–21
Uniform Domain Name Dispute Resolution
  Policy (UDRP), 293
United States
  Agent Orange case, 261
  alternative dispute resolution, 11, 36
  American Arbitration Association, 34, 173,
    178
  American Bar Association, 150, 178
  appellate courts, 199
  arbitration, 36
    court-annexed, 216, 254
  Chinatowns, 33
  compulsory arbitration, 216, 267–8
  compulsory mediation, 254, 259
  court-annexed arbitration, 266–8
  early neutral evaluation (ENE), 263–6
  Freedmen's Bureau, 36
  Hopewell Baptists, 26
  informal justice, 38–40, 44–6
  Knights of Labour, 27, 318
  med-arb, 237
  Middlesex Multi-Door Courthouse
    (MMDC), 204–5
  neighbourhood justice centres, 46
  ombuds, 280
  rent-a-judge, 268–70
  San Francisco Community Boards, 38–40
  Society of Professionals in Dispute
    Resolution (SPIDR), 62
  special masters, 259–62
  summary jury trials, 262–3
  United States v Michigan case, 261
unperceived injurious experience (unPIE), 103,
  311
Ury, William, 141, 144
utopianism, 25

Van Caenegem, R. C., 193–4
Van Wezel Stone, Katherine, 37
Verkuil, Paul, 274
vigilantism, 115
violence. See self-help

Wang Yueying, 297
Weber, Max, 77
Weinstein, Jack B., 259, 261–2

White, James, 149
Wiegand, Shirley, 274
witchcraft, 74
witness statements, 221
Woodburn, James, 79
Woodley, Ann, 263
Woolf Report, 5, 38, 65, 67, 308, 312, 314, 320, 323
World Bank, 199
World Intellectual Property Organisation (WIPO), 294

worst alternative to a negotiated agreement (WATNA), 126
WTO, 218

Ye Jian, 297
Yilmaz, Ihsan, 47

Zammit, Joseph P., 239
Zhao Yan, 291
Zhao Yixian, 333